- buttermilk use evap. milk -

Better Homes and Gardens.

classic RECIPES

Classic Recipes

Editor: Carrie E. Holcomb
Contributing Editor: Staci Bailey, Jessica Saari
Contributing Designer: Craig Hanken, Studio P2
Copy Chief: Terri Fredrickson
Publishing Operations Manager: Karen Schirm
Senior Editor, Asset and Information Manager: Phillip Morgan
Edit and Design Production Coordinator: Mary Lee Gavin
Editorial Assistant: Cheryl Eckert
Book Production Managers: Pam Kvitne, Marjorie J. Schenkelberg, Rick von Holdt, Mark Weaver
Contributing Copy Editors: Gretchen Kauffman, Susan Kling
Test Kitchen Director: Lynn Blanchard
Test Kitchen Home Economists: Paige Boyle, Marilyn Cornelius, Juliana Hale, Laura Harms, R.D., Maryellyn Krantz, Jill Moberly, Dianna Nolin, Colleen Weeden, Lori Wilson, Charles Worthington

Meredith® Books
Executive Director, Editorial: Gregory H. Kayko
Executive Director, Design: Matt Strelecki
Senior Editor/Group Manager: Jan Miller
Marketing Product Manager: Gina Rickert
Managing Editor: Amy Tincher-Durik

Publisher and Editor in Chief: James D. Blume
Editorial Director: Linda Raglan Cunningham
Executive Director, New Business Development: Todd M. Davis
Executive Director, Sales: Ken Zagor
Director, Operations: George A. Susral
Director, Production: Douglas M. Johnston
Director, Marketing: Amy Nichols
Business Director: Jim Leonard

Vice President and General Manager: Douglas J. Guendel

Better Homes and Gardens® Magazine
Editor in Chief: Karol DeWulf Nickell
Deputy Editor, Food and Entertaining: Nancy Hopkins

Meredith Publishing Group
President: Jack Griffin
Executive Vice President: Bob Mate

Meredith Corporation
Chairman and Chief Executive Officer: William T. Kerr
President and Chief Operating Officer: Stephen M. Lacy

In Memoriam: E.T. Meredith III (1933-2003)

All of us at Meredith® Books are dedicated to providing you with the information and ideas you need to create delicious foods. We welcome your comments and suggestions. Write to us at: Meredith Books, Cookbook Editorial Department, 1716 Locust St., Des Moines, IA 50309-3023.

If you would like to purchase any of our cooking, crafts, gardening, home improvement, or home decorating and design books, check wherever quality books are sold. Or visit us at: meredithbooks.com

First Edition.

ISBN: 0-696-22838-6

Our seal assures you that every recipe in Better Homes and Gardens® Classic Recipes has been tested in the Better Homes and Gardens® Test Kitchen. This means that each recipe is practical and reliable, and meets our high standards of taste appeal. We guarantee your satisfaction with this book for as long as you own it.

welcome!

Food is all about celebration! Most momentous occasions spent with family and friends are marked by a spread of delicious treats to share. Whether it's a graduation or a family reunion, a baby shower or a wedding, we relish the food that is offered almost as much as we do the company. Celebrations that highlight food can be held on a much smaller scale too. A quick breakfast opens the day up for possibilities, the lunch hour is a break in a busy schedule, and a hearty family dinner celebrates the end of another successful day. All of these moments with food—whether shared with large groups of loved ones, or cherished in moments of solitude—are important to our lives.

Better Homes and Gardens® magazine has shared in these treasured moments of celebration for more than 80 years. Offering tried and true recipes to generations of families, we have become a trusted name in homes across the country. Every recipe that has ever appeared on the pages of our magazines and books has gone through extensive testing and taste panels with our talented home economists and editors. Too much salt? The recipe goes back for another test. Not enough flavor? The recipe goes back again. Not until the flavor, taste, appearance, and method are perfected does the panel approve the recipe.

In this book we've collected more than 600 treasured recipes that have appeared in Better Homes and Gardens® magazine. From soups to salads, and entrees to desserts, no matter what menu your next celebration—or family dinner—calls for, you'll be sure to find it here. So pull up a chair and have a taste of these favorites. Stamped with the Test-Kitchen seal of approval, each one is guaranteed to be a winner.

contents

196

Mango Whip

Zesty Ravioli Salad

94

Nutty Cucumber Sandwich
269

Valentine Granita
54

121 Easter Rings

January

WITH GET-TOGETHERS RANGING FROM INTIMATE TO GRAND, RING IN THIS NEW YEAR IN STYLISH SIMPLICITY.

Fennel-Lime-Crusted Beef Tenderloin

Roasted Red Pepper and Black Olive Tapenade

Simple Gatherings

Sweet Potato Chowder

Orange-Champagne Cakes

Filled-Up Phyllo Logs

Bloody Mary Swizzlers

Nibbles 'n' Bits

Plus...

THE NEW YEAR SPURS VOWS TO EAT BETTER, EVEN AS WE TURN TO COZY GATHERINGS, MADE FUN WITH INDOOR GAMES AND TASTY MORSELS.

Caesar Salad Cracker Cups

Bacon 'n' Cheese Stuffed Dates

Horseradish-Radish Sandwiches

Corn-Relish Crisps

Simple Gatherings for the New Year

KEEP THE FOOD EASY AND THE CONVERSATION LIVELY, AND THE MOOD WILL BE DELICIOUS. SERVE ONE STAR DISH TO ANCHOR THE GATHERING, THEN SURROUND IT WITH PROVOCATIVE ACCOMPANIMENTS. HERE ARE FOUR EASY IDEAS THAT INVITE EVERYONE TO DIG IN.

Soup's on!

The most memorable casual occasions often start with "Come on over." With the right menu, you can count on these friendly gatherings to be remembered for years ahead. The trick to impromptu parties is keeping them simple: White everyday dinnerware looks comfortable in any setting; layer on a touch of color with linens or tumblers. Advance prep keeps stress levels low. Make a pot of Sweet Potato Chowder ahead of time. The red curry, lemon grass, and coconut flavors of India put a spicy perspective on this warming winter party starter.

Sweet Potato Chowder

Sweet Potato Chowder

Sweet Potato Chowder beckons guests to a comfy-cozy night. They can top off mini bowls of this chunky soup appetizer as they wish—by sweetening it with sliced mango, coconut, and golden raisins; strengthening it with turmeric, cilantro, or roasted unsalted cashews; or sharpening it with paprika or toasted cumin seeds.

PREP: 30 minutes **COOK:** 20 minutes

- 1 large onion, chopped (1 cup)
- 2 Tbsp. cooking oil
- 2 cloves garlic, minced
- 1 tsp. red curry paste or 2 to 3 tsp. curry powder
- 6 medium sweet potatoes (about 3 lb.), peeled and cut into 3/4-inch pieces (about 7 cups)
- 2 14-oz. cans chicken broth
- 1 14-oz. can unsweetened coconut milk
- 1 2-inch piece fresh lemon grass
- 2 tsp. grated fresh ginger (optional)
- 1/4 tsp. white pepper
- 1/8 tsp. salt
- 1 recipe Pita Crisps (below)

1. In a 4-quart Dutch oven cook onion in hot oil over medium heat for 3 minutes, stirring occasionally. Add garlic and curry paste; cook for 3 to 5 minutes more or until onion is tender, stirring occasionally. Add sweet potatoes, chicken broth, coconut milk, lemon grass, and ginger; bring to boiling. Reduce heat. Simmer, covered, for 10 to 15 minutes or until sweet potatoes are tender. Cool slightly. Discard lemon grass.

2. Remove half of the mixture (about 4 cups) from the Dutch oven. In small batches, place mixture in a blender container or food processor bowl. Cover; blend until smooth. Return pureed mixture to soup mixture in pot. Add pepper and salt; heat through. Serve with Pita Crisps. Makes 12 appetizer servings.

PITA CRISPS: Preheat oven to 350° F. In a skillet combine 1 teaspoon each cumin seeds, mustard seeds, and black caraway seeds. Heat over low heat for 2 to 4 minutes or until fragrant, stirring occasionally. Cut 2 pita bread rounds into 8 wedges each. Spread in a single layer on a cookie sheet. Brush with melted butter. Sprinkle with toasted seeds; press seeds lightly. Bake for 8 to 10 minutes or until crisp.

Each serving: 179 cal., 9 g total fat (6 g sat. fat), 0 mg chol., 271 mg sodium, 22 g carbo., 3 g fiber, 3 g pro. Daily Values: 280% vit. A, 22% vit. C, 2% calcium, 5% iron.

So glad you're here

Dressed to impress, and looking like it took hours of preparation, this elegant Fennel-Lime-Crusted Beef Tenderloin hors d'oeuvre can be made up to two days ahead. The chilled tenderloin sits atop a bed of crisp green beans. For crunch, offer cucumber spears dressed with gingered vinaigrette and a few graceful strands of chive. Other easy condiments include fresh green onion, sliced fresh fennel, green peppercorn mustard, and extra-large caperberries.

NEW YEAR'S COCKTAIL PARTY

Roasted Mushrooms with Fresh Sage *(page 16)*
Baguette slices or assorted small toasts and crackers
Fennel-Lime-Crusted Beef Tenderloin *(right)*
Orange-Champagne Cakes *(page 19)*
Assorted cheeses, such as Morbier, Stilton, and Manchego
Assorted fruits, including grapes, dried figs, and clementine oranges
Champagne or other sparkling wine, such as Italian Prosecco

Fennel-Lime-Crusted Beef Tenderloin

A rub of fennel seeds, lime peel, tarragon, and lime-infused olive oil crusts a beef tenderloin for this very special cocktail party dish.

PREP: 30 minutes **ROAST:** 45 minutes **STAND:** 10 minutes

- **8 Tbsp. lime-infused olive oil or olive oil (1/2 cup)**
- **1/4 cup fennel seeds**
- **1/4 cup snipped fresh tarragon**
- **1/4 cup fresh lime peel (from about 5 or 6 limes)**
- **2 tsp. ground black pepper**
- **1/2 tsp. salt**
- **1 3-lb. center-cut beef tenderloin**
- **1 lb. peeled onions, such as cipollini, pearl, or boiling onions; or yellow onions cut into 8 wedges**
- **3 cups sliced fennel strips**
- **1/2 cup dry red wine**
- **1 lb. fresh green beans, trimmed**
- **2 small fresh limes, halved**

1. In a bowl combine 6 tablespoons of the oil, fennel seeds, tarragon, lime peel, pepper, and salt; stir well. Coat the tenderloin with seed mixture. Place meat on a nonmetal tray; cover loosely with foil. Refrigerate for 30 minutes or up to 1 hour.

2. Preheat oven to 425° F. Place roast on a rack in a shallow roasting pan. Return any coating left on tray to meat. Insert an oven-safe meat thermometer into center of meat. In a bowl toss together onions and 1 tablespoon of the remaining olive oil. Place onions on half of the roasting pan alongside meat. Roast, uncovered, for 30 minutes. Meanwhile, toss together fennel and remaining oil. Stir onions; add fennel to other half of roasting pan alongside meat. Roast for 15 to 20 minutes more or until thermometer registers 135° F for medium-rare doneness.

3. Remove roast from oven. Transfer roast to cutting board; cover with foil. Let stand 10 to 15 minutes (temperature should register 145° F for medium-rare). Wrap roast tightly in plastic wrap; refrigerate until serving time. Meanwhile, transfer onions and fennel to separate bowls. Cover tightly; refrigerate until serving time.

4. Place roasting pan on stove top over low heat. Add red wine, stirring constantly to loosen browned bits. Transfer sauce to bowl. Cover; refrigerate until serving time.

5. Cook green beans in a small amount of boiling salted water about 5 minutes or until crisp-tender. Drain. Cover; chill until serving time.

6. To serve, toss beans with reserved sauce; arrange on a platter. Slice tenderloin into thin slices; arrange on beans. Serve with roasted onion and fennel and lime halves. Makes 12 appetizer servings.

Each serving: 288 cal., 17 g total fat (4 g sat. fat), 57 mg chol., 165 mg sodium, 7 g carbo., 8 g fiber, 25 g pro. Daily Values: 2% vit. A, 15 vit. C, 6% calcium, 21% iron.

Fennel-Lime-Crusted Beef Tenderloin

Fresh chives *(far left)* accent cucumber spears to go along with Fennel-Lime-Crusted Beef Tenderloin. Purchased green peppercorn mustard *(left)* is a spicy and colorful complement.

Horseradish-Sour Cream Dip

Relaxed, easy entertaining

Serve Roasted Mushrooms with Fresh Sage for a homey get-together where settling in for plenty of conversation is expected. Add even more flavors and textures with Horseradish-Sour Cream Dip and Red Pepper and Black Olive Tapenade. Serve it all with red endive leaves for scooping and a wedge of crumbly pecorino cheese.

Roasted Mushrooms with Fresh Sage

PREP: 30 minutes **ROAST:** 30 minutes

- 1 recipe Roasted Red Pepper and Black Olive Tapenade (below)
- 3 lb. assorted mushrooms, such as chanterelle, shiitake, button, cremini, brown and alba clamshell, morel, and/or oyster*
- 3 heads garlic
- 3 Tbsp. butter, melted
- 3 Tbsp. olive oil
- 1/2 tsp. salt
- 1/2 tsp. ground black pepper
- Dry sherry, port, or brandy
- 1/4 cup fresh sage leaves, coarsely torn (leaving small leaves whole)
- 1 recipe Horseradish-Sour Cream Dip (below)

1. Prepare Roasted Red Pepper and Black Olive Tapenade; set aside. Preheat oven to 450° F. Remove stems from shiitake and oyster mushrooms. Brush any dirt off mushrooms, leaving mushrooms whole (should have about 16 cups). Remove loose outer skins of garlic heads. Trim stem ends to expose cloves; break apart cloves.

2. Place mushrooms and garlic in a large roasting pan. Combine melted butter and olive oil; drizzle over mushrooms and garlic. Toss to coat. Sprinkle with salt and pepper. Roast about 30 minutes or until mushrooms are tender and garlic cloves are soft, stirring twice.

3. Remove roasted mushrooms and garlic from pan; place on a platter. Splash with sherry; sprinkle with fresh sage. Prepare Horseradish-Sour Cream Dip. Serve mushrooms with dip, tapenade, and assorted dippers. Makes 8 to 10 appetizer servings.

ROASTED RED PEPPER AND BLACK OLIVE TAPENADE: In a bowl combine 1/2 cup coarsely chopped pitted ripe olives, 1/3 cup coarsely chopped roasted red sweet pepper, 2 tablespoons olive oil, 1 tablespoon snipped fresh rosemary, 2 teaspoons snipped fresh oregano, and 1 1/2 teaspoons finely shredded lemon peel. Let stand at room temperature for 2 to 6 hours to allow flavors to blend. Serve at room temperature.

HORSERADISH-SOUR CREAM DIP: Combine one 8-ounce carton dairy sour cream and 2 to 3 tablespoons prepared horseradish; top with coarsely crushed pink peppercorns and snipped rosemary leaves.

***NOTE:** Wild mushrooms are available at gourmet and specialty markets. The clamshell mushroom is distinguished by its crunchy texture even after cooking.

Each serving: 254 cal., 23 g total fat (8 g sat. fat), 25 mg chol., 301 mg sodium, 11 g carbo., 2 g fiber, 7 g pro. Daily Values: 9% vit. A, 37% vit. C, 8% calcium, 9% iron.

Roasted Mushrooms with Fresh Sage

Roasted Red Pepper and Black Olive Tapenade

Red Belgian endive leaves *(far left)* are handy scoopers for Roasted Mushrooms with Fresh Sage. Serve the mushrooms with Roasted Red Pepper and Black Olive Tapenade *(left)* and Horseradish-Sour Cream Dip.

Orange-Champagne Cakes

Choose an assortment of hard and soft cheeses *(far left)* as partners to polenta-based individual Orange-Champagne Cakes. Then drizzle a favorite fruit liqueur *(left)* over the small cakes to add a note of concentrated fruit.

Orange-Champagne Cakes

A tumble of individual Orange-Champagne Cakes perches on a pedestal with room left over for fruity indulgences. The cakes' tender crumb stands alone or provides a good foundation for piling on shards of piquant cheese or a spoonful of ginger-zapped mascarpone and marmalade.

PREP: 30 minutes **BAKE:** 30 minutes **COOL:** 10 minutes + 1 hour

- **1½ cups polenta cornmeal or yellow cornmeal**
- **1 cup all-purpose flour**
- **2 tsp. baking powder**
- **⅛ tsp. salt**
- **1½ cups unsalted butter, softened**
- **2 cups sugar**
- **6 eggs**
- **1 cup orange juice**
- **3 cups finely ground almonds**
- **1 Tbsp. finely shredded orange peel**
- **1½ cups champagne or sparkling wine**
- **¼ cup sugar**
- **Finely shredded orange peel (optional)**

1. Preheat oven to 325° F. Grease and flour two small angel cake pans or twelve 4-inch muffin cups; set aside. In a bowl combine polenta, flour, baking powder, and salt; set aside.

2. In a large mixing bowl beat butter with an electric mixer on medium to high speed for 30 seconds. Add the 2 cups sugar; beat until combined. Add eggs; beat until combined. Beat in orange juice (mixture may appear curdled). Beat in polenta mixture just until combined. Fold in ground almonds and 1 tablespoon finely shredded orange peel.

3. Spoon batter into pans (about ⅔ cup batter each). Bake about 30 minutes or until a wooden pick inserted near the centers comes out clean. Cool in pans on wire racks for 10 minutes.

4. Meanwhile, in a saucepan combine champagne and the ¼ cup sugar. Bring to boiling, stirring to dissolve sugar. Reduce heat; simmer, uncovered, about 10 minutes or until mixture is reduced to 1 cup.

5. Remove cakes from pans. Transfer cakes to a large platter, placing cakes bottoms up. Prick cakes with wooden toothpick. Carefully spoon or brush champagne syrup onto cakes. Immediately cover cakes with plastic wrap; cool completely. Serve cakes at room temperature. If desired, garnish with additional orange peel. Makes 12 cakes or 24 servings.

Each serving: 358 cal., 22 g total fat (9 g sat. fat), 85 mg chol., 64 mg sodium, 34 g carbo., 3 g fiber, 7 g pro. Daily Values: 12% vit. A, 9% vit. C, 8% calcium, 9% iron.

Orange-Champagne Cakes

Cause for celebration

Celebrate simply, but with spirit. A late-evening dessert party needs only one star: Orange-Champagne Cakes. To serve, add Tuscan touches with a bunch of grapes, dried figs, walnuts, clementine oranges, and honey. Match sweet and savory by adding chopped crystallized ginger to softened mascarpone and topping it with orange marmalade, then pair it with grand cheeses, including a wedge of Parmesan. Finally, sprinkle the cake with a favorite liqueur, such as Grand Marnier, B&B, or cassis, and orange Muscatel dessert wine.

Nibbles 'n' bits

PICK A LITTLE, TALK A LITTLE, PICK A LITTLE, TALK A LITTLE. THAT'S WHAT'LL HAPPEN WHEN A ROOMFUL OF FRIENDS SAYS HELLO TO A TABLE FILLED WITH AMAZING APPETIZERS.

Bloody Mary Swizzlers

Bloody Mary Swizzlers

Vodka-flavored veggies will remind you of the classic cocktail.

PREP: 30 minutes **MARINATE:** Overnight

- 24 cherry tomatoes
- 1 cup lemon-flavored vodka
- 24 almond-stuffed green olives or vermouth-marinated green olives
- 3 or 4 stalks celery with tops removed, bias-sliced into 3/4- to 1-inch pieces (24 pieces total)
- 24 cocktail picks or skewers
- Celery salt

1. Using a plastic or wooden pick or a sharp skewer, pierce the skins of the tomatoes in several places. Place tomatoes in a self-sealing, food-safe plastic bag; add vodka. Seal bag. Turn bag to coat tomatoes. Marinate in refrigerator overnight.

2. Drain tomatoes; discard vodka. Skewer an olive, a piece of celery, and a cherry tomato on each pick. Sprinkle lightly with celery salt. Transfer to serving platter. Makes 24 skewers.

Each serving: 21 cal., 1 g total fat (0 g sat. fat), 0 mg chol., 92 mg sodium, 1 g carbo., 0 g fiber, 0 g pro. Daily Values: 2% vit. A, 6% vit. C, 1% calcium, 1% iron.

Caesar Salad Cracker Cups

Caesar Salad Cracker Cups

Roasting the beets and baking the cracker cups in advance will save time on party day.

PREP: 30 minutes

BAKE: 10 minutes for cracker cups; 45 minutes for beets

- 3/4 cup all-purpose flour
- 1/4 cup whole wheat flour
- 1 tsp. sugar
- 1/4 tsp. baking soda
- 1/8 tsp. coarse salt or salt
- 1/8 tsp. freshly ground black pepper
- 1 Tbsp. butter (no substitutes)
- 1/4 cup finely shredded Parmesan cheese
- 1 clove garlic, minced
- 1/3 cup buttermilk
- Nonstick cooking spray
- 4 cups chopped romaine lettuce
- 2 to 3 Tbsp. bottled Caesar salad dressing
- 1 hard-cooked egg, chopped
- 1 recipe Roasted Beets (below)
- Shaved Parmesan cheese

1. Preheat oven to 375° F. In a medium bowl stir together all-purpose flour, whole wheat flour, sugar, baking soda, salt, and pepper. Using a pastry blender, cut in butter until mixture resembles coarse crumbs. Stir in shredded Parmesan cheese and garlic. Make a well in center of flour mixture. Add buttermilk. Using a fork, stir until mixture can be shaped into a ball.

2. Turn dough out onto a lightly floured surface. Knead for 8 to 10 strokes or until dough is almost smooth. Divide dough in half. Roll each portion into a 12×9-inch rectangle. Use a pastry wheel or knife to cut rectangles into 3-inch squares. Use a fork to prick squares several times. Coat the bottom side of a mini muffin pan with cooking spray. Lay dough squares over muffin cup bottoms, making sure edges of squares don't overlap. Place inverted muffin pan on a shallow baking pan.

3. Bake about 10 minutes or until golden brown. Remove cracker cups from muffin pan; cool on a wire rack. (Cracker cups may be made up to 3 days ahead. Store in an airtight container at room temperature. Or freeze the baked cracker cups in a freezer container for up to 3 months.)

4. In a medium bowl toss romaine with salad dressing. To serve, sprinkle some chopped egg in the bottom of each cracker cup. Fill with romaine mixture and top with Roasted Beets and shaved Parmesan cheese. Makes 24 appetizers.

ROASTED BEETS: Preheat oven to 375° F. Scrub one medium beet (or 12 baby beets); trim off stem and root ends. Peel the medium beet and cut into 3/4-inch pieces or halve the baby beets. Place beets in an 8×8×2-inch baking pan. In a small bowl combine 1 tablespoon olive oil, 1 1/2 teaspoons balsamic vinegar, 1 small clove minced garlic, 1/8 teaspoon salt, and 1/8 teaspoon freshly ground black pepper. Drizzle over beets; toss to coat. Cover pan with foil; roast for 35 minutes. Uncover; roast for 10 minutes more or until tender. Cool to room temperature.

Each serving: 49 cal., 2 g total fat (1 g sat. fat), 11 mg chol., 80 mg sodium, 5 g carbo., 1 g fiber, 2 g pro. Daily Values: 6% vit. A, 4% vit. C, 2% calcium, 2% iron.

Thai Spinach Dip

This stir-together treat delivers big peanut flavor with a hit of heat. The dip takes just minutes to prepare.

PREP: 15 minutes **CHILL:** 2 hours

- **1 cup chopped fresh spinach**
- **1 8-oz. carton dairy sour cream**
- **1 cup plain fat-free yogurt**
- **1/4 cup snipped fresh mint**
- **1/4 cup finely chopped peanuts**
- **1/4 cup peanut butter**
- **1 Tbsp. honey**
- **1 Tbsp. soy sauce**
- **1 to 2 tsp. crushed red pepper**
- **Peeled baby carrots or other vegetables for dipping**

1. In a medium bowl combine the spinach, sour cream, and yogurt. Stir in mint, peanuts, peanut butter, honey, soy sauce, and crushed red pepper.

2. Cover and chill for 2 to 24 hours. Serve with baby carrots or other vegetable dippers. Makes about 2½ cups.

Each serving: 34 cal., 3 g total fat (1 g sat. fat), 3 mg chol., 41 mg sodium, 2 g carbo., 0 g fiber, 1 g pro. Daily Values: 2% vit. A, 1% vit. C, 2% calcium, 1% iron.

WARMING WINTER PARTY MENU

Pork and Chicken Barbecue Sticks *(page 28)*
Filled-Up Phyllo Logs *(page 27)*
Thai Spinach Dip *(left)*
Assorted vegetables and crackers
Bloody Mary Swizzlers *(page 21)*

Horseradish-Radish Sandwiches

Horseradish-Radish Sandwiches

Take a shortcut by placing the herbed cheese mixture into a plastic sandwich bag, snipping a small hole in one corner, then piping the mixture onto the puff pastry circles.

PREP: 45 minutes **BAKE:** 10 minutes

- **1⅓ cups herbed goat cheese (chèvre) or two 5-oz. containers semisoft cheese with garlic and herbs**
- **6 to 8 tsp. hot-style prepared horseradish**
- **2 Tbsp. finely chopped green onion**
- **1 17¼-oz. pkg. frozen puff pastry (2 sheets), thawed**
- **1 Tbsp. milk**
- **Coarse salt (optional)**
- **1 large English cucumber, very thinly sliced**
- **10 radishes, very thinly sliced**

1. In a medium bowl combine goat cheese, horseradish, and green onion. Cover and chill until ready to use.

2. Preheat oven to 375° F. Unfold one of the puff pastry sheets on a lightly floured surface. With the tines of a fork, generously prick pastry. Use a 2-inch round cutter to cut pastry into circles. Transfer circles to an ungreased baking sheet. Brush pastry lightly with milk. Sprinkle with salt, if desired. Bake for 10 to 12 minutes or until golden brown. Cool on wire rack. Repeat with remaining puff pastry.

3. To assemble, use a knife to split the baked pastries horizontally. Spread about 1 teaspoon of the cheese mixture onto the cut side of each bottom pastry. Top with several cucumber slices and radish slices. Spread the cut side of each top pastry with about 1 teaspoon of the cheese mixture. Place on top of radish slices. Makes 32 appetizers.

Each serving: 94 cal., 7 g total fat (1 g sat. fat), 4 mg chol., 94 mg sodium, 6 g carbo., 0 g fiber, 2 g pro. Daily Values: 2% vit. A, 1% vit. C, 2% calcium, 1% iron.

Thai Spinach Dip

No excuses

PICK UP THE PHONE, INVITE THE FRIENDS, AND PARTY ON.

Corn-Relish Crisps

Keep them small

AND YOU CAN HAVE ANOTHER, AND ANOTHER, AND ANOTHER.

Corn-Relish Crisps

Shape each cilantro-flecked crisp into a mini taco shell by draping a warm crisp over a rolling pin. Or, keep crisps flat by cooling on a flat surface.

PREP: 30 minutes **BAKE:** 6 minutes per batch

- 3/4 cup all-purpose flour
- 2 Tbsp. snipped fresh cilantro
- 1 Tbsp. sugar
- 1/2 tsp. salt
- 1/4 tsp. ground red pepper
- 1/2 cup butter, softened
- 3 egg whites
- Pointed rolled sugar ice-cream cones or metal cone shapes
- 3/4 cup crème fraîche or dairy sour cream
- 4 tsp. snipped fresh chives
- 1/2 cup purchased corn relish

1. Preheat oven to 375° F. In a small bowl stir together the flour, cilantro, sugar, salt, and ground red pepper; set aside. In a medium mixing bowl beat butter with an electric mixer on medium to high speed until fluffy. Beat in egg whites until combined. Beat in flour mixture until combined.

2. Line a baking sheet with parchment paper. For each shell, drop one heaping teaspoon of batter onto the prepared sheet. Using the back of a spoon, spread batter into a 3-inch circle. Repeat with the remaining batter, baking only five or six crisps at a time.

3. Bake 6 to 7 minutes or until bubbly and golden brown on edges. Remove from oven. Allow to cool 15 seconds. Working quickly, roll each warm crisp around pointed ice-cream cone or metal cone. Allow to cool; remove from cones and set aside. Or transfer flat crisps to a wire rack to cool.

4. To serve, in a small mixing bowl combine crème fraîche and chives. Spoon 1 to 2 teaspoons of the crème fraîche mixture into each shell. Top with 1 teaspoon corn relish. Arrange on a serving platter. Makes 24 appetizers.

MAKE-AHEAD DIRECTIONS: Bake, shape, and cool crisps as directed. Arrange in a single layer in a freezer container and freeze for up to 1 month. To serve, thaw crisps for 15 minutes.

Each appetizer: 76 cal., 6 g total fat (4 g sat. fat), 17 mg chol., 107 mg sodium, 4 g carbo., 0 g fiber, 1 g pro. Daily Values: 4% vit. A, 1% vit. C, 1% calcium, 1% iron.

Deviled Eggs with Spicy Crab

Deviled Eggs with Spicy Crab

Crab and chutney atop deviled eggs make a favorite appetizer doubly delightful.

START TO FINISH: 25 minutes

- 8 hard-cooked eggs
- 1/4 cup mayonnaise or salad dressing
- 1 Tbsp. finely chopped green onion
- 1 to 2 tsp. flavored mustard, such as Dijon-style mustard or horseradish mustard
- 1/4 tsp. salt
- 1/4 tsp. ground red pepper
- 1 to 2 Tbsp. mango chutney
- 3 Tbsp. mayonnaise or salad dressing
- 1/2 tsp. curry powder
- 1/2 cup cooked crabmeat (about 2 3/4 oz.)

1. Halve the hard-cooked eggs lengthwise and remove yolks. Place egg yolks, the 1/4 cup mayonnaise, the green onion, mustard, and 1/8 teaspoon each of the salt and red pepper in a quart-size, self-sealing, food-safe plastic bag. Seal bag; squeeze to mash the egg yolks and combine the ingredients. Snip one corner of the bag; pipe mixture into egg halves.

2. Cut up any large pieces of mango chutney. In a bowl combine the chutney, the remaining 3 tablespoons mayonnaise, curry powder, and remaining salt and red pepper. Gently fold in crabmeat. Top each deviled egg with a spoonful of crab mixture. Cover and chill up to 2 hours. Makes 16 appetizers.

Each appetizer: 91 cal., 8 g total fat (1 g sat. fat), 113 mg chol., 119 mg sodium, 1 g carbo., 0 g fiber, 4 g pro. Daily Values: 4% vit. A, 1% vit. C, 2% calcium, 2% iron.

Filled-Up Phyllo Logs

CALL THEM TAPAS,

HORS D'OEUVRES, OR APPETIZERS. OR CALL THEM A DARN GOOD SUBSTITUTE FOR DINNER TONIGHT.

Bacon 'n' Cheese Stuffed Dates

Warren Weekes, executive chef at Rio Rico Resort and Country Club in Arizona, tweaked his mother's recipe to create this sweet-tangy blend of flavors.

PREP: 25 minutes **BAKE:** 5 minutes

- 2 slices bacon, crisp-cooked, drained, and finely crumbled, or 1/4 cup chopped prosciutto
- 1/4 cup thinly sliced green onion
- 2 cloves garlic, minced
- 1/2 cup Cambazola cheese or crumbled blue cheese
- 1 3-oz. pkg. cream cheese, softened
- 2 tsp. Dijon-style mustard
- 1/8 tsp. pepper
- 24 Medjool dates (about 16 oz. unpitted)

1. Preheat oven to 350° F. In a medium bowl stir together the bacon or prosciutto, green onion, and garlic. Add Cambazola or blue cheese, cream cheese, mustard, and pepper to bacon mixture. Stir to combine.

2. Using a knife, make a lengthwise slit in each date. Spread each date open slightly. Remove pits. Fill each date with a rounded teaspoon of the bacon mixture. Place dates, filling side up, on a baking sheet. Bake for 5 to 8 minutes or until heated through. Serve warm. Makes 24 appetizers.

MAKE-AHEAD DIRECTIONS: Stuff dates, cover, and chill up to 24 hours. Just before serving, uncover and bake as directed.

Each appetizer: 77 cal., 2 g total fat (1 g sat. fat), 6 mg chol., 55 mg sodium, 14 g carbo., 1 g fiber, 1 g pro. Daily Values: 2% vit. A, 2% calcium, 2% iron.

Bacon 'n' Cheese Stuffed Dates

Filled-Up Phyllo Logs

Chef/owner Jeremy Morrow of the 43 Restaurant and Bar in Des Moines, Iowa, inspired these crispy snacks.

PREP: 45 minutes **BAKE:** 18 minutes

- 1 recipe Spinach-White Bean Filling (below)
- 1 recipe Mushroom-Onion Filling (below)
- 12 sheets frozen phyllo dough, thawed
- 1/2 cup butter or margarine, melted
- Shredded Parmesan cheese
- Pepper
- Chives (optional)

1. Prepare the Spinach-White Bean Filling and Mushroom-Onion Filling. Preheat oven to 375° F. Lightly brush a sheet of phyllo with some of the melted butter. Top with another sheet of phyllo and brush with more melted butter. (Keep remaining phyllo covered with plastic wrap to prevent drying.) Using a sharp knife or rotary blade, cut the stacked phyllo in half lengthwise and then crosswise to make four equal rectangles.

2. Spread about 2 tablespoons of the bean filling in a 3/4-inch-wide strip on a long side and to within 1 inch of short ends of each rectangle. Tightly roll the phyllo dough into a thin log, starting with the filled side. Brush seam side with butter. Place log, seam side down, on a baking sheet; brush with butter and sprinkle with shredded Parmesan cheese.

3. Repeat with remaining bean filling and four more phyllo sheets. Fill remaining six sheets of phyllo with the mushroom-onion filling, following the same procedure, except use 4 teaspoons filling per log and sprinkle logs with pepper.

4. Bake about 18 minutes or until logs are golden brown. Cool on wire racks. Tie ends with chive strands, if desired. Serve warm or cool. Makes 24 logs.

SPINACH-WHITE BEAN FILLING: Thaw and thoroughly drain one 10-ounce package frozen chopped spinach; finely chop. Set aside. Drain one 15-ounce can white beans (cannellini); rinse and drain. In a food processor bowl or blender container combine beans, 1 tablespoon water, and 3 cloves minced garlic. Cover and process or blend until smooth. Transfer bean mixture to a medium bowl. Add spinach; mix well.

Each serving: 92 cal., 5 g total fat (3 g sat. fat),11 mg chol., 211 mg sodium, 11 g carbo., 3 g fiber, 4 g pro. Daily Values: 40% vit. A, 5% vit. C, 5% calcium, 6% iron.

MUSHROOM-ONION FILLING: In a large skillet heat 1 tablespoon cooking oil until hot. Cook 2 cups finely diced fresh cremini and/or shiitake mushrooms, 1 finely chopped large onion, and 1 clove minced garlic over medium-high heat for 5 to 7 minutes or until liquid has evaporated. Stir occasionally.

Each serving: 84 cal., 6 g total fat (3 g sat. fat), 11 mg chol., 113 mg sodium, 7 g carbo., 1 g fiber, 1 g pro. Daily Values: 3% vit. A, 1% vit. C, 1% calcium, 2% iron.

Hot Ribeye Bites

Pork and Chicken BBQ Sticks

An indoor grill makes speedy work of these meaty treats, but an oven broiler also offers a quick option.

PREP: 20 minutes **CHILL:** 15 minutes **GRILL:** 5 minutes

- **12 oz. pork tenderloin**
- **12 oz. skinless, boneless chicken thighs**
- **16 6-inch wooden skewers**
- **Salt**
- **Black pepper**
- **1 recipe Chipotle Barbecue Sauce (below)**

1. Trim fat from pork. Cut pork into 1-inch cubes. Cut chicken into 1-inch pieces. Thread three pork pieces onto eight of the skewers, leaving 1/4 inch between pieces. Thread three chicken pieces on each of the remaining eight skewers, leaving 1/4 inch between pieces. Place skewers on a tray.

2. Sprinkle salt and pepper evenly over pork and chicken. Cover with plastic wrap; refrigerate 15 minutes to 2 hours.

3. Lightly grease the rack of an indoor electric grill or lightly coat with nonstick cooking spray. Preheat grill. Place the pork kabobs on the grill rack. (Keep chicken kabobs covered and refrigerated). If using a covered grill, close lid. Grill until meat is slightly pink in center and juices run clear, brushing generously with Chipotle Barbecue Sauce halfway through cooking. (For a covered grill, allow 5 to 7 minutes, giving kabobs a quarter turn once halfway through grilling. For an uncovered grill, allow 12 to 15 minutes, turning kabobs occasionally to cook evenly.) Remove from grill and keep warm.

4. Place chicken kabobs on the grill rack. If using a covered grill, close lid. Grill until chicken is tender and no longer pink, brushing generously with the remaining sauce halfway through cooking. (For a covered grill, allow 3 to 5 minutes, giving kabobs a quarter turn once halfway through grilling. For an uncovered grill, allow 10 to 12 minutes, turning occasionally to cook evenly.) Makes 16 appetizers.

BROILER METHOD: Arrange all of the kabobs on the rack of an unheated broiler pan. Broil 4 to 5 inches from the heat for 8 to 10 minutes or until pork and chicken are done, turning occasionally. Brush generously with sauce the last 5 minutes.

CHIPOTLE BARBECUE SAUCE: In a small saucepan combine 1/2 cup bottled barbecue sauce, 1 tablespoon chopped canned chipotle peppers in adobo sauce, 1 tablespoon honey, and 2 cloves minced garlic. Bring to boiling; reduce heat. Boil gently, uncovered, about 5 minutes or until slightly thickened. Set aside to cool slightly. Makes about 1/2 cup.

Each appetizer: 63 cal., 2 g total fat (0 g sat. fat), 31 mg chol., 116 mg sodium, 2 g carbo., 0 g fiber, 9 g pro. Daily Values: 2% vit. A, 2% vit. C, 1% calcium, 3% iron.

Hot Ribeye Bites

Make sure the pickled peppers you use are a mild variety or your guests will really feel the burn.

PREP: 15 minutes **BROIL:** 12 minutes

- **1/4 cup jalapeño pepper jelly**
- **2 Tbsp. Kansas City steak seasoning or steak seasoning**
- **2 boneless beef ribeye steaks, cut 1 inch thick (about 1 1/4 lb.)**
- **24 pickled baby banana chile peppers, jalapeño peppers, or other mild baby chile peppers**

1. For glaze, in a small saucepan stir together pepper jelly and steak seasoning. Cook and stir for 1 to 2 minutes over low heat or until jelly is melted. Set aside.

2. Preheat broiler. Place steaks on the unheated rack of a broiler pan. Broil steaks 3 to 4 inches from the heat to desired doneness, turning the steaks once. Allow 12 to 14 minutes for medium rare (center of meat is 145° F) or 15 to 18 minutes for medium doneness (center of meat is 160° F). Brush steaks with glaze during the last 5 minutes and turn again to glaze other side.

3. Cut steak into 1-inch cubes. Top each cube with a pickled pepper. Makes about 24 appetizers.

Each appetizer: 47 cal., 1 g total fat (1 g sat. fat), 11 mg chol., 179 mg sodium, 3 g carbo., 0 g fiber, 5 g pro. Daily Values: 4% vit. C, 1% calcium, 3% iron.

Lemony Oven Fries

PULL TOGETHER A FEW TASTY TIDBITS AND A FEW CLOSE FRIENDS AND BASK IN THE CAMARADERIE.

Soy-Glazed Squash

Soy-Glazed Squash

The tan rind of bell-shaped butternut squash is easy to remove with a vegetable peeler.

PREP: 25 minutes **ROAST:** 20 minutes

- **1½ lb. butternut squash, peeled, seeded, and cut into ¾-inch cubes**
- **1 tsp. finely shredded blood orange peel or orange peel**
- **½ cup blood orange juice or orange juice**
- **2 scallions or green onions, finely chopped**
- **3 Tbsp. soy sauce**
- **1 Tbsp. brown sugar**
- **2 tsp. chili oil**

1. Preheat oven to 425° F. Place squash cubes in a lightly greased 13×9×2-inch baking pan. In a bowl combine orange peel, orange juice, scallions or green onions, soy sauce, brown sugar, and chili oil. Drizzle over squash, tossing to coat. Roast, uncovered, 20 to 25 minutes or until squash is tender, stirring twice.

2. Stir cubes again before serving. Place a toothpick in each squash cube. Serve warm. Makes about 48 appetizers.

Each appetizer: 10 cal., 0 g total fat (0 g sat. fat), 0 mg chol., 58 mg sodium, 2 g carbo., 0 g fiber, 0 g pro. Daily Values: 11% vit. A, 5% vit. C, 1% calcium, 1% iron.

Lemony Oven Fries

Wow! Adding a zap of lemon to frozen french fries before baking makes for a surprising burst of fresh flavor.

PREP: 10 minutes **BAKE:** 30 minutes

- **⅓ cup olive oil**
- **1 large lemon, thinly sliced**
- **¼ cup fresh Italian flat-leaf parsley sprigs**
- **1 20-oz. pkg. frozen french-fried shoestring potatoes (about 5 cups)**
- **Coarse sea salt**
- **Lemon wedges**

1. In a large skillet heat olive oil over medium heat. Carefully add lemon slices. Cook for 3 to 5 minutes or until lemon begins to brown. Use tongs to turn lemon slices. Add the parsley to the oil. Cook for 20 to 30 seconds more or until parsley is crisp. Remove lemon slices and parsley with slotted spoon; drain on paper towels. Reserve the lemon-flavored oil (you should have about 3 tablespoons).

2. In a large bowl toss frozen shoestring potatoes with the reserved oil until well coated. Place potatoes in a 15×10×1-inch baking pan. Bake according to package directions or until the potatoes are browned and crisp, stirring occasionally.

3. To serve, toss lemon and parsley with the hot potatoes. Sprinkle generously with sea salt. Squeeze lemon wedges over fries. Serve immediately. Makes about 5 cups.

Each serving: 126 cal., 7 g total fat (1 g sat. fat), 0 mg chol., 72 mg sodium, 14 g carbo., 1 g fiber, 2 g pro. Daily Values: 2% vit. A, 20% vit. C, 1% calcium, 1% iron.

Eat Your Broccoli

Broccoli Raab
Until recently, broccoli raab *(below)* was pretty scarce outside of Italian neighborhoods. Now you'll spot it in most supermarkets. Be sure to cook broccoli raab to help tame its radishlike bite. Try it chopped and stirred into your favorite spicy sausage soup or creamy risotto.

Baby Broccoli
These bitsy buds *(below)* are a cross between broccoli and gai lan *(far right)*. The slender stalks cook quickly. We love sautéing these babies in olive oil and garlic for 5 minutes or so, then adding a generous splash of chicken broth before covering and cooking for a few minutes more.

Broccoli Romanesco
With its chartreuse color and pinecone-shaped flowerets *(below)*, this is the most exotic-looking of the broccoli family. But it tastes more like cauliflower. Show it off by steaming it until crisp tender, or serve it raw with a bit of garlic-mayo or a yogurt-herb dip.

Broccoli IN ALL ITS glorious, green form

is a nutritional powerhouse packed with vitamin C, heart-protecting beta-carotene, and plant chemicals that may keep breast cancer at bay. That's why it's good to "stalk" up on this winter-friendly vegetable. As you can see from the photographs, you have a lot to choose from when scouting for broccoli at the supermarket. Just look for firm stalks with deep green or purplish green heads that are tightly packed. Heads that are light green or those that have tiny yellow flowers are past their prime, so avoid them. To store fresh broccoli, keep it in a plastic bag in the refrigerator for up to 4 days. You can also blanch or steam broccoli slightly and freeze it for up to a year. If broccoli stems seem tough, use a sharp knife to peel away the tough outer skin to use the more tender center portion of the stems.

Gai Lan

Look for this green *(left)*, also called Chinese broccoli, in Asian food stores. To cook, separate leaves from stalks. Cook stalks in boiling water until tender. Add leaves; cook until wilted. Stir-fry cooked greens in peanut oil; add ginger, chili peppers, and/or hoisin sauce.

Broccoli

You can't miss this familiar green *(below)* in the produce aisles because it's there nearly year-round. For a change, finely chop raw broccoli, mix with shredded carrot, and sprinkle with an herbed salt. Use the crunchy mix to fill a sandwich of whole-grain bread slathered with cream cheese.

Pacific Rim Stir-Fry

PREP: 25 minutes **COOK:** 15 minutes

- **3 oz. rice sticks, rice noodles, or thin vermicelli, broken**
- **12 oz. skinless, boneless chicken thighs or breast halves**
- **$\frac{1}{2}$ cup chicken broth**
- **2 Tbsp. soy sauce**
- **2 tsp. cornstarch**
- **$\frac{1}{2}$ tsp. crushed red pepper**
- **$\frac{1}{2}$ tsp. ground turmeric**
- **1 Tbsp. cooking oil**
- **2 medium carrots, cut into short strips or thinly sliced (1 cup)**
- **2 cups broccoli flowerets**
- **1 red or green sweet pepper, cut into 1-inch strips ($\frac{1}{2}$ cup)**
- **2 Tbsp. snipped fresh basil**
- **$\frac{1}{4}$ cup cashew halves or peanuts**

1. In a saucepan cook rice sticks or noodles in boiling water for 3 minutes. (Or cook vermicelli according to package directions.) Drain; keep warm.

2. Meanwhile, cut chicken into thin, bite-size strips. For sauce, combine broth, soy sauce, cornstarch, crushed red pepper, and turmeric; set aside.

3. Add oil to wok or skillet. Preheat over medium-high heat (add more oil if necessary during cooking). Cook and stir carrots in hot oil for 1 minute. Add broccoli; cook and stir 2 minutes. Add sweet pepper; cook and stir $1\frac{1}{2}$ to 2 minutes more or until crisp-tender. Remove.

4. Add chicken; cook and stir 2 to 3 minutes or until no longer pink. Push from center. Stir sauce; add to center. Cook and stir until bubbly. Return vegetables; add basil. Cook and stir 2 minutes or until heated through. Serve over rice sticks; sprinkle with nuts. Makes 4 servings.

Each serving: 313 cal., 13 g total fat (2 g sat. fat), 70 mg chol., 703 mg sodium, 30 g carbo., 3 g fiber, and 22 g pro. Daily Values: 201% vit. A, 146% vit. C, 5% calcium, 13% iron.

Oat Cuisine

Seared Peppers, Black Beans, and Groats

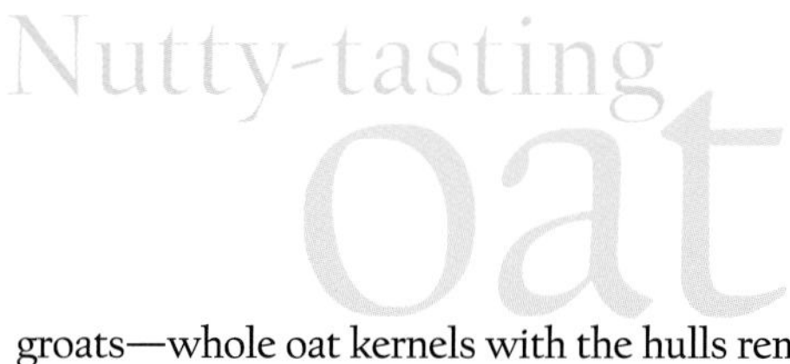

Nutty-tasting oat

groats—whole oat kernels with the hulls removed—go beyond the basic breakfast oatmeal. In fact, they're main-dish delicious, as this recipe (right) shows. "People, especially those at risk for heart disease, should consider eating oats regularly," says Dr. David Katz, Yale School of Medicine. A small Yale study led by Katz showed that oatmeal consumed immediately after a fat-laden milk shake kept participants' arteries from narrowing, which happens to some people after eating foods high in saturated fats.

"A bowl of oatmeal showed the same ability to keep blood vessels open as 800 IU of vitamin E. It looks like oats may be comfort food for our blood vessels," Katz says. Whole grains, such as oats, wheat, and brown rice, are so nutritionally powerful that the USDA urges you to use them for half of the suggested six daily servings of grain-based products.

Oats are packed with soluble fiber, which helps remove cholesterol and reduces blood pressure. For diabetics, fiber may slow digestion—preventing steep rises in blood sugar levels. Fiber also gives the body long-lasting energy and helps keep you feeling full longer.

Seared Peppers, Black Beans, and Groats

START TO FINISH: 25 minutes

- 2 cups water
- 3/4 cup oat groats
- 1/4 tsp. salt
- 1 Tbsp. olive oil or cooking oil
- 1 large sweet green pepper, cut into strips
- 1 1/2 tsp. Cajun seasoning
- 1 15-oz. can black beans, rinsed and drained
- 1 cup cherry tomatoes, halved
- 1/4 cup sliced green onion
- 2 Tbsp. crumbled kasseri or farmer cheese

1. In a saucepan bring water, groats, and salt to boiling; reduce heat. Cover and simmer about 15 minutes or until the groats are tender. Drain excess liquid.

2. Meanwhile, in a large nonstick skillet heat oil. Add pepper strips. Cook and stir over medium-high heat for 4 minutes or until peppers begin to brown. Add Cajun seasoning; cook and stir for 30 seconds. Reduce heat to medium. Add beans. Cook and stir for 2 minutes more or until heated through. Stir in tomatoes. Remove from heat.

3. To serve, place groats in bowl. Top with sweet pepper mixture, green onions, and cheese. Makes 3 servings.

Each serving: 343 cal., 10 g total fat (3 g sat. fat), 7 mg chol., 718 mg sodium, 53 g carbo., 13 g fiber, and 18 g pro. Daily Values: 14% vit. A, 85% vit. C, 13% calcium, 24% iron.

The mighty oat

Take your pick from the oat family. Look in natural foods stores if you don't see them on your grocer's shelves.

GROATS: Whole oat kernels with hulls removed; wild rice texture, nutty taste.

STEEL-CUT OATS: Groats that are thinly sliced; hearty, chewy consistency.

ROLLED OATS: Groats that are steamed and rolled flat.

QUICK-COOKING: Sliced rolled oats.

INSTANT OATS: Precooked and dried rolled oats.

February

FOR THOSE WHOSE PASSIONS INCLUDE AN ABIDING LOVE OF CHOCOLATE, PREPARE FOR A DEEPER RELATIONSHIP.

Dark Chocolate Brownies

Chocolate Sherbet

Milk Chocolate Mini Cookies

A Great Time for Chocolate

Chocolate-Crusted Chocolate Tarts

Chocolate-Cherry Cheesecake

Lavender Crème Brûlée

Desserts

Plus...

Double-Deck Chocolate Custard

Displaying two-toned chocolate splendor, this dessert looks best when served in a parade of small, mismatched glasses.

PREP: 15 minutes **COOL:** 5 minutes **CHILL:** 2 + 4 hours

- 2 cups whipping cream
- 3 oz. 30- to 40-percent-cocoa milk chocolate, chopped
- 6 Tbsp. sugar
- 4 egg yolks
- 1 tsp. vanilla
- 3 oz. 60- to 70-percent-cocoa dark chocolate or bittersweet chocolate, chopped

1. In a small heavy saucepan combine 1 cup of the whipping cream, the 3 ounces milk chocolate, and 3 tablespoons of the sugar. Cook and stir over medium heat about 5 minutes or until mixture comes to a full boil and thickens. (If chocolate flecks remain, use a wire whisk to beat mixture until blended.)

2. In a medium bowl beat 2 of the egg yolks until blended. Gradually stir all of the hot mixture into the beaten egg yolks; stir in 1/2 teaspoon of the vanilla. If using glasses, cool slightly. Divide chocolate mixture evenly into 8 small glasses, dishes, pot de crème cups, or ramekins. Cover and chill for 2 hours.

3. Make second layer of dessert using the same method with the remaining whipping cream, the 3 ounces dark chocolate, remaining sugar, egg yolks, and vanilla. Divide dark chocolate mixture among chilled glasses. Cover and chill about 4 hours or until firm. Makes 8 servings.

Each serving: 384 cal., 32 g total fat (17 g sat. fat), 191 mg chol., 37 mg sodium, 23 g carbo., 1 g fiber, 4 g pro. Daily Values: 21% vit. A, 1% vit. C, 8% calcium, 4% iron.

Double-Deck Chocolate Custard

Start light

We live in tempting times, the very heart of a chocolate renaissance. Chocolatiers all over the world are turning out slabs, bars, and squares that manage to embody sublime, but surprisingly different, tastes. A single bite may reveal a refined, subdued sweetness that seems to melt into earthier flavors springing from cocoa's origins deep in equatorial jungles.

Experience this transformation by hosting a chocolate tasting party for friends. Gather the four or five people who've been nicest to you lately, and serve them some of the desserts on these pages, along with samples of the chocolate that went into each. It's just like a wine or cheese tasting. Start by trying mild chocolates, then move up the scale to a finale of the darkest, richest ones.

41-percent-cocoa milk chocolate

38-percent-cocoa milk chocolate

FAMILIAR JOYS

To begin your tasting, offer two or three samples of milk chocolate from different makers *(above)*; alongside, set out Double-Deck Chocolate Custard. It beckons with a cloudlike layer of milk chocolate perched atop or nestled below a darker, bittersweet layer. Milk chocolate is notable for such great flavors as caramel, soda-fountain chocolate malt, chocolate milk, brown sugar, and vanilla.

A great time for Chocolate

Frozen Chocolate Nougat Mousse

DEEPER, RICHER, DARKER–A NEW GENERATION OF CHOCOLATES HAS ARRIVED! SO GATHER YOUR FRIENDS AND HOST A TASTING PARTY. IT PROMISES TO BE ABOUT THE MOST FUN ANYONE'S TASTE BUDS WILL HAVE ALL YEAR.

TREAT YOURSELF TO YOUR HEART'S DESIRE THIS MONTH WITH DELECTABLE DESSERTS AND HEART-HEALTHY SOUPS AND SIDES.

Valentine Granita

Chocolate Tartlettes

Jam Roly-Polys

Winter Fruit Soup

Build to medium

Be sure to have plenty of coffee or a lusciously soft and fruity wine or two on hand. And don't leave out one of the great joys in life—icy glasses of milk served with a plate of Milk Chocolate Mini Cookies *(page 46)*.

Take time to break off samples of raw chocolate. The sensation of pure pleasure melting on the tongue will delight your guests. They will experience surprising flavors such as cherry, jasmine, rose, almond, and raisin.

All the flavor nuances will make an invitation to your chocolate-tasting party a thing to toast.

61-percent-cocoa bittersweet chocolate

62-percent-cocoa bittersweet chocolate

NUTTY, EARTHY

When your tasting gets to midpoint, set up small plates with two or three varieties of medium (around 60 percent) chocolate. As you sample these chocolates, you'll begin entering unfamiliar territory. These are the woodsy, nuttier, darker chocolates that adults often prefer. This variety is used in these desserts: Simple Fudge *(right)*, Ultimate Chocolate Sundaes *(page 49)*, Chocolate Sherbet *(page 50)*, and Frozen Chocolate Nougat Mousse *(page 46)*.

Simple Fudge

PREP: 10 minutes **COOK:** 12 minutes **CHILL:** 3 hours

- Butter
- 1½ cups sugar
- ⅔ cup half-and-half or light cream
- ½ cup butter
- 2 cups tiny marshmallows or 14 large marshmallows
- 6 oz. 60-percent-cocoa chocolate, chopped, or 6 oz. (1 cup) semisweet chocolate pieces
- ½ cup slivered almonds or chopped walnuts, toasted (optional)
- 1 tsp. vanilla
- Unsweetened cocoa powder (optional)

1. Line an 8×8×2-inch baking pan with foil, extending foil over edges of pan. Butter foil; set aside.

2. Butter sides of a heavy 2-quart saucepan. (Without a heavy pan, the mixture will overcook and separate.) In saucepan combine sugar, cream, and ½ cup butter. Cook and stir over medium-high heat for 2 to 3 minutes or until mixture boils. Reduce heat to medium; continue cooking for 10 minutes. Boil slowly and stir constantly (mixture should not brown).

3. Remove pan from heat. Add marshmallows, chocolate, nuts (if desired), and vanilla. Stir until mixture is melted and combined. Beat by hand for 1 minute.

4. Spread fudge evenly in prepared pan. Score into squares while warm. Cover and chill for 3 to 4 hours or until firm. When firm, use foil to lift from pan. Cut fudge into squares, then cut each in half to make triangles. Store tightly covered in the refrigerator for up to 1 month. If desired, lightly sift cocoa powder over fudge before serving. Makes about 2 pounds (64 pieces).

Each piece: 53 cal., 3 g total fat (2 g sat. fat), 5 mg chol., 19 mg sodium, 8 g carbo., 0 g fiber, 0 g pro. Daily Values: 1% iron.

Simple Fudge

Dark Chocolate Torte

Dark Chocolate Torte

PREP: 45 minutes **BAKE:** 30 minutes **COOL:** 2 hours **CHILL:** 30 minutes

- 5 oz. 90- to 99-percent-cocoa chocolate or unsweetened chocolate, coarsely chopped
- 1/2 cup butter
- 6 egg whites
- 2/3 cup all-purpose flour
- 1/2 tsp. baking powder
- 6 egg yolks
- 1 1/2 tsp. vanilla
- 1 1/4 cups sugar
- 3/4 cup strawberry-balsamic jam* or apricot preserves
- 1 recipe Chocolate Ganache (below)

1. In a medium saucepan melt chocolate and butter over low heat; transfer to a bowl and cool completely. In a large mixing bowl let egg whites stand at room temperature for 30 minutes. Grease and lightly flour a 9-inch springform pan. In a small bowl stir together the flour and baking powder. Set aside.

2. Preheat oven to 350° F. Stir egg yolks and vanilla into the cooled chocolate mixture (mixture will become stiffer); set aside.

3. Beat egg whites with an electric mixer on medium speed until soft peaks form (tips curl). Gradually add the sugar, about 1 tablespoon at a time, beating on high speed about 4 minutes or until stiff peaks form (tips stand straight).

4. Fold about one-third of the egg white mixture into chocolate mixture. Fold chocolate mixture into remaining egg white mixture. Sift about one-third of the flour mixture over egg mixture; gently fold in. Repeat twice, sifting and folding in one-third of the flour mixture at a time. Spread batter into prepared pan. Bake about 30 minutes or until wooden toothpick inserted near center comes out clean. Cool cake completely in pan on wire rack.

5. Meanwhile, stir jam to thin; set aside. Prepare Chocolate Ganache; set aside. Loosen cake from sides of pan; remove sides. Carefully remove bottom of pan from cake by loosening the cake with a knife.

6. To assemble, cut cake horizontally into 2 even layers. Place bottom layer, cut side up, on a wire rack set over waxed paper. Spread jam onto top of this layer. Top with second layer, cut side down. Pour Chocolate Ganache over torte, spreading to glaze top and sides. (If glaze drips onto the waxed paper, spoon it onto torte.) Chill cake on rack about 30 minutes or until glaze sets. Carefully transfer cake to a platter. Makes 14 to 16 servings.

CHOCOLATE GANACHE: Coarsely chop 6 ounces 70-percent-cocoa chocolate or semisweet or bittersweet chocolate; set aside. In a medium saucepan bring 1/2 cup whipping cream to boiling over medium-high heat; remove from heat. Add chocolate (do not stir). Let stand 5 minutes. Stir until smooth. Cool 10 minutes.

***NOTE:** Find strawberry-balsamic jam at kitchen shops. Or combine 3/4 cup strawberry jam and 1 tablespoon balsamic vinegar.

Each serving: 375 cal., 21 g total fat (12 g sat. fat), 122 mg chol., 122 mg sodium, 44 g carbo., 3 g fiber, 6 g pro. Daily Values: 11% vit. A, 3% vit. C, 4% calcium, 11% iron.

Finish dark

At some point during the party, give your guests a little overview on what they're tasting. Here's a short course: Artisanal chocolatiers follow the milk, semisweet, and bittersweet labeling that larger chocolate makers use, but artisans also denote the percentage of cocoa and cocoa butter (or cacao). The higher the number, the less sweet and the more bitter and intense the chocolate. Cocoa percentages range from about 30 to 45 percent in milk chocolate to 50 to 60 percent for semisweet. Above that is bittersweet—from 61 to 80 percent. Unsweetened is 99 percent cocoa.

A big bite of 85-percent-cocoa chocolate is overwhelming, but a tiny piece melting on your tongue is a fun way to discover chocolate's complexity. These chocolates have little or no sugar and offer such aromas and flavors as cedar and coffee. The effect is an intense, lingering, but not unpleasant, bitter sensation.

85-percent-cocoa dark chocolate

85-percent-cocoa dark chocolate

BITTERSWEET AND BEYOND

Now for the tasting finale. Bring out the stoutest chocolates of all—the really dark chocolates. Offer samples of two types for tasting, followed by one last dessert. In Vienna, the locals sit at little marble tables in cafes drinking tiny cups of coffee and eating a low, dense layer cake very much like this Dark Chocolate Torte. The taste is subtle but irresistible. It is made with the most intensely complex of all chocolates: unsweetened.

Frozen Chocolate Nougat Mousse

Nougat is a crispy white confection that can be found in Italian and other European import stores as well as the candy section of some supermarkets.

PREP: 30 minutes **CHILL:** 30 minutes
FREEZE: 3 hours **STAND:** 10 minutes

- **3½ to 4 oz. 69- to 73-percent-cocoa chocolate or bittersweet chocolate, finely chopped**
- **¼ cup milk**
- **¾ tsp. unflavored gelatin**
- **4 egg yolks, slightly beaten**
- **½ cup sugar**
- **1¼ cups whipping cream**
- **½ tsp. vanilla**
- **⅓ cup chopped Italian nougat candy or almond toffee bits**

1. Place finely chopped chocolate in a large bowl; set aside. In a small saucepan combine milk and gelatin. Let stand for 5 minutes. Add egg yolks, sugar, and ½ cup of the whipping cream. Cook and stir over medium heat about 5 minutes or until mixture coats a metal spoon (160° F).

2. Pour mixture over finely chopped chocolate. Let stand for 5 minutes. Gently stir to incorporate chocolate. Stir in vanilla. Place in freezer; chill for 30 minutes or until mixture thickens and cools, stirring after 15 minutes.

3. Meanwhile, place six 3-ounce small cups or soufflé dishes on a tray (or use 4-ounce dessert dishes and do not add collars). To prepare collars, cut six 12×6-inch pieces of foil. Fold lengthwise into thirds to form 12×2-inch strips. Wrap each collar tightly around the cups with one edge extending 1 inch above the top of the cups. Secure with tape. Place cups in freezer to chill.

4. Meanwhile, beat chocolate mixture with an electric mixer on high speed about 3 minutes or until light and fluffy. In a small bowl beat the remaining ¾ cup whipping cream until soft peaks form (tips curl). Gently fold whipped cream and nougat candy or toffee bits into chocolate mixture. Divide chocolate mixture evenly among the chilled cups, filling ½ to 1 inch over the top of each dish, if collar is present. Cover and freeze for 3 to 24 hours or until firm.

5. To serve, remove tape and gently peel away collars. Let mousse stand for 10 to 15 minutes at room temperature before serving. Makes 6 servings.

Each serving: 395 cal., 29 g total fat (16 g sat. fat), 212 mg chol., 0 mg sodium, 33 g carbo., 1 g fiber, 5 g pro. Daily Values: 20% vit. A, 1% vit. C, 8% calcium, 5% iron.

Milk Chocolate Mini Cookies

For an extra dose of tangy sweetness, fill the cookies with the optional Milk Chocolate-Sour Cream Frosting.

PREP: 45 minutes **FREEZE:** 25 minutes **BAKE:** 9 minutes per batch

- **¾ cup all-purpose flour**
- **¾ tsp. baking powder**
- **⅛ tsp. salt**
- **6 oz. 30- to 40-percent-cocoa chocolate or milk chocolate**
- **3 Tbsp. butter, softened**
- **½ cup sugar**
- **1 egg**
- **¾ tsp. vanilla**
- **1 recipe Milk Chocolate-Sour Cream Frosting (below) (optional)**

1. In a medium bowl combine flour, baking powder, and salt; set aside.

2. In a small heavy saucepan heat the chocolate over low heat until melted, stirring constantly; set aside.

3. In a medium mixing bowl beat butter with electric mixer on medium speed for 30 seconds. Beat in sugar until fluffy. Beat in melted chocolate, egg, and vanilla until combined.

4. Gradually beat in the flour mixture. Divide dough into 4 equal portions. Wrap each portion in plastic wrap. Chill in the freezer for 20 to 30 minutes or until firm enough to handle. (Or, chill in the refrigerator for 1 hour.)

5. Preheat oven to 350° F. Removing 1 portion of dough from freezer at a time, roll each portion into a 10-inch-long roll.* Cut each roll crosswise into ¼-inch-thick slices. Place slices 1 inch apart on ungreased cookie sheets. Bake for 9 to 10 minutes or until edges are set. Let cool on cookie sheet for 2 minutes. Gently remove from sheets (cookies will be brittle). Transfer to a wire rack to cool completely.

6. If desired, spread ½ teaspoon of frosting on half of the cookies; top with remaining cookies. Serve the same day. To store, place plain cookies in airtight containers at room temperature for up to 3 days or freeze in a freezer container for up to 3 months. Thaw, then fill, if desired. Makes 72 sandwich cookies or 144 unfrosted cookies.

MILK CHOCOLATE-SOUR CREAM FROSTING: In a medium saucepan melt 3 ounces chopped 30- to 40-percent-cocoa chocolate or milk chocolate and 2 tablespoons butter over low heat, stirring frequently. Cool for 5 minutes. Stir in ¼ cup dairy sour cream. Gradually stir in 1 to 1¼ cups sifted powdered sugar until spreadable.

***NOTE:** It helps to place the dough on a sheet of waxed paper and use the paper to help shape the roll. If dough becomes too sticky, return it to freezer for a few minutes.

Each sandwich cookie: 45 cal., 2 g total fat (1 g sat. fat), 6 mg chol., 21 mg sodium, 6 g carbo., 0 g fiber, 0 g pro. Daily Values: 1% vit. A, 1% calcium, 1% iron.

Milk Chocolate Mini Cookies

THE ART OF THE BUNNY SNIFF

Here's how to get the most out of your chocolate-tasting experience.

LOOK: Chocolate should be shiny, but sometimes has a slightly grayish cast. This is called "bloom" and indicates that the chocolate has experienced temperature fluctuations. Luckily, bloom doesn't usually affect flavor. Examine the color of chocolate, but don't let hue be your only guide; darkness varies by the type of beans used and how they're processed.

BUNNY SNIFFS: Break off a small piece and rub gently until the chocolate just begins to soften. Then take tiny sniffs. In addition to chocolate, you'll discover such aromas as apple pie, flowers, caramel, citrus, berries, grass, and cedar.

TASTE: Pop the piece into your mouth, but don't chew! Let it melt on your tongue for 20 seconds. Some of the flavors you'll encounter include vanilla, fruit, and nuts. Other words that might come to mind: fudgy, smoky, malty, earthy, and tart. Savor the balance of nuttiness, acidity, sweetness, and bitterness.

TEXTURE: Is it smooth, velvety, creamy, soft? Or is it a little gritty? All these textures can be wonderful in chocolate because of the way they interact with the flavors. Smooth chocolates emphasize the fruity, flowery flavors, while gritty chocolates bring out the earthy, nutty side.

Ultimate Chocolate Sundaes

Chocolate-Crusted Chocolate Tarts

STORING CHOCOLATE

- Chocolate must be stored below 70° F—which means in your refrigerator or freezer, especially in summer. It has to be tightly wrapped and kept away from strong-smelling foods.
- When you remove it from the fridge, leave it in its wrapping until it's at room temperature. Water condensing on the surface can cause problems in melting and cooking.
- Dark chocolate candy will keep in the refrigerator for up to one year; milk chocolate will keep for six months. Filled chocolate candy can be stored for up to three months. All chocolate will keep in the freezer up to one year.

Chocolate-Crusted Chocolate Tarts

Work carefully to get an even layer of crust in the muffin tins.

PREP: 20 minutes **BAKE:** 25 minutes

- **1 recipe Chocolate-Hazelnut Tart Shells (below)**
- **10 to 10½ oz. 85-percent-cocoa chocolate or bittersweet chocolate, finely chopped**
- **¾ cup whipping cream**
- **½ cup milk**
- **3 Tbsp. flavored honey (raspberry, cinnamon, or ginger)**
- **1 egg**
- **Halved or chopped hazelnuts (filberts) (optional)**

1. Prepare Chocolate-Hazelnut Tart Shells; set aside to cool.

2. Preheat oven to 325° F. In a 1-quart casserole combine chocolate, whipping cream, and milk. Microwave, uncovered, on 100 percent power (high) for 3 to 4 minutes or until chocolate is melted and mixture is smooth, stirring once each minute. Stir in honey. (Or, place chocolate in a medium bowl. Set aside. In a small saucepan combine cream and milk. Bring to boiling. Pour over chocolate. Stir until chocolate is melted. Stir in honey.)

3. In another medium bowl beat egg. Gradually stir in hot chocolate mixture. Pour into tart shells.

4. Bake for 25 minutes. Cool slightly on a wire rack. Serve warm. If desired, garnish with nuts. Makes 8 servings.

CHOCOLATE-HAZELNUT TART SHELLS: Preheat oven to 375° F. Lightly coat twelve 2½-inch muffin pans with nonstick cooking spray. In a small bowl stir together 1 cup crushed chocolate wafer crumbs, ⅓ cup ground hazelnuts (filberts), ⅓ cup melted butter, and 1 tablespoon sugar. Press onto the bottom and sides of prepared muffin cups. Bake for 5 minutes. Cool on a wire rack.

Each tart: 378 cal., 28 g total fat (14 g sat. fat), 60 mg chol., 217 mg sodium, 33 g carbo., 3 g fiber, 5 g pro. Daily Values: 11% vit. A, 1% vit. C, 4% calcium, 10% iron.

CHOCOLATE DESSERT TASTING

Double-Deck Chocolate Custard *(page 39)*
Milk Chocolate Mini Cookies *(page 46)*
Chocolate Sherbet *(page 50)*
Dark Chocolate Torte *(page 45)*
Assorted broken pieces of 40- to 80-percent-cocoa chocolate
Cold milk and dark-roast coffee, such as French or Italian roast

Ultimate Chocolate Sundaes

It is essential that the water and chocolate are together from the very beginning of cooking; otherwise, they won't blend properly when heated.

START TO FINISH: 30 minutes

- **8 oz. 65-percent-cocoa chocolate or bittersweet chocolate, coarsely chopped**
- **⅓ cup water**
- **¼ cup sugar**
- **¼ cup pear liqueur or pear nectar**
- **4 small fresh Forelle or Bosc pears (1 lb. total)**
- **3 Tbsp. butter**
- **2 Tbsp. sugar**
- **1 qt. vanilla ice cream**

1. For chocolate sauce, in a small saucepan combine chocolate, water, and the ¼ cup sugar. Melt chocolate over low heat, stirring slowly and constantly. Stir in pear liqueur or nectar. Set aside to cool slightly.

2. Peel pears, if desired; cut into halves and remove cores.* Leave stem on one portion, if desired. In a large skillet melt butter. Add pear halves; cook over medium heat about 12 minutes or until brown and tender, turning once. Add the 2 tablespoons sugar, stirring gently until sugar is dissolved and pears are glazed.

3. To assemble, place scoops of ice cream in 8 bowls. Spoon a pear half and some butter mixture around the ice cream in each bowl. Top with the chocolate sauce. Makes 8 servings.

***NOTE:** If using large pears, use only 2 pears and cut them into fourths.

Each serving: 538 cal., 33 g total fat (20 g sat. fat), 132 mg chol., 119 mg sodium, 56 g carbo., 3 g fiber, 7 g pro. Daily Values: 19% vit. A, 4% vit. C, 17% calcium, 6% iron.

Dark Chocolate Brownies

Chocolate Sherbet

The chocolate mixture needs to chill overnight in order to freeze properly. What differentiates a sherbet from a sorbet is the use of a milk product—in this case it's cream.

PREP: 25 minutes **CHILL:** overnight **FREEZE:** 30 minutes + 4 hours

- **6 to 7 oz. 60-percent-cocoa chocolate or bittersweet chocolate, chopped**
- **2 cups water**
- **2/3 cup sugar**
- **1/2 cup whipping cream**
- **1 tsp. vanilla**
- **Pomegranate seeds (optional)**

1. In a medium saucepan stir together chopped chocolate, water, sugar, and whipping cream. Bring to boiling, whisking constantly. Boil gently for 1 minute. Remove from heat; stir in vanilla. Cover and chill overnight.

2. Freeze mixture in a 1-quart ice cream freezer according to manufacturer's directions. Allow to firm up in freezer for 4 hours before serving. To serve, scoop into 12 bowls. If desired, garnish with pomegranate seeds. Makes 12 servings.

Each serving: 157 cal., 9 g total fat (6 g sat. fat), 14 mg chol., 6 mg sodium, 20 g carbo., 1 g fiber, 1 g pro. Daily Values: 3% vit. A, 1% calcium, 3% iron.

Dark Chocolate Brownies

As our recipe demonstrates, it's OK to melt chocolate in a microwave oven. The key is to heat it for a short time, then to stir to complete the melting process.

PREP: 25 minutes **FREEZE:** 2 hours
BAKE: 25 minutes **COOL:** 30 minutes

- **1 recipe Frozen Coffee Whipped Cream (below)**
- **7 oz. 99-percent-cocoa chocolate or unsweetened chocolate, coarsely chopped**
- **3/4 cup butter**
- **1/4 cup water**
- **1 cup granulated sugar**
- **3/4 cup packed brown sugar**
- **2 eggs**
- **1 tsp. vanilla**
- **1 1/3 cups all-purpose flour**
- **1/8 tsp. salt**
- **1/8 tsp. ground cinnamon**

1. Prepare Frozen Coffee Whipped Cream. For brownies, lightly grease a 9×9×2-inch baking pan; set pan aside. Preheat oven to 350° F.

2. In a large microwave-safe mixing bowl combine chocolate, butter, and water. Microwave, uncovered, on 100 percent power (high) for 2 to 3 minutes or until butter is melted, stirring once or twice. Remove bowl from microwave oven. Stir until chocolate is completely melted. (Or, combine chocolate, butter, and water in a medium saucepan; cook and stir over low heat until chocolate is melted. Transfer to a mixing bowl.)

3. Beat in granulated sugar and brown sugar with an electric mixer on low to medium speed until combined. Add eggs and vanilla; beat on medium speed for 2 minutes. Add flour, salt, and cinnamon. Beat on low speed until combined. Spread batter in prepared pan.

4. Bake about 25 minutes or until a toothpick inserted near center comes out clean. Cool on a wire rack about 30 minutes (or until brownies hold a cut edge). Cut into bars.

5. To assemble, while brownie is still warm, place a bar on each plate. Top with a scoop of Frozen Coffee Whipped Cream. Makes 20 to 25 brownies.

FROZEN COFFEE WHIPPED CREAM: Chill a medium mixing bowl and the beaters of an electric mixer. In the chilled bowl combine 2/3 cup whipping cream, 4 teaspoons sugar, and 4 teaspoons cooled brewed espresso or 1/2 teaspoon vanilla. Beat on medium speed until soft peaks form (tips curl). Cover and freeze for 2 to 3 hours or until firm. Let stand at room temperature for 10 minutes to soften slightly. Using 2 teaspoons, shape small ovals of frozen whipped cream, dipping spoons into hot water if necessary.

Each brownie with whipped cream: 304 cal., 19 g total fat (10 g sat. fat), 52 mg chol., 121 mg sodium, 35 g carbo., 2 g fiber, and 3 g pro. Daily Values: 9% vit. A, 4% calcium, 8% iron.

Chocolate Sherbet

HOW TO MEASURE CHOCOLATE

All the recipes in this story were created and tested to be made with either standard 1-ounce squares or 3.5-ounce (100-gram) bars. Recipes work equally well with either. If you buy 250-gram (8.75-oz.) bars or 275-gram (9.7-oz. bars), fear not. They're usually scored in convenient measurements that will allow you to break off what you need. In these recipes, there's some wiggle room, so you can be off by a square or two without affecting the final product.

AS THE CURTAIN RISES ON DINNER'S FINALE, THE SPOTLIGHT IS ON A COMPANY-FRIENDLY SWEET SOUFFLÉ, A JEWEL-LIKE GRANITA, OR PIXIE-SIZE CHOCOLATE PIES.

Encore! DESSERTS

Strawberry Soufflé

Strawberry Soufflé

Plan ahead so you can prepare this airy dessert with minimal fuss at dinnertime. Before sitting down to dine, prepare the soufflé dishes, separate the egg whites, blend the strawberries, and preheat the oven. After dinner, just whip the egg whites, fold in the strawberries, and bake.

PREP: 20 minutes **BAKE:** 15 minutes

- 5 egg whites
- Margarine or butter
- Sugar
- 2 cups sliced fresh strawberries
- 1/4 to 1/3 cup sugar
- 4 tsp. cornstarch
- 1/2 cup sugar
- Strawberry or chocolate syrup

1. Let egg whites stand at room temperature for 30 minutes. Using margarine or butter, grease six 1-cup soufflé dishes or 10-ounce custard cups. Sprinkle with sugar, shaking out any excess sugar. Place on a shallow baking pan or baking sheet.

2. Meanwhile, in a medium bowl combine strawberries and the 1/4 to 1/3 cup sugar. Let stand 15 minutes until strawberries become juicy. In a blender container or food processor bowl combine strawberry mixture and cornstarch. Cover and blend or process until smooth. Set aside.

3. Preheat oven to 350° F. In a large mixing bowl beat egg whites until soft peaks form (tips curl). Gradually add the 1/2 cup sugar, beating for 2 to 3 minutes or until stiff glossy peaks form *(see photo below)*.

4. With a rubber spatula, push beaten egg whites to the side of the bowl. Pour strawberry mixture into bottom of the bowl. Carefully stir a little of the beaten egg whites into strawberry mixture. Then gently fold the two mixtures together (there should be a few white streaks remaining). Divide mixture evenly among prepared dishes.

5. Bake for 15 to 18 minutes or until a knife inserted near the center comes out clean. Serve immediately with strawberry or chocolate syrup. Makes 6 individual soufflés.

Each soufflé: 248 cal., 2 g total fat (1 g sat. fat), 4 mg chol., 70 mg sodium, 57 g carbo., 1 g fiber, 3 g pro. Daily Values: 1% vit. A, 45% vit. C, 1% calcium, 1% iron.

Egg whites are considered stiff when they form peaks that stand up straight and form a curl as you lift the beaters.

Jam Roly-Polys

Jam Roly-Polys

We chose apricot and raspberry jam because we love them together, but feel free to substitute other fruit preserves.

PREP: 25 minutes **BAKE:** 20 minutes

- 1 cup all-purpose flour
- 1 1/2 tsp. baking powder
- 1/4 tsp. salt
- 3 Tbsp. shortening
- 1/3 cup milk
- 2 Tbsp. apricot or peach preserves or jam
- 2 Tbsp. seedless raspberry or strawberry jam
- 1 recipe Lemon-Sour Cream Sauce (below)

1. Preheat oven to 375° F. In a medium bowl stir together the flour, baking powder, and salt. Cut in the shortening until mixture resembles coarse crumbs. Make a well in the center. Add milk all at once. Using a fork, stir just until moistened. Turn dough out onto a lightly floured surface. Quickly knead dough 10 to 12 strokes or until nearly smooth.

2. Roll dough to a 12×8-inch rectangle. Spread apricot or peach preserves lengthwise over half of the dough, leaving a 1/2-inch border around the edges. Spread raspberry or strawberry jam lengthwise over remaining half of dough, leaving a 1/2-inch border around edges. Roll the two long sides, scroll fashion, to meet in the center. Where the rolls come together, brush with water and lightly squeeze together.

3. Line a baking sheet with foil; grease the foil. Transfer the roll to the baking sheet. Bake for 20 minutes or until golden. Cool for 10 minutes on the baking sheet. Cut roll into 1-inch-thick slices. Place two warm slices in each shallow bowl and pass Lemon-Sour Cream Sauce. Makes 5 servings.

LEMON-SOUR CREAM SAUCE: In a small saucepan combine 2/3 cup lemon curd and 1/3 cup dairy sour cream. Heat over low heat just until warm (do not boil).

Each serving: 374 cal., 13 g total fat (5 g sat. fat), 39 mg chol., 288 mg sodium, 63 g carbo., 5 g fiber, 4 g pro. Daily Values: 3% vit. A, 3% vit. C, 12% calcium, 8% iron.

Caramel-Bourbon Upside-Down Cake

As a shortcut, use the pre-peeled, pre-cored, fresh pineapple that's now available in many grocery stores.

PREP: 30 minutes **BAKE:** 20 minutes **COOL:** 35 minutes

- 1/4 cup butter or margarine
- 1/2 cup packed brown sugar
- 1/4 cup bourbon or orange juice
- 1 cup chopped fresh pineapple, well drained, or one 8-oz. can pineapple chunks or tidbits, drained
- 1/2 cup snipped dried apricots
- 1/4 cup golden raisins
- 1/4 cup toasted slivered almonds, pine nuts, or chopped macadamia nuts
- 1 cup all-purpose flour
- 1/2 cup cornmeal
- 2 Tbsp. granulated sugar
- 1 1/2 tsp. baking powder
- 1/4 tsp. salt
- 1/8 tsp. ground nutmeg
- 2 eggs, beaten
- 1/2 cup milk
- 2 Tbsp. cooking oil

1. Preheat oven to 400° F. Melt the butter or margarine in a 9×9×2-inch baking pan in the oven about 5 minutes. Stir in brown sugar and bourbon or orange juice. Spoon pineapple, apricots, raisins, and nuts into the pan. Stir together to mix, then spread out to form an even layer. Set pan aside.

2. In a medium mixing bowl stir together flour, cornmeal, granulated sugar, baking powder, salt, and nutmeg. Make a well in the center of the flour mixture. Set aside.

3. In another bowl combine the eggs, milk, and oil. Add all at once to flour mixture. Stir just until moistened. Carefully spoon batter in mounds over fruit mixture in pan; spread evenly.

4. Bake about 20 minutes or until a wooden toothpick inserted near center comes out clean. Cool on a wire rack for 5 minutes. Loosen sides; invert onto a plate. Spoon on any topping that falls off. Serve warm. Makes 8 servings.

TEST KITCHEN TIP: To reheat, place on a microwave-safe plate. Microwave on 100 percent power (high) for 20 seconds.

Each serving: 327 cal., 11 g total fat (3 g sat. fat), 62 mg chol., 210 mg sodium, 50 g carbo., 3 g fiber, 6 g pro. Daily Values: 17% vit. A, 6% vit. C, 11% calcium, 14% iron.

VALENTINE'S DAY MENU

Mixed greens and fruit salad
Garlicky Steak and Asparagus *(page 85)*
Baked potatoes and sour cream
Valentine Granita *(below)* or
Chocolate-Cherry Cheesecake *(page 58)*
Cabernet or Merlot wine

Valentine Granita

A granita is an Italian ice, similar to sorbet, only icier. This raspberry-mango combination flies the color of the day.

PREP: 20 minutes **FREEZE:** 9 hours **STAND:** 5 minutes

- 1 cup water
- 1/2 cup sugar
- 1 12-oz. pkg. frozen lightly sweetened red raspberries
- 1 medium fresh mango, peeled, seeded, and chopped
- Fresh red raspberries (optional)

1. In a medium saucepan combine water and sugar. Cook over medium heat just until mixture boils, stirring to dissolve sugar. Remove from heat and add the frozen raspberries and mango. Pour into a blender container or food processor bowl. Cover and blend or process until smooth. Strain through a fine mesh sieve (should have about 2 cups sieved fruit mixture).

2. Pour sieved mixture into a 13×9×2-inch baking pan or freezer container. Cover and freeze for 1 to 2 hours or until mixture is nearly frozen. Stir well, scraping frozen mixture from sides of pan or container *(see photo, below)*. Spread mixture to evenly cover bottom of pan or container. Cover and freeze at least 8 hours or overnight.

3. To serve, let stand at room temperature for 5 to 10 minutes. Use an ice cream scoop to spoon into four demitasse cups or dessert dishes. If desired, garnish with fresh berries. Makes 4 servings.

Each serving: 214 cal., 0 g total fat (0 g sat. fat), 0 mg chol., 4 mg sodium, 56 g carbo., 2 g fiber, 0 g pro. Daily Values: 41% vit. A, 48% vit. C, 2% calcium, 3% iron.

Stir the granita when it is still slushy. If you wait too long, it may freeze solid.

Valentine Granita

Lavender Crème Brûlée

Lavender Crème Brûlée

Caramelizing sugar in a pan means you don't have to place cold dishes under a hot broiler, which can cause them to shatter.

PREP: 20 minutes **BAKE:** 30 minutes **CHILL:** 1 hour

- **2 cups half-and-half or light cream**
- **2 to 3 tsp. dried lavender flowers or 1 Tbsp. snipped fresh basil**
- **5 egg yolks, slightly beaten**
- **1/3 cup sugar**
- **1 tsp. vanilla**
- **1/8 tsp. salt**
- **1 recipe Caramelized Sugar**

1. Preheat oven to 325° F. In a heavy small saucepan heat half-and-half or light cream and lavender or basil over medium-low heat just until bubbly. Remove from heat. Strain through a fine mesh sieve; discard lavender or basil. Set cream aside.

2. Meanwhile, in a medium bowl combine egg yolks, sugar, vanilla, and salt. Beat with a wire whisk or rotary beater just until combined. Slowly whisk the hot half-and-half or light cream into the egg mixture.

3. Place eight 4-ounce ramekins or six 6-ounce custard cups in a 13×9×2-inch baking pan. Place baking pan on the oven rack. Pour custard mixture evenly into the dishes or cups. Pour boiling water into baking pan around dishes, reaching halfway up the sides of dishes (about 1 inch deep).

4. Bake the custards for 30 to 35 minutes or until a knife inserted near the center of each custard comes out clean. Remove custards from baking pan; cool on wire rack. Cover and chill at least 1 hour or up to 8 hours.

5. Before serving, remove custards from refrigerator; let stand at room temperature for 20 minutes. Meanwhile, prepare Caramelized Sugar. Quickly drizzle the caramelized sugar over custards in desired pattern. If sugar starts to harden, return skillet to heat, stirring until melted. Makes 8 servings.

CARAMELIZED SUGAR: Place 1/3 cup sugar in a heavy skillet. Heat sugar over medium-high heat until it begins to melt. Do not stir. Once the sugar starts to melt, reduce heat to low and cook about 5 minutes more or until all of the sugar is melted and golden, stirring as needed with a wooden spoon.

Each serving: 178 cal., 10 g total fat (5 g sat. fat), 155 mg chol., 65 mg sodium, 19 g carbo., 0 g fiber, 4 g pro. Daily Values: 9% vit. A, 1% vit. C, 8% calcium, 2% iron.

Pear Ginger Flan

Pear Ginger Flan

To make sure all the flans are done, check one in the middle and one that's in the back of the oven.

PREP: 45 minutes **BAKE:** 50 minutes **CHILL:** 4 hours

- **3 cups chopped, peeled pears**
- **1/2 cup sugar**
- **1/3 cup water**
- **2 Tbsp. shredded fresh ginger**
- **3 eggs, beaten**
- **1 1/2 cups half-and-half or light cream**
- **1/3 cup sugar**
- **1 recipe Cheese Crisps (below)**

1. In a heavy medium saucepan combine pears, the 1/2 cup sugar, the 1/3 cup water, and ginger. Bring to boiling; reduce heat. Cover and cook until pears are tender. Drain, reserving liquid. Discard pears and ginger. Return liquid to saucepan. Cook over medium-high heat about 10 minutes or until liquid is syrupy and reduced to 1/4 cup. Quickly pour the syrup into four 6-ounce custard cups.

2. Preheat oven to 325° F. Place custard cups in a 2-quart square baking dish. Combine eggs, half-and-half or cream, and the 1/3 cup sugar. Pour over syrup in cups. Place baking dish on oven rack. Pour boiling water into dish around cups, reaching halfway up sides of cups (about 1 inch deep). Bake for 40 to 45 minutes or until a knife inserted near centers comes out clean. Remove cups from baking dish. Cool slightly on wire rack. Cover and chill for 4 to 24 hours.

3. To serve, unmold the flans onto dessert plates, scraping any remaining syrup in cups onto flans. Serve with cooled Cheese Crisps. Makes 4 servings.

CHEESE CRISPS: In a small bowl combine 2 tablespoons shredded white cheddar cheese and 2 tablespoons finely shredded Parmesan cheese. Using 1 tablespoon cheese mixture for each, place the shredded cheese on a nonstick baking sheet. Spread into 2-inch circles, spacing the circles about 2 inches apart. Bake in a 325° F oven for 10 to 12 minutes or just until the cheese begins to brown. Allow to cool on the baking sheet for 30 seconds, and then remove. Cool on a wire rack.

Each serving: 356 cal., 16 g total fat (9 g sat. fat), 200 mg chol., 129 mg sodium, 44 g carbo., 0 g fiber, 9 g pro. Daily Values: 14% vit. A, 1% vit. C, 16% calcium, 4% iron.

Caramel Clementines

Clementines, tangerines, and Dancy tangerines are all types of Mandarin oranges that you can use interchangeably.

PREP: 10 minutes **COOK:** 20 minutes

- 6 clementines or other tangerine variety
- 1 $14\frac{1}{2}$-oz. can apricot nectar ($1\frac{3}{4}$ cups)
- $\frac{1}{2}$ cup sugar
- Dash ground red pepper (optional)
- 2 Tbsp. Southern Comfort, orange liqueur, or orange juice
- Pomegranate seeds (optional)

1. Peel clementines and remove any of the fibrous strands of pith on the fruit. In a medium saucepan place clementines, apricot nectar, sugar, and, if desired, ground red pepper. Bring to boiling; reduce heat. Cover and simmer for 5 minutes. Using a slotted spoon, transfer fruit to six individual serving bowls.

2. Continue to gently boil apricot nectar mixture about 15 minutes or until thick and syrupy. Remove from heat. Stir Southern Comfort, orange liqueur, or juice into syrupy mixture. Spoon over fruit. If desired, sprinkle each serving with pomegranate seeds. Serve warm. Makes 6 servings.

Each serving: 151 cal., 0 g total fat (0 g sat. fat), 0 mg chol., 3 mg sodium, 36 g carbo., 2 g fiber, 1 g pro. Daily Values: 35% vit. A, 44% vit. C, 2% calcium, 2% iron.

Caramel Clementines

SIMPLE TOUCHES

- After everyone finishes dessert, bring out a bowl of lusciously ripe fruit and a pair of cheeses—maybe a soft Camembert and a divine farmhouse cheddar.
- Before conversation begins to flag—sneak back into the kitchen and reappear with your best serving platter stacked with a selection of luxurious chocolates.
- Showmanship is everything. Go beyond the basics and serve dessert on pedestals or in saucers, teacups, or glassware.

Chocolate-Cherry Cheesecake

To crush the cookies for the crust, put them into a resealable plastic bag, then press with a rolling pin.

PREP: 30 minutes **BAKE:** 25 minutes
COOL: 2 hours **CHILL:** 4 hours

- $\frac{1}{2}$ cup dried cherries
- $\frac{1}{4}$ cup chocolate liqueur
- 1 8-oz. pkg. cream cheese, softened
- 1 $4\frac{1}{2}$-oz. round Brie cheese, rind removed and cut up
- $\frac{1}{3}$ cup sugar
- 1 Tbsp. all-purpose flour
- 1 egg
- 1 egg yolk
- 2 Tbsp. milk
- 1 recipe Almond Crust (below)

1. Preheat oven to 375° F. In a small bowl combine dried cherries and chocolate liqueur. Set aside.

2. For filling, in a large mixing bowl beat cream cheese, Brie, sugar, and flour with an electric mixer on medium speed until combined. Add egg and yolk all at once, beating on low speed just until combined. Stir in milk and undrained cherries.

3. Pour filling into Almond Crust-lined pan. Place on a shallow baking pan in the oven. Bake about 25 minutes or until center appears nearly set when gently shaken.

4. Cool in pan on a wire rack for 15 minutes. Loosen the crust from side of pan; cool 30 minutes more. Remove the side of the pan; cool cheesecake completely. Cover and chill at least 4 hours before serving. Makes 8 servings.

ALMOND CRUST: In a medium bowl combine 1 cup crushed shortbread cookies (about 13 cookies) and $\frac{1}{2}$ cup ground almonds. Stir in 3 tablespoons melted butter. Press the crumb mixture onto the bottom and about 2 inches up the side of a 7-inch springform pan or about 1 inch up the side of an 8-inch springform pan (use a measuring cup to press crumbs onto pan). Set pan aside.

Each serving: 400 cal., 27 g total fat (13 g sat. fat), 115 mg chol., 294 mg sodium, 28 g carbo., 2 g fiber, 10 g pro. Daily Values: 16% vit. A, 9% calcium, 8% iron.

Chocolate-Cherry Cheesecake

Chocolate Tartlettes

Chocolate Tartlettes

If you're running a little behind, skip the petite tart shells and spoon the mousse onto shortbread cookies.

PREP: 35 minutes **BAKE:** 20 minutes **CHILL:** 1 hour

- 2/3 cup whipping cream
- 3 oz. semisweet or bittersweet chocolate, chopped
- 3 oz. milk chocolate, chopped
- 1 recipe Cream Cheese Tart Shells (below)
- Unsweetened cocoa powder (optional)

1. Preheat oven to 325° F. For filling, in a small saucepan bring the cream just to simmering over medium heat. Remove from heat. Add semisweet or bittersweet chocolate and milk chocolate; let stand for 2 minutes. Using a wooden spoon, stir until smooth and melted. Transfer to a medium bowl; cover and chill for 1 hour.

2. Beat chilled chocolate mixture with an electric mixer on medium speed until soft peaks form. Spoon into Cream Cheese Tart Shells. Cover and chill about 2 hours or until serving time.

3. If desired, just before serving, sprinkle tartlettes lightly with unsweetened cocoa powder. Makes 24 servings.

CREAM CHEESE TART SHELLS: For pastry, in a medium mixing bowl combine 1/2 cup softened butter and one 3-ounce package softened cream cheese; beat until combined. Stir in 2/3 cup all-purpose flour. Press a slightly rounded teaspoon of pastry evenly onto the bottom and up the side of 24 ungreased 1 3/4-inch muffin cups. Bake for 20 to 25 minutes or until pastry is golden. Cool in pans for 5 minutes. Remove from pans. Carefully transfer to wire racks; cool completely.

Each serving: 139 cal., 11 g total fat (6 g sat. fat), 29 mg chol., 59 mg sodium, 8 g carbo., 0 g fiber, 2 g pro. Daily Values: 7% vit. A, 2% calcium, 3% iron.

WHAT TO DRINK?

- After-dinner coffee, decaf or regular, becomes infinitely more compelling when you make it a bit stronger than usual and serve it in tiny demitasse cups.
- Or, pour hot chocolate, again a little stronger, dusted with cocoa powder or powdered sugar.
- Use petite glasses to serve liqueurs or sweet wines, such as Moscato or Vin Santo.

Winter Fruit Soup

No tricky timings to worrry about. Just cut up the fruit, cook a little while, and serve.

PREP: 20 minutes **COOK:** 12 minutes **STAND:** 1 hour

- 1 cup Pinot Gris wine or white grape juice
- 1 cup water
- 1/2 cup sugar
- 1/4 cup dried cranberries
- 1 3-inch piece vanilla bean, split, or 1 tsp. vanilla
- 1/4 to 1/2 tsp. ground white pepper (optional)
- 2 cups cut-up mixed fruit, such as fresh orange sections, halved kumquats, tangerine sections, and/or cored sliced pears
- 4 scoops lemon sorbet (optional)

1. In a small saucepan combine wine or juice, water, sugar, dried cranberries, vanilla bean (if using), and, if desired, white pepper. Cook and stir over medium heat until sugar dissolves and mixture comes to a boil. Remove from heat. If using, add vanilla. Cover and let stand 1 hour. Remove vanilla bean. Scrape seeds from vanilla bean pod and stir into soup mixture.

2. To serve, warm soup slightly. Divide fruit among four bowls. Divide warmed soup among bowls. If desired, add a small scoop of sorbet to each serving. Makes 4 servings.

Each serving: 228 cal., 0 g total fat (0 g sat. fat), 0 mg chol., 7 mg sodium, 48 g carbo., 3 g fiber, 1 g pro. Daily Values: 2% vit. A, 43% vit. C, 3% calcium, 3% iron.

Winter Fruit Soup

Sweetheart Shakes and Chocolate Shortbread Bites

Sweetheart Shakes

Crème fraîche adds a creamy smoothness and tang.

START TO FINISH: 10 minutes

- $^1/_2$ cup purchased crème fraîche or dairy sour cream
- $^1/_4$ cup dark, bittersweet, or triple chocolate-flavored syrup or ice cream topping
- $1^1/_2$ pints chocolate ice cream, softened
- Ground cinnamon (optional)

1. Place crème fraîche or sour cream and chocolate syrup or ice cream topping in a blender container. Cover and blend until smooth, stopping blender and scraping down sides as necessary.

2. Add ice cream and blend until smooth, scraping down sides. Divide among four small glasses. If desired, sprinkle with cinnamon. Serve immediately. Makes 4 servings.

Each serving: 337 cal., 20 g total fat (12 g sat. fat), 60 mg chol., 106 mg sodium, 40 g carbo., 2 g fiber, 5 g pro. Daily Values: 8% vit. A, 2% vit. C, 14% calcium, 7% iron.

Chocolate Shortbread Bites

Savor these with a great pot of coffee.

PREP: 15 minutes **BAKE:** 12 minutes

- 1 cup all-purpose flour
- $^1/_3$ cup packed brown sugar
- $^1/_4$ cup unsweetened cocoa powder
- 1 tsp. instant coffee crystals or $^1/_2$ tsp. instant espresso coffee powder
- $^1/_2$ tsp. ground cinnamon
- $^1/_2$ cup butter
- 1 recipe Chocolate Glaze (below) (optional)

1. Preheat oven to 325° F. In a medium bowl combine flour, brown sugar, cocoa powder, coffee powder, and cinnamon. Using a pastry blender, cut in butter until mixture resembles fine crumbs. With hands, knead dough until it forms a smooth ball.

2. On a lightly floured surface, roll dough $^1/_4$ inch thick (about 9×8-inch rectangle). Use various sizes of heart-shaped cookie cutters to cut out dough. Place 1 inch apart on an ungreased cookie sheet. Reroll as necessary.

3. Bake for 12 to 15 minutes or until edges are set and tops appear dry. Transfer cookies to a wire rack and let cool. If desired, dip one corner of each cookie into Chocolate Glaze. Transfer to a waxed-paper-lined cookie sheet. Let stand until chocolate sets. Makes about eighty 1-inch cookies.

CHOCOLATE GLAZE: In a small saucepan combine $^1/_2$ cup semisweet chocolate pieces and 1 teaspoon shortening. Cook and stir over low heat until melted. Cool.

Each cookie: 21 cal., 1 g total fat (1 g sat. fat), 3 mg chol., 13 mg sodium, 2 g carbo., 0 g fiber, 0 g pro. Daily Values: 1% iron.

Vanilla-Fudge Marble Cake

PREP: 25 minutes **BAKE:** 50 minutes **COOL:** 15 minutes

- $^3/_4$ cup butter, softened
- 2 eggs
- $2^3/_4$ cups all-purpose flour
- $1^1/_2$ tsp. baking powder
- $^1/_2$ tsp. baking soda
- $^1/_2$ tsp. salt
- $1^1/_2$ cups sugar
- 2 tsp. vanilla
- $1^1/_4$ cups buttermilk or sour milk
- $^2/_3$ cup chocolate-flavored syrup
- 1 recipe Semisweet Chocolate Icing (below)

1. Allow butter and eggs to stand at room temperature for 30 minutes. Meanwhile, grease and lightly flour a 10-inch fluted tube pan. In a medium bowl stir together flour, baking powder, baking soda, and salt. Set aside.

2. Preheat oven to 350° F. In large mixing bowl beat butter with an electric mixer on low to medium speed about 30 seconds. Add sugar and vanilla; beat until fluffy. Add eggs, 1 at a time, beating on low to medium speed, for 1 minute after each addition and scraping bowl frequently. Alternately add flour mixture and buttermilk to butter mixture, beating on low speed after each addition just until combined. Reserve 2 cups batter. Pour remaining batter into the prepared pan.

3. In a small mixing bowl combine chocolate syrup and reserved 2 cups batter. Beat on low speed until combined. Pour chocolate batter over vanilla batter in pan. Do not mix.

4. Bake about 50 minutes or until wooden toothpick inserted near center comes out clean. Cool for 15 minutes on a wire rack. Remove from pan; cool completely on rack. Drizzle with Semisweet Chocolate Icing. Makes 12 servings.

SEMISWEET CHOCOLATE ICING: In a small saucepan heat $^1/_2$ cup semisweet chocolate pieces, 2 tablespoons butter, 1 tablespoon light-colored corn syrup, and $^1/_4$ teaspoon vanilla over low heat, stirring until chocolate is melted and mixture is smooth. Use immediately.

Each serving: 416 cal., 18 g total fat (10 g sat. fat), 75 mg chol., 400 mg sodium, 59 g carbo., 2 g fiber, 5 g pro. Daily Values: 12% vit. A, 7% calcium, 9% iron.

There's something about dairy

ADDING SOME LIGHT DAIRY PRODUCTS TO A SMART DIET WAS FIRST SEEN AS A WAY TO LOWER blood pressure. Then researchers recognized a bounty of extra benefits as they developed and tested a diet plan for hypertension.

Rewards of the DASH (Dietary Approaches to Stop Hypertension) plan—based on a diet rich in low-fat dairy foods, whole grains, fruits, and vegetables—included the expected drop in blood pressure. As a bonus, the plan also improved levels of cholesterol and homocysteine—possible risk factors for heart disease and stroke. The DASH diet may also help people to stay lean, according to University of Tennessee (UT) studies.

Researchers, supported by the National Heart, Lung, and Blood Institute (NHLBI) of the National Institutes of Health, have been looking at the diet and its impact on health. But they still have questions about where all the DASH benefits come from.

"Dairy means increased protein, riboflavin, and calcium, so it's hard to key out which nutrients did the job. Any of those dairy components may have contributed to the blood-pressure effect," says Eva Obarzanek, Ph.D., research nutritionist with the NHLBI.

"The svelte factor may be linked to the calcium in dairy products," says UT's Michael Zemel, Ph.D. "Lack of calcium triggers the production of calcium-preserving hormones. Unfortunately, these hormones prevent your body from breaking down fat, plus they stimulate the production of more fat," Zemel says. "Non-dairy sources of calcium, such as white beans and broccoli, also may fight fat, but factors in dairy products besides calcium markedly enhance this effect. We have not yet identified the factors," he says.

DINE AND "DASH"

For a brochure detailing the DASH diet—with sample menus—call the National Heart, Lung, and Blood Institute (NHLBI) of the National Institutes of Health, 301/592-8573. The information also is available at the NHLBI Internet site at www.nhlbi.nih.gov/hbp/prevent/h_eating/h_eating.htm. The heart-healthy DASH eating plan includes the following recommendations:

Grains	7 to 8 servings / day
Vegetables	4 to 5 servings / day
Fruits	4 to 5 servings / day
Low-fat or fat-free dairy	2 to 3 servings / day
Meat/fish/poultry	2 or less servings / day
Nuts, seeds, dry beans	4 to 5 servings / week
Fats and oils	2 to 3 servings / day
Sweets	5 servings / week

Curried Sweet Potato Chowder

Salmon Confetti Chowder

START TO FINISH: 25 minutes

- 2 cups frozen pepper stir-fry vegetables (yellow, green, and red peppers and onion)
- 2 Tbsp. minced seeded jalapeño pepper
- 1 Tbsp. butter or margarine
- 2 Tbsp. all-purpose flour
- 2 cups fat-free milk
- 1 cup fat-free half-and-half
- 2 cups refrigerated diced potatoes with onions
- 1 15-oz. can salmon, drained and flaked
- 1/4 cup snipped watercress
- 1/2 tsp. finely shredded lemon peel
- 1/2 tsp. salt
- 1/2 tsp. ground black pepper

1. In a large saucepan cook stir-fry vegetables and jalapeño pepper in hot butter or margarine for 3 to 5 minutes or until tender. Stir in flour. Stir in milk and half-and-half. Cook and stir until slightly thickened. Cook and stir 2 minutes more.

2. Stir in diced potatoes, salmon, watercress, shredded lemon peel, salt, and black pepper. Cook and stir until chowder is heated through. Makes 4 servings.

Each serving: 349 cal., 10 g total fat (2 g sat. fat), 61 mg chol., 1,174 mg sodium, 33 g carbo., 3 g fiber, 29 g pro. Daily Values: 11% vit. A, 25% vit. C, 42% calcium, 8% iron.

Curried Sweet Potato Chowder

START TO FINISH: 30 minutes

- 2 tsp. butter or margarine
- 1 1/3 cups 1/2-inch cubes peeled sweet potatoes
- 1/3 cup minced shallot (1 large)
- 1/2 tsp. curry powder
- 1 Tbsp. all-purpose flour
- 1 1/2 cups fat-free milk
- 1 cup frozen baby peas
- 1/2 cup fat-free half-and-half
- 4 tsp. curried pumpkin seeds or pumpkin seeds
- Crackers (optional)

1. In a saucepan melt butter. Add sweet potatoes and shallot. Cook and stir over medium heat for 2 minutes. Add curry powder; cook and stir for 30 seconds. Stir in flour. Gradually stir in milk until smooth. Add peas and half-and-half; season with salt and pepper to taste. Cover and simmer about 15 minutes or until potatoes are tender.

2. Spoon the soup into four bowls. Sprinkle each serving with pumpkin seeds. If desired, serve with crackers. Makes 4 servings.

Each serving: 173 cal., 3 g total fat (0 g sat. fat), 2 mg chol., 293 mg sodium, 28 g carbo., 4 g fiber, 8 g pro. Daily Values: 174% vit. A, 22% vit. C, 16% calcium, 9% iron.

Bringing Out the Best in Beans

SOAK 'EM IF YOU'VE GOT 'EM.

That's the secret to unlocking the soul-bracing, velvety richness hidden within dry beans. There's no problem that water can't solve, and you'll give the H_2O a head start if you begin by presoaking your beans. You can soak them overnight in cold water, but boiling and soaking lets you proceed more quickly with your recipe. And, the boiling/soaking method has the added benefit of making the beans more digestible, say some cooking experts.

Once the soaked beans are in the pot and cooking is underway, keep an open ear. What you want to hear is silence, because the beans need to cook slowly to retain their shape and texture. If the lid is rattling or the water is boiling, they're cooking too fast and you run the danger of the beans sticking to the bottom of the pan and burning (something you really want to avoid).

The Beans and Greens recipe (opposite) calls for Great Northern beans, but the kind of beans you'll find on your supermarket shelf depends on where you live. That's why this recipe lets you use nearly any variety of dry bean. Keep in mind though, the darker the bean, the stronger the flavor. Begin testing for doneness after an hour of cooking. As long as you've presoaked them, the beans shouldn't have to cook more than 90 minutes.

When it comes to serving, it's strictly up to you and your family how much of the cooking liquid to serve with the beans. In the South, beans get ladled up with lots of the broth and served with a square of corn bread.

Beans and Greens

PREP: 10 minutes **STAND:** 1 hour **COOK:** 1¼ hours

- ½ lb. dry Great Northern beans, navy beans, pinto beans, or kidney beans (1 cup plus 2 Tbsp.)
- 6½ cups cold water
- 1 14-oz. can reduced-sodium chicken broth
- 1 bay leaf
- 1 tsp. dried thyme, crushed
- ¼ tsp. salt
- ¼ tsp. ground black pepper
- 4 slices bacon
- 1 medium onion, chopped (½ cup)
- 1 clove garlic, minced
- ¼ tsp. crushed red pepper (optional)
- 4 cups torn fresh mustard greens or spinach
- 2 cups chopped tomato (optional)

1. Rinse beans. In a large saucepan combine beans and 4 cups of the cold water. Bring to boiling; reduce heat. Simmer 2 minutes. Remove from heat. Cover; let stand 1 hour.

2. Drain and rinse beans. Return beans to the saucepan and add the 2½ cups fresh cold water, the chicken broth, bay leaf, thyme, salt, and black pepper. Bring to boiling; reduce heat. Cover and simmer about 1¼ hours or until beans are tender, stirring occasionally *(see photo, below)*. (Add more water if needed to prevent the beans from sticking or burning.)

3. Meanwhile, in a skillet cook bacon over medium heat until crisp. Drain on paper towels, reserving 1 tablespoon drippings in skillet. Add onion, garlic, and, if desired, crushed red pepper. Cook and stir over medium heat until onion is tender.

4. Add greens and, if desired, tomato to skillet. Cover and cook for 1 to 2 minutes.

5. Drain beans; if desired, reserve liquid. Discard bay leaf. Return beans to saucepan. Add onion mixture, tossing gently to combine. Season with additional salt and black pepper. Spoon into serving bowl. Crumble bacon over top. If desired, pass reserved liquid. Makes 6 servings.

Each serving: 176 cal., 3 g total fat (1 g sat. fat), 4 mg chol., 355 mg sodium, 27 g carbo., 9 g fiber, 2 g pro. Daily Values: 19% vit. A, 30% vit. C, 10% calcium, 13% iron.

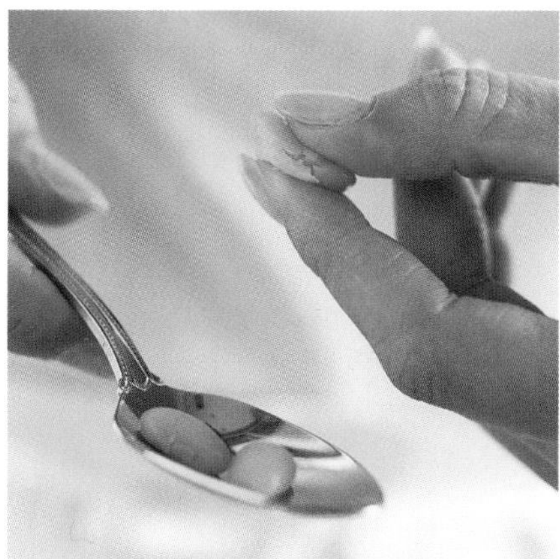

How do you know if beans are done? Pinch one, or try biting one (after cooling it under cold water). Either way, if you feel a hard core, cook an additional 10 to 15 minutes and try again.

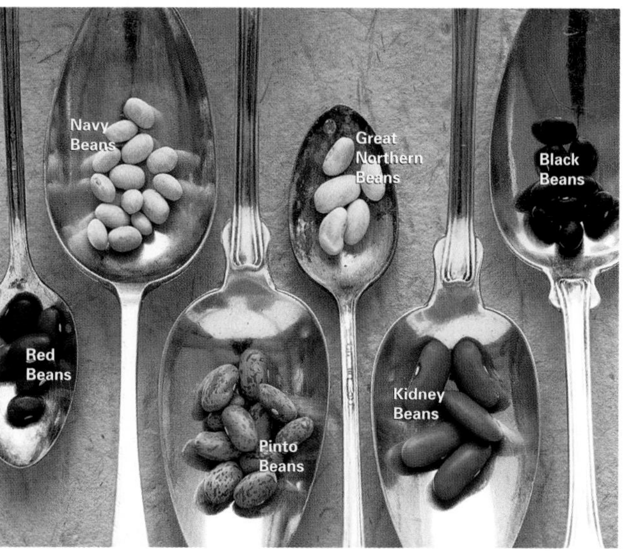

A GUIDE TO BEANS

RED BEANS. Like the more familiar kidney bean, reds have a robust, full-bodied flavor and soft texture. They hold their shape and firmness when cooked.

NAVY BEANS. The name reflects the fact that it's been served to United States Navy sailors for more than 100 years. The bean has a mild flavor with powdery texture (and yes, it's still on ships' menus, says a Navy spokesperson).

PINTO BEANS. This relative of the kidney bean has a rich flavor. ("Pinto" is the Spanish word that means painted.)

GREAT NORTHERN BEANS. Popular in the Midwest, this medium-sized, white oval bean has a mild flavor with powdery texture. Navy beans are the best substitute.

LIGHT RED AND DARK RED KIDNEY BEANS. Kidney beans are noted for their robust, full-bodied flavor and soft texture. Lights and darks can be used interchangeably.

BLACK BEANS. The black's earthy sweet flavor comes with a hint of mushroom. These are also called Turtle beans.

March

SPRING IS HERE, SO MAKE A LITTLE TIME FOR COOKING WITH FAMILY AND FRIENDS, AND TAKE A FRESH LOOK AT THE SIGNATURE INGREDIENTS OF THE COMING SEASON.

Jicima Slaw with Jalapeño Dressing

Banana Split Sundaes

Spring Greens with Shortcut Lemon Sauce

The Comforts of Home

Plus...

Smoked Trout with Mango-Avocado Salsa

Quick Grilled Herb Ratatouille and Polenta

Busy Lives Easy Meals

Plus...

HOT, HEARTY, AND COMFORTING–THOSE ARE THE FOODS WE SHARE AT HOME WHILE WE WAIT FOR THE LION TO TURN INTO A LAMB.

Beef and Red Bean Chili

Deluxe Chicken and Roasted Pepper Sandwiches

Spicy Lamb Shanks

Pan-Seared Lamb Chops with Mint Salad

The Comforts of HOME

COMFORT FOOD'S FAMILIARITY AND HOMEY APPEAL MAKE IT PERFECT FOR COOKING TOGETHER WITH FAMILY—A LESSON CHEF-IN-TRAINING MATTHEW BUCHANAN TOOK TO HEART AT AN EARLY AGE.

Pan-Seared Lamb Chops with Mint Salad

To achieve optimum color and flavor, let the chops sizzle in the skillet without moving or stirring—except when it's time to turn them.

START TO FINISH: 30 minutes

- 1/4 cup snipped fresh mint
- 1/4 cup snipped fresh Italian flat-leaf parsley
- 1/4 cup crumbled feta cheese (1 oz.)
- 1/4 cup toasted chopped pecans
- 8 lamb rib chops or loin chops, cut 1 inch thick (about 2 lb.)
- 2 tsp. olive oil
- 1/4 tsp. salt
- 1/8 tsp. ground black pepper
- Olive oil (optional)
- Lemon juice (optional)
- Mixed salad greens (optional)

1. In a small bowl combine mint, parsley, feta cheese, and pecans; set aside.

2. Trim fat from chops. Rub chops with 2 teaspoons olive oil, salt, and pepper. Preheat a large heavy skillet over medium-high heat until very hot. Add chops. For medium-rare doneness, cook over medium-high heat for 8 to 10 minutes or until brown and an instant-read thermometer inserted in thickest portion registers 145° F, turning chops once halfway through cooking.

3. To serve, sprinkle chops with mint mixture. If desired, drizzle with oil and lemon juice; serve with salad greens. Makes 4 servings.

Each serving: 252 cal., 17 g total fat (5 g sat. fat), 72 mg chol., 311 mg sodium, 2 g carbo., 1 g fiber, 22 g pro. Daily Values: 6% vit. A, 9% vit. C, 7% calcium, 12% iron.

Kitchen comfort

There's comfort to be found in the kitchen. Matthew Buchanan discovered that at age 10 or so when he first began bumping elbows with his mother, Missy, during meal preparations. He was the potato kid, often in charge of spuds for dinner.

"Boy, did my family have to eat 100 varieties of au gratin," says Matthew (shown at left with his mother). Now Matthew's alchemy continues as he transforms a cup of this and a dash of that into nouveau comfort food.

Even when he takes over the kitchen during visits to his parents' home near Dallas, Missy doesn't mind at all. "Matthew is so inventive with food," she says. When Matthew was a boy, he and his mom shared a lot of kitchen time. Meals tended to be simple and quick—something to eat together as a family before it was time to rush off. Matthew's sisters, Mindy and Beth, and father, Barry, were part of the dine-and-dash whirlwind. But Matthew loved helping out in the kitchen. He got upset when his mom went grocery shopping while he was in school.

Puttering in the kitchen at an early age led to advanced puttering in college. While a student at Texas A&M University, Matthew cooked for his roommates. And every year he concocted a "gigantic" post-Thanksgiving feast for his friends. "It was our last hurrah before finals and the Christmas break," he said. After graduating with a degree in psychology, he decided he'd rather be a chef. So, after a year in Italy with his wife, Rachel, he headed for the CIA.

But there's no place like home. Visiting his parents sparks the familiar mom-and-son sessions in the kitchen. Matthew takes his family favorites to new levels, punching up the freshness and adding zings of flavor. See for yourself by trying Matthew's recipes on the following pages.

COOKING FISH

Fish cooks pretty quickly, but just how quick depends on the thickness of the fillet. Measure the height at the thickest part of the fillet before you put the fish on the grill. Expect a 1/2-inch-thick piece to cook in 4 to 6 minutes over direct heat. Indirect heat will take a little longer. To see if fish is done, insert a fork into the thickest part and twist gently. If the fish flakes, it is done. If it doesn't separate into flakes and is still translucent, cook it a little longer.

Smoked Trout with Mango-Avocado Salsa

Wood chips come in several varieties, including apple, cherry, maple, and mesquite. They may be large or could be ground to a fine consistency. Larger wood chips work in most smokers, but must be soaked in water before they're used.

PREP: 20 minutes **COOK:** 20 minutes

- **Wood chips for smoking**
- **1 lb. fresh trout fillets, 1/2 to 1 inch thick**
- **Salt**
- **Ground black pepper**
- **1 recipe Mango-Avocado Salsa (below)**
- **Tortilla chips**

1. At least 1 hour before smoke cooking, soak 1 cup wood chips in enough water to cover. Drain wood chips. In a charcoal grill arrange medium-hot coals around a drip pan. Test for medium heat above the pan. Sprinkle the drained wood chips over the coals.

2. Rinse fish and pat dry with paper towels. Sprinkle fish with salt and pepper. Place fish on foil on the grill rack over drip pan. Cover and smoke for 25 to 30 minutes or until fish flakes easily when tested with a fork. Cool.

3. Meanwhile, prepare Mango-Avocado Salsa. Use a fork to break trout into large chunks. Serve trout pieces on tortilla chips with salsa. Makes 4 servings.

MANGO-AVOCADO SALSA: In a medium bowl combine 1 medium mango,* seeded, peeled, and chopped (1 cup); 1 small avocado, seeded, peeled, and chopped (3/4 cup); 1/4 cup chopped red sweet pepper; 2 tablespoons chopped red onion (a quarter of a small onion); 1/2 of a fresh jalapeño pepper,** seeded and finely chopped; 1 clove garlic, minced; 2 teaspoons lime juice; 1 teaspoon sugar; 1/4 teaspoon salt; and 1/4 teaspoon ground cumin. Cover and chill for up to 2 hours.

***NOTE:** To cut a mango, start on one of the wider sides of the mango and cut from the stem down, following the curve of the pit. Repeat on other sides. With pieces skin sides down, make cross-hatch cuts through the flesh and down to the peel. Slice close to peel to remove fruit.

****NOTE:** Because hot chile peppers contain volatile oils that can burn your skin and eyes, wear plastic or rubber gloves when working with chile peppers. If your bare hands do touch the chile peppers, wash your hands well with soap and water.

Each serving: 408 cal., 19 g total fat (3 g sat. fat), 65 mg chol., 370 mg sodium, 33 g carbo., 4 g fiber, 27 g pro. Daily Values: 56% vit. A, 62% vit. C, 10% calcium, 14% iron.

Smoked Trout with Mango-Avocado Salsa

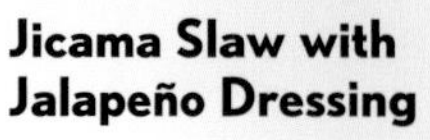

Jicama Slaw with Jalapeño Dressing

Pasta with Mushrooms and Aged Jack Cheese

PERFECT PASTA

To get the best flavor from your pasta, cook it only until it is *al dente* (al DEN-tay), which means it is still slightly firm and a little chewy. In Italian, *al dente* means "to the tooth" and describes the doneness of pasta and other foods, such as vegetables. For the best results, carefully follow the cooking directions on the package of dried or fresh pasta.

Pasta with Mushrooms and Aged Jack Cheese

Aged Jack cheese is not to be confused with Monterey Jack cheese, which is mild and semisoft. The aged version has a pale buttery color, a rich flavor, and a dry texture.

START TO FINISH: 35 minutes

- **8 oz. dried penne or campanelle pasta (2½ cups)**
- **1 Tbsp. butter**
- **1 large Walla Walla onion or other sweet onion, cut into thin wedges**
- **4 cloves garlic, minced**
- **2 Tbsp. butter**
- **3 cups fresh spring mushrooms, such as whole or halved morel mushrooms*, sliced shiitake mushrooms, and/or sliced oyster mushrooms**
- **½ cup whipping cream**
- **¼ cup chicken broth**
- **4 oz. aged Jack cheese, finely shredded (1 cup firmly packed)**
- **Salt**
- **Ground black pepper**
- **Fresh thyme leaves (optional)**

1. In a large saucepan cook pasta according to package directions. Drain; return to saucepan. Stir in the 1 tablespoon butter. Cover and keep warm.

2. In a large skillet cook and stir the onion and the garlic in the 2 tablespoons hot butter over medium heat for 4 to 5 minutes or until tender. Stir in mushrooms; cook about 3 minutes more or until tender.

3. Meanwhile, in a small saucepan heat whipping cream and broth over medium heat just to boiling. Reduce heat to low; stir in cheese. Continue stirring until cheese is almost melted.

4. Add mushroom mixture and cream mixture to pasta. Toss gently to combine; heat through. Season to taste with salt and pepper. If desired, sprinkle with thyme leaves before serving. Makes 4 servings.

***NOTE:** To clean morel mushrooms, set the mushrooms in a pan or bowl. Cover with water; add a dash of salt. Soak for 10 to 15 minutes. Drain and rinse. Repeat twice. Pat mushrooms dry.

Each serving: 586 cal., 36 g total fat (18 g sat. fat), 76 mg chol., 352 mg sodium, 50 g carbo., 4 g fiber, 19 g pro. Daily Values: 24% vit. A, 5% vit. C, 25% calcium, 15% iron.

Jicama Slaw with Jalapeño Dressing

Great as a solo side dish, this slaw is also adaptable. Pile the jicama mixture onto chicken sandwiches, use it to make spring rolls, or place a spoonful on top of tortilla soup or other thick soups.

PREP: 20 minutes **CHILL:** 1 hour

- **2 cups peeled jicama,* cut into thin matchstick strips (about 6½ oz.)**
- **3 small red, yellow, and/or green sweet peppers, cut into thin matchstick strips (1½ cups)**
- **1 small red onion, thinly sliced and halved**
- **1 recipe Jalapeño Dressing (below)**

1. In a large salad bowl combine jicama strips, sweet pepper strips, and onion slices. Prepare Jalapeño Dressing. Pour dressing over jicama mixture; toss gently to coat. Cover; chill for 1 to 6 hours, stirring occasionally. Makes 6 servings.

JALAPEÑO DRESSING: In a screw-top jar combine ¼ cup peanut oil or olive oil; ⅓ cup snipped fresh cilantro; 2 tablespoons red wine vinegar; 1 small fresh jalapeño chile pepper (see note, page 74), seeded and finely chopped; 1 clove garlic, minced; 1 teaspoon sugar; ⅛ teaspoon black pepper; and a dash each of salt and ground red pepper. Cover and shake well.

***NOTE:** You can make cutting up a large jicama less daunting if you cut it in half after you peel it. Place the flat side down on your cutting board so it won't wobble. (All round vegetables are easier to work with when you cut them in half.) Next, cut each jicama half vertically into thin slices. Stack several slices. Cut the stack vertically into thin strips, then trim the strips so you have matchstick-size pieces.

Each serving: 120 cal., 9 g total fat (2 g sat. fat), 0 mg chol., 27 mg sodium, 9 g carbo., 1 g fiber, 1 g pro. Daily Values: 46% vit. A, 146% vit. C, 1% calcium, 5% iron.

FLAVORS OF SPRING DINNER

Pan-Seared Lamb Chops with Mint Salad *(page 73)*
Spring Greens with Shortcut Lemon Sauce *(page 78)*
Pita Crisps *(page 13)*
Banana Split Sundaes *(page 78)*
Iced tea

Banana Split Sundaes

For a special touch, Matthew likes to caramelize the bananas to achieve a brittle brûlée-like crunch. He works with a chef's torch to achieve the effect, but you can also caramelize sugar in a skillet and quickly pour it over the bananas.

START TO FINISH: 35 minutes

- **3 1-inch-thick slices angel food cake, purchased or homemade (right), torn into 1/2- to 1-inch cubes**
- **2 Tbsp. butter, melted**
- **3/4 cup packed brown sugar**
- **4 tsp. cornstarch**
- **1/3 cup water**
- **1/2 cup half-and-half or light cream**
- **3 Tbsp. light-colored corn syrup**
- **1 Tbsp. butter**
- **1/2 tsp. vanilla**
- **1 recipe Caramelized Sugar (below) (optional)**
- **2 bananas**
- **1 pt. vanilla, chocolate, and/or strawberry ice cream**

1. Preheat oven to 400° F. Place cake cubes in an 8×8×2-inch baking pan. Drizzle with the 2 tablespoons melted butter; toss gently to coat. Bake, uncovered, for 10 minutes, stirring twice. Cool. (The cake croutons will crisp as they cool.)

2. For caramel sauce, in a large skillet combine brown sugar and cornstarch. Stir in the water. Stir in cream, corn syrup, and the 1 tablespoon butter. Cook and stir over medium heat until bubbly (mixture may appear curdled). Cook and stir for 2 minutes more. Remove from heat; stir in vanilla. Meanwhile, begin preparing Caramelized Sugar, if using.

3. Cut each banana in half both vertically and horizontally so you have four equal pieces from each. Place bananas in an even layer in the skillet, turning to coat with sauce; cook for 1 to 2 minutes.

4. Scoop ice cream into 4 bowls; top with bananas, cake croutons, and remaining caramel sauce. If desired, drizzle with Caramelized Sugar. Makes 4 servings.

CARAMELIZED SUGAR: Place 1/3 cup sugar in an 8-inch heavy skillet. Heat over medium-high heat until sugar begins to melt, shaking skillet occasionally. Do not stir. Once the sugar starts to melt, reduce heat to low. Cook about 5 minutes more or until sugar is melted and golden, stirring as necessary.

Each serving: 628 cal., 25 g total fat (15 g sat. fat), 81 mg chol., 343 mg sodium, 101 g carbo., 2 g fiber, and 6 g pro. Daily Values: 20% vit. A, 10% vit. C, 19% calcium, 7% iron.

Spring Greens with Shortcut Lemon Sauce

START TO FINISH: 25 minutes

- **1 lb. baby broccoli and/or asparagus spears and/or pea pods**
- **2 oz. mascarpone cheese**
- **2 Tbsp. dairy sour cream**
- **2 Tbsp. milk**
- **3/4 tsp. snipped fresh thyme**
- **1/2 tsp. finely shredded lemon peel**
- **1 1/2 tsp. lemon juice**
- **Salt**
- **Ground white pepper**

1. In a Dutch oven or large saucepan bring a small amount of salted water to boiling. Cook vegetables, covered, until crisp-tender, allowing 5 to 7 minutes for baby broccoli, 3 to 5 minutes for asparagus, and 2 to 4 minutes for pea pods. Drain.

2. For the lemon sauce, in a small bowl combine mascarpone cheese, sour cream, milk, thyme, lemon peel, and lemon juice. Season sauce to taste with salt and pepper. To serve, spoon lemon sauce over the vegetables. Makes 4 servings.

Each serving: 111 cal., 8 g total fat (5 g sat. fat), 21 mg chol., 117 mg sodium, 8 g carbo., 3 g fiber, 7 g pro. Daily Values: 33% vit. A, 135% vit. C, 7% calcium, 6% iron.

Angel Food Cake

Loosen the cooled cake from the pan by sliding a metal spatula between the pan and cake in a continuous—not sawing—motion.

PREP: 50 minutes **BAKE:** 40 minutes **COOL:** 2 hours

- **1 1/2 cups egg whites (10 to 12 large)**
- **1 1/2 cups sifted powdered sugar**
- **1 cup sifted cake flour or sifted all-purpose flour**
- **1 1/2 tsp. cream of tartar**
- **1 tsp. vanilla**
- **1 cup granulated sugar**

1. In a very large mixing bowl let egg whites stand at room temperature for 30 minutes. Meanwhile, sift powdered sugar and flour together 3 times; set aside.

2. Preheat oven to 350° F. Add cream of tartar and vanilla to egg whites. Beat with an electric mixer on medium speed until soft peaks form (tips curl). Gradually add granulated sugar, 2 tablespoons at a time, beating until stiff peaks form (tips stand straight).

3. Sift about one-fourth of the flour mixture over beaten egg whites; fold in gently. (If bowl is too full, transfer to a larger bowl.) Repeat, folding in remaining flour mixture by fourths. Pour into an ungreased 10-inch tube pan. Gently cut through batter to remove any large air pockets.

4. Bake on lowest rack for 40 to 45 minutes or until top springs back when lightly touched. Immediately invert cake (in pan); cool thoroughly. Loosen sides of cake from pan; remove cake. Makes 12 servings.

Each serving: 161 cal., 0 g total fat (0 g sat. fat), 0 mg chol., 51 mg sodium, 36 g carbo., 0 g fiber, 4 g pro. Daily Values: 4% iron.

Spring Greens with Shortcut Lemon Sauce

KEEPING GREENS BRIGHT

To keep green vegetables vivid, avoid overcooking them. Give the veggies a quick dip in a large pot of boiling salted water. Stop the bright color from cooking away by plunging the vegetables into ice water as soon as they're crisp-tender. Cover and store in the refrigerator until serving time. Reheat by dropping them briefly into boiling water.

Banana Split Sundae

EXCELLENT Eggplant

Baby White Eggplant

Japanese Eggplant

Chinese Eggplant

Thai Eggplant

Historically, the 5th-century Chinese were the first to write about eggplants. No wonder the ancient Chinese found eggplant useful—its mild flavor adds a harmonious accent to the spicy overtones of Asian cooking. When eggplants eventually found their way to the Mediterranean, they fit well with the equally zesty cuisines of Spain, Italy, and Greece and became part of many recipes we know today, such as Lemon-Scented Eggplant Tart.

For best results with the tart and other recipes, choose the right eggplant and handle it with care. Select small to medium sizes or try one of the small varieties pictured *left*. The skin of young eggplant is very flavorful but gets bitter as it ages. Small varieties are also more tender than the large types. Store eggplants in a cool, dry place and use them within two days. Because they soak up oils during cooking, bread them to keep them from becoming mushy. Cook small varieties the same way you would cook regular eggplant, but for shorter lengths of time.

Western Eggplant

Lemon-Scented Eggplant Tart

If it's available, substitute white eggplant for purple.

PREP: 45 minutes **BAKE:** 22 minutes

- 1 recipe Butter Pastry (below)
- 12 oz. Japanese eggplant
- Salt
- 1⁄3 cup snipped fresh cilantro
- 4 tsp. shredded lemon peel
- 1 1⁄2 tsp. minced fresh garlic (3 large cloves)
- 2 Tbsp. olive oil
- 1⁄4 cup purchased black olive pâté
- 2 Tbsp. lemon juice

1. Preheat oven to 450° F. For crust, on a lightly floured surface roll the Butter Pastry to a 16×5-inch rectangle. Ease pastry into an ungreased 13 3⁄4×4-inch tart pan with a removable bottom, pressing into sides of pan and trimming to edge of pan to remove excess. Generously prick the bottom of the pastry. Line with a double thickness of foil. Bake for 10 minutes. Remove foil; bake for 4 to 5 minutes more or until golden brown. Cool on a wire rack.

2. Halve eggplant lengthwise and slice into 1⁄4-inch-thick slices. Sprinkle slices with salt on both sides; set between two paper towels. Place a cookie sheet on top of the paper towel. Weigh down with a heavy bowl for 20 minutes. Meanwhile, in a bowl combine cilantro, lemon peel, and garlic; set aside.

3. Place eggplant slices in a colander; rinse and drain well. In a skillet heat 1 tablespoon of the oil over medium-high heat. Cook and stir eggplant, half at a time, for 3 to 5 minutes or until eggplant has softened and is light brown. Remove slices from skillet; drain on paper towels. Repeat with remaining oil and eggplant.

4. Stir together the olive pâté and 1 tablespoon of the lemon juice. Spread olive mixture onto baked pastry. Arrange eggplant on top. Sprinkle evenly with cilantro mixture. Bake, uncovered, about 8 minutes or until heated through.

5. Remove from oven; cool slightly on a wire rack. Remove sides of pan. Cut into 1-inch-thick slices; drizzle with remaining lemon juice. Serve warm. Makes 12 appetizer servings.

BUTTER PASTRY: In a mixing bowl combine 1 cup all-purpose flour and 1⁄4 teaspoon salt. Using a pastry blender, cut in 1⁄3 cup unsalted butter until pieces are pea-size. Sprinkle 1 teaspoon cold water over part of the mixture; gently toss with a fork. Push the moistened dough to side of bowl. Repeat with additional cold water, using 1 tablespoon at a time, until all the dough is moistened. Form dough into a ball.

Each serving: 117 cal., 8 g total fat (4 g saturated fat), 14 mg chol., 106 mg sodium, 10 g carbo., 1 g fiber, 1 g protein. Daily Values: 10 % vit. C, 1 % calcium, 3 % iron.

Lemon-Scented Eggplant Tart

EGGPLANT EXAMPLES

BABY WHITE EGGPLANT: Small, firm, and with a sweet flesh. Its thick skin should be peeled before use. A quick glance at this variety lets one know the probable derivation of eggplant's name.

JAPANESE EGGPLANT: Long, slender, and a deep purple color. Its flesh is tender and slightly sweet. This delicate variety is specified for use in Lemon-Scented Eggplant Tart.

CHINESE EGGPLANT: Resembles a small zucchini. This version has a thin, pleasant-tasting skin, so there's no need to peel it. Its slender shape and size make this eggplant practical and easy to use.

THAI EGGPLANT: Look for golf-ball-size fruits, although occasionally, grape-sized Thai eggplants have been spotted. This one is a natural for grilling, stir-frying, or frying in tempura.

WESTERN EGGPLANT: This larger version is the one most of us know. Look for a smooth, glossy surface and a heavy-in-the-hand weight. Seek out the very freshest eggplant for the sweetest, least bitter flavor.

Egg-Poaching PANS

Poached Eggs with Grainy Mustard Vinaigrette

In a world of kitchen multitaskers, here's a pan designed to do just one thing: poach an egg. Because poached egg dishes are popular again, the *Better Homes and Gardens®* Test Kitchen decided to put a slew of poaching pans through their paces. Here are some tips for picking a great pan.

- Look for nonstick egg cups, although you should coat these cups with butter or oil before filling.
- Cups with perforated bottoms let water enter cups for even poaching.
- Be sure cups can be easily removed from a hot pan, either with easy-access handles on the individual cups or with a knob or handle for lifting out the entire tray.
- Most pans are made of good quality 18/10 stainless steel. Some have a copper or an aluminum disc on the bottom for better heat conduction. Heavier pans typically have thicker discs (a plus) and better heat distribution. However, when considering choices, be sure you're comparing the same kind of pans: copper to copper and aluminum to aluminum.
- A glass lid lets you monitor cooking.
- The dishwasher-safe capabilities of poaching pans differ from manufacturer to manufacturer. Choose the pan that best meets your needs.
- Avoid microwave poachers. During our cooking tests, the pans repeatedly popped open.
- When you are ready to poach, break eggs one at a time into a measuring cup. Pour the egg into a poaching cup and proceed with cooking according to manufacturer's directions.

Poached Eggs with Grainy Mustard Vinaigrette

Put your poaching pan to the test with this quick preparation. Fresh mixed greens provide a cozy nest.

START TO FINISH: 20 minutes

- 1 Tbsp. coarse-grain brown mustard
- 2 Tbsp. vinegar
- 2 Tbsp. olive oil
- 4 large eggs
- 2 cups fresh assorted greens; or 8 cups torn spinach, sautéed in 1 Tbsp. butter
- 2 slices dark rye bread, toasted and halved diagonally
- Salt
- Ground black pepper

1. In a small saucepan combine mustard, vinegar, and olive oil. Bring to boiling, stirring to combine. Reduce heat and keep warm, stirring again just before serving.

2. Grease 4 cups of an egg-poaching pan with oil. Place poacher cups over pan of boiling water (water should not touch the bottoms of the cups). Reduce heat to simmering. Break one of the eggs into a measuring cup. Carefully slide egg into a poacher cup. Repeat with remaining eggs. Cover and cook for 6 to 9 minutes or until the whites are completely set and yolks begin to thicken but are not hard.

3. To serve, loosen eggs by running a knife around poaching cups. Place greens or sautéed spinach over toasted rye bread. Top with poached egg by inverting poaching cups. Drizzle with warm mustard vinaigrette. Season to taste with salt and pepper. Makes 4 servings.

Each serving: 183 cal., 13 g total fat (3 g sat. fat), 213 mg chol., 257 mg sodium, 10 g carbo., 1 g dietary fiber, 8 g protein. Daily Values: 8% vit. A, 2% vit. C, 5% calcium, 8% iron.

Eggs Benedict

STAND: 45 minutes **PREP:** 30 minutes **COOK:** 20 minutes

- 4 eggs
- 1 recipe Hollandaise Sauce (below)
- 2 English muffins, split
- 4 slices Canadian-style bacon
- Paprika (optional)

1. Grease 4 cups of an egg-poaching pan with oil. Place poacher cups over pan of boiling water (water should not touch the bottoms of the cups). Reduce heat to simmering. Break one of the eggs into a measuring cup. Carefully slide egg into a poacher cup. Repeat with remaining eggs. Cover and cook 6 to 9 minutes or until the whites are completely set and yolks begin to thicken but are not hard.

2. Loosen eggs by running a knife around poaching cups. Remove eggs with a slotted spoon; place in a large pan of warm water to keep them warm. Prepare Hollandaise Sauce.

3. Meanwhile, place muffin halves, cut sides up, on a baking sheet. Broil 3 to 4 inches from the heat about 2 minutes or until toasted. Top each muffin half with a slice of Canadian-style bacon; broil about 1 minute more or until meat is heated.

4. To serve, top each bacon-topped muffin half with an egg; spoon Hollandaise Sauce over eggs. If desired, sprinkle with paprika. Makes 4 servings

HOLLANDAISE SAUCE: Cut 1/2 cup unsalted butter into thirds and bring it to room temperature (allow about 45 minutes). In the top of a double boiler combine 3 beaten egg yolks, 1 tablespoon lemon juice, and 1 tablespoon water. Add a piece of the butter. Place over gently boiling water (upper pan should not touch water). Cook, stirring rapidly with a whisk, until butter melts and sauce begins to thicken. (Sauce may appear to curdle at this point but will smooth out when remaining butter is added). Add remaining butter, a piece at a time, stirring constantly until melted. Continue to cook and stir for 2 to 2 1/2 minutes more or until sauce thickens. Immediately remove from heat. If sauce is too thick or curdles, immediately whisk in 1 to 2 tablespoons hot water. Season to taste with salt and ground white pepper. Makes 3/4 cup sauce.

Each serving: 442 cal., 36 g total fat (19 g sat. fat), 451 mg chol., 836 mg sodium, 14 g carbo., 1 g fiber, 16 g pro. Daily Values: 30% vit. A, 3% vit. C, 10% calcium, 12% iron.

Busy Lives Easy Meals

PSST. WANT THE SECRET TO QUICK MEAL PREP? SMART KITCHEN APPLIANCES. THESE COOKING WORKHORSES ARE EASIER THAN EVER TO USE. AND, WE'VE CREATED CONVENIENT, GREAT-TASTING RECIPES TO PROVE IT.

Garlicky Steak and Asparagus

Garlicky Steak and Asparagus

One steak, a handful of fresh asparagus, and less than five minutes on the grill are all it takes to whip up this feast for two.

PREP: 15 minutes **GRILL:** 3 minutes

- 1 12- to 14-oz. boneless beef top loin (strip) steak, cut about 3/4 inch thick
- 1 or 2 large cloves garlic, coarsely chopped
- 1/2 tsp. cracked or coarsely ground black pepper
- 1/4 tsp. salt
- 8 to 10 thin asparagus spears, trimmed (6 oz.)
- 2 tsp. garlic-flavored olive oil or olive oil
- 1/2 cup beef broth
- 1 Tbsp. dry white wine
- 1/4 tsp. Dijon-style mustard

INDOOR GRILL METHOD:

1. Rub steak on both sides with a mixture of garlic, pepper, and salt. Place asparagus in shallow dish; drizzle with the oil.

2. For sauce, in medium skillet stir together broth and wine. Cook over high heat for 4 to 5 minutes or until mixture is reduced to 1/4 cup. Whisk in mustard; keep warm.

3. Preheat an indoor electric grill. Place steak on grill rack. If using a covered grill, close lid. Grill until steak is desired doneness. (For a covered grill, allow 3 to 4 minutes for medium rare or 5 to 7 minutes for medium. For an uncovered grill, allow 6 to 8 minutes for medium rare or 8 to 10 minutes for medium, turning steak once.) If space allows, add asparagus to covered grill for the last 2 to 3 minutes of grilling. Or, for uncovered grill, add asparagus for the last 4 to 5 minutes. Cook the asparagus just until crisp-tender.*

4. Spoon sauce onto plate. If desired, cut steak in half crosswise; stack atop sauce. Top with asparagus. Makes 2 servings.

CONVENTIONAL METHOD: Prepare steak and asparagus as in Step 1. Place steak on unheated rack of a broiler pan. Broil 3 to 4 inches from heat for 8 to 10 minutes for medium rare or 10 to 12 minutes for medium, turning once and adding asparagus the last 2 minutes of broiling. Serve as above.

***NOTE:** For smaller grills, you can grill the asparagus after the steak. Grill for 2 to 5 minutes or until crisp tender.

Each serving: 458 cal., 32 g total fat (11 g sat. fat), 110 mg chol., 549 mg sodium, 3 g carbo., 1 g fiber, 37 g pro. Daily Values: 2% vit. A, 37% vit. C, 3% calcium, 19% iron.

Deluxe Chicken and Roasted Pepper Sandwich

INDOOR GRILL

Portable, table-top indoor grills may be covered or uncovered. Below are some of the differences you may find.

COVERED INDOOR GRILL

Covered grills typically have a hinged lid, and foods are cooked with the lid closed. Therefore, foods are heated from the top and bottom, and cook more quickly than they would on an uncovered grill. Boneless cuts of meat work best on these grills because you can cover them tightly.

From our Test Kitchen expert, Marilyn Cornelius: "I didn't think I would like this appliance when we first got one in the Test Kitchen, but I found out how easy and quick it was for grilling and I fell in love with it."

UNCOVERED INDOOR GRILL

Just as it sounds, the uncovered grill is open. Foods are heated from the bottom only, so tend to cook slower than on a covered grill. You'll find interchangeable grill and griddle plates on some models; others feature extras such as heat indicators that light up when the grill reaches the ideal cooking temperature. You can use these timings for stove-top grills as well.

From our Test Kitchen expert, Colleen Weeden: "Once the grill is preheated, you can grill just about anything small. I love using my indoor grill to toast bread for sandwiches—no messing with lighting coals and setting up the grill."

Quick Grilled Herbed Ratatouille and Polenta

This dish is a whole meal when spooned over grilled polenta slices. For a meatier supper, grill smoked sausages along with the vegetables.

PREP: 25 minutes **GRILL:** 17 minutes

- 1/2 of a small eggplant (about 6 oz.)
- 1 small zucchini (about 4 oz.)
- 1 small fennel bulb (about 6 oz.)
- 1/4 cup olive oil
- 2 tsp. snipped fresh rosemary
- 1/2 tsp. salt
- 1/2 tsp. cracked black pepper
- 1 16-oz. tube plain refrigerated cooked polenta, cut into 12 slices
- 1 14 1/2-oz. can diced tomatoes with garlic and onion

INDOOR GRILL METHOD:

1. If desired, peel eggplant. Slice eggplant, zucchini, and fennel crosswise into 1/4-inch-thick slices *(see photo, below)*. In a small bowl combine oil, rosemary, salt, and pepper. Brush vegetables with about half of the oil mixture, reserving remaining oil mixture.

2. Preheat an uncovered indoor electric grill. Arrange half of the vegetables on grill rack. Grill for 6 to 8 minutes or until crisp-tender and grill marks appear, turning once. Remove from grill rack; set aside. Repeat with remaining vegetables.

3. Brush polenta with reserved oil mixture. Place polenta on grill rack. Grill for 5 to 10 minutes or until heated through and lightly browned, turning once.

4. Meanwhile, in saucepan heat undrained tomatoes until boiling. Add grilled vegetables. Simmer, uncovered, 5 minutes or until desired consistency, stirring occasionally.

5. To serve, place polenta slices in four shallow bowls; spoon the vegetable mixture over polenta. Makes 4 servings.

CONVENTIONAL METHOD: Prepare vegetables and oil mixture as in Step 1. Preheat a grill pan or skillet over medium-high heat. Cook half of the vegetables as in Step 2; repeat with remaining vegetables. Use the grill pan to grill polenta slices as in Step 3. Continue as in Step 4. Serve as above.

Each serving: 275 cal., 14 g total fat (2 g sat. fat), 0 mg chol., 1,247 mg sodium, 33 g carbo., 13 g fiber, 6 g pro. Daily Values: 3% vit. A, 23% vit. C, 4% calcium, 9% iron.

For fennel, carefully cut about 1 inch above the bulb. Discard the stalks, saving some of the feathery leaves for a garnish.

Deluxe Chicken and Roasted Pepper Sandwich

This recipe works well on either a covered or uncovered indoor grill since the chicken cooks quickly and remains juicy.

PREP: 15 minutes **MARINATE:** 15 minutes **GRILL:** 4 minutes

- 1/4 cup olive oil
- 4 tsp. red wine vinegar
- 1 Tbsp. snipped fresh thyme
- 1/2 tsp. salt
- 1/4 tsp. crushed red pepper
- 4 skinless, boneless chicken breast halves (about 1 1/4 lb.)
- 4 1-inch-thick bias-cut slices Italian bread
- 1/4 cup semisoft cheese with herbs or semisoft goat cheese (chèvre)
- 1 cup roasted red sweet peppers (about one 7-oz. jar), cut into strips
- 1/2 cup fresh basil, watercress, or baby spinach leaves

INDOOR GRILL METHOD:

1. For marinade, whisk together oil, vinegar, thyme, salt, and crushed red pepper. Reserve 2 tablespoons; set aside.

2. Place chicken between two sheets of plastic wrap; pound lightly with a meat mallet to about 1/2-inch thickness *(see photo, page 149)*. Place in a plastic bag; add remaining marinade. Seal bag; marinate at room temperature about 15 minutes or in the refrigerator for up to 1 hour.

3. Lightly grease the rack of an indoor electric grill or lightly coat with nonstick cooking spray. Preheat grill. Brush cut sides of bread with reserved marinade. Place bread, cut sides down, on grill rack. If using a covered grill, close the lid. Grill until lightly toasted. (For a covered grill, allow 1 to 2 minutes. For an uncovered grill, allow 2 to 4 minutes, turning once halfway through grilling.) Remove bread from grill; set aside.

4. Drain chicken, discarding marinade. Place chicken on grill rack. If using a covered grill, close the lid. Grill until chicken is tender and no longer pink. (For covered grill, allow 3 to 4 minutes. For an uncovered grill, allow 8 to 10 minutes, turning once halfway through grilling.) Remove from grill; spread or sprinkle with semisoft cheese.

5. To serve, place one chicken breast on each bread slice. Top with roasted pepper strips and basil. Makes 4 servings.

CONVENTIONAL METHOD: Prepare marinade and chicken as in Steps 1 and 2. Toast bread slices in a skillet or grill pan or on a griddle over medium heat for 2 to 4 minutes, turning once. Remove bread from pan or griddle. Place chicken in the skillet, grill pan, or on the griddle. Cook over medium heat for 8 to 10 minutes or until tender and no longer pink, turning once. Remove from pan; spread or sprinkle with cheese. Serve as above.

Each serving: 418 cal., 20 g total fat (5 g sat. fat), 82 mg chol., 629 mg sodium, 21 g carbo., 2 g fiber, 37 g pro. Daily Values: 5% vit. A, 177% vit. C, 5% calcium, 14% iron.

Quick Grilled Herbed Ratatouille and Polenta

Beef and Red Bean Chili

Tangy Barbecue Beef

Beef and Red Bean Chili

Chipotle (smoked jalapeño peppers) in adobo sauce is doubly delicious. The jalapeño provides a direct hit of heat, while the adobo sauce is a slow burn. Together, they leave a warm glow.

PREP: 1¼ hours **COOK:** 5 or 10 hours

- 1 cup dry red beans or kidney beans
- 1 Tbsp. olive oil
- 2 lb. boneless beef chuck, cut into 1-inch cubes
- 1 large onion, coarsely chopped
- 1 15-oz. can tomato sauce
- 1 14½-oz. can diced tomatoes with mild chiles
- 1 14-oz. can beef broth
- 1 or 2 chipotle chile peppers in adobo sauce, finely chopped, plus 2 tsp. adobo sauce
- 2 tsp. dried oregano, crushed
- 1 tsp. ground cumin
- ½ tsp. salt
- 1 medium red sweet pepper, chopped
- ¼ cup snipped fresh cilantro

CROCKERY COOKER METHOD:

1. Rinse beans; place in large saucepan. Add water to cover. Bring to boiling; reduce heat. Simmer, uncovered, for 10 minutes. Remove from heat. Cover and let stand 1 hour.

2. In a skillet heat oil over medium-high heat. Cook half of the beef and all of the onion until mixture is lightly browned. Transfer to a 3½- or 4-quart crockery cooker. Repeat with remaining beef. Add tomato sauce, undrained tomatoes, broth, chipotle peppers and adobo sauce, oregano, cumin, and salt. Stir until combined. Drain and rinse beans. Stir into cooker.

3. Cover and cook on low-heat setting for 10 to 12 hours or high-heat setting for 5 to 6 hours or until meat and beans are tender *(see photo, page 67)*. Serve with red sweet pepper and cilantro. Makes 6 servings.

CONVENTIONAL METHOD: Prepare beans as in Step 1, except use a 4- to 5-quart Dutch oven. Drain and rinse beans; set aside. Brown beef and onion as in Step 2, except use Dutch oven. Return all meat to pan. Stir in the tomato sauce, undrained tomatoes, broth, chipotle peppers and adobo sauce, oregano, cumin, salt, and beans. Bring to boiling; reduce heat. Cover and simmer for 1½ to 2 hours or until meat and beans are tender *(see photo, page 67)*. Serve as above.

Each serving: 516 cal., 26 g total fat (9 g sat. fat), 98 mg chol., 1,162 mg sodium, 32 g carbo., 8 g fiber, 38 g pro. Daily Values: 34% vit. A, 91% vit. C, 7% calcium, 34% iron.

CROCKERY COOKERS

Today, most crockery cookers are continuous slow cookers—they cook foods slowly and continuously at a low wattage via heating coils that wrap around the sides and remain on during cooking. Continuous cookers have fixed settings: low (200° F) or high (300° F). Our recipes are designed for continuous cookers and will not work in intermittent cookers. (Intermittent cookers have dials indicating the temperature in degrees and heat with coils below the food that cycle on and off.) Crockery cookers range in size from 1 to 6 quarts. Be sure your crockery cooker is the right size for the recommendation in the recipe so the food will cook properly. For best results, fill the crockery cooker at least half full, but no more than two-thirds full. For most recipes, you do not need to stir. Lifting the lid to stir can lower the cooker temperature and prolong the cooking time.

From our Test Kitchen expert, Judy Comstock: "The crockery cookers with removable liners are my favorite. They're so easy to clean."

MOROCCAN MENU

Fruit Salad with Cranberry Dressing *(page 109)*
Spicy Lamb Shanks *(right)*
Hot cooked couscous
Warm pita bread
Caramel Clementines *(page 58)*

Tangy Barbecue Beef

Freeze any remaining beef in a tightly covered freezer container for up to three months.

PREP: 25 minutes **COOK:** 10 hours **STAND:** 15 minutes

- 2 Tbsp. chili powder
- 1 tsp. celery seeds
- 1/2 tsp. salt
- 1/2 tsp. ground black pepper
- 1 3-lb. fresh beef brisket, trimmed of fat
- 2 onions, thinly sliced
- 1 cup bottled smoke-flavored barbecue sauce
- 1/2 cup beer or ginger ale
- 8 large sandwich buns or Portuguese rolls, split and toasted
- Bottled hot pepper sauce (optional)
- Mango slices

CROCKERY COOKER METHOD:

1. In a small bowl combine chili powder, celery seeds, salt, and pepper. Rub the spice mixture onto all sides of the brisket. Scatter half of the sliced onions in the bottom of a $3^{1}/_{2}$- to 6-quart crockery cooker. Place the brisket on the onions, cutting the meat to fit the cooker, if necessary. Scatter remaining onions on top of the brisket. In small bowl stir together barbecue sauce and beer or ginger ale. Pour over brisket and onions.

2. Cover and cook on low-heat setting for 10 to 12 hours or until meat is fork-tender. Transfer meat to cutting board; let stand 15 minutes. Halve meat crosswise. Using 2 forks, pull meat into shreds. Return meat to sauce mixture in cooker. Heat sauce through using the high-heat setting.

3. To serve, use a slotted spoon to fill buns with beef mixture. If desired, season with bottled hot pepper sauce. Top with mango. Makes 8 servings.

CONVENTIONAL METHOD: Preheat oven to 325° F. Combine the seasoning mixture and rub onto brisket as in Step 1. Place meat in a shallow roasting pan. Top with all the sliced onions; pour a mixture of barbecue sauce and beer over meat. Cover and roast about 3 hours or until meat is fork tender. Remove meat; let stand 15 minutes. Halve meat crosswise and shred. Pour sauce into saucepan; add meat. Heat through. Serve as above.

Each serving: 442 cal., 11 g total fat (3 g sat. fat), 98 mg chol., 971 mg sodium, 41 g carbo., 3 g fiber, 41 g pro. Daily Values: 36% vit. A, 16% vit. C, 9% calcium, 28% iron.

Spicy Lamb Shanks

Infused with orange and aromatic spices, this dish is the perfect warming supper for chilly March days.

PREP: 25 minutes **COOK:** 8 hours

- 2 large oranges
- $1^{1}/_{4}$ cups beef broth
- $1^{1}/_{2}$ tsp. ground cardamom
- 1 tsp. ground cumin
- 1/2 tsp. salt
- 1/2 tsp. ground turmeric
- 1/2 tsp. pepper
- 5 carrots, cut into 2-inch lengths
- $1^{1}/_{2}$ cups boiling onions, peeled*
- 4 large cloves garlic, thinly sliced
- 4 lb. lamb foreshanks (3 or 4)
- 2 3-inch cinnamon sticks
- 2 Tbsp. water
- 4 tsp. cornstarch
- 1/3 cup pitted kalamata or other black olives, halved, if desired
- 1 Tbsp. snipped fresh cilantro

CROCKERY COOKER METHOD:

1. Using a vegetable peeler, remove orange part of peel from an orange. Cut into thin strips (about 1/4 cup); set aside. Squeeze juice from oranges to make about 2/3 cup. Stir together juice, broth, cardamom, cumin, salt, turmeric, and pepper. Set aside.

2. Place carrots, onions, and garlic in 5- to 6-quart crockery cooker. Top with lamb shanks, cinnamon sticks, and orange peel. Pour orange juice mixture over all. Cover and cook on low-heat setting for 8 to 9 hours or until lamb pulls easily from bone.

3. To serve, use a slotted spoon to transfer lamb shanks and vegetables to serving dish. Skim fat from cooking liquid. Remove and discard cinnamon sticks. Measure $1^{1}/_{2}$ cups juices; transfer to small saucepan. Combine water and cornstarch; add to juices. Cook and stir over medium heat until thickened and bubbly. Cook and stir 2 minutes more. Spoon sauce over lamb. Sprinkle with olives and cilantro. Makes 4 to 6 servings.

CONVENTIONAL METHOD: Prepare orange peel and orange juice mixture as in Step 1. Place lamb shanks in bottom of 5- to 6-quart Dutch oven. Top with cinnamon sticks and orange peel. Pour the orange juice mixture over all. Bring to boiling; reduce heat. Cover and simmer for 1 hour. Top with carrots, onions, and garlic. Cover and simmer for 30 minutes to 1 hour longer or until meat and vegetables are tender. Continue as in Step 3, except prepare and thicken the sauce using a Dutch oven. Serve as directed.

***TEST KITCHEN TIP:** To make it easier to peel boiling onions, place the onions in a saucepan with water. Bring to boiling and cook for 30 seconds. When cool enough to handle, slice off the root ends of onions and squeeze the onions from their peels.

Each serving: 461 cal., 21 g total fat (8 g sat. fat), 150 mg chol., 760 mg sodium, 22 g carbo., 6 g fiber, 44 g pro. Daily Values: 538% vit. A, 38% vit. C, 9% calcium, 24% iron.

Spicy Lamb Shanks

Jamaican Pork Stew

Sicilian Artichokes

PRESSURE COOKERS

In these pots, food cooks on the stove top in a sealed environment, trapping steam and building up pressure so liquids become about 38° F hotter than boiling, or 250° F. The higher temperature translates to faster cooking. In a pressure cooker, foods actually cook three to ten times faster than ordinary cooking methods. Follow the manufacturer's directions when filling and opening the pan. You don't want the release of steam to burn you. The best kinds of foods to cook in a pressure cooker are those that cook well in moist heat at a fairly high temperature without losing quality: pot roasts, vegetables, chicken, and stews.

From our Test Kitchen expert, Jennifer Kalinowski: "I was always afraid of pressure cookers, because of the steam. But, after using one, I discovered how safe and easy they are to use. Our recipes are flavorful and cook in minutes."

Jamaican Pork Stew

Until recently, plantains and yuca were produce items found only in Latino markets and American border towns. With the interest in foods of Central and South America, these starches are now in practically every well-stocked supermarket.

PREP: 40 minutes **COOK:** 6 minutes (at pressure)

- 1 small yuca or white potato (about 12 oz.), peeled
- 2 Tbsp. olive oil
- 1½ lb. boneless pork loin, cut into 1-inch cubes
- 1 plantain, peeled and cut into ¾-inch-thick slices
- 1 large onion, sliced
- 3 cloves garlic, minced
- 1 to 1½ tsp. Jamaican jerk seasoning
- ½ tsp. salt
- 2 large sweet potatoes (about 24 oz. total), peeled and cut into ½- to 1-inch cubes
- 1¼ cups chicken broth
- ½ cup dried apricots, halved

PRESSURE COOKER METHOD:

1. Halve yuca lengthwise; discard fibrous center. Cut into 1-inch pieces; set aside.

2. Remove rack from a 6-quart pressure cooker. Heat oil in pressure cooker. Cook and stir pork, plantain, and onion, half at a time, in hot oil over medium-high heat until lightly browned. Return all pork mixture to pan. Add garlic, jerk seasoning, and the ½ teaspoon salt. Cook and stir for 30 seconds. Add yuca, sweet potatoes, broth, and apricots to cooker.

3. Cover and lock lid in place. Bring up to pressure over high heat. Reduce heat just enough to maintain pressure. Cook 6 minutes. Quick-release pressure. Carefully remove lid. Season to taste with salt and pepper. Makes 6 servings.

CONVENTIONAL METHOD: Prepare yuca as in Step 1. Heat oil in Dutch oven; cook and stir pork, plantain, and onion, half at a time, in hot oil over medium-high heat until lightly browned. Return all of the pork mixture to pan. Add garlic, jerk seasoning, and ½ teaspoon salt; cook and stir for 30 seconds. Add only 1 cup broth. Bring to boiling; reduce heat. Cover and simmer for 30 minutes. Stir in yuca, sweet potatoes, and apricots. Return to boiling; reduce heat. Cover and simmer for 20 to 30 minutes or until meat is tender.

Each serving: 480 cal., 11 g total fat (3 g sat. fat), 62 mg chol., 566 mg sodium, 65 g carbo., 6 g fiber, 31 g pro. Daily Values: 434% vit. A, 91% vit. C, 6% calcium, 14% iron.

Sicilian Artichokes

This is a classic Sicilian Lenten dish, both because it is meatless and because artichokes are in season during this time of year.

PREP: 45 minutes **COOK:** 8 minutes (at pressure)

- 3 cups onion and/or garlic croutons
- ½ cup finely chopped red or yellow sweet pepper
- ½ cup shredded mozzarella cheese (2 oz.)
- ¼ cup finely shredded Parmesan cheese
- 4 anchovy fillets, rinsed, patted dry, and finely chopped (optional)
- 2 Tbsp. olive oil
- 1 Tbsp. snipped fresh oregano or 1 tsp. dried oregano, crushed
- 1 Tbsp. balsamic vinegar
- ¼ tsp. salt
- ¼ tsp. freshly ground black pepper
- ¼ to ⅓ cup chicken broth
- 4 large artichokes (about 10 oz. each)
- 2 Tbsp. lemon juice
- 1 cup water

PRESSURE COOKER METHOD:

1. For filling, in a large bowl coarsely crush croutons. Add sweet pepper, mozzarella and Parmesan cheeses, and, if desired, anchovies. In small bowl combine oil, oregano, vinegar, salt, and pepper; drizzle over crouton mixture. Stir in enough broth for desired moistness. Set aside.

2. Wash artichokes; trim stems and remove loose outer leaves. Cut off 1 inch from top of each artichoke; snip off leaf tips with kitchen scissors. Brush edges with some of the lemon juice. Thump artichokes, point sides down, on countertop and centers will open to expose yellow center leaves and chokes. Pull outer leaves away from center leaves. Scoop out inner yellow leaves and fuzzy centers. Brush insides with remaining lemon juice. Spoon filling into artichokes, packing lightly.

3. Pour water into a 6-quart pressure cooker. (Recipe works best in a stainless-steel pressure cooker. Artichokes tend to discolor with aluminum.) Place artichokes, stuffing sides up, on rack in pressure cooker.

4. Cover and lock lid in place. Bring up to pressure over high heat (allow about 10 minutes). Adjust heat for moderate cooking. Cook 8 minutes. Quick-release pressure. Carefully remove lid. Pass additional oil for drizzling. Makes 4 servings.

CONVENTIONAL METHOD: Prepare artichokes as through Step 2. Place artichokes, stuffing sides up, in a 4- to 5-quart stainless-steel or enamel-coated Dutch oven. Add 1½ cups water to pan. Bring to boiling; reduce heat. Cover and simmer for 25 to 30 minutes or until leaf pulls out easily. Carefully remove with tongs. Serve as above.

Each serving: 418 cal., 16 g total fat (4 g sat. fat), 14 mg chol., 1,089 mg sodium, 55 g carbo., 19 g fiber, 24 g pro. Daily Values: 24% vit. A, 113% vit. C, 29% calcium, 19% iron.

DEEP FRYERS

What's not to like? Today's deep fryers are easy to use and, better yet, easy to clean. Tightly sealing covers eliminate the messy spatters and reduce the odors of regular frying. Many models even have extra-large viewing windows, so you can watch foods fry without opening the cover.

From our Test Kitchen expert, Jill Moberly: "I never liked frying until I tried the newer fryers. Once your oil is preheated, you simply add the food, shut the lid, and you're frying. I also love not having to use a thermometer to monitor the heat."

Egg Rolls

PREP: 25 minutes **COOK:** 2 minutes per batch

- 8 egg roll skins
- 1 recipe Pork Filling (below)
- Cooking oil for deep frying
- 1⅓ cups bottled sweet-and-sour sauce or ½ cup prepared Chinese-style hot mustard

DEEP FRYER METHOD:

1. For each egg roll, place an egg roll skin on a flat surface with a corner pointing toward you. Spoon about ¼ cup of the Pork Filling across and just below center of egg roll skin. Fold bottom corner over filling, tucking it under on the other side. Fold the side corners over filling, forming an envelope shape. Roll egg roll toward remaining corner. Moisten top corner with water; press firmly to seal.

2. Heat oil in electric deep-fryer according to manufacturer's directions. Fry egg rolls, a few at a time, for 2 to 3 minutes or until golden brown. Remove with slotted spoon; drain on paper towels. Keep warm in 300° F oven while frying remaining egg rolls. Serve with sweet-and-sour sauce or hot mustard. Makes 8 egg rolls.

CONVENTIONAL METHOD: Prepare egg rolls as in Step 1. For frying, use heavy 3-quart saucepan filled with about 2 inches cooking oil. Attach a deep-fat frying thermometer to side of saucepan. Heat oil over medium heat to 365° F. Fry egg rolls as in Step 2. Serve as above.

PORK FILLING: In skillet cook ½ pound ground pork, 1 teaspoon grated fresh ginger, and 1 clove minced garlic for 2 to 3 minutes or until meat is brown; drain fat. Add ½ cup finely chopped bok choy or cabbage, ½ cup chopped water chestnuts, ½ cup shredded carrot, and ¼ cup finely chopped onion. Cook and stir for 2 minutes. In a small bowl combine 2 tablespoons soy sauce, 2 teaspoons cornstarch, ½ teaspoon sugar, and ¼ teaspoon salt; add to skillet. Cook and stir for 1 minute more. Cool slightly.

Each egg roll: 240 cal., 3 g total fat (1 g sat. fat), 16 mg chol., 794 mg sodium, 44 g carbo., 1 g fiber, 9 g pro. Daily Values: 46% vit. A, 17% vit. C, 8% calcium, 10% iron.

Zesty Ravioli Salad

Any flavor ravioli tastes great. Your choice. We especially like the ones with multiple cheeses.

PREP: 25 minutes **COOK:** 2 minutes per batch

- 1 9-oz. pkg. refrigerated ravioli (any flavor)
- 1 cup seasoned fine dry bread crumbs
- ¼ cup whole milk, half-and-half, or light cream
- 1 egg, slightly beaten
- Cooking oil for deep frying
- 6 cups torn mixed salad greens
- 1 cup halved or quartered cherry tomatoes
- ¼ cup torn fresh basil
- ¼ cup bottled balsamic vinaigrette or Italian vinaigrette
- Finely shredded Parmesan cheese

DEEP FRYER METHOD:

1. In a large saucepan cook ravioli in salted boiling water for 3 minutes; drain well. Place bread crumbs in a shallow dish. In another shallow dish stir together milk and egg until combined. Dip ravioli into egg mixture, then into bread crumb mixture. Cover and chill while oil heats.

2. Heat oil in electric deep-fryer according to manufacturer's directions. Fry ravioli, half at a time, about 2 minutes or until golden. Remove with slotted spoon; drain on paper towels. Keep warm in 300° F oven.

3. Meanwhile, for salad, in a large bowl combine greens, tomatoes, and basil. Add vinaigrette; toss to coat. Divide among serving plates. Top with ravioli. Sprinkle with Parmesan cheese. Pass additional vinaigrette. Makes 4 main-dish servings.

CONVENTIONAL METHOD: Prepare ravioli as in Step 1. For frying, use heavy 3-quart saucepan filled with about 2 inches cooking oil. Attach deep-fat frying thermometer to side of pan. Heat oil over medium heat to 365° F. Carefully add ravioli to oil, 4 or 5 at a time (do not add too many at once or oil temperature will drop). Fry about 2 minutes or until golden. Remove with a slotted spoon; drain on paper towels and keep warm. Continue as in Step 3.

Each serving: 520 cal., 28 g total fat (6 g sat. fat), 118 mg chol., 1,215 mg sodium, 49 g carbo., 2 g fiber, 19 g pro. Daily Values: 17% vit. A, 22% vit. C, 17% calcium, 18% iron.

Zesty Ravioli Salad

MAKING A "BIG" PURCHASE OF SMALL APPLIANCES

▪ Do your homework. Check out the housewares department of any large retailer or specialty kitchen shop. Often, the appliances are lined up side by side, where you can see and touch the differences. Many manufacturers offer helpful information on their Web sites.

▪ Determine how often you're likely to use the appliance. This will help you determine how much money to spend.

▪ Still unsure? Give an appliance a test run in your own kitchen. Borrow one from a friend or relative and try a favorite recipe.

Oriental Cashew Asparagus

PREP: 20 minutes **COOK:** 6 minutes

- 1 lb. asparagus spears
- 1½ cups quartered fresh button mushrooms
- 1 medium red onion, cut into thin wedges
- ¼ cup chopped red sweet pepper
- 1 Tbsp. butter or margarine
- 1 tsp. cornstarch
- ¼ tsp. ground black pepper
- 2 Tbsp. teriyaki sauce
- 1 Tbsp. water
- 2 Tbsp. cashew halves

TABLETOP STEAMER METHOD:

1. Snap off and discard woody bases from asparagus. If desired, scrape off scales. Bias-slice asparagus into 1-inch pieces (you should have 3 cups).

2. Place asparagus in bottom of steamer basket. Steam the asparagus according to manufacturer's directions for 2 minutes. Carefully add mushrooms, onion, and sweet pepper. Steam for 2 to 5 minutes more or until vegetables are crisp-tender.

3. Meanwhile, in a medium saucepan melt butter or margarine; stir in cornstarch and black pepper. Add the teriyaki sauce and water. Cook and stir until thickened and bubbly. Add vegetables to saucepan; toss gently to coat. Top with cashews. Makes 4 servings.

CONVENTIONAL METHOD: Prepare asparagus as in Step 1. In a medium saucepan bring 1 cup water to boiling; reduce heat. Place asparagus in a steamer basket. Place steamer basket in saucepan. Cover and steam asparagus, and then mushrooms, onion, and sweet pepper as in Step 2. Remove basket; discard liquid. In the same saucepan melt butter or margarine. Continue as in step 3. Serve as above.

Each serving: 105 cal., 6 g total fat (2 g sat. fat), 8 mg chol., 381 mg sodium, 11 g carbo., 3 g fiber, 5 g pro. Daily Values: 23% vit. A, 46% vit. C, 3% calcium, 9% iron.

Lime-Steamed Salmon

PREP: 15 minutes **COOK:** 12 minutes

- 2 limes
- 1 1-lb. salmon fillet (about 1 inch thick), skinned and cut into 3 pieces
- 1 Tbsp. grated fresh ginger
- ⅛ tsp. salt
- ⅛ tsp. black pepper
- 2 Tbsp. toasted sesame oil
- 2 cups trimmed small green beans (about 8 oz.) or one 9-oz. pkg. frozen French-cut green beans

TABLETOP STEAMER METHOD:

1. Shred 2 teaspoons of peel from limes; set aside. Thinly slice limes; place slices in bottom of steamer basket. Rinse fish; pat dry. Place fish in a single layer on top of lime slices. Stir reserved lime peel, ginger, salt, and pepper into oil; brush onto fish.

2. Place the fresh or frozen beans in the upper section of steamer container. Steam the fish and beans according to manufacturer's directions for 12 to 15 minutes or until fish flakes easily when tested with a fork and beans are crisp-tender. Arrange beans in serving dish; top with fish. Makes 3 servings.

CONVENTIONAL METHOD: Prepare limes, fish, and oil mixture as in Step 1. In a medium saucepan cover and cook fresh or frozen green beans in a small amount of boiling salted water about 15 minutes for fresh beans (5 to 6 minutes for frozen beans). Drain. Meanwhile, in a very large skillet bring 4 cups water to boiling; reduce heat. Place lime slices and fish in a steamer basket. Brush fish with oil mixture. Place steamer basket in skillet. Cover and steam about 10 minutes or until fish flakes easily when tested with a fork. Serve as above.

Each serving: 293 cal., 14 g total fat (2 g sat. fat), 78 mg chol., 204 mg sodium, 11 g carbo., 4 g fiber, 32 g pro. Daily Values: 13% vit. A, 42% vit. C, 6% calcium, 12% iron.

TABLETOP STEAMERS

These machines feature a multitude of cooking benefits, so read the owner's manual to get the most from your steamer. In a nutshell, foods cook as steam circulates inside the appliance. Since steam is hotter than dry oven air, foods cook quicker than they do during baking, but hold their shape better than during boiling. Depending on the model, you'll find you can magically steam entire meals, vegetables, rice, fish, and even traditional puddings. If the steamer has two racks, you can cook a couple of different foods at once.

From our Test Kitchen expert, Maryellyn Krantz: "Until now, I'd always thought a steamer was just for cooking rice, but I've discovered that this handy appliance can be used to prepare the whole meal. It's a cinch to clean up."

Lime-Steamed Salmon

Quick Cioppino

Flex Your Mussels

DON'T BE SHY; SHOW YOUR MUSSELS.

Steamed fresh mussels, that is. Fresh mussels are becoming more available throughout the country and are especially popular in soups, appetizers, and pastas. If you buy fresh mussels, scrub them well and remove the beards that are visable between the shells. Then try them in this simple appetizer and favorite seafood soup.

Mediterranean

Prince Edward

Green Lip

Quick Cioppino

This version of San Francisco's delicious fish stew is very easy to make.

START TO FINISH: 50 minutes

- 6 oz. fresh or frozen cod fillets
- 6 oz. fresh or frozen peeled and deveined shrimp
- 8 oz. live mussels
- 4 qt. cold water
- 1/3 cup salt
- 1 medium green sweet pepper, cut into thin bite-size strips
- 1 cup chopped onion (1 large)
- 2 cloves garlic, minced
- 1 Tbsp. olive oil or cooking oil
- 2 14 1/2-ounce cans Italian-style stewed tomatoes, undrained
- 1/2 cup water
- 3 Tbsp. snipped fresh basil

1. Thaw cod and shrimp, if frozen. Discard mussels with broken shells. Pull off "beards." Using a stiff brush, scrub mussels under cold running water.

2. In a Dutch oven combine the 4 quarts cold water and the 1/3 cup salt; add mussels. Soak for 15 minutes. Drain and rinse. Soak, drain, and rinse twice more in unsalted water.

3. Rinse cod and shrimp; pat dry. Cut cod into 1-inch pieces.

4. In the same Dutch oven cook sweet pepper, onion, and garlic in hot oil until tender. Stir in undrained tomatoes and the 1/3 cup water. Bring to boiling. Stir in cod, shrimp, and mussels. Return to boiling; reduce heat. Cover and simmer for 3 to 4 minutes or until cod flakes easily when tested with a fork, shrimp turn opaque, and mussel shells open. Discard any unopened mussel shells. Stir in basil. Makes 4 main-dish servings.

Each serving: 268 cal., 7 g total fat (1 g sat. fat), 99 mg chol., 684 mg sodium, 22 g carbo., 3 g fiber, 26 g pro. Daily Values: 8% vit. A, 51% vit. C, 11% calcium, 24% iron.

BETWEEN THE SHELLS

- Mussels are available year-round. They may come from either coast, Europe, or New Zealand (Green Lip).
- Allow 1/4 to 1/2 pound mussels per person to serve as an appetizer, 1/2 to 1 pound as a main course.
- Buy mussels only from reputable, licensed seafood dealers.
- When you purchase mussels, they should be alive, with shells slightly agape. To check, tap the mussel hard with your fingertip. If the shell closes, even slightly, that means the mussel is alive, fresh, and okay to cook.
- Store live mussels in the refrigerator, uncovered, for up to two days.
- Before cooking, soak mussels in salt water for 15 minutes, then rinse twice.

Mussels Steamed in Wine

Use any leftovers as a delicious stir-in for marinated salads, pastas, or fish stews.

PREP: 1 hour **COOK:** 6 minutes

- 1 lb. live mussels
- 4 qt. cold water
- 1/3 cup salt
- 1 medium onion, finely chopped (about 1/2 cup)
- 3 cloves garlic, minced
- 2 Tbsp. olive oil
- 1/2 cup dry white wine, chicken broth, or vegetable broth
- 1/2 cup water
- 2 bay leaves
- 1/4 tsp. salt
- 2 Tbsp. snipped fresh parsley
- Freshly cracked black pepper
- Lemon wedges (optional)

1. Discard mussels with broken shells. Pull off "beards." Using a stiff brush, scrub mussels under cold running water.

2. In a Dutch oven combine 4 quarts cold water and the 1/3 cup salt; add mussels. Soak for 15 minutes. Drain and rinse. Soak, drain, and rinse twice more in unsalted water.

3. In the same Dutch oven cook onion and garlic in hot olive oil over medium heat for 3 to 4 minutes or just until tender. Carefully add wine, water, bay leaves, and the 1/4 teaspoon salt. Bring to boiling. Place the mussels in a steamer basket. Set basket in Dutch oven. Cover and steam for 3 to 5 minutes or until shells open.

4. Lift steamer basket from Dutch oven, reserving steaming liquid. Discard any unopened mussels and the bay leaves. Divide the mussels among four large, shallow soup bowls. Pour the steaming liquid over each portion. Sprinkle with parsley and pepper. If desired, serve with lemon wedges. Makes 4 appetizer servings.

MUSSELS WITH TOMATO: Prepare recipe as directed, except add 1 ripe tomato, seeded and finely chopped, along with the wine.

Each serving: 114 cal., 7 g total fat (1 g sat. fat), 8 mg chol., 231 mg sodium, 4 g carbo., 1 g fiber, 4 g pro. Daily Values: 3% vit. A, 10% vit. C, 2% calcium, 9% iron.

Asparagus

TEN IDEAS FOR SERVING UP THE SPEARS

- Dress up a melted cheese-and-bacon sandwich by adding stalks of blanched or roasted asparagus.
- Toss cooked asparagus pieces with cooked pasta, grated Parmesan, olive oil, and lemon juice.
- Wrap cooked spears in prosciutto for a simple hors d'oeuvre.
- Roll thin fish fillets around spears of blanched asparagus, then bake.
- Marinate uncooked asparagus in balsamic vinegar, then grill.
- Toss cooked, chopped asparagus into cooked risotto or wild rice.
- Add asparagus and fresh herbs, such as tarragon, to soup broths.
- Fold cooked asparagus and smoked salmon into an omelet.
- Roast asparagus drizzled with orange juice, olive oil, and orange peel in a 450° F oven.
- Puree cooked stalks with a small amount of water, lemon juice, and olive oil for an asparagus sauce.

Asparagus

THE APPEARANCE OF THIN, YOUNG ASPARAGUS SPEARS

in the market is a surefire sign of spring. While available year-round, asparagus is at its peak in March and April. But don't just grab any bunch in the produce aisle. Check out how it's stocked. Ideally, asparagus should be standing upright in a container filled with a couple of inches of water.

To store asparagus at home, wrap the stalk bottoms in a damp paper towel, then wrap that in foil. The shoots will stay crisp and tender in the fridge for two to four days before they start to lose their flavor.

When cooked to crisp-tender, asparagus has a distinctive, pleasantly pungent flavor. And cooking asparagus is a snap, really. To know exactly where the tender, edible part begins, hold the stalk at the bottom and just below the tip. Bend the spear several times until you find the place that is most flexible; snap it off there. Then, tidy up the end with a knife.

Lay the stalks in a skillet filled with about 1/2 inch of boiling water and cook 3 to 4 minutes (depending on the thickness of the stalks) or until the stalks turn bright green. Don't overcook; asparagus will become woody and fibrous, with an assertive odor and a wilted appearance. To serve asparagus cold, place cooked, drained asparagus in a colander under cold water or place in an ice bath.

To ensure you get tender and flavorful stalks, follow these guidelines for selecting fresh asparagus spears at your market:

- Tightly closed tips.
- Deep green and/or purplish color (not sage or grayish green).
- Taut skin. You don't want to see any wrinkling along the stalk, which is a sure sign of age.
- Firm stalks. Here's an easy test: Hold a stalk from the bottom and it should stand up straight—even if it's pencil thin.

One last word on the finished product: According to today's etiquette experts, it's ok to eat asparagus with your fingers as long as the stalks are firm and not dripping with a sauce or melted butter. Otherwise, use a knife and fork.

Asparagus with Almond Sauce

Start to Finish: 15 minutes

- 1 lb. asparagus spears or one 10-oz. pkg. frozen asparagus spears
- 1 Tbsp. butter or margarine
- 2 Tbsp. sliced almonds
- 1 1/4 tsp. cornstarch
- 1/2 cup water
- 2 tsp. lemon juice
- 1/2 tsp. instant chicken bouillon granules
- Dash black pepper

1. Snap off and discard woody bases from fresh asparagus. If desired, scrape off scales. Cover and cook fresh asparagus in a small amount of boiling lightly salted water for 3 to 5 minutes or until crisp-tender. (Or cook frozen asparagus according to package directions.) Drain well; transfer asparagus to a serving platter.

2. Meanwhile, for sauce, in a small saucepan melt butter or margarine; add almonds. Cook and stir over medium-low heat for 3 to 5 minutes or until golden. Stir in cornstarch. Stir in water, lemon juice, bouillon granules, and pepper. Cook and stir until thickened and bubbly. Cook and stir for 2 minutes more. Spoon over asparagus. Makes 4 servings.

Eachr serving: 73 cal., 6 g total fat (2 g sat. fat), 8 mg chol., 179 mg sodium, 3 g carbo., 1 g fiber, 3 g pro. Daily Values: 4% vit. A, 26% vit. C, 2% calcium, 4% iron.

Measuring Up

TWO TYPES OF MEASURING CUPS–LIQUID AND DRY MEASURES–ARE ESSENTIAL IN THE KITCHEN.

The main difference between the two? A liquid measure filled to capacity leaves room to move the cup without spilling the liquid. A dry measure is designed to be filled, then leveled to get a precise reading. Leveling with a knife blade works best.

A trip up the housewares aisle of major department stores or specialty kitchen shops is an easy way to buy measuring tools. The sturdy glass or plastic liquid measures you'll find are hard to beat. Most liquid measures require that you check the amount at eye level.

For dry ingredients, pick a set of 1/4-, 1/3-, 1/2-, and 1-cup measures. If they nest, you'll save on storage space. With measuring spoons, you'll want to have more than one set (in 1/8 teaspoon to 1 tablespoon increments) so you don't have to wash spoons in mid-recipe. Leave spoons attached to the ring they come on so they won't get lost in action.

Pack solid vegetable shortening or butter into dry measures to eliminate air spaces. Level the top with a knife blade.

Measuring spoons should be dry when used. Scoop your ingredient to overflowing, then level with a table knife. Narrow spoons that fit easily into spice jars are a wise choice.

Measure flour by gently spooning it into your cup. Don't pack down the flour. Slide a knife blade over the rim to level, letting excess fall back into the bag.

Place the liquid measuring cup on a level surface; bend down to read at eye level while pouring to the correct mark. Select glass cups for easier reading; a 2-cup measure is standard, and a 4-cup measure is helpful to have on hand.

Dino Kale Sauté

All Hail the Mighty Kale

IT'S TIME TO STEP OUTSIDEOF YOUR COMFORT ZONE AND VENTURE INTO

the green unknown. We're talking about eating kale, collards, turnip greens, and mustard greens. These veggies are nutritionally supercharged and bursting with plant chemicals that medical studies indicate we should consume to prevent cancer, heart disease, and even vision problems.

Ruffly bluish-green kale leads the leafy group in phyto-chemicals—the substances that give plants color, flavor, and health-boosting abilities. Researchers are constantly uncovering more health benefits of these plant chemicals. For instance, the hefty load of lutein in kale is linked to a reduced risk of eye problems. Other components of kale make it a cancer-fighting vegetable, especially against cancers of the colon, stomach, lung, and breast. Kale also is high in vitamin A, has almost as much calcium as milk, and contains a burst of potassium.

Before cooking greens, wash them well. Soil likes to hide amid their ruffles. Remove tough stems, and cook leaves in a bit of boiling broth or salted water until tender—two to four minutes—before using in a recipe. Serve cooked greens in soups, tossed with garlic-flavored olive oil and a splash of vinegar, or in these recipes *(right)*.

Dino Kale Sauté

Prep: 5 minutes **Cook:** 3 minutes

- 12 oz. dinosaur kale or regular kale, cut or torn into 1- to 2-inch pieces (about 12 cups)
- 2 Tbsp. olive oil
- 1/4 cup soft sourdough or French bread crumbs
- 1/8 tsp. pepper
- 1 tsp. white wine Worcestershire sauce
- Lemon wedges (optional)

1. Rinse kale thoroughly under cold running water. Drain well; set aside.

2. In a small skillet heat 2 teaspoons of the oil over medium heat. Cook and stir bread crumbs in hot oil for 1 to 2 minutes or until browned. Sprinkle with pepper; set aside.

3. In a large nonstick skillet heat the remaining 4 teaspoons oil. Add kale. Cover and cook for 1 minute. Uncover. Cook and stir for 1 minute more or just until wilted.

4. Transfer kale to a serving dish. Drizzle with Worcestershire sauce. Sprinkle with browned bread crumbs. If desired, squeeze lemon wedges over all. Makes 4 side-dish servings.

Each serving: 89 cal., 5 g total fat (1 g sat. fat), 0 mg chol., 53 mg sodium, 9 g carbo., 4 g fiber, 3 g pro. Daily Values: 96% vit. A, 94% vit. C,8% calcium, 8% iron.

Lamb and Orzo Soup

PREP: 15 minutes **COOK:** 1½ hours

- 2½ lb. lamb shanks
- 4 cups water
- 4 cups chicken or vegetable broth
- 2 bay leaves
- 1 Tbsp. snipped fresh oregano or 1 tsp. dried oregano, crushed
- 1½ tsp. snipped fresh marjoram or ½ tsp. dried marjoram, crushed
- ¼ tsp. pepper
- 2 medium carrots, cut into short thin strips (1 cup)
- 1 cup sliced celery (2 stalks)
- ¾ cup dried orzo (rosamarina) pasta
- 3 cups torn fresh kale, mustard greens, turnip greens, collard greens, or spinach
- Finely shredded Parmesan cheese (optional)

1. In a large Dutch oven combine lamb shanks, water, broth, bay leaves, oregano, marjoram, and pepper. Bring to boiling; reduce heat. Cover and simmer for 1¼ to 1¼ hours or until meat is tender.

2. Remove shanks from Dutch oven. When cool enough to handle, cut meat off bones; coarsely chop meat. Discard bones. Strain broth through a large sieve or colander lined with double thickness of 100-percent-cotton cheesecloth; discard bay leaves and herbs. Skim fat; return broth to Dutch oven.

3. Stir chopped meat, carrots, celery, and orzo into Dutch oven. Return to boiling; reduce heat. Cover and simmer about 15 minutes or until vegetables and orzo are tender. Stir in kale or spinach. Cook for 1 to 2 minutes more or just until kale is cooked. If desired, serve with Parmesan cheese. Makes 6 servings.

Each serving: 258 cal., 6 g total fat (2 g sat. fat), 82 mg chol., 635 mg sodium, 17 g carbo., 2 g fiber, 33 g pro. Daily Values: 163% vit. A, 71% vit. C, 8% calcium, 22% iron.

Mustard greens are more tender than kale, so they can be used raw in salads. They have a zesty mustard bite. The leaves mellow with simmering. Or you can steam them, sauté them, or stir-fry them.

Turnip greens, as you probably guessed, are simply the tops of turnips. Young greens are tender enough to eat raw in salads. Mature greens should be cooked like other leafy greens. Six ounces of cooked turnip greens contain 220 mg of calcium. By comparison, an 8-ounce glass of milk has 300 mg.

Collard greens, like kale, are related to the cabbage family. The deep-colored leaves have an irregular shape and torn-looking edges. Cook collards as you would kale.

Kale is often used as a garnish because of its frilly edges and varying colors of white, green, or purple. But it's a garnish you should eat because it's loaded with nutrients—phytochemicals, lutein, vitamin A, calcium, and potassium.

Hash Browns

MOST FOLKS HAVE AN OPINION ON HOW THEY LIKE THEIR HASH-BROWN potatoes—divided between those who like a crispy jumble of chopped golden nuggets and those who prefer long delicate shreds fried into an orderly, soul-fortifying cake.

We'll teach you both methods. But whichever camp you belong to, the secret to perfect hash browns is patience. Let hash browns cook for the full time called for in the recipe before turning so they'll develop a nice brown crust (peek after about 4 minutes to make sure they don't burn). Then, if making the shredded style, turn carefully—using two spatulas or a spatula and a fork—to keep the potatoes together. Turn chopped potatoes the same way, keeping them together as much as you can.

We've discovered that plain russet potatoes work the best for creating incredible shredded hash browns. You can also use whites or Yukon golds, if that's what you have on hand. For the chopped style, any potato works well.

Chopped Hash Browns

Russet potatoes (the brown ones) have a slightly drier, crumblier texture; the whites and reds are firmer and smoother in texture (*see bottom photo, page 106*).

PREP: 15 minutes **COOK:** 25 minutes

- 1/4 tsp. salt
- 4 to 5 small russet, white, or red potatoes (1 lb.)
- 1/4 cup finely chopped onion
- 1 small jalapeño or banana pepper, seeded and cut into thin strips (optional)
- 1/4 tsp. salt
- 1/8 tsp. coarsely ground black pepper (optional)
- 3 Tbsp. butter, cooking oil, or margarine

1. Fill a medium saucepan one-third full of water; add 1/4 teaspoon salt. Coarsely chop unpeeled potatoes by slicing lengthwise into strips, then cutting crosswise (see lower right opposite). Place potatoes in the saucepan. Bring water to boiling over high heat; reduce heat. Cook, uncovered, for 5 minutes. Drain well.

2. In a medium bowl combine potatoes, onion, jalapeño pepper strips (if desired), the remaining 1/4 teaspoon salt, and, if desired, black pepper.

3. In a large nonstick skillet melt butter. Add potato mixture; cook over medium heat about 20 minutes or until potatoes are soft and browned, turning occasionally. Makes 4 servings.

Each serving: 159 cal., 8 g total fat (8 g sat. fat), 21 mg chol., 280 mg sodium, 19 g carbo., 3 g fiber, 3 g pro. Daily Values: 6% vit. A, 27% vit. C, 2% calcium, 5% iron.

Shredded Hash Browns

PREP: 10 minutes **COOK:** 13 minutes

- 3 to 4 small russet or white potatoes (about 3/4 lb.)
- 1/4 cup finely chopped onion
- 1 small jalapeño, banana, or Anaheim pepper, seeded and chopped (optional)
- 1/4 tsp. salt
- 1/8 tsp. coarsely ground black pepper
- 2 Tbsp. butter, cooking oil, or margarine

1. Peel potatoes and coarsely shred using the coarsest side of the grater (see photo, bottom left)—you should have about 2 cups. Rinse shredded potatoes in a colander; drain well and pat dry. In a medium bowl combine shredded potatoes, onion, jalapeño pepper (if desired), salt, and black pepper.

2. In a large nonstick skillet heat butter over medium heat. Carefully add potatoes, pressing into an even pancake-like round (7 to 8 inches in diameter). Using a spatula, press potato mixture firmly. Cover and cook over medium heat about 8 minutes or until golden brown. Check occasionally; reduce heat, if necessary, to prevent overbrowning.

3. Turn the hash browns using two spatulas or a spatula and fork. (If you're not sure you can turn the potatoes in a single flip, cut into quarters and turn by sections. See photo, bottom middle.) Cook, uncovered, for 5 to 7 minutes more or until golden brown and crisp. Remove from skillet; serve in wedges. Makes 2 or 3 servings.

Eacj serving: 168 cal., 9 g total fat (1 g sat. fat), 0 mg chol., 197 mg sodium, 19 g carbo., 2 g fiber, 3 g pro. Daily Values: 27% vit. C, 1% calcium, 5% iron.

Shredded Hash Browns

Pineapple Short & Sweet

WE ALL LOVE THE KING OF PINEAPPLES, CROWNED WITH A PLUME OF VIBRANT GREENERY. But the king has some short and chubby cousins that are well worth the slicing. See if you can find these fresh gems in your supermarket. As for regular pineapples, look for fresh-looking fruits that are plump, slightly soft to the touch, and heavy for their size. You can refrigerate an uncut pineapple for 1 to 2 days. Peeled pineapples will hold for a few days longer. Eat them plain or try one in our colorful salad.

Golden pineapple:
This big guy looks like the standard fresh pineapple, but take a bite of its succulent flesh and you'll notice the difference. The fruit is sweeter and more brilliant in color than the common variety. Golden is ready to eat when you buy it, so there's no waiting for it to ripen. The core is edible, but is a tad tougher than the baby varieties.

South African baby pineapple:
Topping off at 4 inches tall, this cutie is super sweet. It's dense with rich-textured fruit and low in acid. When purchasing, look for a golden color and use the sniff test; when ripe, these are very aromatic. South African baby pineapples are available year-round in major markets. Can't find them? Ask your produce manager to order some.

Baby Hawaiian pineapple:

This one hails from the islands of aloha and stands about an inch taller than the South African baby pineapple. A mini version of the flavorful Sugar Loaf, the baby Hawaiian has a mild sweetness with a slightly crunchy but edible core. The fruit is low in acid. Like the South African variety, it can be found all year at most major markets.

QUICK PINEAPPLE TIPS

- Lop off the top and bottom of the pineapple. Slice remaining fruit into thin wedges. Nibble around the rind. Or, cut off the top and scoop out fruit.
- Use the hollow shell to serve pineapple salsa or exotic tropical drinks.

Fruit Salad with Cranberry Dressing

PREP: 25 minutes **CHILL:** 2 hours

- 2 cups cranberries
- 1/3 cup water
- 1 cup sugar
- 1/4 cup orange juice
- Bibb lettuce leaves
- 2 large seedless oranges, peeled and sectioned
- 1/2 of a large pineapple, peeled, cored, sliced, and cut into wedges
- 2 large ripe pears, cored and sliced into wedges*
- 2 kiwifruit and/or golden kiwifruit, peeled and sliced lengthwise into wedges

1. For dressing, in a medium saucepan combine cranberries and water. Bring to boiling; reduce heat. Cover and simmer for 4 to 5 minutes or just until berries begin to pop.

2. Remove saucepan from heat; stir in sugar and orange juice. When cool, press mixture through a sieve. Discard cranberry skins. Cover and refrigerate about 2 hours or until well chilled. (The dressing will thicken slightly as it chills.)

3. To serve, line six small bowls with lettuce leaves. Arrange fruit on lettuce. Drizzle with dressing. Makes 6 servings.

***TEST KITCHEN TIP:** To prevent pears from darkening, brush the cut edges with lemon juice.

Each serving: 231 cal., 1 g total fat (0 g sat. fat), 0 mg chol., 4 mg sodium, 58 g carbo., 5 g fiber, 2 g pro. Daily Values: 11% vit. A, 113% vit. C, 5% calcium, 5% iron.

April

CELEBRATE SPRING'S RENEWED SUNSHINE AND WARMTH WITH A FRESH APPROACH TO ITS BEST-LOVED FLAVORS.

Lemon Muffins

Garden Bunnies

Corn Bread Cassata

Orange-Saffron Bread

A Parade of Easter Breads

Plus...

Toasted Walnut Bread

Tandoori Chicken Burger

Spring Chicken

Plus...

Coconut Chicken Salad

LET APRIL SHOWERS MUSHROOM INTO FRESH IDEAS FOR FAMILY CHICKEN DINNERS.

Provençal Herb-Rubbed Roaster

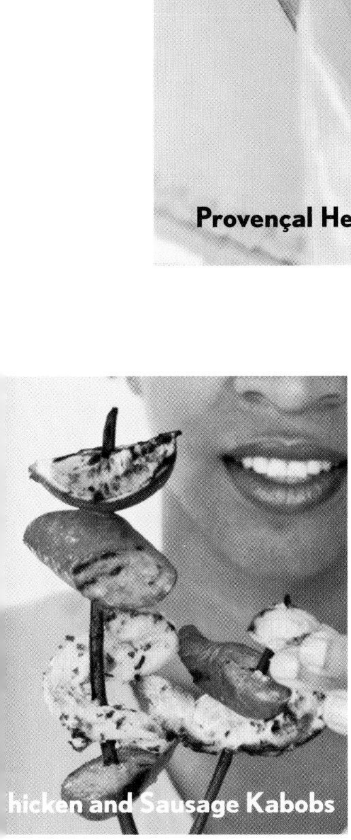

hicken and Sausage Kabobs

Ravioli Chicken Soup

Guava-Glazed Chicken

A Parade of Easter Breads

THERE'S AS MUCH TRADITION IN OUR HOT CROSS BUNS AS THERE IS PLAYFULNESS IN OUR GARDEN BUNNY BREAD. HOP TO THE BEST IN SPRING BAKING.

Hot Cross Buns

Hot Cross Buns

Soaking the currants in balsamic vinegar gives them a slightly tangy flavor that contrasts well with the rich dough.

Prep: 45 minutes **Rise:** 2 hours
Chill: 6 hours **Bake:** 12 minutes

- 2/3 cup dried currants or raisins
- 2 Tbsp. balsamic vinegar
- 3 1/4 to 3 3/4 cups all-purpose flour
- 1 pkg. active dry yeast
- 1 tsp. ground cardamom
- 1/8 tsp. ground cloves
- 2/3 cup milk
- 1 1/2 cups mascarpone cheese (12 oz.)
- 1/3 cup sugar
- 1/2 tsp. salt
- 3 eggs
- 1 egg white
- 1 Tbsp. water
- 1/4 cup sugar
- Milk

1. Place the currants in a small bowl; add vinegar. Cover; let stand. In a large mixing bowl stir together 2 cups of the flour, the yeast, cardamom, and cloves; set aside.

2. In a saucepan heat and stir 2/3 cup milk, 1/2 cup of the mascarpone cheese, 1/3 cup sugar, and salt just until warm (120° F to 130° F) and mascarpone almost melts. Add milk mixture to flour mixture along with eggs. Beat with an electric mixer on low to medium speed for 30 seconds, scraping sides of bowl constantly. Beat on high speed for 3 minutes. Using a wooden spoon, stir in currant mixture and as much of the remaining flour as you can.

3. Turn dough out onto a lightly floured surface. Knead in enough remaining flour to make a moderately soft dough (3 to 5 minutes). (The dough will be sticky.) Shape into a ball. Place in a lightly greased bowl; turn once to grease the surface. Cover; let rise in a warm place until double (about 1 hour). Chill dough for 6 hours. (Or, omit rising time and chill dough for 12 to 24 hours.)

4. Punch dough down; turn out onto a lightly floured surface. Cover; let rest for 10 minutes. Meanwhile, lightly grease 2 baking sheets; set aside. Divide dough into 24 portions. Gently shape each portion into a ball, tucking edges under to make smooth tops. Arrange balls on prepared baking sheets so edges are almost touching. Cover; let rise until nearly double (1 to 1 1/2 hours).

5. Preheat oven to 375° F. Using a sharp knife, make a crisscross slash across the top of each bun. In a small bowl beat egg white; stir in water. Brush onto rolls. Bake for 12 to 15 minutes or until golden brown. Immediately remove buns from baking sheets. Cool slightly on a wire rack.

6. In a small bowl stir together remaining mascarpone cheese, 1/4 cup sugar, and enough milk to make a frosting of a thick drizzling consistency. Drizzle icing into a cross on each bun. Pass additional icing for dipping. Serve warm. Makes 24 buns.

Each bun: 168 cal., 7 g total fat (4 g sat. fat), 45 mg chol., 71 mg sodium, 22 g carbo., 1 g fiber, 6 g pro. Daily Values: 1% vit. A, 2% calcium, 6% iron.

History of bread

Whether they're crusty loaves that tug apart into a dozen fragrant portions or trays stacked high with sweet muffins, breads are meant as a communal blessing—particularly at this time of year. People have long gathered to share and celebrate the dawn of spring. Ever since we began reckoning that the dark days of winter were over and nature was reawakening, we've enjoyed spring feasts.

We're especially lucky in America because we're adept at striking a respectful balance between observing Easter and pursuing a day of whimsical fun to celebrate the beginning of spring. Thankfully, bread has been a staple of both occasions.

The breads presented here—many with long traditions and deep connections to our culture—strike a similar balance. Take Hot Cross Buns, for example. The cross imagery may appeal to devout Christians, while children just love to giggle and recite "one a penny, two a penny, hot cross buns."

Historians believe these rolls predate Christianity and were enjoyed by ancient Greeks, Romans, and Britons. To them, the round shape represented the sun. The cross stood for the four seasons or the moon's four phases.

As the centuries passed, Hot Cross Buns became associated with Good Friday and its community meals. The rest of the year, the buns were used as a kind of magical talisman to ward off everything from fires to shipwrecks.

Regardless of historical context, anytime is a good time to bake bread with family. A sunny spot in the kitchen and a new bag of flour are God's gifts to the baker. And never are these blessings more welcome than at Eastertime. The pace of life slows, the yearning for connection grows, and the prospect of a quiet hour or two of baking seems suddenly irresistible.

HOW TO TELL BREAD IS DONE

To tell when bread is ready to come out of the oven, you can tap the bottom and listen for a hollow sound, something like knocking on a wooden box. Or you can take the bread's temperature with an instant-read thermometer. Insert it into the thickest part of the loaf and look for a temperature of 195° F to 200° F.

"Using a thermometer is an excellent way to tell when bread is done," says Glenna Vance, spokesperson for Red Star Yeast, "especially for younger bakers who don't know how that thump on the bottom sounds."

Red Star also has a baker's help line: 800/445-4746.

CREATING THE EASTER LATTICE

With hands lightly floured, and working on a lightly floured surface, weave strips together by crossing short strips of dough under and over long strips. Try not to stretch the dough too much as you work.

PURCHASING QUAIL EGGS

Find quail eggs in Asian grocery stores, farmers' markets, health food stores, and some supermarkets. You can also call Rosi's Game Bird Farm at 800/969-9970.

EASTER BRUNCH

Asparagus-Salmon Scramble *(page 168)*
Hot Cross Buns *(page 115)* or Easter Lattice *(right)*
Assorted fresh fruit such as sliced melon, kiwifruit, strawberries, and pineapple
Coffee or tea

Easter Lattice

PREP: 45 minutes **RISE:** 1 3/4 hours **BAKE:** 25 minutes

- 4 1/4 to 4 3/4 cups all-purpose flour
- 1 pkg. active dry yeast
- 1 cup milk
- 1/3 cup sugar
- 1/4 cup butter
- 1 1/4 tsp. salt
- 2 eggs
- 3 Tbsp. flaxseeds, poppy seeds, and/or toasted sesame seeds
- 2 tsp. fennel seeds, toasted and crushed
- Cooking oil
- Hard-cooked and dyed quail eggs* (see tip, left), eggs, or egg-shaped colored candies, such as Jordan almonds or malted milk eggs
- Crème fraîche or butter

1. In a large mixing bowl stir together 2 cups of the flour and the yeast; set aside. In a medium saucepan heat and stir milk, sugar, the 1/4 cup butter, and salt just until warm (120° F to 130° F) and butter almost melts. Add milk mixture to flour mixture along with eggs. Beat with an electric mixer on low to medium speed for 30 seconds, scraping sides of bowl constantly. Beat on high speed for 3 minutes. Stir in seeds. Using a wooden spoon, stir in as much of the remaining flour as you can.

2. Turn dough out onto a lightly floured surface. Knead in enough remaining flour to make a moderately stiff dough that is smooth and elastic (6 to 8 minutes). Shape dough into a ball. Place in a lightly greased bowl; turn once to grease the surface. Cover; let rise in a warm place until double in size (about 1 hour).

3. Punch dough down; turn onto a lightly floured surface. Divide in half. Cover and let rest for 10 minutes. Meanwhile, lightly grease a large baking sheet. Roll half of dough into a 12×6-inch rectangle. Cut into three 12×2-inch strips; arrange 1 inch apart on the prepared baking sheet. Roll remaining dough into a 10×8-inch rectangle; cut into five 8×2-inch strips. Arrange shorter strips crosswise over longer ropes, weaving under and over longer strips (see photo, *left*). Cover; let rise in warm place until nearly double (45 minutes).

4. Preheat oven to 350° F. Bake for 25 to 30 minutes or until bread is brown and sounds hollow when tapped. Lightly brush bread with cooking oil. Cool on a wire rack. Arrange eggs on top of bread. Serve with crème fraîche or butter. Makes 15 servings.

BREAD MACHINE METHOD: Use 4 1/2 cups all-purpose flour. In a 2-pound bread machine combine first 9 ingredients. Select dough cycle according to manufacturer's directions. When cycle finishes, remove dough. Shape and bake as in Steps 3 and 4, *above.*

***NOTE:** To hard-cook quail eggs, place eggs in a single layer in a medium saucepan. Cover eggs with cold water. Bring to a rapid boil over high heat (water will have large, rapidly breaking bubbles). Cook for 3 minutes; remove from heat. Drain; cool.

Each serving (bread): 201 cal., 6 g total fat (3 g sat. fat), 38 mg chol., 245 mg sodium, 31 g carbo., 2 g fiber, 5 g pro. Daily Values: 4% vit. A, 4% calcium, 11% iron.

Easter Lattice

Garden Bunnies

Garden Bunnies

Rosemary and sage are strong-flavored herbs. If using them alone, add only 2 tablespoons fresh or 2 teaspoons dried.

PREP: 30 minutes **RISE:** 1¼ hours **BAKE:** 40 minutes

- **5½ to 6 cups all-purpose flour**
- **1 pkg. active dry yeast**
- **2¼ cups milk or buttermilk**
- **¼ cup mixed snipped fresh herbs such as sage, rosemary, parsley, and thyme; or 3 to 4 tsp. dried herbs, crushed**
- **2 Tbsp. sugar**
- **1 Tbsp. butter**
- **1½ tsp. salt**
- **1 recipe Sugar-Sage Topping or Rosemary-Cheese Topping (right)**
- **1 egg white**
- **1 Tbsp. water**

1. In a large mixing bowl combine 2½ cups of the flour and the yeast; set aside. In a medium saucepan heat and stir milk, herbs, sugar, butter, and salt just until warm (120° F to 130° F) and butter almost melts. Add milk mixture to flour mixture. Beat with an electric mixer on low to medium speed for 30 seconds, scraping sides of bowl constantly. Beat on high speed for 3 minutes. Using a wooden spoon, stir in as much of the remaining flour as you can.

2. Turn dough out onto a lightly floured surface. Knead in enough of the remaining flour to make a moderately stiff dough that is smooth and elastic (6 to 8 minutes). Shape into a ball. Place in a lightly greased bowl; turn once to grease surface. Cover; let rise in a warm place until double (45 to 60 minutes).

3. Punch dough down; turn out onto a lightly floured surface. Divide in half; cover and let rest for 10 minutes. Meanwhile, lightly grease a baking sheet; set aside.

4. To form bunnies, roll a portion of dough into an 8-inch circle. With a sharp knife, cut into 6 wedges (see photo 1, *above right*). From 4 wedges, snip a small amount of dough to make tails for bunnies. Gently shape the 4 wedges into ovals by pulling edges under and pinching together. Place ovals, pinched side down, on prepared baking sheet. Flatten slightly to 4 inches long.

5. Form snipped pieces of dough into tails; press onto one end of dough ovals. To make heads and ears, divide the remaining 2 wedges in half, making 4 small wedges total. Shape each wedge into a teardrop shape, about 4 inches long. With kitchen shears, cut into the pointed end of each, making cuts about 2½ inches long (see photo 2, *above center*). Lay each set of ears on top of an oval shape, near end opposite tail (see photo 3, *above right*). If necessary, brush with water to help dough stick together. Gently give the ears a half twist so the cut edge is facing up.

6. Repeat rolling and shaping with the other portion of dough. Cover and let rise in a warm place until nearly double in size (about 30 minutes).

7. Preheat oven to 350° F. Prepare Sugar-Sage Topping or Rosemary-Cheese Topping; set toppings aside. In a small bowl beat together egg white and water. Brush bunnies with egg mixture. Sprinkle (or rub) with topping. Bake for 15 to 20 minutes or until done, covering with foil the last half of baking to prevent overbrowning. Serve warm. Makes 8 bunnies.

SUGAR-SAGE TOPPING: In a small bowl stir together ⅓ cup fine sanding sugar or granulated sugar and 1 tablespoon finely snipped fresh sage.

ROSEMARY-CHEESE TOPPING: In a small bowl stir together ⅓ cup grated Parmesan cheese and 1 tablespoon finely snipped fresh rosemary.

Each serving: 390 cal., 4 g total fat (2 g sat. fat), 18 mg chol., 495 mg sodium, 75 g carbo., 2 g fiber, 12 g pro. Daily Values: 6% vit. A, 3% vit. C, 9% calcium, 24% iron.

MAKING THE BUNNIES

Cut two of the six wedges in half to make four small and four big wedges (photo 1) from each half of the dough. Create the ears by snipping the point of the triangle of the small wedges (photo 2). To give the ears surface texture, twist slightly outward (photo 3).

EASTER BUNNY BRUNCH

Scrambled eggs
Sausage
Garden Bunnies *(left)* or Lemon Muffins *(page 126)*
Strawberries or grapes
Fruit juice

Easter Rings

This rich Easter bread hails from Bologna, Italy. The round shape is said to represent the unity of the family.

PREP: 30 minutes **RISE:** 1½ hours + 40 minutes
STAND: 10 minutes **BAKE:** 25 minutes

- 3¼ to 3¾ cups all-purpose flour
- 1 pkg. active dry yeast
- ½ tsp. ground cinnamon (optional)
- ¾ cup milk
- ¼ cup butter
- ¼ cup sugar
- 1 tsp. salt
- 2 eggs
- ¾ cup chopped almonds, toasted
- ¼ cup sugar
- ¼ cup almond toffee pieces
- 2 egg yolks, slightly beaten
- 1 egg white, slightly beaten

1. In a large mixing bowl combine 1½ cups of the flour, the yeast, and cinnamon, if desired; set aside. In a small saucepan heat and stir together the milk, butter, ¼ cup sugar, and salt just until warm (120° F to 130° F) and butter almost melts. Add milk mixture to flour mixture along with eggs. Beat with an electric mixer on low speed for 30 seconds, scraping sides of bowl constantly. Beat on high speed for 3 minutes. Using a wooden spoon, stir in as much of the remaining flour as you can.

2. Turn dough out onto a lightly floured surface. Knead in enough of the remaining flour to make a moderately soft dough that is smooth and elastic (3 to 5 minutes total). Shape dough into a ball. Place in a lightly greased bowl; turn once to grease surface. Cover; let rise in a warm place until double in size (about 1½ hours).

3. Punch dough down. Turn dough out onto a lightly floured surface. Cover and let rest for 10 minutes. Meanwhile, lightly grease a baking sheet; set aside.

4. Divide dough in half. Roll each dough half into a rope about 20 inches long. Shape each half into 2 rings; place on prepared baking sheet. Pinch ends to seal. Cover and let rise in a warm place until nearly double in size (about 40 minutes).

5. Preheat oven to 350° F. In a small bowl combine almonds, ¼ cup sugar, and toffee bits; stir in egg yolks. Brush rings with egg white. Sprinkle almond mixture evenly onto the tops and sides of rings, lightly pressing almond mixture into sides as necessary. Bake about 25 minutes until golden brown and a thermometer registers 195° F in the thickest part of the bread. Serve warm. Makes 4 rings (20 to 24 servings).

Each serving: 177 cal., 7 g total fat (2 g sat. fat), 51 mg chol., 172 mg sodium, 24 g carbo., 1 g fiber, 5 g pro. Daily Values: 4% vit. A, 3% calcium, 8% iron.

Orange-Saffron Bread

PREP: 1 hour **RISE:** 1¾ hours **BAKE:** 35 minutes

- 1 recipe Candied Orange Slices (below)
- 4¼ cups all-purpose flour
- 1 pkg. active dry yeast
- ¾ cup water
- ½ cup packed brown sugar
- ½ cup orange juice
- ⅓ cup butter
- ½ tsp. salt
- ¼ tsp. thread saffron, ⅛ tsp. ground saffron, or ¼ tsp. ground turmeric
- 1 egg
- ½ cup pine nuts or chopped almonds, toasted
- ½ cup Candied Orange Syrup (below)

1. Prepare Candied Orange Slices; set aside.

2. In a large mixing bowl, combine 1½ cups of the flour and the yeast, set aside. In a medium saucepan heat and stir water, brown sugar, orange juice, butter, salt, and saffron just until warm (120° F to 130° F) and butter almost melts. Add to flour mixture along with egg. Beat with an electric mixer on low to medium speed for 30 seconds, scraping sides of bowl constantly. Beat on high speed for 3 minutes. Using a wooden spoon, stir in the remaining flour and pine nuts. Cover and let rise in a warm place until double in size (about 1 hour).

3. Grease a 9×1½-inch round or 8×8×2-inch square baking pan; set aside. Lightly grease a spoon; stir dough down. Transfer batter to pan; use back of spoon to pat dough into corners. Cover; let rise in a warm place until double in size (about 45 minutes).

4. Preheat oven to 350° F. Bake about 35 minutes or until bread sounds hollow when lightly tapped and a thermometer registers 195° F in the thickest part of bread. Cover with foil after 20 minutes of baking to prevent overbrowning. Remove from pan; cool on a wire rack.

5. To serve, place half of the candied orange slices on top of the bread; drizzle with ½ cup of the candied orange syrup. Remove remaining orange slices from syrup; coarsely chop. Pass chopped orange slices with bread. (Reserve remaining syrup to brush onto chicken, turkey, or pork during the last 5 minutes of broiling or grilling.) Makes 12 servings.

CANDIED ORANGE SLICES AND SYRUP: Cut 3 oranges crosswise into ¼-inch-thick slices; remove seeds. In a large skillet that's at least 2 inches deep combine 3½ cups water, 3 cups sugar, one 1-inch piece of peeled fresh ginger, and ¼ teaspoon crushed red pepper. Bring to boiling. Add orange slices. Simmer, uncovered, about 1 hour until rinds become very tender. Transfer slices and syrup to a glass bowl. Remove ginger. Cool.

Each serving: 367 cal., 10 g total fat (4 g sat. fat), 32 mg chol., 163 mg sodium, 65 g carbo., 2 g fiber, 7 g pro. Daily Values: 6% vit. A, 38% vit. C, 4% calcium, 17% iron.

Orange-Saffron Bread

WOODEN MOLDS ADD CHARM

Baking Orange-Saffron Bread in wooden molds gives it a timeless, old-world appearance. Line three $5\frac{1}{8}\times3\frac{3}{4}\times2$-inch wooden bread molds with parchment paper. Prepare the dough through Step 3, then turn it onto a lightly floured surface. With a floured knife, divide the dough into three portions. With floured hands, transfer the dough to prepared molds; cover and let rise in a warm place until double (about 45 minutes). Bake as directed in Step 4.

Easter Rings

Fig-Nutmeg Coffee Cake

Rhubarb-Strawberry Coffee Cake

The tantalizing filling of strawberries and rhubarb makes a scarlet ribbon in this rich and tangy coffee cake.

PREP: 35 minutes **BAKE:** 40 minutes

- 1 recipe Rhubarb-Strawberry Filling (below)
- 3 cups all-purpose flour
- 1 cup sugar
- 1 tsp. baking soda
- 1 tsp. baking powder
- 1 tsp. salt
- 1 cup butter
- 2 eggs
- 1 cup buttermilk or sour milk*
- 1 tsp. vanilla
- 1/2 cup sugar
- 1/2 cup all-purpose flour
- 1/4 cup butter

1. Prepare Rhubarb-Strawberry Filling; set aside to cool.

2. Preheat oven to 350° F. In a large mixing bowl stir together the 3 cups flour, the 1 cup sugar, the baking soda, baking powder, and salt. Cut in the 1 cup butter until mixture resembles fine crumbs. In a small bowl beat eggs; stir in buttermilk or sour milk and vanilla. Add to flour mixture; stir to moisten.

3. Lightly grease a 13×9×2-inch baking pan; spread half of the batter in pan. Spread cooled filling over batter in pan. Spoon remaining batter in small mounds on filling.

4. In a small bowl combine the 1/2 cup sugar and the 1/2 cup flour. Cut in the 1/4 cup butter until mixture resembles fine crumbs. Sprinkle crumb mixture over batter in pan. Bake for 40 to 45 minutes or until golden. Serve warm. Makes 15 servings.

RHUBARB-STRAWBERRY FILLING: In a medium saucepan combine 3 cups fresh rhubarb or one 16-ounce package frozen unsweetened sliced rhubarb, and 4 cups hulled fresh strawberries or one 16-ounce package frozen unsweetened whole strawberries, thawed and halved. Cook fruit, covered, for 5 minutes. Add 2 tablespoons lemon juice. Combine 1 cup sugar and 1/3 cup cornstarch; add to rhubarb mixture. Cook and stir for 4 to 5 minutes until thickened and bubbly; cool.

***NOTE:** For each cup of sour milk needed, place 1 tablespoon lemon juice or vinegar in a glass measuring cup. Add enough milk to make 1 cup total liquid; stir. Let mixture stand for 5 minutes before using.

Each serving: 410 cal., 17 g total fat (10 g sat. fat), 73 mg chol., 458 mg sodium, 60 g carbo., 2 g fiber, 5 g pro. Daily Values: 14% vit. A, 41% vit. C, 7% calcium, 9% iron.

Fig-Nutmeg Coffee Cake

For fresh nutmeg flavor, use whole nutmeg and grate it yourself.

PREP: 20 minutes **BAKE:** 65 minutes **COOL:** 10 + 30 minutes

- 2 cups all-purpose flour
- 1 Tbsp. freshly grated nutmeg or 1 1/2 tsp. ground nutmeg
- 1 tsp. baking powder
- 1/4 tsp. salt
- 1/2 cup butter, softened
- 1 1/2 cups sugar
- 2 eggs
- 1 8-oz. carton dairy sour cream
- 1 1/2 cups snipped dried figs
- 1 recipe Lemon-Honey Glaze (below)

1. Preheat oven to 350° F. Grease and lightly flour a 9-inch springform pan with flat-bottom tube insert or an 8- to 10-cup fluted tube pan; set aside. In a medium bowl stir together flour, nutmeg, baking powder, and salt; set aside.

2. In a large bowl beat butter with an electric mixer on medium speed for 30 seconds. Add sugar; beat until combined. Add eggs, 1 at a time, beating well after each addition. Alternately add the flour mixture and the sour cream, beating after each addition until combined (batter will be thick). Stir in figs. Spoon batter into prepared pan, spreading evenly.

3. Bake for 65 to 70 minutes or until a wooden toothpick inserted near center comes out clean. Cool in pan on a wire rack over waxed paper for 10 minutes. Remove from pan. Cool slightly on the rack, about 30 minutes.

4. Prepare Lemon-Honey Glaze. Drizzle glaze onto slightly cooled cake, spooning any glaze that drips onto waxed paper back onto the cake. Serve warm or at room temperature. Makes 10 to 12 servings.

LEMON-HONEY GLAZE: In a small bowl combine 1/3 cup honey and 1/2 teaspoon finely shredded lemon peel.

Each serving: 465 cal., 16 g total fat (10 g sat. fat), 79 mg chol., 227 mg sodium, 78 g carbo., 4 g fiber, 6 g pro. Daily Values: 13% vit. A, 1% vit. C, 11% calcium, 12% iron.

Toasted Walnut Bread

Blueberry Rolls

Although shaped and baked like cinnamon rolls, this recipe offers a richer dough. Blueberry Rolls are scrumptious alone for breakfast or brunch or with ice cream for dessert.

PREP: 25 minutes **BAKE:** 20 minutes

- 2 16 1/2-oz. cans blueberries
- 1 recipe Rich Shortcake (below)
- 1 Tbsp. butter, melted
- 2 Tbsp. sugar
- 1/2 tsp. ground cinnamon
- 1/4 cup sugar
- 2 Tbsp. all-purpose flour
- 2 tsp. lemon juice
- Vanilla ice cream (optional)

1. Drain blueberries, reserving juice; set aside. Grease a 2-quart square baking dish; set aside.

2. Prepare Rich Shortcake dough. On a lightly floured surface roll dough into an 11×9-inch rectangle. Brush dough with melted butter. In a small bowl combine the 2 tablespoons sugar and the cinnamon; sprinkle onto dough. Sprinkle with 1 cup of the drained blueberries. Roll up, starting from a short side. Seal seam. Slice roll into 9 equal pieces.

3. Preheat oven to 425° F. In a small saucepan combine the 1/4 cup sugar and the flour. Add remaining blueberries and reserved juice. Cook and stir until thickened and bubbly. Remove from heat; stir in lemon juice.

4. Pour blueberry mixture into prepared baking dish. Place rolls, cut sides down, on top of blueberry mixture. Bake about 20 minutes or until rolls are golden. Invert rolls onto a round platter; remove pan. If desired, serve warm with vanilla ice cream. Makes 9 servings.

RICH SHORTCAKE: In a medium mixing bowl stir together 2 cups all-purpose flour, 4 teaspoons baking powder, 1 tablespoon sugar, and 1/2 teaspoon salt. Using a pastry blender, cut in 1/3 cup shortening until mixture resembles coarse crumbs. Make a well in the center. Add 2/3 cup milk and 1 beaten egg all at once. Stir just until dough clings together. On a heavily floured surface coat the dough lightly with flour. Knead gently for 10 to 12 strokes.

Each serving: 284 cal., 10 g total fat (3 g sat. fat), 29 mg chol., 339 mg sodium, 44 g carbo., 2 g fiber, 5 g pro. Daily Values: 157% vit. A, 2% vit. C, 145% calcium, 2% iron.

Toasted Walnut Bread

Toasting the walnuts before adding them to the dough intensifies their flavor, providing greater richness and depth to the finished bread.

PREP: 20 minutes **BAKE:** 50 + 20 minutes

- 2 cups all-purpose flour
- 1/3 cup sugar
- 1 Tbsp. baking powder
- 1/2 tsp. salt
- 1 egg
- 1 cup milk
- 1/3 cup cooking oil
- 2 cups coarsely chopped walnuts, toasted*
- Slices of firm cheese, such as white or orange farmhouse cheddar, Appenzell, Edam, or Gouda (optional)

1. Preheat oven to 350° F. Grease the bottom and 1/2 inch up sides of an 8×4×2-inch loaf pan; set aside. In a large bowl stir together flour, sugar, baking powder, and salt. Make a well in center of flour mixture; set aside.

2. In a medium bowl beat egg; stir in milk and oil. Add egg mixture all at once to flour mixture. Stir just until moistened (batter should be lumpy). Fold in nuts. Spoon batter into prepared pan; spreading evenly.

3. Bake for 50 to 55 minutes or until a wooden toothpick inserted near center comes out clean. Cool in pan on a wire rack for 10 minutes. Remove from pan. Cool on the wire rack.

4. Preheat oven to 375° F. Cut bread into 3/4-inch-thick slices. Arrange slices in a single layer on a baking sheet. Bake about 20 minutes or until brown on both sides, turning once. If desired, serve warm with cheese slices. Makes 1 loaf (10 servings).

***NOTE:** To toast nuts, bake in a 350° F oven for 5 to 10 minutes or until golden, stirring once or twice.

Each serving (without cheese): 355 cal., 24 g total fat (3 g sat. fat), 23 mg chol., 256 mg sodium, 30 g carbo., 2 g fiber, 8 g pro. Daily Values: 2% vit. A, 1% vit. C, 14% calcium, 11% iron.

EASTER DINNER

Roasted Asparagus Soup *(page 133)*
Baked ham
Zucchini-Olive Couscous *(page 544)*
Toasted Walnut Bread *(above)*
Corn Bread Cassata *(page 126)*
Coffee or tea

Lemon Muffins

Lemon curd is a smooth, sweet spread popular in Britain. You can find it in the preserves section of grocery stores or specialty food shops. Spread any leftover curd onto toasted English muffins.

PREP: 25 minutes **BAKE:** 18 minutes **COOL:** 5 minutes

- 1½ cups all-purpose flour
- ½ cup sugar
- ¼ cup whole wheat flour
- 2 tsp. baking powder
- ¼ tsp. salt
- 1 egg
- ¾ cup milk
- ¼ cup cooking oil
- ⅔ cup purchased lemon curd
- 2 Tbsp. toasted coconut

1. Preheat oven to 400° F. Grease 6 popover pans and line with paper bake cups; set aside. (See directions for baking in muffin cups, below.) In a medium bowl stir together all-purpose flour, sugar, whole wheat flour, baking powder, and salt. Make a well in the center of the flour mixture; set aside.

2. In a small mixing bowl beat the egg; stir in milk and oil. Add egg mixture all at once to flour mixture. Stir just until moistened (batter should be lumpy).

3. Spoon half of the batter into the prepared popover pans (2 rounded tablespoons in each cup). Spoon 2 rounded teaspoons lemon curd into each cup. (There will be some remaining for topping.) Spoon remaining batter into popover pans, filling each cup two-thirds full.

4. Bake for 18 to 20 minutes or until golden. Cool in popover pans on a wire rack for 5 minutes. Remove from popover pans. Spread with remaining lemon curd; top with toasted coconut. Serve warm, or cool on a wire rack. If desired, slip muffins into fresh paper bake cups and tie with string. Makes 6 tall muffins.

NOTE: To bake in muffin cups, grease twelve 2½-inch muffin cups and line with paper bake cups; set aside. Prepare muffin batter through Step 2. Spoon half the batter into prepared muffin cups (a rounded tablespoon in each muffin cup). Spoon a rounded teaspoon of lemon curd onto the batter in each cup. (There will be some remaining for topping.) Spoon remaining batter into muffin cups, filling each cup two-thirds full. Bake, cool, and serve as directed. Makes 12 muffins.

Each tall muffin: 419 cal., 13 g total fat (4 g sat. fat), 65 mg chol., 291 mg sodium, 47 g carbo., 5 g fiber, 6 g pro. Daily Values: 2% vit. A, 1% vit. C, 13% calcium, 9% iron.

Corn Bread Cassata

PREP: 30 minutes **BAKE:** 20 minutes **COOL:** 2 hours

- 2 8½-oz. pkg. corn muffin mix
- 1 8-oz. can crushed pineapple (juice pack)
- 2 Tbsp. rum or brandy
- 1½ cups chopped, dried cherries and/or golden raisins
- 1½ cups whipping cream
- 1 Tbsp. packed brown sugar
- ½ cup chopped white chocolate chunks
- Dried cherries (optional)
- White chocolate chunks (optional)

1. Preheat oven to 350° F. Chill a large mixing bowl and beaters of an electric mixer. Grease and flour 8 nonstick popover or 2½-inch muffin cups or two 9×1½- or 8×1½-inch round cake pans. Line pans with waxed paper or parchment paper; set aside.

2. In 2 medium bowls prepare each muffin mix according to package directions, except stir half of the undrained pineapple into each bowl along with the milk and egg. Spoon a scant ½ cup batter into each popover or muffin cup* or spread the batter into prepared 8- or 9-inch pans, using 1 pan for each mix.

3. Bake until a wooden toothpick inserted near the center comes out clean, allowing 20 minutes for popover pans, 2½-inch muffin cups, or 9-inch pans, and 20 to 22 minutes for 8-inch pans. Cool in pans on a wire rack for 5 minutes for smaller pans and 10 minutes for larger pans. Remove cakes from pans; remove paper. Cool for 2 hours on the wire rack.

4. Meanwhile, in a small saucepan heat rum over low heat until warm. Add the 1½ cups dried fruit. Let stand for 20 minutes; drain off any excess liquid.

5. In the chilled mixing bowl beat whipping cream and brown sugar with chilled beaters of an electric mixer on medium speed until soft peaks form (tips curl). Fold in fruit mixture and the ½ cup white chocolate chunks. Cover and chill for up to 2 hours.

6. Trim rounded cake tops so inverted cakes will be flat. Split cakes horizontally at a slight diagonal. Place 1 layer on a dessert plate. Top with some of the filling, cake top, and more filling. If desired, top with additional cherries and white chocolate chunks. Makes 8 to 12 servings.

***NOTE:** You have enough batter to make 8 individual cakes. If you don't have 8 of the smaller pans, refrigerate the remaining batter while the first cakes bake. Cool pans; wash and prepare pans as above to bake remaining cakes.

Each serving: 604 cal., 30 g total fat (13 g sat. fat), 104 mg chol., 510 mg sodium, 76 g carbo., 1 g fiber, 9 g pro. Daily Values: 13% vit. A, 5% vit. C, 15% calcium, 7% iron.

Lemon Muffins

Corn Bread Cassata

Tuna, Fennel, and Rotini Casserole

COUNT ON Casseroles

HERE ARE THREE HOMESPUN CASSEROLES TO FEED CROWD-SIZE APPETITES. JUST ADD A SALAD AND A LOAF OF CRUSTY BREAD.

Remember the good old days when Mom would say to friends, "We'd love to have you over. I've got a casserole in the oven"? It sounded so simple and inviting, and tasted so good. Now, with the help of these updated classics, you can serve your family and friends an impromptu feast with the same ease. Consider these delicious spins on tried-and-true favorites. They're big on flavor and perfect for those days when carpool conversation turns into an invitation for supper. Plus, they go together with a minimum of effort and require only ingredients you probably have on hand. Even better, they're out of the oven in 30 minutes or less and register a big 10 in the flavor department. And while you're at it, why not make an extra casserole and tuck it in the freezer so you're always ready for company?

Tuna, Fennel, and Rotini Casserole

It's tuna-noodle casserole like your mom never made, tossed with fennel and capers and coated in a creamy light Alfredo sauce.

PREP: 20 minutes **BAKE:** 20 minutes

- 1½ cups dried rotini
- 2 Tbsp. butter
- ¾ cup seasoned croutons, slightly crushed
- 2 small fennel bulbs, sliced (2 cups)
- 1 10-oz. container refrigerated light Alfredo sauce
- 2 Tbsp. capers, drained (optional)
- 2 6-oz. cans tuna (packed in oil), drained and broken into chunks

1. Preheat oven to 375° F. Cook rotini according to package directions; drain.

2. Meanwhile, in a medium saucepan melt butter. In a bowl combine croutons with 1 tablespoon of the melted butter; toss gently to coat.

3. Add fennel to remaining butter in saucepan. Cover; cook for 6 to 8 minutes or until fennel is just tender, stirring occasionally. Stir in Alfredo sauce, cooked rotini, and capers, if desired. Fold in tuna.

4. Transfer tuna mixture to an ungreased 1½-quart casserole. Top with croutons. Bake, uncovered, about 20 minutes or until heated through. Serve warm. Makes 6 servings.

Each serving: 306 cal., 11 g total fat (6 g sat. fat), 44 mg chol., 527 mg sodium, 29 g carbo., 9 g dietary fiber, 20 g protein. Daily Values: 4% vit. A, 6% vit. C, 13% calcium, 10% iron.

Chicken and Orzo Casserole

Chicken and Orzo Casserole

To boost the heat, choose the serrano peppers. They provide more kick than jalapeño peppers.

PREP: 15 minutes **BAKE:** 20 minutes **STAND:** 10 minutes

- 2 tsp. cumin seeds
- 1 14-oz. can chicken broth
- 1 14½-oz. can Mexican-style stewed tomatoes or one 10-oz. can diced tomatoes and green chile peppers
- ¼ cup oil-packed dried tomatoes, drained and cut up
- 1 cup dried orzo pasta
- 2 9-oz. pkg. frozen cooked southwest-flavored chicken breast strips, thawed, or two 6-oz. pkg. refrigerated cooked southwest-flavored chicken breast strips
- Seeded and chopped jalapeño or serrano chile peppers (optional)*
- Paprika (optional)

1. Preheat oven to 350° F. In a large saucepan heat cumin seeds over medium heat for 3 to 4 minutes or until fragrant and toasted, shaking pan occasionally. Carefully stir in broth, undrained tomatoes, dried tomatoes, and orzo. Bring to boiling. Transfer mixture to an ungreased 2-quart baking dish. Top with chicken breast strips.

2. Bake, covered, for 20 minutes or until orzo is tender. Let casserole stand, covered, for 10 minutes. If desired, top with jalapeño peppers; sprinkle with paprika. Serve warm. Makes 4 to 6 servings.

***NOTE:** Because hot chile peppers, such as jalapeños, contain volatile oils that can burn your skin and eyes, avoid direct contact with chiles as much as possible. When working with chile peppers, wear plastic or rubber gloves. If your bare hands do touch the chile peppers, wash your hands well with soap and water.

Each serving: 388 cal., 7 g total fat (2 g sat. fat), 60 mg chol., 1,227 mg sodium, 44 g carbo., 3 g dietary fiber, 35 g protein. Daily Values: 14% vit. A, 15% vit. C, 9% calcium, 24% iron.

MAKE-AHEAD TIPS

Make-ahead cooking—whether you're stashing leftovers in the freezer or baking ahead for busy days—is a great way to get the most out of your time in the kitchen. You can store most casseroles in the fridge for three to four days or in the freezer up to three months.

SEAL IT TIGHTLY

Most food-storage containers that have tight-fitting lids—even disposables—provide adequate protection in the refrigerator. However, when you're shopping for freezer-safe containers, look for a phrase or icon indicating the container is designed for freezer use. Be sure to use freezer-to-oven dishes when you want to store an entire casserole in its baking dish. If your casserole doesn't have its own tight-fitting lid, cover the surface with heavy-duty foil or plastic freezer wrap. Do not use foil to wrap foods that contain acidic ingredients. To freeze a casserole that contains tomatoes or other acidic ingredients, cover with plastic freezer wrap, then with foil. Remove the plastic wrap before reheating in the oven.

COOL IT QUICKLY

Hot casseroles bound for the refrigerator or freezer must be cooled rapidly. A quick chill decreases the chance that harmful bacteria will grow. Cooling food quickly before popping the sealed containers into the freezer allows the food to freeze faster. This also helps to prevent the formation of large ice crystals that may ruin the flavor and texture. When freezing leftovers, the quickest way to cool down a casserole is to divide it into individual portions and place them in shallow containers. Put these into the refrigerator. Once thoroughly chilled, transfer the cold containers to the freezer. Arrange the containers in a single layer until frozen. Stack after they're frozen solid.

KEEP IT COLD

When you store casseroles in the refrigerator or freezer, it's important to make sure they are kept cold enough. Maintain a refrigerator temperature of 40° F or below. Freezers should be kept at a temperature of 0° F or below.

Creamy Macaroni and Cheese

You can use cavatelli or campanelle pasta instead of the elbow macaroni called for in this hearty macaroni and cheese.

PREP: 10 minutes **BAKE:** 30 minutes
COOK: 10 minutes **STAND:** 10 minutes

- **4 slices bacon**
- **1 large sweet onion, thinly sliced**
- **6 oz. dried elbow macaroni**
- **8 oz. mozzarella cheese, shredded (2 cups)**
- **2 to 4 oz. blue cheese, crumbled (1/2 to 1 cup)**
- **1 cup half-and-half or light cream**
- **1/8 tsp. ground black pepper**

1. Preheat oven to 350° F. In a large skillet cook bacon over medium heat until crisp, turning once. Drain bacon on paper towels; crumble. Reserve bacon drippings in skillet.

2. Cook onion in reserved bacon drippings for 5 to 8 minutes or until onion is tender and golden brown. Set aside.

3. Cook elbow macaroni according to package directions. Drain and place in an ungreased 1 1/2-quart casserole. Add the crumbled bacon, onion, 1 1/2 cups of the mozzarella cheese, the blue cheese, half-and-half, and pepper. Toss gently to combine.

4. Bake, uncovered, for 20 minutes. Stir gently. Top with the remaining mozzarella cheese. Bake for 10 minutes more or until top is brown and bubbly. Let stand for 10 minutes. Serve warm. Makes 6 servings.

Each serving: 331 cal., 18 g total fat (9 g sat. fat), 45 mg chol., 280 mg sodium, 26 g carbo., 1 g dietary fiber, 16 g protein. Daily Values: 8% vit. A, 3% vit. C, 30% calcium, 6% iron.

COMFORTING CASSEROLE SUPPER

Creamy Macaroni and Cheese *(above)*
Apple wedges
Dinner rolls
Ultimate Chocolate Sundaes *(page 49)*
Milk

Creamy Macaroni and Cheese

Roasted Asparagus Soup

SOUPED UP AND READY TO GO

USE APRIL'S SHOWER OF TENDER GREENS TO THEIR BEST ADVANTAGE IN THESE LIGHT-AS-AIR SPRING SOUPS.

Soups are the best way to bridge this changeable season. Caught between winter's last gasp and springtime's first fertile breath, we turn to soups to both warm chilled souls and rejuvenate spirits still caught in the winter doldrums. Thankfully, as we start to pick up the threads of outdoor life again, these soups are ready. They're quick to prepare and use a minimum number of ingredients, with a big nod toward spring's tenderest greens—spinach, asparagus, baby green beans, green onions, chives, and fresh herbs.

Spring Carrot Soup

Spring Carrot Soup

You'll find *haricots vert,* which are tiny French green beans, in the specialty section of the produce aisle.

Start to Finish: 25 minutes

- 1 14-oz. can vegetable broth
- 8 to 10 small carrots with tops, trimmed, scrubbed, halved lengthwise, and cut in half crosswise (4 oz.)
- ½ cup haricots verts or baby green beans, trimmed
- 6 oz. fresh or frozen peeled, deveined medium shrimp
- 1 12-oz. can carrot juice
- ¼ tsp. bottled hot pepper sauce
- Salt
- Ground black pepper

1. In a large saucepan bring vegetable broth to boiling. Add carrots.* Bring to boiling; reduce heat. Cover and simmer for 4 minutes.

2. Add haricots verts and shrimp. Bring to boiling; reduce heat. Cover and simmer about 3 minutes or until shrimp turn pink.

3. Add carrot juice and hot pepper sauce; heat through (do not boil). Season to taste with salt and pepper. To serve, ladle soup into 4 to 6 bowls. Makes 4 to 6 appetizer servings.

***NOTE:** If you prefer green beans to be more than crisp-tender, add them with the carrots.

Each serving: 104 cal., 1 g total fat (0 g sat. fat), 65 mg chol., 586 mg sodium, 13 g carbo., 2 g fiber, 11 g pro. Daily Values: 351% vit. A, 21% vit. C, 6% calcium, 9% iron.

Roasted Asparagus Soup

Roasted green onions give this soup smoky depth. Their dark green tops, along with fresh dill, brighten the soup with a splash of color.

Start to Finish: 25 minutes

- 2 bunches green onions
- 1½ lb. asparagus, trimmed and cut into 2- to 3-inch pieces
- 1 medium onion, cut into thin wedges
- 2 Tbsp. olive oil
- 2 14-oz. cans reduced-sodium chicken broth
- ¼ tsp. kosher salt
- ¼ tsp. ground black pepper
- ½ cup half-and-half, light cream, or milk
- 1 Tbsp. snipped fresh dill

1. Preheat oven to 450° F. Trim root ends from green onions. Cut white parts into 1-inch lengths. Cut green tops into 1-inch lengths and reserve. Place the white parts of green onions, asparagus, and onion wedges in an even layer in a shallow large roasting pan. Drizzle vegetables with olive oil. Roast, uncovered, for 15 to 20 minutes or until vegetables are charred and tender.

2. Place half of the roasted vegetables in a food processor bowl or blende container. Add half a can of broth. Cover; process or blend until smooth. Transfer to a large saucepan. Repeat with remaining asparagus, onion wedges, and half a can of broth.

3. Stir in remaining can of broth, salt, and pepper. Bring to boiling; reduce heat. Stir in half-and-half and snipped fresh dill; heat through but do not boil.

4. To serve, ladle soup into 6 bowls. Top with green onion tops and dill sprigs, if desired. Makes 6 appetizer servings.

Each serving: 128 cal., 8 g total fat (3 g sat. fat), 9 mg chol., 598 mg sodium, 10 g carbo., 3 g fiber, 6 g pro. Daily Values: 14% vit. A, 28% vit. C, 8% calcium, 8% iron.

Country Potato Soup with Chives and Garlic Olive Oil

This soup is equally delicious hot or chilled. Garlic Olive Oil is not only great in the soup, it's marvelous as a dipper for crusty bread.

START TO FINISH: 20 minutes

- 1½ cups refrigerated diced red-skinned potatoes or new potatoes, peeled and quartered
- ½ cup chopped leek*
- 1 clove garlic, minced
- 2 14-oz. cans reduced-sodium chicken broth
- 6 fresh chives, cut into 1-inch pieces
- ⅛ tsp. ground white pepper
- 1 cup half-and-half, light cream, or milk
- Snipped fresh chives
- 1 recipe Garlic Olive Oil (below)

1. In a large saucepan combine potatoes, leek, garlic, and 1 cup of the broth. Bring to boiling; reduce heat. Cover and simmer until potatoes are tender, allowing 5 minutes for diced potatoes or 10 minutes for quartered potatoes.

2. Using a hand-held mixer, puree undrained potato mixture. (Or, add potato mixture to a blender. Cover; blend on low speed until nearly smooth, adding additional broth if necessary. Return mixture to saucepan.)

3. Add cut chives and white pepper. Whisk in remaining broth and half-and-half. Heat through.

4. To serve, ladle soup into 6 bowls. Top with snipped chives and a few drops of Garlic Olive Oil. Makes 6 appetizer servings.

GARLIC OLIVE OIL: In a small skillet heat 1 clove minced garlic in 2 tablespoons olive oil until garlic begins to brown. Strain to remove garlic. Discard any unused oil (do not store).

***NOTE:** Use the white part of the leek plus a little of the green top to give the soup a pleasant hint of color.

Each serving: 96 cal., 5 g total fat (3 g sat. fat), 15 mg chol., 424 mg sodium, 10 g carbo., 1 g fiber, 4 g pro. Daily Values: 4% vit. A, 8% vit. C, 5% calcium, 2% iron.

Spring Salmon Chowder

This broth-based chowder sings with spring flavors. Baby spinach, thyme, and green onions nicely accent sweet new potatoes and salmon.

START TO FINISH: 25 minutes

- 6 tiny new potatoes, quartered
- 2 14-oz. cans vegetable broth
- 1 ear fresh corn, kernels removed and reserved, or ½ cup frozen whole kernel corn, thawed
- 6 2-inch sprigs fresh thyme, or ½ tsp. dried thyme, crushed
- 12 oz. fresh or frozen skinless, boneless salmon, cut into 1-inch chunks
- 1 cup packed baby spinach leaves
- ¼ cup sliced green onion
- Salt
- Ground black pepper

1. In a large saucepan cook potatoes, covered, in boiling vegetable broth about 5 minutes or until potatoes are tender but not cooked through.

2. Add corn and thyme. Return to boiling; reduce heat. Cover and cook about 4 minutes or until vegetables are crisp-tender; reduce heat.

3. Carefully add salmon to saucepan. Simmer, uncovered, for 3 to 5 minutes or until salmon flakes easily with a fork.

4. Remove thyme sprigs, if desired. Stir in spinach and green onion; cook about 1 minute or until spinach begins to wilt.

5. To serve, ladle chowder into 6 cups or bowls. Season to taste with salt and pepper. Makes 6 main-dish servings.

Each serving: 169 cal., 7 g total fat (1 g sat. fat), 37 mg chol., 639 mg sodium, 14 g carbo., 2 g fiber, 14 g pro. Daily Values: 14% vit. A, 22% vit. C, 3% calcium, 9% iron.

A SOUPER SUPPER

Spring Salmon Chowder *(above)*
Tossed green salad
Mom's Bread *(page 540)*
Nutty Berry-Chip Squares *(page 553)*
Sparkling water

Country Potato Soup with Chives and Garlic Olive Oil

SOUP TOPPERS

Sometimes a quick little sprinkle of something special can bring a soup to life—not only its flavor but also its appearance. To find ideal toppers and garnishes, start by looking at the soup recipe itself.

First, consider classic complements such as shredded cheese, snipped herbs, croutons or toast, or coarsely cracked peppercorns—in fact, a colorful mix of peppercorns is often pretty and peppy. But if none of the classic toppers sounds appealing, take one more look at the recipe's ingredient list. Is there something you can chop, slice, or julienne into a garnish—and perhaps even use in a different form than in the recipe?

In a soup featuring cooked carrots, you can float a simple sprinkling of raw, julienne-cut carrot for contrasting color and flavor. In a beet soup, you might do the same with blanched or even pickled beets.

Don't be afraid of a mess when garnishing wide-rimmed soup bowls—many garnishes, particularly herbs, look great sprinkled not only on the soup but on the bowl rim as well.

Spring Salmon Chowder

Alesia Lacina *(left)* and her sister, Francene Coons, stand in their Iowa field of soybeans. The sisters follow their soybeans from field to factory, where they make tofu that they include in recipes such as Thai Noodles. The young green soybeans *(below left)* look similar to peas in a pod.

The Soy SISTERS

TWO SISTERS—WHO ADMIT TO BEING SOY NUTS—ADD A HEALTHY BOOST OF SOY FOODS TO NEARLY EVERYTHING THEY EAT.

Thai Noodles

Featuring soy in three ways—soy nut butter, soy sauce, and tofu—this dish showcases the delicious versatility of the nutritious bean.

PREP: 15 minutes **COOK:** 15 minutes

- ½ cup soy nut butter or creamy peanut butter
- ⅓ cup water
- ⅓ cup reduced-sodium soy sauce
- 3 Tbsp. lime juice
- 3 cloves garlic, quartered
- 1 Tbsp. grated fresh ginger
- 1 Tbsp. sesame oil
- 1 14- to 16-oz. pkg. firm tofu
- 1 Tbsp. cooking oil
- 8 oz. Chinese egg noodles or fine egg noodles
- 2 Tbsp. snipped fresh cilantro
- ¼ tsp. crushed red pepper
- ¼ cup chopped unsalted peanuts

1. In a food processor or blender combine soy nut butter, water, soy sauce, lime juice, garlic, ginger, and sesame oil. Cover and process or blend until smooth; set aside.

2. Drain tofu; pat dry with paper towels. Cut tofu into ½-inch-thick slices. In a 12-inch nonstick skillet heat cooking oil over medium-high heat. Add tofu; cook for 5 minutes or until brown. Turn slices. Cook for 5 minutes more. Remove from heat. Transfer slices to a cutting board. Cut each slice into 1½- to 2-inch triangles or squares; set aside.

3. Meanwhile, cook noodles according to package directions; drain and add to skillet.

4. Add soy nut butter mixture to skillet; heat through. Add tofu, noodles, cilantro, and crushed red pepper to skillet. Toss gently to coat. Sprinkle with peanuts. Serve warm. Makes 4 to 6 main-dish servings.

Each serving: 582 cal., 28 g total fat (4 g sat. fat), 54 mg chol., 972 mg sodium, 58 g carbo., 3 g fiber, 27 g pro. Daily Values: 4% vit. A, 12% vit. C, 6% calcium, 18% iron.

Thai Noodles

Sisters' story

It all began when Alesia Lacina and her husband, Tom, an attorney and Iowa soybean farmer, experienced a "eureka" moment one evening. At the time, they were growing and shipping food-grade soybeans to Japan, where the beans were used to make tofu.

"We thought—why can't we do that here?" says Alesia. So she and Tom teamed up with her sister, Francene Coons, and Francene's husband, Dave, to immerse themselves in everything tofu. Alesia and Francene—they call themselves the Soy Sisters—tried making tofu in their kitchens, but it "was a real mess," Alesia says. So they studied with soy experts at Iowa State University and the University of Illinois at Urbana-Champaign.

In 1999, the family-run company, Midwest Harvest, started producing organic tofu. The sisters' tofu consumption skyrocketed as their knowledge of the health benefits of soy foods increased. The sisters say they consume 25 grams of soy protein daily—the amount reported to reduce the risk of heart disease. Soy foods, which are high in protein and low in saturated fat, also may alleviate hot flashes and other menopausal symptoms, as well as reduce the risk of osteoporosis. Research also shows soy foods may fight prostate, colon, and breast cancers.

The Soy Sisters compiled their recipes into *A Tofu Cookbook* in an effort to move tofu into the mainstream. "There's a tremendous misconception about soy," says Francene. "You don't have to go vegetarian. The recipes may not be low in fat, but they are comfort foods with the added benefits of soy." Recipes for some of their favorite dishes begin here. Their cookbook, $20 including shipping, is available by calling 888/766-0051 or by sending e-mail requests to: orders@wildwoodharvestfoods.com.

"THE RECIPES MAY NOT BE LOW IN FAT, BUT THEY'RE COMFORT FOODS WITH THE ADDED BENEFITS OF SOY."

Francene Coons

Chocolate Chip Cookies

Chocolate Chip Cookies

What better way to introduce tofu to your diet than through chocolate chip cookies?

PREP: 30 minutes **BAKE:** 8 minutes per batch

- 2½ cups quick-cooking rolled oats
- 2 cups all-purpose flour
- 1 tsp. baking powder
- 1 tsp. baking soda
- 8 oz. soft tofu
- 1 cup butter or margarine, softened
- 1 cup packed brown sugar
- 1 cup granulated sugar or maple sugar
- 1 tsp. vanilla
- 1 12-oz. pkg. semisweet chocolate pieces
- 4 oz. semisweet chocolate, coarsely chopped

1. Preheat oven to 375° F. Process oats in small batches in a food processor bowl until oatmeal resembles coarse flour. In a medium bowl stir together the oatmeal, flour, baking powder, and baking soda; set aside. Place tofu in food processor bowl; cover and process until smooth. Set aside.

2. In a very large bowl beat butter with an electric mixer on medium to high speed for 30 seconds. Add sugars; beat until combined. Beat in vanilla and tofu until combined. Beat in as much of the flour mixture as you can with the mixer. Stir in any remaining flour mixture. Stir in chocolate pieces and chopped chocolate.

3. Form dough into 1½-inch balls. Place 3 inches apart on an ungreased cookie sheet. Slightly flatten dough. Bake for 8 to 10 minutes or until cookies are golden brown around the edges; cool on a wire rack. Makes about 52 cookies.

Each cookie: 131 cal., 6 g total fat (4 g sat. fat), 10 mg chol., 70 mg sodium, 19 g carbo., 1 g fiber, 2 g pro. Daily Values: 3% vit. A, 1% calcium, 4% iron.

Garlic Mashed Potatoes with Tofu and Feta

TOFU IS SOY GOOD

Besides being good for you—cholesterol-free, low-calorie, high-protein—tofu is surprisingly fun and easy to use in cooking. Originating in China as early as the 2nd century B.C., tofu is made from soy bean curd in a process similar to cheesemaking. In fact, many of the historic uses of tofu in Asia compare well to Western uses of dairy products. Tofu is easy to use because it takes on the flavors of other ingredients. Yet, because tofu is available in textures ranging from soft to extra firm, it's important to select the texture specified in the recipe you're preparing.

Garlic Mashed Potatoes with Tofu and Feta

Tofu lends smooth creaminess while feta cheese and garlic add flavorful accents to comfy mashed potatoes.

PREP: 20 minutes **COOK:** 20 minutes

- 8 oz. soft tofu, drained
- ½ cup crumbled basil-and-tomato feta cheese
- 6 medium red potatoes (about 2 lb.)
- 8 cloves garlic, peeled
- 1 Tbsp. olive oil
- ½ tsp. salt
- ¼ tsp. ground black pepper
- Milk (optional)
- 2 Tbsp. finely shredded Parmesan cheese

1. Let tofu and feta cheese stand at room temperature while preparing the potatoes. Quarter potatoes. In a large saucepan cook potatoes and garlic, covered, in lightly salted boiling water for 20 to 25 minutes or until tender.

2. Meanwhile, place tofu in a blender container or food processor bowl. Cover; blend or process tofu until smooth. Set aside.

3. Drain potatoes and garlic; transfer to a large bowl. Mash potatoes and garlic with a potato masher or beat with an electric mixer on low speed. Stir in pureed tofu, olive oil, salt, and pepper. If needed, add milk, 1 tablespoon at a time, until potatoes are light and fluffy. Stir in feta and Parmesan cheeses. Makes 6 servings.

Each serving: 229 cal., 9 g total fat (4 g sat. fat), 16 mg chol., 499 mg sodium, 28 g carbo., 3 g fiber, 11 g pro. Daily Values: 2% vit. A, 39% vit. C, 22% calcium, 14% iron.

Flourless Chocolate Torte with Apricot Filling

KEEPING THE Passover SPIRIT

COOKBOOK AUTHOR JOAN NATHAN'S PASSOVER SEDER SETS THE STAGE FOR A HARMONIOUS BLEND OF RITUAL AND FAMILY TRADITION.

Flourless Chocolate Torte with Apricot Filling

Joan's chocolate torte is made with potato starch instead of flour, which is forbidden for use during the eight days of Passover.

PREP: 40 minutes **BAKE:** 30 minutes
STAND: 30 minutes **COOL:** 2 hours

- 6 egg yolks
- 8 egg whites
- 1 Tbsp. unsweetened cocoa powder
- 8 oz. bittersweet chocolate, chopped
- 1 cup unsalted butter or parve margarine, softened
- 1 cup sugar
- 2 Tbsp. potato starch
- 1 recipe Apricot Filling (below)
- 1/2 cup toasted chopped almonds
- 1 cup fresh red raspberries
- 1/2 cup sliced, pitted, fresh apricots or dried apricots, cut into slivers

1. Let egg yolks and whites stand at room temperature for 30 minutes. Meanwhile, grease two 9-inch round cake pans. Line the bottoms of the pans with waxed paper; grease the waxed paper. Dust the insides of the pans with the cocoa powder; set aside.

2. In a small saucepan cook and stir bittersweet chocolate over low heat until melted. Let cool for 10 minutes.

3. Preheat oven to 350° F. In a large bowl beat butter with an electric mixer on medium to high speed for 30 seconds. Add sugar and potato starch; beat until combined. Beat in the melted chocolate until combined. Add egg yolks, 2 at a time, beating well after each addition until combined.

4. Thoroughly wash beaters. In another large bowl beat the egg whites with an electric mixer on medium speed until stiff peaks form (tips stand straight).

5. Stir some of the egg white into the chocolate mixture to lighten. Fold remaining egg white into chocolate mixture. Divide batter evenly between prepared pans. Bake for 30 to 35 minutes or until tops spring back when lightly touched and a toothpick inserted near the centers comes out clean. Cool in pans on a wire rack for 10 minutes. Remove from pans; cool completely. (Centers will sink slightly as cakes cool.) Remove waxed paper.

6. Meanwhile, prepare Apricot Filling. To assemble, place one cake layer on a plate, top side up. Top with half of the filling and half of the almonds. Top with remaining cake layer, filling, and almonds. Mound raspberries and fresh or dried apricot slivers on top. Chill to store for up to 3 days. Makes 12 to 16 servings.

APRICOT FILLING: In a small saucepan combine one 18-ounce jar apricot preserves (1 1/2 cups), 1/2 cup snipped dried apricots, and 3 tablespoons lemon juice. Cook and stir over low heat until melted. Set aside to cool.

Each serving: 549 cal., 31 g total fat (15 g sat. fat), 150 mg chol., 58 mg sodium, 66 g carbo., 4 g fiber, 8 g pro. Daily Values: 27% vit. A, 15% vit. C, 7% calcium, 12% iron.

Passover tradition

"The seder is absolutely my favorite night of the year," says Joan Nathan, award-winning author of cookbooks on Jewish cooking. "The most important part of the holiday is to relate the story of Passover to your children. It provides a direct connection to ancient Israel—and could be the oldest theatrical event in history. We put on a Passover play every year, a tradition that started 23 years ago when my eldest daughter was two."

In addition to hosting the annual play, Joan creates a happy medley of dishes for her Passover seder guests, incorporating everything from recipes that are hundreds of years old to her own version of Flourless Chocolate Torte with Apricot Filling. On the first night of Passover, you'll find at least 40 relatives and friends gathering at the Nathans' table for seder. The event combines food, ritual, and storytelling to commemorate the flight from Egypt by Moses and the people of Israel, as told in the Book of Exodus.

Joan is shy when asked to talk about her writing accomplishments, but her expertise and enthusiasm for cooking and her faith are plain to see. Her book *Jewish Cooking in America* won the Julia Child Cookbook Award and the James Beard Award for Food of the Americas. She also has written *The Jewish Holiday Baker* and *The Jewish Holiday Kitchen*.

Good Ol' Buttermilk Fried Chicken

Spring Chicken

THAT GIDDY GRIN IS CONTAGIOUS. ONE SURE WAY TO CATCH IT IS BY CRUNCHING INTO THE ULTIMATE FINGER FOOD: FRIED CHICKEN. OR, FIND BLISS BY MUNCHING ON TANDOORI, KABOBS, OR SCALLOPINI.

Good Ol' Buttermilk Fried Chicken

An electric skillet works wonders for fried chicken, but be careful when adding the chicken because the oil can splatter. A Dutch oven or large pot produces crispy chicken too.

PREP: 25 minutes **MARINATE:** 30 minutes **COOK:** 20 minutes

- 3 lb. small meaty chicken pieces (drumsticks, thighs, and/or breast halves)
- 1½ tsp. salt
- 1½ cups buttermilk
- 1¼ cups all-purpose flour
- 2 tsp. paprika
- ½ tsp. ground black pepper
- 2 eggs, beaten
- 4 cups cooking oil
- 1 recipe Vinegar Splash(below) or malt vinegar

1. If desired, remove skin from chicken. Place chicken pieces into a self-sealing plastic bag set in a large bowl. Sprinkle chicken with ½ teaspoon of the salt. Pour buttermilk over chicken. Seal bag. Marinate in the refrigerator for 30 minutes or overnight, turning bag occasionally to coat chicken.

2. Drain chicken, reserving ½ cup of the buttermilk. In a shallow dish combine flour, paprika, the remaining 1 teaspoon salt, and pepper. In another shallow dish combine the eggs and the reserved buttermilk. Coat chicken with the flour mixture, then dip into egg mixture, then dip into flour mixture again. Place chicken pieces on a tray; set aside while oil heats.

3. In a 12-inch electric skillet heat ½ inch of oil (about 3 cups) to 350° F (about 10 to 15 minutes). Using tongs, carefully add chicken to the skillet. Reduce temperature setting to 325° F. Cook, uncovered, for 10 minutes. Turn chicken and cook for 10 to 12 minutes more or until coating is golden, chicken is no longer pink, and an instant-read thermometer registers 170° F for breasts or 180° F for thighs and drumsticks. Drain on paper towels. Transfer chicken to a serving platter. Sprinkle with Vinegar Splash or malt vinegar. Makes 6 servings.

VINEGAR SPLASH: In a small bowl whisk together ½ cup cider vinegar, 1 tablespoon snipped fresh cilantro, and several dashes bottled hot pepper sauce.

DUTCH-OVEN METHOD: In a Dutch oven heat 1½ inches of oil (about 6½ cups) over medium heat to 350° F. Using tongs, carefully add a few pieces of chicken to Dutch oven. (Oil temperature will drop; maintain at 325° F.) Cook for 12 to 15 minutes or until coating is golden, chicken is no longer pink, and an instant-read thermometer registers 170° F for breasts or 180° F for thighs and drumsticks, turning once. Drain on paper towels. Keep warm in a 300° F oven while cooking remaining.

Each serving: 390 cal., 18 g total fat (3 g sat. fat), 169 mg chol., 625 mg sodium, 22 g carbo., 1 g fiber, 34 g pro. Daily Values: 13% vit. A, 6% vit. C, 7% calcium, 15% iron.

Ravioli Chicken Soup

Ravioli Chicken Soup

Just a pinch of saffron goes a long way in adding flavor and more intense color to food. The aromatic spice is a tad expensive, so feel free to leave it out. This soup is terrific with or without it.

START TO FINISH: 25 minutes

- Nonstick cooking spray
- 12 oz. skinless, boneless chicken breast halves, cut into ½-inch cubes
- 6 cups reduced-sodium chicken broth
- ½ cup sliced leek or chopped onion
- 1 Tbsp. finely chopped fresh ginger
- ¼ tsp. saffron threads, slightly crushed (optional)
- 1 9-oz. pkg. vegetable ravioli or herb chicken tortellini
- ½ cup fresh baby spinach leaves or shredded fresh spinach

1. Lightly coat a large saucepan with cooking spray. Heat saucepan over medium-high heat. Add chicken; cook and stir for 3 minutes. Carefully add broth, leek or onion, ginger, and, if desired, saffron.

2. Bring to boiling. Add ravioli or tortellini. Return to boiling; reduce heat. Simmer, uncovered, for 5 to 9 minutes or until ravioli is tender, stirring occasionally. Remove from heat. To serve, ladle into four small bowls. Top with spinach. Makes 4 main-dish servings.

Each serving: 222 cal., 3 g total fat (0 g sat. fat), 59 mg chol., 1,221 mg sodium, 21 g carbo., 3 g fiber, 29 g pro. Daily Values: 18% vit. A, 9% vit. C, 6% calcium, 13% iron.

Chicken and Sausage Kabobs

Go ahead and make your own skewers from apple tree sticks. Twigs from oak, maple, or hickory trees will work too. Just be sure those trees have not been sprayed with pesticides or other chemicals.

PREP: 25 minutes **MARINATE:** 2 hours **GRILL:** 12 minutes

- 4 medium skinless, boneless chicken breast halves (about 1 lb. total)
- 2 Tbsp. finely chopped green onion
- 2 Tbsp. olive oil
- 1 Tbsp. snipped fresh Italian flat-leaf parsley
- 1 Tbsp. snipped fresh oregano
- 1 Tbsp. lime juice
- 1 clove garlic, minced
- 8 oz. apple-flavored smoked chicken sausage or other smoked sausage, halved lengthwise and cut into 3/4-inch pieces
- 1 recipe Herbed Dipping Sauce (below)
- Grilled lime wedges

1. Cut chicken into 1/2-inch-thick strips. Place in a bowl. For marinade, combine green onion, olive oil, parsley, oregano, lime juice, and garlic. Pour marinade over chicken; stir to coat. Cover and marinate in the refrigerator for 2 to 8 hours.

2. Drain chicken, discarding marinade. Thread strips of chicken and sausage onto six long skewers.

3. For a charcoal grill, place the kabobs on the rack of an uncovered grill directly over medium coals. Grill for 12 to 14 minutes or until chicken is no longer pink, turning to brown evenly. (For a gas grill, preheat grill. Reduce heat to medium. Place kabobs on grill rack over heat. Cover and grill as directed.) Remove kabobs from grill. Serve with Herbed Dipping Sauce and lime wedges. Makes 6 servings.

HERBED DIPPING SAUCE: In a bowl combine 1/4 cup dairy sour cream, 1/4 cup mayonnaise or salad dressing, 2 tablespoons finely chopped green onion and/or chives, 1 tablespoon snipped fresh Italian flat-leaf parsley, 1 tablespoon snipped fresh oregano, 1 tablespoon lime juice, and 1 clove minced garlic.

Each serving: 262 cal., 18 g total fat (4 g sat. fat), 61 mg chol., 347 mg sodium, 1 g carbo., 0 g fiber, 23 g pro. Daily Values: 3% vit. A, 8% vit. C, 3% calcium, 5% iron.

CHICKEN TIPS

- When you can't even wait that long, start with deli-roasted chicken or precooked, seasoned chicken pieces. Use them in main-dish salads, in pastas, or on pizza.
- Check chicken doneness with a meat thermometer. The internal temperature of a whole bird or drumsticks and thighs should reach 180° F; breasts, 170° F; and ground chicken, 165° F.
- Visit the National Chicken Council Web site: www.EatChicken.com for more tips and information.

Chicken and Sausage Kabobs

Provençal Herb-Rubbed Roaster

Prepare this bird for the oven the night before you plan to serve it. The next day, just pile the potatoes around the chicken and pop the whole dish into the oven.

PREP: 20 minutes **MARINATE:** 2 hours
ROAST: 1 1/4 hours **STAND:** 10 minutes

- 1 3- to 4-lb. whole broiler-fryer chicken
- 1/4 cup olive oil
- 2 Tbsp. herbes de Provence
- 1 tsp. smoked salt or salt
- 1 tsp. crushed red pepper
- 3/4 tsp. coarsely ground black pepper
- 1 1/2 lb. tiny yellow and purple potatoes and/or fingerling potatoes, halved

1. Remove neck and giblets from chicken. Skewer neck skin to back; tie legs with 100-percent-cotton string. Twist wings under back. Brush chicken with 2 tablespoons of the olive oil.

2. In a small bowl stir together herbes de Provence, salt, crushed red pepper, and black pepper. Rub 2 tablespoons of the herb mixture onto the bird. Cover the remaining herb mixture; set aside. Place chicken in a large self-sealing plastic bag. Seal bag. Marinate in the refrigerator for 2 to 24 hours.

3. Preheat oven to 375° F. Remove chicken from bag. Place chicken, breast side up, on a rack in a shallow roasting pan. Insert a meat thermometer into center of an inside thigh muscle. Do not allow thermometer bulb to touch bone.

4. In a large bowl combine the remaining 2 tablespoons oil and remaining herb mixture. Add potatoes; toss to combine. Arrange potatoes around chicken. Roast chicken, uncovered, for 1 1/4 to 1 3/4 hours or until drumsticks move easily in their sockets and meat thermometer registers 180° F. Remove chicken from oven; cover. Let stand 10 minutes before carving.

5. To serve, place chicken and potatoes on a large serving platter. Makes 6 servings.

Each serving: 543 cal., 35 g total fat (9 g sat. fat), 134 mg chol., 492 mg sodium, 18 g carbo., 3 g fiber, 37 g pro. Daily Values: 6% vit. A, 31% vit. C, 5% calcium, 16% iron.

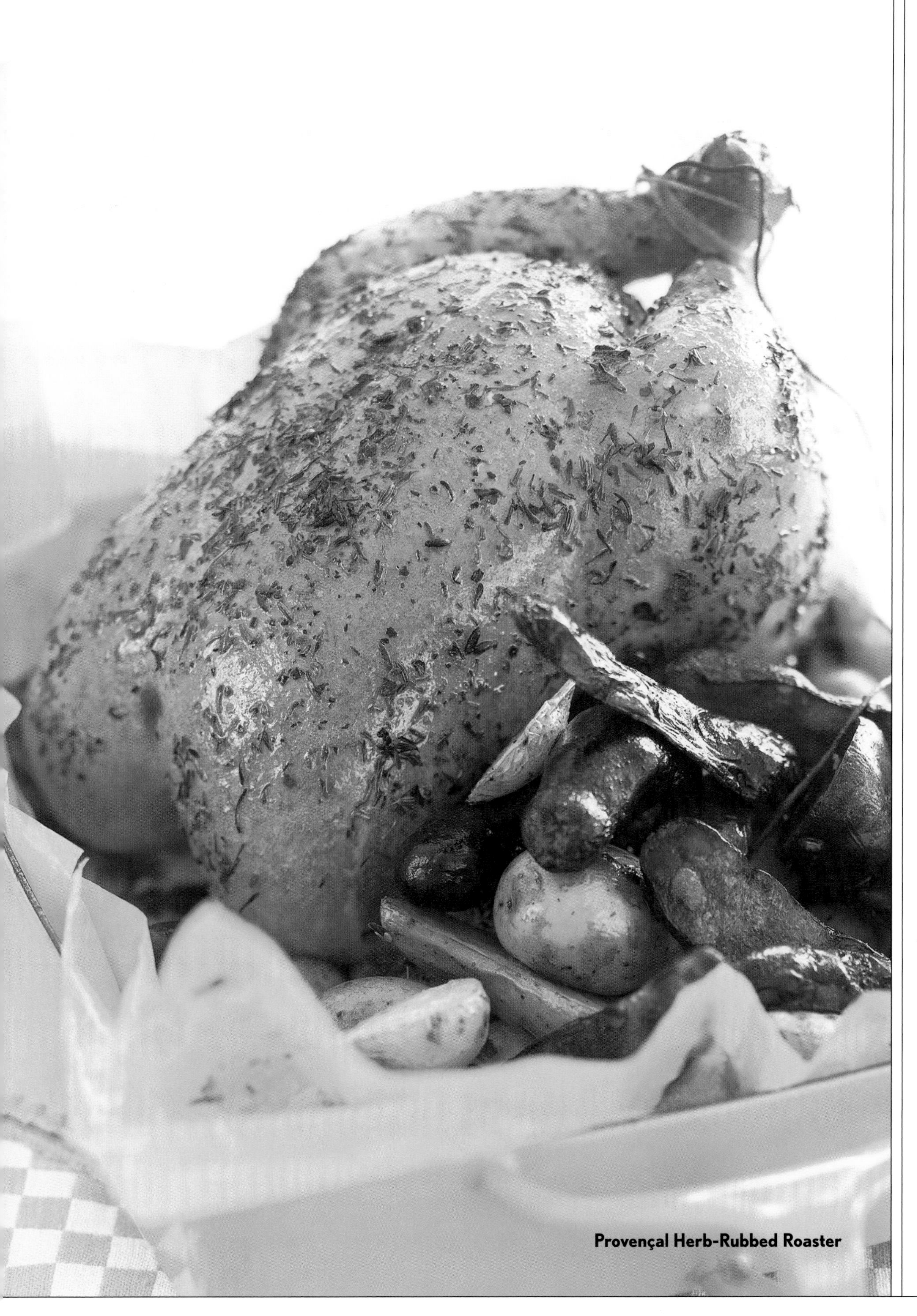

Provençal Herb-Rubbed Roaster

Mushroom-Smothered Chicken

Mushroom-Smothered Chicken

The mushroom sauce is swooning material as is, but a splash of cream sends it over the top. There's plenty of sauce to ladle over the chicken on a toasted baguette. We also love it with hot cooked potato gnocchi.

PREP: 20 minutes **COOK:** 30 minutes

- 1/4 cup all-purpose flour
- 1/2 tsp. salt
- 1/4 tsp. pepper
- 2 1/2 to 3 lb. meaty chicken pieces (breast halves, thighs, and drumsticks), skinned
- 2 Tbsp. olive oil or cooking oil
- 6 cups halved fresh mushrooms, such as morel, chanterelle, shiitake, and/or button
- 2 large onions, chopped (2 cups)
- 2 cloves garlic, minced
- 3/4 cup dry white wine or chicken broth
- 3/4 cup chicken broth
- 2 Tbsp. snipped fresh basil or 1 tsp. dried basil, crushed
- 1 Tbsp. snipped fresh thyme or 1 tsp. dried thyme, crushed
- 2 Tbsp. whipping cream (optional)
- Toasted baguette slices (optional)

1. In a plastic bag combine flour, salt, and pepper. Add chicken pieces, a few at a time, shaking to coat. In a 12-inch skillet brown chicken in hot oil over medium-high heat for 8 minutes, turning occasionally. Remove from skillet; set aside.

2. Add mushrooms, onions, and garlic to skillet. Cook for 4 minutes, stirring occasionally and scraping up any browned bits. Return chicken to pan. Add wine, broth, basil, and thyme. Bring to boiling; reduce heat. Cover and simmer for 25 to 30 minutes or until chicken is no longer pink and an instant-read thermometer registers 170° F for breasts or 180° F for thighs and drumsticks. Remove chicken; cover and keep warm.

3. Increase heat to medium and gently boil sauce, uncovered, for 5 minutes. If desired, stir in whipping cream. If desired, serve chicken and sauce over toasted baguette slices. Season to taste with salt and pepper. Makes 6 servings.

Each serving: 293 cal., 13 g total fat (3 g sat. fat), 77 mg chol., 368 mg sodium, 12 g carbo., 2 g fiber, 30 g pro. Daily Values: 1% vit. A, 7% vit. C, 4% calcium, 12% iron.

SPRING CHICKEN MENU

Leaf lettuce and strawberry salad with red wine vinaigrette
Mushroom-Smothered Chicken *(above)*
Steamed sugar snap peas
Toasted baguette slices
Pear Ginger Flan *(page 57)*

Tandoori Chicken Burger

Tandoori Chicken Burger

Feel free to separate the onions from the cucumbers before piling them onto your burgers. That way, those who aren't fond of onions can share with those who are.

PREP: 30 minutes **GRILL:** 14 minutes

- 1/4 cup fine dry bread crumbs
- 2 tsp. garam masala or curry powder
- 1/4 tsp. salt
- 1/4 tsp. ground red pepper
- 1 lb. uncooked ground chicken*
- 2 Tbsp. plain yogurt
- 4 seeded hamburger buns or kaiser rolls, split and toasted
- 1 recipe Minty Cucumbers (below)
- Kale or lettuce

1. In a large mixing bowl combine bread crumbs, garam masala or curry powder, salt, and ground red pepper. Add ground chicken and yogurt; mix well. Shape chicken mixture into four 3/4-inch-thick patties.

2. For a charcoal grill, place patties on the rack of an uncovered grill directly over medium coals. Grill for 14 to 18 minutes or until no longer pink (165° F), turning once halfway through grilling. (For a gas grill, preheat grill. Reduce heat to medium. Place patties on grill rack over heat. Cover and grill as above.) Remove from grill. Serve burgers on toasted buns with Minty Cucumbers and kale or lettuce. Makes 4 servings.

MINTY CUCUMBERS: Combine 1 cup thinly sliced cucumber, 1/2 cup thinly sliced red onion, 1/4 cup snipped fresh mint, 1 tablespoon balsamic vinaigrette, and 1/4 teaspoon salt.

***TEST KITCHEN TIP:** If you ask your butcher to prepare ground chicken for you, be sure to request it coarsely ground.

Each serving: 383 cal., 13 g total fat (1 g sat. fat), 0 mg chol., 841 mg sodium, 37 g carbo., 2 g fiber, 27 g pro. Daily Values: 2% vit. A, 10% vit. C,12% calcium, 25% iron.

Coconut Chicken Salad

Spring Chicken Scallopini

Spring Chicken Scallopini

A buttery white wine sauce and a little heap of herbs dress up the chicken and add incredibly fresh flavor. Best of all, it's fast and flashy.

START TO FINISH: 25 minutes

- 4 medium skinless, boneless chicken breast halves (about 1 lb. total)
- 1/4 cup all-purpose flour
- 1 1/4 tsp. salt
- 1/4 cup butter
- 1/2 cup dry white wine (such as Sauvignon Blanc) and/or chicken broth
- 1/4 cup sliced green onions
- 1/2 cup mixed snipped fresh herbs (such as oregano, thyme, lemon thyme, and/or mint)
- 1/4 tsp. coarsely ground black pepper
- 1/8 tsp. salt
- Steamed asparagus* (optional)

1. Place each chicken piece between two pieces of waxed paper or plastic wrap. Pound lightly with the flat side of a meat mallet, working from the center to the edges until pieces are an even 1/4-inch thickness (*see photo, below*). Remove the plastic wrap. In a shallow dish combine flour and the 1/4 teaspoon salt. Coat chicken pieces with flour mixture.

2. In a 12-inch skillet heat 2 tablespoons of the butter over medium heat. Add chicken; cook for 6 to 8 minutes or until chicken is tender and no longer pink, turning once. Remove chicken from skillet. Transfer chicken to a serving platter; cover and keep warm.

3. Add white wine and/or broth and green onions to the skillet. Cook and stir for 1 minute, scraping up any browned bits in skillet, if necessary. Cook 1 minute more or until reduced to 1/3 cup. Remove from heat. Whisk in remaining 2 tablespoons butter until melted. Stir in 2 tablespoons of the snipped fresh herbs, the pepper, and the 1/8 teaspoon salt. (If using chicken broth, omit the 1/8 teaspoon salt.)

4. If desired, serve chicken with steamed asparagus. Drizzle wine sauce over all. Pile remaining fresh herbs onto each serving. Makes 4 servings.

***TEST KITCHEN TIP:** To steam asparagus spears, snap off and discard woody bases from asparagus. Steam for 4 to 6 minutes or until tender.

Each serving: 320 cal., 14 g total fat (8 g sat. fat), 115 mg chol., 422 mg sodium, 7 g carbo., 0 g fiber, 34 g pro. Daily Values: 12% vit. A, 8% vit. C, 4% calcium, 8% iron.

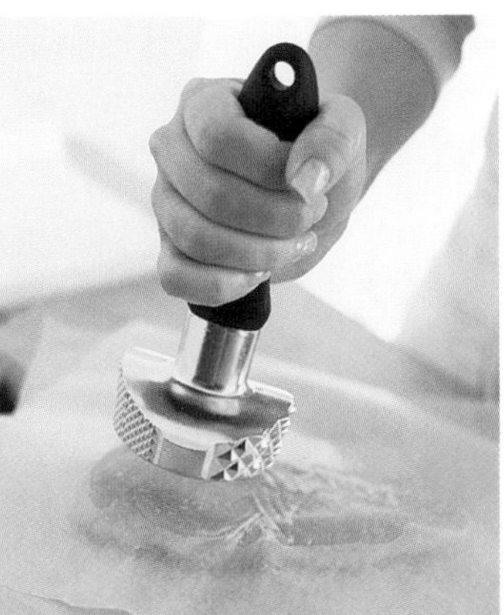
Use a meat mallet to lightly pound chicken to 1/4-inch thickness.

Coconut Chicken Salad

To give the Indian flatbread a sculptured look, use a pair of kitchen tongs to carefully hold bread a few inches above the open flame of a gas burner. As the bread heats up, it softens and curls. Or let it stay flat and serve it at room temperature.

PREP: 10 minutes **COOK:** 12 minutes **CHILL:** 1 hour

- 12 oz. skinless, boneless chicken breast halves and/or thighs
- 1 14-oz. can unsweetened light coconut milk
- 1/4 tsp. salt
- 1/8 tsp. ground black pepper
- 1/4 cup thinly sliced red onion or Vidalia onion
- 2 Tbsp. lime juice
- 2 red chile peppers, seeded and finely chopped, (optional)
- 1 cup shredded lettuce
- 1/2 cup coconut chips, toasted
- Indian flatbread (papadam or naan) or 3-inch rounds Armenian cracker bread

1. In a large skillet place chicken, coconut milk, the 1/4 teaspoon salt, and the 1/8 teaspoon black pepper. Bring to boiling; reduce heat. Cover and simmer for 12 to 14 minutes or until chicken is no longer pink and an instant-read thermometer registers 170° F for breasts or 180° F for thighs. Drain well; discard milk mixture. Cool chicken slightly; cut into bite-size pieces.

2. In a medium bowl combine chicken pieces, onion, lime juice, and chile peppers. Cover and chill in the refrigerator for 1 hour. Just before serving, gently stir shredded lettuce and half of the toasted coconut chips into the chicken mixture. Season to taste with additional salt and black pepper. Sprinkle with remaining coconut chips. Serve with Indian flat bread (pappadam or naan). Makes 4 servings.

Each serving: 201 cal., 10 g total fat (7 g sat. fat), 49 mg chol., 294 mg sodium, 7 g carbo., 1 g fiber, 20 g pro. Daily Values: 8% vit. A, 17% vit. C, 2% calcium, 10% iron.

Guava-Glazed Chicken

The technique may be unfamiliar, but removing the backbone and flattening the chicken shortens the cooking time for a whole bird. Great on the grill, this chicken also can be oven-roasted.

PREP: 20 minutes **COOK:** 15 minutes **GRILL:** 50 minutes

- 1 3- to 4-lb. whole broiler-fryer chicken
- 1/2 tsp. salt
- 1/4 tsp. pepper
- 1 recipe Guava Sauce (below)
- Sliced fresh guava (optional)
- Green onion (optional)

1. Remove the neck and giblets from chicken. Place the chicken, breast side down, on a cutting board. Use kitchen shears to make a lengthwise cut down one side of the backbone, starting from the tail end. Repeat the lengthwise cut on the opposite side of the backbone. Remove and discard backbone.

2. Turn chicken cut side down. Flatten chicken with your hands. (Try to make it as flat as possible.) Use kitchen shears to remove the wing tips. Sprinkle the salt and pepper over chicken.

3. For direct grilling, place chicken, cut side up, on the rack of an uncovered grill directly over medium coals. Grill for 25 minutes. Turn, using tongs. Grill for 20 minutes more. To glaze, brush with some Guava Sauce. Grill 5 minutes more or until an instant-read thermometer inserted in the thigh portion registers 180° F. (For indirect grilling, arrange medium-hot coals around a drip pan. Test for medium heat above the pan. Place chicken, cut side up, on grill rack over drip pan. Cover and grill for 45 minutes. Turn; brush with some of the sauce. Grill 5 minutes more or until an instant-read thermometer inserted in the thigh portion registers 180° F.)

4. Bring remaining sauce to boiling; pass with chicken. If desired, serve with sliced guava and onions. Makes 6 servings.

GUAVA SAUCE: In a small saucepan combine 1 cup guava, mango, peach, or apricot nectar; 1/4 cup bottled hoisin sauce; 2 cloves minced garlic; and, if desired, several dashes bottled hot pepper sauce. Bring to boiling; reduce heat. Boil gently, uncovered, about 15 minutes or until thickened and sauce is reduced to about 3/4 cup.

OVEN-ROASTING METHOD: Prepare the chicken and sauce as through Step 2. Place chicken on a rack in a shallow baking pan. Roast, uncovered, in a 425° F oven for 35 minutes. To glaze, brush chicken with some of the sauce. Roast for 5 to 10 minutes more or until an instant-read thermometer inserted in the thigh portion registers 180° F.

Each serving: 272 cal., 12 g total fat (3 g sat. fat), 79 mg chol., 478 mg sodium, 13 g carbo., 0 g fiber, 25 g pro. Daily Values: 12% vit. C, 2% calcium, 7% iron.

Chicken Cobbler

To really show off this all-in-one dish, cut a 16x2½-inch strip of parchment paper and wrap it around each dish. Tie it in place with 100-percent-cotton string before baking (see photo, below).

PREP: 15 minutes **BAKE:** 45 minutes

- 6 skinless, boneless chicken thighs (3 oz. each)
- Salt
- Pepper
- 1 cup shelled fresh peas or frozen peas
- 1/2 cup chopped Vidalia, Maui, or other sweet onion
- 2 Tbsp. butter
- 1/3 cup all-purpose flour
- 1/2 tsp. snipped fresh tarragon or 1/4 tsp. dried tarragon, crushed
- 2 cups chicken broth
- 1 recipe Carrot Cobbler Topping (below)

1. Preheat oven to 400° F. Arrange chicken in a 13×9×2-inch baking pan. Season with salt and pepper. Bake about 20 minutes or until chicken is no longer pink and juices run clear; set aside.

2. Meanwhile, if using fresh peas, cook peas in a small amount of boiling salted water for 2 minutes; drain.

3. For sauce, in a saucepan cook and stir onion in hot butter over medium heat about 5 minutes or until onion is tender. Stir in flour and tarragon. Add broth all at once. Cook and stir until thickened and bubbly. Stir in peas. Cover; keep warm while preparing cobbler topping.

4. Place a baked chicken thigh in each of six individual ungreased 10-ounce ramekins, custard cups, or baking dishes. Pour warm sauce over the chicken. Dollop Carrot Cobbler Topping over sauce. Place dishes in a 15×10×1-inch baking pan. Bake about 25 minutes or until topping is golden brown and a wooden toothpick inserted in the center of topping comes out clean. Makes 6 servings.

CARROT COBBLER TOPPING: In a medium mixing bowl stir together 2 cups all-purpose flour, 1 cup coarsely shredded carrot, 2 tablespoons sugar, 1 tablespoon baking powder, and 1/2 teaspoon salt. Stir in 1⅓ cups milk and 2 tablespoons melted butter until all is moistened.

Each serving: 425 cal., 13 g total fat (7 g sat. fat), 85 mg chol., 943 mg sodium, 48 g carbo., 4 g fiber, 28 g pro. Daily Values: 115% vit. A,11% vit. C, 22% calcium, 19% iron.

Fill each ramekin before wrapping in parchment paper.

Chicken Cobbler

PICKING CHICKEN

Chicken is packaged in a variety of ways, including with or without skin and bones.

- Broiler-fryer: A young chicken weighing between 3 and 5 pounds. It may be packaged whole or in parts, such as breasts, thighs, and wings.
- Roaster: Large and meaty, this whole bird weighs about 6 to 8 pounds.
- Ground chicken: Typically made from thigh meat, this makes a great burger. Ask your butcher to coarsely grind some for you if it's not available in the display cases.
- The weight of the chicken helps determine how many people it will serve. Twelve ounces of raw skinless, boneless chicken will serve about four people. If you're starting with one pound of raw bone-in chicken with skin, you'll have enough to feed two to three people.

Guava-Glazed Chicken

Down to Earth Granola

Down to Earth Granola

LESS IS OFTEN MORE.

Take granola, for instance. If you keep it simple, kids will launch into it. Start padding it with grits, groats, and other UFOs and they'll quickly depart for Planet Apathy. The aroma of granola baking is tantalizing, but wait until you taste these recipes. Out of this world!

Wholly granola!

Nuts About Granola

PREP: 15 minutes **BAKE:** 40 minutes

- 2 cups regular rolled oats
- 1 cup coarsely chopped walnuts or pecans
- ½ cup shelled sunflower seeds
- ½ cup coconut (optional)
- ¼ cup toasted wheat germ
- ¼ cup honey or maple-flavored syrup
- 2 Tbsp. cooking oil

1. Preheat oven to 300° F. In a large bowl mix oats, nuts, sunflower seeds, coconut (if desired), and wheat germ. Stir together honey and cooking oil; stir into oat mixture.

2. Spread oat mixture evenly in a 15×10×1-inch baking pan. Bake, uncovered, for 30 to 35 minutes or until lightly browned, stirring after 20 minutes.

3. Spread on a large piece of foil to cool. Break into clumps. Store in an airtight container for up to 1 week or in freezer for 2 months. Makes 6 cups (12 servings).

Each ½-cup serving: 234 cal., 12 g total fat (1 g sat. fat), 0 mg chol., 1 mg sodium, 27 g carbo., 4 g fiber, 7 g pro. Daily Values: 5% calcium, 9% iron.

Down to Earth Granola

PREP: 15 minutes **BAKE:** 40 minutes

- 4 cups regular rolled oats
- 1½ cups sliced almonds
- ½ cup packed light brown sugar
- ½ tsp. salt
- ½ tsp. ground cinnamon
- ¼ cup cooking oil
- ¼ cup honey
- 1 tsp. vanilla
- 1½ cups raisins or dried cranberries

1. Preheat oven to 300° F. In a bowl mix oats, almonds, brown sugar, salt, and cinnamon. In a saucepan warm oil and honey. Whisk or stir in vanilla. Carefully pour liquid over oat mixture. Stir gently with a wooden spoon; finish mixing by hand.

2. Spread evenly in a 15×10×1-inch baking pan. Bake for 40 minutes or until lightly browned, stirring every 10 minutes. Cool in pan on a wire rack. Stir in raisins or dried cranberries. Store in an airtight container for up to 1 week or in freezer for 3 months. Makes 8 cups (24 servings).

Each ⅓-cup serving: 186 cal., 8 g total fat (1 g sat. fat), 0 mg chol., 52 mg sodium, 27 g carbo., 3 g fiber, 4 g pro. Daily Values: 1% vit. C, 4% calcium, 7% iron.

Just What Is It?

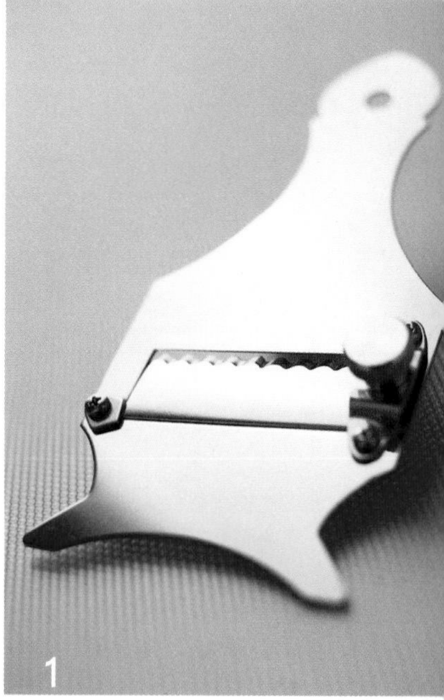

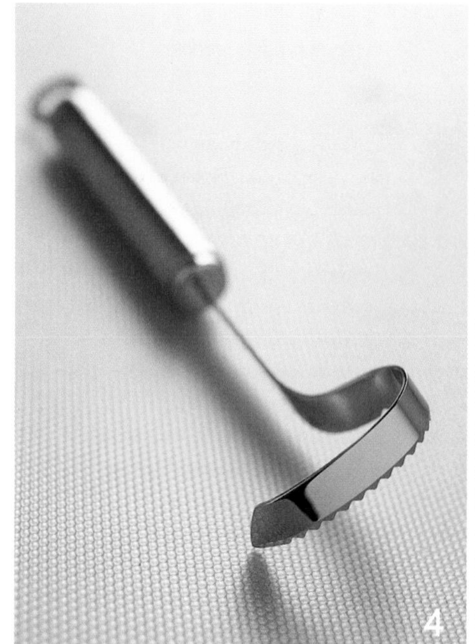

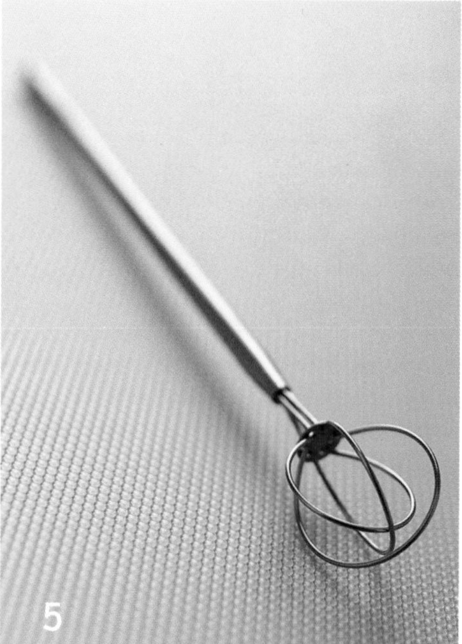

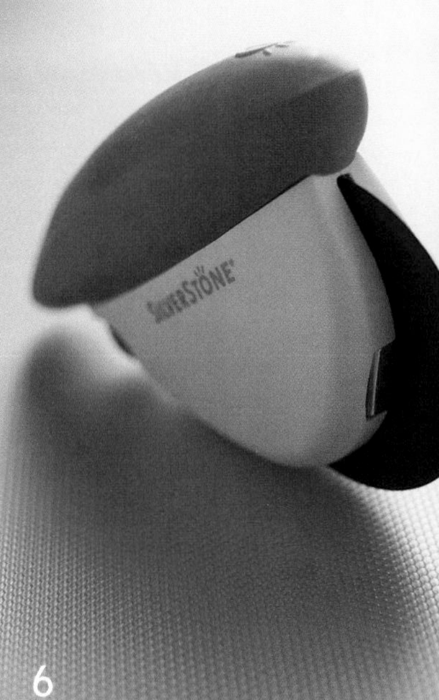

THE KITCHEN GADGET AISLE CAN HOLD A CURIOUS SELECTION OF TOOLS THAT DEFY DESCRIPTION.

What can all these do-hickeys and thingamajigs accomplish? We took a closer look and turned up some useful options. See if you can guess what each one does before you read the description—a point for each correct guess. The prize? An opportunity to try your gadgets by making a delicious salmon dish for dinner. You can use your fish scaler, your utility cutter, your grater, and your citrus reamer. And while you're at it, use your cocktail whisk to make a drink for quenching your thirst while cooking.

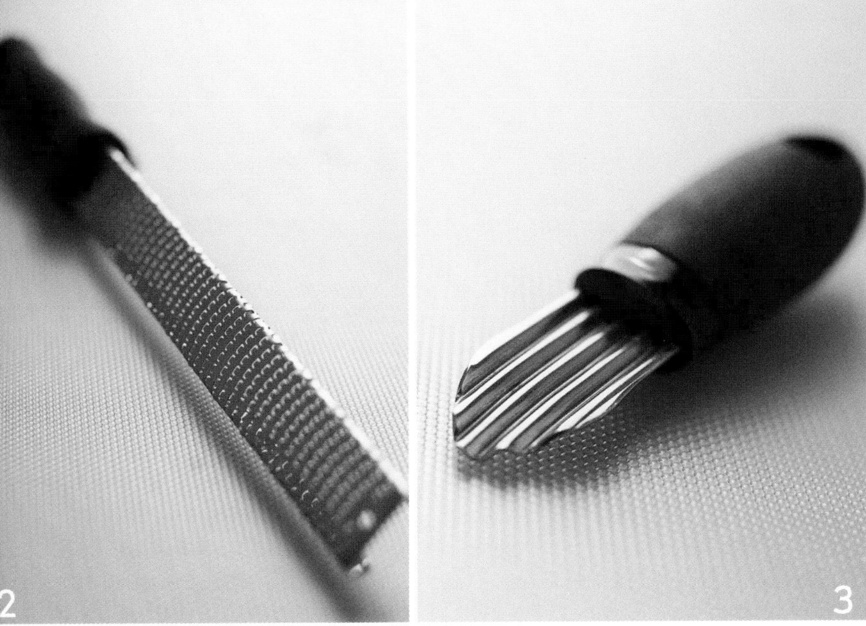

1. The blade on this chocolate shaver adjusts to different widths; use it for cutting chocolate into chunks or delicate swirls.
2. Yes, the microplane grater had its origins in the wood shop. However, this kitchen version finely shreds citrus peel perfectly and does wonders shaving hard cheeses.
3. The pleats in this citrus reamer gently pull the fruit away from the skin to make peeling your favorite citrus decidedly easier.
4. This simply designed fish scaler cleans your catch without digging into the fish's flesh.
5. A wandlike cocktail whisk whips up any libation served in an extra-tall glass—it's cute to boot.
6. The retractable blade on this utility cutter is a safety feature we like. We also like the way this tool minces herbs and slices through pizza and pastry dough with ease.
7. A tenderizing roller rolls along on chicken, beef, or pork.
8. Sleek and stylish, this wired cheese slicer performs elegantly on soft and semisoft cheeses.

Salmon-Veggie Bake

Use your utility cutter to slice the vegetables and snip the herbs.

PREP: 30 minutes **BAKE:** 30 minutes

- **1 lb. fresh or frozen salmon, orange roughy, cod, flounder, or sea bass fillets, about 3/4 inch thick**
- **2 cups thinly sliced carrots**
- **2 cups sliced fresh mushrooms**
- **1/2 cup sliced green onions**
- **2 tsp. grated orange peel**
- **2 tsp. snipped fresh oregano or 1/2 tsp. dried oregano, crushed**
- **4 cloves garlic, halved**
- **1/4 tsp. salt**
- **1/4 tsp. ground black pepper**
- **4 tsp. olive oil**
- **Salt**
- **Ground black pepper**
- **2 medium oranges, thinly sliced**
- **Fresh oregano sprigs (optional)**

1. Thaw fish, if frozen. Use a fish scaler to remove any scales. Rinse fish; pat dry. Cut into four serving-size pieces.

2. In a small saucepan cover and cook carrots in a small amount of boiling water for 2 minutes. Drain and set aside.

3. Tear off four 24-inch pieces of 18-inch-wide heavy foil. Fold each in half to make four 18×12-inch rectangles.

4. In a large bowl combine carrots, mushrooms, green onions, orange peel, oregano, garlic, the 1/4 teaspoon salt, and 1/4 teaspoon pepper; toss gently.

5. Divide vegetables among foil. Add fish. Drizzle with oil; sprinkle with salt and pepper. Top with orange slices and, if desired, oregano sprigs. Bring together two opposite edges of foil; seal with a double fold. Fold remaining ends to enclose food, allowing space for steam. Place in a single layer on a baking pan.

6. Bake in a 350° F oven about 30 minutes or until carrots are tender and fish flakes easily with a fork. Open packets slowly to allow steam to escape. Makes 4 servings.

Each serving: 252 cal., 10 g total fat (1 g sat. fat), 59 mg chol., 393 mg sodium, 18 g carbo., 4 g fiber, 26 g pro. Daily Values: 314% vit. A, 73% vit. C, 8% calcium, 10% iron.

The Power of Mushrooms

LOVERS OF MUSHROOMS KNOW THE MAGIC THESE EARTHY DELIGHTS BRING TO JUST ABOUT ANY DISH.

Now, scientists are learning that mushrooms may deserve a spot on the list of cancer-fighting foods.

Cancer researchers are beginning to uncover the potential of mushrooms, including the common white button. Components of button mushrooms may help prevent breast cancer by reducing the activity of an enzyme that makes estrogen, according to a study in the *Journal of Nutrition*. "Estrogen promotes breast cancer cell growth in 60 percent of breast cancer patients," says lead researcher Shiuan Chen, Ph.D., of the City of Hope's Beckman Research Institute in California. Other mushrooms provide similar effects.

Additional anticancer properties of mushrooms may come from their ability to inhibit tumor growth by boosting the immune system. Plant chemicals called beta-glucans—found heavily in maitake and shiitake mushrooms—are believed to activate immune cells that fight infection.

Mushrooms are rich in potassium and selenium, known for its antioxidant properties and tested recently for its ability to combat prostate cancer and cardiovascular disease. They are also rich in riboflavin, niacin, and pantothenic acid, which promote healthy skin and help regulate the nervous system. Dried mushrooms have a more intense flavor than fresh mushrooms, making them a terrific seasoning. Before using dried mushrooms, soak them in warm water until they're soft.

Dancing Mushrooms

This dish is a major hit as an appetizer, but it can also be the start of so much more. Toss it with cooked spring peas, serve over pasta, or pile it on a burger.

PREP: 15 minutes **COOK:** 12 minutes

- **3 cloves garlic, minced**
- **3 shallots, peeled and cut into thin wedges**
- **2 Tbsp. olive oil or cooking oil**
- **1 1/4 lb. fresh mushrooms (such as maitake, oyster, white button, or shiitake), broken into clusters or sliced (about 8 cups)**
- **1/4 cup snipped mixed fresh herbs (such as tarragon, rosemary, basil, oregano, and/or parsley)**
- **1/4 tsp. coarse salt or salt**
- **1/4 tsp. cracked black pepper**

1. In a large skillet cook the garlic and shallots in hot oil over medium-high heat for 2 minutes.

2. Add maitake mushrooms. Cook, stirring occasionally, for 10 to 12 minutes or until tender. If using oyster or button mushrooms, add them during the last 6 to 8 minutes. Add shiitakes during last 4 minutes. Stir in herbs, salt, and pepper. Makes 6 to 8 servings.

Each serving: 74 cal., 5 g total fat (1 g sat. fat), 0 mg chol., 86 mg sodium, 6 g carbo., 1 g fiber, 3 g pro. Daily Values: 3% vit. A, 5% vit. C, 1% calcium, 6% iron.

Shiitake (shee-TAH-kay)
These have a rich, earthy taste with a hint of smokiness. Let them strut in more intensely flavored dishes.

Maitake (my-TAH-kay)
A meaty texture with a woodsy taste makes these a good match for pasta, smoked meats, or risotto.

Enoki (eh-NO-key)
Heat tends to wilt and toughen these tiny mild mushrooms. Best to serve them raw on salads.

Oyster
With their mild flavor, these do best in subtle soups or sautés.

Portobello
These are the big humdingers that make good meat substitutes. Great on the grill or sautéed.

White button
You'll have no trouble finding this common variety. Slice them for nibbling raw, or toss them in sauces or soups.

May

SAVOR THE GENTLE, SWEET DAYS OF MAY WITH SIMPLE MEALS SHARED OUTDOORS WITH FRIENDS AND FAMILY.

Flash-Roasted Vegetables and Pasta

Spring Pea Soup

Pork and Porcini Bolognese

Game Hens with Rhubarb Barbecue Glaze

Together on Sunday

Plus ...

Grilled Pork with Melon-Tomato Tumble

White Beans, Spiral Pasta, and Lobster

4 Chefs, Great Pasta, Happy Families

Spring Garlic Pesto Perciatelli

Plus...

TOSS AROUND A FEW FUN IDEAS THIS MONTH—GREAT PASTA DISHES AND SOME FRESH LOOKS FOR SPRING GREENS AND FRUITS. IT'S TIME TO PLAY!

Fusilli with Prosciutto and Fava Beans

Pappardelle alla Pepolino

Free-Form Basil Lasagna

Together on Sunday

Quick-Fried Chicken Salad with Strawberries

SUNDAY DINNER HAS A COMFY MOOD OF ITS OWN. WE PILE PLATES HIGH WITH FAMILY FAVORITES AND SERVE THEM WITH HEAPS OF LOVE AND MAYBE A GOOFY JOKE OR TWO. IT'S A TRADITION THAT FEEDS THE HEART AND SOUL.

Quick-Fried Chicken Salad with Strawberries

Chicken breast strips double-dipped in a lemon-and-herb flour, then flash-fried in a skillet have all the crunch of the traditional fried chicken. And it's ready in half the time.

Start to Finish: 30 minutes

- 3/4 cup all-purpose flour
- 4 Tbsp. snipped fresh purple or green basil
- 1 Tbsp. finely shredded lemon peel
- 2 eggs, slightly beaten
- 1 lb. skinless, boneless chicken breast strips
- 2 Tbsp. cooking oil
- 4 cups mixed spring salad greens
- 1 head radicchio, torn into bite-size pieces
- 2 cups sliced fresh strawberries
- 1/2 cup bottled balsamic vinaigrette salad dressing
- 6 Bibb or butterhead lettuce leaves
- Purple or green basil leaves (optional)

1. In a shallow dish combine flour, 2 tablespoons of the basil, and the lemon peel. Place eggs in another shallow dish. Dip chicken into flour mixture, then into the eggs, and then again into flour mixture to coat.

2. In a 12-inch heavy skillet heat cooking oil over medium-high heat. Add chicken breast strips to skillet. Cook, uncovered, for 6 to 8 minutes or until chicken is no longer pink, turning once. (If necessary, reduce heat to medium to prevent overbrowning and add more oil as needed during cooking.) Cool slightly.

3. Meanwhile, in a large bowl toss together greens, radicchio, strawberries, and remaining 2 tablespoons basil. Drizzle vinaigrette over salad mixture; toss gently to coat.

4. To serve, line 6 bowls with lettuce leaves. Add salad mixture. Top with chicken and, if desired, basil leaves. Makes 6 main-dish servings.

Each serving: 261 cal., 13 g total fat (2 g sat. fat), 79 mg chol., 295 mg sodium, 16 g carbo., 2 g fiber, 21 g pro. Daily Values: 14% vit. A, 60% vit. C, 5% calcium, 10% iron.

SUNDAY DINNER

Salt-and-Pepper Trout with
Caramelized Red Onion Polenta *(page 168)*
Steamed peas
Biscuits
Good Thyme Lemon Cups *(page 548)*
Iced tea

Dinner Traditions

It doesn't seem to matter whether supper is pasta, fried chicken, rack of lamb, or even hot dogs. The Sunday tradition of puttering together in the kitchen and sharing a relaxing family meal holds meaning beyond the menu. If you haven't yet started your own Sunday family dinner tradition, now's the time. The pace is more leisurely than the grab-and-go weeknight dinner and the food can be more carefully planned. It's the perfect combination to draw the family together.

As you might discover, when your family eats together, you share more than just a meal. Sitting down for dinner together nourishes body and soul. Indeed, psychologists have confirmed what most of us have always known in our hearts: Dinnertime rituals are associated with better health, both physical and mental. Such rituals even provide a beneficial boost to marriages. (That information comes from a review of 50 years' worth of studies scrutinized by a group of psychologists led by Barbara Fiese, Ph.D., professor and chair of psychology at Syracuse University in New York.)

The ritual of Sunday dinner gives families an opportunity to bond in ways that often only make sense to members of that family. "There are inside jokes. A lot of shorthand communication tends to go on. It helps you feel like you belong to something bigger than yourself," Fiese says.

Although food links the family in a special way on Sunday, your meal doesn't have to be a major production. Our spring-fresh recipes will help you. Each recipe is a fairly complete meal in itself. The only things you may want to go with Quick-Fried Chicken Salad with Strawberries are tall glasses of icy lemonade or tea and bakery-fresh rolls slathered with honey butter. And you'll be in comfort-food nirvana if you add some homemade mashed potatoes to Grilled Pork with Melon-Tomato Tumble on *page 171*. Just remember: The more relatives you can squeeze around the table, the more memories you'll be making.

New Potato Simmer

Spring Pea Soup

A subtle touch of tarragon enhances the flavor of this chunky pea soup—a hearty spring meal when you top it with a baguette slice piled high with prosciutto and feta cheese.

PREP: 25 minutes **COOK:** 10 minutes

- 5 cups fresh shelled peas or two 1-lb. pkg. frozen baby peas
- 2 14-oz. cans chicken broth
- 2 small heads butterhead or Bibb lettuce, ribs discarded and torn into small pieces
- 12 green onions, sliced
- 3 Tbsp. snipped fresh tarragon
- 1½ to 2 cups half-and-half or milk
- Salt
- Ground black pepper
- 6 slices French bread or baguette, brushed with olive oil and oven-toasted or grilled
- 2 oz. prosciutto, cut into thin strips
- ⅓ cup crumbled feta cheese
- Fresh tarragon sprigs (optional)

1. If using fresh peas, in a 4-quart Dutch oven combine peas and broth. Bring to boiling; reduce heat. Cover and simmer for 6 minutes. Add lettuce and green onions. Bring to boiling; reduce heat. Cover and simmer for 4 to 6 minutes more or until peas are tender. If desired for garnish, use a slotted spoon to remove ⅓ cup peas. (If using frozen peas, thaw ⅓ cup of peas; set aside for garnish. In a Dutch oven combine remaining frozen peas, lettuce, green onions, and broth. Bring to boiling; reduce heat. Cover and simmer for 4 to 6 minutes or until peas are tender.)

2. Stir tarragon into soup mixture in Dutch oven. Cool slightly. Place one-fourth of the soup mixture in a blender container or food processor bowl. Cover and blend or process until nearly smooth. Repeat with remaining soup mixture, blending or processing one-fourth at a time. Return all of the soup to the Dutch oven. Stir in enough half-and-half to reach desired consistency; heat through, but do not boil. Add salt and pepper to taste.

3. To serve, ladle soup into 6 bowls. Top each serving with a slice of French bread, some prosciutto, and some feta cheese. Sprinkle with reserved peas and add a tarragon sprig, if desired. Makes 6 main-dish servings.

Each serving: 341 cal., 12 g total fat (6 g sat. fat), 36 mg chol., 1,120 mg sodium, 41 g carbo., 9 g fiber, 20 g pro. Daily Values: 41% vit. A, 63% vit. C, 20% calcium, 22% iron.

New Potato Simmer

There's nothing complicated about this savory potato soup enhanced with a splash of cream for a rich flavor. We love the bright yellow-green color of napa cabbage on each serving, but a little pile of baby spinach leaves is a great option.

PREP: 10 minutes **COOK:** 20 minutes

- 1½ lb. tiny new potatoes
- 1 lb. smoked turkey or chicken breast, shredded
- 2 14-oz. cans reduced-sodium chicken broth
- 1 medium leek, sliced
- ⅓ cup whipping cream
- 3 Tbsp. Dijon-style mustard
- 1 Tbsp. snipped fresh lemon thyme
- 1½ cups napa cabbage, cut into ¼-inch-wide strips
- Breadsticks (see tip, page 167) (optional)

1. Cut any large potatoes in half. In a 4-quart Dutch oven combine potatoes, turkey, broth, and leek. Bring to boiling; reduce heat. Simmer, covered, for 15 minutes.

2. In a small bowl stir together cream and mustard. Add cream mixture and thyme to Dutch oven. Simmer, uncovered, for 5 minutes more or until potatoes are tender, stirring occasionally.

3. To serve, ladle soup into 6 bowls. Top each serving with ¼ cup of cabbage. If desired, serve with breadsticks. Makes 6 main-dish servings.

Each serving: 243 cal., 8 g total fat (4 g sat. fat), 57 mg chol., 1,297 mg sodium, 23 g carbo., 3 g fiber, 19 g pro. Daily Values: 9% vit. A, 41% vit. C, 5% calcium, 13% iron.

Spring Pea Soup

Flash-Roasted Vegetables and Pasta

Flash-Roasted Vegetables and Pasta

Pappardelle pasta is a fantastically wide (about 1-inch) egg noodle, while mafalda pasta is narrower with rippled edges similar to lasagna. In a pinch, you can use any wide noodle, such as fettuccine.

PREP: 20 minutes **ROAST:** 35 minutes

- 2 Tbsp. Fennel-Spice Mix (below)
- 2 lb. assorted fresh mushrooms, such as chanterelles, cremini, and/or oyster, cut into chunks
- 2 medium fennel bulbs, trimmed and cut into wedges (about 1 lb. trimmed)
- 1 large red onion, cut into 6 or 8 wedges
- 8 oz. baby carrots with tops, trimmed
- 1/4 cup olive oil
- 8 oz. dried pappardelle or mafalda pasta
- 3/4 cup dry white wine
- Shredded Parmesan cheese (optional)

1. Prepare Fennel-Spice Mix; set aside. Preheat oven to 425° F. Place mushrooms, fennel, onion, and carrots in a large roasting pan. Combine oil and Fennel-Spice Mix; drizzle over vegetables. Toss gently to coat.

2. Roast, uncovered, for 35 minutes or until vegetables are tender, stirring twice. Transfer roasted vegetables to a very large bowl, leaving juices in pan.

3. Meanwhile, cook pasta according to package directions; drain well.

4. Add pasta to roasted vegetables. Add wine to roasting pan. Cook and stir over medium-high heat, scraping up any browned bits, about 3 minutes or until wine is slightly reduced. Pour wine over pasta mixture; toss well to coat. Top with cheese. Makes 6 to 8 main-dish servings.

FENNEL-SPICE MIX: In a small skillet over medium heat toast 1/4 cup fennel seeds, 1 tablespoon coriander seeds, and 1/4 teaspoon cracked peppercorns about 1 minute or until fragrant, shaking the pan occasionally. Cool thoroughly. When completely cool, grind in a spice grinder or blender container with 1 teaspoon coarse sea salt or kosher salt.

Each serving: 336 cal., 13 g total fat (2 g sat. fat), 0 mg chol., 197 mg sodium, 45 g carbo., 24 g fiber, 12 g pro. Daily Values: 213% vit. A, 24% vit. C, 9% calcium, 15% iron.

DO-IT-YOURSELF BREADSTICKS

Dressing up breadsticks with a twist of your own is a simple technique that produces impressively tasty results.

Here's how you can create your own: Start with purchased breadstick dough. Preheat the oven according to package directions. Separate breadstick dough and lay flat. Brush the dough with melted butter or olive oil. Add a generous sprinkling of toasted seeds, such as sesame or poppy; snipped parsley and thyme; and/or coarse sea salt and cracked peppercorns. Twist dough strips; transfer twisted strips to a foil-lined baking sheet. Bake as directed.

Spaghetti Pie

PREP: 30 minutes **BAKE:** 20 minutes

- 4 oz. dried spaghetti
- 1 Tbsp. butter or margarine
- 1 egg, beaten
- 1/4 cup grated Parmesan cheese
- 8 oz. ground beef
- 1/2 cup chopped onion (1 medium)
- 1/2 cup chopped green sweet pepper
- 1 clove garlic, minced
- 1/2 tsp. fennel seeds, crushed
- 1 8-oz. can tomato sauce
- 1 tsp. dried oregano, crushed
- Nonstick cooking spray
- 1 cup low-fat cottage cheese, drained
- 1/2 cup shredded part-skim mozzarella cheese

1. Cook spaghetti according to package directions; drain.

2. Return spaghetti to warm saucepan. Stir butter into hot pasta until melted. Stir in egg and Parmesan cheese; set aside.

3. Preheat oven to 350° F. In a medium skillet cook ground beef, onion, sweet pepper, garlic, and fennel seeds until meat is brown and onion is tender. Drain off fat. Stir in tomato sauce and oregano; heat through.

4. Coat a 9-inch pie plate with nonstick cooking spray. Press spaghetti mixture onto bottom and up sides of pie plate to form a crust. Spread cottage cheese on the crust, spreading it up the sides. Spread meat mixture onto cottage cheese. Sprinkle with shredded mozzarella cheese.

5. Bake for 20 to 25 minutes or until bubbly and heated through. To serve, cut into wedges. Makes 6 servings.

Each serving: 270 cal., 11 g total fat (6 g sat. fat), 76 mg chol., 500 mg sodium, 20 g carbo., 1 g fiber, 21 g pro. Daily Values: 7% vit. A, 17% vit. C, 16% calcium, 11% iron.

Asparagus-Salmon Scramble

PREP: 25 minutes **STAND:** 1 hour **BAKE:** 18 minutes per batch

- 1 17-oz. pkg. (2 sheets) frozen puff pastry
- 1 egg yolk
- 1 lb. fresh asparagus, trimmed
- 8 eggs
- 1/2 cup milk, half-and-half, or light cream
- 1 tsp. snipped fresh dill or 1/4 tsp. dried dillweed
- 1/2 tsp. salt
- 1/8 tsp. ground black pepper
- 1 Tbsp. butter
- 4 oz. Havarti cheese with dill, shredded (1 cup)
- 1 4-oz. piece smoked salmon, broken into chunks, with skin and bones removed
- Fresh dill sprigs (optional)

1. Thaw the pastry sheets at room temperature for 1 hour.

2. Preheat oven to 400° F. In a small bowl mix egg yolk with 1 teaspoon water; set aside. Unfold pastry sheets on a lightly floured surface. Roll gently to flatten creases (you should have a 10-inch square). Cut 1/2-inch-wide strips from all 4 sides of each pastry sheet. Brush edges of pastry sheets with egg mixture. Place the cut strips along edges on top of the pastry sheets, gently pressing in place to form a raised rim; trim ends. Place pastries on 2 baking sheets. Prick centers with a fork. Brush pastries with egg mixture. Bake, 1 sheet at a time, about 15 minutes or until puffed and golden brown. Cool on baking sheets on wire racks.

3. Meanwhile, in a large skillet bring 1 cup water and a dash salt to boiling. Add asparagus and cook, covered, for 1 minute. Drain. Rinse asparagus with cold water; drain well. Transfer the asparagus to a cutting board. Slice 3-inch pieces from the tips of asparagus; set aside. Cut remaining asparagus into 2-inch pieces.

4. In a large mixing bowl whisk together eggs, milk, snipped dill, salt, and pepper until combined. In the large skillet melt butter over medium heat. Add egg mixture to skillet. Cook over medium heat, without stirring, until mixture begins to set on bottom and around edges. With a spatula or a large spoon, lift and fold the partially cooked egg mixture so the uncooked portion flows underneath. Continue cooking over medium heat for 2 to 3 minutes or until egg mixture is cooked but still glossy. Remove from heat; fold in 1/2 cup of the cheese.

5. Spoon egg mixture into baked pastry shells on baking sheets. Top with the 2-inch asparagus pieces, salmon, and remaining 1/2 cup cheese. Arrange asparagus tips over all. Return 1 baking sheet at a time to oven and bake 3 to 5 minutes or until cheese is melted and filling is heated through. If desired, garnish with fresh dill sprigs. Makes 8 main-dish servings.

Each serving: 524 cal., 37 g total fat (9 g sat. fat), 266 mg chol., 567 mg sodium, 30 g carbo., 2 g fiber, 18 g pro. Daily Values: 13% vit. A, 6% vit. C, 14% calcium, 15% iron.

Salt-and-Pepper Trout with Caramelized Red Onion Polenta

For a splash of color, rescue a few red onions from the skillet after they've softened slightly, but while they still have a pretty tint. Let the rest of the onions cook until they're caramelized and golden brown. Stir all of the onions into the creamy soft polenta and use it as a bed for the broiled trout.

PREP: 30 minutes **COOK:** 30 minutes **BROIL:** 8 minutes

- 1 medium red onion, cut into 1/4-inch-thick slices and separated into rings (3/4 cup)
- 4 tsp. butter
- 2/3 cup stone-ground cornmeal
- 2 1/2 cups chicken broth
- 3 Tbsp. grated Parmesan cheese
- 1/8 tsp. ground black pepper
- 4 fresh or frozen boned, pan-dressed trout (6 to 7 oz. each) or 4 fresh trout fillets (about 4 oz. each)
- Citrus-flavored olive oil (such as lime, lemon, or grapefruit) or olive oil
- Coarse sea salt
- Ground black pepper
- 1 bunch watercress

1. In a medium covered skillet cook onion in hot butter over medium-low heat for 13 to 15 minutes or until onion is tender. Uncover and stir over medium-high heat for 4 to 5 minutes or until onions are golden brown. Set aside.

2. In a small bowl combine cornmeal and 1 cup of the chicken broth; set aside. In a medium saucepan bring the remaining 1 1/2 cups chicken broth to boiling over medium-high heat. Slowly add cornmeal mixture, stirring constantly. Return to boiling; reduce heat to low. Cook for 10 to 15 minutes or until mixture is very thick, stirring occasionally. Add the caramelized onion, Parmesan cheese, and the 1/8 teaspoon pepper; stir until the cheese is melted. Set aside and keep warm.

3. Preheat broiler. If using pan-dressed trout, spread open fish; brush with olive oil and sprinkle with salt and pepper. Close fish and place on greased, unheated rack of a broiler pan. Measure thickness of fish at the thickest spot. Broil 4 inches from the heat for 4 to 6 minutes per 1/2-inch thickness or until fish flakes easily when tested with a fork, turning after 4 minutes. (If using fillets, place fish, skin side down, on ungreased rack of broiler pan. Measure thickness of fish at the thickest spot. Brush with flavored olive oil and sprinkle with salt and pepper. Broil 4 inches from the heat for 4 to 6 minutes per 1/2-inch thickness or until fish flakes easily when tested with a fork.)

4. To serve, spoon polenta onto 4 plates. Top with fish and some watercress. Makes 4 main-dish servings.

Each serving: 425 cal., 18 g total fat (6 g sat. fat), 114 mg chol., 859 mg sodium, 21 g carbo., 2 g fiber, 43 g pro. Daily Values: 18% vit. A, 12% vit. C, 18% calcium, 7% iron.

Asparagus-Salmon Scramble

"SUNDAY DINNER IS THE ESSENCE OF THE DINNERS WE HAVE THE REST OF THE WEEK. I MAKE THINGS THE FAMILY REALLY LOVES. THE KIDS MIGHT HELP ME COOK. DINNER IS MUCH MORE LEISURELY."

SARA MOULTON, TV CHEF, COOKBOOK AUTHOR

Salt-and-Pepper Trout with Caramelized Red Onion Polenta

Grilled Pork with Melon-Tomato Tumble

Grilled Pork with Melon-Tomato Tumble

Although the colorful pear-shape cherry tomatoes make a stunning statement in the melon-tomato mixture, chopped roma tomatoes work well too. The mixture makes a standout accompaniment to a simple grilled pork tenderloin.

PREP: 20 minutes **GRILL:** 30 minutes **STAND:** 10 minutes

- 3 Tbsp. olive oil
- 3 Tbsp. white wine vinegar
- 1/4 tsp. salt
- 1/8 tsp. ground black pepper
- 1 1-lb. pork tenderloin
- 1 recipe Melon-Tomato Tumble (below)

1. In a small mixing bowl whisk together oil, vinegar, salt, and pepper. Remove 1 tablespoon of the mixture for pork. Reserve remaining oil-and-vinegar mixture for Melon-Tomato Tumble.

2. Brush reserved 1 tablespoon oil-and-vinegar mixture onto pork. Place pork tenderloin on a grill rack directly over medium coals. Grill, uncovered, about 30 minutes or until an instant-read thermometer inserted into the center of meat registers 160° F, turning every 5 to 6 minutes.

3. Meanwhile, prepare Melon-Tomato Tumble. Transfer the pork to a cutting board. Cover and let pork rest for 10 minutes. Slice meat diagonally; serve with Melon-Tomato Tumble spooned onto melon wedges. Makes 4 main-dish servings.

MELON-TOMATO TUMBLE: Cut 1 small cantaloupe or honeydew melon in half. Cut one of the melon halves into bite-size pieces. Cut remaining melon half into 4 wedges; cover and chill wedges in the refrigerator until serving time. In a medium bowl combine melon pieces; 1 cup yellow, red, and/or orange pear-shape cherry and/or grape tomatoes, halved or quartered; 1 small red onion, thinly sliced and halved; and 1/3 cup small fresh mint leaves. Add remaining oil-and-vinegar mixture; toss gently to coat.

Each serving: 292 cal., 14 g total fat (3 g sat. fat), 73 mg chol., 211 mg sodium, 15 g carbo., 2 g fiber, 26 g pro. Daily Values: 88% vit. A, 122% vit. C, 3% calcium, 19% iron.

FAMILY DINNER ALFRESCO

Chive-Yogurt Cheese Spread *(page 175)*
Grilled Pork with Melon-Tomato Tumble *(above)*
Grilled corn on the cob
Angel Food Cake *(page 78)* with strawberries
Iced tea or Watermelon Lemonade *(page 218)*

Campfire-Style Pot Roast

PREP: 30 minutes **GRILL:** 2 1/2 hours

- 1 3 1/2- to 4-lb. boneless beef chuck pot roast
- 1 Tbsp. cooking oil
- Salt
- Ground black pepper
- Nonstick cooking spray
- 1 recipe Mustard Barbecue Sauce (below)
- 2 stalks celery, bias-sliced into 1-inch pieces
- 6 small whole carrots, peeled and halved
- 1 medium green sweet pepper, cut into rings
- 2 medium onions, quartered
- 2 medium tomatoes, cut into wedges

1. Trim fat from roast. In a 4-quart Dutch oven brown pot roast in hot oil on all sides. Season with salt and pepper.

2. Meanwhile, fold two 5-foot lengths of heavy foil in half crosswise. Place one on top of the other, forming a cross shape. Lightly coat center of foil with cooking spray. Top with meat. Spread 3/4 cup sauce onto meat (cover and chill remaining sauce). Top with vegetables. Season with salt and pepper. Seal each piece of foil securely, allowing room for expansion.

3. For a charcoal grill, arrange medium coals around edge of grill. Test for medium heat in the center of the grill. Place foil packet on grill rack in center of grill. Cover and grill for 2 1/2 hours, adding additional charcoal as needed to maintain heat. (For a gas grill, preheat grill. Reduce heat to medium-low. Adjust for indirect cooking. Grill as above, except place packet in a roasting pan.)

4. To serve, transfer meat and vegetables to a platter. Heat remaining sauce; pass with meat. Makes 8 main-dish servings.

OVEN METHOD: Preheat oven to 350° F. Trim fat from roast and brown as above. Drain off fat; season roast with salt and pepper. Spread 3/4 cup of the sauce on meat in Dutch oven; add vegetables. Cover Dutch oven; roast for 2 1/2 hours. Serve as above.

MUSTARD BARBECUE SAUCE: In a medium saucepan stir together 2 tablespoons dried minced onion; 2 tablespoons packed brown sugar; 1 tablespoon mustard seeds, slightly crushed; 2 teaspoons paprika; 1 teaspoon dried oregano, crushed; 1 teaspoon chili powder; 1 teaspoon cracked black pepper; 1/2 teaspoon salt; 1/2 teaspoon ground cloves; 1 bay leaf; 1 clove garlic, minced. Stir in 1 cup catsup, 1/2 cup water, 2 tablespoons olive oil or cooking oil, 2 tablespoons red wine vinegar or cider vinegar, 2 tablespoons Worcestershire sauce, and 2 or 3 drops liquid smoke. Bring to boiling; reduce heat. Simmer, uncovered, for 20 to 25 minutes or until desired consistency, stirring often. Remove bay leaf.

Each serving: 395 cal., 14 g total fat (3 g sat. fat), 118 mg chol., 790 mg sodium, 24 g carbo., 4 g fiber, 44 g pro. Daily Values: 251% vit. A, 47% vit. C, 6% calcium, 41% iron.

Game Hens with Rhubarb Barbecue Glaze

Game Hens with Rhubarb Barbecue Glaze

Bottled barbecue sauce gets taken in a grand new direction when simmered with chopped rhubarb. The garden-fresh tangy sauce provides a spectacular glaze of flavor and color for Cornish game hens.

PREP: 30 minutes **COOK:** 20 minutes **ROAST:** 55 minutes

- **3 1¼- to 1½-lb. Cornish game hens**
- **Olive oil**
- **Salt**
- **Ground black pepper**
- **3½ to 4 cups chopped fresh or frozen rhubarb**
- **1 cup bottled tomato-based barbecue sauce**
- **¼ cup water**
- **8 oz. dried orzo (rosamarina)**
- **1 cup shredded carrots**
- **¼ cup sliced green onions**

1. Preheat the oven to 375° F. Using a long, heavy knife or kitchen shears, halve Cornish hens lengthwise, cutting through the breast bone, just off-center, and through the center of the backbone. (Or, ask the butcher to cut hens into halves.) Twist wing tips under back. Rub the olive oil onto the surface and in the cavity of each hen half; sprinkle generously with salt and pepper. Place hen halves, cut side down, in a 15×10×1-inch baking pan. Roast, uncovered, for 40 minutes.

2. Meanwhile, for sauce, in a medium saucepan bring rhubarb, barbecue sauce, and water to boiling over medium-high heat. Reduce heat to medium-low and cook, covered, for 20 minutes or until rhubarb loses its shape. Remove from heat; coarsely mash rhubarb. Remove and reserve 1 cup of the sauce.

3. Brush surface of game hens with some of the remaining sauce. Roast for 15 to 20 minutes more, brushing every 5 minutes, or until hens are glazed, tender, no longer pink, and an instant-read thermometer inserted into thigh muscle registers 180° F.

4. Meanwhile, cook orzo according to package directions; drain. Transfer orzo to a large bowl. Stir in the additional reserved sauce, carrots, and green onions. Season to taste with salt and pepper. Spoon orzo mixture onto a large platter; top with hen halves. Pass the remaining sauce. Makes 6 main-dish servings.

Each serving: 375 cal., 10 g total fat (2 g sat. fat), 111 mg chol., 609 mg sodium, 39 g carbo., 4 g fiber, 31 g pro. Daily Values: 124% vit. A, 18% vit. C, 10% calcium, 17% iron.

German Meatballs with Spaetzle

If you've never made pasta from scratch, consider spaetzle a good place to start. These chewy homemade egg noodles are easy to make and worth the effort.

PREP: 20 minutes **COOK:** 25 minutes **STAND:** 5 minutes

- **1 egg**
- **¼ cup milk**
- **¼ cup fine dry bread crumbs**
- **1 Tbsp. snipped fresh parsley**
- **½ tsp. salt**
- **Dash ground black pepper**
- **1 lb. ground beef**
- **1⅓ cups beef broth**
- **1 4-oz. can mushroom pieces and stems, drained**
- **½ cup chopped onion**
- **1 8-oz. carton dairy sour cream**
- **2 Tbsp. all-purpose flour**
- **½ to 1 tsp. caraway seeds**
- **1 recipe Spaetzle (below)**
- **Snipped fresh parsley (optional)**

1. In a large bowl beat egg; stir in milk, bread crumbs, the 1 tablespoon parsley, salt, and pepper. Add ground meat; mix well. Shape mixture into twenty-four 1½-inch meatballs.

2. In a large nonstick skillet brown meatballs; drain off fat. Add broth, mushrooms, and onion. Simmer, covered, about 20 minutes or until an instant-read thermometer inserted into meatballs registers 160° F.

3. In a small bowl combine sour cream, flour, and caraway seeds; stir into broth. Cook and stir until mixture is thickened and bubbly. Cook and stir for 1 minute more.

4. Meanwhile, prepare Spaetzle. To serve, spoon Spaetzle onto 6 plates; top with meatballs and sauce. If desired, sprinkle with snipped parsley. Makes 6 servings.

SPAETZLE: In a medium bowl combine 2 cups all-purpose flour and 1 teaspoon salt. Add 2 slightly beaten eggs and 1 cup milk; beat well. Let rest for 5 minutes. Bring a large pot of lightly salted water to boiling. Holding a coarse-sieved colander (such as the basket for a deep-fat fryer) over rapidly boiling water, pour batter into colander. Press batter through colander with back of wooden spoon or rubber spatula. Cook and stir for 5 minutes; drain.

Each serving: 465 cal., 21 g total fat (10 g sat. fat), 175 mg chol., 1,049 mg sodium, 40 g carbo., 2 g fiber, 26 g pro. Daily Values: 12% vit. A, 5% vit. C, 14% calcium, 23% iron.

GO FOR YOGURT

GOBBLING GOOD BACTERIA MAY HEAL STOMACH WOES.

Foods you already know are good for your bones are proving to be good for your digestive tract as well. Eating certain calcium-rich dairy products, such as yogurt, provides you with a boost of "good" bacteria that may prevent a host of health problems. These good bacteria, called probiotics, bind to intestinal tissues and crowd out less-friendly bugs that might be present. A daily helping of foods enhanced with probiotics could keep you from suffering some stomach and gastro-intestinal problems. Yogurt that contains added probiotics can improve the balance between good bacteria and bad bacteria in the gut.

At Johns Hopkins Children's Center in Baltimore, Maryland, researchers have found that children with symptoms of lactose intolerance (the inability to break down lactose, the sugar in many dairy products) experience fewer side effects when they eat yogurt containing *Lactobacillus bulgaricus* and *Streptococcus thermophilus*. After eating the bacteria-enhanced yogurt, children in the study could drink milk with less pain and discomfort. However, despite the potential health benefits, people with health problems should consult their doctors before consuming products enhanced with probiotics.

Orange-Yogurt Cheese Spread

PREP: 5 minutes **CHILL:** 24 hours

- 1 recipe Yogurt Cheese (below)
- ¼ cup orange marmalade or lemon curd
- 1 tsp. finely shredded orange or lemon peel
- Thin spice cookies
- Fresh or canned mandarin orange slices or fresh berries

1. In a small bowl combine Yogurt Cheese, orange marmalade, and orange peel. Stir to combine. Place cheese spread on cookie; top with orange slices.

YOGURT CHEESE: Line a sieve or small colander with 3 layers of 100-percent-cotton cheesecloth or a clean paper coffee filter. Suspend lined sieve or colander over a bowl. (Or use a yogurt strainer.) Spoon in one 16-ounce carton plain yogurt.* Cover with plastic wrap. Chill for at least 24 hours. Remove from refrigerator. Discard liquid. Transfer yogurt cheese to a bowl. Cover and store in the refrigerator for up to 1 week.

***NOTE:** Use a brand of yogurt that contains no gums, gelatin, or fillers. These ingredients may prevent the whey from separating from the curd to make cheese.

Each tablespoon of orange-yogurt spread: 27 cal., 1 g total fat (0 g sat. fat), 4 mg chol., 19 mg sodium, 2 g carbo., 0 g fiber, 1 g pro. Daily Values: 1% vit. C, 4% calcium.

ONE A DAY

Researchers say one to two 1-cup daily servings of yogurt with probiotics are enough to be beneficial for adults. Children should stick to 1 cup of yogurt each day. "I think a probiotic a day is like a multi-vitamin a day. It offers protection against viruses," says Rosemary Young, pediatric gastroenterology nurse specialist at the University of Nebraska Medical Center in Omaha.

Studies show that probiotics also prevent diarrhea. "From human studies, we know that probiotics are very effective for diarrhea from viral illnesses. Seventy percent of all traveler's diarrhea is viral in nature," says Rosemary.

Probiotics are added to—or found in—such foods as some rice and soy "milks" as well as acidophilus milks, yogurt, and some cottage cheeses. If the products contain probiotics, they will be listed on the label, typically as acidophilus or bifidus.

Yogurt, drinkable yogurt, and fermented milk that list probiotics on the label are among the best food sources of the helpful bacteria.

Besides being in foods, probiotics are sold in pills, powders, and suppositories. But experts caution that dietary supplements are not closely regulated, so there is no guarantee that labels are accurate.

Chive-Yogurt Cheese Spread

PREP: 5 minutes **CHILL:** 24 hours

- 1 recipe Yogurt Cheese (left)
- 2 Tbsp. chopped dried tomatoes
- 2 Tbsp. finely snipped fresh chives
- 1 small clove garlic, minced (optional)
- ¼ tsp. salt
- Crackers or fresh vegetables, such as carrots, broccoli, and cucumber spears (optional)

1. In a small bowl combine Yogurt Cheese, dried tomatoes, chives, garlic (if desired), and salt. Stir to combine. Spoon the spread onto crackers or use it as a dip for fresh vegetables.

Each tablespoon of chive-yogurt spread: 15 cal., 0 g total fat (0 g sat. fat), 1 mg chol., 52 mg sodium, 2 g carbo., 0 g fiber, 1 g pro. Daily Values: 1% vit. A, 1% vit. C, 4% calcium.

BY DAY, THEY'RE THE SUPERSTARS OF AMERICA'S CULINARY UNIVERSE, BUT AT NIGHT, THEY'RE JUST DADS WHO FACE THE CHALLENGE OF CREATING DINNERS THEIR FAMILIES WILL LOVE.

4 chefs great pasta happy families

Orecchiette with Pancetta and Broccoli Rabe

Orecchiette with Pancetta and Broccoli Rabe

To prepare broccoli rabe, Chef Michael Chiarello trims away any wilted leaves and the woody ends of stems. In case you were wondering, pancetta is unsmoked Italian bacon.

Start to Finish: 35 minutes

- **4 oz. pancetta, coarsely chopped**
- **6 oz. dried orecchiette pasta (1¾ cups) or small shell pasta**
- **2 tsp. olive oil**
- **4 cloves garlic, minced**
- **¼ tsp. crushed red pepper**
- **3 cups cut-up broccoli raab or broccoli (see page 32)**
- **⅓ cup reduced-sodium chicken broth**
- **¼ cup pitted Greek black olives or ripe olives, or 2 Tbsp. drained capers or caper berries**
- **¼ cup finely shredded Parmesan cheese**

1. In a large skillet cook the pancetta over medium heat about 10 minutes or until browned and crisp. Drain on paper towels, reserving 1 tablespoon drippings in skillet. Set aside.

2. Cook pasta according to package directions. Drain; return to pan. Toss with olive oil; cover and keep warm.

3. In the same skillet heat the reserved drippings over medium heat. Add garlic and crushed red pepper; cook and stir for 30 seconds. Add broccoli raab or broccoli and broth. Bring to boiling; reduce heat. Cover and simmer about 3 minutes or until broccoli raab is tender. Stir in pancetta and olives or capers; heat through.

4. Add broccoli raab mixture to pasta in saucepan. Add half of the Parmesan cheese and toss to combine. Transfer to a serving dish. Sprinkle with remaining cheese. Makes 6 servings.

Each serving: 211 cal., 9 g total fat (3 g sat. fat), 11 mg chol., 244 mg sodium, 25 g carbo., 2 g fiber, 8 g pro. Daily Values: 14% vit. A, 59% vit. C, 7% calcium, 7% iron.

"A good bowl of pasta is like getting a hug from the inside."

—Michael Chiarello

CHEFS' SPECIALTIES

For more great recipes from our featured chefs, try these cookbooks available at book stores everywhere.

Michael Chiarello's ***The Tra Vigne Cookbook: Seasons in the California Wine Country*** is a behind-the-scenes look at recipes from his Napa Valley restaurant. Lush photos and a contemporary design show off such seasonal dishes as Roasted Asparagus, Pumpkin Polenta, and Italian Holiday Cookies. The 215-page hardcover book is from Chronicle Books.

Pino Luongo's ***Simply Tuscan*** shares the cooking of the author's native land and helps to satisfy America's appetite for all things Tuscan. Recipes include Upside-Down Warm Apple Tart, Trout Roasted Porchetta-Style, and Carrot and Apple Puree. The 292-page hardcover book is from Random House.

Todd English became a star in the culinary world with his distinctive style of layering flavors and textures. ***The Olives Dessert Table*** is not a cookbook for those fearful of fat or short on time. Desserts such as Mango Tarte Tatin with Pastry Cream and Chocolate Pastry or Blue Cheese Danish with Port-Poached Pears combine familiar and comfortable flavors in unique and unexpected ways. The 256-page hardcover book is from Simon and Schuster.

Alfred Portale's ***12 Seasons Cookbook*** takes the home cook on a journey through the year in food. Using the best of seasonal ingredients, he includes recipes for Lamb Chops and Truffled Mashed Potatoes, Grilled Soft-Shell Crabs with Asparagus, and Coconut Panna Cotta. The 400-page hardcover book is from Random House.

PERFECT PASTA MENU

Asparagus Finger Salad *(page 191)*
Pork and Porcini Bolognese*(right)*
Anytime Breadsticks *(page 188)*
Keen Nectarine *(page 197)*

Spring Garlic Pesto Perciatelli

This is a milder version of regular pesto. Spring garlic is garlic that has been picked when the plant is young and the flavor is mild. Look for it from February through the end of spring.

START TO FINISH: 35 minutes

- **15 cloves garlic or 6 oz. spring garlic**
- **1/3 cup fresh basil leaves**
- **3/4 cup olive oil**
- **1/3 cup pine nuts, toasted**
- **4 tsp. finely shredded pecorino Romano (a hard sheep's milk cheese) or Parmesan cheese**
- **3/4 tsp. sea salt or salt**
- **1/8 tsp. freshly ground black pepper**
- **1 Tbsp. olive oil**
- **1 lb. dried perciatelli or spaghetti**
- **1/4 cup freshly grated pecorino Romano or Parmesan cheese**
- **Small basil leaves**
- **Basil flowers**

1. Bring a 4-quart Dutch oven or large pot of salted water to boiling. If using spring garlic, trim off the green part of garlic. Add garlic to the water and cook for 8 minutes. Remove garlic with a slotted spoon and immerse in a bowl of ice water. Add the 1/3 cup basil leaves to the boiling water and cook for 5 seconds; remove basil with a slotted spoon and drain well on paper towels. Peel garlic when cool enough to handle. Don't drain water; it is needed for cooking pasta.

2. For pesto, in a blender container or food processor bowl combine the garlic, briefly cooked basil, and the 3/4 cup olive oil; cover and blend or process just until combined. Add 2 tablespoons of the pine nuts, 4 teaspoons cheese, salt, and pepper. Cover; blend or process mixture until nearly smooth.

3. Meanwhile, add the 1 tablespoon olive oil to the boiling water in which garlic and basil were cooked. Add pasta and cook according to package directions. Drain and return to pot. Toss pasta with the pesto mixture. Transfer to a serving bowl. Sprinkle with the remaining pine nuts, the 1/4 cup cheese, small basil leaves, and basil flowers. Makes 6 to 8 servings.

Each serving: 461 cal., 27 g total fat (4 g sat. fat), 3 mg chol., 193 mg sodium, 46 g carbo., 2 g fiber, 10 g pro. Daily Values: 6% vit. A, 5% vit. C, 7% calcium, 15% iron.

Pork and Porcini Bolognese

You can substitute dried fettuccine for the refrigerated pasta.

START TO FINISH: 45 minutes

- **8 cups water**
- **2 1/4 tsp. sea salt or salt**
- **1 oz. dried porcini mushrooms**
- **1 bunch escarole, core removed, or 8 cups fresh spinach**
- **12 oz. bulk pork sausage**
- **1/2 cup chopped onion**
- **6 cloves garlic, minced**
- **1 Tbsp. snipped fresh sage**
- **1/3 cup dry white wine**
- **3/4 cup beef broth**
- **1/2 cup purchased chunky marinara sauce**
- **1 Tbsp. snipped fresh parsley**
- **1 Tbsp. olive oil**
- **1/4 tsp. freshly ground black pepper**
- **2 9-oz. pkg. refrigerated tagliatelle or fettuccine**
- **1/3 cup shaved Parmesan cheese**

1. In a 4-quart Dutch oven or large pot bring the 8 cups water and 2 teaspoons of the salt to boiling. Place mushrooms in a small bowl; add 1 cup of the boiling water. Let stand for 15 minutes.

2. Meanwhile, add escarole or spinach to the remaining boiling water. Return water to boiling; immediately drain escarole or spinach in a colander and rinse with cold water. Drain well, pressing out extra liquid. Chop greens and set aside. Drain mushrooms, reserving 2 tablespoons of the liquid. Chop mushrooms; set mushrooms and liquid aside.

3. In a large skillet cook sausage, onion, garlic, and sage until meat is brown, stirring to break up sausage. Drain off fat. Stir in white wine and reserved mushroom liquid. Bring to boiling; reduce heat. Boil gently, uncovered, about 7 minutes or until most of the liquid is evaporated. Add broth, marinara sauce, parsley, oil, pepper, and remaining 1/4 teaspoon salt. Bring to boiling; reduce heat. Simmer, uncovered, for 2 minutes.

4. Meanwhile, cook pasta in the Dutch oven or pot according to package directions using fresh water. Drain pasta, reserving 1/4 cup pasta water. Add pasta water, mushrooms, and cooked escarole or spinach to pork mixture. Heat through; spoon over cooked pasta. Toss before serving. Top with Parmesan cheese. Makes 6 servings.

Each serving: 540 cal., 23 g total fat (9 g sat. fat), 128 mg chol., 688 mg sodium, 56 g carbo., 5 g fiber, 21 g pro. Daily Values: 31% vit. A, 16% vit. C, 14% calcium, 18% iron.

Spring Garlic Pesto Perciatelli

MICHAEL CHIARELLO

"Try this" is high on the list of favorite phrases for Michael Chiarello (key-a-rello). It's a constant refrain from the father of Margaux, Felicia, and Giana. He views every meal as an opportunity to broaden the girls' taste buds and pass on values he learned growing up in his extended Italian-American family in Turlock, California. His enthusiasm for Italian cuisine is secondary to his real mission: Teaching people that the surest route to great food is through their heritage. "If you're not from a family rich in tradition, start your own," he says. Besides Italian, Chiarello is known for using seasonal foods on his PBS cooking series *Michael Chiarello's Napa*. The theme continues at NapaStyle, a company that includes his TV shows, Web site, and specialty foods. His cookbooks include *Casual Cooking (2002), Napa Stories (2001), The Tra Vigne Cookbook (1999), Flavored Vinegars (1996)*, and *Flavored Oils (1995)*.

Pork and Porcini Bolognese

Pappardelle alla Pepolino

PINO LUONGO

Great pasta is only half of the recipe for a successful dinnertime at the home of Pino Luongo. The author and restaurateur works hard to create a great atmosphere—an attitude he grew up with during his boyhood in Tuscany.

Pasta sets the mood when Luongo sits down with his wife, Jessie, and children Marcoantonio, Jacobella, and Lorenzo.

"Pasta is a dish that's meant to be shared," he says. "It's the smell of the sauce, the cheese, the big bowl in the middle of the table, of everyone serving themselves. In Italy, we all learn to cook pasta dishes—everybody takes pride in shopping for food, and in buying only the best ingredients."

Pino has turned his first-hand knowledge of Italian cooking into a line of specialty foods and three books: *Simply Tuscan* (2000), *Fish Talking* (1994), and *A Tuscan in the Kitchen* (1988).

"Cooking pasta isn't about ego, it's about sharing."

—Pino Luongo

Fettuccine with Baby Artichokes and Shrimp

Fettuccine with Baby Artichokes and Shrimp

Fresh baby artichokes are available mid-March through May.

PREP: 30 minutes **COOK:** 20 minutes

- 8 oz. dried fettuccine or spaghetti
- 8 baby artichokes or one 9-oz. pkg. frozen artichoke hearts, thawed and halved lengthwise
- 4 cloves garlic, minced
- 3 Tbsp. olive oil
- 1 lb. shrimp in shells, peeled and deveined (reserve shells for broth)
- 1/2 cup dry white wine
- 2 Roma tomatoes, finely chopped
- 1 cup Shrimp Broth (below) or chicken broth
- 1 Tbsp. butter
- 1 tsp. finely shredded lemon peel
- 1/2 tsp. salt
- 1/2 tsp. ground nutmeg
- 1 Tbsp. snipped fresh Italian flat-leaf parsley
- 4 slices Italian country bread or other hearty bread, toasted
- Lemon halves or wedges

1. In a large saucepan cook the pasta according to package directions; drain well and set aside.

2. Meanwhile, if using baby artichokes, cut off the bases of artichokes. Snap off outer leaves until pale green petals are reached. Cut off top third of an artichoke; trim the artichoke stem. Quarter the artichoke lengthwise and remove fuzzy "choke," if necessary. Repeat with remaining artichokes.

3. In a large skillet cook garlic in 2 tablespoons of the hot olive oil for 30 seconds; remove from skillet. Add artichokes to skillet and cook for 1 minute. Add shrimp and wine to skillet. Cook and stir for 2 minutes. Stir in tomatoes, Shrimp Broth, butter, lemon peel, salt, nutmeg, and cooked pasta; heat through. Stir in the parsley; drizzle with remaining olive oil.

4. To serve, place bread slices in four shallow soup bowls. With a slotted spoon, divide pasta mixture among bowls. Add additional Shrimp Broth as desired. Squeeze lemon halves over pasta mixture. Makes 4 servings.

SHRIMP BROTH: In a large saucepan combine 3 cups water, the reserved shells from the 1 pound of shrimp, 4 sprigs fresh Italian flat-leaf parsley, 1 slice lemon, and 1/4 teaspoon black pepper. Bring to boiling over high heat; reduce heat. Simmer, uncovered, for 10 minutes. Strain broth.

Each serving: 564 cal., 17 g total fat (4 g sat. fat), 137 mg chol., 477 mg sodium, 66 g carbo., 6 g fiber, 30 g pro. Daily Values: 10% vit. A, 21% vit. C, 12% calcium, 28% iron.

Pappardelle alla Pepolino

To turn this recipe into a main dish, add cooked shrimp or cooked tuna just before heating through.

START TO FINISH: 40 minutes

- 12 oz. dried pappardelle, mafalda, or fettuccine
- 1 clove garlic, minced
- 2 Tbsp. olive oil
- 1 8-oz. can tomato sauce
- 1 Tbsp. snipped fresh thyme
- 1/4 tsp. crushed red pepper
- 1 recipe Roasted Tomatoes (below)
- 1/4 tsp. freshly ground black pepper
- 1/4 cup coarsely shaved pecorino Romano or Parmesan cheese*

1. In a large saucepan cook pasta according to package directions; drain and set aside.

2. In the same pan cook garlic in hot olive oil for 30 seconds. Stir in tomato sauce, half of the thyme, and the crushed red pepper. Bring to boiling; reduce heat. Simmer, uncovered, for 2 minutes.

3. Add pasta, Roasted Tomatoes, remaining thyme, and black pepper. Heat through. Season to taste with additional salt and black pepper. Transfer to a serving dish. Sprinkle with cheese. Makes 8 side-dish or 4 main-dish servings.

ROASTED TOMATOES: Preheat oven to 450° F. Line a 15×10×1-inch baking pan with foil. Halve 8 Roma tomatoes; place, cut sides up, on the prepared pan. Drizzle with 1 tablespoon olive oil; sprinkle with salt and black pepper. Roast, uncovered, for 20 to 25 minutes or until bottoms of tomatoes are dark brown. Remove from pan; carefully halve each piece.

***TEST KITCHEN TIP:** To shave cheese into strips, draw a vegetable peeler across the block of cheese.

Nutrition facts per side-dish serving: 234 cal., 7 g total fat (1 g sat. fat), 2 mg chol., 248 mg sodium, 36 g carbo., 2 g fiber, and 7 g pro. Daily Values: 7% vit. A, 19% vit. C, 4% calcium, and 10% iron.

Quick Tomato Sauce

Pino Luongo stirs up this sauce when fresh tomatoes are not at their best. He uses canned tomatoes imported from Italy.

START TO FINISH: 20 minutes

1. In a food processor bowl or blender container puree one 28-ounce can whole tomatoes. Cover and blend or process until smooth. Add 3 tablespoons snipped fresh basil; blend or proceess until mixed.

2. In a medium saucepan, cook 2 minced cloves garlic in 2 tablespoons hot olive oil over medium heat until garlic is just lightly browned. Remove garlic. Add pureed tomatoes, 1/4 teaspoon salt, and 1/4 teaspoon freshly ground black pepper. Bring to boiling; reduce heat. Simmer, uncovered, for 10 minutes. Remove from heat. Serve over cooked pasta. Makes 3 cups, enough for 4 to 6 servings.

Each 3/4-cup sauce: 98 cal., 7 g total fat (1 g sat. fat), 0 mg chol., 439 mg sodium, 9 g carbo., 2 g fiber, and 2 g pro.

White Beans, Spiral Pasta, and Lobster

This dish works well with any firm-fleshed white fish or, if you prefer, substitute peeled cooked shrimp.

START TO FINISH: 30 minutes

- 8 oz. dried cavatappi, fusilli, or rotini (corkscrew) pasta
- 1 15- to 19-oz. can cannellini (white kidney) beans, rinsed and drained
- 1/2 cup chicken broth
- 3 cloves garlic, thinly sliced
- 1 Tbsp. olive oil
- 6 plum tomatoes, coarsely chopped (about 2 cups)
- 12 oz. cooked lobster* or 12 oz. fresh or frozen cod fillets, cooked and cut into 1-inch pieces
- 1/4 cup snipped fresh Italian flat-leaf parsley
- 1/2 to 1 tsp. cracked black pepper
- 1/2 tsp. salt
- Fresh Italian flat-leaf parsley sprigs (optional)
- Olive oil (optional)

1. In a large saucepan cook the pasta according to package directions; drain well and set aside.

2. In a blender container or food processor bowl combine 3/4 cup of the drained beans and the chicken broth; cover and blend or process until smooth. Add to the pan used for cooking the pasta; bring to boiling. Return pasta to pan.

3. Meanwhile, in a large skillet cook garlic in 1 tablespoon hot olive oil for 1 minute. Add tomatoes; cook for 1 minute. Add the remaining beans, cooked lobster or cod, snipped parsley, pepper, and salt. Heat through.

4. Add the tomato mixture to hot pasta; toss to coat. Top with parsley sprigs and additional olive oil. Serve immediately. Makes 4 servings.

***TEST KITCHEN TIP:** If cooked lobster is not available, cook 3 lobster tails; remove meat from shells and cut up. To broil lobster, use a large knife to cut through top shell, cutting just to bottom shell; press lobster open. Place, cut side up, on broiler pan. If desired, brush with melted butter. Broil 4 to 5 inches from heat for 12 to 15 minutes or until meat is opaque.

Each serving: 450 cal., 7 g total fat (1 g sat. fat), 77 mg chol., 786 mg sodium, 65 g carbo., 7 g fiber, 37 g pro. Daily Values: 16% vit. A, 41% vit. C, 10% calcium, 26% iron.

Free-Form Basil Lasagna

If you have no pasta machine and you're a very patient person, you can roll the homemade lasagna with a rolling pin on a lightly floured surface. Or, use dried noodles (see below).

PREP: 1 hour **ROAST:** 50 minutes **BAKE:** 30 minutes

- 1 cup unbleached all-purpose flour or all-purpose flour
- 1/8 tsp. salt
- 1 egg
- 2 Tbsp. water
- 1 tsp. olive oil
- 8 oz. fresh mozzarella cheese, cubed
- 6 oz. fontina cheese, shredded
- 1/2 cup ricotta cheese
- 1/2 cup finely shredded Parmesan cheese
- 1/2 cup snipped fresh basil or 1/4 cup snipped fresh oregano or sage
- 1/8 tsp. freshly ground black pepper
- 1 recipe Roasted Tomato Sauce (below) or 2 1/4 cups purchased meatless spaghetti sauce
- Fresh sage sprigs (optional)

1. For pasta*, in a medium bowl combine flour and salt. Beat together egg, water, and olive oil. Pour into flour mixture; stir until combined. Knead on a lightly floured surface until smooth and elastic (8 to 10 minutes). Cover; let rest for 10 minutes. For filling, stir together cheeses, desired herb, and pepper.

2. Preheat oven to 350° F. Divide dough into 5 pieces. Roll out in a pasta machine according to manufacturer's directions. Sheets should be 15×4 1/2 inches. Trim each sheet to a 12×4-inch rectangle. Spread about 2/3 cup filling over each rectangle, leaving a 1-inch border along long sides. Fold the two long sides over edges of filling, then roll up from a short side to enclose filling. Place in individual au gratin dishes or shallow casseroles. Top each with about 1/2 cup Roasted Tomato Sauce, covering pasta. Bake, uncovered, about 30 minutes or until sauce is bubbly. If desired, garnish with sage sprigs. Makes 5 servings.

ROASTED TOMATO SAUCE: Preheat oven to 375° F. In a large roasting pan toss together 1 1/2 pounds tomatoes, cored and halved; 1 medium onion, sliced; 1/3 cup water or chicken broth; 1/4 cup fresh basil leaves; 2 tablespoons cooking oil; 1 teaspoon kosher salt; and 1/4 to 1/2 teaspoon freshly ground black pepper. Bake 50 minutes or until skins are slightly charred. Cool slightly. With a slotted spoon, remove tomatoes; coarsely chop. In a medium bowl combine tomatoes and juices and herbs from pan. Cover; chill until ready to use. Makes 2 1/4 cups.

***TEST KITCHEN TIP:** You can use 10 dried lasagna noodles instead of fresh pasta. Cook noodles according to package directions; drain well and cool. Spread about 1/3 cup filling onto each noodle; roll up from a short side and place two rolls, seam sides down, in each au gratin dish. Cover with sauce, being careful to cover edges so they won't dry out. Bake as above.

Each serving: 540 cal., 34 g total fat (17 g sat. fat), 139 mg chol., 1,046 mg sodium, 29 g carbo., 3 g fiber, 29 g pro. Daily Values: 41% vit. A, 37% vit. C, 60% calcium, 13% iron.

White Beans, Spiral Pasta, and Lobster

"It's wonderful cooking pasta for kids; it's something they'll always remember."

—Todd English

Free-Form Basil Lasagna

TODD ENGLISH

The aroma of olive oil, garlic, and onions sizzling in a pan for pasta sauce is one of chef Todd English's favorite memories of growing up—an experience he tries to re-create for his kids Oliver, Isabelle, and Simon.

He believes simplicity is crucial to success in pasta cooking with—or without—children in mind.

"Try not to be too fussy—the pasta should be as important as the sauce; it should never be too heavy," he says.

English developed his philosophy on his long and wandering route from captain of his Connecticut high school baseball team through the prestigious Culinary Institute of America, to head a company that now operates 16 restaurants in seven states.

His practical approach has served him well as host of *Cooking In with Todd English* on PBS and as author of three books: *The Olives Dessert Table (2000), The Figs Table (1998),* and *The Olives Table (1997).*

Fusilli with Prosciutto and Fava Beans

"Pasta is the consummate comfort food. It's easy, it's versatile, it's satisfying."

—Alfred Portale

ALFRED PORTALE

Pasta topped with a favorite little something is the key to Alfred Portale's success in getting daughters Olympia, and Victoria to enjoy dinner.

"I pair it with foods they like," says the chef of Gotham Bar and Grill restaurant in New York City. Though Portale (por-TAL-ee) uses his restaurant magic at home, cooking for family is different from being a chef. "With my children," he says, "I'm trying to expand their horizons. I talk about how to taste, about texture and flavor, and when one is eating too fast, I try to teach her to slow down and savor it."

Portale trained first as a jewelry designer, then enrolled at the Culinary Institute of America, graduating first in his class. After stints in other restaurants, he became chef at Gotham in 1984. He offers up lessons from his two decades in the kitchen in his two books: *The 12 Seasons Cookbook (2000)* and *The Gotham Bar and Grill Cookbook (1997)*.

Chicken Soup with Ham and Orzo

Fusilli with Prosciutto and Fava Beans

You can prepare Herbed Garlic Butter up to a week in advance and freeze it until you're ready to use it.

START TO FINISH: 25 minutes

- 12 oz. dried fusilli or bow-tie pasta
- 1 recipe Herbed Garlic Butter
- 1 19-oz. can fava or cannellini (white kidney) beans, rinsed and drained
- 2 cups grape tomatoes or halved cherry tomatoes
- 4 oz. thinly sliced prosciutto, torn into bite-size pieces
- 1/8 cup coarsely shredded pecorino Toscano cheese or grated Parmesan cheese
- 1 1/2 cups loosely packed torn arugula or watercress
- 3 Tbsp. snipped fresh chives
- Coarse salt
- Freshly ground white pepper
- Coarsely shredded pecorino Toscano cheese or grated Parmesan cheese

1. In a 4-quart Dutch oven cook pasta in 3 quarts of lightly salted boiling water according to package directions. Just before draining pasta, remove 1/2 cup of the pasta cooking water and set aside. Drain pasta; return to warm pan.

2. Immediately add Herbed Garlic Butter to pasta along with beans, tomatoes, prosciutto, and the 1/4 cup cheese. Gradually add 1/3 to 1/2 cup of the reserved cooking liquid while tossing constantly over low heat, as the butter and cheese melt to form a sauce. Add the arugula and chives; toss again. Season to taste with salt and pepper. Serve immediately. Top with additional coarsely shredded cheese. Makes 8 servings.

HERBED GARLIC BUTTER: In a small bowl combine 1/3 cup softened butter, 4 cloves minced garlic, 2 teaspoons snipped fresh thyme, 1 teaspoon lemon juice, and 1/4 teaspoon freshly ground black pepper; stir until smooth. Wrap tightly and refrigerate until ready to use.

Each serving: 331 cal., 12 g total fat (6 g sat. fat), 74 mg chol., 722 mg sodium, 41 g carbo., 8 g fiber, 15 g pro. Daily Values: 15% vit. A, 22% vit. C, 8% calcium, 11% iron.

SPRING GARDEN MENU

Mesclun with Pears and Blue Cheese *(page 192)*
Fusilli with Prosciutto and Fava Beans *(above)*
Crusty Italian Bread
Rhubarb Crisp *(page 199)*

Chicken Soup with Ham and Orzo

Chef Portale suggests drizzling each portion with a little extra-virgin olive oil.

START TO FINISH: 35 minutes

- 7 cups White Chicken Stock or four 14-oz. cans reduced-sodium chicken broth
- 2 bone-in chicken breast halves (1 lb.)
- 1 cup dried orzo (rosamarina) pasta (small, rice-shaped pasta)
- 3/4 lb. asparagus spears
- 4 cups lightly packed, thinly sliced Swiss chard
- 4 plum tomatoes, seeded and chopped
- 2 oz. cooked ham, cut into 1/2-inch cubes
- Coarse salt
- Freshly ground black pepper
- Snipped fresh chives
- Snipped fresh Italian flat-leaf parsley

1. In a 4-quart Dutch oven combine White Chicken Stock or broth and chicken. Bring to boiling; reduce heat. Cover and simmer about 20 minutes or until chicken is no longer pink. Remove chicken from broth; cool slightly. Discard skin and bones. Shred chicken into bite-size pieces.

2. Return broth to boiling; add orzo. Return to boiling; reduce heat. Cook, uncovered, for 7 minutes. Meanwhile, wash asparagus; break off woody bases where spears snap easily. Cut the asparagus diagonally into 1 1/4-inch pieces. Add asparagus to broth in Dutch oven. Cook for 3 minutes more.

3. Stir Swiss chard, tomatoes, ham, and shredded cooked chicken into broth in Dutch oven. Heat through. Season to taste with salt zzand pepper.

4. To serve, top individual portions with snipped chives and parsley. Makes 6 servings.

WHITE CHICKEN STOCK: In a very large pot combine 6 pounds chicken bones, cut up (substitute wings if bones or carcasses are unavailable), and 4 quarts cold water (water should cover chicken by about 2 inches). Bring to boiling. Skim any foam that rises to the surface. Add 1 large onion, chopped; 1 small carrot, coarsely chopped; 1 small stalk celery; 1 bulb garlic, halved crosswise; 2 sprigs fresh thyme; 2 sprigs fresh Italian flat-leaf parsley; 1 bay leaf; and 1 teaspoon whole pepper. Reduce heat. Simmer, uncovered, about 6 hours. Strain the stock through a sieve into a large bowl. Cool completely. Cover and refrigerate. Skim off and discard fat on the surface. Makes 15 cups.

Each serving: 286 cal., 8 g total fat (2 g sat. fat), 44 mg chol., 1,115 mg sodium, 26 g carbo., 2 g fiber, 25 g pro. Daily Values: 25% vit. A, 32% vit. C, 4% calcium, 6% iron.

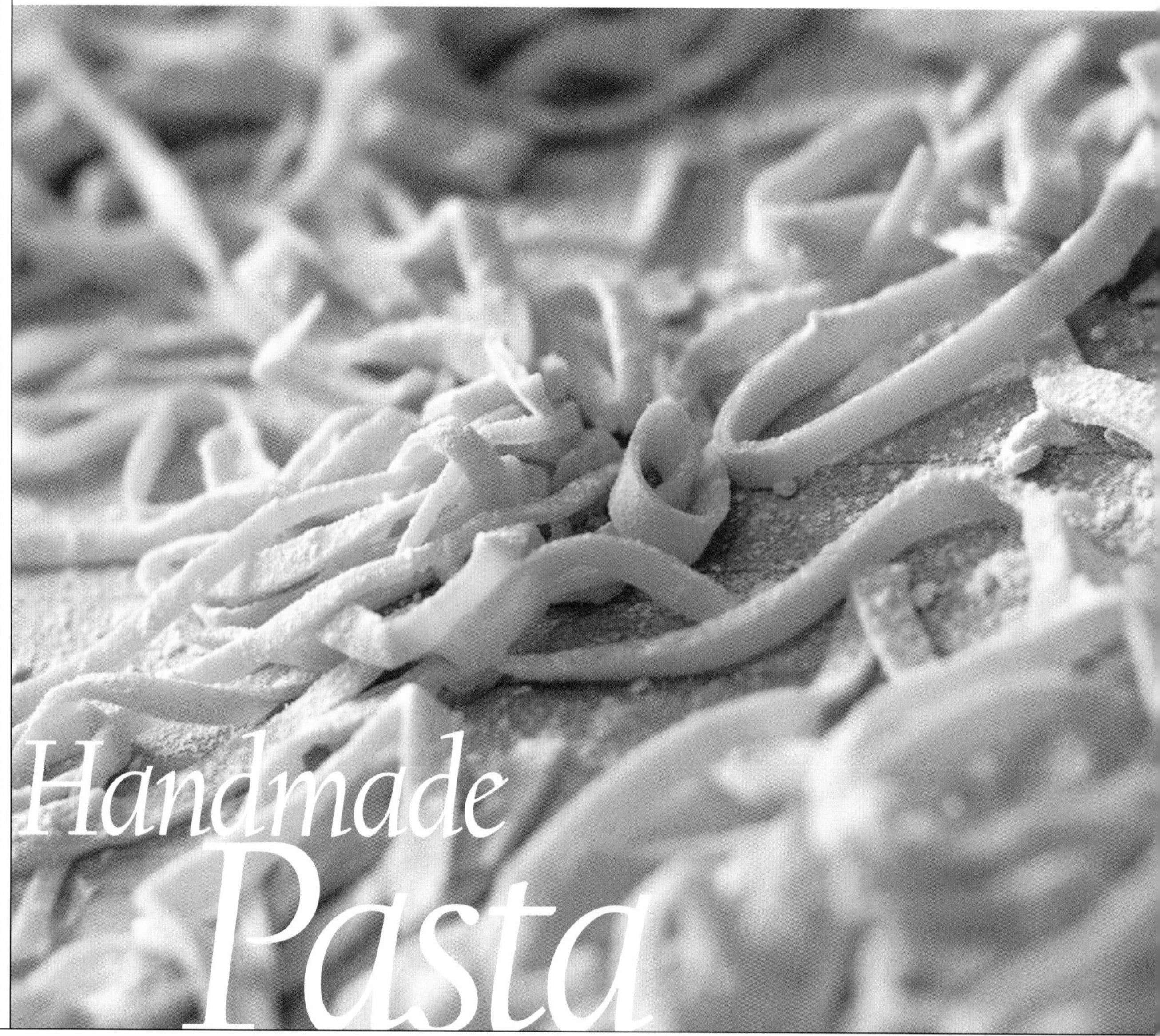

Handmade Pasta

THIS IS ONE OF THOSE RECIPES WHERE JOY IS AS MUCH IN THE MIXING, KNEADING, AND ROLLING AS IT IS IN THE DELIGHT YOU AND YOUR FAMILY SHARE WHEN YOU FINALLY SIT DOWN TO EAT IT.

Your hands, not your brain, are in charge on this job. "Pasta is a feel, not a recipe," says Chef Michael Chiarello, who bases his recipe on one he helped his mother and aunts make countless times as a child in the California farm belt. His mother taught him to appreciate the pairing of pasta and fresh vegetables.

These noodles—enriched by egg yolks—taste great with extra virgin olive oil, a shower of herbs, Parmesan cheese, and a quick tomato sauce. "Make a vinaigrette with shallots, garlic, parsley, lemon juice, basil oil, salt, and pepper, and toss in whatever's in season: zucchini, roasted peppers, or vine-ripe tomatoes," Michael says.

Little additions with big impact are the foundation of Chiarello's pasta dishes. His shelves are packed with foods he has either made or holds close to his heart—cans of Italian tuna, homemade pickled vegetables, home-canned tomato sauce, and his favorite red peppers.

Michael's Family Handmade Pasta

START TO FINISH: 1 hour

- $2\frac{1}{2}$ cups all-purpose flour
- 1 tsp. gray or kosher salt
- 6 egg yolks
- $1\frac{1}{2}$ Tbsp. olive oil
- 4 to 6 Tbsp. water

1. On a work surface, heap flour and make a large well in the center. Sprinkle flour with salt, and place egg yolks and oil in the well. With your fingertips, mix yolk mixture into flour. Sprinkle with water, and mix with hands until it forms a ball.

2. Knead 10 minutes or until dough feels smooth (it will still appear slightly lumpy). Flatten into a disk, wrap, and refrigerate for 20 minutes.

3. On a lightly floured surface, roll dough to $\frac{1}{16}$-inch-thick circle. Dust top lightly with flour. Roll up from one edge.

4. Cut crosswise into $\frac{1}{4}$-inch-wide strips. Unroll and separate strips.

5. Allow to dry (about 5 minutes).

6. To cook, drop pasta into a large pot containing a large amount of boiling salted water. Cook 5 to 8 minutes or until tender. Makes 4 to 6 servings.

Each serving: 289 cal., 10 g total fat (2 g sat. fat), 213 mg chol., 330 mg sodium, 40 g carbo., 1 g fiber, 8 g pro.

Making Michael's Pasta

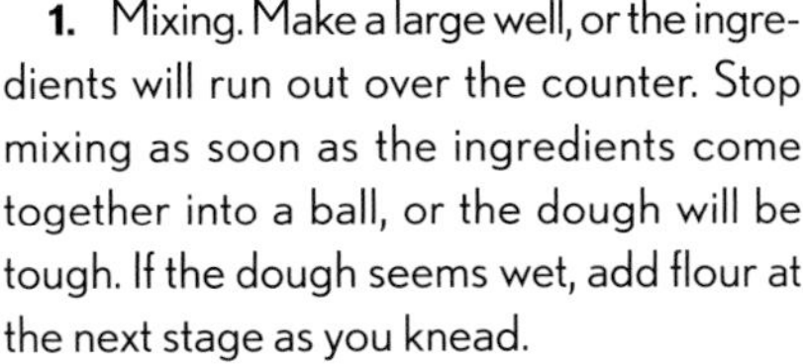

1. Mixing. Make a large well, or the ingredients will run out over the counter. Stop mixing as soon as the ingredients come together into a ball, or the dough will be tough. If the dough seems wet, add flour at the next stage as you knead.

2. Kneading. Push dough down with the heels of your hands, give it a quarter turn, fold, and do it again—for about 10 minutes. "This is the meditative side of cooking," says Michael.

3. Rolling. Patience is the key to successful rolling—steady work will get the dough to about the thickness of a penny. To help the dough relax and soften, roll each time in a different direction. If the dough shrinks back when you roll, cover with plastic wrap and let rest about 10 minutes. To prevent noodles from getting too thin on the edges, ease up on the pin as you reach the edge of the dough.

4. Slicing. After you roll up the dough, use a sharp, thin knife to cut noodles.

5. Drying. Allow the noodles to dry slightly before cooking. Part of their charm is their irregularity. "I could make them perfect," says Michael. "But what would I have gained? You want people to be able to see you took the time to make pasta."

Anytime Breadsticks

PARMESAN-PROSCIUTTO
Spread dough with Dijon-style mustard. Layer with thinly sliced, snipped prosciutto and grated Parmesan cheese or sliced Swiss cheese.

PILE-ON-PESTO
Slather dough with a generous amount of prepared pesto sauce. Add a few pine nuts, if you like.

HERBAL BLEND
Brush dough with olive oil. Heap on a handful each of coarsely chopped thyme and parsley. Drizzle top with additional olive oil. Sprinkle with coarse salt.

TRAIL MIX
Coat dough with honey; sprinkle with cinnamon. Press raisin-nut trail mix lightly into dough. (Some mix will fall out when you twist.) Brush top with melted butter.

CHEESE-STUFFED
Brush dough with your favorite Italian salad dressing. Add fresh Parmesan cheese or spread with Boursin cheese. Spoon additional dressing on top.

OLIVE-ROSEMARY
Press pitted, chopped kalamata olives into dough. Twist to enclose olives. (Expect some olives to spill out.) Scatter top with snipped fresh rosemary.

COME ON, BABY, DO THE TWIST.
Refrigerated breadstick dough turns into rustic bakery-fresh snacks for any time of day. Start with a 10-ounce package of refrigerated breadstick dough and choose from the flavor options to the left. Depending on the flavor, the sticks make great dinnertime serve-alongs, especially with pasta, salads, and soups. Or, serve them as an after-school or picnic snack. Fill and roll, grab and go!

Start with a 10-ounce package of refrigerated breadstick dough. Preheat oven according to the breadstick dough package directions. Separate dough into strips. Flavor each one as you please (*suggestions, left*).

Twist the breadstick dough around the fillings. Don't worry if the breadsticks aren't perfect or if some of the filling falls out.

Place breadsticks on a baking sheet. Brush with olive oil or melted butter. Sprinkle with salt or fresh or dried herbs. Bake as package directs.

Don't Forget Folate

IT'S A NO-BRAINER.

Get enough of the vitamin B folate and you may prevent some of the forgetfulness that occurs with aging. Folate and its manmade version, folic acid, play a key role in brain function.

Forget where you put your cell phone again? Chow down on a handful of folate-rich peanuts. Actually it's not as simple as all that, but "keeping folate levels high is extremely important to memory," says scientist Martha Morris, Ph.D., of Tufts University in Boston.

Folate and other B vitamins also assist the body in lowering levels of homocysteine, an amino acid that increases the risk of heart disease. In fact, this finding appears to be closely related to claims of a poor memory.

In a report published in the *American Journal of Clinical Nutrition*, Morris and her colleagues found a link between poor recall and high homocysteine. Further digging provided evidence that high levels of folate seemed to offer some protection against memory loss.

REMEMBER THIS.

So if you find yourself at a party fumbling for the name of that person you just met, maybe you need to alter your diet a bit.

Black beans and other dried beans and peas are full of folate. So are deepgreen leafy vegetables, asparagus, strawberries, artichokes, and citrus fruits (see chart, opposite). Enriched grain products, including bread, flour, rice, breakfast cereal, and pasta, have been fortified with folic acid since 1998. That requirement—set by the U.S. Food and Drug Administration—came about when it was determined that adequate folate taken by women in their child-bearing years reduced the risk of certain birth defects affecting the brain and spinal cord.

YOUR DAILY DOSE

The recommended daily intake of folate is 400 micrograms (mcg). Pregnant women should take in 800 mcg. Most people get adequate folate in their diets, Morris says, but pregnant women may be advised to take a vitamin supplement with folic acid.

A serving of most breakfast cereals, for instance, provides about 25 percent of the daily folate requirement for the average person in the country. Check the nutrition label on the package to find the exact amount of folate.

The latest folate buzz also has researchers looking at the nutrient's impact on Parkinson's disease and Alzheimer's disease. Trials by the National Institute on Aging to see if a regimen of folate and other B vitamins slows the rate of progression of Alzheimer's disease. Studies on mice have shown that a group that got less folic acid had higher levels of homocysteine in their bodies and were more susceptible to Parkinson's-like abnormalities.

Folate also reduces your risk of colon cancer. Several studies have shown that high levels of folate in the body lower the risk of colon cancer. Folic acid commonly found in vitamin supplements appears to offer the same protection.

FINDING FOLATE

Here are some of your best folate choices:

FOOD	SERVING SIZE	FOLATE AMOUNT (MICROGRAMS)
Breakfast cereal	1/2 cup to 1 1/2 cups	100-400 mcg
Lentils	1/2 cup cooked	179 mcg
Black beans	1/2 cup cooked	178 mcg
Artichoke	1 medium boiled	153 mcg
Asparagus	1/2 cup cooked	131 mcg
Turnip greens	1/2 cup boiled, chopped	85 mcg
Orange juice, fresh	1 cup	75 mcg
Kidney beans	1/2 cup cooked	65 mcg

Asparagus Finger Salad

Aparagus is a good source of folate to enjoy as a snack or side dish.

PREP: 15 minutes **COOK:** 2 minutes

- **8 oz. fresh asparagus spears**
- **4 large butterhead lettuce or romaine lettuce leaves**
- **1 small carrot, halved lengthwise**
- **2 tsp. finely shredded lemon peel**
- **1 recipe Tarragon Dipping Sauce (below)**

1. Snap off and discard woody bases from asparagus. If desired, scrape off scales. Cover and cook asparagus in a small amount of boiling water for 2 to 4 minutes or until crisp-tender. Transfer asparagus to a bowl filled with ice water. Set aside.

2. To serve, cut center vein from each lettuce leaf, keeping each leaf in one piece. Place lettuce leaves on a serving plate. Pat asparagus dry with paper towels. Cut each carrot half into four equal lengthwise strips.

3. Divide asparagus and carrot strips evenly across the middle of the lettuce. Sprinkle each serving with finely shredded lemon peel. Wrap lettuce around asparagus and carrots. Place each asparagus salad upright in a small cup. Serve or drizzle with Tarragon Dipping Sauce. Makes 4 servings.

TARRAGON DIPPING SAUCE: In a small bowl combine 1/3 cup light dairy sour cream, 1 tablespoon fresh snipped chives, 2 teaspoons lemon juice, 1 teaspoon fresh snipped tarragon, 1/8 teaspoon salt, and 1/8 teaspoon freshly ground black pepper. Cover and chill until serving time.

Each serving: 49 cal., 3 g total fat (2 g sat. fat), 8 mg chol., 93 mg sodium, 5 g carbo., 2 g fiber, 2 g pro. Daily Values: 96% vit. A, 19% vit. C, 4% calcium, 3% iron.

Mesclun with Pears and Blue Cheese

micro Greens

LITTLE LETTUCES MIMIC THEIR MATURE FAMILY MEMBERS IN FLAVOR–BUT IN A SWEETLY MILD MANNER.

Add them to just about anything for a bite of freshness. You can look for these baby greens on their own or buy a mixture of greens called mesclun, which may be sold in a package or loose. The greens in mesclun may vary, but can include arugula, dandelion, frissée, greens, mâche, mizuna, oak leaf lettuce, radicchio, sorrel, and tatsoi. For mesclun or any green, look for crisp leaves with no signs of wilting. Before serving, wash leaves in cold water, drain in a colander, and pat dry with paper towels. Store in a plastic bag lined with paper towels for up to 5 days.

Mesclun with Pears and Blue Cheese

In a real rush? Substitute your favorite balsamic vinaigrette for the dressing.

START TO FINISH: 25 minutes

- 10 cups mesclun and/or baby greens
- 3 medium red and/or green pears, cored and thinly sliced
- 1 recipe Pear-Ginger Vinaigrette (below)
- 1/2 cup broken walnuts, toasted, or
- 1 recipe Candied Nuts (below)
- 1/2 cup crumbled blue cheese

In a large salad bowl combine mesclun and pear slices. Toss gently to combine. Pour Pear-Ginger Vinaigrette over salad; toss gently to coat. Divide the salad evenly among eight salad plates. Sprinkle with nuts and blue cheese. Makes 8 servings.

PEAR-GINGER VINAIGRETTE: In a screw-top jar combine 1/4 cup pear nectar, 2 tablespoons walnut oil or salad oil, 2 tablespoons white wine vinegar, 1 teaspoon Dijon-style mustard, 1/8 teaspoon ground ginger, and 1/8 teaspoon ground black pepper. Cover and shake well to mix.

CANDIED NUTS: Line a baking sheet with foil; butter foil. In a 10-inch heavy skillet combine 1 1/8 cups raw or roasted cashews, peanuts, almonds, and pecan or walnut halves; 1/2 cup sugar; 2 tablespoons butter; and 1/2 teaspoon vanilla. Cook over medium-high heat, shaking skillet occasionally, until sugar begins to melt. Do not stir. Reduce heat to low. Continue cooking until sugar is golden brown, stirring occasionally. Remove from heat. Pour nut mixture onto the prepared baking sheet. Cool completely. Break into clusters. Store nuts, tightly covered, in the refrigerator for up to 3 weeks. Makes 1 1/2 cups.

Each serving with walnuts: 152 cal., 11 g total fat (2 g sat. fat), 5 mg chol., 110 mg sodium, 13 g carbo., 3 g fiber, 4 g pro. Daily Values: 6% vit. A, 10% vit. C, 7% calcium, 4% iron.

You'll see micro greens in trendy restaurants and upscale food markets. They're just basic greens snipped while the leaves are still tiny. Typically, you'll find them packaged as a mix of miniatures. Don't see them in the store? Beg your produce manager to order some. They're available year-round. Or grow your own. Call Johnny's Seeds for guidance, 207/437-4301, or check the Web site: www.johnnyseeds.com and do a search for "greens."

Red Mustard Greens | **Micro Red Mustard Greens**

Tatsoi | **Micro Tatsoi**

Mizuna

Micro Mizuna

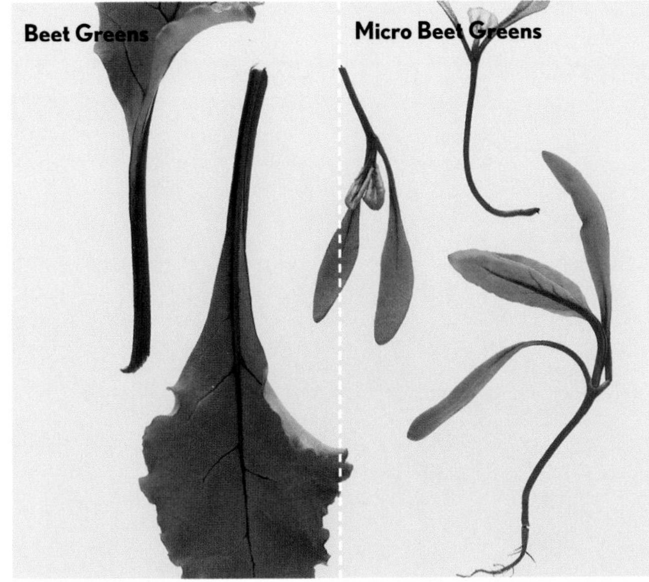

Beet Greens | **Micro Beet Greens**

RED MUSTARD GREENS

The teeny version is tangy and tender. Its horseradish-like bite gives sandwiches some snap.

TATSOI

These small spoon-shaped leaves will remind you of Swiss chard with a little zip.

MIZUNA

A jaggedy shape and a sharp-but-mellow taste make this bitsy green a dressy topper for just about anything.

BEET GREENS

Its purplish-red veins and stem add great color. These mild-mannered fellas have a very subtle beet flavor. They're delicately delicious floating on a light soup.

APPLE MINT
Lightly scented with apple.

PINEAPPLE MINT
Fragrant multicolor leaves of green and cream.

PEPPERMINT
Widely available; a bit more pungent and peppery than spearmint.

LIME MINT
Very aromatic with a full flavor.

SPEARMINT
A mild-tasting variety, commonly found in supermarkets and garden shops.

GINGER MINT
A mingling of two warm flavors.

A Touch of Mint

MINT CAN DO MUCH MORE THAN DRESS UP A JULEP OR A LAMB CHOP.

This flavorful, internationally popular herb is a tasty player with a variety of foods.

Mint's pronounced effect shows up immediately in dishes, making it a worthwhile last-minute stir-in. Smelling and tasting are the best ways to judge how much mint to use. Start with a small amount, then add more as needed. If a recipe calls for dried mint, substitute three times the amount of fresh.

When adding snipped fresh mint to hot mixtures, stir it in just before serving; its flavor lessens during long cooking. Try it a number of ways:

- **STEEP IT:** Add 1/2 cup of fresh mint leaves when you make a pot of tea.
- **SOAK IT:** Combine slightly crushed fresh mint leaves in a saucepan with 2 parts water and 1 part sugar; bring to boiling. Stir to dissolve sugar. Cool; spoon over ice cream or fresh fruit.
- **ROLL IT:** Stir together equal amounts of tahini paste and mayonnaise. Spread on top of a flour tortilla; layer with deli roast beef, mint leaves, and mesclun salad mix. Roll up and serve.
- **WHIP IT:** Combine snipped fresh mint and cooked fresh asparagus in a blender container. Add enough of the vegetable cooking water to blend until smooth. Chill for a refreshing summer soup.
- **TOSS IT:** Stir a generous amount of snipped fresh mint into cooked couscous with grilled chicken and vegetables. Drizzle with olive oil.

To store fresh mint, rinse it well and place the stems in a vase of water; don't immerse the leaves. The sprigs will stay fresh for 2 to 3 days at room temperature. For longer storage, place a plastic bag over the leaves and refrigerate for up to a week, changing the water every two days.

Spearmint is the variety you'll find most often in the grocery store. However, the common garden types (pictured) can be used interchangeably in recipes.

AROMATIC GARDENING

When planting your garden, consider tucking in a few mint plants. This perennial is easy to grow, but it spreads quickly and can overtake a garden. Use a permanent barrier to separate it from other plants, or grow it in big pots. The flavor of mint is strongest just before it begins to flower. Pick mint early in the morning because the sun draws out some of the plant's essential oils.

Tabbouleh

There is no need to cook the bulgur for this salad—the mint-lemon dressing softens it while the salad chills.

PREP: 25 minutes **CHILL:** 4 hours

- 3/4 cup bulgur
- 1 small cucumber, peeled, seeded, and chopped
- 3 Tbsp. snipped fresh parsley
- 2 Tbsp. snipped fresh mint or 2 tsp. dried mint, crushed
- 2 Tbsp. thinly sliced green onion
- 1 recipe Mint-Lemon Vinaigrette (below)
- 1/2 cup chopped, seeded tomato (1 small)

1. Place bulgur in a colander; rinse with cold water and drain. In a medium bowl combine bulgur, cucumber, parsley, mint, and green onion. Pour Mint-Lemon Vinaigrette over bulgur mixture. Toss gently to coat. Cover and chill for 4 to 24 hours.

2. Before serving, bring tabbouleh to room temperature. Just before serving, stir in tomato. Makes 4 to 6 servings.

LEMON VINAIGRETTE: In a screw-top jar combine 1/4 cup olive oil or salad oil, 3 tablespoons lemon juice, 2 tablespoons water, 1/4 teaspoon salt, and 1/8 teaspoon pepper. Cover and shake well to mix. Makes 1/2 cup.

Each serving: 228 cal., 14 g total fat (2 g sat. fat), 0 mg chol., 156 mg sodium, 24 g carbo., 6 g fiber, 4 g pro. Daily Values: 8% vit. A, 31% vit. C, 3% calcium, 9% iron.

Luscious, Fast Fruit Desserts

WITH A LITTLE DRESSING UP,

you can turn fresh fruit into light, showstopper desserts that use just four ingredients or less. These three easy ideas take advantage of what's in favor for summer—mangoes, peaches, cherries, and nectarines. They're perfect for a refreshing ending to a spicy backyard cookout because you just cut 'em up, add a little of this and a little of that, and bring 'em out on a tray.

MANGO WHIP

Seed and peel two mangoes or peaches. Cut into wedges. Divide fruit between two chilled dessert bowls. In a mixing bowl beat together 1/4 cup softened light cream cheese and 2 tablespoons white grape or orange juice. Spoon over mangoes. Top with chopped pistachios.

Mango Whip

Cherry Dream

CHERRY DREAM

Mound 1/4 cup prepared vanilla custard, vanilla pudding, or tapioca pudding into a chilled dessert bowl. Spoon about 1/2 cup pitted, halved dark sweet cherries over custard. Drizzle with a cherry liqueur, such as Kirsch.

KEEN NECTARINE

Scoop 1/3 cup vanilla or peach-flavored frozen yogurt (or vanilla or peach-flavored ice cream) into a chilled dessert bowl. Add half of a pitted ripe nectarine or peach. Sprinkle with crumbled amaretti cookies or gingersnaps.

Keen Nectarine

Tomato-Rhubarb Chutney

Ready for Rhubarb

RHUBARB IS NATURE'S LITTLE SWEET-TART VEGETABLE.

It has a not-so-demure flavor that sends some fans into a swoon, while others just pucker up to its sassy taste. Hothouse rhubarb (found almost year-round in grocery stores) has pink to pale red stalks. The more assertively flavored field-grown rhubarb sports ruby red stalks and is available from late winter to early summer. The leaves of both varieties are highly toxic and should never be eaten.

When purchasing rhubarb, look for stalks that are crisp and brightly hued. Refrigerate it tightly wrapped in plastic, and use within three days of purchase.

Rhubarb is also known as "pieplant," because of its most obvious association. Try it in our pie, crisp, and bold chutney.

Rhubarb Crisp

PREP: 30 minutes **BAKE:** 30 minutes

- **5 cups fresh or frozen unsweetened sliced rhubarb, thawed**
- **3/4 cup granulated sugar**
- **1/2 cup regular rolled oats**
- **1/2 cup packed brown sugar**
- **1/3 cup all-purpose flour**
- **1/4 tsp. ground nutmeg, ginger, or cinnamon**
- **1/4 cup butter**
- **1/4 cup chopped nuts or coconut**
- **Vanilla ice cream (optional)**

1. Preheat oven to 375° F. Place rhubarb in a 2-quart square baking dish. Stir in the granulated sugar.

2. For topping, in a medium bowl combine oats, brown sugar, flour, and nutmeg. Cut in butter until mixture resembles coarse crumbs. Stir in the nuts. Sprinkle topping over filling.

3. Bake 30 to 35 minutes (40 minutes for thawed rhubarb) or until rhubarb is tender and topping is golden. Serve warm. If desired, serve with vanilla ice cream. Makes 6 servings.

MICROWAVE DIRECTIONS: Prepare filling as in Step 1. Microwave filling, covered with vented plastic wrap, on 100 percent power (high) for 4 to 6 minutes or until rhubarb is tender, stirring twice. Prepare topping as in Step 2. Sprinkle over filling. Cook, uncovered, on high 2 to 4 minutes or until topping is heated through, giving the dish a half-turn once.

Each serving: 360 cal., 13 g total fat (6 g sat. fat), 22 mg chol., 92 mg sodium, 61 g carbo., 4 g fiber, 4 g pro. Daily Values: 8% vit. A, 12% vit. C, 12% calcium, 8% iron.

Tomato-Rhubarb Chutney

Serve this chutney with grilled beef or chicken, spread it on a cold pork sandwich, or top a round of Brie cheese and serve with crackers for a party snack.

PREP: 20 minutes **COOK:** 40 minutes

- **3 medium tomatoes, cored, seeded, and chopped (about 1 1/2 cups)**
- **1/3 cup chopped onion**
- **1/3 cup coarsely chopped red sweet pepper**
- **1/3 cup dried cherries, cranberries, or raisins**
- **1/3 cup white vinegar**
- **1/4 cup granulated sugar**
- **1/4 cup packed brown sugar**
- **1/4 cup water**
- **1 Tbsp. lime or lemon juice**
- **2 cloves garlic, minced**
- **1 tsp. grated fresh ginger or 1/4 tsp. ground ginger**
- **1/4 tsp. salt**
- **1 cup fresh rhubarb cut into 1/2-inch pieces or 1 cup frozen cut rhubarb, thawed and drained**

1. In a saucepan combine tomatoes, onion, sweet pepper, dried cherries, vinegar, sugars, water, lime juice, garlic, ginger, and salt. Bring to boiling; reduce heat. Cover and simmer for 25 minutes, stirring occasionally. Stir in rhubarb.

2. Cover and simmer for 10 minutes. Uncover. Simmer about 5 minutes more for fresh rhubarb (15 minutes more for frozen rhubarb) or until thickened. Cool. To store, cover and refrigerate up to 1 week or freeze up to 3 months. Makes about 2 3/4 cups.

Each 2 tablespoons chutney: 30 cal., 0 g total fat (0 g sat. fat), 0 mg chol., 29 mg sodium, 8 g carbo., 0 g fiber, 0 g pro. Daily Values: 11% vit. C, 1% calcium, 1% iron.

Rhubarb Pie

Serve with ice cream, of course.

PREP: 30 minutes **BAKE:** 45 minutes

- **3/4 cup sugar**
- **1/3 cup all-purpose flour**
- **1/2 tsp. ground cinnamon**
- **6 cups fresh or frozen unsweetened sliced rhubarb, thawed**
- **1 15-oz. package folded refrigerated unbaked piecrust (2 crusts)**

1. Preheat oven to 375° F. For filling, in a large bowl stir together sugar, flour, and cinnamon; stir in undrained rhubarb.

2. Line a 9-inch pie plate with pastry; trim. Transfer filling to pastry. Trim bottom pastry to edge of plate. Cut slits in remaining pastry; place on filling and seal. Crimp edge as desired. If desired, brush with milk; sprinkle with sugar.

3. Cover edge of plate with foil. Bake for 25 minutes; remove foil. Bake for 20 to 30 minutes more or until filling is bubbly in center and pastry is golden. Cool on a wire rack. Makes 8 servings.

Each serving: 365 cal., 13 g total fat (5 g sat. fat), 12 mg chol., 129 mg sodium, 58 g carbo., 24 g fiber, 4 g pro. Daily Values: 5% vit. A, 10% vit. C, 10% calcium, 10% iron.

Cookies and Ice Cream

GATHER THE FAMILY 'ROUND to try a fondue-inspired dessert that combines the best of fudge and hot cocoa—a dip for dunking or a sauce for spooning. Then pair it with ice cream, fruit, and cookies. You can make everything from scratch or take the supermarket shortcut and buy readymade. Either way, it's a taste of summer, any time of year.

No-Drip Chocolate Dip

PREP: 5 minutes **COOK:** 10 minutes

- 8 oz. unsweetened chocolate, chopped
- 1 14-oz. can (1¼ cups) sweetened condensed milk
- 2 Tbsp. light-colored corn syrup
- ½ cup milk
- 1 tsp. vanilla
- ½ tsp. ground cinnamon
- Milk

1. In a medium saucepan melt chocolate over low heat, stirring constantly.

2. Stir in the sweetened condensed milk and corn syrup until combined. Gradually stir in the ½ cup milk until combined. Stir in vanilla and cinnamon. Serve warm, stirring in additional milk, as necessary until of dipping consistency. Makes 2 cups.

Each 1 tablespoon: 83 cal., 5 g total fat (3 g sat. fat), 4 mg chol., 20 mg sodium, 10 g carbo., 1 g fiber, 2 g pro. Daily Values: 1% vit. A, 1% vit. C, 5% calcium, 3% iron.

Shortbread

PREP: 15 minutes **BAKE:** 20 minutes

- 1¼ cups all-purpose flour
- 3 Tbsp. granulated sugar
- ½ cup butter

1. Preheat oven to 325° F. In a small mixing bowl combine flour and sugar; cut in butter until mixture resembles fine crumbs and starts to cling. Form mixture into a ball; knead until smooth.

2. On a lightly floured surface roll dough into an 8x6-inch rectangle about ½ inch thick. Using a knife, cut into twenty-four ½-inch strips. Place 1 inch apart on an ungreased cookie sheet.

3. Bake for 20 to 25 minutes or until bottoms just starts to brown. Transfer to a wire rack; cool. Makes 24 cookies.

SPICED SHORTBREAD: Prepare as above, except substitute brown sugar for the granulated sugar and stir ½ teaspoon ground cinnamon, ¼ teaspoon ground ginger, and ⅛ teaspoon ground cloves into the flour mixture.

Each cookie: 98 cal., 6 g total fat (4 g sat. fat), 16 mg chol., 62 mg sodium, 10 g carbo., 0 g fiber, 1 g pro. Daily Values: 5% vit. A 3% iron.

Vanilla Ice Cream

PREP: 5 minutes **FREEZE:** per directions **RIPEN:** 4 hours

- 4 cups half-and-half, light cream, or milk
- 1½ cups sugar
- 1 Tbsp. vanilla
- 2 cups whipping cream

1. In a large bowl combine half-and-half, sugar, and vanilla. Stir until sugar dissolves. Stir in whipping cream.

2. Freeze ice cream mixture in a 4- or 5-quart ice cream freezer according to the manufacturer's directions. Ripen for 4 hours. Makes 2 quarts (15 servings).

STRAWBERRY OR PEACH ICE CREAM: Prepare as above, except in a blender container place 4 cups fresh strawberries; frozen unsweetened strawberries, thawed; or cut-up, peeled peaches. Cover and blend until nearly smooth (you should have 2 cups). Stir fruit into cream mixture before freezing.

Each serving: 253 cal., 18 g total fat (11 g sat. fat), 63 mg chol., 36 mg sodium, 22 g carbo., 0 g fiber, 2 g pro. Daily Values: 14% vit. A, 1% vit. C, 8% calcium.

No-Drip Chocolate Dip

June

ENJOY THE MAGICAL SEASON OF BACKYARDS, BARBECUES, AND RELAXED GOOD TIMES, BY CASTING FAMILIAR FAVORITES IN ENTICING NEW GUISES.

Slow-Simmered Pork Sandwiches with Roasted Tomato-Jalapeño Vinaigrette

Hibiscus Tea

Polka-Dot Angel Food Cupcakes

Bacon-Avocado Deviled Eggs

Easy-Does-It Summer

Fruit Wands

Plus ...

Turtle Pretzels

Lumpy PB&J Roosters

A Cherry Jubilee

Plus...

SCHOOL'S OUT AND SUMMER'S ON. PICK THE PERFECT PICNIC SPOT AND PACK YOUR BASKET HIGH.

Wild Blueberry Pies and Just Cherries

Green Goddess Dip

Easy-does-it Summer

A SPIRIT OF SPONTANEITY, A MOOD OF PLENTY, WILLING HANDS, AND A BIT OF PLANNING MAKE IT ALL HAPPEN AT A CASUAL GATHERING FOR FRIENDS.

Green Goddess Dip

A 1920s San Francisco chef gave the name "green goddess" to a unique salad dressing to honor an actor appearing in a play of the same name.

Start to Finish: 30 minutes

- 1/3 cup refrigerated or frozen egg product, thawed
- 3 Tbsp. lemon juice
- 2 tsp. Dijon-style mustard
- 1 clove garlic, minced
- 1 cup canola oil
- 4 to 5 anchovy fillets, drained and chopped (1 Tbsp.)
- 1 cup loosely packed fresh parsley leaves
- 1/4 cup loosely packed fresh tarragon leaves
- 1/4 cup snipped fresh chives
- 2 green onions, chopped
- 4 oz. cream cheese, cubed and softened
- 1/4 cup tarragon vinegar
- Salt
- Vegetable dippers such as Belgian endive, baby romaine lettuce leaves, asparagus spears, radishes, and/or green onions

1. In a large food processor or blender combine egg product, lemon juice, mustard, and garlic; cover and process or blend until combined. With the processor or blender running, add oil in a thin, steady stream. (When necessary, stop and scrape down sides of blender.)

2. Add anchovies, parsley, tarragon, chives, and green onion; pulse until blended. Add the softened cream cheese and vinegar; pulse to combine. Season to taste with salt.

3. Serve dip with vegetable dippers. Any leftover dip may be stored, covered, in the refrigerator for up to 1 week. Makes 2 1/4 cups.

Each tablespoon: 69 cal., 7 g total fat (2 g sat. fat), 4 mg chol., 45 mg sodium, 1 g carbo., 0 g fiber, 1 g pro. Daily Values: 3% vit. A, 6% vit. C, 1% calcium, 1% iron.

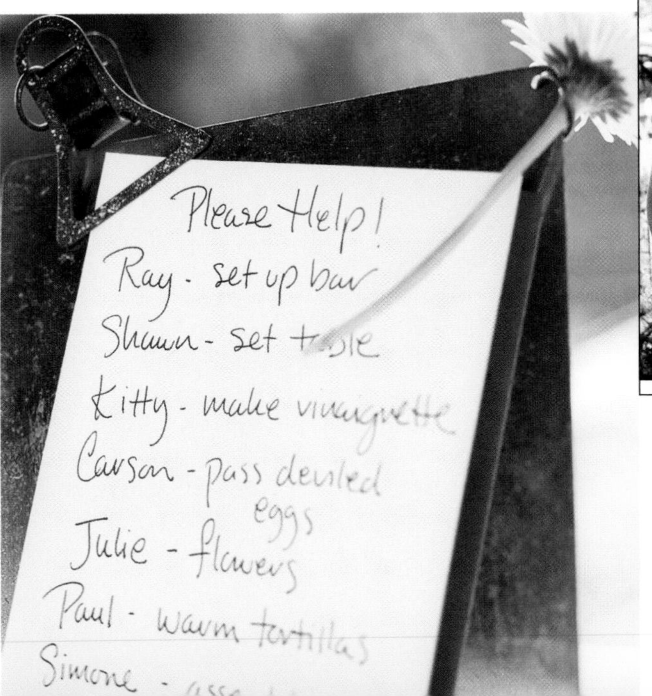

Summer gatherings

A great summer gathering is the sum of its sensations: Afternoon sun alighting on tall skewers of the freshest summer fruit, the taste of deviled eggs topped with bacon and avocado, and the laughter of familiar voices gathered around the grill.

Making wonderful moments happen for guests is simple when you understand that your life, at least your backyard life, is not a one-person show. Even if you're like Carrie Brown *(below right)*—who owns a restaurant, specialty food company, and general store—when you let guests help, the day is elevated from merely entertaining to truly enchanting others.

"I used to try to make everything perfect and flawless, but I didn't enjoy my own parties," says Carrie, whose Jimtown Store sits alongside a rural highway in the Sonoma County wine country north of San Francisco. "Then I learned to loosen up and let everyone help so we could all sit back and enjoy the chaos of the moment."

Carrie's key to successful delegation is giving people specific, but fun, assignments. Before her gatherings, she creates a to-do list for the close friends who come to the party. When they're working for their supper, she tries to make sure they're supplied with all the tools needed for the task at hand. Carrie also posts notes on serving bowls and platters to designate which goes with each recipe.

Grilled Salmon Tacos

Make the salsa and crème fraîche one or two days ahead. Then you can devote your full attention to preparing the salmon.

PREP: 1 hour **GRILL:** 8 minutes

- 2 lb. fresh or frozen skinless salmon fillets
- 1 lb. medium round red or white potatoes (2 cups)
- 1 Tbsp. ground chipotle chile pepper
- 1½ tsp. sugar
- 1 tsp. kosher salt or ¾ tsp. salt
- 2 cups Lupe's Tomatillo Salsa (right) or purchased green salsa
- ⅓ cup lime juice
- 1 tsp. kosher salt or ¾ tsp. salt
- 12 green onions, thinly sliced
- 1 cup snipped fresh cilantro
- 32 4-inch corn tortillas or twenty-four 6-inch corn tortillas, warmed
- 1 cup Crème Fraîche (below right)
- Lime wedges

1. Thaw fish, if frozen. Peel and cube potatoes. Cook potatoes, covered, in enough boiling salted water to cover about 15 minutes or until tender. Drain and cool.

2. Rinse fish; pat dry. Measure thickness of fish in the thickest spot. In a small bowl combine chipotle pepper, sugar, and 1 teaspoon salt; rub onto both sides of fish. Place fish on greased grill rack directly over medium coals. Grill, uncovered, for 4 to 6 minutes per ½-inch thickness or until fish flakes easily when tested with a fork. Cool slightly. Break salmon into chunks.

3. In a large bowl stir together Lupe's Tomatillo Salsa, lime juice, and 1 teaspoon salt. Add the salmon, potatoes, green onions, and cilantro; stir gently.

4. Divide the salmon mixture among tortillas. Top each with a dollop of Crème Fraîche. Serve immediately with lime wedges. Makes 24 to 32 tacos.

Each taco: 161 cal., 5 g total fat (2 g sat. fat), 29 mg chol., 316 mg sodium, 19 g carbo., 2 g fiber, 10 g pro. Daily Values: 12% vit. A, 28% vit. C, 8% calcium, 7% iron.

Lupe's Tomatillo Salsa

This salsa is named for one of Carrie's first employees. Canned tomatillos, though great in other dishes, are not successful in this particular recipe.

PREP: 30 minutes **ROAST:** 20 minutes

- 3 lb. fresh tomatillos
- 6 fresh serrano chile peppers
- 2 cups fresh cilantro leaves
- ⅓ cup finely chopped yellow or white onion
- 3 cloves garlic, minced
- 1½ tsp. kosher salt or 1 tsp. salt
- ⅓ cup finely chopped green onions

1. Preheat oven to 425° F. Remove husks, stems, and cores from tomatillos. Cut any large tomatillos in half. Place tomatillos in a foil-lined shallow roasting pan. Remove stems and, if desired, seeds from serrano peppers*. Place peppers in roasting pan with tomatillos. Roast, uncovered, for 20 minutes or until tomatillos are soft. Drain tomatillos and cool. (Save some of the drained liquid from roasting pan to use in blender, if necessary.)

2. In a blender or food processor combine half of the tomatillos, peppers, cilantro, yellow onion, and garlic. Cover and blend or process until almost smooth. (If necessary, add a bit of the reserved cooking liquid to the blender to help blend.) Pour mixture into a medium bowl. Repeat with remaining tomatillos, peppers, cilantro, yellow onion, and garlic.

3. Stir salt and the green onions into the salsa mixture. Serve immediately or cover and chill for up to 2 days. Makes about 3¼ cups.

***NOTE:** Because hot peppers contain oils that can burn your eyes, lips, and skin, when working with chile peppers, wear plastic or rubber gloves.

Each ¼-cup serving: 33 cal., 1 g total fat (0 g sat. fat), 0 mg chol., 230 mg sodium, 6 g carbo., 1 g fiber, 1 g pro. Daily Values: 10% vit. A, 40% vit. C, 2% calcium, 4% iron.

Crème Fraîche

PREP: 5 minutes **STAND:** 5 hours

- 1 8-oz. carton dairy sour cream
- 1 cup whipping cream (not ultrapasteurized)

1. In a medium mixing bowl whisk together sour cream and whipping cream. Cover with plastic wrap. Let stand at room temperature for 5 to 8 hours or until mixture is thickened.

2. When thickened, cover and chill until serving time or for up to 48 hours. Stir before serving. Makes about 2 cups.

Each tablespoon serving: 41 cal., 4 g total fat (3 g sat. fat), 13 mg chol., 7 mg sodium, 1 g carbo., 0 g fiber, 0 g pro. Daily Values: 3% vit. A, 1% calcium.

Grilled Salmon Tacos
"IT'S THOUGHTFUL FOOD; I'VE TAKEN
A TRIED-AND-TRUE RECIPE
AND MADE IT A LITTLE BIT SPECIAL."
CARRIE BROWN

Baked Bean Quintet

This crowd-pleasing recipe is perfect for potlucks and picnics. Tote it to your next summertime bring-a-dish gathering—everyone will be glad you did.

PREP: 10 minutes **BAKE:** 1 hour

- 1 cup chopped onion (1 large)
- 6 slices bacon, cut up
- 1 clove garlic, minced
- 1 16-oz. can lima beans, drained
- 1 16-oz. can pork and beans in tomato sauce
- 1 15½-oz. can red kidney beans, drained
- 1 15-oz. can butter beans, drained
- 1 15-oz. can garbanzo beans, drained
- ¾ cup catsup
- ½ cup molasses
- ¼ cup packed brown sugar
- 1 Tbsp. prepared mustard
- 1 Tbsp. Worcestershire sauce
- Cooked bacon (optional)

1. Preheat oven to 375° F. In a skillet cook onion, bacon, and garlic until bacon is crisp and onion is tender; drain. In a bowl combine onion mixture, lima beans, pork and beans, kidney beans, butter beans, garbanzo beans, catsup, molasses, brown sugar, mustard, and Worcestershire sauce.

2. Transfer bean mixture to a 3-quart casserole. Bake, covered, for 1 hour. If desired, top with additional cooked bacon. Makes 12 to 16 side-dish servings.

SLOW COOKER DIRECTIONS: Prepare bean mixture as above. Transfer to a 3½- or 4-quart electric slow cooker. Cover and cook on low-heat setting for 10 to 12 hours or on high-heat setting for 4 to 5 hours.

Each serving: 245 cal., 3 g total fat (1 g sat. fat), 5 mg chol., 882 mg sodium, 47 g carbo., 9 g fiber, 10 g pro. Daily Values: 5% vit. A, 13% vit. C, 10% calcium, 22% iron.

Slow-Simmered Pork Sandwiches with Roasted Tomato-Jalapeño Vinaigrette

Like coffee beans, cumin seeds retain more flavor when kept whole and ground just before use. Toasting further enhances the flavor.

PREP: 40 minutes **COOK:** 4½ hours on high; 9 hours on low

- 1 4-lb. boneless pork shoulder roast
- 5 tsp. cumin seeds, toasted*
- 2 Tbsp. packed brown sugar
- 1 tsp. kosher salt or ¾ tsp. salt
- ½ tsp. cayenne pepper
- ½ tsp. ground black pepper
- 1 medium onion, sliced
- 3 cloves garlic, minced
- 1 cup chicken broth
- 1 12-oz. can cola
- ¼ cup cooking oil
- 1 lb. roma tomatoes, cored, seeded, and chopped
- 1 12- to 16-oz. jar pickled jalapeño chile peppers or jalapeño chile pepper slices
- ⅔ cup coarsely snipped fresh cilantro
- 1 tsp. kosher salt or ¾ tsp. salt
- ¼ tsp. ground black pepper
- 12 hoagie buns, Mexican torta rolls, or other hard rolls, split and toasted, if desired
- 2 limes, cut into wedges

1. Trim fat from meat. Remove netting, if present. If necessary, cut meat into 2 or 3 pieces that will fit into a 3½- to 5-quart electric slow cooker; set aside. Use a mortar and pestle or a blender to grind cumin seeds. In a small bowl combine the cumin seeds, brown sugar, the 1 teaspoon salt, the cayenne pepper, and ½ teaspoon black pepper. Rub mixture onto meat.

2. In the slow cooker combine onion and garlic; add meat. Pour broth and cola over meat. Cover and cook on low-heat setting for 9 to 10 hours or on high-heat setting for 4½ to 5 hours or until meat is fork tender.

3. Meanwhile, in a large skillet heat the oil over medium heat. Add tomatoes and cook, uncovered, for 4 minutes, stirring occasionally. Drain jalapeños, reserving ½ cup juice; set jalapeños aside. Add reserved juice to tomatoes along with cilantro, 1 teaspoon salt, and ¼ teaspoon black pepper. Bring to boiling; reduce heat. Cook, uncovered, 3 to 4 minutes more or until slightly thickened, stirring occasionally; set aside.

4. Use a slotted spoon to transfer meat from liquid to cutting board; remove onions with a slotted spoon and discard remaining liquid. Shred meat; stir onion into shredded meat mixture.

5. To assemble, spoon meat and tomato mixture onto split buns. Serve with jalapeños and lime wedges. Makes 12 servings.

***NOTE:** To toast cumin seeds, place seeds in small skillet. Cook over medium heat about 2 minutes or until fragrant, shaking pan occasionally to toast seeds evenly.

Each serving: 683 cal., 22 g total fat (6 g sat. fat), 98 mg chol., 1,354 mg sodium, 80 g carbo., 5 g fiber, 42 g pro. Daily Values: 10% vit. A, 26% vit. C, 16% calcium, 37% iron.

Slow-Simmered Pork Sandwiches with Roasted Tomato-Jalapeño Vinaigrette

Her friends insist that dinner in the garden is such a memorable event because of the way Carrie pays attention to the smallest details. For Carrie, "It's about the bonding and laughing and spending time together."

Sweet Corn, Red Pepper, and Cheese Salad

Bacon-Avocado Deviled Eggs

Bacon-Avocado Deviled Eggs

Deviled eggs are traditional favorites for outdoor summer gatherings. This innovative variation makes a great thing even better.

START TO FINISH: 45 minutes

- 12 **eggs**
- 5 **slices thick-sliced bacon, chopped**
- 1/2 **cup mayonnaise**
- 1 **Tbsp. grainy (country) Dijon-style mustard**
- 2 **tsp. caper juice**
- **Few dashes bottled hot pepper sauce**
- 1/4 **tsp. ground black pepper**
- 1 **ripe but firm avocado, halved, seeded, and peeled**
- 2 **tsp. lemon juice**
- **Snipped fresh chives (optional)**

1. Place eggs in a single layer in a large saucepan or 4-quart Dutch oven. Add enough cold water to just cover the eggs. Bring to a rapid boil over high heat (water will have large rapidly breaking bubbles). Remove from heat; cover. Let stand for 15 minutes; drain. Run cold water over eggs or place in ice water until cool enough to handle; drain. Peel eggs; slice in half lengthwise. Remove yolks; place in a medium bowl. Set whites aside.

2. Meanwhile, cook bacon in a small skillet over medium heat until crisp. Drain on paper towels; set aside.

3. Use a fork to mash egg yolks. Stir in mayonnaise, mustard, caper juice, hot pepper sauce, and black pepper until combined.

4. Chop the avocado into 1/2-inch pieces; toss with lemon juice. Place pieces of avocado in the hollow of each egg white. Spoon or pipe egg yolk mixture into egg white halves. Sprinkle with bacon pieces, any remaining avocado pieces, and snipped chives. Cover and chill for up to 4 hours. Makes 24 servings.

Each serving: 109 cal., 9 g total fat (2 g sat. fat), 110 mg chol., 112 mg sodium, 1 g carbo., 0 g fiber, 4 g pro. Daily Values: 4% vit. A, 1% vit. C, 1% calcium, 2% iron.

CUTTING KERNELS

To cut kernels from a fresh ear of corn, place the cob on a steady surface and saw downward with a sharp knife.

FILLING EGGS

Use one teaspoon to scoop the egg yolk mixture and another to gently push the mixture into the halved egg whites.

Sweet Corn, Red Pepper, and Cheese Salad

This recipe also works with frozen corn; cook it briefly, then chill.

START TO FINISH: 40 minutes

- 8 **ears of sweet corn**
- 2/3 **cup finely chopped red sweet pepper**
- 8 **oz. manchego, Teleme, or Monterey Jack cheese with jalapeño peppers, cut into 1/4-inch cubes**
- 1 **recipe Sherry Vinaigrette (below)**
- 2 **Tbsp. snipped fresh flat-leaf parsley**
- **Salt or kosher salt**
- **Ground black pepper**

1. Remove husks from ears of corn. Scrub ears with a stiff brush to remove silks; rinse. Cut kernels from cobs; scrape cobs with knife to release juices. In a large bowl combine corn and juices, sweet pepper, and cheese. Prepare Sherry Vinaigrette; add to corn mixture. Stir gently to coat; stir in parsley. Season to taste with salt and pepper. Makes 12 servings.

SHERRY VINAIGRETTE: In a medium mixing bowl combine 3 tablespoons sherry wine vinegar, 2 teaspoons Dijon-style mustard, and 1/2 teaspoon salt or kosher salt; whisk until smooth. Gradually add 2/3 cup extra-virgin olive oil, whisking constantly until dressing thickens slightly. Season to taste with ground black pepper. Cover and chill for up to 3 days. Makes about 3/4 cup.

Each serving: 233 cal., 18 g total fat (5 g sat. fat), 17 mg chol., 209 mg sodium, 12 g carbo., 2 g fiber, 7 g pro. Daily Values: 17% vit. A, 35% vit. C, 14% calcium, 3% iron.

SKEWER ART

Carrie suggests spearing the fruit so it rests toward the blunt end of the skewer. This keeps the sharp end free for poking into more fruit, as well as making the fruit on the skewer safer to eat.

Fruit Wands

There's an art to making great fruit skewers; use a few fruit varieties, but vary shapes and sizes for maximum visual and flavor impact.

START TO FINISH: 30 minutes

- **8 cups assorted fresh fruit, such as kiwifruit pieces, strawberry halves, watermelon chunks, and/or thin honeydew melon strips**
- **2 cups Crème Fraîche, (page 208)**
- **1/4 cup snipped fresh herbs, such as lemon verbena or basil**
- **Raw sugar**

1. On eight 8- to 10-inch skewers thread some of the fruit. Place any remaining fruit in a serving bowl.

2. For dip, in a small bowl stir together Crème Fraîche and herb. Serve fruit with crème fraîche dip. Makes 8 servings.

Each serving: 242 cal., 18 g total fat (11 g sat. fat), 54 mg chol., 31 mg sodium, 21 g carbo., 2 g fiber, 2 g pro. Daily Values: 20% vit. A, 63% vit. C, 7% calcium, 3% iron.

Trilevel Brownies

Who doesn't love chocolate and brownies? This recipe boasts three sweet layers—a chewy oatmeal cookie crust, a fudgy layer, and a creamy frosting—for one solid-gold treat.

PREP: 15 minutes **BAKE:** 35 minutes

- **1 cup quick-cooking rolled oats**
- **1/2 cup all-purpose flour**
- **1/2 cup packed brown sugar**
- **1/4 tsp. baking soda**
- **1/2 cup butter, melted**
- **1 egg**
- **3/4 cup granulated sugar**
- **2/3 cup all-purpose flour**
- **1/4 cup milk**
- **1/4 cup butter, melted**
- **1 oz. unsweetened chocolate, melted and cooled**
- **1 tsp. vanilla**
- **1/4 tsp. baking powder**
- **1/2 cup chopped walnuts**
- **1 oz. unsweetened chocolate**
- **2 Tbsp. butter**
- **1 1/2 cups sifted powdered sugar**
- **1/2 tsp. vanilla**
- **Walnut halves (optional)**

1. Preheat oven to 350° F. For the bottom layer, stir together oats, the 1/2 cup flour, the brown sugar, and baking soda. Stir in the 1/2 cup melted butter. Pat mixture onto the bottom of an ungreased 11×7×1 1/2-inch baking pan. Bake for 10 minutes.

2. Meanwhile, for the middle layer, beat egg; stir in granulated sugar, the 2/3 cup flour, the milk, the 1/4 cup melted butter, the 1 ounce melted chocolate, the 1 teaspoon vanilla, and the baking powder until smooth. Fold in chopped walnuts. Spread batter evenly over baked layer in pan. Bake for 25 minutes more. Place on a wire rack while preparing top layer.

3. For the top layer, in a medium saucepan heat and stir the 1 ounce chocolate and the 2 tablespoons butter until melted. Stir in the powdered sugar and the 1/2 teaspoon vanilla. Stir in enough hot water (1 to 2 tablespoons) to make a mixture that is almost pourable. Spread onto brownies. If desired, garnish with walnut halves. Cool in pan on a wire rack. Cut into bars. Makes 24 brownies.

Each brownie: 199 cal., 11 g total fat (6 g sat. fat), 28 mg chol., 96 mg sodium, 25 g carbo., 1 g fiber, 2 g pro. Daily Values: 6% vit. A, 2% calcium, 4% iron.

WAYS WITH WATERMELON

The reverse twist from using watermelon to hold skewers *(above)* is to hollow it into a bowl or basket. This makes a decorative vessel for foods such as salads and bite-sized fruits and veggies. Reserve some of the watermelon to shape into balls, freezing them for several hours in a single layer on a cookie sheet. The frozen fruit is delicious added to cold drinks, including teas, lemonades, and sweet sparkling wines.

Polka-Dot Angel Food Cupcakes

Polka-Dot Angel Food Cupcakes

The berries become unexpected bursts of jamlike flavor in these light popovers or cupcakes. The popover version is pictured on the cover.

PREP: 1 hour **BAKE:** 15 minutes

- 1½ cups egg whites (10 to 12)
- 1 cup sifted cake flour
- ½ cup sugar
- 1½ tsp. cream of tartar
- 1 tsp. vanilla
- ½ tsp. almond extract
- ½ tsp. salt
- ¾ cup sugar
- 1 cup assorted fresh red raspberries, blueberries, blackberries, and strawberries, diced

1. In a very large mixing bowl let egg whites stand at room temperature for 30 minutes. Meanwhile, sift cake flour and ½ cup sugar together 3 times; set aside. Grease 12 popover pans, if using. Line popover pans or 12 jumbo (3¼-inch) muffin cups with large paper bake cups. Preheat oven to 350° F.

2. Add cream of tartar, vanilla, almond extract, and salt to egg whites. Beat with an electric mixer on medium speed until soft peaks form (tips curl). Gradually add ¾ cup sugar, about 2 tablespoons at a time, beating until stiff peaks form (tips stand straight).

3. Sift one-fourth of the cake flour mixture over beaten egg whites; fold in gently. Repeat, folding in the remaining flour mixture by fourths.

4. Spoon half of the batter into popover or muffin pans, filling about half full. Sprinkle a few berry pieces onto each, then top with another large dollop of batter and remaining berries. Mound remaining batter over fruit pieces (the cups will be very full).

5. Bake for 15 to 18 minutes or until tops are golden and spring back when lightly touched. Cool on a wire rack in the pan. To remove, run a knife around edges. If desired, wrap with new paper bake cups and tie with ribbon. Makes 12 cupcakes.

Each cupcake: 134 cal., 0 g total fat (0 g sat. fat), 0 mg chol., 143 mg sodium, 29 g carbo., 1 g fiber, 4 g pro. Daily Values: 2% vit. C, 4% iron.

SUMMER PICNIC

Bacon-Avocado Deviled Eggs *(page 213)*
Sweet Corn, Red Pepper, and Cheese Salad *(page 213)*
Slow-Simmered Pork Sandwiches with Roasted Tomato-Jalapeño Vinaigrette *(page 210)*
Polka-Dot Angel Food Cupcakes *(above)*
Hibiscus Tea or Lavender Coolers *(page 218)*

Fudge Ribbon Pie

This pie, with its combination of rich chocolate sauce, refreshing peppermint ice cream, and airy meringue, is sure to dazzle and impress. If making a meringue sounds too fussy, replace the meringue topping with sweetened whipped cream.

PREP: 50 minutes **BAKE:** 3 minutes **FREEZE:** Several hours

- 1 cup sugar
- 1 5-oz. can (⅔ cup) evaporated milk
- 2 Tbsp. butter or margarine
- 2 oz. unsweetened chocolate, cut up
- 1 tsp. vanilla
- 2 pt. (4 cups) peppermint ice cream
- 1 9-inch baked pastry shell, cooled
- 1 recipe Peppermint Meringue (below)
- 1 Tbsp. crushed peppermint stick candy

1. For fudge sauce, in a small saucepan combine the 1 cup sugar, the evaporated milk, butter, and chocolate. Cook and stir over medium heat until bubbly. Reduce heat; boil gently for 4 to 5 minutes, stirring occasionally, until thickened and reduced to 1½ cups. Remove from heat; stir in vanilla. If necessary, beat until smooth with wire whisk or rotary beater. Set aside to cool.

2. In a chilled bowl stir 1 pint of the ice cream until softened. Spread into cooled pastry shell. Cover with half of the cooled fudge sauce. Freeze until nearly firm. Repeat with remaining ice cream and fudge sauce. Return to freezer.

3. Prepare Peppermint Meringue. Spread meringue onto fudge sauce layer, sealing to edge. Sprinkle with crushed candy. Freeze for several hours or overnight or until firm.

4. Preheat oven to 475° F. Bake frozen pie for 3 to 4 minutes or just until meringue is golden. Cover loosely; freeze for a few hours or overnight before serving. Makes 8 servings.

PEPPERMINT MERINGUE: In a medium mixing bowl dissolve ¾ cup sugar in ½ cup boiling water. Cool to room temperature. Add ¼ cup meringue powder. Beat on low speed until combined; beat on high speed until stiff peaks form (tips stand straight). By hand, fold 3 tablespoons crushed peppermint stick candy into the meringue.

Each serving: 564 cal., 24 g total fat (12 g sat. fat), 43 mg chol., 198 mg sodium, 83 g carbo., 2 g fiber, 6 g pro. Daily Values: 3% vit. A, 1% vit. C, 10% calcium, 7% iron.

Lavender Cooler

Look for unsprayed, organic lavender flowers in health food stores, or purchase them either online at www.matanzascreek.com or by calling 800/590-6464.

PREP: 30 minutes **COOL:** 2 hours

- **3 cups sugar**
- **3 cups water**
- **½ cup dried lavender flowers**
- **4 cups lemon juice**
- **8 cups cold water**
- **Ice**
- **Sprigs of Spanish lavender or other edible flowers (optional)**

1. For syrup, in a medium saucepan combine sugar and the 3 cups water. Bring to boiling; reduce heat, stirring often until the sugar is dissolved.

2. Place lavender flowers in a large bowl. Pour syrup over dried flowers. Let cool to room temperature.

3. Strain the syrup through a fine sieve, pressing the flowers with the back of a wooden spoon to extract all the liquid. Cover and chill for up to 1 week.

4. To serve, in a very large pitcher or crock measure 4 cups of the syrup. Add the lemon juice and 8 cups cold water. Stir to combine. Serve over ice in tall glasses. If desired, garnish with sprigs of lavender. Makes about 20 servings.

Each serving: 124 cal., 0 g total fat (0 g sat. fat), 0 mg chol., 5 mg sodium, 33 g carbo., 0 g fiber, 0 g pro. Daily Values: 37% vit. C, 1% calcium.

Watermelon Lemonade

The sweetness of watermelon along with a splash of apple juice make this version of lemonade unexpectedly delightful.

PREP: 10 minutes

- **2 cups cubed watermelon, seeded**
- **½ cup apple or white grape juice**
- **⅓ cup lemon or lime juice**
- **1 to 2 Tbsp. honey**

1. In a blender combine watermelon, apple juice, lemon juice, and honey. Cover and blend until smooth. Serve over ice in tall glasses. Makes 2 to 3 servings.

Each serving: 120 cal., 1 g total fat (0 g sat. fat), 0 mg chol., 6 mg sodium, 30 g carbo., 1 g fiber, 1 g pro. Daily Values: 11% vit. A, 56% vit. C, 2% calcium, 3% iron.

Hibiscus Tea

Find hibiscus, also called Flor de Jamaica, in the Mexican section of supermarkets, Latin markets, and health food stores.

PREP: 10 minutes **COOL:** 2 hours

- **1 medium lemon**
- **1 medium orange**
- **2 cups dried hibiscus flowers**
- **1 cup sugar**
- **6 inches stick cinnamon**
- **12 whole cloves**
- **4 cardamom pods or ¼ tsp. ground cardamom**
- **12 cups boiling water**
- **Ice**
- **Lemon wedges**

1. Using a vegetable peeler, remove the peel from the lemon and orange. In a large bowl combine lemon peel, orange peel, hibiscus flowers, sugar, cinnamon sticks, cloves, and cardamom pods. Add boiling water and stir. Let cool to room temperature.

2. Strain tea into a pitcher and serve. Or cover and chill for up to 24 hours. Serve over ice in tall glasses. Garnish with lemon wedges. Makes 12 servings.

Each serving: 62 cal., 0 g total fat (0 g sat. fat), 0 mg chol., 7 mg sodium, 16 g carbo., 0 g fiber, 0 g pro.

Lime-Pineapple Punch

Make the syrup for this punch ahead of time. But once you add the sherbet and carbonated beverage, serve it right away.

PREP: 10 minutes **CHILL:** 4 hours

- **1 cup sugar**
- **2 cups water**
- **2 tsp. finely shredded lime peel**
- **½ cup lime juice (about 4 limes)**
- **1 pt. lime sherbet**
- **1 pt. pineapple sherbet**
- **3½ cups lemon-lime carbonated beverage, chilled**

1. In a medium saucepan, combine sugar and 1 cup of the water; cook and stir until sugar is dissolved. Add the remaining 1 cup water and the lime peel and juice. Cover and chill for at least 4 hours.

2. Before serving, strain syrup mixture. Pour strained mixture into a chilled punch bowl; add scoops of lime sherbet and pineapple sherbet, stirring until partially melted. Slowly pour in carbonated beverage, stirring with up-and-down motion. Serve punch immediately. Makes about 10 servings.

Each serving: 240 cal., 2 g total fat (1 g sat. fat), 4 mg chol., 63 mg sodium, 57 g carbo., 0 g fiber, 1 g pro. Daily Values: 12% vit. C, 4% calcium, 1% iron.

Hibiscus Tea and Lavender Cooler

Country French Ribeyes

WHAT'S THE CUT?

LOOK FOR STANDARD INDUSTRY CUT NAMES ON MEAT LABELS. HERE ARE A FEW CLUES FOR CLARIFICATION.

It's a familiar scene: Your recipe calls for a certain cut of beef and the butcher in your new neighborhood gives you a blank stare. "Never heard of it," he says. Chances are, that cut of meat is simply known by a different name than the one you've used before. Across the country, the names of meat cuts vary from region to region.

For example, a Kansas City steak and New York strip steak are the same cut. Until recently, asking for Kansas City steak in Kansas City or a New York strip steak in New York earned you only a blank stare. Regardless of your location, a top loin steak is what you want.

Look for beef short plate in Chicago, and you'll get skirt steak. Order skirt steak in other parts of the Midwest, and the butcher-paper-wrapped package may bear the label "steak for fajitas." You'll also find skirt steak labeled as Philadelphia steak or London broil. London broil has nothing to do with London or skirt steak. It's a recipe name for marinated flank steak, so purchase flank steak when you want London broil.

Don't let Swiss steak fool you. It has no relation to bank accounts, the Alps, or Heidi and her goats. The name is said to originate in Britain, where "swissing" is a method of smoothing bolts of cloth with huge rollers. When you want Swiss steak, look for beef chuck arm steak, round steak, or steak for swissing—meaning the meat is intended to be pounded thin.

Swiss Steak

With this version of Swiss Steak, you can choose the cooking method—range-top or oven—that best fits your schedule.

PREP: 25 minutes **COOK:** 1¼ hours

- 1 lb. boneless beef round steak, cut ¾ inch thick
- 2 Tbsp. all-purpose flour
- ¼ tsp. salt
- ¼ tsp. ground black pepper
- 1 Tbsp. cooking oil
- 1 14½-oz. can diced tomatoes with basil, oregano, and garlic, undrained
- 1 small onion, sliced and separated into rings
- ½ cup sliced celery (1 stalk)
- ½ cup sliced carrot (1 medium)
- 2 cups hot cooked noodles or mashed potatoes

1. Trim fat from meat. Cut into 4 serving-size pieces. Combine flour, salt, and pepper. Use the notched side of a meat mallet to pound the flour mixture into the meat.

2. In a large skillet brown meat on both sides in hot oil. Drain off fat. Add undrained tomatoes, onion, celery, and carrot. Bring to boiling; reduce heat. Simmer, covered, about 1¼ hours or until meat is tender. Skim off fat. Serve with noodles or mashed potatoes. Makes 4 main-dish servings.

OVEN DIRECTIONS: Prepare and brown meat in skillet as above. Transfer meat to a 2-quart casserole. In the same skillet combine undrained tomatoes, onion, celery, and carrot. Bring mixture to boiling, scraping up any browned bits. Pour over meat. Cover and bake in a 350° F oven about 1 hour or until tender. Serve as above.

Each serving: 340 cal., 9 g total fat (2 g sat. fat), 82 mg chol., 459 mg sodium, 35 g carbo., 3 g fiber, 28 g pro. Daily Values: 78% vit. A, 26% vit. C, 7% calcium, 26% iron.

FATHER'S DAY DINNER

Country French Ribeyes *(right)*
Steak Fries *(right)*
Coleslaw
Macaroon Fruit Tart *(page 547)*
Iced coffee

Country French Ribeyes

Harvested abundantly in the French region of Provence, lavender is a key ingredient in the seasoning blend known as herbes de Provence. When used as a rub, as it is here, lavender imbues meats with an enticing flavor and aroma that is at once herbal and floral.

PREP: 5 minutes **GRILL:** 16 minutes

- 5 green onions
- 2 tsp. dried lavender, crushed
- 2 tsp. dried thyme, crushed
- 1 tsp. ground black pepper
- ½ tsp. ground rock sea salt or coarse salt
- 4 6- to 8-oz. beef ribeye steaks, cut 1 inch thick
- 1 Tbsp. olive oil
- 4 to 8 roma tomatoes
- 1 recipe Steak Fries (below) (optional)

1. Clean and trim green onions. Finely chop 1 green onion; set remaining onions aside. In a small bowl combine chopped onion, lavender, thyme, pepper, and salt. Rub mixture onto steaks. Brush steaks with half of the olive oil. Brush tomatoes and remaining green onions with remaining olive oil.

2. Place steaks on the lightly-oiled rack of a grill directly over medium-high heat. Grill for 8 to 10 minutes. Place tomatoes and onions on grill. Turn steaks; grill 8 to 10 minutes more or until desired doneness. Grill tomatoes and onions for 8 to 10 minutes or until slightly charred, turning several times. If desired, serve steaks with Steak Fries. Makes 4 servings.

STEAK FRIES: Slice 2 medium potatoes into ¼-inch-thick wedges. In a large mixing bowl toss potatoes with 2 teaspoons olive oil. Add seasoned salt to taste; stir. Fold a 36×18-inch piece of heavy foil in half to form an 18-inch square. Arrange potatoes evenly in center of square. Bring up opposite edges of foil; seal with a double fold. Place packet on the rack of a grill directly over medium heat. Grill for 25 minutes or until potatoes are tender.

Each serving: 433 cal., 18 g total fat (5 g sat. fat), 94 mg chol., 422 mg sodium, 18 g carbo., 3 g fiber, 46 g pro. Daily Values: 19% vit. A, 5% vit. C, 48% calcium, 29% iron.

Simple Salmon Spread

SOCKEYE SALMON

Look at this old friend in a new way. Once thought of only as a convenient food-budget stretcher, canned red sockeye salmon does an amazing Cinderella act when it's wearing the right glass slipper. For example, Simple Salmon Spread is an elegant party starter that pulls together in minutes. Cool, crunchy kohlrabi slices, endive leaves, or daikon rounds partner well with the spread's slightly grainy texture; celery is a nice option too.

Before using canned sockeye salmon, drain it well, remove the skin, and be sure to pick out the little bones—a necessary but quick job. Flake fish into large pieces before adding to your recipe. Sockeye salmon can be a little salty, so adjust the salt level in your recipe to suit your personal taste.

Simple Salmon Spread

Anchovy paste adds maximum depth of flavor to this dish. For a slightly less salty spread, however, feel free to omit it.

START TO FINISH: 20 minutes

- 1 14¾-oz. can red sockeye salmon, drained, skin and bones removed
- ¼ cup snipped oil-packed dried tomatoes, drained
- 2 Tbsp. lemon juice
- 2 Tbsp. mayonnaise
- 2 cloves garlic, minced
- 1 tsp. capers, drained
- 1 tsp. anchovy paste (optional)
- ¼ tsp. ground white pepper

1. In a food processor*, combine all ingredients. Cover; process until smooth, adding additional mayonnaise, if necessary, for desired consistency. Transfer mixture to a serving dish. Cover; chill for up to 24 hours. Makes about 1¾ cups.

***NOTE:** If you don't have a food processor, combine ingredients in a medium bowl and mash with a potato masher until combined, adding additional mayonnaise, if necessary, for desired consistency.

Each serving: 67 cal., 4 g total fat (1 g sat. fat), 12 mg chol., 189 mg sodium, 1 g carbo., 0 g fiber, 6 g pro. Daily Values: 2% vit. A, 5% vit. C, 8% calcium, 2% iron.

Salmon-Sauced Mostaccioli

PREP: 15 minutes **COOK:** 15 minutes

- 8 oz. dried mostaccioli or rigatoni (about 3 cups)
- 1 small green or red sweet pepper, cut into bite-size strips
- ½ cup chopped onion (1 medium)
- 2 Tbsp. butter or margarine
- 1½ cups chicken broth
- 2 tsp. snipped fresh dill or ½ tsp. dried dill
- ½ cup plain low-fat yogurt
- 3 Tbsp. all-purpose flour
- 1 15½-oz. can salmon, drained, broken into large chunks, and skin and bones removed
- 2 Tbsp. snipped fresh parsley

1. Cook pasta according to package directions. Drain pasta and keep it warm.

2. Meanwhile, for sauce, in a medium saucepan cook sweet pepper and onion in hot butter until tender but not brown. Stir in 1 cup of the broth and the dill. Bring to boiling; reduce heat. Stir together remaining ½ cup broth, the yogurt, and flour. Add yogurt mixture to saucepan. Cook and stir until thickened and bubbly. Cook and stir for 1 minute more. Gently stir in salmon; heat through. Serve sauce over hot pasta. Sprinkle with parsley. Makes 4 servings.

Each serving: 471 cal., 13 g total fat (6 g sat. fat), 78 mg chol., 964 mg sodium, 53 g carbo., 2 g fiber, 30 g pro. Daily Values: 9% vit. A, 30% vit. C, 9% calcium, 20% iron.

DELIVER THE (CANNED) GOODS

With its firm and delicious red flesh, wild Pacific red sockeye salmon has long been a favorite variety of salmon for canning. In addition to the recipes here, try it as a flavorful substitute for canned tuna in recipes. Here are a few more quick ideas to help you start enjoying canned sockeye's incredible versatility:

- Asian Salmon Salad: Combine canned red sockeye salmon with mayonnaise, sliced green onion, sliced bok choy, crushed red pepper, unsalted roasted peanuts, and peanut sauce.
- New Salmon Cakes: Substitute canned red sockeye salmon for the crab in your favorite crab cake recipe. Cook until golden brown and heated through; serve with lemon wedges and tartar sauce.

Salmon Mousse

PREP: 30 minutes **CHILL:** 4½ hours

- 1 14¾- to 15½-oz. can red salmon
- 2 envelopes unflavored gelatin
- 1 tsp. sugar
- 1¼ cups mayonnaise or salad dressing
- ¼ cup tomato sauce
- 2 Tbsp. lemon juice
- 2 tsp. Worcestershire sauce
- ½ cup finely chopped celery
- 2 hard-cooked eggs, chopped
- 2 Tbsp. snipped fresh chives
- ¼ tsp. ground black pepper
- ½ cup whipping cream
- Lettuce leaves
- Thin cucumber slices
- Assorted crackers

1. Chill a small bowl and beaters of electric mixer. Drain salmon, reserving the liquid. Bone and flake salmon; set aside. Add enough water to the reserved salmon liquid to equal 1 cup; pour into a small saucepan. Sprinkle unflavored gelatin and sugar over the salmon liquid mixture; let stand for 3 minutes to soften gelatin. Heat over medium-low heat until gelatin is dissolved, stirring constantly. Remove from heat.

2. In a large bowl combine mayonnaise, tomato sauce, lemon juice, and Worcestershire sauce; stir in gelatin mixture. Chill until partially set, about 30 minutes. Fold in salmon, celery, chopped hard-cooked eggs, chives, and pepper.

3. In chilled bowl beat cream with chilled beaters until soft peaks form; fold into gelatin mixture. Pour into a 6-cup fish-shape or ring mold. Cover and chill until firm, about 4 hours.

4. To serve, line a tray with lettuce. Unmold mousse onto tray. Serve with cucumber slices and crackers. Makes 16 servings.

Each serving: 211 cal., 20 g total fat (4 g sat. fat), 58 mg chol., 280 mg sodium, 2 g carbo., 0 g fiber, 7 g pro. Daily Values: 6% vit. A, 4% vit. C, 8% calcium, 3% iron.

Really Red Coleslaw

PICNIC SALADS

The first promise of a warm summer day gets us right into the mood: Let's eat outside! The park, the beach, the backyard, the bike trail—they're all beckoning for an impromptu outdoor feast. Here are six essential picnic salads you can toss together in less time than it takes to plan where to go.

You won't need gourmet ingredients—the recipes call for readily available items, such as convenient bagged slaws or jarred stir-ins—but the flavors are anything but ordinary. Cabbage slaw dresses up in a single color with a blend of textures; pineapple salad revs up with a dash of heat; macaroni salad trades its mayonnaise base for pesto; and potato salad turns Thai. Best of all, you can make these salads ahead and chill until departure time if you have a premonition that the day may hold an outdoor adventure in store.

Really Red Coleslaw

Well, purple, actually, but you get the idea. Make sure you use a vinegar-and-oil-based dressing.

START TO FINISH: 15 minutes

- **1 10-oz. pkg. red cabbage slaw (about 6 cups)**
- **1 medium red onion, slivered (1 cup)**
- **½ cup dried tart red cherries**
- **½ cup red raspberry vinaigrette**
- **1 Tbsp. seedless red raspberry preserves**

1. In a large bowl combine slaw, red onion, and dried cherries; set aside. Combine vinaigrette and preserves; pour over slaw mixture and toss gently to coat. Serve at room temperature or chill for up to 6 hours. Makes 8 side-dish servings.

Each serving: 108 cal., 6 g total fat (1 g sat. fat), 0 mg chol., 5 mg sodium, 12 g carbo., 1 g fiber, 1 g pro. Daily Values: 1% vit. A, 36% vit. C, 2% calcium, 1% iron.

GET THERE, STAY THERE, EAT THERE

Packing and serving picnic fare in a food-safe manner is essential for a happy and healthy outing. Follow these guidelines:

- Move salads directly from the refrigerator to the cooler. To avoid a soggy lettuce salad, pack dressings and ingredients separately, then toss together at the picnic site.
- Place cooked meats and raw items for the barbecue, as well as items more likely to be used last, on the bottom of the cooler close to the cooling source.
- Pack the cooler with ice packs or blocks of ice; they last longer than ice cubes. Once the cooler is packed, avoid opening it as much as possible.
- The shadier the spot you find to set up your picnic, the better. Foods will warm up quickly when placed in the hot sun, even if they are in a cooler.
- Remove foods from coolers as close as possible to the time you plan to eat. Rather than setting out all the food at once, put out starters first, then main courses and side dishes, and desserts last. If possible, set salads and other foods in bowls of ice for serving.
- Dispose of any leftover foods on-site. Food that still looks appealing but was exposed to sunshine and warm temperatures for more than one hour can be harmful.

Hot-and-Sweet Pineapple Slaw

Hot-and-Sweet Pineapple Slaw

PREP: 10 minutes **CHILL:** 1 hour

- **1 16-oz. pkg. shredded broccoli (broccoli slaw mix)**
- **2 cups fresh pineapple chunks or one 20-oz. can pineapple chunks, drained**
- **2 cups broccoli florets**
- **½ cup mayonnaise or salad dressing**
- **1 to 2 Tbsp. adobo sauce from canned chipotle peppers in adobo sauce**
- **¼ tsp. salt**

1. Rinse and drain shredded broccoli; dry thoroughly. In a bowl combine shredded broccoli, pineapple, and broccoli florets. In a small bowl stir together mayonnaise, adobo sauce, and salt. Add mayonnaise mixture to broccoli mixture. Toss gently to coat. Cover and chill for 1 to 4 hours. Toss before serving. Makes 10 side-dish servings.

Each serving: 112 cal., 11 g total fat (1 g sat. fat), 6 mg chol., 145 mg sodium, 7 g carbo., 2 g fiber, 2 g pro. Daily Values: 20% vit. A, 106% vit. C, 3% calcium, 4% iron.

Pesto Macaroni Salad

To add even more freshness and flavor, you stir an extra dose of basil into the salad before chilling and serving.

START TO FINISH: 30 minutes

- 3 cups dried elbow macaroni
- 5 oz. fresh green beans, trimmed and cut into 1-inch pieces (about 1 cup)
- 1 lb. small fresh mozzarella balls, drained and sliced
- 1 7-oz. container purchased refrigerated basil pesto
- 1/2 cup fresh basil leaves, torn
- 1/2 tsp. salt

1. Cook macaroni according to package directions; drain. Rinse with cold water; drain again. In a saucepan cook green beans, covered, in a small amount of boiling lightly salted water for 10 to 15 minutes or until crisp-tender; drain. Rinse with cold water; drain again.

2. In a large bowl combine macaroni, green beans, mozzarella, and pesto. Stir in basil and salt. Cover and chill for up to 2 hours before serving. Makes 14 side-dish servings.

Each serving: 249 cal., 14 g total fat (4 g sat. fat), 26 mg chol., 255 mg sodium, 20 g carbo., 1 g fiber, 11 g pro. Daily Values: 8% vit. A, 18% vit. C, 18% calcium, 5% iron.

Southwestern-Style Three-Bean Salad

PREP: 20 minutes **CHILL:** 3 hours

- 1 15-oz. can garbanzo beans, rinsed and drained
- 1 15-oz. can black beans, rinsed and drained
- 1 15-oz. can red kidney beans, rinsed and drained
- 1 cup thinly sliced celery
- 3/4 cup chopped red onion
- 1 recipe Cilantro Lime Dressing (below)

1. In a large mixing bowl stir together garbanzo beans, black beans, kidney beans, celery, and onion.

2. Prepare Cilantro Lime Dressing; pour over bean mixture. Toss gently to coat. Cover and chill for 3 to 24 hours, stirring occasionally. Serve with a slotted spoon. Makes 8 side-dish servings.

CILANTRO LIME DRESSING: In a screw-top jar combine 1/4 cup salad oil, 1/4 cup vinegar, 1 minced garlic clove, 2 tablespoons snipped fresh cilantro, 2 tablespoons lime juice, 1 tablespoon sugar, 1/2 teaspoon chili powder, 1/2 teaspoon ground cumin, and 1/4 teaspoon salt. Cover and shake well.

Each serving: 202 cal., 8 g total fat (1 g sat. fat), 0 mg chol., 562 mg sodium, 27 g carbo., 9 g fiber, 9 g pro. Daily Values: 3% vit. A, 9% vit. C, 7% calcium, 11% iron.

Thai Beef-Potato Salad

PREP: 20 minutes **CHILL:** 4 hours

- 2 20-oz. pkg. refrigerated diced potatoes with onions
- Cooking oil
- 1/2 lb. medium-rare deli roast beef, cut into thin strips
- 3/4 cup 1-inch bias-sliced green onion
- 1/2 tsp. salt
- 2/3 cup purchased Thai peanut sauce
- 1 large lime

1. In a very large skillet cook potatoes in hot oil according to package directions; cool slightly. In a large bowl combine potatoes, roast beef, green onion, and salt. Stir in peanut sauce.

2. Finely shred enough peel from lime to equal 1 tablespoon. Squeeze juice from lime. Add peel and 2 to 3 tablespoons lime juice to salad; stir gently. Cover; chill for 4 to 24 hours. Stir before serving. Makes 12 to 16 side-dish servings.

Each serving: 157 cal., 3 g total fat (1 g sat. fat), 13 mg chol., 473 mg sodium, 24 g carbo., 3 g fiber, 9 g pro. Daily Values: 1% vit. A, 21% vit. C, 1% calcium, 5% iron.

Citrus-Avocado Salad

START TO FINISH: 30 minutes

- 4 medium oranges
- 2 ruby red grapefruit
- 4 small ripe avocados, peeled and seeded
- 1/4 cup pomegranate seeds
- 1 recipe Celery Seed Dressing (below)
- 8 leaves red leaf lettuce

1. Peel and section the oranges and grapefruit, working over a bowl to catch juices; set juices aside. Reserve 24 orange sections; dice the remaining sections.

2. Slash rounded end of each avocado 3 times, cutting about three-quarters of the way to the opposite end each time. Turn flat sides up and insert an orange section in each slash. Brush avocados with reserved fruit juices. Heap diced oranges and grapefruit sections into avocados; garnish with pomegranate seeds. Prepare Celery Seed Dressing; serve over avocados on lettuce. (Chill any remaining dressing for another use.) Makes 8 side-dish servings.

CELERY SEED DRESSING: In a small mixing bowl, blender, or food processor combine 1/2 cup sugar, 1/3 cup lemon juice, 1 teaspoon celery seeds, 1 teaspoon dry mustard, 1 teaspoon paprika, and 1/2 teaspoon salt. With mixer, blender, or food processor running, slowly add 3/4 cup salad oil in a thin, steady stream. (This should take 2 to 3 minutes.) Continue mixing, blending, or processing until mixture reaches desired consistency. Makes about 1 1/4 cups.

Each serving: 335 cal., 28 g total fat (4 g sat. fat), 0 mg chol., 152 mg sodium, 23 g carbo., 4 g fiber, 2 g pro. Daily Values: 15% vit. A, 67% vit. C, 3% calcium, 5% iron.

Thai Beef-Potato Salad

TAKING CARE OF FRESH GREENS

Proper washing and storing of lettuce and other greens makes a big difference in how long they remain at peak freshness and flavor. This is crucial in summer, when high temperatures can accelerate their decline.

- First, remove and discard any leaves that are discolored, bruised, or wilted. Wash the greens under cold running water by separating the leaves from each other, then rinsing them in a colander.
- Next, get rid of any excess water—wet greens make soggy salads. Salad spinners can do a good job of drying greens as long as they are filled no more than two-thirds full—overfilling can cause the spinner to bruise the leaves. You can also place wet greens on a clean kitchen towel or several layers of paper towels to dry.
- To store, layer or wrap greens in a clean, dry kitchen towel or paper towels. Seal them in a resealable plastic bag or airtight container and chill for 30 minutes or up to several hours to crisp before serving.

Pesto Macaroni Salad

Chocolate Ice Cream Roll

A Chocolate-Coated HEART

Chocolate is good for your heart—according to researchers at the University of California at Davis who reviewed a number of studies. Single studies conducted previously have suggested this, but it's the first time the issue has been analyzed from a broad perspective. It appears that certain compounds in chocolate called flavan-3-ols are responsible for the decreased risk of cardiovascular disease among people who regularly eat chocolate. Flavan-3-ols are antioxidants that give chocolate most of its beloved flavor. Studies suggest that chocolate has an aspirinlike effect—it thins your blood slightly, reducing the inflammation that may lead to heart attacks and strokes. No one is recommending that you throw your aspirin away, but the American Dietetic Association (ADA) says that chocolate can be a part of a heart-healthy diet. The association does say you should take your "medicine" in moderation and make sure your diet includes other antioxidant-rich foods, such as fruits, vegetables, tea, and red wine.

Chocolate Ice Cream Roll

This do-ahead dessert is spectacular enough to serve as a grand finale to your most elegant dinner. (P.S.: Kids will like it too.)

BAKE: 12 minutes **FREEZE:** 4 hours

- 4 egg whites
- 1/3 cup all-purpose flour
- 1/4 cup unsweetened cocoa powder
- 1 tsp. baking powder
- 1/4 tsp. salt
- 4 egg yolks
- 1/2 tsp. vanilla
- 1/3 cup granulated sugar
- 1/2 cup granulated sugar
- Sifted powdered sugar
- 1 qt. fat-free vanilla ice cream, softened
- 1/4 cup broken pecans, toasted
- 1 recipe Raspberry Sauce (below) (optional)
- Fresh red raspberries (optional)
- Fresh mint sprigs (optional)

1. Let egg whites stand at room temperature for 30 minutes. Grease and flour a 15×10×1-inch baking pan. In a large bowl stir together flour, cocoa powder, baking powder, and salt. Set aside.

2. Preheat oven to 375° F. In a small mixing bowl beat egg yolks and vanilla with an electric mixer on high speed for 5 minutes or until lemon-colored. Gradually add the 1/3 cup sugar, beating on medium speed about 5 minutes or until sugar is almost dissolved. Wash and dry beaters.

3. In a large mixing bowl beat egg whites on high speed until soft peaks form (tips curl). Add the 1/2 cup sugar, beating until stiff peaks form (tips stand straight). Fold yolk mixture into egg white mixture. Sprinkle flour mixture over egg mixture; fold in gently. Spread batter into prepared pan.

4. Bake for 12 to 15 minutes or until top springs back when touched. Loosen edges of hot cake from pan; turn out onto a clean dish towel sprinkled with powdered sugar. Starting with a narrow end, roll up cake and towel together. Cool.

5. Unroll cake. Spread ice cream onto cake to within 1 inch of edges. Sprinkle with pecans. Reroll cake without towel. Wrap and freeze for at least 4 hours.

6. Meanwhile, prepare Raspberry Sauce, if desired. To serve, drizzle Raspberry Sauce onto 10 plates. Slice cake; place slices on plates. If desired, garnish with fresh raspberries and mint. Makes 10 servings.

RASPBERRY SAUCE: In a small saucepan combine 2/3 cup seedless red raspberry spreadable fruit, 1 tablespoon lemon juice, and 1/4 teaspoon almond extract; heat and stir until spreadable fruit is melted. Cool slightly.

Each serving: 214 cal., 4 g total fat (1 g sat. fat), 85 mg chol., 211 mg sodium, 37 g carbo., 0 g fiber, 7 g pro. Daily Values: 5% vit. A, 18% calcium, 4% iron.

CHOCOLATE TASTING TIPS

While all chocolate contains some heart-healthy compounds, dark chocolate has the most (with fewer calories than lighter varieties). No matter which kind you choose, the ADA offers these hints:

- Chocolate tastes best on an empty stomach. The delicate flavors of chocolate are easily overwhelmed by competing flavors.
- Serve chocolate at room temperature (66° to 77° F). If too hot, chocolate melts and separates. If too cold, the flavors deaden.
- Finally, let the chocolate linger in your mouth. Like wine, chocolate has a host of primary and secondary flavors. You'll eat less chocolate and it enjoy more if you slow down to savor all the nuances.

Chocolate-Cream Cheese Cupcakes

PREP: 15 minutes **BAKE:** 25 minutes **COOL:** 30 minutes

- 1/2 of an 8-oz. package fat-free cream cheese, softened
- 1 1/3 cups sugar
- 1/4 cup refrigerated or frozen egg product, thawed
- 1/3 cup miniature semisweet chocolate pieces
- 1 1/2 cups all-purpose flour
- 1/4 cup unsweetened cocoa powder
- 1 tsp. baking powder
- 1/4 tsp. baking soda
- 1/8 tsp. salt
- 1 cup water
- 1/3 cup cooking oil
- 1 Tbsp. vinegar
- 1 tsp. vanilla
- 1/2 cup low-fat granola

1. Line 18 muffin cups with paper bake cups; set aside.

2. In a small mixing bowl beat cream cheese with an electric mixer on medium speed until smooth. Add 1/3 cup of the sugar and the egg product. Beat on medium speed for 1 minute or until smooth. Stir in the semisweet chocolate pieces; set aside.

3. Preheat oven to 350° F. In a large mixing bowl stir together remaining 1 cup sugar, the flour, cocoa powder, baking powder, baking soda, and salt. Add water, oil, vinegar, and vanilla. Beat with an electric mixer on medium speed for 2 minutes, scraping sides of bowl occasionally. Spoon batter into the prepared muffin cups, filling each half full. Spoon about 1 tablespoon of the cream cheese mixture over each. Sprinkle with granola.

4. Bake for 25 to 30 minutes or until tops spring back when touched. Cool cupcakes in pan on a wire rack for 10 minutes. Remove cupcakes from pan; cool thoroughly on the wire rack. Makes 18 cupcakes.

Each serving: 162 cal., 5 g total fat (1 g sat. fat), 1 mg chol., 69 mg sodium, 27 g carbo., 1 g fiber, 3 g pro. Daily Values: 1% vit. A, 5% calcium, 5% iron.

A cherry jubilee

A BABY BLUE SKY THAT GOES ON AND ON AND ON. COMFY SOFT BLANKETS ON THE GRASS. A PLUMP DRIPPY SANDWICH NEARLY TOO BIG TO BITE. YOU KNOW WHAT IT ALL MEANS: AN OLD-FASHIONED OUTDOOR SUMMER FEAST.

Cheery Cherry-Lemon Cake

Tote the frosting separately in a cooler until you're ready to serve this lemony cake flecked with chopped cherries. Then just plop a big spoonful of the fluffy stuff onto each serving of cake and add a jaunty cherry.

PREP: 40 minutes **BAKE:** 30 minutes

- 1½ cups coarsely chopped pitted sweet cherries
- 2½ cups all-purpose flour
- 2½ tsp. baking powder
- ½ tsp. salt
- ¾ cup butter, softened
- 1¾ cups sugar
- 1½ tsp. vanilla
- 3 eggs
- 1¼ cups milk
- 2 tsp. finely shredded lemon peel
- 1 recipe Cream Cheese Frosting (below)
- Sweet cherries with stems (optional)
- Fresh mint leaves (optional)

1. Preheat oven to 375° F. Grease a 13×9×2-inch baking pan; set aside. Pat the coarsely chopped cherries as dry as possible with paper towels to prevent bleeding. In a medium bowl combine flour, baking powder, and salt; set aside.

2. In a large mixing bowl beat butter with an electric mixer on medium to high speed for 30 seconds. Add sugar and vanilla; beat until combined. Add eggs, one at a time, beating for 1 minute after each. Add dry mixture and milk alternately to beaten mixture, beating on low speed after each addition just until combined. Stir lemon peel into batter. Pour batter into the prepared pan. Sprinkle the chopped cherries evenly over top of batter. (The cherries will sink during baking.)

3. Bake for 30 to 35 minutes or until a wooden toothpick inserted near center comes out clean. Place cake in pan on a wire rack; cool thoroughly.

4. To serve, cut cake into 12 pieces. Top each piece with a generous dollop of Cream Cheese Frosting. If desired, add a cherry and mint leaf. Makes 12 large servings.

CREAM CHEESE FROSTING: In a large bowl combine one 8-ounce package cream cheese, softened; ⅔ cup butter, softened; 2 teaspoons finely shredded lemon peel; and 2 tablespoons lemon juice. Beat with an electric mixer on medium speed until light and fluffy. Gradually add 3 cups sifted powdered sugar, beating well. Gradually beat in about 1½ cups more sifted powdered sugar to reach a spooning consistency.

Each serving: 676 cal., 32 g total fat (20 g sat. fat), 138 mg chol., 498 mg sodium, 94 g carbo., 1 g fiber, 8 g pro. Daily Values: 26% vit. A, 8% vit. C, 12% calcium, 10% iron.

Hit-the-Spot Lemon Water

Hit-the-Spot Lemon Water

You'll be amazed at the subtle flavors that pop out when you soak lemons and fresh herbs in water for a few hours. It's pure, thirst-quenching goodness—no sugar needed.

PREP: 15 minutes **CHILL:** 1 hour

- 4 lemons, sliced
- 1½ cups firmly packed fresh mint or basil leaves
- 6 to 8 cups water
- 6 to 8 cups ice cubes
- Fresh mint or basil sprigs

1. Place lemon slices in a large pitcher. Carefully rub the 1½ cups mint or basil leaves between the palms of your hands to slightly bruise the leaves. Add to the pitcher with lemon. Pour in water. Cover and chill for 1 to 8 hours.

2. Strain lemon-water mixture. Discard herbs. Divide lemon slices and additional fresh mint or basil leaves equally among six to eight pint-sized canning jars (or plastic water bottles). For each serving, add 1 cup of ice cubes; fill with the lemon water. Add lids when transporting the jars. Makes 6 to 8 servings.

Each serving: 11 cal., 0 g total fat (0 g sat. fat), 0 mg chol., 8 mg sodium, 4 g carbo., 1 g fiber, 0 g pro. Daily Values: 34% vit. C, 1% calcium, 1% iron.

Potato Gnocchi Salad

Look for small fresh gnocchi in sealed plastic pouches.

PREP: 25 minutes **COOK:** 5 minutes **CHILL:** 4 hours

- **2 cups sugar snap peas (8 oz.), ends trimmed and halved crosswise**
- **8 oz. potato gnocchi or tiny new potatoes, quartered**
- **1/2 of a 4-oz. pkg. (1/2 cup) crumbled garlic-and-herb feta cheese**
- **1/4 cup thin wedges red onion**
- **1 recipe Herb Vinaigrette (below)**

1. In a large saucepan cook peas in lightly salted boiling water for 1 minute. Remove with slotted spoon; rinse and drain.

2. Add gnocchi to the boiling water in saucepan; cook according to package directions or until tender but firm. (Or, add potatoes to boiling water; cook, covered, for 10 minutes or until just tender.) Drain and rinse with cold water; drain again.

3. In a large bowl toss together sugar snap peas, gnocchi or potatoes, feta cheese, and onion. Cover and chill 4 to 24 hours.

4. Before serving, shake Herb Vinaigrette; pour over salad. Toss lightly to coat. Makes 8 servings.

HERB VINAIGRETTE: In a screw-top jar combine 3 tablespoons olive oil, 3 tablespoons lemon juice, 1 tablespoon snipped fresh dill, 1 tablespoon snipped fresh chives, 1/4 teaspoon salt, and 1/8 teaspoon pepper. Cover; chill. Makes 1/2 cup.

Each serving: 114 cal., 7 g total fat (2 g sat. fat), 6 mg chol., 282 mg sodium, 12 g carbo., 1 g fiber, 3 g pro. Daily Values: 1% vit. A, 19% vit. C, 4% calcium, 2% iron.

Cantaloupe and Tomato Salad

Carry the dressing and other ingredients in separate containers and keep them in the cooler. Toss everything together just before it's time to summon picnickers to the table.

PREP: 25 minutes

- **1/4 cup olive oil**
- **2 Tbsp. balsamic vinegar**
- **1 green onion, finely chopped**
- **1/4 tsp. salt**
- **1/4 tsp. pepper**
- **2 cups lightly packed watercress**
- **1 medium cantaloupe, halved, seeded, peeled, and cut into thin wedges**
- **2 cups red and/or yellow pear or cherry tomatoes, halved or quartered**
- **4 oz. crumbled goat cheese with garlic and herbs**

1. For dressing, in a screw-top jar combine olive oil, balsamic vinegar, green onion, salt, and pepper. Cover and shake well.

2. In a large bowl carefully toss together watercress, cantaloupe wedges, and tomatoes. Sprinkle with goat cheese. Drizzle with dressing. Toss gently to coat. Makes 8 servings.

Each serving: 149 cal., 11 g total fat (4 g sat. fat), 11 mg chol., 160 mg sodium, 9 g carbo., 1 g fiber, 4 g pro. Daily Values: 62% vit. A, 70% vit. C, 6% calcium, 4% iron.

PICNIC MENU

Salmon Picnic Sandwiches *(page 235)*
Gingered Salt with Cukes and Radishes *(page 235)*
Potato Gnocchi Salad *(left)*
Cantaloupe and Tomato Salad *(left)*
Peachy Baked White Beans *(below)*
Cheery Cherry Lemon Cake *(page 231)*
Hit-the-Spot Lemon Water *(page 231)*

Peachy Baked White Beans

Tote these summertime baked beans to the feast in an insulated carrier to keep them hot.

PREP: 20 minutes **STAND:** 1 hour **COOK:** 1 hour **BAKE:** 1 1/2 hours

- **1 lb. dry white beans, such as great northern, cannellini, or navy beans (about 2 1/3 cups)**
- **1 to 1 1/3 lb. meaty smoked pork hocks**
- **3 medium peaches, pitted and cut into wedges (about 3 cups)**
- **1 cup chopped onion (1 large)**
- **1 cup peach nectar or apple juice**
- **1/4 cup packed brown sugar**
- **2 Tbsp. snipped fresh sage or 2 tsp. dried sage, crushed**
- **1/2 tsp. salt**
- **1/2 tsp. pepper**
- **1 or 2 medium peaches, pitted and sliced**
- **Fresh sage sprig (optional)**

1. Rinse beans. In a large Dutch oven or pot combine beans and 8 cups water. Bring to boiling; reduce heat. Simmer for 2 minutes. Remove from heat. Cover and let stand for 1 hour. (Or, place beans in water in Dutch oven. Cover and let soak in a cool place overnight.)

2. Drain and rinse beans. Return beans to Dutch oven. Add pork hocks. Stir in 8 cups water. Bring to boiling; reduce heat. Cover; simmer for 1 to 1 1/2 hours or until beans are tender, stirring occasionally. Remove hocks; set aside. Drain beans. When cool enough to handle, cut meat from bones; coarsely chop meat.

3. Preheat oven to 300° F. In a 2 1/2- to 3-quart casserole combine beans, meat, the 3 cups peach wedges, and onion. Stir in peach nectar, brown sugar, sage, salt, and pepper.

4. Bake, covered, for 1 hour. Uncover and bake about 15 minutes more or until desired consistency, stirring occasionally. Before serving, top with remaining peach slices and fresh sage sprig, if desired. Makes 10 to 12 servings.

Each serving: 229 cal., 2 g total fat (1 g sat. fat), 6 mg chol., 139 mg sodium, 43 g carbo., 10 g fiber, 12 g pro. Daily Values: 6% vit. A,11% vit. C, 8% calcium, 12% iron.

Potato Gnocchi Salad

Cantaloupe and Tomato Salad

Peachy Baked White Beans

THIS OVER-THE-TOP ALFRESCO feast is worth a little extra fuss. Roomy baskets and tubs make charming carryalls for plates, napkins, and other essentials. And fresh cherries go everywhere. Turn them into fanciful table weights—with the help of some wooden clothespins—to keep your tablecloth from flapping skyward in the breeze. Just bunch up the dangling tablecloth at each corner and tie it with a ribbon. Then use clothespins to clip a couple of cherries by their stems to the ribbon or cloth.

BRIGHT BEAMS OF SUNSHINE BURSTING

from a sleepy morning sky are all the incentive you need to kick off your picnicking hoopla. Food is the focus here, but the setting—and the setup—adds the fun. Get a little hype going by hand-delivering a delicious invitation, in this case on a jar of jaunty red Just Cherries or preserves like the ones pictured at right. Try our recipe on page 236, or pick up some cherry preserves at the store. On picnic day, tote it all to the park—or just step outside your back door. Take along your favorite flea-market finds—an old chair or two, chunky go-anywhere dishes, and reliable Mason jars. And remember to toss in big, cushy pillows and blankets.

Just Cherries

Gingered Salt with Cukes and Radishes

Salmon Picnic Sandwiches

Avoid last-minute scurrying by putting together these two-fisted sandwiches in advance.

PREP: 30 minutes **COOK:** 10 minutes **CHILL:** 1 hour

- 1 lb. fresh or frozen skinless salmon fillets, cut 1 inch thick
- 1 cup Chardonnay, other dry white wine, or chicken broth
- 1 medium Vidalia or other sweet onion, cut into thin wedges (1/2 cup)
- 1/2 tsp. coarse-grain sea salt or kosher salt
- 1/2 tsp. cracked black pepper
- 2 sprigs fresh oregano
- 1 8- to 12-oz. loaf ciabatta or baguette-style French bread
- Olive oil
- 1 recipe Olive-and-Onion Relish (below)
- Lemon wedges (optional)

1. Thaw fish, if frozen. Rinse fish. In a large skillet or fish poacher combine wine or broth, onion, salt, pepper, and oregano. Bring to boiling; add salmon. Reduce heat and simmer, covered, for 10 to 12 minutes or until fish flakes easily when tested with a fork.

2. Use a slotted spatula to transfer salmon and onion to a large bowl. Discard cooking liquid. Cover and refrigerate about 1 hour or until chilled.

3. Cut bread into quarters; slice in half horizontally. Drizzle cut sides lightly with olive oil. Cut salmon into 4 equal pieces. Place a piece of salmon on bread bottoms. Top with Olive-and-Onion Relish and bread tops. Wrap securely in plastic wrap. Refrigerate for up to 4 hours. Before serving, squeeze lemon over salmon and relish, if desired. Makes 4 sandwiches.

OLIVE-AND-ONION RELISH: In a small bowl combine reserved onion wedges (from poaching liquid); 1/2 cup pitted green olives, halved; 1/2 cup pitted kalamata olives, halved; 2 tablespoons snipped fresh Italian flat-leaf parsley; and 2 teaspoons snipped fresh oregano.

Each sandwich: 398 cal., 17 g total fat (2 g sat. fat), 70 mg chol., 1,269 mg sodium, 32 g carbo., 3 g fiber, 29 g pro. Daily Values: 7% vit. A, 6% vit. C, 7% calcium, 15% iron.

Salmon Picnic Sandwiches

Gingered Salt with Cukes and Radishes

Candied ginger, which you can buy in major markets or specialty stores, adds a spicy snap to this dipping salt.

PREP: 10 minutes **STAND:** 24 hours

- 1/2 cup coarse sea salt or kosher salt
- 2 to 3 Tbsp. chopped crystallized ginger
- Radishes
- Baby cucumbers, halved lengthwise, or medium cucumbers, halved crosswise and cut lengthwise into wedges, peeled, if desired

1. In a screw-top jar combine salt and ginger. Screw on the lid. Shake well to combine. Let stand for 24 hours or up to 1 month.

2. To serve, pass salt with radishes and cucumbers. Makes 2/3 cup salt (48 servings).

Each 1/2 teaspoon salt: 12 cal., 0 g total fat (0 g sat. fat), 0 mg chol., 804 mg sodium, 3 g carbo., 1 g fiber, 1 g pro. Daily Values: 3% vit. A, 10% vit. C, 1% calcium, 1% iron.

Just Cherries

These lemongrass-infused cherries are refreshingly tart, so they're perfect to pair with sweeter companions, such as chocolate or vanilla ice cream.

PREP: 45 minutes **COOK:** 35 minutes

- **2 1/2 lb. fresh tart red cherries or two 1-lb. pkg. frozen unsweetened pitted tart red cherries**
- **1 cup sugar**
- **1/2 cup water**
- **4 large stalks fresh lemongrass, trimmed and cut into 2-inch pieces, or 4 tsp. finely shredded lemon peel**
- **1 1/2 tsp. vanilla**

1. If using fresh cherries, rinse and drain cherries; remove stems and pits. Measure 6 cups. In a large saucepan combine cherries, sugar, water, and lemongrass or lemon peel. Bring to boiling; reduce heat. Simmer, uncovered, for 35 minutes. Remove from heat. Stir in vanilla.

2. Ladle the fruit mixture into clean half-pint jars or storage containers. Cover and store for up to 3 weeks in the refrigerator. About 1 week before serving, remove lemongrass, if using. Makes 4 half-pint jars.

Each 1/4-cup serving: 79 cal., 0 g total fat (0 g sat. fat), 0 mg chol., 2 mg sodium, 20 g carbo., 1 g fiber, 1 g pro. Daily Values: 16% vit. A, 11% vit. C, 1% calcium, 1% iron.

Carrots with Dried Fruit Confetti

Cut the get-ready time to nearly nothing by buying carrot sticks.

PREP: 15 minutes **CHILL:** 1 hour

- **12 small carrots with tops or 6 medium carrots (1 lb.)**
- **1 8-oz. tub flavored cream cheese, such as honey-nut or apple-cinnamon**
- **2 to 3 tsp. milk**
- **1 1/2 cups dried blueberries, dried cranberries, and/or golden raisins**

1. Peel carrots. If using small carrots, serve whole. Cut medium carrots into sticks about 3 inches long and 1/2 inch wide. Pat dry with paper towels.

2. In a medium bowl combine cream cheese and milk, stirring until smooth; spread onto half of each carrot.

3. Sprinkle dried blueberries onto the cream cheese mixture. Cover and chill for 1 to 4 hours. Makes 12 snack servings.

Each serving: 139 cal., 5 g total fat (3 g sat. fat), 18 mg chol., 76 mg sodium, 21 g carbo., 2 g fiber, 1 g pro. Daily Values: 192% vit. A, 6% vit. C, 4% calcium, 3% iron.

Lumpy PB&J Roosters

Thick slices of firm bread work best to support the lollipop sticks. Pile finished sandwiches on a "nest" of shoestring potatoes (which come in a variety of kid-pleasing flavors).

PREP: 25 minutes **CHILL:** 1 hour

- **1 10-oz. jar raspberry or strawberry spreadable fruit**
- **1/4 cup chopped peanuts**
- **1/4 cup shredded coconut**
- **3 Tbsp. orange juice**
- **12 slices firm-textured white or whole wheat sandwich bread**
- **3/4 cup peanut butter**
- **1/2 cup chopped strawberries, bananas, and/or pineapple**
- **6 4- to 5-inch lollipop sticks**
- **6 dried currants or miniature semisweet chocolate pieces or 3 raisins, snipped in half**

1. In a small bowl combine spreadable fruit, chopped peanuts, coconut, and orange juice. Set aside.

2. Cut 12 shapes from bread slices using 3- to 4-inch rooster or other shaped cutters. (Reserve bread you've cut away for another use.)

3. Spread 1 tablespoon of the peanut butter onto one side of each shape, making sure that shapes will match up when placed together. Sprinkle chopped fruit over peanut butter on 6 of the shapes. Top each fruit-covered shape with matching top, peanut butter side down. Press shapes together, forming a sandwich. Insert a lollipop stick into the filling of sandwich. Press slightly to secure stick. Repeat with remaining shapes and sticks.

4. Spread a small amount of peanut butter onto bottom of a currant. Place a currant "eye" on each rooster sandwich. Wrap and chill for up to 1 hour. Serve with spreadable fruit mixture as a dipping sauce. Makes 6 sandwiches.

Each sandwich: 486 cal., 24 g total fat (5 g sat. fat), 0 mg chol., 421 mg sodium, 64 g carbo., 3 g fiber, 14 g pro. Daily Values: 18% vit. C, 6% calcium, 13% iron.

KIDS' PICNIC

Lumpy PB&J Roosters (above)
Carrots with Dried Fruit Confetti (left)
Turtle Pretzels (page 239)
Wild Blueberry Pies (page 239)
Just Cherries with ice cream (left)
Lemonade or fruit punch

Lumpy PB&J Roosters and Carrots with Dried Fruit Confetti

ALLOW WIDE OPEN SPACES FOR PLAY.

All the whooping and hollering and zigzagging between the trees will stir up kids' appetites. Bring a favorite red wagon, hula hoops, and a net for chasing butterflies. Even the grown-ups might join in on a giddy game of "Ring Around the Rosey." And when appetites are ready, give the small-fry their very own lunch baskets and a kid-size dining nook far enough from the adults to encourage general silliness and goofy gobbling.

Wild Blueberry Pies

Wild Blueberry Pies

Prepare the pastry first and have the cutouts ready before making either fruit filling so the filling doesn't get too juicy.

PREP: 30 minutes **BAKE:** 18 minutes

- 2 cups all-purpose flour
- 1/2 tsp. salt
- 1/2 tsp. ground cardamom
- 2/3 cup shortening
- 6 to 7 Tbsp. cold water
- 1 recipe Wild Blueberry Filling or Raspberry Filling(below)
- 1 beaten egg
- Coarse sugar or sugar

1. Line a large baking sheet with foil; set aside. In a medium mixing bowl stir together flour, salt, and cardamom. Using a pastry blender, cut in shortening until pieces are pea-size.

2. Sprinkle 1 tablespoon of the water over part of the mixture; gently toss with a fork. Push moistened dough to side of bowl. Repeat, using 1 tablespoon water at a time, until dough is moistened. Divide dough in half. Form into 2 balls.

3. On a lightly floured surface flatten 1 ball of dough; roll into a 16×8-inch rectangle. Use a 3 3/4- to 4-inch scalloped or round cutter to cut 8 circles. Stack cutouts between pieces of waxed paper. Repeat with remaining dough to make 16 cutouts.

4. Preheat oven to 375° F. Prepare Wild Blueberry Filling or Raspberry Filling. Place 8 pastry cutouts 2 inches apart on the prepared baking sheet. Spoon about 2 tablespoons filling onto each cutout. Moisten edges with water. Top with remaining cutouts. Seal edges with tines of a fork. Prick tops of pies two or three times to allow steam to escape. Brush with beaten egg; sprinkle with sugar.

5. Bake for 18 to 20 minutes or until golden brown. Remove from pan; cool on a wire rack. Makes 8 pies.

WILD BLUEBERRY FILLING: In a medium bowl stir together 2 to 3 tablespoons sugar, 1 tablespoon all-purpose flour, and 1/2 teaspoon finely shredded lemon peel. Stir in 1 1/2 cups fresh or frozen wild or cultivated blueberries. (If berries are frozen, do not thaw before using.)

RASPBERRY FILLING: In a mixing bowl stir together 3 to 4 tablespoons sugar, 4 teaspoons all-purpose flour, and 1/2 teaspoon finely shredded lemon peel. Stir in 1 1/2 cups raspberries.

Each serving: 305 cal., 17 g total fat (4 g sat. fat), 27 mg chol., 156 mg sodium, 33 g carbo., 2 g fiber, 4 g pro. Daily Values: 1% vit. A, 7% vit. C, 2% calcium, 11% iron.

Use scalloped or round cutters to make these individual mini pies. Pressing the tines of a fork onto the edges will seal in the filling.

Turtle Pretzels

Turtle Pretzels

Enjoy these pretzels the same day they're prepared because the pretzels may soften on standing.

PREP: 45 minutes **CHILL:** 20 minutes

- Butter
- 1 14-oz. pkg. vanilla caramels (about 48)
- 1 Tbsp. water
- 15 to 20 large pretzel twists (4 inches wide and 1/2 inch thick)
- 4 oz. semisweet chocolate, chopped
- 1 tsp. shortening
- Chopped pecans, snipped dried cranberries or dried blueberries, or miniature candy-coated semisweet chocolate pieces

1. Lightly butter a large cookie sheet; set aside. In a small saucepan combine unwrapped caramels and 1 tablespoon water. Cook and stir over low heat until caramels are just melted and smooth. Remove from heat.

2. Dip top portions of pretzels into caramel mixture, tilting pan as necessary to help coat each pretzel and letting excess caramel drip off. Arrange on prepared cookie sheet. (If caramel mixture is running off pretzels, wait a few minutes to let it cool and thicken slightly.) Cool until caramel is set.

3. Place chocolate and shortening in another small saucepan. Cook and stir over low heat until chocolate is just melted and smooth. Cool slightly. Spoon melted chocolate mixture into a small plastic bag; snip a small hole in one corner. Squeeze chocolate onto pretzels, forming decorative lines. Sprinkle with nuts, dried fruit, or chocolate pieces. Chill pretzels in refrigerator about 20 minutes or until chocolate is firm. Transfer to waxed paper or cellophane bags. Makes 15 to 20 pretzels.

Each serving: 283 cal., 10 g total fat (3 g sat. fat), 4 mg chol., 503 mg sodium, 46 g carbo., 2 g fiber, 5 g pro. Daily Values: 6% calcium ,5% iron.

Roasted Garlic Steak

Steak on the Grill

GRAB YOUR TONGS AND GET READY TO PUT SOME FIRE INTO YOUR BACKYARD COOKING CAREER.

1. Pick the right cut. The route to a great steak begins at the meat counter. The six best-for-grilling cuts are shown opposite. Buy steaks that measure 3/4 to 1 1/2 inches thick—any thinner and the inside may overcook. The most tender and flavorful steaks are those with the most marbling—tiny white flecks and veins of fat within the meat. The grades reflect the amount of marbling. Select-grade meat has less fat, choice has more, and prime has the most.

2. Read before you cook. Your grill owner's manual has all the information you need to be the best backyard chef on your block. And the best chefs keep it clean. Scrub the grill with a wire brush when it's still hot after grilling.

3. Season. Shake your favorite seasoning blend or pepper onto the steaks, then brush or rub with olive oil or cooking oil to lessen sticking and help create steak-house-style grill marks.

4. Keep the fire moderate. A steady, medium temperature is the key to success. If using charcoal, put in enough coals to make one layer on the bottom. After you light the coals, let them burn until covered with gray ash.About 5 minutes before adding the meat, preheat the cooking grill over the coals. The coals will stay at the right cooking temperature for 45 minutes. For gas grills, adjust controls to the manufacturer's recommendation.

5. Follow the chart. Cook steaks for the minimum time suggested on our chart, turning them once halfway through cooking. If they stick, leave them on for another minute, then gently lift until they release from the grill.

To check doneness, cut into one of the steaks for a peek (that's the steak you'll give yourself) or use an instant-read thermometer inserted horizontally into the meat. The USDA doesn't recommend serving steaks that are less than medium rare, and well-done steaks are usually drier and less tender. A steak is rare at 140° F and well-done at 170° F.

For steaks thicker than 1 1/2 inches, remove from the grill when a thermometer registers 5° F under the desired doneness. Cover loosely with foil and the steak will cook to the proper degree of doneness. If thinner steaks are not quite done, pop them back over the coals for 2 or 3 more minutes. Once you take meat off the grill, cover it with foil and let it stand for 5 to 10 minutes.

Roasted Garlic Steak

PREP: 15 minutes **GRILL:** 30 minutes

- 1 or 2 whole garlic bulb(s)
- 3 to 4 tsp. snipped fresh basil or 1 tsp. dried basil, crushed
- 1 Tbsp. snipped fresh rosemary or 1 tsp. dried rosemary, crushed
- 2 Tbsp. olive oil or cooking oil
- 1½ lb. boneless beef ribeye steaks or sirloin steak, cut 1 inch thick
- 1 to 2 tsp. cracked pepper
- ½ tsp. salt

1. With a sharp knife, cut off the top ½ inch from garlic bulb(s) to expose the ends of the individual cloves. Leaving garlic bulb(s) whole, remove any loose, papery outer layers.
2. Fold a 20×18-inch piece of heavy foil in half crosswise. Trim into a 10-inch square. Place garlic bulb(s), cut sides up, in center of foil square. Sprinkle garlic with basil and rosemary; drizzle with oil. Bring up opposite edges of foil; seal with a double fold. Fold remaining edges together to completely enclose garlic, leaving space for steam to build.
3. For a charcoal grill, grill garlic on the rack of an uncovered grill directly over medium coals about 30 minutes or until garlic feels soft when packet is squeezed, turning occasionally.
4. Meanwhile, trim fat from steaks. Sprinkle the pepper and salt evenly onto both sides of steaks; rub in. Add steaks to grill. Grill to desired doneness, turning once halfway through grilling. For ribeye steaks, allow 11 to 15 minutes for medium rare (145° F) and 14 to 18 minutes for medium (160° F). For sirloin steak, allow 14 to 18 minutes for medium rare (145° F) and 18 to 22 minutes for medium (160° F). (For a gas grill, preheat grill. Reduce heat to medium. Place garlic, then steaks on grill rack over heat. Cover and grill as above.)
5. To serve, cut steaks into 6 serving-size pieces. Remove garlic from foil, reserving the oil mixture. Squeeze garlic pulp onto steaks; mash pulp slightly and spread onto steaks. Drizzle with the reserved oil mixture. Makes 6 servings.

Each serving: 189 cal., 9 g total fat (2 g sat. fat), 52 mg chol., 139 mg sodium, 4 g carbo., 0 g fiber, 22 g pro. Daily Values: 1% vit. A, 6% vit. C, 3% calcium, 14% iron.

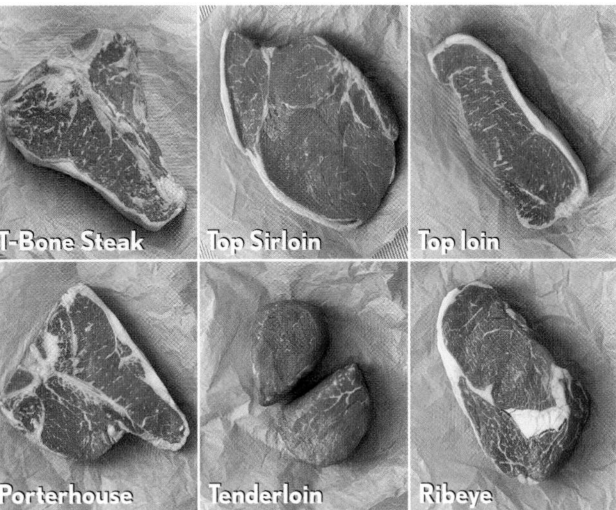

CHOOSING MEAT

- The **T-bone** and the **porterhouse** are very similar. They're both made up of two other cuts—a top loin and a tenderloin—with the t-shape bone in the middle. (The porterhouse has a larger tenderloin).
- Top **sirloin** is firmer and slightly lower in fat than the other four steak cuts.
- The **top loin**, also called a New York or Kansas City strip, among other names, is tender and among the leanest.
- As the name implies, **tenderloin** is often singled out as a very tender cut. It also has the mildest taste of the steaks shown here. It tastes best if not cooked beyond medium.
- A **ribeye** is a very flavorful steak, almost like eating grilled roast beef. This is a good cut for those who prefer well-done.

HOW LONG WILL IT TAKE?

These timings produce steaks that are medium rare at an internal temperature of 145° F. The actual grilling times will vary according to the air temperature and wind. Cover thicker steaks with the grill lid to cook evenly.

CUT	THICKNESS	TIME
Ribeye	¾ inch	6 to 8 minutes
	1 inch	11 to 14 minutes
	1½ inches	17 to 22 minutes (covered)
T-bone, Top loin, Porterhouse	¾ inch	10 to 12 minutes
	1 inch	14 to 18 minutes
	1½ inches	20 to 24 minutes (covered)
Top sirloin	¾ inch	13 to 16 minutes
	1 inch	17 to 21 minutes
	1½ inches	22 to 26 minutes (covered)
Tenderloin	1 inch	13 to 15 minutes
	1½ inches	14 to 16 minutes (covered)

Cocktail cool

GRAB A JIGGER AND A SHAKER for the latest libations from the cocktail circuit. Whether you're sipping to the beat of lounge music CDs or hitting the hammock with glass in hand, relax and say cheers!

Basil Martini
Fill a shaker with ice, add a dash of vermouth, shake, and strain. Add 2 jiggers basil-infused vodka (for infusion tips, see opposite). Shake vigorously; strain. Note: 1 jigger equals approximately $1\frac{1}{2}$ fluid ounces.

Mojito Sparkler
Samba, anyone? Crush 6 fresh mint leaves in the bottom of a glass. Pour in $1\frac{1}{2}$ to 2 jiggers gold rum, 2 teaspoons extra-fine granulated sugar, and 1 teaspoon lime juice. Add ice, stir, and top with soda.

Mai Tai Me
Fill a shaker with ice. Add 1 jigger each of dark rum and orange liqueur, $\frac{1}{3}$ cup pineapple juice, 2 tablespoons grenadine syrup, a dash of lime juice, and sugar. Shake and serve. Umbrella required.

Dandy Shandy
This British tradition is just smashing, mate. Top a good dark stout or porter (or nonalcoholic beer) with an equal amount of ginger ale or ginger beer.

Clove Julep
Spice up the Derby classic. Crush 5 fresh mint sprigs along with 3 teaspoons of extra-fine granulated sugar in the bottom of a glass. Add ice and clove-infused vodka. Stir and serve.

Ultra Alexander
Dessert in a glass. In a shaker filled with ice, add $1\frac{1}{3}$ jiggers brandy, $\frac{1}{3}$ jigger crème de cacao, and 1 tablespoon each of whipping cream and chocolate syrup. Shake, strain, and serve. Sprinkle with chocolate shavings.

INFUSION MIXOLOGY

Infused vodkas, or vodkas that have had a flavoring agent added, are popular on restaurant bar menus. Infusing subtle flavor is easy. Start with a half-pint bottle of vodka. For basil-infused vodka, gently crush six basil leaves and immerse in the bottle. Try mint as an alternative. For clove-infused vodka, place eight whole cloves in a piece of cheesecloth; tie into a bundle. Gently crush some of the cloves. Insert the bundle into the vodka. Peppercorns or anise seed lend their flavors nicely too. Or, insert slices of fresh gingerroot, cucumber, or citrus peel. Store the infused vodka in the freezer for at least four days. Strain and discard the solids before serving.

Take 5 at the very least

EAT FIVE SERVINGS A DAY OF FRUITS AND VEGETABLES. HOW HARD CAN THAT BE?

It's not. And we're here to show you how easy it is.

"In fact, five is just the starting point," says Lorelei DiSogra, R.D., director of the 5 a Day for Better Health program at the National Cancer Institute. "Women should be eating closer to seven. And men should be eating nine."

Research shows that the more fruits and vegetables you eat, the lower your risk of developing chronic diseases, including cancer, heart disease, diabetes, and macular degeneration. "The brighter the color of what you eat, the better," DiSogra says. "The natural plant chemicals that make cherries a vivid red and blueberries so blue also take on double-duty as disease fighters."

The best colors to pick when you're purchasing produce? Red, orange, yellow, green, and blue-purple. So go ahead and color your world, using the easy ideas opposite.

Snow Peas and Tomatoes

Look for tiny tomatoes available in a rainbow of colors and shapes.

START TO FINISH: 10 minutes

- **6 cups fresh pea pods (1 lb.)**
- **1 large shallot, sliced**
- **2 tsp. peanut oil**
- **1/4 tsp. toasted sesame oil**
- **1 Tbsp. teriyaki sauce**
- **1/4 cup grape, cherry, and/or pear-shape red and/or yellow tomatoes**
- **2 tsp. sesame seed, toasted**

1. Remove strings and tips from the pea pods; set aside. In a 12-inch skillet cook shallot in hot peanut oil and sesame oil over medium heat until tender. Stir in pea pods and teriyaki sauce. Cook and stir for 2 to 3 minutes or until the pea pods are crisp-tender.

2. Add tomatoes; cook for 1 minute more. Sprinkle with sesame seed. Makes 6 servings.

Each serving: 115 cal., 3 g total fat (2 g sat. fat), 8 mg chol., 53 mg sodium, 17 g carbo., 4 g fiber, 4 g pro. Daily Values: 2% vit. A, 47% vit. C, 6% calcium, 10% iron.

5 FROM YOUR KITCHEN

1. Sneak more fruit into peanut butter and jelly sandwiches by making your own easy blender jam. Blend well-drained canned apricots, peaches, or pineapple until smooth, then slather onto whole wheat bread.

2. Pile grilled veggies onto one side of a flour tortilla. Sprinkle with shredded cheese. Fold over and heat in a skillet until both sides are golden brown, turning once. Serve with salsa.

3. Blend blueberries or strawberries into milk. Try 1/2 cup berries with 3/4 cup milk. Sweeten with a little honey.

4. Cook chopped mushrooms and onion in olive oil. Add a handful or two of fresh baby spinach and toss together. Stuff the mixture into pockets cut in chicken breast halves and bake. Or pile it onto baked potatoes.

5. Build a stack of mini pancakes, piling chopped fresh strawberries or peaches between each layer. Add fresh blueberries to a favorite pancake syrup, and spoon on top.

5 TO BOOKMARK

Better Homes and Gardens® Eating for Life, Kristi Fuller, R.D., Editor (2001). Big flavors with little effort is a recurring theme in this book. Each recipe includes a tidbit explaining its health benefits.

The Color Code, by James A. Joseph, Ph.D.; Daniel A. Nadeau, M.D.; and Anne Underwood (2002). Two nutrition pros at Tufts University teamed up with Newsweek reporter Underwood to provide an easy-to-read rainbow of reasons to eat colorful plant foods. The book is packed with good information and includes recipes.

5 a Day, by Dr. Elizabeth Pivonka and Barbara Berry (2002). Think it's tough to to meet your fruit and veggie quota? This book's recipe for a mango, banana, grapefruit-juice shake alone has 3 1/2 servings. We tested a few recipes in the Better Homes and Gardens® Test Kitchen. Good stuff.

www.aboutproduce.com. This great site serves anyone who wants to eat "in season." An A-to-Z produce guide pinpoints availability dates, gives health information, features a nutrition dictionary, and offers a recipe search engine.

www.5aday.com or **www.5aday.gov** Both sites have great information and some fun interactive tools. The first is sponsored by the Produce for Better Health Foundation; the second by the National Cancer Institute. They spread the word about the 5 a Day for Better Health program.

July

ENTERTAIN FRIENDS AND FAMILY WITH
SIZZLING-HOT IDEAS ALL SUMMER LONG.

Sweet Layers of Red, White, and Blue

Corn-on-the-Cob Salad

Peaches and Ice Cream Sandwich Bars

Watermelon Salad with Watercress

Celebrate Summer in a Big Way

Plus...

Oven-Fried Buttermilk Chicken

Stuffed Caprese

Chilled Thai Tenderloin and Pasta with Tons of Basil

Big Easy

Plus...

SUMMER BRINGS WITH IT WARM WEATHER THAT INSISTS WE ENJOY THE OUTDOORS, BE IT SNOOZING IN THE HAMMOCK, GRILLING ON THE DECK, OR DINING ALFRESCO.

Mad Mad Martian Juice

Smooth and Chunky Melon Soup

Watermelon Salad with Watercress

celebrate summer

in a big way

FAMILY REUNIONS. BACKYARD BARBECUES. BLOCK PARTIES. PICNICS IN THE PARK. HERE'S HOW TO STAGE THE SEASON'S TASTIEST OUTDOOR BASHES.

Corn-on-the-Cob Salad

Potluck for a crowd

You might be tempted to take the easy way out when you're preparing a potluck dish for a crowd. Well, so are we. Let's face it: Necessity is the mother of shortcuts, especially when it's summertime. With our cut-to-the-chase techniques and big-batch recipes, you'll be able to put together incredible dishes and still have plenty of hammock time left before the party.

When everyone brings a dish to pass and Mother Nature contributes a generous portion of sunshine, the food is bound to taste good. We've infused the typical tote-along classics with fresh flourishes bold enough to stand up to the fireworks to come. Success relies on an easy three-step strategy: Plan ahead. Depend on good-to-the-last-crumb recipes. And keep everything simple.

When it comes to presentation, think hassle-free and practical. Go ahead and use foil pans or toss-away plastic containers. Big punch bowls make supersize serving vessels. Grab inexpensive white painter's dropcloths from the hardware store to cover tables. Have everyone bring a vintage linen or favorite place mat to add pizzazz. Be sure to have plenty of heavy-duty paper plates that won't buckle and spill when they're piled high.

Whether you're hosting the picnic or simply bringing a dish, do as much as you can ahead of time. As you plan and shop, bear in mind that repetition makes for an awesome display. A platter full of red berries or a big tray piled with mounds of carrots can be dazzling. Get vivid. It's the season for flaunting garden-fresh bursts of color.

Magically transform any basic buffet table into a vivid summer show-off with a massive watermelon split down the center. When melon shopping, go ahead and thump away if you have aspirations to be a drummer, but professional watermelon pickers say it's better to check the bottom of the melon to determine whether it is ripe. The underside should be pale green to light yellow, or just beginning to turn white.

Corn-on-the-Cob Salad

Prep: 40 minutes **Grill:** 20 minutes **Chill:** 2 hours

- 8 fresh ears of corn
- 1 recipe Herb Vinaigrette (below)
- 1 lb. fresh or frozen shelled baby lima beans
- 1 medium red, yellow, or orange sweet pepper, chopped
- 1 medium sweet onion, such as Vidalia or Walla Walla, chopped
- 1 to 2 fresh jalapeño chile peppers,* seeded and chopped

1. Remove husks and silk from corn. Break or cut each ear of corn in half (leave some whole, if desired); set aside.

2. Prepare Herb Vinaigrette; brush some onto corn. Grill corn on the rack of an uncovered gas grill on medium or a charcoal grill directly over medium coals about 20 minutes or until tender, turning often. Let cool. Remove kernels from 4 grilled corn halves; set aside. Brush remaining corn with some of the remaining vinaigrette. Cover ears of corn and chill.

3. Meanwhile, in a medium saucepan cook lima beans in a small amount of lightly salted boiling water for 10 to 15 minutes or until beans are crisp-tender; drain. Rinse with cold water; drain again.

4. In a large bowl combine lima beans, corn kernels, sweet pepper, onion, and jalapeño pepper. Add remaining vinaigrette; toss to coat. Cover and chill for 2 to 24 hours. To serve, spoon lima bean mixture into a serving container. Top with remaining ears of corn. Makes 12 side-dish servings.

HERB VINAIGRETTE: In a small bowl whisk together ½ cup olive oil, ½ cup cider vinegar, 2 tablespoons snipped fresh oregano, ¼ teaspoon salt, and ⅛ teaspoon ground black pepper.

***NOTE:** Because hot chile peppers, such as jalapeños, contain volatile oils that can burn your skin and eyes, avoid direct contact with chiles as much as possible. When working with chile peppers, wear plastic or rubber gloves. If your bare hands do touch the chile peppers, wash your hands well with soap and water.

Each serving: 190 cal., 10 g total fat (1 g sat. fat), 0 mg chol., 76 mg sodium, 23 g carbo., 4 g fiber, 5 g pro. Daily Values: 5% vit. A, 59% vit. C, 2% calcium, 7% iron.

Watermelon Salad with Watercress

Chunky Mustard Potato Salad

Purchased precooked potato wedges give this salad a quick start. For an even faster version, substitute a 9-ounce jar of mustard pickle relish for the pickles, mustard, and roasted red pepper. This recipe can easily be doubled to serve 24, but be sure to start with a Dutch oven for cooking the bigger batch of potatoes.

PREP: 35 minutes **CHILL:** 2 + 4 hours

- **2 20-oz. pkg. refrigerated new potato wedges**
- **1/4 tsp. salt**
- **1/2 cup coarsely chopped dill pickles**
- **1/4 cup Dijon-style mustard**
- **1/4 cup chopped, roasted red sweet pepper**
- **1 cup chopped celery (2 stalks)**
- **1/2 cup sliced green onions**
- **1/3 cup chopped radishes**
- **4 hard-cooked eggs, peeled and coarsely chopped**
- **1/2 tsp. salt**
- **1/4 tsp. ground black pepper**
- **3/4 cup mayonnaise or salad dressing**

1. Place potatoes in a large saucepan. Add enough water to cover the potatoes and the 1/4 teaspoon salt. Bring to boiling; reduce heat. Cover and simmer for 5 minutes. Drain well; cool for 10 minutes.

2. In a very large serving bowl combine warm potatoes, pickles, mustard, and roasted pepper; stir gently. Cover and chill for 2 hours. Add celery, green onions, radishes, eggs, the 1/2 teaspoon salt, and black pepper. Add mayonnaise; mix gently. Cover and chill for 4 to 24 hours. Makes 12 side-dish servings.

Each serving: 194 cal., 13 g total fat (2 g sat. fat), 76 mg chol., 521 mg sodium, 13 g carbo., 3 g fiber, 5 g pro. Daily Values: 3% vit. A, 22% vit. C, 2% calcium, 4% iron.

Watermelon Salad with Watercress

In this fruit salad, the peppery bite of watercress and onion is quickly mellowed by the sweet, cool watermelon and a refreshing hint of mint. Half of a large watermelon will disappear quickly if you put it in front of about 12 guests. If you're expecting double that number, use both halves of the melon and double the remaining ingredients. You'll have plenty to serve a crowd of 24.

PREP: 45 minutes **CHILL:** up to 6 hours

- **1 13- to 14-lb. oval watermelon**
- **4 cups snipped fresh watercress**
- **1 medium red onion, cut into thin wedges**
- **1/4 cup snipped fresh mint**
- **2 Tbsp. olive oil flavored with red pepper or plain olive oil**
- **1/4 tsp. sea salt or salt**
- **1/4 tsp. ground black pepper**

1. Cut watermelon in half horizontally. Reserve half for another use. With remaining half, use a small paring knife or grapefruit knife to carefully cut around the fruit, just inside the rind. Cut fruit in the melon crosswise into 1-inch-thick slices (leaving the rind intact). Cut underneath each slice and remove from the shell. Pile slices into the shell. Cover and chill up to 6 hours.

2. Just before serving, in a large bowl combine watercress, onion, mint, olive oil, salt, and pepper; toss to coat. Sprinkle mixture over watermelon slices. Makes 12 side-dish servings.

Each serving: 64 cal., 3 g total fat (0 g sat. fat), 0 mg chol., 41 mg sodium, 10 g carbo., 1 g fiber, 1 g pro. Daily Values: 20% vit. A, 29% vit. C, 3% calcium, 2% iron.

FOURTH OF JULY PICNIC

Watermelon Salad with Watercress *(left)*
Chunky Mustard Potato Salad *(above)*
Oven-Fried Buttermilk Chicken *(page 258)*
Biscuits with red, white, and blue sprinkles
Sweet Layers of Red, White, and Blue *(page 260)*
Madeline's Lemonade *(page 266)*

Chunky Mustard Potato Salad

Veggies with a Splash

Veggies with a Splash

Three pounds of veggies will feed about 12 people. Serving 24? Just double everything. If your guest list grows to three dozen, prepare a 3-pound platter of carrots, a 3-pound platter of green beans, and a 3-pound platter of pea pods. Steamed asparagus is a good option too.

PREP: 25 minutes **CHILL:** 4 hours

- **3 lb. baby maroon carrots (Beta Sweet), baby carrots with tops, carrot sticks, Chinese long beans or whole green beans, and/or pea pods, washed and trimmed**
- **1/2 cup olive oil**
- **1/3 cup lime juice**
- **2 Tbsp. snipped fresh dill**
- **2 Tbsp. snipped fresh garlic chives or chives**
- **Salt**
- **Ground black pepper**
- **Coarse sea salt**
- **Black or red radishes, thinly sliced (optional)**

1. If using baby maroon carrots, wash and cut off all but about 1 1/2 inches of the green top. In a Dutch oven or large saucepan bring a small amount of salted water to boiling. Add baby carrots, carrot sticks, and/or green beans; cook, covered, about 5 minutes or until crisp-tender. Cook pea pods, covered, for 2 to 4 minutes or until crisp-tender. Drain. Immediately transfer vegetables to a large bowl of ice water to stop cooking; drain. Cover and chill for 4 to 24 hours.

2. For vinaigrette, in a screw-top jar combine olive oil, lime juice, dill, and chives. Season to taste with salt and pepper. Cover and shake well.

3. Just before serving, toss vegetables with half of the vinaigrette. Arrange vegetables on a tray or platter and drizzle with remaining vinaigrette. Sprinkle with coarse sea salt. If desired, serve with thinly sliced radishes. Makes 12 side-dish servings.

Each serving: 122 cal., 9 g total fat (1 g sat. fat), 0 mg chol., 186 mg sodium, 9 g carbo., 3 g fiber, 2 g pro. Daily Values: 195% vit. A, 46% vit. C, 4% calcium, 7% iron.

KEEPING VEGETABLES FRESH

Picking the prettiest produce from your garden, the farmer's market, or the grocery store is a big part of presentation. However, you've got to treat your tender gems right at home to keep them beautiful.

- Wash greens in cold water, then dry in a salad spinner or pat with paper towels. Store in an airtight container wrapped in moist paper towels in the refrigerator.
- Trim ends of fresh herbs and asparagus. Store unwashed stalks in a container of water or wrapped in moist paper towels. Keep in an airtight container in the refrigerator. Wash and trim before using.
- Store carrots, green beans, pea pods, zucchini, and peppers unwashed in resealable bags in the refrigerator. Wash and trim before using.

Strawberry-Spinach Salad

For this potluck favorite, you can easily double, triple, or quadruple the ingredients to serve the number of people you need. Just be sure to pack the pecans and dressing separately from the spinach mixture, then toss it all together at your picnic. That way, the greens stay crisp and fresh and the nuts are nice and crunchy.

START TO FINISH: 30 minutes

- **1 lb. asparagus spears**
- **1/3 cup bottled poppy seed salad dressing or Italian salad dressing**
- **1 tsp. finely shredded orange peel**
- **1 Tbsp. orange juice**
- **8 cups fresh baby spinach or assorted salad greens**
- **2 cups sliced fresh strawberries and/or blueberries**
- **3/4 to 1 lb. cooked turkey, cut into 1/2-inch cubes**
- **1/4 cup pecan halves, toasted**

1. Snap off and discard woody bases from asparagus. If desired, scrape off scales. Cut into 1-inch pieces. Cook asparagus, covered, in a small amount of boiling lightly salted water for 3 to 5 minutes or until crisp-tender. Drain asparagus. Rinse with cold water. Let stand in cold water until cool; drain.

2. Meanwhile, for dressing, in a small mixing bowl stir together poppy seed dressing, orange peel, and orange juice; set aside.

3. In a salad bowl combine asparagus, spinach, berries, and turkey. Top with pecans. Serve with dressing. Makes 4 to 6 main-dish servings.

Each serving: 329 cal., 19 g total fat (3 g sat. fat), 65 mg chol., 299 mg sodium, 10 g carbo., 9 g fiber, 30 g pro. Daily Values: 71% vit. A, 25% vit. C, 10% calcium, 37% iron.

Zucchini Pilaf

Zucchini Pilaf

Fresh summer color comes to this warm rice side dish from vivid tomatoes and your pick of green zucchini or sunny yellow summer squash. This pilaf is easily made the day before your gathering. Just reheat it before serving.

PREP: 20 minutes **COOK:** 25 minutes **BAKE:** 35 minutes

- **1 cup chopped onion**
- **3 cloves garlic, minced**
- **3 Tbsp. olive oil**
- **4½ cups water**
- **2 6-oz. pkg. long grain and wild rice mix or rice pilaf mix**
- **8 oz. semisoft goat cheese, cubed**
- **3 to 4 medium assorted fresh summer tomatoes (red, yellow, and/or orange), seeded and coarsely chopped**
- **1 lb. medium zucchini or yellow summer squash, quartered lengthwise and sliced ½ inch thick (cut some thin strips of peel for garnish, if desired)**
- **2 tsp. snipped fresh rosemary**
- **¼ tsp. salt**
- **⅛ tsp. ground black pepper**

1. In a large saucepan cook onion and garlic in 2 tablespoons of the hot olive oil until tender. Add water; bring to boiling. Stir in rice mix (including seasoning packet). Cover; reduce heat to low. Simmer about 25 minutes or until most of the water is absorbed. Add cheese; stir until melted and combined.

2. Preheat oven to 350° F. Transfer rice mixture to a large bowl. Stir in tomatoes, zucchini, rosemary, salt, and pepper. Transfer to a greased 3-quart rectangular baking dish or a 13×9×2-inch foil pan. If desired, top with strips of zucchini peel. Bake, covered, for 35 to 45 minutes or until heated through. Drizzle with remaining 1 tablespoon olive oil. Makes 12 side-dish servings.

MAKE-AHEAD DIRECTIONS: Prepare as directed, except cover and chill for up to 24 hours before baking. Bake, covered, in a 350° F oven for 50 to 60 minutes or until heated through.

Each serving: 212 cal., 9 g total fat (4 g sat. fat), 15 mg chol., 542 mg sodium, 26 g carbo., 2 g fiber, 7 g pro. Daily Values: 13% vit. A, 18% vit. C, 8% calcium, 7% iron.

GET THE LOOK

The mix-and-match look is part of the ambience of a great potluck. To make the setting even better, tie it all together with the help of white tablecloths and vintage linens and napkins.

- Tell guests to use disposable cookware and toss-away foil pans for the food they're toting. But have them bring their favorite summer linens or big napkins.
- Start with plain white tablecloths as your base. Use the linens to emphasize each dish—as stand-out mats beneath each item or as wrap-around color for the cookware and pans.

Farm-Style Green Beans

This recipe was published in a 1976 *Better Homes and Gardens®* magazine story that featured specialties from the tables of Wisconsin dairy farmers. Try it when fresh green beans and homegrown tomatoes are in season and you'll really understand why it ranks as one of the best ways ever to prepare green beans.

PREP: 20 minutes **COOK:** 10 minutes

- **4 thick slices bacon, cut up**
- **2 medium onions, sliced**
- **3 medium tomatoes, peeled, seeded, and chopped (2 cups)**
- **½ tsp. salt**
- **1 lb. green beans, washed, stemmed, and cut up (4 cups)**

1. In a large skillet cook bacon until crisp. Remove bacon, reserving 3 tablespoons of the drippings. Drain bacon and set aside. Cook the onions in the reserved drippings over medium heat until onions are tender. Add the tomatoes and salt; cook, uncovered, about 5 minutes more or until most of the liquid is absorbed.

2. Meanwhile, in a medium saucepan cook the beans in small amount of boiling salted water for 10 to 15 minutes or until crisp-tender; drain. Transfer beans to a serving bowl. Top beans with tomato mixture and bacon pieces. Makes 8 side-dish servings.

Each serving: 86 cal., 5 g total fat (2 g sat. fat), 6 mg chol., 217 mg sodium, 8 g carbo., 3 g fiber, 3 g pro. Daily Values: 13% vit. A, 29% vit. C, 3% calcium, 5% iron.

Poor Boy Filets

In the late 1970s and early 1980s, as men became more interested in cooking, *Better Homes and Gardens®* magazine ran a monthly feature entitled "He Cooks," with recipes sent in from men all over the country. The bachelor cook who concocted this recipe said, "My guests love the filets, and they're a great way to dress up ground beef." These days, the topic of men in the kitchen doesn't merit any special mention because so many men love to cook.

PREP: 30 minutes **GRILL:** 20 minutes

- 10 slices bacon
- 1 lb. lean ground beef
- 1/4 tsp. lemon-pepper seasoning
- 1/8 tsp. salt
- 1/4 cup grated Parmesan cheese
- 1 4-oz. can mushroom stems and pieces, drained and chopped
- 3 Tbsp. finely chopped pimiento-stuffed olives
- 2 Tbsp. finely chopped onion
- 2 Tbsp. finely chopped green sweet pepper
- Halved cherry tomatoes (optional)

1. In a very large skillet partially cook bacon just until light brown, but still soft. Drain on paper towels. Set aside.

2. Pat ground beef on waxed paper to a 12×7½-inch rectangle that is ¼ inch thick. Sprinkle with lemon-pepper seasoning and salt. Top with Parmesan cheese. Combine mushrooms, olives, onion, and sweet pepper; sprinkle evenly over meat. Lightly press into meat.

3. Carefully roll meat into a spiral, starting from a short side. Cut into 1½-inch-thick slices. Wrap the edge of each slice with 2 strips of partially cooked bacon, overlapping as needed and securing ends with wooden picks.

4. Grill meat on the rack of uncovered gas grill on medium or a charcoal grill directly over medium coals for 10 minutes. Turn meat over and grill about 10 minutes more or until meat is done (instant-read thermometer registers 160° F). Serve on a platter. If desired, garnish with cherry tomatoes. Makes 5 servings.

Each serving: 273 cal., 18 g total fat (7 g sat. fat), 74 mg chol., 673 mg sodium, 2 g carbo., 1 g fiber, 24 g pro. Daily Values: 3% vit. A, 10% vit. C, 7% calcium, 12% iron.

Oven-Fried Buttermilk Chicken

It's easy to add "wow" to oven-fried chicken by creating two different crushed-cracker coatings. A deep brown coating with rye crackers adds great flavor. A second batch coated with pepper-flavored water crackers yields a light brown color. Two tones. Two fantastic flavors. It's delicious cold, too, if you want to make it the night before.

PREP: 20 minutes **MARINATE:** 4 hours **BAKE:** 45 minutes

- 5 to 6 lb. meaty chicken pieces (small bone-in breast halves, thighs, and drumsticks), skinned, if desired
- 2 cups buttermilk
- 1½ tsp. salt
- 1 8-oz. pkg. crisp rye crackers
- 2 Tbsp. Greek seasoning blend
- ½ cup butter, melted
- 3 eggs
- 2 Tbsp. water

1. Place chicken pieces in a plastic bag set in a bowl. (If breast halves are large, cut in half before marinating.) For marinade, stir together buttermilk and salt. Pour over chicken; seal bag. Chill for 4 to 24 hours, turning bag occasionally.

2. Meanwhile, place half of the crackers and half of the Greek seasoning blend in a blender or food processor. Cover and blend or process until crackers are crushed.* Repeat with remaining crackers and Greek seasoning blend. In a shallow dish toss together crushed crackers and melted butter. Set aside.

3. Preheat oven to 400° F. In another shallow dish beat eggs; stir in water. Drain chicken pieces, discarding marinade. Dip chicken pieces, one at a time, into egg mixture; roll in cracker mixture to coat. Arrange chicken in 2 lightly greased 13×9×2-inch foil baking pans, making sure pieces do not touch.

4. Bake, uncovered, for 45 to 50 minutes or until chicken pieces are tender and no longer pink (170° F for breast pieces and 180° F for thighs or drumsticks). Serve warm or cover and chill for up to 24 hours. Makes 12 servings.

Each serving: 388 cal., 20 g total fat (8 g sat. fat), 162 mg chol., 476 mg sodium, 18 g carbo., 5 g fiber, 33 g pro. Daily Values: 8% vit. A, 5% calcium, 10% iron.

PEPPER FRIED CHICKEN: You can substitute two 4¼-ounce packages water crackers with cracked pepper for the crisp rye crackers and the Greek seasoning. Continue as directed above.

***NOTE:** If you like, you can crush the crackers in a resealable plastic bag with a rolling pin.

Each serving: 344 cal., 17 g total fat (7 g sat. fat), 153 mg chol., 612 mg sodium, 17 g carbo., 1 g fiber, 30 g pro. Daily Values: 8% vit. A, 1% vit. C, 7% calcium, 7% iron.

Oven-Fried Buttermilk Chicken

Sweet Layers of Red, White, and Blue

This patriotic dessert includes berries, an herb-flavored whipped cream, and purchased small meringue cookies.

PREP: 20 minutes **CHILL:** 24 hours

- 1 recipe Rosemary-Lemon Cream (below)
- 1 8-oz. carton dairy sour cream
- 1⁄3 cup sifted powdered sugar
- 6 cups fresh blueberries
- 6 cups fresh red raspberries and/or strawberries, halved
- 1 5.1-oz. container bite-size vanilla meringue cookies
- Fresh herbs (optional)

1. Prepare Rosemary-Lemon Cream; strain to remove herbs and lemon peel. Discard herbs and peel.

2. In a large mixing bowl combine strained whipping cream, sour cream, and powdered sugar. Beat with an electric mixer on medium speed until soft peaks form (tips curl). Serve immediately or cover and chill for up to 24 hours. (The cream may thicken upon chilling. Stir before serving.)

3. To serve, alternate layers of berries with layers of meringue cookies and whipped cream in twelve 16-ounce glasses or bowls. (The cream helps soften the crunch of the cookies, so keep this in mind when layering.) If desired, garnish with fresh herbs. Makes 12 servings.

ROSEMARY-LEMON CREAM: In a 2-cup glass measuring cup combine 1 1⁄3 cups whipping cream, five 4-inch sprigs of fresh rosemary (stems removed), and one 2×1-inch piece of lemon peel. (If desired, 1⁄4 cup torn basil leaves may be substituted for the rosemary.) Cover with plastic wrap; chill for 24 hours.

Each serving: 232 cal., 14 g total fat (9 g sat. fat), 45 mg chol., 28 mg sodium, 25 g carbo., 5 g fiber, 3 g pro. Daily Values: 12% vit. A, 81% vit. C, 6% calcium, 3% iron.

Peaches and Ice Cream Sandwich Bars

Purchased ice cream sandwiches form the base for this frozen dessert. You can change the toppings at whim. For instance, eliminate the sorbet, mound with whipped cream, and cap it off with a massive pile of whatever fresh fruit calls to you from the produce stand.

PREP: 25 minutes **FREEZE:** 4 hours **STAND:** 10 minutes

- 10 to 14 rectangular ice cream sandwiches, unwrapped
- 2 pt. peach or mango sorbet, softened
- 1 8-oz. carton dairy sour cream
- 1 cup whipping cream
- 3⁄4 cup sifted powdered sugar
- 2 cups fresh blueberries or red raspberries

1. Place ice cream sandwiches in the bottom of a 13×9×2-inch baking pan, cutting to fit. Spread sorbet onto top of ice cream sandwiches. Freeze about 15 minutes or until sorbet is firm.

2. Meanwhile, in medium bowl combine sour cream, whipping cream, and powdered sugar. Beat with an electric mixer on medium speed until soft peaks form (tips curl). Spread onto sorbet.

3. Cover and freeze for 4 to 24 hours or until firm. Let stand at room temperature for 10 minutes before serving. Sprinkle berries over whipped cream mixture. Makes 12 servings.

Each serving: 354 cal., 16 g total fat (10 g sat. fat), 52 mg chol., 49 mg sodium, 51 g carbo., 1 g fiber, 3 g pro. Daily Values: 15% vit. A, 10% vit. C, 9% calcium, 2% iron.

Butter Pecan Ice Cream

Our taste panel's response to this rich treasure was unanimous—you just can't buy ice cream like this, not even as a gourmet brand.

PREP: 20 minutes **FREEZE:** per freezer's directions **RIPEN:** 4 hours

- 1 cup chopped pecans
- 1⁄2 cup sugar
- 2 Tbsp. butter
- 4 cups half-and-half or light cream
- 2 cups packed brown sugar
- 1 Tbsp. vanilla
- 4 cups whipping cream

1. In heavy 8-inch skillet combine nuts, sugar, and butter; heat over medium heat, stirring constantly, for 6 to 8 minutes or until sugar melts and turns a rich brown color. Quickly spread on buttered foil; separate into clusters. Cool; break into small chunks.

2. In a large bowl combine half-and-half, brown sugar, and vanilla; stir until sugar is dissolved. Stir in whipping cream.

3. Freeze in a 4- to 5-quart ice cream freezer according to manufacturer's directions. Stir in pecan mixture. Ripen for 4 hours. Makes 16 servings.

Each serving: 354 cal., 16 g total fat (10 g sat. fat), 52 mg chol., 49 mg sodium, 51 g carbo., 1 g fiber, 3 g pro. Daily Values: 15% vit. A, 10% vit. C, 9% calcium, 2% iron.

Peaches and Ice Cream Sandwich Bars

ICE CREAM DELIGHTS

A potluck is bound to end happily ever after when you serve ice cream—homemade or otherwise. Dress up plain ice cream with one of these easy-does-it fix-ups.

- Roll scoops of ice cream in miniature semisweet chocolate pieces or grated semisweet chocolate and freeze until dessert time.
- Fold crushed peppermint candies or crushed toffee into thawed frozen whipped dessert topping and spoon it over chocolate ice cream.
- Top sliced cantaloupe or strawberries with scoops of your favorite sherbet or ice cream and sprinkle with toasted coconut.
- Mix equal parts of apricot or peach nectar with lemon-lime or grapefruit carbonated beverage. Float vanilla ice cream or fruit-flavored sherbet on top.

Sweet Layers of Red, White, and Blue

Tuna Salad Niçoise

TAKE Fish TO HEART

SEAFOOD IS GOOD FOR YOU, BUT CONCERNS ABOUT MERCURY IN FISH MEAN YOU MUST PICK WISELY.

When it comes to your heart, a few servings of fish go a long, long way. But government warnings about high methylmercury levels in some fish have people worried about adding more fish to their diet. Although rare in the United States, too much methylmercury in a diet can cause nerve damage and blood pressure problems. It can also harm an unborn child's developing nervous system.

According to the U.S. Department of Agriculture, most fish are safe to eat because they contain methylmercury only in trace amounts. The species of concern are larger fish that feed on other fish. Fish lovers should dine only once a week on swordfish, shark, tilefish, and king mackerel, which contain the highest levels of mercury. Young children and women who are pregnant, planning to become pregnant, or who are breastfeeding should avoid these fish altogether. Those women and young children also should limit their intake of lower-mercury seafood to 12 ounces per week. Tuna steaks also can contain high levels of mercury, but not as high as those fish listed above.

Seafood lower in methylmercury and considered safe to eat include clams, cod, crab, flounder, haddock, halibut, herring, lobster, mahi mahi, oysters, scallops, shrimp, canned tuna and other canned fish, whitefish, and farm-raised fish.

Don't avoid fish because of the mercury issue. Medical experts still highly recommend making fish a regular part of your diet (two 3-ounce servings per week) because the oil in fish (omega-3 fatty acids) has heart-healthy benefits: lowering blood pressure, reducing fat levels in blood, and helping to prevent sudden cardiac death.

Tuna Salad Niçoise

PREP: 45 minutes **MARINATE:** 4 hours

- 1½ cups cut fresh green beans
- 8 oz. whole tiny new potatoes (4 to 6)
- 1 recipe Caper Vinaigrette (below)
- 1 9¼-oz. can chunk white tuna (water pack), drained and broken into chunks, or 12 oz. cooked tuna
- 1 medium green sweet pepper, cut into strips
- 1 cup cherry tomatoes, halved
- ¾ cup pitted ripe olives
- 4 cups torn romaine and/or Bibb or Boston lettuce
- ½ of a 2-oz. can anchovy fillets, drained and halved

1. In a medium covered saucepan cook beans in lightly salted boiling water for 10 minutes. Add potatoes; cook about 15 minutes more or until tender. Drain; rinse with cold water. Drain again.

2. Prepare Caper Vinaigrette. Place tuna chunks in a small bowl; top with ⅔ cup vinaigrette. Quarter potatoes. In a medium bowl combine potatoes, beans, green pepper, tomatoes, olives, and ⅔ cup vinaigrette. Cover each bowl; chill for 4 hours.

3. To serve, line 4 plates with lettuce. Using a slotted spoon, top with tuna and bean mixture. Top with anchovies; pass remaining vinaigrette. Makes 4 main-dish servings.

CAPER VINAIGRETTE: In a screw-top jar combine 1 cup olive oil or salad oil, ½ cup white wine vinegar or white vinegar, 1 tablespoon dry mustard, 1 tablespoon drained and chopped capers, 2 minced garlic cloves, 1 tablespoon snipped fresh basil or 1 teaspoon crushed dried basil, and 1 tablespoon snipped fresh oregano or 1 teaspoon crushed dried oregano. Cover and shake well to mix.

Each serving: 404 cal., 23 g total fat (3 g sat. fat), 55 mg chol., 551 mg sodium, 19 g carbo., 5 g fiber, 31 g pro. Daily Values: 37% vit. A, 94% vit. C, 11% calcium, 21% iron.

Lime Seafood Salad

THE TUNA CHOICE: CANNED OR FRESH?

Believe it or not, canned is better. The tuna used for canning are typically younger than the tuna sold in the fresh and frozen market and have not accumulated high levels of mercury in their bodies.

- Also, canned tuna is often composed of smaller species of tuna, such as albacore and skipjack, both of which have lower levels of mercury. The Food and Drug Administration recommends that tuna lovers eat white albacore tuna because it's from smaller fish and contains minimal traces of mercury.
- Be sure to buy water-pack tuna rather than the type packed in oil. The oil used to preserve canned tuna extracts all the good fatty acids, says longtime fish oil researcher Alexander Leaf, M.D., professor emeritus of clinical medicine at Harvard Medical School.

Lime Seafood Salad

START TO FINISH: 30 minutes

- 1 lb. sea scallops, skinless salmon fillet, whitefish fillet, or mahi mahi fillet
- 2 Tbsp. all-purpose flour
- ½ tsp. ground black pepper
- 2 Tbsp. butter or margarine
- ¼ cup orange marmalade
- 2 Tbsp. lime juice
- 1 Tbsp. soy sauce
- ½ tsp. grated fresh ginger
- ¼ tsp. cayenne pepper
- 4 cups sliced bok choy or Chinese cabbage
- ½ cup coarsely shredded carrot
- 1 lime, cut into wedges

1. If using scallops, in a plastic bag combine flour and black pepper. Add scallops; toss to coat. If using fish, cut into 4 serving-size portions; sprinkle with black pepper (omit flour).

2. In a large skillet heat butter. Add scallops or fish. Cook scallops about 2 minutes per side or until golden brown. (Cook fish pieces 4 to 6 minutes per side or until the fish flakes easily when tested with a fork.) Use a slotted spatula to remove fish from skillet, reserving drippings in skillet.

3. Add orange marmalade, lime juice, soy sauce, ginger, and cayenne pepper to skillet; heat through. Remove from heat. Add bok choy and carrot to skillet. Toss to coat. Serve with scallops and lime wedges. Makes 4 main-dish servings.

Each serving: 250 cal., 7 g total fat (4 g sat. fat), 54 mg chol., 864 mg sodium, 25 g carbo., 3 g fiber, 23 g pro. Daily Values: 180% vit. A, 88% vit. C, 20% calcium, 14% iron.

Flower Cookies with Cardamom

SWEET DREAMS COME TRUE

MADELINE CALLAHAN'S CREATIVITY IN THE KITCHEN HAS TURNED HER INTO A FOOD MOGUL.

Flower Cookies with Cardamom

Ground cardamom loses much of its flavor if it is stored for a long time. Make sure your supply smells fresh before you begin baking.

PREP: 1 hour **CHILL:** 2 hours **BAKE:** 5 minutes per batch
STAND: 1 hour

- 1 cup butter, softened
- 1½ cups granulated sugar
- ¾ tsp. ground cardamom
- ½ tsp. baking powder
- ½ tsp. salt
- 2 eggs
- ¼ cup milk
- 1½ tsp. vanilla
- 3 cups all-purpose flour
- 1 recipe Powdered Sugar Frosting (below)
- Colored sprinkles or colored sugar (optional)

1. In a large bowl beat butter with an electric mixer on medium to high speed for 30 seconds. Add granulated sugar, cardamom, baking powder, and salt. Beat until combined. Add eggs, milk, and vanilla. Beat until combined. Beat in as much of the flour as you can with the mixer. Stir in any remaining flour. Divide dough in half. Cover and chill about 2 hours or until easy to handle.

2. Preheat oven to 425° F. On a lightly floured surface roll half of the dough to an ⅛-inch thickness. Cut cookie dough using 1¾-, 2½-, and 4-inch flower-shape cookie cutters. (By rerolling the dough you should get 12 to 15 cutouts of each size from each dough half.) Place cutouts 1 inch apart on ungreased cookie sheets. Bake about 5 minutes or until edges just start to brown. Remove and cool cookies on a wire rack.

3. Spread cookies with Powdered Sugar Frosting.* While still moist, stack cookies together, placing a 2½-inch cookie in the center of a 4-inch cookie and a 1¾-inch cookie in the center of the 2½-inch cookie. If desired, add sprinkles or colored sugar. Allow cookies to stand for 1 to 2 hours to set before serving. Makes 24 to 30 stacked cookies.

POWDERED SUGAR FROSTING: In a large mixing bowl stir together 6 cups powdered sugar, ⅓ cup milk, and 1 tablespoon vanilla. Add additional milk, 1 tablespoon at a time, until frosting is of a spreading consistency. Tint as desired with food coloring.

***NOTE:** Store unfrosted cookies in the freezer for up to 3 months.

Each cookie: 280 cal., 9 g total fat (5 g sat. fat), 40 mg chol., 148 mg sodium, 49 g carbo., 0 g fiber, 2 g protein. Daily Values: 7% vit. A, 2% calcium, 4% iron.

Uniquely together

It seems every time teenager Madeline Callahan steps into the kitchen, her creative taste buds kick into high gear. Her first attempt at baking, however, wasn't exactly success. The Illinois teen decided to bake a cake when she was 7 years old. Without measuring, Madeline stirred together lots of yeast, plus flour, sugar, butter, and eggs. She poured the mixture into a pan, popped it in the oven, and watched it rise and overflow. "We decorated it with sprinkles, but it still tasted pretty gross," Madeline says. That failure didn't keep the self-confident girl from experimenting. After tasting a biscuit flavored with cardamom, "I thought, 'What is that mysterious taste?' " Madeline says. "It intrigued me." So she added cardamom to a sugar cookie recipe and loved it.

Although her family's interest has helped to spark Madeline's love of cooking, her mother, Anne, says she comes by her culinary flair naturally. "Madeline is extremely creative and always has been," says Anne. Her greatest idea (so far) came at a party her family hosted. "My parents were getting ready for the adults, and I thought, 'There's nothing for the kids to drink,' " Madeline says. Looking for inspiration, Madeline spied bowls of limes and lemons. So she squeezed, stirred, and tasted. Still not satisfied with the pale color of the finished product, she pulled some fresh raspberries from the fridge and tossed them into the pitcher. Madeline's Lemonade *(page 266)* was such a hit, a family friend—a buyer for Crate&Barrel—snapped it up. Madeline's Lemonade is now featured in Crate&Barrel stores.

Madeline's Lemonade

Madeline's Lemonade

In a 2-quart pitcher combine the juice from 6 large lemons ($1\frac{1}{2}$ cups juice) and 2 large limes ($\frac{1}{3}$ cup juice). Add 6 cups water and 1 cup sugar; stir to dissolve sugar. Add 1 cup fresh red raspberries; cover and chill overnight. Serve over ice. Garnish with lemon and lime slices. Makes 8 or 9 servings.

Grilled Cheese Sandwich with Sautéed Onions and Mushrooms

Grilled Cheese Sandwich with Sautéed Onions and Mushrooms

To make 4 sandwiches, slice a large onion. In a skillet cook onion slices in 2 tablespoons butter over medium heat about 10 minutes or until onion is soft and golden brown, stirring occasionally. Stir in about 1 cup sliced fresh mushrooms. Cook and stir for 2 minutes more. Remove from heat. Sprinkle with sea salt and about 1 teaspoon berry-balsamic vinegar. Place slices of desired cheese onto 4 slices sourdough bread. Top each with some of the onion-mushroom mixture and another slice of sourdough bread. Butter bread and cook on a griddle or in a skillet over medium heat for 2 to 3 minutes per side or until the cheese is melted.

Super-Quick Ice Cream Sandwiches

Stir 1/2 cup chopped malted milk balls into a pint of softened strawberry ice cream. Spoon ice cream onto the flat side of 6 soft cookies (such as chocolate, oatmeal, or chocolate chip). Spread about 1 tablespoon fudge ice cream topping onto flat side of each of 6 additional cookies. Place cookies, fudge sides down, on ice cream. Wrap and freeze at least 6 hours or until firm. Let frozen sandwiches stand about 10 minutes before eating.

Super-Quick Ice Cream Sandwiches

big easy

HAVE FUN PLAYING IN THE KITCHEN. THESE RECIPES ARE FRESH, SIMPLE, AND QUICK. THIS IS WHAT MAKES THEM SO GREAT.

Stuffed Caprese

Stuffed Caprese

Go beyond red tomatoes, if you can. Yellow tomatoes will be sweeter; green a little more tart.

Prep: 25 minutes **Chill:** up to 2 hours

- 4 small tomatoes (3 to 4 oz. each)
- 1/3 tsp. sea salt or salt
- 1/8 tsp. pepper
- 3 Tbsp. olive oil
- 3 Tbsp. white wine vinegar
- 1/2 tsp. sugar
- 3 oz. fresh mozzarella or fresh buffalo mozzarella, drained and cut into small chunks (about 1/2 cup)
- 1/4 cup slivered red onion
- 1/4 cup snipped fresh basil

1. Cut a 1/4-inch slice from the stem end of each tomato. Using a spoon, carefully scoop out core, seeds, and pulp, leaving up to a 1/2-inch-thick shell. Discard pulp. Sprinkle tomato shells with salt and pepper. Stand tomato shells on a plate; set aside.

2. For dressing, in a screw-top jar combine olive oil, vinegar, and sugar. Cover; shake well. Reserve 1 1/2 tablespoons of dressing. Spoon remaining dressing into tomato shells.

3. In a bowl combine mozzarella, red onion, basil, and reserved dressing; toss to mix. Spoon cheese mixture into shells. Cover; refrigerate until ready to serve or up to 2 hours.

4. To serve, place stuffed tomatoes on plates. Sprinkle with additional salt and pepper. Makes 4 servings.

Each serving: 177 cal., 15 g total fat (4 g sat. fat), 16 mg chol., 187 mg sodium, 6 g carbo., 1 g fiber, 5 g pro. Daily Values: 29% vit. C, 12% calcium, 4% iron.

Small tomatoes are the best size to choose for this salad. Take care not to break the shell when scooping; the curved bowl of a soup spoon is a helpful tool.

Nutty Cucumber Sandwich

Select chèvre that has been rolled in cracked black pepper to add another flavor dimension to this sandwich.

Start to Finish: 15 minutes

- 1/2 cup fresh snow pea pods, trimmed
- 1/2 medium cucumber
- 8 thin slices rye bread
- 3 to 4 oz. soft goat cheese (chèvre)
- 1/3 cup seasoned roasted soy nuts (such as ranch or garlic)
- 1 medium tomato, thinly sliced
- Salt

1. In a saucepan cook pea pods in lightly salted boiling water for 2 minutes. Drain; rinse with cold water. Drain again. Place pea pods in a small bowl; chill.

2. Use a vegetable peeler to remove a few lengthwise strips of peel from cucumber. Thinly slice cucumber.

3. Spread one side of each bread slice with goat cheese. Sprinkle 4 bread slices with soy nuts, gently pressing nuts into the cheese. Top with cucumber slices, tomato slices, and pea pods. Sprinkle with salt. Top with remaining bread slices. Makes 4 sandwiches.

Each serving: 276 cal., 9 g total fat (4 g sat. fat), 10 mg chol.,540 mg sodium, 36 g carbo., 6 g fiber, 14 g pro. Daily Values: 24% vit. C, 10% calcium, 17% iron.

DINNER ON THE DECK

Smooth and Chunky Melon Soup *(page 274)*
Grilled Halibut with Blueberry-Pepper Jam *(left)*
Roasted Potato Salad *(page 289)*
Fill-the-Grill Nectarine Toss *(page 277)*
Sourdough bread
White wine or iced tea

Grilled Halibut with Blueberry-Pepper Jam

A drizzle of olive oil just before serving keeps the sage-crouton topping moist. If some topping tumbles off, so be it, because that's just the way crunchy crust crumbles.

PREP: 25 minutes **GRILL:** 12 minutes

- **4 5- to 6-oz. fresh or frozen halibut steaks or fillets or sea bass or salmon fillets, cut 1 inch thick**
- **1 cup garlic croutons, coarsely crushed**
- **1/4 cup snipped fresh sage**
- **1 tsp. finely shredded orange peel**
- **1/4 tsp. pepper**
- **2 Tbsp. orange juice**
- **1 Tbsp. olive oil**
- **1 recipe Blueberry-Pepper Jam (below)**

1. Thaw fish, if frozen. Rinse fish; pat dry.

2. For topping, in a small bowl combine crushed croutons, sage, orange peel, and pepper. Stir in orange juice and olive oil until lightly moistened; set aside.

3. Lightly grease the rack of a grill. For a charcoal grill, cook fish, skin side up if using fillets, on the rack of the grill, uncovered, directly over medium coals for 5 minutes. Turn fish; top evenly with crouton topping, pressing onto fish. Grill for 7 to 10 minutes more or until fish flakes easily when tested with a fork. (For a gas grill, preheat grill. Reduce heat to medium. Place fish on greased grill rack over heat. Cover and cook as above.)

4. To serve, place fish on a serving platter. Drizzle fish with additional olive oil. If desired, garnish with additional sage leaves. Serve with Blueberry-Pepper Jam. Makes 4 servings.

BLUEBERRY-PEPPER JAM: In a bowl place 3/4 cup fresh blueberries; mash with a potato masher or fork. Stir in 3/4 cup blueberries, 1 teaspoon snipped fresh sage, and 1/2 teaspoon freshly ground black pepper. Cover; chill until ready to serve.

Each serving: 222 cal., 7 g total fat (1 g sat. fat), 45 mg chol., 101 mg sodium, 8 g carbo., 1 g fiber, 30 g pro. Daily Values: 16% vit. C, 9% calcium, 8% iron.

Soy-Lime Scallops with Leeks

When purchasing fresh sea scallops, look for color between pale beige and pink, a sweet smell, and a moist sheen.

PREP: 10 minutes **MARINATE:** 30 minutes **GRILL:** 8 minutes

- **1 lb. fresh or frozen sea scallops**
- **1 small leek or 4 baby leeks**
- **8 medium green or red scallions**
- **1/4 cup soy sauce**
- **1/4 cup rice vinegar**
- **1 medium lime, halved**
- **Black sesame seed (optional)**
- **1/4 cup butter, melted***

1. Thaw scallops, if frozen. Rinse scallops; pat dry with paper towels. Set aside.

2. Trim root end and green tops of leek and scallions. Rinse leek thoroughly to remove any grit. Cut the small leek lengthwise into quarters; insert a wooden toothpick crosswise through each leek quarter to hold layers together when grilling. Or trim the baby leeks.

3. Place scallops, leeks, and scallions in a plastic bag set in a shallow bowl. For marinade, in a small bowl whisk together soy sauce and rice vinegar; add to bag. Seal bag; turn to coat scallops and vegetables. Marinate in refrigerator for 30 minutes.

4. Remove scallops, leeks, and scallions from the bag. Discard the marinade. For a charcoal grill, place scallops, leeks, scallions, and lime halves, cut side down, on the rack of an uncovered grill directly over medium coals. Grill for 8 to 10 minutes or until scallops are opaque, turning scallops and vegetables occasionally. Remove scallions before they overbrown. (For a gas grill, preheat grill. Reduce heat to medium. Place scallops, leeks, scallions, and lime halves on rack over heat. Grill as above.)

5. To serve, transfer leeks and scallions to four serving plates. Top with scallops. Using grilling tongs, remove limes from grill; squeeze over scallops. Sprinkle with black sesame seed. Serve with melted butter. Makes 4 servings.

***TEST KITCHEN TIP:** Melt butter in heat-resistant bowl or ramekin on grill alongside scallops and leeks.

Each serving: 229 cal., 13 g total fat (8 g sat. fat), 70 mg chol., 467 mg sodium, 8 g carbo., 1 g fiber, 20 g pro. Daily Values: 24% vit. C, 6% calcium, 6% iron.

Grilled Halibut with Blueberry-Pepper Jam

Soy-Lime Scallops with Leeks

Chilled Thai Tenderloin and Pasta with Tons of Basil and Curried Green and Yellow Bean Salad

Chilled Thai Tenderloin and Pasta with Tons of Basil

This recipe can be made two days in advance of a party. Tying the tenderloin butcher-style helps keep its shape during cooking. Just follow the tying directions below.

PREP: 30 minutes **GRILL:** 1 hour **CHILL:** 8 hours

- 1 3-lb. center-cut beef tenderloin
- Pepper
- 1/2 cup purchased Thai peanut sauce
- 3 cups packed purple or green basil sprigs (do not remove leaves from stems)
- 2 lb. angel hair pasta, cooked according to package directions
- 1 1/2 cups purchased Thai peanut sauce
- 2 cups sliced fennel strips
- 1 cup slivered fresh purple or green basil
- 2 Tbsp. olive oil

1. Butcher-wrap the beef tenderloin (see instructions, below). Season with pepper. Spread the 1/2 cup peanut sauce onto the beef until coated. Tuck basil sprigs under string, covering as much of the beef as possible.

2. For a charcoal grill, arrange preheated coals around a drip pan. Test for medium-high heat above pan. Place beef on grill rack over drip pan. Cover; grill to desired doneness. Allow 1 to 1 1/4 hours for medium rare (135° F) or 1 1/4 to 1 1/2 hours for medium (150° F). (For a gas grill, preheat grill. Reduce heat to medium. Adjust for indirect cooking. Grill as above, except place beef on rack in a roasting pan.)

3. Remove beef from grill; cover with foil and let stand for 40 minutes. (The temperature of the meat should rise 10° F during cooking.) Wrap beef tightly in plastic wrap; cover and store in refrigerator at least 8 hours or up to 2 days until ready to serve.

4. In a very large bowl toss cooked angel hair pasta with the 1 1/2 cups peanut sauce and fennel. Add slivered basil. Cover and chill until ready to serve.

5. To serve, toss pasta mixture with olive oil; arrange on a serving platter. Cut string from tenderloin; remove basil sprigs and discard. Slice tenderloin into 1/4-inch-thick slices. To serve, arrange sliced tenderloin beside pasta. Makes 10 servings.

Each serving: 670 cal., 19 g total fat (5 g sat. fat), 62 mg chol., 828 mg sodium, 83 g carbo., 7 g fiber, 37 g pro. Daily Values: 9% vit. C, 6% calcium, 33% iron.

Curried Green and Yellow Bean Salad

The snap of curry complements the crunch of chilled beans in this salad and the flavors of Chilled Thai Tenderloin.

PREP: 25 minutes **COOK:** 10 minutes **CHILL:** 2 hours

- 12 oz. green beans, trimmed
- 12 oz. yellow wax beans, trimmed
- 2 Tbsp. white wine vinegar
- 2 Tbsp. olive oil
- 1 1/2 tsp. sugar
- 1 tsp. grated fresh ginger
- 1 tsp. curry powder
- 1/2 tsp. ground turmeric
- 1/4 tsp. salt
- 1/4 tsp. pepper

1. In a saucepan cook beans, covered, in a small amount of boiling salted water for 10 minutes or until crisp-tender. Drain and immerse in a bowl half-filled with ice water. Drain again. Return beans to bowl. Cover and refrigerate until serving.

2. Meanwhile, for salad dressing, in a screw-top jar combine vinegar, olive oil, sugar, ginger, curry powder, turmeric, salt, and pepper. Cover; shake well. Refrigerate until serving time.

3. To serve, pour salad dressing over beans. Toss gently to coat. Makes 8 to 10 servings.

Each serving: 60 cal., 4 g total fat (0 g sat. fat), 0 mg chol., 78 mg sodium, 7 g carbo., 3 g fiber, 2 g pro. Daily Values: 17% vit. C, 3% calcium, 5% iron.

BUTCHER-WRAP A TENDERLOIN

1. Slide an 8-foot-long, 100-percent-cotton string under meat about 2 inches from end. Pull to top. Make a knot, keeping one end short.

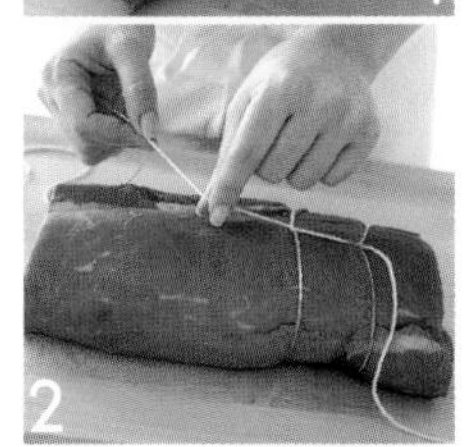

2. Pull long end toward other end. About 2 inches from first tie, loop string under; bring up and around. Insert long end under top string to secure; pull to tighten. Repeat, making a loop every 2 inches to the end.

3. Bring the string lengthwise around the underside of the roast and back to the starting point at the top side of the tenderloin, twisting the string around each loop as you go. Knot it around the initial loop. Cut the string.

Smooth and Chunky Melon Soup

Soymilk, an increasingly popular alternative to milk, is now available at most grocery stores.

PREP: 15 minutes **CHILL:** 3 hours

- **6 cups cubed cantaloupe**
- **$1\frac{1}{2}$ cups mango nectar**
- **1 tsp. freshly ground dried whole green or black peppercorns**
- **$1\frac{1}{2}$ cups vanilla-enriched soy-based beverage (soymilk) or $1\frac{1}{2}$ cups plain yogurt**
- **2 cups cubed cantaloupe and/or honeydew melon (optional)**
- **1 recipe Peppered Yogurt (below) (optional)**
- **1 recipe Prosciutto Gremolata (below) (optional)**
- **Yellow sweet pepper spears (optional)**

1. Place 3 cups of the cantaloupe, half of the mango nectar, and $\frac{1}{2}$ teaspoon of the pepper in a blender container or food processor bowl. Cover and blend or process until cantaloupe is smooth. Transfer to a large bowl with a spout. Repeat with remaining 3 cups cantaloupe, nectar, and pepper.

2. Stir soy milk into the cantaloupe mixture in bowl. Cover and refrigerate until serving time, up to 3 hours.

3. To serve, pour soup into eight soup bowls. Top with cantaloupe cubes. If desired, garnish with Peppered Yogurt and/or Prosciutto Gremolata. Makes 8 servings.

PEPPERED YOGURT: In a small bowl stir $\frac{1}{2}$ teaspoon freshly cracked whole dried green or black peppercorns into $\frac{1}{2}$ cup plain yogurt. Cover; store in the refrigerator. Makes $\frac{1}{2}$ cup.

PROSCIUTTO GREMOLATA: In a bowl combine 2 ounces chopped prosciutto, $1\frac{1}{2}$ teaspoons snipped fresh parsley, and 1 teaspoon finely shredded lemon peel. Makes about $\frac{1}{2}$ cup.

Each serving: 99 cal., 1 g total fat (0 g sat. fat), 38 mg sodium, 21 g carbo., 1 g fiber, 2 g pro. Daily Values: 94% vit. C, 7% calcium, 4% iron.

Mad Mad Martian Juice

Chill this herbal concoction in the refrigerator for at least one hour before serving to let the flavors blend.

PREP: 15 minutes **CHILL:** 1 hour

- **$\frac{1}{2}$ cup snipped fresh mint or basil or $\frac{1}{4}$ cup snipped fresh tarragon**
- **1 recipe Simple Syrup (below)**
- **$1\frac{1}{2}$ cups water**
- **2 cups ice cubes**
- **Lavender sprigs (optional)**
- **Lemon wedges (optional)**

1. In a blender container combine herb, Simple Syrup, and water. Cover; blend until nearly smooth.

2. With blender running, gradually add ice cubes through hole in lid, blending until slushy. To serve, pour into three or four glasses. If desired, garnish with lavender sprigs and/or lemon wedges. Makes 3 or 4 servings.

SIMPLE SYRUP: In a small saucepan combine $\frac{1}{4}$ cup sugar and $\frac{1}{4}$ cup water. Bring just to boiling, stirring to dissolve sugar. Cool; cover and chill for at least 1 hour before using. Makes about $\frac{1}{3}$ cup.

Each serving: 65 cal., 0 g total fat (0 g sat. fat), 0 mg chol.,8 mg sodium, 16 g carbo., 0 g fiber, 0 g pro. Daily Values: 15% vit. C, 2% calcium, 14% iron.

Smooth and Chunky Melon Soup

Mad Mad Martian Juice

Afternoon Coffee Vodka Cooler

Fill-the-Grill Nectarine Toss

If your mother begged you to eat fresh fruit, here's your answer: Have it with a big bowl of ice cream.

PREP: 15 minutes **GRILL:** 8 minutes

- 6 medium nectarines, halved and pitted
- 2 Tbsp. olive oil
- Ground cinnamon or nutmeg (optional)
- 3 cups vanilla ice cream
- Coarsely chopped chocolate chunks

1. Brush nectarines with olive oil. Sprinkle with cinnamon. Place a grill wok or grill basket on the rack of an uncovered grill directly over medium coals; heat for 5 minutes. Place nectarine halves in the wok or basket. Grill for 8 to 10 minutes or until heated through, turning gently halfway through cooking time. (For gas grill, preheat grill. Reduce heat to medium. Place grill wok or basket on grill rack over heat. Cover; grill as above.)

2. To serve, scoop ice cream into a serving bowl. Top with grilled nectarines. Sprinkle with chocolate. Makes 6 servings.

Each serving: 312 cal., 19 g total fat (9 g sat. fat), 46 mg chol., 46 mg sodium, 36 g carbo., 2 g fiber, 4 g pro. Daily Values: 13% vit. C, 10% calcium, 1% iron.

Fill-the-Grill Nectarine Toss

Afternoon Coffee Vodka Cooler

Prepare the Coffee Bean Vodka (see instructions, right) at least four days in advance. Save some of the morning coffee—the stronger the better—to make these afternoon refreshers.

PREP: 5 minutes

- Ice cubes
- 1/2 cup cold brewed coffee
- 2 Tbsp. Coffee Bean Vodka (right)
- 1 Tbsp. whipping cream, half-and-half, or light cream
- 1 tsp. extra-fine or regular granulated sugar

1. To serve, fill a short glass with ice cubes. Add coffee, Coffee Bean Vodka, whipping cream, and sugar to glass. Stir gently. Makes 1 cooler.

ESPRESSO MARTINI: Fill a martini shaker with ice. Add 2 tablespoons Coffee Bean Vodka. Shake vigorously. Strain vodka into a well-chilled martini glass. Add 1/2 cup cold brewed coffee; stir gently. Add a splash of cream or cream-based liqueur, if you like. Makes 1 martini.

Each serving: 143 cal., 6 g total fat (3 g sat. fat), 21 mg chol., 8 mg sodium, 5 g carbo., 0 g fiber, 0 g pro. Daily Values: 1% calcium.

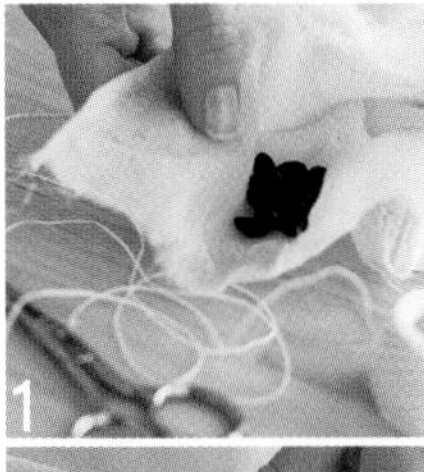

1

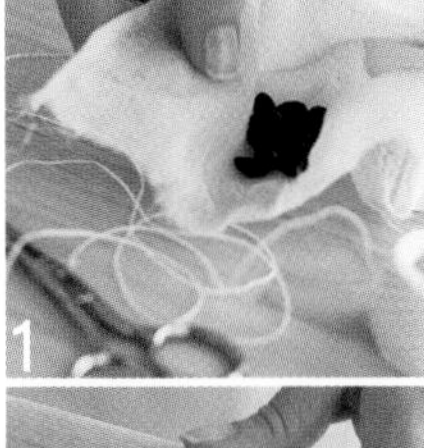

2

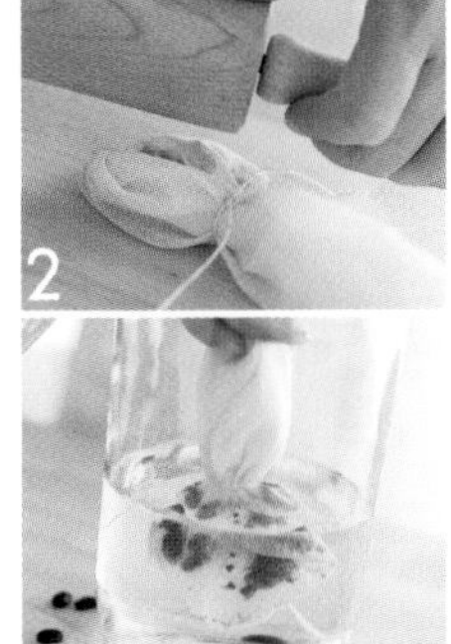

3

HOW TO MAKE COFFEE BEAN VODKA

1. Place 16 whole espresso or coffee beans on a piece of 100-percent-cotton cheesecloth and tie into abundle with clean 100-percent-cotton string.

2. Gently crush a few beans by tapping the tied coffee bean bundle lightly with a rolling pin.

3. Pour a 750-milliliter bottle of vodka into a plastic freezer container; add bean bundle. Cover; store in the freezer for at least four days or up to two weeks. To chill longer, remove the coffee bean bundle.

You Say Tomato

A SPELL-BINDING BLUSH MAY BE THE tomato's seductive lure, but its wholesome nutrition is the best reason to keep coming back for more. An average-size tomato supplies about 40 percent of the vitamin C, 20 percent of the vitamin A, and 10 percent of the potassium you should get in a day.

Red tomato varieties are rich in lycopene too. This plant chemical, which puts the red color in tomatoes, also acts as a powerful antioxidant in the body. A Harvard study of men who consumed a tomato-rich diet (at least 10 servings a week) showed that they may have reduced their risk of prostate cancer by 45 percent. Researchers also are looking at lycopene's role in protecting against other cancers, as well as heart disease. Since the body absorbs lycopene more easily from heat-processed tomatoes, cooked tomato dishes and canned tomato products will give you a boost of the antioxidant—two to four times more than fresh tomatoes.

With all this going for tomatoes, is it any wonder the French originally called them the fruit of love? To savor the of the end-of-summer tomato harvest, cook up a quick sauté (right)—terrific over pasta or wilted greens—or stir together a great gazpacho (far right) that's a meal in itself.

Go-with-Anything Tomato Sauté

Prep: 12 minutes **Cook:** 3 minutes

- 2½ cups whole red grape and yellow teardrop tomatoes and/or cherry tomatoes
- Nonstick olive oil cooking spray
- ¼ cup finely chopped shallots
- 1 clove garlic, minced
- 1 tsp. snipped fresh lemon-thyme or thyme
- ¼ tsp. salt
- ¼ tsp. pepper
- 1 cup fresh mozzarella cut into ½-inch cubes (4 oz.)

1. Halve about 1½ cups of the tomatoes; set aside. Lightly coat a 10-inch nonstick skillet with olive oil cooking spray. Add shallots, garlic, and thyme. Cook and stir over medium heat for 2 to 3 minutes or until shallots are tender.

2. Add remaining tomatoes, salt, and pepper. Cook and stir for 1 to 2 minutes more or until tomatoes are just warmed. Remove from heat. Stir in mozzarella cubes. Makes 4 side-dish servings.

Each serving: 107 cal., 5 g total fat(3 g sat. fat), 16 mg chol., 289 mg sodium, 9 g carbo., 1 g fiber, 8 g pro. Daily Values: 14% vit. A, 43% vit. C, 19% calcium, 5% iron.

Go-with-Anything Tomato Sauté

HOT LITTLE TOMATOES

You'll see this sweetie linked on the vine with other little ones. Bite through its slightly thick skin, and this mild tomato bursts.

Stunning color and a voluptuous shape make this babe irresistible. The yellow teardrop is meaty with a mild flavor.

Just like the yellow teardrop, the pear shape is alluring. It tastes like a vine-ripened tomato with an extra hint of sweetness.

Popular in home gardens, this hybrid has a rich orange color and a sweet-as-candy taste.

This itsy-bitsy cutie is among the tiniest of tomatoes. Its flavor has a bit of a tomato tang.

Loaded with vitamin C, this sugary, grape-size version of the cherry tomato was first cultivated in China.

Some people pop this super-sweet, 1-inch wonder into their mouths like candy. There's a yellow variety too.

Red and Green Gazpacho

Red and Green Gazpacho

PREP: 30 minutes **CHILL:** 1 hour

- 3 cups chopped red and/or partially green tomatoes (3 large)
- 1/2 cup chopped tomatillo (2 medium)
- 1 16-oz. can tomato juice (2 cups)
- 1/2 cup chopped cucumber
- 1 large jalapeño pepper, seeded and finely chopped
- 1/4 cup finely chopped green onion
- 1 clove garlic, minced
- 1/4 tsp. bottled hot green pepper sauce
- 1 Tbsp. olive oil
- 1 Tbsp. lime juice
- 1/4 cup finely snipped cilantro
- 6 oz. peeled, cooked medium shrimp (12 to 15)
- Fat-free dairy sour cream (optional)
- Green onion curl (optional)

1. In a bowl combine tomatoes, tomatillo, tomato juice, cucumber, jalapeño pepper, green onion, garlic, pepper sauce, olive oil, lime juice, and cilantro. Cover; chill at least 1 hour.

2. To serve, reserve 6 shrimp. Coarsely chop remaining shrimp. Stir chopped shrimp into gazpacho. Spoon gazpacho into six chilled soup bowls. Top each serving with a dollop of sour cream, a whole shrimp, and a green onion curl, if desired. Makes 6 side-dish servings.

Each serving: 90 cal., 3 g total fat (0 g sat. fat), 55 mg chol., 371 mg sodium, 10 g carbo., 2 g fiber, 8 g pro. Daily Values: 27% vit. A, 64% vit. C, 3% calcium, 11% iron.

August

MIDSUMMER'S THE PERFECT TIME TO THROW A GARDEN PARTY. HERE'S HOW TO DO IT WITH STYLE.

Watermelon-Berry Sorbet

Maine Vichyssoise with Chive Oil

Gathering Herbs & Friends

Rosemary Lamb Chops

Plus...

Tomato Bread Pudding

Summer Ripe

Plus...

AH!!! AUGUST. HOT DAYS OF GARDEN TRADING, FARMER'S MARKET STROLLING, AND RELISHING SUMMER'S MOST COLORFUL GEMS.

Cornmeal-Crusted Onion Rings

nion Dip

Fresh Corn Fritters

Square Summer Pie

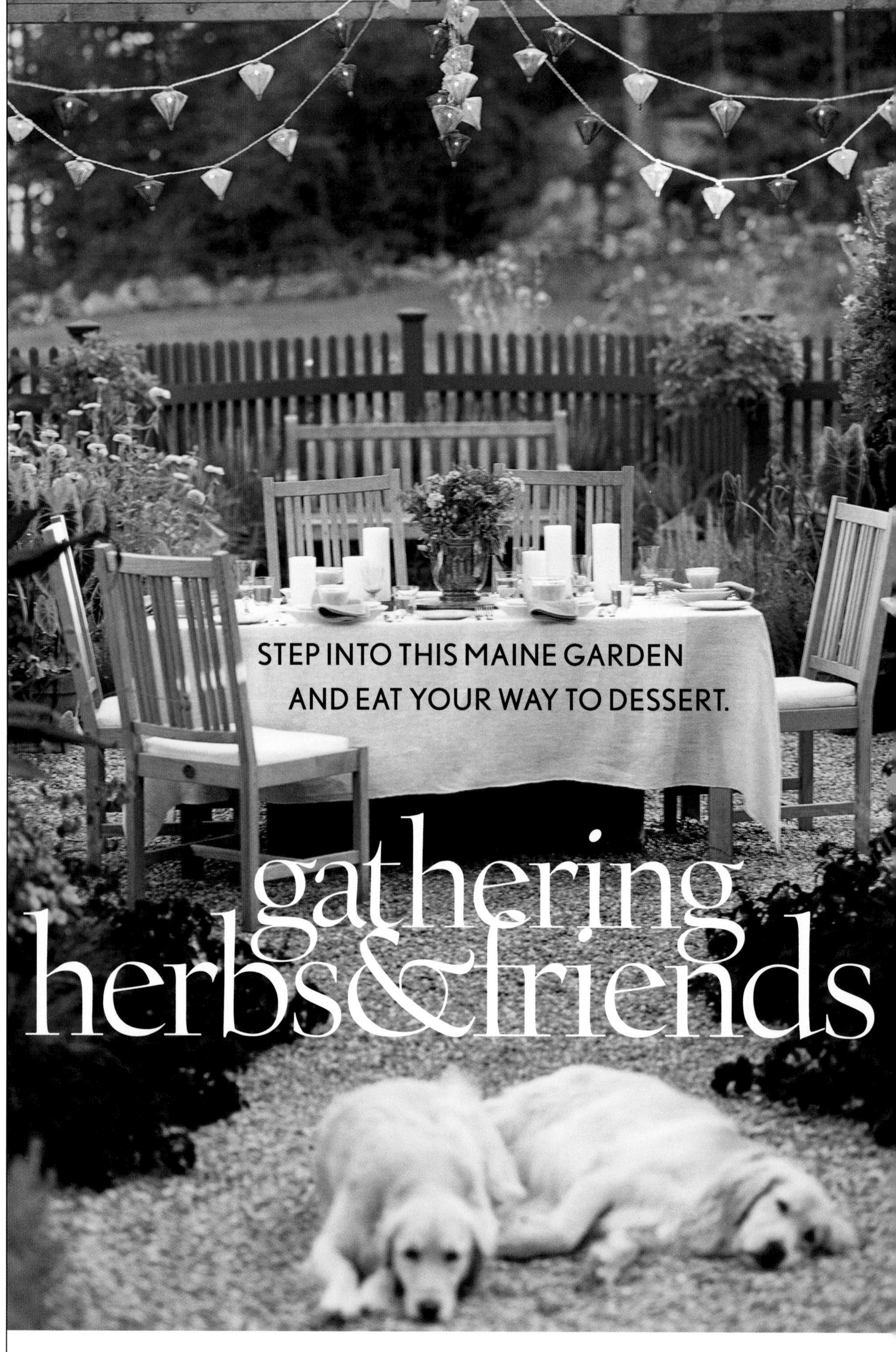
STEP INTO THIS MAINE GARDEN
AND EAT YOUR WAY TO DESSERT.
gathering
herbs&friends

Figs with Herbed Goat Cheese

Fig fanciers tend to be a selfish lot. Once you taste fresh figs, you'll understand why. The season is short, making them a precious commodity. Their soft skin means they should be handled with care, and their delicate nature and sweet flavor make them all the more desired. Fresh figs need little embellishment, but pairing them with goat cheese and herbs makes a tasty exclamation point.

Start to Finish: 15 minutes

- **3 oz. soft goat cheese (chèvre)**
- **1½ tsp. snipped fresh chives**
- **1½ tsp. snipped fresh parsley**
- **½ tsp. snipped fresh rosemary**
- **Salt**
- **Ground black pepper**
- **6 fresh figs or apricots**
- **Fresh rosemary sprigs (optional)**

1. In a small bowl combine goat cheese, chives, parsley, snipped rosemary, salt, and pepper.

2. Cut the figs in half. If using apricots, cut in half; remove and discard pits. Top fig halves with herbed cheese. Cover and chill for up to 1 hour before serving. If desired, top with rosemary sprigs just before serving. Makes 6 appetizer servings.

Each serving: 75 cal., 3 g total fat (2 g sat. fat), 7 mg chol., 150 mg sodium, 10 g carbo., 2 g fiber, 3 g pro. Daily Values: 5% vit. A, 3% vit. C, 4% calcium, 3% iron.

Figs with Herbed Goat Cheese

A passion for herbs

Jonathan King's passion for herbs began as a love affair with rosemary. It grew to encompass herbs in all forms, which is evident in nearly everything he does. The fragrant bounty of summer thrives on the grounds surrounding his picturesque home not far from the southern coast of Maine. The homegrown herbs star in his impromptu outdoor dinners. His basil patch alone fills a 12×12-foot waist-high raised bed. If he's fixing a salad, he steps outside the back door and snips from the beds of lemon thyme, garlic chives, parsley, and mint to add to the mix of lettuces he grows from spring to fall.

Jonathan's interest in gardening began as a high school student and eventually evolved into a business. Jonathan and Jim Stott run Stonewall Kitchen, a specialty food company in York, Maine, known for bottling up the bounty in fresh ways. "It's amazing to me that we started by putting herbs in a few bottles of vinegar and now we're producing 50,000 jars a day," he says.

Jonathan loves to entertain, much to the delight of friends, family, and coworkers. Spontaneous meals are common at his home in the summer. When he's cooking, friends often gather around the kitchen island. "If you're standing at the island, you'd better be prepared to pitch in, because I'll put you to work," Jonathan says. "I love cooking with family and friends. The food always seems to taste better that way."

Summer Tomato Salad

Maine Vichyssoise with Chive Oil

When making this creamy-smooth soup, it's important to pick the proper potatoes for the best results. Starchy potatoes—such as russets, a favorite baking potato—work better than waxy potatoes, which have skin that's smooth and thin. Waxy potatoes tend to get a little gummy when mashed or puréed in a blender.

PREP: 30 minutes **COOK:** 30 minutes
COOL: 20 minutes **CHILL:** 8 hours

- 4 medium leeks
- 1 Tbsp. olive oil
- 1½ lb. Maine potatoes, Yukon gold potatoes, or russet potatoes, peeled and cut into 2-inch pieces (about 5 medium potatoes)
- 4 cups chicken broth
- ¼ tsp. salt
- ⅛ tsp. ground black pepper
- ⅓ cup milk
- 3 Tbsp. finely snipped fresh chives
- 2 Tbsp. finely snipped fresh thyme
- 1 recipe Chive Oil (below)
- Fresh chives

1. Trim leeks, separating the dark green stems from the white leek. Discard green section. Cut the white part of the leek in half lengthwise and clean out the dirt between the layers. Cut the leek into 2-inch-long pieces.

2. In a Dutch oven heat the olive oil over medium-low heat. Add leeks. Cook, covered, for 10 minutes, stirring occasionally. Stir in potato pieces; cook 2 minutes. Increase the heat to high. Add the broth, salt, and pepper. Bring to boiling; reduce heat to medium-low. Simmer, covered, about 15 minutes or until the potatoes are tender. Remove from heat. Let cool slightly.

3. Place the mixture in batches in a food processor or blender. Cover and process or blend until smooth. Place in a large bowl; stir in the milk and snipped herbs. Cover and chill at least 8 hours or until cold.

4. About 20 minutes before serving, prepare Chive Oil. Serve vichyssoise in small glasses or bowls. Drizzle each serving with 2 teaspoons Chive Oil. Top with chives. Makes 6 appetizer servings.

CHIVE OIL: In a small saucepan combine ¼ cup very finely snipped fresh chives and ¼ cup olive oil. Place over low heat for 5 minutes, stirring occasionally. Remove from heat. Add ⅛ teaspoon coarse sea salt and a dash ground black pepper; let cool for 20 minutes. (Use chive oil immediately. Discard any remaining.) Makes about ¼ cup.

Each serving: 232 cal., 13 g total fat (2 g sat. fat), 1 mg chol., 821 mg sodium, 25 g carbo., 3 g fiber, 5 g pro. Daily Values: 5% vit. A, 36% vit. C, 6% calcium, 12% iron.

Summer Tomato Salad

This tarragon-touched salad offers a tasting of different colors and types of tomatoes. Let the selection at your farmer's market or your garden be your guide.

START TO FINISH: 30 minutes

- 1 recipe Tarragon-Dijon Vinaigrette (below)
- 3 cups mesclun salad greens
- 2 medium red tomatoes, cut into wedges or sliced
- 2 medium yellow or heirloom green tomatoes, cut into 8 wedges each
- 1 cup red or yellow cherry tomatoes, halved if desired
- 1 small red onion, cut into thin slices
- ¼ tsp. coarse salt
- ¼ tsp. ground black pepper

1. Prepare Tarragon-Dijon Vinaigrette; set aside.

2. Divide the greens among 6 individual salad plates. Arrange the tomatoes on and around the greens. Top each serving with onion slices. Sprinkle with salt and pepper. Drizzle with desired amount of dressing. Store any remaining dressing, covered, in the refrigerator for up to 1 week. Makes 6 side-dish servings.

TARRAGON-DIJON VINAIGRETTE: In a small bowl whisk together ½ cup olive oil, ¼ cup red or white wine vinegar, 1 tablespoon finely snipped fresh tarragon, 1 tablespoon finely snipped fresh chives, and ¼ teaspoon Dijon-style mustard.

Each serving: 192 cal., 19 g total fat (3 g sat. fat), 0 mg chol., 109 mg sodium, 7 g carbo., 2 g fiber, 2 g pro. Daily Values: 14% vit. A, 37% vit. C, 3% calcium, 5% iron.

Maine Vichyssoise with Chive Oil

Rosemary Lamb Chops

Orzo and Corn Off the Cob

Rosemary Lamb Chops

Rosemary thrives in rocky sunny spots, much like the islands of Greece. There, lamb and rosemary are an inseparable pair.

PREP: 35 minutes **MARINATE:** 2 hours **GRILL:** 12 minutes

- **6 lamb chops, cut about 1 inch thick (about 1¾ lb. total)**
- **¾ cup dry red wine**
- **3 Tbsp. finely snipped fresh rosemary**
- **2 cloves garlic, finely chopped**
- **1 Tbsp. balsamic vinegar**
- **½ tsp. ground black pepper**
- **¼ tsp. salt**
- **1 Tbsp. butter**
- **Fresh rosemary sprigs (optional)**

1. Trim fat from lamb chops. Place chops in a resealable plastic bag set in a shallow dish. Add red wine, 2 tablespoons of the snipped rosemary, the garlic, balsamic vinegar, the ½ teaspoon pepper, and the ¼ teaspoon salt. Seal the bag. Marinate in the refrigerator for 2 to 48 hours, turning bag occasionally.

2. Drain the chops, reserving the marinade. Grill chops on the rack of an uncovered gas grill on medium or a charcoal grill directly over medium coals until desired doneness, turning once halfway through grilling. Allow 12 to 14 minutes for medium-rare (instant-read thermometer registers 145° F) or 15 to 17 minutes for medium doneness (instant-read thermometer registers 160° F). Season to taste with additional salt and pepper.

3. Meanwhile, strain reserved marinade into a small saucepan; discard solids. Simmer, uncovered, over medium heat about 5 minutes or until reduced to ⅓ cup. Add butter and the remaining 1 tablespoon snipped rosemary; cook for 1 minute. Serve sauce with the chops. If desired, top with rosemary sprigs. Makes 6 servings.

Each serving: 134 cal., 7 g total fat (3 g sat. fat), 43 mg chol., 154 mg sodium, 1 g carbo., 0 g fiber, 11 g pro. Daily Values: 2% vit. A, 1% calcium, 6% iron.

Orzo and Corn Off the Cob

Fresh corn and orzo can be cooked together in the same pot. Orzo is a quick-cooking pasta that looks like large grains of rice. Feel free to substitute other small types of pasta, such as acini de pepe.

PREP: 30 minutes **COOK:** 8 minutes

- **4 fresh ears of corn**
- **1¼ cups orzo (rosamarina)**
- **1 cup kalamata olives, pitted and halved**
- **1 medium red sweet pepper, chopped (¾ cup)**
- **¼ cup thinly sliced green onions**
- **¼ cup finely snipped fresh basil**
- **¼ cup finely snipped fresh parsley**
- **¼ cup olive oil**
- **2 Tbsp. white wine vinegar**
- **¼ tsp. salt**
- **¼ tsp. ground black pepper**

1. Cut corn kernels off cob (you should have about 2 cups). Set aside. Bring a large pot of lightly salted water to boiling. Add the orzo and cook, stirring occasionally, for 8 to 9 minutes or until just tender, adding corn for the last 3 minutes of cooking. Drain well; place in a large serving bowl.

2. Add olives, sweet pepper, and onions; toss well. Add basil, parsley, oil, vinegar, salt, and black pepper. Toss gently to combine. Serve at room temperature. Makes 6 to 8 side-dish servings.

Each serving: 308 cal., 13 g total fat (1 g sat. fat), 0 mg chol., 361 mg sodium, 42 g carbo., 4 g fiber, 7 g pro. Daily Values: 30% vit. A, 75% vit. C, 2% calcium, 12% iron.

JONATHAN'S GARDEN DINNER

Maine Vichyssoise with Chive Oil *(page 286)*
Rosemary Lamb Chops *(above left)*
Orzo and Corn Off the Cob *(above)*
Peach Crostada with Herb-Scented Ice Cream *(page 294)*
Double-Mint Brandy Cooler *(page 296)*

Grilled Beef Tenderloin with Mediterranean Relish

This favorite calls on two rediscovered old-world ingredients—kalamata olives and balsamic vinegar—for a new-world take on grilled beef tenderloin.

PREP: 25 minutes **GRILL:** 10 + 25 minutes **STAND:** 15 minutes

- 2 tsp. dried oregano, crushed
- 2 tsp. cracked black pepper
- 1½ tsp. finely shredded lemon peel
- 3 cloves garlic, minced
- 1 3- to 4-lb. center-cut beef tenderloin
- 2 Japanese eggplants, halved lengthwise
- 2 red or yellow sweet peppers, halved lengthwise and seeded
- 1 sweet onion, such as Walla Walla or Vidalia, cut into ½-inch-thick slices
- 2 Tbsp. olive oil
- 2 plum tomatoes, chopped
- 2 Tbsp. chopped, pitted kalamata olives
- 2 Tbsp. snipped fresh basil
- 1 Tbsp. balsamic vinegar
- ¼ to ½ tsp. salt
- ⅛ tsp. ground black pepper

1. In a small bowl combine oregano, cracked pepper, lemon peel, and 2 cloves of the garlic. Use your fingers to rub the mixture onto all sides of the meat.

2. For a charcoal grill, arrange hot coals around a drip pan. Test for medium-hot heat above the pan. Place meat on grill rack over drip pan. For a gas grill, place meat adjacent to heat source. Brush eggplants, sweet peppers, and onion slices with olive oil. Arrange vegetables on edges of grill rack directly over coals. Cover and grill for 10 to 12 minutes or until vegetables are tender, turning once. Remove vegetables from grill; set aside. Cover grill and continue grilling meat for 25 to 30 minutes more or until medium-rare doneness (instant-read thermometer registers 135° F). Cover meat; let stand for 15 minutes before slicing.

3. Meanwhile, for relish, coarsely chop grilled vegetables. In a medium bowl combine grilled vegetables, tomatoes, olives, basil, the remaining garlic clove, the vinegar, salt, and the ground black pepper. Serve the beef with relish. Makes 10 servings.

Each serving: 240 cal., 12 g total fat (4 g sat. fat), 77 mg chol., 133 mg sodium, 6 g carbo., 2 g fiber, 27 g pro. Daily Values: 12% vit. A, 49% vit. C, 1% calcium, 25% iron.

Chicken with Lemon Thyme Pesto

This recipe will make twice as much pesto as you need for the chicken. Save the rest to toss with pasta for a light dinner or to drizzle over sliced summer tomatoes.

PREP: 1 hour **GRILL:** 50 minutes

- 3½ lb. meaty chicken pieces (breast halves, thighs, and drumsticks)
- Salt
- Ground black pepper
- 1⅓ cups lemon thyme*
- ½ cup salted pistachio nuts
- ½ cup olive oil
- ¼ tsp. ground black pepper
- Lemon wedges (optional)

1. If desired, skin chicken. Season with salt and pepper.

2. In a food processor or blender combine lemon thyme and pistachio nuts; cover and process or blend with several on/off turns until finely chopped. With processor or blender running, gradually drizzle in oil, stopping to scrape down sides as necessary. Stir in pepper to taste. Set aside half to brush on chicken. Reserve remaining pesto for another use.

3. For a charcoal grill, arrange medium-hot coals around a drip pan. Test for medium heat above pan. Place chicken, bone side down, on grill rack over drip pan. For gas grill, place chicken adjacent to heat source. Cover and grill for 50 to 60 minutes or until chicken is no longer pink (instant-read thermometer registers 170° F for breasts or 180° F for thighs and drumsticks), turning chicken and brushing with pesto during the last 5 minutes of grilling. If desired, serve chicken with lemon wedges. Makes 6 servings.

***NOTE:** If you don't have lemon thyme, use 1⅓ cups fresh thyme plus 2 teaspoons finely shredded lemon peel.

Each serving: 414 cal., 26 g total fat (6 g sat. fat), 121 mg chol., 225 mg sodium, 3 g carbo., 1 g fiber, 40 g pro. Daily Values: 5% vit. A, 12% vit. C, 4% calcium, 15% iron.

JONATHAN'S GARDEN LUNCH

Figs with Herbed Goat Cheese *(page 285)*
Chicken with Lemon Thyme Pesto *(above)*
Summer Tomato Salad *(page 286)*
Watermelon-Berry Sorbet *(page 293)*
Lavender Cooler *(page 218)*

Rosemary Lamb Chops and Chicken with Lemon Thyme Pesto

PRESERVING FRESH HERBS

Because fresh herbs are highly perishable, it's important to take a few minutes to store your precious supply properly. To keep fresh herbs at their peak in the refrigerator, cut off ends of the stems and place the herbs in a container with about 2 inches of water. Cover the leaves loosely with a plastic bag or plastic wrap and refrigerate for up to several days.

To dry fresh herbs, hang them in bunches, upside down by the stems, in a dry, warm spot out of direct sunlight. Be sure air circulates freely around the bunches. Dry the herbs until the leaves are brittle. This can take anywhere from a few days to a week, depending on the thickness of the leaves. Then remove the leaves from the stems and store the leaves in a tightly covered container.

HERBAL ACCENTS

This bouquet garni *(right)* has an American accent. Jonathan ties fresh thyme, garlic chives, rosemary, and fennel blossoms with a name tag and uses them as a place marker. During dinner, the mini bouquets are combined in a vase for an instant centerpiece *(pages 281 and 284)*. "You can literally create a bouquet garni with whatever herbs suit your taste," Jonathan says. "Dill, tarragon, chervil, and parsley make a light combination for poaching fish."

Watermelon-Berry Sorbet

Watermelon-Berry Sorbet

Your berry choice determines the color of this icy refresher. Using all blueberries with the watermelon will give you a purply-blue sorbet. Skip the blues and focus on raspberries and strawberries and you'll get a vivid red hue.

PREP: 25 minutes **FREEZE:** 1½ + 1 hour

- 1 cup water
- ½ cup sugar
- 2 cups seeded watermelon cubes
- 2 cups fresh berries (red raspberries, strawberries, and/or blueberries)
- Snipped fresh lemon balm or snipped fresh mint
- Fresh lemon balm sprigs or fresh mint sprigs (optional)
- Fresh red raspberries and/or blueberries (optional)

1. In a medium saucepan combine the water and sugar; bring to boiling, stirring frequently. Boil gently, uncovered, for 2 minutes. Remove from heat; cool slightly.

2. Place the watermelon and the 2 cups berries in a blender or large food processor; cover and blend or process for 30 seconds. Add the warm syrup and blend until almost smooth. Transfer the mixture to a 3-quart rectangular baking dish or a 13×9×2-inch baking pan. Place in freezer, uncovered, about 1½ hours or until almost solid.

3. Remove sorbet from freezer. Using a fork, break up the frozen fruit into a somewhat smooth mixture. Stir in snipped lemon balm. Freeze for 1 hour more.* Break up the ice with a fork and serve in shallow bowls. If desired, top with lemon balm sprigs and a few blueberries and/or raspberries. Makes 6 to 8 servings.

***NOTE:** If the mixture is frozen longer than the final hour, let it stand at room temperature for 20 minutes before breaking it up and serving.

Each serving: 98 cal., 0 g total fat (0 g sat. fat), 0 mg chol., 2 mg sodium, 24 g carbo., 3 g fiber, 1 g pro. Daily Values: 5% vit. A, 25% vit. C,1% calcium, 2% iron.

Lemon-Berry Cobbler-Puff

The golden soufflélike topping on this fresh-tasting dessert just melts in your mouth.

PREP: 30 minutes **BAKE:** 30 minutes **COOL:** 30 minutes

- 3 egg whites
- 4 cups sliced fresh strawberries
- 2 cups fresh red raspberries
- ¼ cup granulated sugar
- 2 Tbsp. cornstarch
- 1 Tbsp. snipped fresh basil
- 1½ tsp. finely shredded lemon peel
- 2 Tbsp. lemon juice
- 3 egg yolks
- ⅓ cup dairy sour cream
- 1 Tbsp. all-purpose flour
- ¼ cup granulated sugar
- Sifted powdered sugar (optional)

1. Let egg whites stand at room temperature for 30 minutes. Preheat oven to 350° F. Lightly grease a 2-quart square baking dish; set aside.

2. In a medium saucepan combine strawberries, raspberries, ¼ cup sugar, the cornstarch, basil, ½ teaspoon of the lemon peel, and 1 tablespoon of the lemon juice. Bring to boiling, stirring constantly; remove from heat. Set aside.

3. In a small mixing bowl beat egg yolks until thick and lemon colored. Beat in sour cream, the remaining lemon peel, the remaining lemon juice, and the flour.

4. In a large mixing bowl beat egg whites until soft peaks form (tips curl). Gradually add remaining ¼ cup sugar, beating until stiff peaks form (tips stand straight). Fold in egg yolk mixture.

5. Transfer fruit mixture to prepared baking dish; spoon egg mixture on top.

6. Bake for 30 minutes (fruit mixture will bubble in the corners). Cool for 30 to 40 minutes. If desired, sprinkle with sifted powdered sugar. Serve warm. Makes 8 servings.

Each serving: 144 cal., 4 g total fat (2 g sat. fat), 83 mg chol., 29 mg sodium, 25 g carbo., 3 g fiber, 4 g pro. Daily Values: 5% vit. A, 85% vit. C, 4% calcium, 4% iron.

Peach Crostada

You'll taste the essence of summer in this dessert. Super-fresh peaches need little embellishment beyond piling them on top of a slab of pastry, tucking in the sides, and baking.

PREP: 1 hour **CHILL:** 1 hour **BAKE:** 35 minutes

- **1 recipe Butter Pastry (below)**
- **6 ripe medium peaches (about 2 lb.)**
- **1/4 cup packed brown sugar**
- **1 Tbsp. all-purpose flour**
- **1/2 tsp. vanilla**
- **1 Tbsp. packed brown sugar**
- **1/4 cup orange blossom honey***
- **1 recipe Herb-Scented Ice Cream (right) (optional)**

1. Prepare Butter Pastry; chill until needed. To peel peaches, bring a medium saucepan of water to boiling. Add peaches, one at a time; heat for 20 seconds. Remove from boiling water and immediately place peaches in a bowl of ice water. Peel, pit, and slice peaches (should have about 6 cups).

2. For filling, in a large bowl combine peach slices, the 1/4 cup brown sugar, the 1 tablespoon flour, and the vanilla; toss gently to coat. Set aside.

3. Preheat oven to 425° F. On a lightly floured surface, roll pastry from center to edges into a 16×12-inch oval. (If chilled pastry is too firm, let stand at room temperature for 10 to 15 minutes before rolling.) Transfer to a very large ungreased baking sheet. Mound the peach filling in the center of the dough, leaving an outside border of 2 inches. Drape the edges of dough over the filling. (The dough won't cover the filling completely.) Sprinkle the filling with the 1 tablespoon brown sugar.

4. Bake for 35 to 40 minutes or until the filling is bubbly. Cover loosely with foil if necessary to prevent overbrowning. Remove from oven and drizzle fruit with honey. Cool on a wire rack. Serve warm or at room temperature with Herb-Scented Ice Cream, if desired. Makes 8 servings.

BUTTER PASTRY: In a medium bowl combine 2 cups all-purpose flour and 1/4 teaspoon salt. Cut 3/4 cup cold butter into cubes. Using a pastry blender, cut butter into flour mixture until pieces are pea-size. Sprinkle 6 to 7 tablespoons cold water, 1 tablespoon at a time, over flour-butter mixture, tossing with a fork until all of the dough is moistened. Gently knead the dough just until a ball forms. If necessary, wrap pastry in plastic wrap; chill for 1 to 24 hours.

***NOTE:** If you don't have orange blossom honey, use 1/4 cup honey combined with 1/4 teaspoon finely shredded orange peel.

Each serving (without ice cream): 386 cal., 19 g total fat (11 g sat. fat), 50 mg chol., 263 mg sodium, 52 g carbo., 3 g fiber, 5 g pro. Daily Values: 24% vit. A, 11% vit. C, 2% calcium, 10% iron.

Peach Crostada with Herb-Scented Ice Cream

Herb-Scented Ice Cream

This is one of those experiment-at-will recipes. Snip whatever fresh herb beckons to be sampled and stir it into softened ice cream.

PREP: 10 minutes **FREEZE:** 4 hours

- **1 pt. vanilla ice cream**
- **2 Tbsp. coarse sugar**
- **4 tsp. snipped fresh lemon thyme, cinnamon basil, pineapple sage, or lemon verbena**
- **Fresh herb sprigs (optional)**

1. In a chilled medium bowl stir ice cream just enough to soften, using a wooden spoon to press ice cream against side of bowl. Quickly stir in coarse sugar and herbs. Cover and freeze about 4 hours or until firm. Store, covered, for up to 1 week. Serve alone or with Peach Crostada. If desired, garnish with small herb sprigs. Makes 6 servings.

Each serving: 104 cal., 5 g total fat (3 g sat. fat), 19 mg chol., 35 mg sodium, 15 g carbo., 0 g fiber, 2 g pro. Daily Values: 4% vit. A, 2% vit. C, 6% calcium, 1% iron.

Peach Crostada

Herbed Leek Tart

PREP: 15 minutes **BAKE:** 7 + 8 minutes **STAND:** 5 minutes

- 1 10-oz. pkg. refrigerated pizza dough
- 6 medium leeks, thinly sliced
- 3 cloves garlic, minced
- 2 Tbsp. olive oil
- 1 Tbsp. snipped fresh savory, marjoram, and/or thyme
- 3 Tbsp. creamy Dijon-style mustard blend
- 1 cup shredded Gruyère or Swiss cheese (4 oz.)
- 1/4 cup pine nuts or chopped almonds, toasted

1. Preheat oven to 425° F. Grease a baking sheet. Unroll pizza dough onto prepared baking sheet; press dough to form a 12×9-inch rectangle. Bake for 7 minutes.

2. Meanwhile, in a large skillet cook leeks and garlic in olive oil about 5 minutes or until tender. Remove from heat. Stir in snipped herb(s). Spread mustard blend onto prebaked crust. Top with leek mixture, cheese, and nuts.

3. Bake about 8 minutes more or until cheese is bubbly. Let stand for 5 minutes before serving. Cut into 24 squares. Makes 24 appetizer servings.

Each serving: 53 cal., 3 g total fat (0 g sat. fat), 0 mg chol., 66 mg sodium, 6 g carbo., 0 g fiber, 1 g pro. Daily Values: 2% vit. C, 1% calcium, 3% iron.

Toasted Almonds with Rosemary and Cayenne

START TO FINISH: 15 minutes

- 8 oz. unblanched almonds or pecan halves (about 2 cups)
- 1½ tsp. butter
- 1 Tbsp. finely snipped fresh rosemary
- 1½ tsp. packed brown sugar
- 1/4 to 1/2 tsp. salt
- 1/4 tsp. cayenne pepper

1. Preheat oven to 350° F. Spread almonds in a single layer on a baking sheet. Bake about 10 minutes or until almonds are lightly toasted and fragrant.

2. Meanwhile, in a medium saucepan melt butter over medium heat until sizzling. Remove from heat. Stir in rosemary, brown sugar, salt, and cayenne. Add almonds to butter mixture; toss gently to coat. Cool slightly before serving. If desired, seal cooled nuts in an airtight container and store for up to 1 month in refrigerator or up to 3 months in freezer. Makes 16 servings.

Each serving: 80 cal., 7 g total fat (1 g sat. fat), 1 mg chol., 37 mg sodium, 3 g carbo., 1 g fiber, 4 g pro. Daily Values: 4% calcium, 5% iron.

Double-Mint Brandy Cooler

Modeled after a Southern specialty traditionally made with bourbon, sugar syrup, mint, and fine-as-snow ice, this version uses brandy and gets a little bubbly with a splash of club soda. You can substitute bourbon, if you prefer.

START TO FINISH: 5 minutes

- 10 large fresh mint leaves
- 2 tsp. sugar
- Crushed ice
- 1/4 cup brandy*
- 1/4 cup carbonated water or club soda*
- Fresh mint sprigs

1. For each drink, place mint leaves in a tall cocktail glass. Add sugar. With an iced-tea spoon or bar spoon, press sugar into leaves to release mint oils. Fill the glass half full with crushed ice.

2. Add brandy and carbonated water. Stir gently to dissolve sugar. Top with fresh mint sprigs. Makes 1 serving.

***NOTE:** For a nonalcoholic version, substitute 1/2 cup lemonade for the brandy and the carbonated water.

Each serving: 160 cal., 0 g total fat (0 g sat. fat), 0 mg chol., 13 mg sodium, 8 g carbo., 0 g fiber, 0 g pro.

Dill Dip

Take a cool and creamy dip to show off the flavors of favorite herbs. Serve this with garden-fresh vegetables or crackers

START TO FINISH: 10 minutes

- 1 8-oz. pkg. cream cheese, softened
- 1 8-oz. carton dairy sour cream
- 2 Tbsp. finely chopped green onion
- 2 Tbsp. snipped fresh dill or 2 tsp. dried dill weed
- 1/2 tsp. seasoned salt or salt
- Milk (optional)
- 4 small fresh dill sprigs

1. In a medium mixing bowl beat cream cheese, sour cream, green onion, snipped dill, and seasoned salt with an electric mixer on low speed until fluffy. Cover and chill for up to 24 hours. If the dip thickens during chilling, stir in 1 to 2 tablespoons milk. If desired, garnish with dill sprigs. Makes about 2 cups.

Each tablespoon: 40 cal., 4 g total fat (2 g sat. fat), 11 mg chol., 49 mg sodium, 1 g carbo., 0 g fiber, 1 g pro. Daily Values: 3% vit. A, 1% calcium, 1% iron.

CREAMY BLUE CHEESE DIP: Prepare dip as above, except omit dill and seasoned salt or salt. Stir 1/2 cup crumbled blue cheese (2 ounces) and 1/3 cup finely chopped walnuts into the beaten cream cheese mixture. Makes about 2 cups.

Each tablespoon: 55 cal., 5 g total fat (3 g sat. fat), 12 mg chol., 50 mg sodium, 1 g carbo., 0 g fiber, 1 g pro. Daily Values: 3% vit. A, 2% calcium, 1% iron.

Double-Mint Brandy Cooler

Salsa GOES FRUITY

Summer is the time for glorious fresh fruits, and there's no better way to enjoy them than in sensational salsas. Here are two exciting fruit medleys to add zip to your warm-weather meals. Double-Duty Salsa starts with fresh strawberries and adds a touch of the tropics, a sweet hint of honey, and the zing of black pepper. This sweet salsa's quite different from the traditional chopped tomato-onion mixture. However, you can go from sweet to savory by switching to the suggested alternative ingredients for a sassy jalapeño-black pepper salsa that adds zest to grilled pork, ham, or turkey. And, when the weather's almost too hot to eat, beat the heat with refreshing Mango Sorbet with Gingered Fruit Salsa. The smooth, luscious sorbet makes the perfect base for a lively ginger-and-mint-accented berry salsa topper.

Double-Duty Salsa

PREP: 15 minutes **CHILL:** 2 hours

- 1 pt. fresh strawberries, hulled and coarsely chopped
- 1 cup coarsely chopped fresh pineapple or avocado
- ½ cup coarsely chopped fresh mango or peach, or seeded cucumber
- 1 tsp. finely shredded lime peel
- 2 Tbsp. lime juice
- 2 Tbsp. honey
- ½ tsp. grated fresh ginger or 1 to 2 Tbsp. seeded and finely chopped jalapeño pepper (see note, page 251)
- ¼ tsp. cracked black pepper

1. For sweet salsa, combine strawberries, pineapple, mango or peach, lime peel, lime juice, honey, fresh ginger, and cracked black pepper.

2. For savory salsa, combine strawberries, avocado, cucumber, lime peel, lime juice, honey, jalapeño pepper, and cracked black pepper.

3. Cover and chill for 2 to 24 hours. Makes about 3 cups.

Each serving sweet salsa (¼ cup): 28 cal., 0 g total fat (0 g sat. fat), 0 mg chol., 1 mg sodium, 7 g carbo., 1 g fiber, and 0 g pro. Daily Values: 3% vit. A, 34% vit. C, 1% calcium, and 1% iron.

Each serving savory salsa (¼ cup): 23 cal., 1 g total fat (0 g sat. fat), 0 mg chol., 1 mg sodium, 5 g carbo., 1 g fiber, and 0 g pro. Daily Values: 30% vit. C, 1% calcium, 1% iron.

STRAWBERRY SAVVY

To make sure the strawberries in your salsas are top-notch, look for plump, fresh-looking berries with bright green caps and a rich red color. Select only fully ripe berries because strawberries do not ripen after picking. Size is not a good indicator of quality, so the largest berries aren't necessarily the most flavorful. Avoid bruised, wet, or mushy berries. To keep the berries at their best once you get them home, don't wash or hull them until you're ready to use them. Store berries loosely covered in a single layer in the refrigerator and use them within a day or two.

Mango Sorbet with Ginger Fruit Salsa

Mango Sorbet with Ginger Fruit Salsa

PREP: 30 minutes **FREEZE:** 8 hours

- 3 cups chopped fresh mango (about 3 large)
- 1 8¼-oz. can crushed pineapple (syrup pack)
- 2 large bananas, sliced (about 2 cups)
- ¼ cup frozen orange juice concentrate, thawed
- 1 Tbsp. finely chopped crystallized ginger
- 1 recipe Ginger Fruit Salsa (below)
- Fresh mint leaves (optional)

1. For sorbet, in a bowl combine mango, undrained pineapple, bananas, and orange juice concentrate. In food processor or blender place 2 cups mixture at a time; cover and process or blend until smooth. Pour all of the mixture into a freezer container; stir in ginger. Cover and freeze about 8 hours or until firm.

2. Meanwhile, prepare Ginger Fruit Salsa; cover and chill for up to 1 hour.

3. Break frozen mango mixture into small chunks. (If necessary, let mixture stand at room temperature for 30 minutes to soften before breaking into chunks.) Place small portions at a time into food processor.* Cover and process until fluffy. If desired, return to freezer container and freeze. Or serve immediately in dessert dishes topped with salsa. If desired, garnish with mint leaves. Makes 10 servings.

***MIXER METHOD:** Break up mango mixture and place all of the mixture in a chilled very large mixing bowl. Beat until fluffy. Proceed as above.

GINGER FRUIT SALSA: In a small bowl combine 1 cup chopped mango, 1 cup chopped fresh strawberries, ½ cup fresh blueberries, 1 tablespoon crystallized ginger, and 1 tablespoon snipped fresh mint.

Each serving: 113 cal., 0 g total fat (0 g sat. fat), 0 mg chol., 3 mg sodium, 29 g carbo., 3 g fiber, and 1 g pro. Daily Values: 53% vit. A, 70% vit. C, 2% calcium, 3% iron.

OPEN YOURSELF TO THE CHARMS OF YOUR FAVORITE GARDEN BEDFELLOWS: GLEAMING PLUMP TOMATOES, SWEET PEPPERS (CRISP, SPICY, OH-SO-AMENABLE), AND ONIONS, THE STRONGMEN OF THE VEGETABLE KINGDOM. THIS TRIO OF VEGETABLES PEAKS IN AUGUST, SO COOK 'EM UP QUICK.

Stand-Up Tomato Salad

summer ripe

Stand-Up Tomato Salad

The tequila dressing echos of a margarita, but, if you prefer, you may substitute your favorite vinaigrette.

PREP: 30 minutes **CHILL:** 2 hours

- 3 small yellow, orange, ripe green, and/or red tomatoes (about 12 oz. total), cored
- 1 recipe Margarita Dressing (below)
- 1 cup peeled jicama, peeled kohlrabi, yellow summer squash, and/or zucchini, coarsely shredded (about 6 oz.)
- 6 large shrimp, peeled, deveined, and cooked

1. Cut each tomato horizontally into 6 slices. Keeping slices together, place in a 2-quart square baking dish. Pour Margarita Dressing over slices. Cover and chill for 2 to 4 hours.

2. Remove tomatoes from dish, reserving dressing. Place a tomato slice on each of six individual salad plates. Top with about 1 tablespoon of the shredded vegetables. Repeat layers, ending with a tomato slice. Top each salad with a cooked shrimp. Drizzle with reserved dressing. Makes 6 servings.

MARGARITA DRESSING: In a screw-top jar combine 2 tablespoons lime juice, 2 tablespoons tequila, 1 tablespoon salad oil, 2 teaspoons snipped fresh marjoram, 1/4 teaspoon salt, and 1/4 teaspoon pepper. Cover and shake well to mix.

Each serving: 75 cal., 3 g total fat (0 g sat. fat), 28 mg chol., 138 mg sodium, 5 g carbo., 0 g fiber, 5 g pro. Daily Values: 1% vit. A, 22% vit. C, 2% calcium, 6% iron.

TOMATOES

Tasty heirloom tomatoes are now more available than ever, as are many newer varieties, making the tomato picking fun.

- Choosing: Look for shiny, smooth skins and a plump shape. The skin of the tomato should just give slightly to thumb pressure.
- Keeping: To ripen tomatoes, put them on the counter in a brown bag to speed the process. After ripening, they'll keep on the counter about seven days. Cold renders tomatoes tasteless, so don't store them in the refrigerator.

Tomato Bread Pudding

Tomato Bread Pudding

For the best results, seek out crusty, firm-textured bread.

PREP: 25 minutes **BAKE:** 15 minutes

- 4 oz. French bread, Italian bread, or Italian Country bread, torn into 1-inch chunks
- 2 cloves garlic, minced
- 2 Tbsp. olive oil
- 2 lb. tomatoes, cored, seeded, and coarsely chopped (about 4 cups)
- 3 Tbsp. snipped fresh dill or 1 tsp. dried dillweed
- 1/4 tsp. pepper
- 1/4 cup reduced-sodium chicken broth
- Finely shredded Parmesan cheese (optional)
- Sprigs of fresh dill (optional)

1. Preheat oven to 350° F. Place bread pieces in a large shallow baking pan. Bake about 15 minutes or until golden brown, stirring once.

2. In a large skillet cook garlic in hot olive oil over medium heat for 30 seconds. Add tomatoes, dill, and pepper. Cook, uncovered, over medium heat for 2 minutes, stirring occasionally. Add broth; bring to boiling. Remove from heat.

3. To serve, place toasted bread pieces in a serving bowl. Pour tomato mixture over bread; toss gently to mix. If desired, top with Parmesan cheese and sprigs of fresh dill. Serve immediately. Makes 4 to 6 servings.

Each serving: 189 cal., 8 g total fat (1 g sat. fat), 0 mg chol., 232 mg sodium, 26 g carbo., 3 g fiber, 5 g pro. Daily Values: 28% vit. A, 73% vit. C, 4% calcium, 10% iron.

ONE OF THE JOYS OF SUMMER EATING IS A SIDE DISH LOADED WITH TOMATOES. THEIR BLEND OF SWEET AND SOUR BRINGS A BRIGHTNESS TO THE TABLE THAT ELEVATES DINNER INTO A FEAST.

Yellow Pepper Soup with Yogurt and Cucumbers

Fennel and cardamom add a spicy niceness to warm or chilled soup. Crush the fennel seeds with the back of a spoon.

PREP: 25 minutes **COOK:** 20 minutes

- **1 cup plain or low-fat yogurt (do not use nonfat)**
- **1 tsp. fennel seeds, crushed**
- **4 to 7 medium yellow sweet peppers (1½ lb.), seeded and coarsely chopped (about 5 cups)**
- **2 medium shallots, chopped (¼ cup)**
- **¾ tsp. ground cardamom**
- **2 Tbsp. olive oil**
- **1 14-oz. can reduced-sodium chicken broth**
- **1 cup water**
- **2 Tbsp. cider vinegar**
- **Plain or low-fat yogurt**
- **¼ cup coarsely chopped cucumber**
- **Fennel seeds**

1. In a bowl stir together the yogurt and fennel seeds. Cover; let stand at room temperature for 30 minutes.

2. Meanwhile, in a large saucepan cook sweet peppers, shallots, and cardamom in hot oil about 15 minutes or until peppers are just beginning to soften, stirring occasionally. Add chicken broth, water, and vinegar. Bring to boiling; reduce heat. Simmer, covered, for 5 minutes more.

3. Remove from heat; cool slightly. In a blender container or food processor bowl blend or process half at a time until smooth. Return all to saucepan; cook and stir until warm.

4. Serve warm or chilled. Ladle soup into four bowls. Top with yogurt, cucumber, and fennel seeds. Makes 4 servings.

Each serving: 154 cal., 9 g total fat (2 g sat. fat), 8 mg chol., 306 mg sodium, 15 g carbo., 2 g fiber, 5 g pro. Daily Values: 10% vit. A,365% vit. C, 10% calcium, 6% iron.

Grilled Pickled Peppers

Serve with an assortment of pickles, olives, chips, and raw vegetables or with grilled sausages or other meats.

PREP: 20 minutes **COOL:** 1 hour **CHILL:** overnight

- **4 medium orange, red, and/or yellow sweet peppers**
- **1 Tbsp. olive oil**
- **1 tsp. mustard seeds, toasted***
- **2 whole cloves**
- **½ cup red wine vinegar**
- **5 sprigs fresh thyme**
- **¼ tsp. salt**
- **¼ tsp. ground black pepper**

1. Halve the sweet peppers; remove the stems, seeds, and membranes. Brush pepper halves with olive oil. Place pepper halves on the rack of an uncovered grill directly over medium coals. Grill about 10 minutes or until crisp-tender and peppers have grill marks, turning once. Remove from grill and cool. Cut into chunks.

2. While peppers cool, place the toasted mustard seeds and cloves on a small square of double thickness 100-percent-cotton cheesecloth. Bring up corners to make a bundle; tie with 100-percent-cotton string. Place the spice bag in a small stainless-steel saucepan with the vinegar and thyme sprigs. Bring to boiling; remove from heat. Cool completely.

3. In a medium glass bowl stir together peppers, vinegar mixture, salt, and black pepper; cover and chill overnight. To serve, remove spice bag. Makes 3 cups.

***TEST KITCHEN TIP:** To toast mustard seeds, place seeds in a small skillet. Heat over medium-high heat for 2 to 3 minutes or until toasted, shaking the skillet occasionally. Watch carefully as the seeds may "pop" in skillet, jumping out when hot.

Each ¼ cup serving: 42 cal., 2 g total fat (0 g sat. fat), 0 mg chol., 67 mg sodium, 5 g carbo., 1 g fiber, 1 g pro. Daily Values: 4% vit. A, 202% vit. C, 1% calcium, 3% iron.

PEPPERS

The mild member of the pepper family comes in many colors. All sweet peppers start out green, then ripen into red, orange, yellow, purple, and even chocolate brown. The riper peppers are sweeter than the greens, but differ only slightly in flavor.

- Choosing: Look for well-shaped peppers with deep color, glossy sheen, relatively heavy weight for their size, and firm sides. Don't buy peppers with very thin walls, those that are are wilted or wrinkly, or those that have cuts or punctures or soft, watery spots on the sides (which would indicate the pepper has started to go bad).
- Keeping: Refrigerate unwashed peppers in a plastic bag for up to five days.

SWEET PEPPERS CAN BE A PUZZLE. HOW DO YOU MAKE THE MOST OF THEIR SWEET, SLIGHTLY SPICY FLAVOR BEYOND CHOPPING FOR PASTA AND SALADS? THE SOLUTION IS THE GENTLE APPLICATION OF HEAT.

Yellow Pepper Soup with Yogurt and Cucumbers

Grilled Pickled Peppers

Square Summer Pie

Square Summer Pie

PREP: 50 minutes **BAKE:** 40 minutes **COOL:** 10 minutes

- 4 medium red or orange sweet peppers, seeded
- 1 medium baking potato
- 8 cloves garlic, sliced
- 2 Tbsp. cooking oil
- 1 9-oz. pkg. frozen artichoke hearts
- 1 cup shredded Swiss cheese (4 oz.)
- 1 Tbsp. coarse-grain brown mustard
- 1/2 tsp. salt
- 1 recipe Pastry for Lattice-Top Pie (below)
- Milk

1. Cut peppers into 1-inch pieces. Peel and slice potatoes 1/4 inch thick. In a 12-inch skillet cook peppers, potato slices, and garlic in hot oil over medium heat for 5 minutes, stirring occasionally. Thaw, drain, and chop artichoke hearts; stir into pepper mixture. Cook, covered, about 4 minutes more or until crisp-tender, stirring occasionally.

2. Transfer vegetable mixture to a large bowl; add cheese, mustard, and salt. Toss gently to coat; spoon into pan lined with Pastry for Lattice-Top Pie.

3. Move oven rack to lowest position in oven. Preheat oven to 450° F. Roll out remaining pastry into an 11-inch square. Cut into 1-inch-wide strips. Arrange strips on filling in a free-form lattice pattern. Press ends into crust edges. Brush with milk. Cover edges with foil. Bake for 20 minutes. Remove foil; bake about 20 minutes more or until crust is brown. Cool in pan on a wire rack 10 minutes; remove sides of pan. Makes 8 servings.

PASTRY FOR LATTICE-TOP PIE: In a bowl stir together 2 cups all-purpose flour and 1/2 teaspoon salt. Using a pastry blender, cut in 2/3 cup shortening until pieces are pea-size. Sprinkle 1 tablespoon cold water over part; gently toss with a fork. Push dough to side. Repeat, using 5 to 6 more tablespoons cold water, until all is moistened. Divide in half; form each half into a ball. (If making ahead, wrap in plastic wrap; seal. Refrigerate up to 24 hours. Bring to room temperature before rolling out.)

On a lightly floured surface slightly flatten one ball. Roll from center to edges to form an 11-inch square. To transfer pastry, roll around rolling pin. Unroll pastry into a 9-inch square tart pan or a 2-quart square baking dish, being careful not to stretch. If necessary, trim edge even with top edge of pan.

Each serving: 392 cal., 25 g total fat (7 g sat. fat), 13 mg chol., 377 mg sodium, 33 g carbo., 4 g fiber, 9 g pro. Daily Values: 68% vit. A, 170% vit. C, 17% calcium, 11% iron.

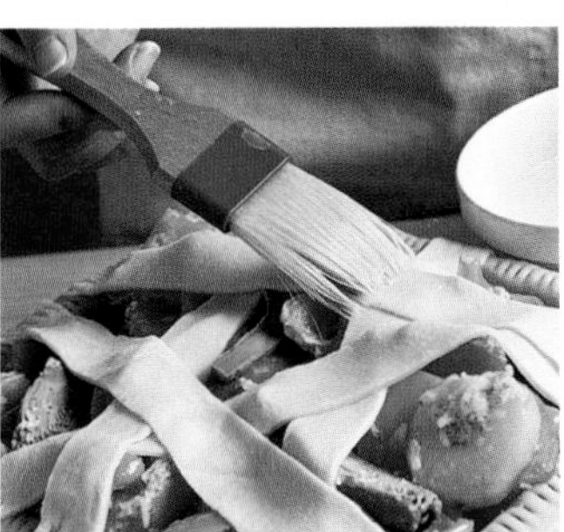

The lattice looks better if you arrange it casually rather than in rigid lines. If the dough does not come up to the rim in a deeper pan, tuck the edges of the strips under the edge of the bottom crust.

GARDEN-STYLE SUPPER

Onion Dip with dippers *(page 308)*
Stand-Up Tomato Salad *(page 301)*
Square Summer Pie *(left)*
Keen Nectarine *(page 197)*
Sparkling water

Peppers Stuffed with Cinnamon Bulgur

For your sweet pepper "bowls," choose from a variety of colors—green, red, yellow, and orange.

START TO FINISH: 30 minutes

- 1 3/4 cups water
- 1/2 cup shredded carrot
- 1/4 cup chopped onion
- 1 tsp. instant chicken bouillon granules
- 1/8 tsp. salt
- 3 inches stick cinnamon or dash ground cinnamon
- 3/4 cup bulgur
- 1/3 cup dried cranberries or raisins
- 2 large or 4 small green, red, yellow, or orange sweet peppers
- 3/4 cup shredded Muenster, brick, or mozzarella cheese (3 oz.)
- 1/2 cup water
- 2 Tbsp. sliced almonds or chopped pecans, toasted

1. In a large skillet stir together the 1 3/4 cups water, carrot, onion, bouillon granules, salt, and cinnamon. Bring to boiling; reduce heat. Simmer, covered, for 5 minutes.

2. Stir in bulgur and cranberries. Remove from heat. Cover and let stand for 5 minutes. If using stick cinnamon, remove from the bulgur mixture. Drain off excess liquid.

3. Meanwhile, halve sweet peppers lengthwise; remove the seeds and membranes.

4. Stir cheese into bulgur mixture; spoon into sweet pepper halves. Place sweet pepper halves in skillet. Add the 1/2 cup water. Bring to boiling; reduce heat. Simmer, covered, for 5 to 10 minutes or until peppers are crisp-tender and bulgur mixture is heated through. Sprinkle with nuts. Makes 4 servings.

Each serving: 253 cal., 9 g total fat (4 g sat. fat), 20 mg chol., 496 mg sodium, 36 g carbo., 8 g fiber, 10 g pro. Daily Values: 83% vit. A, 92% vit. C, 19% calcium, 8% iron.

ONIONS

Spring onions are usually sweeter and milder than fall and winter onions. Both work well in these recipes, although summer onions tend to take a little longer to brown.

Choosing: White onions have a pungent, sharp aroma and flavor. Reds are about as sharp as yellows, but the color fades during cooking. Look for dry outer skins free of spots or blemishes. Onions should be heavy for their size with no scent (scent indicates internal breakdown or bruising).

Keeping: Onions keep about 10 days in a well-ventilated, cool, dry place—not in the refrigerator. You can freeze chopped onion, tightly wrapped, for up to three months.

Glazed Onions

Onion Gratin with Country Ham

Glazed Onions

Sauté pearl onions and walnuts, then splash with fig vinegar.

PREP: 25 minutes **COOK:** 13 minutes

- 1/4 cup broken walnuts
- 1 1/2 lb. pearl onions, peeled (see photo, below)
- 1 Tbsp. cooking oil
- 1/4 tsp. salt
- 1/8 tsp. pepper
- 2 Tbsp. dried currants, raisins, or chopped dried figs
- 3 Tbsp. black fig vinegar*, or red wine vinegar with 1/2 tsp. sugar stirred in
- 1 Tbsp. snipped fresh savory or oregano
- 1 recipe Sherry Whipped Cream (below) (optional)
- Black fig vinegar*

1. In a large skillet cook walnuts over medium-high heat for 4 to 5 minutes or until toasted, stirring occasionally. Remove from skillet; set aside.

2. In the same skillet cook onions in hot oil over medium-low heat for 12 to 15 minutes until golden brown and tender, stirring occasionally. Sprinkle with salt and pepper. Stir in walnuts, currants, and the 3 tablespoons vinegar. Cook and stir about 1 minute until vinegar has evaporated and onions are glazed.

3. Transfer onions to a serving bowl. Sprinkle with savory or oregano. If desired, spoon Sherry Whipped Cream onto onions. Pass additional fig vinegar. Makes 5 to 6 servings.

SHERRY WHIPPED CREAM: Place 2 tablespoons heavy whipping cream (not ultra-pasteurized) and 1 tablespoon dry sherry in a screw-top jar. Cover; shake until cream thickens slightly.

***TEST KITCHEN TIP:** Find fig vinegar in specialty food stores or order it at www.cuisineperel.com or from Gourmet Country, 800/665-9123.

Each serving: 142 cal., 7 g total fat (1 g sat. fat), 0 mg chol., 123 mg sodium, 18 g carbo., 4 g fiber, 3 g pro. Daily Values: 15% vit. C, 4% calcium, 4% iron.

Onion Gratin with Country Ham

We used country-style ham in this recipe for its full flavor and bold saltiness. You can buy 6-ounce steaks from many grocery stores or sliced ham at your store's deli counter, but regular smoked ham works very well as a substitute.

PREP: 30 minutes **BAKE:** 1 1/4 hours **STAND:** 10 minutes

- 1/4 cup butter
- 1/4 cup all-purpose flour
- 1 tsp. salt
- 1/2 tsp. pepper
- 2 cups milk
- 2 lb. large onions. peeled
- 1 15-oz. can cannellini beans or Great Northern beans, rinsed and drained
- 6 oz. cooked, country-style ham or smoked ham, cut into bite-size strips
- 1/2 cup smoked provolone or plain provolone cheese, shredded (about 2 oz.)

1. Preheat oven to 350° F. In a large saucepan melt butter over medium heat. Stir in flour, salt, and pepper. Cook and stir for 2 to 3 minutes until light brown. Add milk all at once. Cook and stir over medium heat until thickened and bubbly.

2. Slice onions 1/2 inch thick; separate into rings. Stir onions, beans, and ham into saucepan. Transfer to a 1 1/2-quart oval or 2-quart rectangular baking dish; place on a baking sheet.

3. Bake, covered, for 1 hour. Uncover and sprinkle with cheese. Bake, uncovered, about 15 minutes more or until onions are tender and top is golden. Let stand for 10 minutes before serving. Makes 6 to 8 servings.

Each serving: 309 cal., 15 g total fat (8 g sat. fat), 54 mg chol., 1,318 mg sodium, 30 g carbo., 6 g fiber, 19 g pro. Daily Values: 11% vit. A, 14% vit. C, 22% calcium, 10% iron.

VEGETABLE MATH

Vegetable sizes and yields vary with growing conditions—peppers especially have a wide range of size and weight. Your best bet is to buy by weight rather than size when possible, but use these guidelines to eliminate some of the guesswork. The "What you get" column is what you have after seeding, trimming, and cutting.

Vegetable	What you buy	What you get
Onions	1 medium (5 oz.)	1/2 cup chopped
Peppers	1 medium (3 oz.)	3/4 cup chopped or 1 cup strips
Tomatoes	1 medium (5 oz.)	1/2 cup chopped

To peel small onions, bring a small saucepan of water to boiling. Cook onions for 30 seconds. Drain and cool. Cut a thin slice off of the root end and squeeze from other end to remove peel.

Onion Dip

Cornmeal-Crusted Onion Rings

Use a saucepan that's taller than it is wide to minimize the oil spattering.

Prep: 30 minutes **Cook:** 3 minutes per batch

- 3 Tbsp. honey
- 1 tsp. snipped fresh rosemary
- 1 48-oz. bottle cooking oil for deep-fat frying
- 1/2 cup buttermilk
- 1 egg, beaten
- 1 cup all-purpose flour
- 1/2 cup cornmeal
- 1/4 cup finely chopped peanuts or pecans
- 1/2 tsp. salt
- 1/4 tsp. pepper
- 1 lb. white onions (3 medium)

1. In a small saucepan heat honey and rosemary over very low heat about 3 minutes or until heated through. Set aside.

2. Preheat oven to 300° F. Line a baking sheet with waxed paper; set aside. In a heavy, deep, 3-quart saucepan or deep-fat fryer, heat oil to 365° F.

3. In a medium bowl combine buttermilk and egg. In a shallow dish combine flour, cornmeal, peanuts or pecans, salt, and pepper.

4. Cut 1 onion in half crosswise; set aside half. Cut remaining onions into 1/2-inch-thick slices; separate into rings.

5. Working in batches, dip onion rings into egg mixture, letting excess drip into bowl. Toss rings into flour mixture until well-coated; gently shake off excess. Place onion rings on prepared baking sheet. Repeat process with remaining onions, egg, and flour mixtures.

6. With long-handled tongs, carefully add onion rings, a few at a time, to hot oil. Fry about 3 minutes, turning rings a few times, until onions are golden brown and cooked through. Drain on paper towels. Transfer to another baking sheet; keep warm in oven. Repeat with remaining onion rings.

7. To serve, place reserved onion half, cut side down, on a plate. Insert a fork into the top so the fork is upright. Stack onion rings on fork handle. Arrange remaining rings on plate around onion. Drizzle with rosemary-honey mixture. Sprinkle with additional salt, if desired. Makes 6 servings.

Each serving: 385 cal., 23 g total fat (3 g sat. fat), 36 mg chol., 229 mg sodium, 41 g carbo., 3 g fiber, 6 g pro. Daily Values: 2% vit. A, 9% vit. C, 5% calcium, 10% iron.

THE GENTLER SIDE OF ONIONS COMES OUT IN THE COOKING—BUT EVEN WHEN THEIR PUNGENCY HAS BEEN TAMED, THEY RETAIN A LITTLE BITE TO REMIND YOU OF THEIR WILD PAST.

Onion Dip

Splurge on a big bag of thick, sea-salt-sprinkled potato chips to serve with this recipe.

Prep: 15 minutes **Cook:** 21 minutes

- 1 1/3 lb. medium onions (4), halved and coarsely chopped (2 cups)
- 1/2 tsp. salt
- 2 Tbsp. cooking oil
- 2 tsp. snipped fresh sage
- 1/3 cup dairy sour cream
- 2 Tbsp. grated Parmesan cheese
- 2 Tbsp. finely chopped red onion
- Potato chips or Armenian cracker bread (lahvosh), broken into serving-size pieces

1. In a large skillet cook the coarsely chopped onions and salt in hot oil, uncovered, over medium-low heat about 20 minutes or until very soft and lightly browned, stirring occasionally.

2. Stir in sage. Cook for 1 minute more. Remove from heat; stir in sour cream and Parmesan cheese. Transfer to a serving bowl. Sprinkle with red onion. Serve with chips or cracker bread. Makes about 1 cup (8 servings).

Each 2 tablespoons dip: 69 cal., 6 g total fat (2 g sat. fat), 5 mg chol., 174 mg sodium, 4 g carbo., 1 g fiber, 1 g pro. Daily Values: 2% vit. A, 4% vit. C, 4% calcium, 1% iron.

Cornmeal-Crusted Onion Rings

Market-Fresh Corn Favorites

NOTHING SAYS SUMMER QUITE LIKE THE crunch of sweet, fresh corn right off the cob. Take corn from the market to the table in the same day for the very best flavor. First, you remove the husks and scrub with a stiff brush to remove the silks. Then, for these delightfully corny classics, you scrape uncooked corn kernels from the cob. Or, for good ol' corn on the cob, plunge the ears into boiling lightly salted water for 5 to 7 minutes or until juicy and tender. Serve with a dollop of butter.

Summer Bounty Salad

For this no-cook salad, combine fresh uncooked corn kernels, slivered red onion, shredded basil leaves, and finely chopped sweet peppers. Toss with balsamic vinegar, olive oil, salt, and pepper. Cover; chill up to 2 hours before serving.

Fresh Corn Fritters

Mix 2 cups fresh uncooked corn kernels with one $8^1/2$-ounce package corn muffin mix, snipped fresh sage, 1 egg, and $^1/4$ cup milk. Drop batter by tablespoons into deep hot oil (365° F). Fry 2 to 3 minutes or until golden brown, turning once. Drain well; serve warm.

Sassy Garden Relish

Stir together 2 cups fresh uncooked corn kernels, $^3/4$ cup chopped sweet peppers, $^1/2$ cup chopped cucumber, $^1/4$ cup sliced green onions, 2 tablespoons snipped fresh cilantro, and 1 chopped, seeded habañero pepper. Add vinegar, sugar, salt, and bottled hot pepper sauce to taste. Cover; chill for up to 2 days.

picnic eggs

POSTPONING SUMMER'S ITCHY CHORES

in favor of an afternoon enjoying the cool breezes off a lake doesn't mean that you have to do your basking on an empty stomach.

Bring sandwiches, of course, but add a plate of deviled eggs. They're everything you want in a hot-weather food: cool, easy, and the right size to sustain you between lunch and dinner.

Follow our recipe and you'll learn a couple of things. The first is a little food science: Too much heat causes a chemical reaction that makes yolks turn gray-green. If you follow our boiling method, right, your eggs won't overcook.

The second lesson is to trust your taste buds. You know what your family loves, so use the kind of mustard they prefer and adjust the balance of mustards, salt, and pepper to suit yourselves.

Deviled Eggs

Prep: 20 minutes **Cook:** 15 minutes

- 7 Hard-Cooked Eggs (right)
- 1/4 cup mayonnaise or salad dressing
- 1 to 2 tsp. Dijon-style mustard, balsamic herb mustard, honey mustard, or other favorite mustard
- 1/2 tsp. dry mustard
- Salt
- Pepper
- Several leaves Italian flat-leaf parsley or paprika (optional)

1. Cut 6 eggs in half lengthwise; gently remove yolks; set whites aside. Coarsely chop the remaining egg.

2. In a resealable plastic bag combine egg yolks, chopped egg, mayonnaise, mustard, and dry mustard. Seal bag; gently squeeze to combine ingredients. Season to taste with salt and pepper.

3. Snip one corner of the bag (see top photo, left). Squeeze bag, pushing egg yolk mixture through hole into egg white halves (*see bottom photo, left*). Top with fresh parsley or paprika. Cover and chill for up to 12 hours. Makes 12 halves.

Each egg half: 72 cal., 6 g total fat (1 g sat. fat), 109 mg chol., 63 mg sodium, 0 g carbo., 0 g fiber, 3 g pro. Daily Values: 3% vit. A, 1% calcium, 2% iron.

THE HARD-BOILED BASICS

■ **Hard-Cooked Eggs:** Place the eggs in a single layer in a large saucepan. Add enough cold water to cover 1 inch above the eggs. Bring to a full rolling boil over high heat. Reduce the heat so the water is just below simmering, then cover and cook for 15 minutes. Remove the eggs from the pan, place them in a colander, and run cold water over them until they're cool enough to handle. To peel, gently tap each egg on the counter. Roll the egg between the palms of your hands. Peel off the eggshell. Cover and refrigerate the eggs until they're thoroughly chilled, about 1 hour.

■ **Italian-Style Deviled Eggs:** Prepare Deviled Eggs as directed left, except omit mayonnaise and mustards. Stir 1/4 cup bottled creamy Italian salad dressing and 2 tablespoons grated Parmesan cheese into mashed yolks; mix well.

■ **Greek-Style Deviled Eggs:** Prepare Deviled Eggs as directed left, except fold 2 tablespoons feta cheese, 1 tablespoon finely chopped pitted kalamata olives or other pitted ripe olives, and 2 teaspoons snipped fresh oregano into yolk mixture. If desired, season with black pepper.

■ **Mexican-Style Deviled Eggs:** Prepare Deviled Eggs as directed left, except omit mayonnaise and mustards. Fold 3 tablespoons dairy sour cream, 1 tablespoon salsa, and 1/2 teaspoon ground cumin into yolk mixture. Top with snipped fresh cilantro.

■ **Indian-Style Deviled Eggs:** Prepare Deviled Eggs as directed at left, except omit mayonnaise and mustards. Fold 3 tablespoons plain low-fat yogurt, 1 tablespoon chopped chutney, and 1/2 teaspoon curry powder into yolk mixture. Sprinkle with chopped peanuts.

counting beans

WITH THEIR COATS OF MANY COLORS, dry beans are more than pretty packages. The skins—in tints of sienna, earthy black, and red—may deliver a potent nutritional boost.

It turns out that beans contain eight flavonoids, plant substances that act as nature's dyes and give many fruits and vegetables their colors. Scientists say those plant chemicals act as antioxidants to provide some protection against certain cancers and heart disease.

"You really have to go for the color," said George Hosfield, Ph.D., geneticist at the U.S. Department of Agriculture's Agricultural Research Service at Michigan State University.

More research may develop beans with more flavonoids and a more powerful antioxidant effect. Meanwhile, Hosfield suggests that you reuse the cooking liquid from beans in soups. When you soak or cook beans, flavonoids leach into the liquids but aren't destroyed.

White Beans and Spinach Ragout

START TO FINISH: 15 minutes

- 2 slices bacon, cut into 1-inch pieces
- 1 medium onion, halved and thinly sliced
- 1 14½-oz. can diced tomatoes
- 1 15-oz. can cannellini or navy beans, rinsed and drained
- 4 cups torn fresh spinach
- 4 tsp. bottled balsamic or red wine vinaigrette

1. In a large skillet cook bacon pieces until crisp. Remove with slotted spoon, reserving 1 tablespoon drippings in skillet. Drain bacon on paper towels.

2. Add onion to skillet; cook about 3 minutes or until just tender. Drain tomatoes, reserving ⅓ cup liquid. Stir tomatoes, reserved liquid, and beans into onion. Cook and stir over medium heat about 2 minutes or until heated through.

3. Stir in 3 cups spinach; cover and cook until just wilted, about 30 seconds. Stir in bacon and remaining spinach. Spoon into four bowls. Drizzle each serving with 1 teaspoon vinaigrette. Makes 4 servings.

Each serving: 131 cal., 3 g total fat (1 g sat. fat), 3 mg chol., 508 mg sodium, 23 g carbo., 9 g fiber, 9 g pro. Daily Values: 20% vit. A, 27% vit. C, 7% calcium, 18% iron.

BEAN BOOSTERS

- To perk up a humble bean dish, add a handful of intensely flavored ingredients, such as Parmesan cheese, bacon, or prosciutto.
- Use canned beans to cut cooking time to minutes. Rinse beans first to trim sodium levels. Rinsing also freshens the taste of canned beans.
- Combine tomatoes, which are high in vitamin C, with plant sources of iron, such as beans. Your body will absorb more of the iron.

Red Beans and Orzo

START TO FINISH: 30 minutes

- 1 14½-oz. can chicken broth (about 1¾ cups)
- 1½ cups water
- 1⅓ cups orzo (rosamarina)
- ¼ cup finely chopped onion
- 1 tsp. herbes de Provence or dried Italian seasoning, crushed
- 1 15-oz. can red beans or pinto beans, rinsed and drained
- 1 oz. prosciutto or cooked ham, cut into thin strips (⅓ cup)
- 2 Tbsp. snipped fresh Italian flat-leaf parsley
- ⅓ cup finely shredded Parmesan cheese

1. In a medium saucepan bring chicken broth and water to boiling. Stir in orzo, onion, and herbes de Provence. Reduce heat. Simmer, uncovered, for 12 to 15 minutes or until orzo is just tender and most of the liquid is absorbed, stirring often.

2. Stir in beans, prosciutto or ham, and parsley; heat through. Spoon into four bowls. Top each serving with Parmesan cheese. Makes 4 servings.

Each serving: 363 cal., 6 g total fat (2 g sat. fat), 7 mg chol., 800 mg sodium, 59 g carbo., 7 g fiber, 22 g pro. Daily Values: 3% vit. A, 5% vit. C, 17% calcium, 19% iron.

Red Beans and Orzo

PUMPING IRON

The flavonoid factors are highest in red, black, and deep-colored beans. But all beans, including cream-colored navy beans and garbanzo beans, contain some iron, folate, zinc, and a bit of calcium.

- **Iron:** Beans supply anywhere from 1 to 4 milligrams of iron in every half-cup serving. That's an amount similar to what you'd get in a serving of beef. Your body does a better job of taking in iron from animal sources, but you can compensate by mixing a little meat in with the beans.
- **Folate:** You probably know that women of childbearing age should eat foods rich in folate to help prevent neural-tube defects in their babies. You also need folate as you age to reduce your blood levels of homocysteine, a substance that puts you at greater risk for heart disease.
- **Zinc:** Some people have trouble getting enough zinc, which is essential for your body's growth, insulin function, and immune system. Beans are an excellent source of zinc.
- **Calcium:** Don't trade in your glass of milk or calcium-fortified orange juice for beans. However, every bit helps, and a half-cup serving of beans supplies 4 to 8 percent of the calcium you should have every day.

The Art of Choosing Fruit

JUST LIKE US OLDER FOLK, KIDS absolutely adore fresh fruit when it is at the top of its game—juicy, plump, and almost as sweet as candy. Consider this quest for the best fruit to be reason enough to hustle your children into the produce section for a quick, easy, and delicious lesson in the art of choosing fruits. After all, peachy peaches, perfect plums, fat sun-kissed berries, and deluxe ripe melons don't just show up on the family table. They're chosen.

Need more reasons? Fresh fruit is an essential part of a healthy kid's diet, a good source of vitamins and fiber. And it's a thrill to handle, like playing with big, brilliant jewels. Read on for a fruit-by-fruit guide and ideas for tossing together a yummy salad.

FRUITY FUN ...

Follow these simple tips to select fruits whose beauty is more than skin deep.

- **Look**

A bright hue, a rosy blush, pretty skin that's blemish free, and a plump shape—these are generally key for ripe fruits. No bruises, bumps, cracks, mold, or oozing, please.

- **Sniff**

Delicious fruits are fragrant and sweetly aromatic. Avoid fruits that have a stale, odd odor. An overly strong smell indicates overripeness.

- **Poke; Push; Lift**

Skip fruits that are hard and overly firm—this is an indication of underripeness. Overly soft fruits indicate overripeness. Most fruits should feel heavy for their size and be well shaped for their variety.

- **Taste**

Sweet, moist, and juicy. Bottom line: Ripe fruit should taste FRESH.

BEST OF SEASON

A street-smart fruit detective uses his or her sight, smell, touch, and taste to spot superior goods. Your kids can too.

- **Apricots**

Look for plump, firm apricots with a pretty red blush. Avoid fruit that is pale yellow or green-yellow, very firm, very soft, or bruised. Availability: late May to mid-August.

- **Blueberries, Strawberries, Raspberries, Blackberries**

Look for blueberries with a rounded shape and a tiny star-shaped cap. They should be firm, plump, and sweet. Strawberries should be plump with bright green caps and a healthy red color. Size does not indicate quality; the largest strawberries aren't necessarily the most flavorful. Raspberries grow in various shades of yellow, red, and black and contain many tiny, edible seeds. Blackberries should have an inviting color, ranging from purplish black to black. Beware of excess juices in the bottom of the containers—this is a sign of spoilage. Sniff for mold too. Availability: all summer long, depending on the region.

- **Melons**

Pick a juicy, heavyweight contender. Cantaloupes should have tightly-netted skin; honeydews should be smooth and unblemished. Poke and whiff the belly-button, or blossom, end; it should give a little and smell melony. Melons will soften but not sweeten further when left to sit at room temperature. Availability: nearly year-round.

- **Peaches and Nectarines**

Watch out for greenish ones; they won't ripen. A rosy blush is nice, but not an indicator of ripeness. Use finger pressure; ripe peaches feel slightly soft, yielding. Ditto on nectarines. Availability: peak from June through September.

- **Plums**

A plump shape, vibrant coloring, smooth skin, and moderately yielding flesh are good signs. Stay away from soft, leaky ones. The bloom (light gray cast) on the skin is natural and doesn't affect quality. Avoid exceptionally hard or soft fruits. Availability: June through September.

Fruit Salad Bowl Turnover

START TO FINISH: 30 minutes

- 4 cups sliced fresh peaches, nectarines, plums, and/or apricots
- 1 to 2 cups assorted fresh berries, such as blueberries, blackberries, raspberries, and/or halved strawberries
- 1 to 2 cups 1-inch chunks honeydew or cantaloupe melon
- 1 to 2 Tbsp. fresh lemon juice
- 1 to 2 Tbsp. sugar (optional)
- 3 small cantaloupes, halved (optional)

1. Refrigerate a large glass serving bowl for 20 to 30 minutes. Add desired fruit to the bowl. Toss gently until fruits are just mixed. Sprinkle with the lemon juice. Sprinkle with sugar to taste; toss gently until sugar is dissolved. To serve, spoon mixed fruits into cantaloupe halves, if desired. Makes 6 to 8 servings.

Each serving: 73 cal., 0 g total fat (0 g sat. fat), 0 mg chol., 4 mg sodium, 19 g carbo., 3 g fiber, 1 g pro. Daily Values: 13% vit. A, 32% vit. C, 1% calcium, 1% iron.

September

AS THE DAYS GROW EVER SHORTER, WE SAVOR SUMMER'S LAST GLOW AND STOW AWAY THE FRUITS OF HER SEASON.

N.Y. Steak with Pear Brandy-Black Pepper Sauce

Pear Roquefort Tart

Spiced Canned Pears

Perfect Pears

Plus...

Pear-Cherry Chutney

Big Green Salad with Two-Pepper Dressing

Steamed Salmon and Swiss Chard Stack

Big Flavor

Plus...

WITH COOLER DAYS COMES A LONGING FOR THE COMFORTABLE AND THE FAMILIAR. SEPTEMBER CALLS FAMILY FAVORITES TO THE DINNER TABLE, WITH SOME CLEVER BACK-TO-SCHOOL TWISTS.

Buttery Sage and Acorn Squash Tart

ear Scones ith Pear Butter

Mediterranean Parsnips

Brined Skillet-Roasted Brussels Sprouts

Perfect Pears

THE REWARDS OF FALL'S ESSENTIAL FRUIT

LOCK UP THE FLAVORS OF FALL BY CANNING, FREEZING, AND DRYING GOLDEN PEARS, READY FOR FABULOUS FALL DINNERS AND DESSERTS.

Spiced Canned Pears

Creamy Pear Soup

Can your own pears for this rosemary-scented soup or purchase pears canned in a light syrup. Our recipe for home-canned pears on page 332 calls for a lighter syrup to suit today's tastes.

PREP: 25 minutes **COOK:** 25 minutes

- 2 cups water
- 1/2 tsp. salt
- 1 fresh rosemary sprig
- 1/2 of a large celery root (8 oz.), peeled and chopped, or 1 1/2 cups chopped celery
- 1 qt. Spiced Canned Pears (page 332) or one 29-oz. can pear halves in light syrup
- 1/4 cup Riesling or other sweet white wine
- 1/4 cup whipping cream
- Fresh Parmesan cheese shards (optional)
- Cracked black pepper (optional)

1. In a large saucepan bring water, salt, and rosemary sprig to boiling. Add celery root. Return to boiling; reduce heat. Simmer, covered, about 20 minutes or until tender.

2. Meanwhile, place undrained pears in a blender (or half of the pears at a time in a food processor). Cover and blend or process until smooth (you should have about 3 1/2 cups).

3. Remove rosemary from hot mixture. Stir in pureed pears, wine, and cream; heat through. Ladle into 6 bowls. If desired, top with Parmesan and pepper. Makes 6 appetizer servings.

Each serving: 222 cal., 6 g total fat (3 g sat. fat), 17 mg chol., 308 mg sodium, 42 g carbo., 3 g fiber, 3 g pro. Daily Values: 4% vit. A, 8% vit. C, 9% calcium, 3% iron.

Creamy Pear Soup

A flavor favorite

It's that abundance of flavor that makes people buy pears by the bushel to put up for later a perfect cook's ally. More than any other fruit, the pear benefits from being preserved. Consider plump halves suspended in thick glass jars; slices simmered into long-lasting chutneys; slivers dried to make intense, chewy fruit leather; and sweet, ice-fast wedges in a deep-freeze slumber.

"In the middle of a dreary winter, there's nothing like opening up a jar of fruit you've canned that summer," says Sydney Blaine, a pear farmer in Mount Hood, Oregon.

Unlike many other fruits, the pear's affinity for preservation comes from the complexity of its flavor and the role that cooking plays in bringing out its best aspects—whether on the stove in preparation for canning or freezing, or the low and slow heat during drying.

"They're perfumy and really unctuous and juicy," says Cathy Whims, a Portland cooking teacher and chef who often incorporates pears into her classes. "It's not a one-hit taste. And their aroma is so amazing. It's flowery, kind of sweet in a way. They have an earthy quality to them, similar to grapes. And cooking intensifies the flavors I really like."

Pears not only taste "unctuous" in our collection of recipes but also lend themselves to improvisation. For example, you can toss dried pears into a salad. Cut up canned pears and skewer them with chicken for a unique kabob. Or, for one of the best tricks around, throw slightly thawed frozen pears into the blender, where they become sorbet. From cheesy appetizer to chocolaty dessert, with dried, canned, and frozen pears, here you'll find a winter's worth of delectable ideas based on the golden fruit of fall.

Spiced Pears
and Lamb Chops
THE MEAT OF THE MOMENT—LAMB—GETS FAMILY-FRIENDLY WITH A JAR OF HOME-CANNED PEARS FOR THIS 30-MINUTE MAIN DISH.

N.Y. Steak with Pear Brandy-Black Pepper Sauce

Pear brandy is available at fine wine and liquor shops. Brandy made with Oregon pears can be found at www.clearcreekdistillery.com.

START TO FINISH: 30 minutes

- ½ cup snipped Oven-Dried Pears (page 330) or purchased dried pears
- ⅓ cup Poire Williams brandy, pear brandy, or pear nectar
- 4 tsp. all-purpose flour
- 1 tsp. cracked black pepper
- ½ tsp. salt
- 4 beef tenderloin steaks or beef top loin steaks, cut 1 inch thick (1 to 1½ lb. total)
- 3 Tbsp. butter or margarine
- ¼ cup finely chopped shallots or green onions
- ¼ cup reduced-sodium beef broth

1. In a small bowl stir together pears and brandy or nectar. Cover; let stand for 15 minutes.

2. Meanwhile, in a shallow dish stir together flour, pepper, and salt. Dip steaks into flour mixture to coat. In a large skillet cook steaks in 2 tablespoons of the hot butter over medium heat to desired doneness, turning once. For tenderloin steaks, allow 10 to 13 minutes for medium rare (145° F) to medium (160° F). For top loin steaks, allow 12 to 15 minutes for medium rare to medium. Transfer steaks to a platter, reserving the drippings in the skillet. Cover and keep warm.

3. For sauce, in the same skillet cook shallots in the drippings over medium heat for 1 minute. Remove from heat. Let stand for 1 minute. Carefully stir in dried pear mixture and beef broth. Bring to boiling. Boil gently, uncovered, over medium heat about 3 minutes or until mixture is slightly thickened, stirring occasionally. Whisk in remaining 1 tablespoon butter. To serve, spoon sauce over steaks. Makes 4 servings.

Each serving: 322 cal., 17 g total fat (8 g sat. fat), 81 mg chol., 465 mg sodium, 6 g carbo., 0 g fiber, 24 g pro. Daily Values: 9% vit. A, 2% vit. C, 2% calcium, 19% iron.

A PEAR-FECT FALL DINNER

Creamy Pear Soup *(page 323)*
N.Y. Steak with Pear Brandy-Black Pepper Sauce *(above)*
French fries
Steamed broccoli
Dried Pear-Chocolate Caramel Pie *(page 334)*
Pinot Noir or other dry red wine
Coffee or tea

N.Y. Steak with Pear Brandy-Black Pepper Sauce

Spiced Pears and Lamb Chops

Simmer pears and pear nectar for a few minutes to concentrate the fruity flavor and thicken the sauce naturally.

PREP: 15 minutes **COOK:** 16 minutes

- 8 lamb rib or loin chops, cut 1 inch thick
- Salt
- Ground black pepper
- 2 tsp. olive oil
- 2 large onions, sliced (2 cups)
- 1 tsp. paprika
- 1 tsp. ground cumin
- ½ tsp. celery seeds
- 2 Tbsp. butter or margarine
- ½ cup pear nectar
- 1 qt. Spiced Canned Pears (page 332) or two 16-oz. cans pear halves, drained
- 2 cups torn radicchio leaves

1. Trim fat from chops. Sprinkle with salt and pepper. In a large skillet cook chops in hot oil over medium heat for 9 to 11 minutes for medium (160° F), turning once. Transfer chops to a platter; cover and keep warm. Drain fat from skillet.

2. For sauce, in the same large skillet cook onions, paprika, cumin, and celery seeds in hot butter about 5 minutes or until tender, stirring occasionally. Add pear nectar and drained pears. Bring to boiling. Boil gently, uncovered, about 2 minutes or until sauce is slightly thickened.

3. To serve, arrange chops on radicchio leaves. Spoon pear sauce over chops. Makes 4 servings.

Each serving: 518 cal., 18 g total fat (7 g sat. fat), 80 mg chol., 209 mg sodium, 72 g carbo., 6 g fiber, 22 g pro. Daily Values: 12% vit. A, 19% vit. C, 7% calcium, 15% iron.

Pears and Brie in Phyllo

Serve this pear-filled cheese spread with assorted crackers or sliced French bread. Ooh-la-la!

PREP: 35 minutes **BAKE:** 40 minutes

- 1 small pear, finely chopped (1/2 cup)
- 2 Tbsp. snipped dried tart cherries
- 1/2 tsp. snipped fresh rosemary
- 3 Tbsp. butter, melted
- 1 recipe Sugar-Coated Walnuts (below)
- 1 8-oz. round Brie cheese
- 4 sheets frozen phyllo dough (9×14-inch rectangles), thawed

1. For filling, in a small saucepan cook pear, cherries, and rosemary in 1 tablespoon hot butter about 3 minutes or until pear is just tender; remove from heat. Cool slightly. Prepare Sugar-Coated Walnuts; set aside.

2. Preheat oven to 400° F. Split Brie round in half horizontally, making 2 rounds. Top a cut side with pear filling and half of the Sugar-Coated Walnuts. Top with the other Brie half, cut side down (Brie will be full).

3. Lightly brush a sheet of phyllo with some of the melted butter. Top with 3 more sheets, brushing each sheet with butter.

4. Place the Brie round in center of phyllo stack. Bring phyllo up and around Brie to enclose, pleating phyllo as necessary. Invert onto a greased 15×10×1-inch baking pan; brush with butter.

5. Bake about 15 minutes or until golden. Transfer to a platter. Top with remaining Sugar-Coated Walnuts. Serve warm. Makes 20 appetizer servings.

SUGAR-COATED WALNUTS: In a small skillet melt 1 tablespoon butter over medium heat. Add 1/2 cup broken walnuts and 1 tablespoon sugar (sugar will not dissolve). Cook and stir over medium heat about 5 minutes or until walnuts are toasted and sugar is brown. Pour mixture onto a piece of foil; let cool. Coarsely crush the nut mixture. Makes about 1/2 cup.

Each serving: 91 cal., 8 g total fat (4 g sat. fat), 18 mg chol., 105 mg sodium, 3 g carbo., 0 g fiber, 3 g pro. Daily Values: 3% vit. A, 3% calcium, 1% iron.

Pear Roquefort Tart

Serve this knife-and-fork appetizer to start off a harvest feast.

PREP: 40 minutes **BAKE:** 12 minutes

- 1 recipe Walnut Tart Pastry (below)
- 1/2 of an 8-oz. pkg. cream cheese, softened
- 2 oz. Roquefort or blue cheese, crumbled (1/2 cup)
- 3/4 cup Pear Butter (page 330)
- 2 Tbsp. butter
- 3 small fresh pears, peeled, cored, and sliced; or 1 pt. Spiced Canned Pears (fennel-flavored) (page 332), drained and sliced; or one 15-oz. can pear slices, drained
- 1/4 cup bite-size strips prosciutto

1. Prepare, bake, and cool Tart Pastry. Meanwhile, in a medium mixing bowl beat cream cheese and blue cheese with an electric mixer on low to medium speed until smooth.

2. Spread cheese mixture onto bottom of the pastry. Top with Pear Butter.

3. In a large skillet melt butter over medium-high heat; add pear slices. Cook until tender and heated through, allowing 5 minutes for fresh pears or 2 minutes for canned pears, turning gently occasionally. Cool slightly in pan for 5 minutes.

4. Arrange pear slices on cheese mixture in crust-lined pan. Top with prosciutto. If desired, cover and chill in the refrigerator up to 4 hours. To serve, cut into squares. Makes 9 servings.

WALNUT TART PASTRY: Preheat oven to 425° F. In a medium bowl stir together 1 1/4 cups all-purpose flour, 1/4 cup chopped walnuts, 2 tablespoons sugar, 1 teaspoon cracked black pepper, and 1 teaspoon snipped fresh thyme. Using a pastry blender, cut 1/2 cup butter into flour mixture until pieces are pea-size. In a small bowl stir together 2 beaten egg yolks and 1 tablespoon ice water; gradually stir into flour mixture. Using your fingers, gently knead the dough just until a ball forms. Pat onto bottom and halfway up the sides of a 9-inch square baking pan. Prick generously with a fork. Bake for 12 to 14 minutes or until golden. Cool on a wire rack.

Each serving: 348 cal., 24 g total fat (13 g sat. fat), 103 mg chol., 307 mg sodium, 30 g carbo., 2 g fiber, 6 g pro. Daily Values: 17% vit. A, 6% vit. C, 7% calcium, 8% iron.

Pear Roquefort Tart

Pear-Cherry Chutney

USE THIS CHUTNEY TO CREATE A GLAZE FOR GRILLED PORK AND TO ADD THE FINAL PIQUANT TOUCH TO ROAST

Pear-Cherry Chutney

For an easy and pretty appetizer, spoon this sweet-tart combo over cheese and serve it with French bread.

PREP: 20 minutes **COOK:** 10 minutes

- 1/2 cup sugar
- 1 cup dried tart red cherries
- 2 tsp. finely shredded lemon peel
- 1/3 cup lemon juice
- 1/2 tsp. ground cinnamon
- 1/2 tsp. ground allspice
- 5 cups chopped, peeled firm fresh pears

1. In a large saucepan combine sugar, dried cherries, lemon peel, lemon juice, cinnamon, and allspice. Bring to boiling; reduce heat. Simmer, uncovered, for 5 minutes, stirring occasionally. Stir in pears; return to boiling. Simmer, uncovered, for 5 minutes or until pears are just tender. Let cool.

2. Transfer chutney to a storage container. Cover and chill in the refrigerator for up to 2 weeks. Or place in a freezer container; cover and freeze up to 6 months. Use a slotted spoon to serve chutney as a topper for cheese or as a condiment with beef, pork, or lamb. Makes 4 1/2 cups chutney (18 servings).

Each 1/4-cup serving: 71 cal., 0 g total fat (0 g sat. fat), 0 mg chol., 0 mg sodium, 18 g carbo., 1 g fiber, 0 g pro. Daily Values: 7% vit. C, 1% calcium, 1% iron.

PICKING PEARS

Thanks to imports and advances in storage, most pear varieties are available year-round. Choose from the kinds listed below.

BOSC: Best for cooking as well as for canning, freezing, and drying is the swan-necked, sandy-skinned Bosc, which many experts consider to be their favorite all-around pear. It holds its shape and flavor well under a variety of cooking, preserving, and baking conditions. The charm of the Bosc—available August through April—is its flowery aroma and spicy, clovelike flavor.

BARTLETT: Equally versatile in the minds of many cooks are the Bartletts, both red and yellow. Available July through December—and canned year-round—they are a little more tender and slightly sweeter than Boscs, with a floral, hint-of-jasmine character.

SECKEL: Maroon-blushed or all-maroon Seckels have been dubbed honey or sugar pears for their lusciously juicy, syrupy quality. These September-to-May pears are less practical for preserving because of their small size, but they are beauties when canned whole. And, for anyone with a little patience, they make outstanding preserves.

ANJOU, COMICE, FORELLE, AND ASIAN: The Anjou (October to June), the Comice (September to March), and the tiny Forelle (September to February) are better appreciated fresh. Both green and red Anjous have all the best of the honey-wine-butter character of pears. Asian pears, which combine the crunchiness of apple with the flavor of pear, are also best fresh.

(below, left to right) Yellow Anjou, Red Anjou, Forelle, Comice, Bosc, Red Bartlett, Seckel, Maroon Seckel

Oven-Dried Pears

Pear Scones

The texture of these scones will vary with the form of pears you use. Fresh and canned pears will make moister scones; for drier scones, use the dried-pear option.

Prep: 25 minutes **Bake:** 14 minutes

- 2 cups all-purpose flour
- 1/3 cup granulated sugar
- 1 1/2 tsp. baking powder
- 1/2 tsp. baking soda
- 6 Tbsp. butter, chilled
- 1/3 cup buttermilk
- 1 egg
- 1 1/2 tsp. vanilla
- 1 cup chopped, peeled fresh pears; canned pears, patted dry; or 1 cup finely chopped Oven-Dried Pears* (right)
- Coarse sugar (optional)

1. Preheat oven to 400° F. In a large bowl combine flour, granulated sugar, baking powder, and baking soda. Using a pastry blender, cut in butter until mixture resembles coarse crumbs. Make a well in center of flour mixture; set aside.

2. In a bowl stir together buttermilk, egg, and vanilla. Add buttermilk mixture to flour mixture. Stir just until combined (mixture may appear dry). Stir in pears. Form dough into a ball.

3. Turn dough out onto a well floured surface (lightly floured if using dried pears). Knead by folding and gently pressing dough for 8 to 10 strokes or until dough holds together and is no longer sticky. Pat or lightly roll dough to 1-inch thickness. Cut with a floured 2- to 2 1/2-inch biscuit cutter. Gather any remaining dough; pat to 1-inch thickness and cut additional scones (handle dough gently; don't overwork).

4. Arrange scones on an ungreased baking sheet. If desired, sprinkle with coarse sugar. Bake for 14 to 18 minutes or until golden. Serve warm. Makes 10 to 12 scones.

***Note:** If using dried pears, increase the buttermilk to 1/2 cup.

Each serving: 205 cal., 8 g total fat (5 g sat. fat), 41 mg chol., 197 mg sodium, 29 g carbo., 1 g fiber, 3 g pro. Daily Values: 6% vit. A, 2% vit. C, 6% calcium, 7% iron.

PEAR-FECT FALL PICNIC

Pear Roquefort Tart *(page 326)*
Pear Scones *(above)*
Pear Butter *(right)*
Spiced Canned Pears *(page 332)*
Pear or apple cider

Oven-Dried Pears

Prep: 20 minutes **Bake:** 3 1/2 hours

- 2 lb. ripe but firm fresh pears, such as Bartlett, Anjou, and Bosc, peeled and cored

1. Preheat oven to 200° F. Line 2 large baking sheets with parchment paper or nonstick foil. Cut pears into 1/4-inch-thick slices. Arrange in a single layer on baking sheets (see photo, *above)*. Bake about 3 1/2 hours or until pears are dry but still slightly chewy, turning pear slices every hour.

2. Let pear slices cool completely. Transfer pear slices to an airtight container. Cover and store in the freezer for up to 6 months. Pears may develop a sugary appearance during storage. Makes 5 to 6 ounces pear slices (about 1 1/2 cups).

Each ounce: 98 cal., 1 g total fat (0 g sat. fat), 0 mg chol., 0 mg sodium, 25 g carbo., 4 g fiber, 1 g pro. Daily Values: 1% vit. A, 8% vit. C, 2% calcium, 2% iron.

Pear Butter

In addition to being a key element in Pear Roquefort Tart, this butter is delicious when spread onto scones or toast or when stirred into plain yogurt or salad dressing.

Prep: 40 minutes **Cook:** 1 3/4 hours

- 4 lb. fresh cooking pears, such as Bosc or Bartlett (about 9 pears)
- 2 1/2 cups water
- 1 1/2 cups sugar
- 1 Tbsp. finely shredded orange peel
- 1/4 cup orange juice

1. Quarter and core pears. In a 6- to 8-quart Dutch oven combine pears and the water. Bring to boiling; reduce heat. Simmer, covered, for 30 minutes, stirring occasionally. Press mixture through a food mill, discarding solids (you should have about 6 cups sieved mixture). Return to Dutch oven.

2. Stir in sugar, orange peel, and orange juice. Bring to boiling; reduce heat. Simmer, uncovered, over medium-low heat for 1 1/4 hours or until very thick. As the mixture thickens, reduce heat to low, if necessary, stirring often.

3. Ladle hot pear butter into hot, sterilized half-pint canning jars, leaving 1/4-inch headspace. Wipe jar rims; adjust lids. Process in a boiling-water canner for 5 minutes (start timing when water returns to boil). Remove jars; cool on racks. Makes 4 half-pints.

Each tablespoon: 38 cal., 0 g total fat, 0 mg chol., 0 mg sodium, 10 g carbo., 1 g fiber, 0 g pro. Daily Values: 3% vit. C.

Pear Scones with Pear Butter

Freezing Pears

Find ascorbic acid in the spice section or canning supplies section of your supermarket.

Prep: 50 minutes **Cook:** 2 minutes **Cool:** 30 minutes

- **4 tsp. ascorbic acid color-keeper**
- **⅓ cup water**
- **4 lb. fresh pears, such as Bartlett, Bosc, or Seckel**
- **4 cups water**
- **1 cup sugar**

1. In a large bowl combine ascorbic acid color-keeper and the ⅓ cup water. Peel, core, and cut pears into ¼-inch-thick slices, adding pears to color-keeper solution as they are sliced. Gently toss the mixture occasionally to prevent fruit from discoloring.

2. In a Dutch oven or kettle bring the 4 cups water to boiling. Add sugar and stir until dissolved. Return sugar-water mixture to boiling. Add pear mixture. Cook for 2 minutes. Drain pears, reserving syrup; cool.

3. Pack pears into resealable freezer bags or clean pint canning jars or freezer containers. Add cooled syrup, completely covering the pears. For wide-top jars or containers, leave a ½-inch headspace; for narrow-top containers, leave a ¾-inch headspace (see photo 3, *opposite*). Seal, label, and freeze. Use pears within 8 months. Makes 3 pints (12 servings).

Each ½-cup serving: 44 cal., 1 g total fat (0 g sat. fat), 0 mg chol., 3 mg sodium, 37 g carbo., 3 g fiber, 1 g pro. Daily Values: 8% vit. C, 2% calcium, 2% iron.

Spiced Canned Pears

When selecting pears for canning, look for fruit that is ripe and still firm to the touch. Avoid pears that are overripe, because canning will make them too soft.

Start to Finish: 2½ hours

- **5 lb. fresh Bartlett or Bosc pears**
- **Ascorbic acid color-keeper**
- **8 cups water**
- **2 cups sugar**
- **Whole cloves, stick cinnamon, or fennel seeds (optional)**

1. Fill an 18- to 20-quart boiling-water canner (with rack) half full of water; cover and heat over high heat until boiling. Heat additional water in another kettle. Wash jars in hot, soapy water. Rinse thoroughly. Prepare screw bands and new flat metal lids with a built-in sealing compound according to manufacturer's directions.

2. Peel, halve, and core pears. Treat with color-keeper solution according to package directions. In a 6- to 8-quart large kettle or Dutch oven combine water and sugar; bring to boiling. Add pear halves. Return to boiling; simmer in syrup for 5 minutes.

3. When the water in the canner is boiling, fill each jar and place it on rack in canner. To fill jars, use a slotted spoon to transfer pear halves to jars. Pack pears tightly in jars to avoid excess air space between pears, leaving about ½-inch headspace at the top of the jar. (If you are using medium-sized pears, you should be able to get 8 to 10 pear halves in a quart jar.)

4. Add desired spices or seeds to each jar. For cloves, add ¼ teaspoon whole cloves per jar. For cinnamon, add one 3-inch stick of cinnamon per quart jar (if canning pints, use one 1½-inch stick per jar). For fennel seeds, add 1 teaspoon per jar.

5. Add syrup to jars using a funnel and small ladle or 1-cup liquid measuring cup (see photo 1, *opposite*). Use a small spatula to release air bubbles and pack pears (photo 2, *opposite*). Adjust liquid to create ½-inch headspace (see photo 3, *opposite*). Wipe jar rims with a clean, damp cloth. Place prepared lids on jars; add screw bands and tighten. Place jars on rack in canner using a jar lifter (photo 4, *opposite*).

6. After the last jar has been added to canner, add enough additional boiling water to put tops of jars 1 inch below the waterline. Cover; heat to a brisk, rolling boil. Keep water boiling gently during canning. If canning quarts, boil for 25 minutes; for pints, boil for 20 minutes. Using a jar lifter, remove jars from canner and place on a wire rack to cool.

7. When jars are completely cool (12 to 24 hours), press the center of each lid to check the seal. If the dip in the lid holds, the jar is sealed. If the lid bounces up and down, the jar isn't sealed. (The contents of unsealed jars can be refrigerated and used within 2 to 3 days.) Store canned pears in a cool, dry place for up to 1 year. Makes 3 quarts (4 or 5 servings per quart).

Each serving: 226 cal., 1 g total fat (0 g sat. fat), 0 mg chol., 5 mg sodium, 58 g carbo., 4 g fiber, 1 g pro. Daily Values: 1% vit. A, 8% vit. C, 2% calcium, 3% iron.

Spiced Canned Pears

The steps necessary to can your own pears, ranging from filling and removing bubbles (see photos 1 and 2, *right*) to measuring headspace and cooking pears in a large kettle called a "canner" (see photos 3 and 4, *right*), ensure both food safety and the maximum flavor.

PIECRUST POINTER

To transfer the pastry for baking, drape it over the rolling pin and unroll pastry into the pie plate.

Caramel Sauce

Serve this silky sauce warm or cool with Dried Pear-Chocolate Caramel Pie or spoon it over ice cream or cake.

START TO FINISH: 20 minutes

- 3/4 **cup packed brown sugar**
- 1/4 **cup water**
- 1 **tsp. lemon juice**
- 1/3 **cup whipping cream**
- 1 **Tbsp. butter**
- 2 **Tbsp. pear brandy (optional)**
- 1/2 **tsp. vanilla**

1. In a heavy small saucepan combine brown sugar, water, and lemon juice. Cook and stir over medium heat until bubbly. Cook and stir about 10 minutes more or until thickened.

2. Carefully stir in cream and butter. Cook and stir until butter is melted. Remove from heat. Stir in pear brandy, if desired, and vanilla. Serve warm or cool. Cover and chill any leftovers in the refrigerator for up to 3 days. Makes 1 cup sauce (8 servings).

Each 2-tablespoon serving: 132 cal., 5 g total fat (3 g sat. fat), 18 mg chol., 28 mg sodium, 22 g carbo., 0 g fiber, 0 g pro. Daily Values: 4% vit. A, 1% vit. C, 3% calcium, 2% iron.

Dried Pear-Chocolate Caramel Pie

You can make your own pastry or use a folded, refrigerated piecrust from the supermarket.

PREP: 45 minutes **BAKE:** 52 minutes
COOK: 15 minutes **COOL:** 4 hours

- 1 **recipe Pastry for Single-Crust Pie (below)**
- 4 **cups Oven-Dried Pears (page 330) or five 3-oz. pkg. dried pears, sliced into 1/4-inch-thick slices**
- 2 **12-oz. cans pear nectar (3 cups)**
- 2 **Tbsp. honey**
- 1/2 **tsp. ground cinnamon**
- 1/4 **tsp. ground nutmeg**
- 1 **Tbsp. butter**
- 1 **recipe Almond Crumb Topping (below)**
- 1 **recipe Caramel Sauce (left) or 3/4 cup prepared caramel ice cream topping**
- 1 **oz. bittersweet chocolate, chopped**

1. Preheat oven to 450° F. Prepare Pastry for Single-Crust Pie. Roll pastry to a 12-inch circle. Transfer pastry to a 9-inch pie plate (see photo, *left*). Trim pastry to 1/2 inch beyond edge of pie plate. Fold under extra pastry. Flute edges high. Do not prick. Line pastry with a double thickness of foil. Bake for 8 minutes. Remove foil. Bake 4 to 5 minutes more or until set and dry. Remove crust from oven; reduce oven temperature to 375° F.

2. Meanwhile, for filling, in a large saucepan combine dried pears and nectar. Bring to boiling; reduce heat. Simmer, covered, for 5 minutes. Stir in honey, cinnamon, and nutmeg. Simmer, uncovered, for 10 minutes (juices will be thick).

3. Add pear filling to pastry shell, spreading evenly. Dot with butter. Prepare Almond Crumb Topping; sprinkle onto pie.

4. Bake for 40 to 45 minutes or until topping is light brown. If needed, cover edge of pie with foil the last 5 to 10 minutes of baking time to prevent overbrowning. Cool on a wire rack for 20 minutes. Drizzle with 1/4 cup of the Caramel Sauce; sprinkle with chocolate. Cool completely. Serve with remaining Caramel Sauce. Makes 8 servings.

PASTRY FOR SINGLE-CRUST PIE: In a medium bowl stir together 1 1/4 cups all-purpose flour and 1/4 teaspoon salt. Using a pastry blender, cut in 1/3 cup shortening until pieces are pea-size. Using a total of 4 to 5 tablespoons cold water, sprinkle 1 tablespoon water over part of the mixture; gently toss with a fork. Push moistened dough to side of bowl. Repeat until all is moistened. Form dough into a ball.

ALMOND CRUMB TOPPING: In a bowl combine 1/2 cup all-purpose flour, 1/4 cup granulated sugar, 1/4 cup packed brown sugar, and 1/4 teaspoon salt. Using a pastry blender or 2 knives, cut in 1/3 cup cold butter until mixture resembles coarse crumbs. Stir in 3/4 cup coarsely chopped almonds.

Each serving: 628 cal., 31 g total fat (12 g sat. fat), 43 mg chol., 278 mg sodium, 86 g carbo., 5 g fiber, 6 g pro. Daily Values: 11% vit. A, 5% vit. C, 8% calcium, 16% iron.

HONEYED PEAR NECTAR BUBBLES AND SOFTENS DRIED PEARS INTO JUICY SLICES OF THIS FABULOUS FALL PIE.

Dried Pear-Chocolate Caramel Pie

Triple Pear Sauce

A WORD ABOUT RIPENESS

Growers pick their pears when the fruit on the trees is mature (full in size and shape) but still unripe. Because of the packing and storing procedures, the pears are often still not quite ripe when you buy them at the supermarket. If that's the case, follow these easy steps and you'll have juicy, drip-down-your-arms pears every time!

- To ripen pears at home, place the fruit, stems up, in a brown paper bag and close the bag.
- Check the fruit daily for ripeness; usually two or three days will do the trick.
- A pear is ripe when the skin is yellow or pink and yields to gentle pressure.
- Once pears are ripe, store them in your refrigerator to keep them as fresh as possible.

Triple Pear Sauce

Try this sauce over slices of vanilla ice cream or pound cake and top with toasted, chopped hazelnuts.

PREP: 20 minutes **COOK:** 11 minutes

- 1 pt. or 1/2 qt. Spiced Canned Pears (page 332) or one 15-oz. can pear halves in light or extra light syrup
- 2 cups snipped Oven-Dried Pears (page 330)
- 1/2 cup butter or margarine
- 1/2 cup sugar
- 2 cups fresh Seckel, Forelle, or Bartlett pears, cored and cut into small chunks

1. Drain pears, reserving 3/4 cup syrup. Cut canned pears into large chunks; set aside.

2. In a large nonstick skillet bring the reserved syrup and the dried pears to boiling; reduce heat. Simmer, uncovered, until the liquid is evaporated. Remove pears from the skillet; set aside.

3. In the same skillet melt butter over medium heat. Add sugar; cook and stir for 1 to 2 minutes until sugar is almost dissolved. Decrease heat to medium-low. Stir in cooked and canned pears. Cook, covered, for 5 minutes, stirring frequently.

4. Add fresh pears. Cover and cook for 5 minutes more, stirring frequently. Cool slightly. Serve warm. Cover and chill any remaining sauce for up to 2 days; heat slightly before serving. Makes 8 (1/2-cup) servings.

Each serving: 252 cal., 13 g total fat (8 g sat. fat), 33 mg chol., 125 mg sodium, 37 g carbo., 3 g fiber, 1 g pro. Daily Values: 10% vit. A, 6% vit. C, 2% calcium, 2% iron.

PEAR-FECT SUNDAY SUPPER

Spiced Pears and Lamb Chops *(page 325)*
Radicchio leaves or steamed red cabbage
Mashed potatoes
Rye rolls
Triple Pear Sauce *(above)* over vanilla ice cream
Iced tea or water

Pear-Pecan Cake with Caramel Topping

You can serve this potluck favorite plain as a coffee cake or top it with whipped cream for a real old-fashioned dessert.

PREP: 20 minutes **BAKE:** 50 minutes **COOL:** 2 hours

- 3 cups all-purpose flour
- 1 tsp. baking soda
- 1/2 tsp. salt
- 3 eggs
- 2 cups sugar
- 1 cup cooking oil
- 2 tsp. vanilla
- 3 medium pears, cored, peeled, and finely chopped (3 cups)
- 1 cup toasted, chopped pecans
- 1 recipe Caramel Topping (below)
- Whipped cream (optional)

1. Preheat oven to 350° F. Lightly grease a 13×9×2-inch baking pan; set aside. In a medium bowl stir together flour, baking soda, and salt; set aside.

2. In a large bowl beat eggs; stir in sugar, oil, and vanilla. Add flour mixture to oil mixture; stir until combined. Stir in pears and pecans (batter will be thick).

3. Spread batter in prepared pan. Bake about 50 minutes or until golden brown and a toothpick inserted near the center comes out clean. Cool in pan on a wire rack.

4. Prepare Caramel Topping; spoon warm topping over cooled cake. Allow topping to cool. Cut into squares to serve. If desired, serve with whipped cream. Makes 20 servings.

CARAMEL TOPPING: In a medium saucepan melt 1/2 cup butter over medium heat. Stir in 1 cup packed brown sugar and 1/4 cup evaporated milk. Bring to boiling over medium-high heat. Reduce heat to medium. Boil, uncovered, for 3 minutes, stirring constantly. Remove from heat.

Each serving with topping: 389 cal., 21 g total fat (5 g sat. fat), 46 mg chol., 189 mg sodium, 49 g carbo., 2 g fiber, 4 g pro. Daily Values: 5% vit. A, 2% vit. C, 3% calcium, 8% iron.

a bit of garlic guidance

GARLIC CAN BE MELLOW OR ASSERTIVE. IT ALL DEPENDS ON HOW YOU HANDLE IT.

Garlic lovers can easily understand why ancient Egyptians worshiped the herb, Confucius wrote ballads to it, and early Vikings toted it with them on voyages. Its pronounced flavor, which mellows sweetly with cooking, adds a taste sensation to nearly any dish.

Whether you're after a sweetly subtle note or a bold and tasty blast, you can control garlic's flavor with a few kitchen tricks. It boils down to timing and cutting. Garlic that is cooked for a long time generally is mild and creamy. Hence, if you toss a whole clove or thick slices of garlic into a long-simmering casserole or soup, you'll get a gentle hint of garlic.

On the other hand, if you wait until just before serving to crush or finely chop fresh garlic before stirring it into your pot, you'll get a much more potent effect. The finer that garlic is minced, the bigger the flavor.

That pesky papery covering you find on garlic will easily slip off if you soak the individual cloves in plain water about an hour before using. Or if you're in a hurry, just drop the cloves into boiling water for 30 seconds, rinse under cold water, and drain. The papery skins pop right off.

GROW YOUR OWN GARLIC

You can reap at least 10 times what you sow if you plant your own garlic. Here's how:

- Order garlic bulbs in in the fall if you live in the North or spring in the South. To order, check a local nursery or try: Johnny's Selected Seeds, 207/437-4301, or Seed Savers Exchange, 563/382-5990.
- Plant garlic in the North at least one month before the soil freezes, usually about mid-September to mid-October. In the South, you can plant in February or March.
- Break open bulbs, separate cloves, and peel away papery layers of skin immediately before planting.
- Plant cloves, pointy tips up, 4 to 6 inches apart and 2 to 4 inches deep (the colder your winters, the deeper you plant).
- As green growth appears, trim off any flower buds that bloom.

Cheesy Garlic Rolls

This bread recipe was inspired by an appetizer created by Jim Powell, chef/owner of Gibson's Restaurant in Grand Rapids, Michigan.

PREP: 25 minutes **BAKE:** 8 minutes
COOK: 25 minutes **COOL:** 20 minutes

- **1/3 cup peeled garlic cloves (24 cloves, 2 to 3 bulbs)**
- **2/3 cup chicken broth**
- **1/2 cup dry white wine**
- **1/2 of a 12-oz. pkg. (6 rolls) Hawaiian sweet rolls or dinner rolls**
- **2 oz. fontina cheese, shredded (1/2 cup)**
- **Olive oil**

1. In a heavy small saucepan combine garlic, broth, and wine. Bring to boiling; reduce heat. Simmer, uncovered, over medium heat about 25 minutes or until garlic is tender and 1/3 cup of the liquid remains. Set aside to cool.

2. Preheat oven to 325° F. Place rolls (do not separate) in a greased 8×8×2-inch baking pan. Cut an "X" about 1/2 inch deep in the top of each roll; spread open slightly. Spoon garlic cloves and cheese into openings, pressing gently into rolls. Drizzle with broth mixture; brush with olive oil.

3. Bake for 8 to 10 minutes until heated through and cheese is melted. Serve warm. Makes 6 appetizer servings.

Each serving: 181 cal., 7 g total fat (3 g sat. fat), 21 mg chol., 275 mg sodium, 19 g carbo., 0 g dietary fiber, 6 g protein. Daily Values: 2% vit. A, 6% vit. C, 8% calcium, 2% iron.

Spicy Garlic Chicken Pizza

PREP: 20 minutes **CHILL:** 30 minutes **BAKE:** 12 + 2 minutes

- **12 oz. skinless, boneless chicken breast halves**
- **1/2 cup sliced green onions**
- **2 cloves garlic, minced**
- **2 Tbsp. rice vinegar**
- **2 Tbsp. reduced-sodium soy sauce**
- **2 Tbsp. olive oil**
- **1/2 tsp. crushed red pepper**
- **1/4 tsp. ground black pepper**
- **1 Tbsp. cornstarch**
- **1 16-oz. Italian bread shell (Boboli)**
- **2 oz. Monterey Jack cheese, shredded (1/2 cup)**
- **2 oz. mozzarella cheese, shredded (1/2 cup)**
- **2 Tbsp. pine nuts or sliced almonds**

1. Cut chicken into 1/2-inch pieces. In a large mixing bowl combine half of the green onions, the garlic, vinegar, soy sauce, 1 tablespoon of the oil, the red pepper, and black pepper. Add chicken pieces; stir to coat. Cover and chill for 30 minutes.

2. Preheat oven to 400° F. Drain chicken, reserving liquid. In a large skillet heat 1 tablespoon of the oil; add chicken mixture. Cook and stir about 3 minutes or until chicken is no longer pink. Stir cornstarch into reserved liquid. Add to chicken mixture in skillet. Cook and stir until thickened and bubbly.

3. Place bread shell on baking sheet. Spread with chicken mixture; sprinkle with cheeses. Bake, uncovered, for 12 minutes. Top with remaining green onions and the nuts. Bake for 2 minutes more. To serve, cut into 6 wedges. Makes 6 servings.

Each serving: 392 cal., 16 g total fat (4 g sat. fat), 50 mg chol., 729 mg sodium, 36 g carbo., 2 g dietary fiber, 28 g protein. Daily Values: 5% vit. A, 5% vit. C, 23% calcium, 14% iron.

Beet Greens with Walnuts and Blue Cheese

Beets FROM TOP TO BOTTOM

BEETS ARE RED-HOT THESE DAYS, BUT BEET GREENS MAY BE THE RUBY ROOT'S BEST-KEPT SECRET. SIMILAR IN FLAVOR TO CHARD AND SPINACH, BEET GREENS ARE SCRUMPTIOUS WHETHER ENJOYED RAW IN SALADS OR LIGHTLY COOKED AS A NUTRITIOUS SIDE DISH.

Beet Greens with Walnuts and Blue Cheese

PREP: 10 minutes **COOK:** 3 minutes

- 8 oz. beet greens*
- 2 tsp. cooking oil
- 2 Tbsp. chopped walnuts
- 1 Tbsp. crumbled blue cheese
- 1/4 tsp. ground black pepper

1. Thoroughly clean greens. Drain well. Cut into 1-inch strips.

2. In a large skillet heat oil over medium-high heat. Add walnuts. Cook and stir for 2 minutes. Add beet greens; cook and stir, uncovered, for 1 minute or until just wilted.

3. Spoon into 4 bowls. Top each serving with crumbled blue cheese and pepper. Makes 4 side-dish servings.

***NOTE:** You can also make this recipe with spinach or chard. Just clean the leaves well under cold running water, drain, and use as directed above.

Each serving: 55 cal., 5 g total fat (1 g sat. fat), 0 mg chol., 109 mg sodium, 3 g carbo., 2 g fiber, 2 g pro. Daily Values: 66% vit. A, 17% vit. C, 7% calcium.

Roasted Vegetables over Salad Greens

PREP: 20 minutes **COOK:** 40 minutes

- 8 oz. baby beets or 3 medium beets
- 12 oz. whole tiny new potatoes, halved
- 4 oz. pearl onions, peeled
- 1/4 cup olive oil
- 6 cloves garlic, minced
- 1 Tbsp. snipped fresh rosemary or basil
- 1/2 tsp. salt
- 1/2 tsp. ground black pepper
- 2 Tbsp. balsamic vinegar
- 1 Tbsp. snipped fresh chives
- 1 Tbsp. water
- 6 cups torn Boston or Bibb lettuce

1. Preheat oven to 375° F. Scrub beets; trim off stem and root ends. (If using medium beets, peel and cut into 1-inch pieces.) Place beets, potatoes, and onions in a 13×9×2-inch baking pan.

2. In a small bowl combine 2 tablespoons of the olive oil, the garlic, rosemary, salt, and pepper. Drizzle over vegetables in pan; toss to coat. Cover; roast for 30 minutes. Uncover; roast for 10 to 20 minutes more or until vegetables are tender. Cool to room temperature; drain, reserving pan drippings.

3. For dressing, in a screw-top jar combine reserved pan drippings, the remaining 2 tablespoons oil, balsamic vinegar, chives, and water. Cover and shake well.

4. Divide lettuce among 6 salad plates. Top lettuce with roasted vegetable mixture; drizzle with dressing. Serve immediately. Makes 6 side-dish servings.

Each serving: 172 cal., 9 g total fat (1 g sat. fat), 0 mg chol., 245 mg sodium, 20 g carbo., 3 g fiber, 3 g pro. Daily Values: 30% vit. C, 4% calcium, 7% iron.

Borsch-Style Casserole

To anyone of Polish descent, beets mean borsch—a red beet soup. In this Test Kitchen favorite, beet soup takes on a heartier tone, beefed up into a main-dish stew. Top each serving with a dollop of sour cream and serve with black bread and frosty mugs of beer.

PREP: 30 minutes **BAKE:** 3 1/2 hours

- 2 lb. beef short ribs, cut up
- 1 Tbsp. cooking oil
- 2 stalks celery, sliced (1 cup)
- 1 medium onion, sliced (1/2 cup)
- 1/2 of 6-oz. can (1/3 cup) tomato paste
- 1 tsp. salt
- 1/8 tsp. ground black pepper
- 1 1/2 tsp. sugar
- 1 1/2 tsp. vinegar
- 1 medium beet, cut into strips (1 cup)
- 2 carrots, sliced (1 cup)
- 1 turnip, cut into strips (3/4 cup)
- 1 small head cabbage, cut into 4 wedges
- Dairy sour cream (optional)

1. Preheat oven to 350°F. Trim fat from ribs. In 4-quart Dutch oven brown ribs in hot oil. Drain off fat. Add celery and onion. In a large bowl combine 3 cups water, the tomato paste, salt, and pepper; pour over vegetables and meat in pan. Cover and bake for 2 1/2 hours.

2. Skim off fat. Combine 1/2 cup water, the sugar, and vinegar; add to meat mixture. Add beet strips, carrot slices, and turnip strips; place cabbage wedges on top of vegetable and meat mixture, pushing cabbage wedges into the liquid. Cover and bake for 1 hour.

3. To serve, spoon stew into bowls. Season to taste with salt and pepper. If desired, top each serving with sour cream. Makes 4 main-dish servings.

Each serving: 272 cal., 11 g total fat (4 g sat. fat), 43 mg chol., 759 mg sodium, 21 g carbo., 6 g fiber, 23 g pro. Daily Values: 157% vit. A, 63% vit. C, 9% calcium, 18% iron.

jewels of Mt. Rainier

THESE PLUMP, SWEET FRUITS GO FAST ONCE THEY HIT THE STORES, SO YOU MAY WANT TO BUY AND FREEZE EXTRAS.

Rainier cherries sparkle gold and blush like the rays of a Northwestern sunset. As these cherries have grown more popular, their season has stretched beyond the summer months. Once available only in July, you can now find Rainiers as late as October.

Still, these fruits go quickly once they hit the stores, so you may want to buy and freeze extras. Wash them, then pat them dry with paper towels. Pit them, if you like, and freeze them, tightly covered, for up to six months.

Rainier Cherry Tart

Almond-Cherry Trifles

This simple dessert showcases cherries in triplicate: juicy cherry preserves, cherry liqueur, and golden Rainier cherries.

START TO FINISH: 20 minutes

- 1 cup plain low-fat yogurt
- 1/4 cup cherry preserves
- 2 Tbsp. cherry liqueur or maraschino cherry juice
- 1/2 of a 10-oz. frozen pound cake, thawed
- 1 cup halved and pitted fresh Rainier or other sweet cherries
- 1/4 cup sliced almonds, toasted

1. In a small bowl stir together yogurt, 2 tablespoons of the cherry preserves, and cherry liqueur. Set aside.

2. Slice the cake in half lengthwise. Spread the cut sides of each cake half with the remaining cherry preserves. Cut each half into 1/2-inch cubes. Place half of the cake cubes in 4 parfait glasses or dessert dishes. Top with half of the cherries, then half of the yogurt mixture. Sprinkle with half of the nuts. Repeat layering with the remaining ingredients.

3. Cover and chill for up to 2 hours. Makes 4 servings.

Each serving: 298 cal., 10 g total fat (5 g sat. fat), 43 mg chol., 177 mg sodium, 44 g carbo., 2 g fiber, 6 g pro. Daily Values: 6% vit. A, 8% vit. C, 13% calcium, 5% iron.

Rainier Cherry Tart

PREP: 45 minutes **BAKE:** 15 minutes

- 1 recipe Almond Tart Shell (below)
- 1/2 cup dairy sour cream*
- 1/4 of an 8-oz. tub cream cheese*
- 3 Tbsp. sifted powdered sugar
- 1 Tbsp. cherry-flavored liqueur or cherry cider
- 3 1/2 cups fresh Rainier cherries or other sweet cherries, pitted
- 1/2 cup apple jelly

1. Prepare Almond Tart Shell. For filling, in a medium bowl combine sour cream, cream cheese, powdered sugar, and liqueur or cider; beat with an electric mixer on low speed until smooth. Cover and chill for up to 60 minutes.

2. To assemble, spread filling evenly onto the bottom of Almond Tart Shell. Arrange cherries on top.

3. In a small saucepan heat apple jelly over low heat just until melted. Cool slightly; drizzle onto cherries. To serve, remove sides of tart pan. Cut into wedges; serve immediately. Makes 8 servings.

ALMOND TART SHELL: Preheat oven to 400° F. In a medium bowl stir together 3/4 cup all-purpose flour, 1/4 cup finely chopped almonds, and 3 tablespoons granulated sugar. Using a pastry blender, cut in 1/3 cup butter until the mixture resembles coarse crumbs. Sprinkle with 2 tablespoons water, working in with a fork until moistened. Form dough into a ball. Press dough evenly onto the bottom and up the sides of a 9-inch tart pan with removable bottom. Bake for 15 minutes or until light brown. Cool in pan on a wire rack.

***NOTE:** For a lighter tart (269 calories, 30 mg cholesterol, 13 g total fat, 6 g saturated fat): Substitute sour cream and cream cheese with equal amounts of light dairy sour cream and light cream cheese.

Each serving: 295 cal., 16 g total fat (8 g sat. fat), 34 mg chol., 113 mg sodium, 36 g carbo., 2 g fiber, 4 g pro. Daily Values: 13% vit. A, 9% vit. C, 3% calcium, 7% iron.

strategies for Big Flavor

SPIRITED COOKING STARTS WITH DON'T-BE-SHY FLAVOR. ONE BIG IDEA CAN ADD ROBUST TASTE AND SIMPLE SOPHISTICATION TO DINNERTIME. HERE ARE OUR EIGHT CLEVER IDEAS, WITH QUICK NOTES ON TERMS AND TECHNIQUES. LET THE LESSON BEGIN!

Steamed Salmon and Swiss Chard Stack

Steamed Salmon and Swiss Chard Stack

Lemon, both oil and fresh, rules in these fanciful phyllo stacks.

PREP: 30 minutes **BAKE:** 12 minutes **COOK:** 8 minutes

- 1 lb. fresh or frozen skinless, boneless salmon fillets, cut 1/2 to 3/4 inch thick
- 5 sheets frozen phyllo dough (18×14-inch rectangles)
- 4 Tbsp. lemon-infused olive oil or other flavored oils, such as garlic- or rosemary-infused olive oil
- 1/2 tsp. kosher salt
- 2 Tbsp. snipped fresh parsley
- Pepper
- 2 medium lemons, very thinly sliced and seeded
- 4 cups torn fresh Swiss chard or spinach leaves
- 1/4 cup thin red onion slivers

1. Thaw salmon and phyllo dough, if frozen. Preheat oven to 350° F. Unroll phyllo dough. Carefully transfer a sheet to a large cutting board. (Keep remaining phyllo covered with plastic wrap.) Set aside 1 tablespoon lemon oil. Brush phyllo sheet with some of the remaining 3 tablespoons oil. Top with a second phyllo sheet; brush with oil. Sprinkle with half of the salt and parsley. Repeat layers. Place remaining phyllo sheet atop phyllo stack. Brush with oil.

2. Trim edges to make a 16×12-inch rectangle (discard trimmings). Cut stack lengthwise into thirds. Cut each third into four squares, making twelve 4×4-inch squares. Place phyllo stacks on an ungreased 15×10-inch baking sheet. Bake for 12 to 14 minutes or until golden. Cool on baking sheet. Set aside.

3. Rinse salmon. Cut salmon into 8 pieces; set aside. Fill a 12-inch skillet with water to a depth of 1 inch. Bring water to boiling; reduce heat. Place salmon pieces in the bottom of a double-tiered bamboo steamer or steamer basket. Sprinkle with pepper; top with one of the sliced lemons. Layer remaining sliced lemon and Swiss chard in top basket of bamboo steamer or on top of salmon in steamer basket. Place over simmering water. Cover and steam for 8 to 12 minutes or until salmon flakes easily with a fork.

4. To serve, place one stack of phyllo on each of four individual serving plates. Divide half of the salmon, lemon, and chard among phyllo stacks. Top each with another phyllo stack and remaining salmon, lemon, and chard. Crumble remaining phyllo stacks over individual servings. Drizzle with the reserved 1 tablespoon oil. Sprinkle with onion. Makes 4 servings.

Each serving: 401 cal., 25 g total fat (4 g sat. fat), 70 mg chol., 489 mg sodium, 20 g carbo., 4 g fiber, 27 g pro. Daily Values: 30% vit. A, 92% vit. C, 7% calcium, 14% iron.

Bacon-Crusted Tri-Tip Roast with Shallots and Figs

We took a spin on the classic wrapped filet by crusting a roast with two cured meats—bacon and prosciutto.

PREP: 30 minutes **ROAST:** 35 minutes **STAND:** 30 + 10 minutes

- 1 lb. fresh or dried Turkish, Mission, or Calimyrna figs, halved
- 1 1 1/2- to 2-lb. boneless beef bottom sirloin roast (tri-tip)
- 4 oz. chopped bacon (about 4 slices)
- 4 oz. chopped prosciutto
- 1 Tbsp. Dijon-style mustard
- 2 cloves garlic, slivered
- 1 lb. shallots or small white onions, skinned, ends trimmed
- Dry red wine

1. If using dried figs, in a bowl combine figs and enough boiling water to cover; let stand 30 minutes or until plump.

2. Preheat oven to 425° F. Place roast, fat side up, on a rack in a roasting pan. Insert thermometer. Combine bacon, prosciutto, mustard, and garlic; divide in half. Press half onto roast.

3. Drain figs. Halve large shallots. In a large bowl toss together figs, shallots, and remaining bacon mixture; scatter in pan.

4. Roast for 35 to 45 minutes or until thermometer registers 140° F for medium-rare doneness and bacon crust is crisp.

5. Transfer roast, figs, and shallots to a platter. Cover with foil; let stand 10 minutes. (The temperature should rise 5° to 10° F.)

6. Meanwhile, remove any drippings from pan; skim fat. Measure juices; add wine to equal 1 1/2 cups total. Return to pan. Bring to boiling, scraping up any brown bits from pan. Simmer, uncovered, for 5 to 10 minutes or until the wine is reduced by half; serve with roast. Makes 6 to 8 servings.

Each serving: 421 cal., 14 g total fat (5 g sat. fat), 75 mg chol., 734 mg sodium, 27 g carbo., 3 g fiber, 35 g pro. Daily Values: 18% vit. A, 12% vit. C, 7% calcium, 22% iron.

Spaghetti and Porcini Meatballs with Cabernet-Tomato Sauce

Porcini mushrooms and a bold Cabernet make this dish sassy enough for company, but still hearty enough for the family.

STAND: 30 minutes **PREP:** 30 minutes **COOK:** 38 minutes

- 3 Tbsp. olive oil
- 1 recipe Porcini Meatballs (below)
- 4 cups chopped, peeled plum tomatoes (10 to 12 tomatoes)
- 1 cup plus 1 to 2 Tbsp. Cabernet Sauvignon or dry red wine
- 1/4 cup finely chopped onion
- 2 Tbsp. snipped fresh parsley
- 2 Tbsp. snipped fresh thyme
- 1 tsp. sugar
- 1/4 tsp. pepper
- Hot cooked spaghetti or fettuccine
- Salt
- Pepper

1. In a large skillet heat olive oil over medium-high heat. Add Porcini Meatballs; cook about 8 minutes or until brown, turning occasionally. Drain on paper towels. Drain off fat.

2. Add tomatoes, 1 cup of the wine, onion, parsley, thyme, sugar, pepper, and the reserved 1/2 cup mushrooms (from the meatball recipe) to the hot skillet; stir well. Bring to boiling; reduce heat. Add meatballs. Simmer, uncovered, about 30 minutes or until sauce is the desired consistency, gently stirring to keep meatballs moistened.

3. Just before serving, add 1 to 2 tablespoons wine. Serve sauce and meatballs over spaghetti or fettuccine. Season to taste with salt and pepper. Makes 6 servings.

PORCINI MEATBALLS: Rinse 2 1/2 ounces dried porcini mushrooms*. In a medium bowl combine dried mushrooms and enough boiling water to cover. Let stand for 30 minutes. Drain. Rinse mushrooms under running water. Drain well, squeezing out excess liquid. Set aside 1/2 cup of the mushrooms for the sauce (see recipe, above). Finely chop remaining mushrooms.

In a large bowl combine 1 beaten egg, finely chopped mushrooms, 1/4 cup onion, 1/4 cup fine dry bread crumbs, 1 tablespoon Cabernet Sauvignon, 2 cloves minced garlic, 2 teaspoons snipped fresh thyme, and 1/2 teaspoon salt. Add 1 pound ground beef; mix well. Shape into 18 meatballs.

***TEST KITCHEN TIP:** September and October are the short peak season months for fresh porcini mushrooms. If you find fresh mushrooms, substitute 10 ounces of fresh for the 2 1/2 ounces of dried. You can order fresh or dried porcini from Melissa's at 800/588-0151 or www.melissas.com.

Each serving: 549 cal., 19 g total fat (5 g sat. fat), 83 mg chol., 374 mg sodium, 64 g carbo., 5 g fiber, 26 g pro. Daily Values: 18% vit. A, 48% vit. C, 5% calcium, 26% iron.

Mediterranean Parsnips

Mediterranean Parsnips

Open a jar of your favorite condiment to zip up plain vegetables, pasta, or salads. Capers, olives, caramelized onions, and flavored mustards are just a few off-the-shelf ideas.

PREP: 20 minutes **COOK:** 7 minutes

- 3 1/2 lb. parsnips
- 3 Tbsp. olive oil
- 1/4 tsp. salt
- 1/4 tsp. pepper
- 1 cup pitted kalamata olives, drained and coarsely chopped
- 1/4 cup capers, drained (3 1/2-oz. jar)

1. Peel and slice the parsnips lengthwise into 1/4-inch-thick slices. In a large saucepan cook parsnips, covered, in a small amount of boiling lightly salted water for 7 to 9 minutes or until tender; drain.

2. Gently toss parsnips with oil, salt, and pepper; transfer to a serving dish. Top with olives and capers. Makes 8 servings.

HONEY-MUSTARD PARSNIPS: Prepare parsnips as above, except omit olive oil. Toss parsnips with 1/4 cup raspberry mustard; drizzle with 2 tablespoons honey.

CARAMELIZED ONION PARSNIPS: Prepare parsnips as above, except omit olives and capers. Top parsnips with 1 cup of caramelized onions from a jar.

Each serving of Mediterranean Parsnips: 234 cal., 8 g total fat (1 g sat. fat), 0 mg chol., 535 mg sodium, 41 g carbo., 9 g fiber, 3 g pro. Daily Values: 44% vit. C, 8% calcium, 7% iron.

Spaghetti and Porcini Meatballs with Cabernet-Tomato Sauce

Big Green Salad with Two-Pepper Dressing

Big Green Salad with Two-Pepper Dressing

You can make Two-Pepper Dressing ahead; just bring it back to room temperature before you toss together the salad.

START TO FINISH: 30 minutes

- 4 cups torn butterhead lettuce (2 medium heads)
- 1 cup fresh mint sprigs
- 1 cup fresh watercress sprigs
- 3/4 cup fresh cilantro sprigs
- 1 cup daikon, peeled and cut into 1-inch strips
- 1 recipe Two-Pepper Dressing(below)

1. Rinse lettuce, mint, watercress, and cilantro in cold water; pat dry. In a salad bowl toss together greens and daikon. Slowly add Two-Pepper Dressing; toss to coat. Makes 6 servings.

TWO-PEPPER DRESSING: In a screw-top jar combine 1/2 cup finely chopped green sweet pepper; 1/3 cup rice vinegar; 3 tablespoons salad oil; 1 fresh anaheim or jalapeño chile pepper, seeded and finely chopped*; 1 clove garlic, minced; 1/2 teaspoon sugar; 1/4 teaspoon salt; and 1/4 teaspoon ground black pepper. Cover and shake well. Refrigerate until ready to use.

***TEST KITCHEN TIP:** Because chile peppers contain volatile oils that can burn your skin and eyes, wear plastic or rubber gloves when working with them. If you do touch the peppers, wash your hands well with soap and water.

Each serving: 86 cal., 7 g total fat (1 g sat. fat), 0 mg chol., 112 mg sodium, 4 g carbo., 1 g fiber, 1 g pro. Daily Values: 26% vit. A, 57%vit. C, 5% calcium, 17% iron.

Brined Skillet-Roasted Brussels Sprouts

HARVEST DINNER

Big Green Salad with Two-Pepper Dressing *(left)*
Bacon-Crusted Tri-Tip Roast with Shallots and Figs *(page 345)*
Steamed green beans
The Mount Everest of Spice Cake *(page 351)*
Dry red wine or sparkling water

Brined Skillet-Roasted Brussels Sprouts

Brining acts as a preservative, but it also enhances flavor. Use intensely flavored kosher and sea salts to bring out the taste.

PREP: 20 minutes **STAND:** 1 hour **ROAST:** 25 minutes

- 1 1/2 lb. brussels sprouts
- 8 cups cold water
- 1/2 cup kosher salt
- 1/4 cup olive oil
- 1 tsp. mustard seeds
- 1/4 tsp. sea salt
- 1/4 tsp. cracked black pepper

1. Trim stems and remove any wilted outer leaves from brussels sprouts; wash. Halve any large brussels sprouts; set aside. In a very large mixing bowl or deep container stir together the cold water and the kosher salt until salt is completely dissolved. Add brussels sprouts to salt mixture, making sure the sprouts are covered (hold sprouts down with a plate if necessary to keep them submerged). Let stand for 1 hour.

2. Preheat oven to 350° F. Drain brussels sprouts; do not rinse. In a large cast-iron skillet or roasting pan toss sprouts with olive oil to coat. Roast, uncovered, for 25 to 30 minutes or until tender, stirring once.

3. Meanwhile, in a skillet heat mustard seeds over medium heat about 5 minutes or until seeds are lightly toasted, shaking skillet occasionally. Remove seeds from skillet; crush slightly. Add crushed seeds, sea salt, and pepper to roasted sprouts; toss well. Makes 6 servings.

Each serving: 131 cal., 10 g total fat (1 g sat. fat), 0 mg chol., 415 mg sodium, 10 g carbo., 5 g fiber, 4 g pro. Daily Values: 18% vit. A, 121% vit. C, 5% calcium, 9% iron.

Buttery Sage and Acorn Squash Tart

The Mount Everest of Spice Cake

Buttery Sage and Acorn Squash Tart

Browning butter to drizzle atop this quichelike appetizer tart gives every bite a toasty, mellow richness.

PREP: 60 minutes **BAKE:** 40 minutes **COOL:** 20 minutes

- 1/2 cup plus 1 Tbsp. unsalted butter, softened
- 3 eggs
- 2 cups mashed, cooked acorn squash
- 1/2 cup milk
- 1/4 cup honey
- 1 Tbsp. snipped fresh sage
- 1/4 tsp. salt
- 1 recipe Butter-Pepper Pastry (below)
- 1/4 cup broken black walnuts or broken walnuts
- 1/2 tsp. pepper

1. Preheat oven to 350° F. For filling, in a large bowl beat 1/4 cup butter with an electric mixer on medium-high speed for 30 seconds. Add eggs, one at a time, beating until combined. Stir in squash, milk, honey, sage, and salt.

2. Spoon filling into Butter-Pepper Pastry, smoothing top (tart will be very full). Place on foil-lined baking sheet. Bake about 40 minutes or until a knife inserted near center comes out clean. Cool for 20 minutes on a wire rack. Remove pan sides; place on platter.

3. Meanwhile, in a small saucepan melt 1/4 cup plus 1 tablespoon butter; set aside 1 tablespoon. Heat remaining butter about 15 minutes until butter turns a delicate brown.

4. In a small bowl combine walnuts, the 1 tablespoon reserved melted butter, and pepper; toss to coat. Sprinkle over tart. Cut tart into wedges; spoon browned butter over each serving. Makes 10 to 12 appetizer servings.

BUTTER-PEPPER PASTRY: Preheat oven to 450° F. In a bowl combine 1 cup all-purpose flour, 1/2 teaspoon salt, and 1/2 teaspoon pepper. Cut in 1/3 cup cold unsalted butter until pieces are pea-size. Sprinkle 1 tablespoon cold water over part of the mixture; toss with a fork. Push to the side. Repeat with 2 to 3 tablespoons more cold water, using 1 tablespoon water at a time, until dough is moistened. Form into a ball. If necessary, cover with plastic wrap; refrigerate for 30 to 60 minutes or until easy to handle.

On a lightly floured surface roll pastry into a 12-inch circle. Ease into an ungreased 10-inch tart pan with a removable bottom. Press pastry into fluted sides of pan; trim edges. Generously prick the bottom of the pastry. Line pastry with a double thickness of foil. Place tart pan on a foil-lined baking sheet. Bake for 10 minutes. Remove foil from pastry; bake for 6 to 8 minutes more or until golden. Cool on a wire rack.

Each serving: 285 cal., 21 g total fat (12 g sat. fat), 112 mg chol., 203 mg sodium, 21 g carbo., 2 g fiber, 5 g pro. Daily Values: 45% vit. A, 7% vit. C, 4% calcium, 6% iron.

The Mount Everest of Spice Cake

To prepare the meringue, use pasteurized egg whites from pasteurized (not regular) eggs. Or use powdered dried egg whites.

PREP: 45 minutes **BAKE:** 30 minutes **COOL:** 2 hours

- 1 1/4 cups buttermilk
- 2 eggs
- 1/4 cup butter
- 2 cups all-purpose flour
- 1 1/2 tsp. baking powder
- 1 1/2 tsp. baking soda
- 1 tsp. ground cinnamon
- 1/4 tsp. ground ginger
- 1/4 tsp. ground nutmeg
- 1/4 tsp. ground cloves
- 1/4 cup shortening
- 1 1/2 cups sugar
- 1/2 tsp. vanilla
- 1 18-oz. jar apricot or peach preserves
- 1 recipe Ginger Meringue* (below)

1. Allow buttermilk, eggs, and butter to stand at room temperature for 30 minutes. Meanwhile, grease and lightly flour two 8×1 1/2-inch round baking pans; set aside. In a bowl stir together flour, baking powder, baking soda, cinnamon, ginger, nutmeg, and cloves; set aside.

2. Preheat oven to 350° F. In a bowl beat butter and shortening for 30 seconds. Add sugar and vanilla, beat on medium speed until combined, scraping side of bowl occasionally. Add eggs, one at a time, beating for 30 seconds after each addition. Alternately add flour mixture and buttermilk, beating on low speed just until combined. Spread batter in prepared pans.

3. Bake for 30 to 35 minutes or until a wooden toothpick inserted in centers comes out clean. Cool cakes in pans on wire racks for 10 minutes. Carefully remove. Cool on wire racks.

4. To assemble, using a serrated knife, carefully split each cake layer horizontally in half. Place bottom layer of cake on serving plate. Spread with about 1/2 cup apricot preserves. Top with second cake layer, 1/2 cup preserves, third layer, remaining preserves, and fourth layer. Top with Ginger Meringue; lightly brown meringue peaks with a small kitchen torch. Serve at once or cover and chill for up to 4 hours. (Chilling firms the meringue and makes cake easier to cut.) Makes 8 to 10 servings.

GINGER MERINGUE: Allow 6 pasteurized egg whites from pasteurized eggs in shell to stand at room temperature for 30 minutes. (Or combine 3 tablespoons dried egg whites and 1/2 cup plus 1 tablespoon warm water; stir about 2 minutes or until powder is completely dissolved.) In a large, non-aluminum mixing bowl combine egg whites, 1/2 teaspoon cream of tartar, and 1/2 teaspoon ground ginger or 1/4 teaspoon ground nutmeg. Beat with an electric mixer on medium speed about 5 minutes or until soft peaks form (tips curl). Gradually add 3/4 cup sugar (1/2 cup for powdered egg whites), 1 tablespoon at a time, beating on high speed about 5 minutes more or until mixture forms soft, glossy peaks (tips stand straight), and sugar is dissolved.

***TEST KITCHEN TIP:** As an alternative to the meringue, you can stir a little ground ginger into 2 cups sweetened whipped cream. Top cake with whipped cream and chill up to 1 hour.

Each serving: 651 cal., 14 g total fat (6 g sat. fat), 71 mg chol., 334 mg sodium, 123 g carbo., 2 g fiber, 9 g pro. Daily Values: 7% vit. A, 10% vit. C, 12% calcium, 11% iron.

Harvest Leg of Lamb

THERE'S MUCH TO BE SAID FOR cooking a lamb roast for a crowd—not the least of which is the vision of you deftly carving slice after juicy slice for an appreciative audience.

Cooking big roasts is not an everyday feat anymore. But with long, slow cooking, there's lots of time to check on the process. That kind of leisurely pace makes creating a crown roast or leg of lamb for a weekend crowd very doable.

For both of these roasts, you rub herbs and seasonings on the outside to let the flavor penetrate into the meat. Be sure to use a meat thermometer so you can cook the meat to the exact degree of doneness you want. (We recommend medium rare.) And make sure the thermometer is not touching fat or bone.

Roast Rack of Lamb

The classic crown shape is made by sewing together two rib roasts. The little paper crowns on each bone are optional.

PREP: 20 minutes **ROAST:** 45 minutes **STAND:** 15 minutes

- **2 1- to 1½-lb. lamb rib roasts (6 to 8 ribs each), with or without backbone**
- **3 Tbsp. Dijon-style mustard**
- **3 Tbsp. lemon juice**
- **1 Tbsp. snipped fresh rosemary or thyme**
- **½ tsp. salt**
- **¾ cup soft bread crumbs**
- **1 Tbsp. butter or margarine, melted**
- **Bottled chutney (optional)**

1. Preheat oven to 325° F. Trim fat from meat. Stir together mustard, lemon juice, rosemary, and salt. Rub onto meat. Toss together crumbs and butter. Sprinkle onto meat.

2. Place meat on a rack in a shallow roasting pan. Insert a meat thermometer into center of meat, without touching fat or bone. Roast, uncovered, until desired doneness. For medium rare, roast for ¾ to 1 hour or until thermometer registers 140° F. For medium, roast for 1 to 1½ hours or until meat thermometer registers 155° F. Cover with foil; let stand 15 minutes. (The temperature of the meat will rise 5° to 10° F during standing.) Serve warm with chutney, if desired. Makes 6 servings.

Each serving: 299 cal., 9 g total fat (3 g sat. fat), 50 mg chol., 332 mg sodium, 41 g carbo., 3 g fiber, 16 g pro. Daily Values: 11% vit. A, 16% vit. C, º5% calcium, 12% iron.

Harvest Leg of Lamb

PREP: 30 minutes **MARINATE:** 12 hours
ROAST: 1¾ hours **STAND:** 15 minutes

- **1 5- to 7-lb. whole lamb leg roast (bone in)**
- **6 cloves garlic, cut into thin slices**
- **2 to 3 Tbsp. lemon juice**
- **3 Tbsp. snipped fresh parsley**
- **2 Tbsp. olive oil or cooking oil**
- **1 Tbsp. dried Italian seasoning or dried oregano, crushed**
- **1 tsp. pepper**

1. Trim fat from meat. With a knife, cut ½-inch-wide slits into roast at 1-inch intervals (approximately 36 holes) inserting a thin slice of garlic in each. Brush with lemon juice. Stir together parsley, oil, Italian seasoning or oregano, and pepper; pat onto meat. Wrap in plastic wrap; chill overnight.

2. Preheat oven to 325° F. Place meat, fat side up, on a rack in a shallow roasting pan. Insert a meat thermometer. Roast, uncovered, until desired doneness. For medium rare, roast for 1¾ to 2¼ hours or until thermometer registers 140° F. For medium, roast for 2 to 2½ hours or until meat thermometer registers 155° F. Cover with foil; let stand 15 minutes. (The temperature of the meat will rise 5° to 10° F during standing.)

3. To carve, cut away large, round side. The opposite side will also come off in a single piece. Cut off the 2 smaller pieces on either side of bone. Slice meat. Makes 12 to 16 servings.

Each serving: 187 cal., 8 g total fat (3 g sat. fat), 79 mg chol., 68 mg sodium, 2 g carbo., 0 g fiber, 25 g pro. Daily Values: 2% vit. A,6% vit. C., 2% calcium, 15% iron.

Make the slits in the meat as you go; don't try to save time by making all the slits first—they close up too quickly. It's fine if some of the garlic cloves stick out slightly.

To spread the herbs evenly, sprinkle them onto meat first, then pat them down so they don't fall off.

October

WITH PUMPKINS ON THE DOORSTEP AND A CHILL IN THE AIR, FALL HAS US YEARNING FOR STEAMING BOWLS OF GOODNESS.

Vegetable-Orzo Soup

The Magic of Soup

Plus...

Dad's Rolls

Zucchini Quiche

Cooking Together

Plus...

FALL WEEKENDS LURE US INTO THE KITCHEN TO COOK AND SHARE OUR FAVORITE COMFORT FOODS.

College Chicken and Pasta

Shortcut Nutty Fruit Cinnamon Rolls

Pumpkin Chocolate Cheesecake Bars

COOK UP A POT OF SOUP TO RESTORE, INVIGORATE, NURTURE, AND EVEN INSPIRE. THESE HEARTY SOUPS MINGLE THE ESSENCE OF BOTH FLAVOR AND SOUL, NOURISHING OUR BODIES AND OUR HEARTS.

THE MAGIC OF SOUP

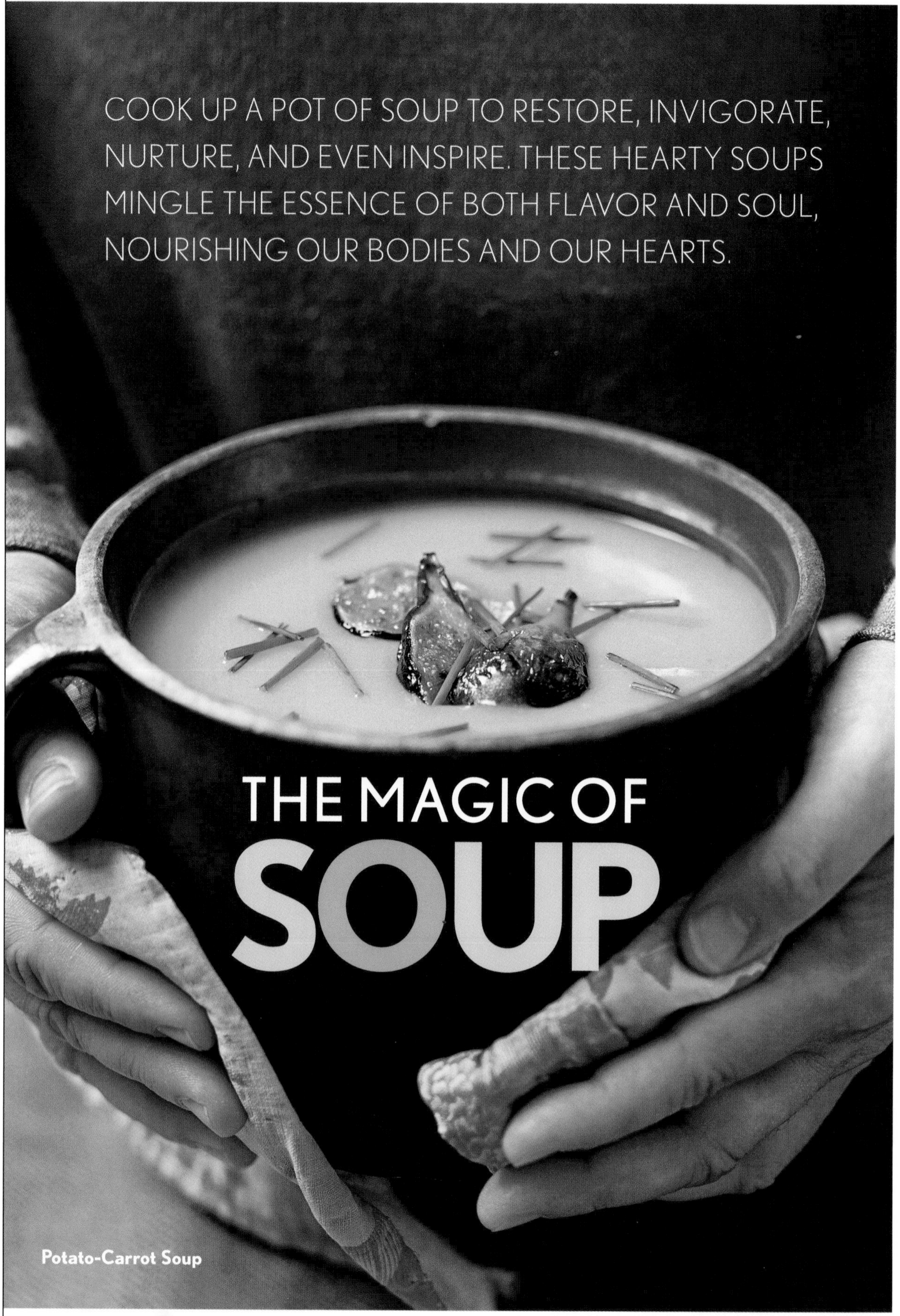

Potato-Carrot Soup

Potato-Carrot Soup

If fresh figs aren't available for topping this soup, rehydrate dried figs by covering them with boiling water. Let them stand for 10 minutes, then drain and cool. Halve the figs and sauté in a little olive oil.

PREP: 15 minutes **COOK:** 20 minutes

- 2 medium garlic bulbs (about 16 cloves)
- 4 14-oz. cans reduced-sodium chicken broth
- 3 medium potatoes, peeled and cut into ½-inch pieces (about 1 lb.)
- 3 medium carrots, peeled and chopped (1½ cups)
- ⅓ cup whipping cream
- Salt
- Ground black pepper
- 1 recipe Roasted Fresh Figs (below) (optional)
- Snipped fresh chives (optional)

1. Separate garlic bulbs into cloves; peel. In a large saucepan combine garlic, broth, potatoes, and carrots. Bring to boiling; reduce heat. Simmer, covered, for 20 to 25 minutes or until vegetables are tender. Cool slightly.

2. In a blender or food processor puree soup, a third at a time, until smooth. Return all of the soup to saucepan. Stir in whipping cream. Season to taste with salt and pepper. Cook and stir until heated through.

3. To serve, spoon into 6 bowls. If desired, garnish with Roasted Fresh Figs and chives. Makes 6 side-dish servings.

ROASTED FRESH FIGS: Preheat oven to 425° F. Halve 6 fresh figs lengthwise. Place fig halves, cut sides up, on a baking sheet lined with parchment or foil. Brush figs with 1 tablespoon olive oil. Bake, uncovered, about 15 minutes or until fig halves are softened and heated through.

Each serving: 163 cal., 7 g total fat (4 g sat. fat), 18 mg chol., 1,172 mg sodium, 21 g carbo., 2 g fiber, 5 g pro. Daily Values: 158% vit. A, 26% vit. C, 4% calcium, 5% iron.

SOUP SUPPER BUFFET

Potato-Carrot Soup *(above)*
Smoked Sausage-Lentil Soup *(page 373)*
Beef and Cabbage Soup *(page 370)*
Assorted crackers and breads
Mixed green salad
Strawberry-Lemon Bars *(page 549)*
Iced tea

Autumn warmth

Soups fill the house with their warmth and aroma as they simmer on the stove, fulfilling a promise greater than just satisfying hunger. With soups, we feel comforted, our spirits revive, a bad day gets better.

Jana Kolpen, cook, painter, and author of the enchantingly illustrated fable and cookbook, *The Secrets of Pistoulet*, knows well the journey from hearth to heart. This month, she contributes a collection of everyday autumn soup recipes that are a graceful blend of cherished standards juxtaposed with clean, honest flavor. Jana has an understanding of the meaning behind ingredients—some are based in folklore, some in mythology. Her instinctual ability to combine them infuses her soups with a soulfulness that says as much about food's vitality as it does about our appetites.

"Soups are the humblest of fares; most are not very complicated. Cooking soup combines ritual, compassion, and fresh ingredients to give back what the harvest has given to us," Jana says. You could almost suspect Jana of spell-casting; in truth, it's her bubbling passion that makes her philosophy so believable.

For example, Jana's Potato-Carrot Soup is heady with garlic, which the ancient Egyptians and Greeks saw as a godlike food. Carrots and potatoes soften its powerful flavor. The soup is satisfying and surprising—roasted end-of-season figs crown it with a touch of sweetness. This soup offers a boost of energy that's especially helpful when you're tired.

For all of us, Jana's soups carry a message that goes beyond their expressive flavors. The spirit of the cook manifests itself in every dish, from simple Tuesday night suppers to holiday dinners or a batch of cookies named for a favorite aunt. We relish the reaction to our cooking as much as we enjoy its taste. The empty bowl and the heartfelt "thank you" give back the love we put in. That is the magic of soup.

SO MANY SOUPS, SO LITTLE TIME

"I love simple foods; there is something pure and honest about them," author Jana Kolpen says. "I just love having people over and watching them enjoy themselves. That's the essence of cooking."

Jana's insight into soups is the result of her stay at the small French farm Pistoulet, which she chronicles in her first book, *The Secrets of Pistoulet*. While visiting there, she started cooking with her hosts—making a variety of soups because the oven didn't work—and watched the effects the soups had on other visitors to the farm. "Guests would arrive worn and withered, and leave refreshed."

Today, Jana prepares her soups for company at her New York City apartment, where she is working on her third book. Most recently, she has designed a full line of dinnerware and serving pieces based on *The Secrets of Pistoulet* and featuring her hand-painted designs.

If you'd like to discover firsthand other secrets and recipes from Pistoulet, you can order the 72-page hardcover book. AF81250, $17.95. TO ORDER: Visit our Web site at www.bhgcatalog.com or call 800/881-4066. Please specify item number. Shipping, handling, and tax, if applicable, will be added to the price shown.

Beet Soup

Jana learned to cook at her Russian-born grandmother's New Jersey farm kitchen, and the rustic beets in her Beet Soup resonate with a grandmother's compassion and caretaking. The flavor of the beets is delivered by preparing them three ways: pureed to give a velvety texture, chopped for a chunky contrast, and roasted for strong, earthy flavor. The recipe is as uncomplicated as the purest emotion. You can add a spoonful of sour cream or crème fraîche to each bowl of soup at serving time.

PREP: 15 minutes **COOK:** 35 + 25 minutes

- **1¾ lb. small beets**
- **1 to 2 cloves garlic, minced**
- **1 Tbsp. olive oil**
- **1 large russet potato, peeled, diced (1½ cups)**
- **2 14-oz. cans chicken broth**
- **Salt**
- **Ground black pepper**
- **1 recipe Roasted Baby Beets (below) (optional)**

1. Cut off all but 1 inch of beet stems and roots; wash. Do not peel. In a large covered saucepan cook beets, covered, in boiling salted water for 35 to 45 minutes or until tender. Drain and cool slightly. Slip skins off beets; dice.

2. In the same saucepan cook garlic in olive oil over medium heat for 1 minute. Add potato; cook and stir for 5 minutes. Add beets and broth; bring to boiling. Simmer, covered, for 20 minutes.

3. Transfer half of the mixture to a blender or food processor (process in batches if using a small food processor). Cover and blend or process until smooth. Return pureed mixture to the saucepan; heat through. Add salt and pepper to taste.

4. To serve, spoon soup into 6 bowls. If desired, add half of a Roasted Baby Beet to each. Makes 6 side-dish servings.

ROASTED BABY BEETS: Preheat oven to 425° F. Wash 3 baby beets and trim tops. Fold a 24×18-inch piece of heavy-duty foil in half. Place beets in center of foil; drizzle with 1 to 2 tablespoons olive oil. Fold foil up and around beets; seal with a double fold, leaving space for steam to build. Place packet on a baking sheet; roast for 35 to 40 minutes or until beets are tender. Cool slightly; cut beets in half.

Each serving: 124 cal., 4 g total fat (1 g sat. fat), 0 mg chol., 700 mg sodium, 20 g carbo., 3 g fiber, 4 g pro. Daily Values: 1% vit. A, 16% vit. C, 2% calcium, 7% iron.

Beet Soup

Potato-Onion Soup

This approach to potato soup—plain and simple—takes its flavor from a bit of crumbled bacon and humble onions.

START TO FINISH: 25 minutes

- **6 slices bacon**
- **5 cups sliced red potatoes**
- **3 cups water**
- **1 Tbsp. instant chicken bouillon granules**
- **3 medium onions, cut into thin wedges (1½ cups)**
- **2 cups milk**
- **¼ tsp. ground black pepper**

1. In a large skillet cook bacon over medium heat until crisp. Remove bacon, reserving 1 tablespoon drippings in skillet. Drain bacon on paper towels. Crumble bacon; set aside.

2. In a large saucepan combine potatoes, water, and chicken bouillon granules. Bring to boiling; reduce heat. Simmer, covered, about 15 minutes or until potatoes are very tender.

3. Meanwhile, cook onions in reserved bacon drippings over medium-low heat for 8 to 10 minutes or until tender and golden brown. Remove from skillet; set aside.

4. Do not drain potatoes. Use a potato masher to mash potatoes slightly. Stir in bacon, onions, milk, and pepper; heat through. If desired, season to taste with additional pepper. To serve, spoon into 6 bowls. Makes 6 side-dish servings.

Each serving: 201 cal., 6 g total fat (3 g sat. fat), 14 mg chol., 600 mg sodium, 27 g carbo., 3 g fiber, 8 g pro. Daily Values: 34% vit. C, 12% calcium, 7% iron.

ITALIAN DINNER

Tomato-Basil Soup *(above right)*
Green Lasagna *(page 529)*
Steamed carrots
Garlic breadsticks
Italian Cheesecake *(page 551)*
Red wine or sparkling water
Espresso

Tomato-Basil Soup

When tomatoes first arrived in France, they were called "pommes d'amour," or "love apples." So Jana is sure her tomato soup will inspire passion. "The rich tomato taste is enhanced by basil, which brings out friendliness, and a touch of cream, which makes anyone happy," she asserts. "Armagnac is a special brandy whose long aging gives the soup depth and is said to arouse age-old passions." If you prefer, let everyone add the cheese, cream, Armagnac, and chopped tomato-basil mixture to taste.

PREP: 30 minutes **COOK:** about 40 minutes

- **3½ lb. ripe beefsteak or globe tomatoes**
- **2 Tbsp. unsalted butter**
- **2 cloves garlic, minced**
- **2 to 3 small onions, diced**
- **1½ cups loosely packed fresh basil leaves**
- **1½ tsp. sea salt or kosher salt**
- **¼ tsp. cracked black pepper**
- **6 oz. Gruyère or Emmentaler cheese, grated**
- **½ cup whipping cream**
- **1 Tbsp. Armagnac or brandy (optional)**

1. Set aside 1 tomato. Peel remaining tomatoes by dipping into boiling water for 30 seconds or until skins start to split. Dip into cold water; when cool enough to handle, remove skins and core tomatoes. Coarsely chop; set aside.

2. In a 4-quart Dutch oven melt butter over high heat. Add garlic; cook for 30 seconds. Add onions; cook for 4 to 5 minutes or until tender. Add chopped tomatoes; bring to boiling. Simmer, covered, for 30 minutes, stirring occasionally.

3. Puree tomato mixture in batches in food processor or food mill (discard tomato seeds and onion pulp if using food mill). Return liquid to pan.

4. Meanwhile, finely chop basil; reserve ¼ cup. Stir basil, salt, and pepper into tomato mixture. Heat through. Add cheese, whipping cream, and Armagnac, if desired. Heat and stir until cheese is just melted (natural or unprocessed cheese may give soup a slightly grainy texture).

5. To serve, spoon soup into 6 bowls. Chop remaining tomato; combine with reserved basil. Sprinkle tomato mixture onto each serving. Makes 6 side-dish servings.

Each serving: 284 cal., 22 g total fat (13 g sat. fat), 70 mg chol., 26 mg sodium, 14 g carbo., 3 g fiber, 12 g pro. Daily Values: 53% vit. A, 71% vit. C, 33% calcium, 9% iron.

Tomato-Basil Soup

Green Bean Soup

COLOR YOUR SOUP

What makes a soup exciting at first glance may not be what's in it, but what's on it. For an attention grabber, float a colorful ingredient on top, such as the green beans above, the tomatoes on page 363 or the beets on page 361. Try some of the ideas below and think of complementary or contrasting colors for your soups.

- Brighten with orange: Curl long shreds of orange peel, carrot, or cheddar cheese on top. Or chop it finely. And if you have 'em, pieces of orange peppers or tomatoes work well.
- Shine with yellow: Strips or pieces of lemon, yellow squash, or yellow pepper lift soup. And remember corn kernels, slices of pear, golden caviar, or yellow edible flowers.
- Splash with red: Beets, radishes, apples, tomatoes, red peppers, red caviar, and pomegranates all have their own shade of red. Chop, shred, julienne, or slice for the right look.
- Go with green: One of the easiest colors to add to soup, green means a sprig of herb, capers, snipped chives or green onion, or snippets of green pepper, zucchini, or lime.

Green Bean Soup

Haricots vert are tiny French green beans, but you can substitute regular-size green beans if you like.

PREP: 25 minutes **COOK:** 15 minutes

- 2 14-oz. cans vegetable broth
- 1 medium onion, chopped (1/2 cup)
- 1/2 of a vanilla bean*, split lengthwise
- 3 Tbsp. butter, softened
- 3 Tbsp. all-purpose flour
- 1 lb. haricots verts or green beans, cut into bit-size pieces (3 to 3 1/2 cups)
- 8 oz. whole haricots vert (optional)
- 1 recipe Herb Sourdough Breadsticks (below) (optional)

1. In a large saucepan combine broth, onion, and vanilla bean. Bring to boiling; reduce heat. Cover and simmer about 10 minutes or until onion is tender. Discard vanilla bean.

2. In a small bowl stir together butter and flour. Whisk into broth mixture. Cook and stir until slightly thickened and bubbly.

3. Add beans; return to boiling. Reduce heat; cover and simmer for 5 to 7 minutes or until beans are crisp-tender. Meanwhile, if desired, place whole haricots verts in a steamer basket. Cover and steam over boiling water about 5 minutes or until tender; drain.

4. To serve, ladle soup into 6 to 8 bowls. If desired, add steamed whole haricots vert; serve with Herbed Sourdough Breadsticks. Makes 6 to 8 side-dish servings.

HERB SOURDOUGH BREADSTICKS: Preheat oven to 375° F. Cut half of a 12-inch sourdough baguette lengthwise into 1/2-inch-thick slices. Cut into 1-inch-wide sticks. Brush cut surfaces with 2 tablespoons olive oil; sprinkle with 1 teaspoon snipped fresh thyme. Place on a baking sheet. Bake about 16 minutes or until golden brown.

***NOTE:** Store the unused half of the vanilla bean in the refrigerator, wrapped in plastic wrap, in an airtight jar for up to 6 months.

Each serving: 94 cal., 7 g total fat (4 g sat. fat), 16 mg chol., 607 mg sodium, 11 g carbo., 3 g fiber, 2 g pro. Daily Values: 13% vit. A, 15% vit. C, 3% calcium, 6% iron.

Root Vegetable and Bean Soup

Underappreciated for decades, the simple technique of roasting has come back into fashion. We love the way roasting adds a caramel color and flavor to fruits and vegetables. Here root vegetables (also making a culinary comeback) get the royal roasting treatment in this utterly satisfying vegetarian soup.

START TO FINISH: 40 minutes

- 2 medium parsnips, peeled and cut into 1/2-inch pieces (1 1/2 cups)
- 1 medium potato, cut into 1/2-inch pieces (1 cup)
- 1 small rutabaga, peeled and cut into 1/2-inch pieces (1 cup)
- 2 medium carrots, sliced 1/2 inch thick
- 1 medium onion, cut into 8 wedges
- 1 Tbsp. olive oil
- 1/2 tsp. sea salt or kosher salt
- 3 cups vegetable or chicken broth
- 1 15-oz. can small red beans, garbanzo beans, or Great Northern beans, rinsed and drained
- 2 tsp. snipped fresh thyme

1. Preheat oven to 450° F. In a large roasting pan combine parsnips, potato, rutabaga, carrots, and onion with oil; sprinkle with salt and toss. Spread in a single layer in the pan. Roast for 15 to 20 minutes or until the vegetables start to brown.

2. In a large saucepan bring broth and beans to boiling; add roasted vegetables. Return to boiling; reduce heat. Simmer, covered, about 5 minutes or until vegetables are tender. Stir in thyme. (For a thicker consistency, mash vegetables and beans slightly.) Makes 4 side-dish servings.

Each serving: 274 cal., 5 g total fat (1 g sat. fat), 0 mg chol., 1,338 mg sodium, 58 g carbo., 13 g fiber, 11 g pro. Daily Values: 150% vit. A, 44% vit. C, 8% calcium, 22% iron.

Cauliflower-Crab Chowder

Creamy seafood chowder reaches beyond the usual potatoes to cauliflower, cream cheese, and a splash of sherry.

START TO FINISH: 35 minutes

- 2 cups frozen cauliflower
- 1/2 cup water
- 3 Tbsp. butter
- 3 Tbsp. all-purpose flour
- 1 14-oz. can vegetable or chicken broth
- 1 1/4 cups milk
- 1 3-oz. pkg. cream cheese, cubed
- 2 Tbsp. snipped fresh parsley
- 2 Tbsp. chopped pimiento or roasted red sweet pepper
- 1 Tbsp. snipped fresh chives
- 1/4 tsp. salt
- 1 6-oz. pkg. frozen crabmeat, thawed and drained
- 1/4 cup dry white wine or dry sherry

1. In a medium saucepan combine cauliflower and water. Bring to boiling; reduce heat. Simmer, covered, about 4 minutes or just until crisp-tender. Do not drain. Cut up large pieces of cauliflower; set aside.

2. Meanwhile, in a large saucepan melt butter. Stir in flour. Add broth and milk. Cook and stir until slightly thickened and bubbly.

3. Stir in undrained cauliflower, cream cheese, parsley, pimiento, chives, and salt. Stir over low heat until cheese is melted. Stir in crab; heat through. Stir in wine. To serve, spoon into 6 soup bowls. Makes 6 appetizer servings.

Each serving: 189 cal., 13 g total fat (8 g sat. fat), 64 mg chol., 589 mg sodium, 9 g carbo., 1 g fiber, 10 g pro. Daily Values: 15% vit. A, 42% vit. C, 12% calcium, 6% iron.

SEAFARER'S SUPPER

Seafood-Melon Cocktail *(page 511)*
Cauliflower-Crab Chowder *(above)*
Dill-buttered rolls
Minty Summer Shortcakes *(page 546)*
Sparkling water

Hearty Pumpkin Soup

The spices in this pumpkin soup all supposedly have healing qualities—cumin, especially, is thought to bring on peace of mind.

START TO FINISH: 50 minutes

- 2 Tbsp. butter
- 2 tsp. ground cumin
- 3/4 tsp. ground turmeric
- 1/2 tsp. ground cinnamon
- 2 leeks, chopped (2/3 cup)
- 2 1/2 lb. pie pumpkin or acorn squash, peeled and cut into 1- to 1 1/2-inch pieces (about 9 cups)
- 7 cups chicken broth
- 1/2 cup long grain white rice
- 4 cups coarsely chopped green cabbage
- Kosher salt or salt
- Ground black pepper
- 1 Tbsp. snipped fresh tarragon

1. In a 5 1/2- to 6-quart stockpot melt butter over medium heat. Add cumin, turmeric, and cinnamon; cook and stir for 1 minute. Add leeks; cook 2 minutes, stirring to coat. Add pumpkin and broth. Bring to boiling; reduce heat. Simmer, covered, for 10 minutes.

2. Add uncooked rice. Simmer, covered, for 10 minutes more. Add cabbage; simmer, covered, for 5 to 10 minutes more or until rice and squash are tender. Season to taste with salt and pepper. Just before serving, add tarragon. To serve, spoon into 10 to 12 bowls. Makes 10 to 12 side-dish or 6 main-dish servings.

Each side-dish serving: 120 cal., 4 g total fat (2 g sat. fat), 7 mg chol., 760 mg sodium, 18 g carbo., 2 g fiber, 4 g pro. Daily Values: 65% vit. A, 30% vit. C, 5% calcium, 8% iron.

Cheesy Chicken-Corn Chowder

PREP: 15 minutes **COOK:** 15 minutes **COOL:** 15 minutes

- 2 small skinless, boneless chicken breast halves (about 8 oz. total)
- 1/4 cup chopped onion
- 1/4 cup chopped celery
- 1 10 3/4-oz. can condensed cream of chicken soup
- 1 cup frozen whole kernel corn
- 1/2 cup milk
- 2 oz. American cheese or cheddar cheese, shredded (1/2 cup)
- 2 Tbsp. chopped pimiento

1. In a medium saucepan combine chicken, onion, celery, and 1 cup water. Bring to boiling; reduce heat. Simmer, covered, for 15 to 20 minutes or until chicken is no longer pink.

2. Remove chicken, reserving cooking liquid. When cool, chop chicken; return to pan. Stir in reserved cooking liquid, soup, corn, milk, cheese, and pimiento. Bring just to boiling, stirring until cheese is melted. To serve, spoon into 4 bowls. Makes 4 main-dish servings.

Each serving: 251 cal., 11 g total fat (5 g sat. fat), 54 mg chol., 868 mg sodium, 18 g carbo., 1 g fiber, 21 g pro. Daily Values: 9% vit. A, 16% vit. C, 14% calcium, 5% iron.

Hearty Pumpkin Soup

Cassoulet-Style Stew

STAND: 1 hour **PREP:** 50 minutes **COOK:** 1¾ hours

- 8 oz. dry navy beans
- 1 meaty lamb shank (1 to 1½ pounds)
- 1 Tbsp. olive oil or cooking oil
- 1 cup chopped celery (including leaves)
- 1 medium potato, peeled and coarsely chopped
- ½ cup coarsely chopped peeled carrot
- ½ cup coarsely chopped peeled parsnip
- 2 cloves garlic, minced
- 1½ cups sliced fresh mushrooms
- ⅔ cup dry black-eyed peas, rinsed and drained
- ½ cup dry red wine or beef broth
- 1¼ tsp. salt
- 1 Tbsp. snipped fresh thyme or 1 tsp. dried thyme, crushed
- 2 tsp. snipped fresh rosemary or ½ tsp. dried rosemary, crushed
- ¼ tsp. ground black pepper
- 1 14½-oz. can diced tomatoes, drained
- Fresh rosemary or thyme sprigs (optional)

1. Rinse beans. In a Dutch oven combine beans and 3 cups water. Bring to boiling; reduce heat. Simmer, uncovered, for 2 minutes. Remove from heat. Cover; let stand for 1 hour. (Or place beans in water in a Dutch oven. Cover and let stand in a cool place for 6 to 8 hours or overnight.) Drain beans; rinse. Set aside.

2. In a 4- to 5-quart Dutch oven or kettle brown lamb shank in hot oil over medium-high heat. Add celery, potato, carrot, parsnip, and garlic. Cook over medium-high heat for 5 minutes, stirring frequently. Add 3½ cups water, mushrooms, black-eyed peas, wine, salt, dried thyme (if using), dried rosemary (if using), pepper, and beans. Bring to boiling; reduce heat. Simmer, covered, about 1½ hours or until beans and peas are tender.

3. Remove shank; let cool. Remove meat from shank; chop meat. Stir meat, tomatoes, fresh thyme (if using), and fresh rosemary (if using) into bean mixture. Return to boiling; reduce heat. Simmer, covered, for 15 minutes more.

4. To serve, spoon stew into 6 bowls. If desired, garnish with fresh rosemary or thyme sprigs. Makes 6 main-dish servings.

MAKE-AHEAD DIRECTIONS: Prepare stew as directed. Let cool for 30 minutes. Place stew in freezer containers; freeze for up to 3 months. To serve, place frozen stew in a saucepan. Heat, covered, over medium-low heat about 45 minutes or until heated through, stirring occasionally to break apart mixture.

Each serving: 295 cal., 7 g total fat (2 g sat. fat), 25 mg chol., 662 mg sodium, 39 g carbo., 12 g fiber, 18 g pro. Daily Values: 55% vit. A, 29% vit. C, 13% calcium, 21% iron.

Vegetable-Orzo Soup

Homemade pistou, a basil-based condiment similar to pesto, garnishes this soup. Basil is known as the herb of friendliness, opening you up to the world around you. Use pistou in other friendly ways: Stir it into pasta, spoon it over vegetables, or serve it on top of a baked potato.

STAND: 1 hour **PREP:** 15 minutes **COOK:** 1½ hours

- ½ cup dry cannellini (white kidney) beans
- ½ recipe Bouquet Garni (page 370)
- 1 medium onion, chopped (½ cup)
- 3 cloves garlic, minced
- 1 Tbsp. extra-virgin olive oil
- 3 cups chicken broth
- 8 oz. green beans, halved
- ½ of a fennel bulb, chopped (about ⅔ cup)
- 1 medium zucchini, chopped
- 2 medium tomatoes
- 2 sprigs fresh thyme
- ½ tsp. salt
- ⅓ cup dried orzo or any small pasta
- 1 recipe Pistou (below)
- Grated Parmigiano-Reggiano cheese (optional)

1. Rinse beans; drain. In a large saucepan combine beans and 2 cups water. Bring to boiling; reduce heat. Simmer, uncovered, for 2 minutes. Remove from heat. Cover; let stand for 1 hour. (Or place beans in water in the saucepan. Cover; soak overnight in a cool place.) Drain beans; rinse. Set aside.

2. Prepare Bouquet Garni; set aside. In a 4-quart Dutch oven cook onion and garlic in the 1 tablespoon olive oil until tender. Add soaked beans and 2 cups water. Add Bouquet Garni; bring to boiling. Reduce heat; simmer, covered, for 55 minutes. Remove Bouquet Garni; discard.

3. Add chicken broth, green beans, fennel, zucchini, tomatoes, thyme, and salt. Bring to boiling; reduce heat. Simmer, covered, for 20 minutes. Add pasta; simmer, covered, for 10 minutes more. Discard thyme sprigs.

4. To serve, spoon soup into 4 or 5 bowls. Top with Pistou and cheese, if desired. Makes 4 or 5 main-dish servings.

PISTOU: In a food processor or blender combine 2 cups firmly packed basil; 6 cloves garlic, halved; 2 tablespoons grated Parmigiano-Reggiano cheese; and 2 tablespoons olive oil. Cover and process or blend until finely chopped. Thin to desired consistency with an additional 1 to 2 tablespoons olive oil.

Each serving: 400 cal., 20 g total fat (5 g sat. fat), 12 mg chol., 1,350 mg sodium, 39 g carbo., 14 g fiber, 18 g pro. Daily Values: 35% vit. A, 52% vit. C, 33% calcium, 24% iron.

Vegetable-Orzo Soup

Beef and Cabbage Soup

A dash of thyme from the bouquet garni supposedly imparts courage to those who eat this hearty soup. A bouquet garni is a useful cook's bag of tricks. It's a variety of herbs and spices wrapped in cheesecloth and simmered to flavor soups and stews.

PREP: 50 minutes **COOK:** 2 hours

- 1 recipe Bouquet Garni (below)
- 1 lb. slab bacon or prosciutto, diced
- 1½ to 2 lb. beef shank cross cuts
- 6 cups water
- 1½ lb. new potatoes, quartered
- 2 medium yellow onions, coarsely chopped (1 cup)
- 4 medium carrots, peeled and quartered crosswise
- 2 medium turnips, peeled and quartered (12 oz. total)
- 1 15- to 19-oz. can navy or cannellini (white kidney) beans
- 4 cloves garlic, minced
- 4 cups coarsely chopped green cabbage
- Kosher salt or salt
- 8 slices French bread, toasted and rubbed with olive oil and garlic

1. Prepare Bouquet Garni; set aside. In a 10- to 12-quart stockpot or Dutch oven, cook bacon or prosciutto until crisp, stirring frequently. Remove with a slotted spoon. Drain on paper towels, reserving 2 tablespoons drippings in stockpot. (If using prosciutto, add oil to equal 2 tablespoons.)

2. Brown beef shanks on both sides in reserved drippings. Add water, potatoes, onions, carrots, turnips, undrained beans, garlic, and Bouquet Garni. Bring to boiling; reduce heat. Simmer, covered, for 1½ hours. Add cabbage. Simmer, covered, about 30 minutes more or until meat is tender.

3. Discard Bouquet Garni. Remove beef shanks; cool slightly. Remove meat from bones. Using 2 forks, shred meat; return to soup. Skim fat from soup. Stir in cooked bacon or prosciutto. Heat through. Season to taste with salt.

4. To serve, place a slice of bread in 8 bowls. Spoon soup over bread. Makes 8 main-dish servings.

BOUQUET GARNI: Cut a 10-inch square of 100-percent-cotton cheesecloth. Place 8 sprigs fresh parsley, 2 bay leaves, 12 lightly crushed whole black peppercorns, and 4 or 5 sprigs each of fresh thyme and marjoram on center of cheesecloth. Draw up corners of square to create a bag; tie with clean kitchen string.

Each serving: 548 cal., 23 g total fat (10 g sat. fat), 45 mg chol., 925 mg sodium, 48 g carbo., 8 g fiber, 26 g pro. Daily Values: 155% vit. A, 52% vit. C, 11% calcium, 27% iron.

Beef and Cabbage Soup

FLAVORED TOASTS FOR SOUP

A toasted slice of French bread or crostini just seems to go with soup, especially when it's flavored. To make your own crostini, cut French bread into 1/2-inch-thick slices. Lightly brush both sides of each slice with olive oil. Arrange the slices on an ungreased baking sheet. If you like, brush on a little garlic, pesto, or olive paste. Or sprinkle with snipped herbs, cracked pepper, or shredded Parmesan cheese. Bake in a 425° F oven for 5 to 7 minutes or until crisp and light brown. Serve warm or cool.

Smoked Sausage-Lentil Soup

Smoked Sausage-Lentil Soup

Lentils are considered to be a symbol of good fortune. In fact, Italians eat lentils at New Year's to bring luck. In addition to lentils, you'll find sausage, carrots, onion, garlic, and anise-like fennel in this lucky soup. Snip the delicate fennel fronds to add a last-minute garnish.

PREP: 20 minutes **COOK:** 25 minutes

- 1 small fennel bulb, fronds reserved
- 4 cloves garlic, minced
- 1 Tbsp. olive oil
- 1 medium onion, chopped (1/4 cup)
- 2 medium carrots, chopped
- 6 cups water
- 1 1/4 cups green lentils, rinsed and drained
- 2 tsp. kosher salt or sea salt
- 1/4 tsp. ground black pepper
- 6 oz. cooked smoked sausage links, cut into 1/4-inch-thick pieces
- 3 Tbsp. red wine vinegar

1. Chop enough of the fennel bulb to measure 1 cup.

2. In a Dutch oven cook garlic in hot oil over medium heat for 1 minute. Add onion; cook until golden brown. Add fennel and carrots; cook until tender, stirring occasionally. Add water, lentils, salt, and pepper; bring to boiling. Reduce heat; simmer, uncovered, for 25 to 30 minutes or until lentils are tender.

3. Meanwhile, in a large skillet brown sausage on all sides. Using a slotted spoon, remove sausage from skillet. Add sausage to soup; stir in red wine vinegar.

4. To serve, spoon soup into 5 or 6 bowls. Top with fennel fronds. Makes 5 to 6 main-dish servings.

Each serving: 347 cal., 14 g total fat (4 g sat. fat), 23 mg chol., 1,314 mg sodium, 34 g carbo., 20 g fiber, 22 g pro. Daily Values: 137% vit. A, 14% vit. C, 6% calcium, 24% iron.

Ham and Bean Stew

PREP: 10 minutes **COOK:** 6 to 8 hours (low), 3 to 4 hours (high)

- 1 28-oz. can diced tomatoes, undrained
- 2 1/2 cups diced cooked ham
- 1 15-oz. can navy beans, rinsed and drained
- 1 14 3/4-oz. can cream-style corn
- 1 cup chopped onion
- 1/4 cup water
- 1/4 tsp. ground black pepper
- Dash bottled hot pepper sauce

1. In a 3 1/2- or 4-quart electric slow cooker combine undrained tomatoes, ham, beans, corn, onion, water, black pepper, and hot pepper sauce. Cover; cook on low-heat setting for 6 to 8 hours or on high-heat setting for 3 to 4 hours. To serve, spoon into 5 bowls. Makes 5 main-dish servings.

Each serving: 368 cal., 8 g total fat (3 g sat. fat), 50 mg chol., 2,190 mg sodium, 45 g carbo., 7 g fiber, 29 g pro. Daily Values: 2% vit. A, 43% vit. C, 12% calcium, 22% iron.

Hearty Hodgepodge

A hodgepodge of four different flavorful meats makes this stick-to-your-ribs simmered supper something to remember. Because the bacon, sausage, beef, and ham are so full of flavor, you need little else in the way of seasoning.

PREP: 20 minutes **BAKE:** 1 1/2 hours + 30 + 15 minutes

- 6 slices bacon
- 1 medium onion, thinly sliced
- 1 lb. beef shank cross cuts
- 3/4 lb. meaty ham bone
- 6 cups water
- 1/2 tsp. salt
- 2 15-oz. cans chickpeas (garbanzo beans), drained
- 3 cups cubed potatoes (4 medium)
- 1 clove garlic, minced
- 1 4-oz. link cooked, smoked Polish sausage, thinly sliced
- 8 French bread slices, toasted and buttered (optional)

1. In a 4- to 6-quart Dutch oven cook bacon until crisp; drain, reserving 2 tablespoons drippings in pan. Add sliced onion to reserved drippings. Cook and stir until onion is tender. Crumble bacon and chill.

2. Add beef shanks, ham hock, water, and salt to pan. Heat to boiling; reduce heat. Cover and simmer about 1 1/2 hours or until beef is tender.

3. Carefully remove meat from beef shanks and ham hock and cut up; discard bones. Carefully skim fat from broth. Return the cut-up meat to soup; add chickpeas, potatoes, and garlic. Return to boiling; reduce heat. Simmer, covered, for 30 minutes more.

4. Add sausage; simmer, covered, for 15 minutes more. Stir in bacon. To serve, spoon into 8 bowls. If desired, serve with toasted French bread. Makes 8 main-dish servings.

Each serving: 390 cal., 16 g total fat (6 g sat. fat), 40 mg chol., 1,008 mg sodium, 40 g carbo., 6 g fiber, 22 g pro. Daily Values: 1% vit. A, 15% vit. C, 8% calcium, 20% iron.

BROWNED BUTTER

WHAT'S SIMPLER THAN A SAUCE BASED ON BUTTER? NOT MUCH.

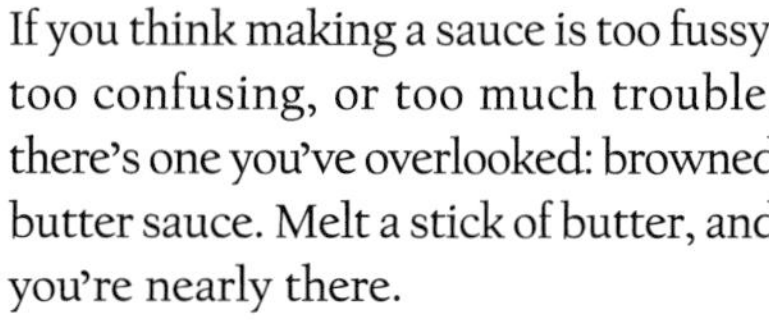

If you think making a sauce is too fussy, too confusing, or too much trouble, there's one you've overlooked: browned butter sauce. Melt a stick of butter, and you're nearly there.

Browned butter is melted butter with a toasted attitude. The taste is bigger and earthier, and the aroma more enticing—much the way a toasted nut compares to a raw one.

Chefs like to make browned butter sauce with butter they've clarified, a process which removes the milk solids from melted butter. You can be more relaxed, though. Instead of clarifying the butter, just pour it through a fine-mesh sieve to get a clearer sauce.

To make a simple browned butter sauce for potatoes, steak, or pasta (far right), melt 1/2 cup butter in a medium skillet over medium-low heat. Continue cooking about 10 minutes, stirring the butter, and lifting and swirling the pan occasionally, until the butter is golden brown. Strain the butter through a fine-mesh sieve over a bowl. Stir in 2 tablespoons lemon juice and 2 tablespoons snipped fresh parsley. The result is a clear winner.

Pumpkin Ravioli with Browned Butter

Start to Finish: 75 minutes

- 1 recipe Pasta Dough (below)
- 1 cup canned pumpkin
- 1/4 cup butter, melted
- 1/3 cup finely shredded Parmesan cheese
- 1/4 tsp. salt
- 1/4 tsp. ground cinnamon
- 1/8 tsp. ground black pepper
- Dash ground nutmeg
- 1 egg, slightly beaten
- 1/3 cup butter
- 4 fresh sage leaves
- Fresh sage leaves (optional)

1. Prepare Pasta Dough. For filling, in a small bowl stir together pumpkin, the 1/4 cup melted butter, Parmesan, salt, cinnamon, pepper, and nutmeg; set aside.

2. Use a sharp knife to cut pasta into 2- to 2½-inch-wide strips. Leaving a ½-inch margin on edges, place 1 slightly rounded teaspoon of filling at 1½-inch intervals on 1 strip of dough.

3. Using a pastry brush, brush dough around mounds of filling with egg. Lay a second strip of dough atop the first. Press pasta around each mound of filling so the dough sticks together. With a fluted pastry wheel or a sharp knife, cut the pasta between the mounds of filling to separate into squares. (To prevent the filled ravioli from tearing or sticking until you are ready to cook them, lay them on a lightly floured surface without touching.)

4. In a Dutch oven cook the ravioli, half at a time, in boiling salted water for 2 minutes or until tender. Use a slotted spoon to transfer to a colander-lined bowl; drain well.

5. Melt the 1/3 cup butter in a large skillet over medium-low heat. Continue cooking about 10 minutes or until butter is golden brown, stirring butter and lifting and swirling the pan occasionally. Add the 4 sage leaves. Cook and stir for 1 minute. Remove from heat.

6. To serve, arrange the ravioli on 6 plates. Top with sage butter. If desired, garnish with additional fresh sage leaves. Serve warm. Makes 6 servings.

PASTA DOUGH: In a large bowl stir together 2 cups all-purpose flour and ½ teaspoon salt. Make a well in the center of the flour mixture. In a small bowl combine 2 eggs, 1/3 cup water, and 1 teaspoon olive oil. Add to flour mixture; stir to combine. Sprinkle a clean kneading surface with 1/3 cup all-purpose flour. Turn dough out onto floured surface. Knead until dough is smooth and elastic (8 to 10 minutes total). Cover; let the dough rest for 10 minutes. Divide dough into 4 equal portions. On a lightly floured surface roll each portion into a 12-inch square (about 1/16 inch thick). Let stand, uncovered, about 20 minutes. Or, if using a pasta machine, pass each portion through the machine according to manufacturer's directions until dough is 1/16 inch thick.

Each serving: 509 cal., 31 g total fat (18 g sat. fat), 178 mg chol., 1,014 mg sodium, 39 g carbo., 2 g fiber, 19 g pro. Daily Values: 201% vit. A, 3% vit. C, 40% calcium, 19% iron.

BUTTER 'EM UP

Try these simple ideas for browned butter or make some traditional ravioli with your own pasta at left.

POTATOES: Spooning browned butter into mashed potatoes is a Pennsylvania Dutch tradition. But don't stop with potatoes. Steamed vegetables taste bolder with a browned butter drizzle.

STEAK: A spoonful of browned butter sauce over steak does double duty: It enhances any topper, such as a quick mushroom sauté, plus gives the steak a shiny, moist glaze.

PASTA: Toss browned butter with hot pasta as an alternative to sauce or olive oil. Take full advantage of the nutty flavor by keeping the accompaniments simple.

SHRED A SALAD
Create a sassy, colorful slaw with cabbages, peppers, carrots, fennel, and radishes.

MAKE A PICKLE
Make short work of bread-and-butter pickles, pickled beets, sauerkraut cabbage, fresh ginger, or zucchini slices.

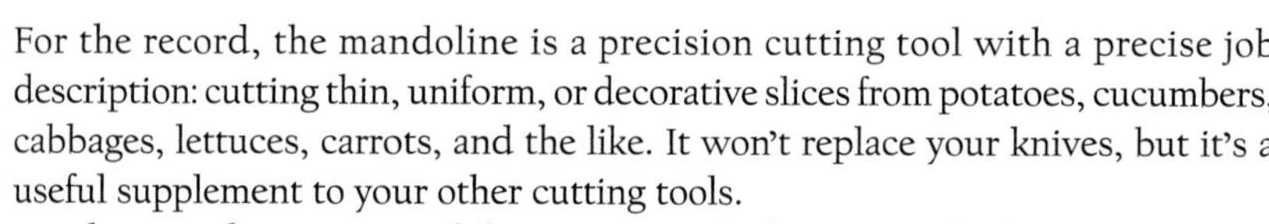

SAVVY SLICING

THE MANDOLINE CUTS A JAZZY TUNE IN THE KITCHEN REPERTOIRE. PLAY IT SAFE, THOUGH.

For the record, the mandoline is a precision cutting tool with a precise job description: cutting thin, uniform, or decorative slices from potatoes, cucumbers, cabbages, lettuces, carrots, and the like. It won't replace your knives, but it's a useful supplement to your other cutting tools.

When purchasing a mandoline, it's a good idea to spend a few extra dollars for one with all the bells and whistles. Check for stability, a comfortable angle for slicing, and blades that are easy to change or adjust for thickness. Blades should give you the cuts you want, such as a ripple cut or wafer-thin slices. Make sure there is a finger guard or food carriage for safety.

The mandoline is a quick and creative tool that brings a level of artistry to a dish's final presentation. But you need a little practice before using it becomes second nature, so pay special attention to the safety tips, *right*.

SLICE A SPUD

Cut potatoes the way you like them for chips and fries—thin, thick, or rippled—or shred them for potato cakes and hash browns.

SAFETY TIPS

- Place the mandoline on a damp tea towel to prevent it from sliding around. If a table clamp comes with your model, use it.
- Dry your hands thoroughly before using your mandoline so you won't slip and cut yourself.
- Let the mandoline do the work. The blades are sharp; slide foods over them—don't push.
- Use the finger guard at all times.
- Preslice the bottom side of the food first to create a flat surface for cutting.
- Always cut away from you, not toward.
- When the finger guard starts to stick or the food becomes difficult to move over the blades, stop slicing. Reserve the remainder of the vegetable or fruit you're cutting for another use.
- Take care to avoid exposed blades when cleaning.
- Keep the mandoline away from children!

Artichoke and Basil Hero

Practice slicing cheese and firm tomatoes for this hearty sandwich. You'll find the mandoline makes quick work of slicing all sorts of sandwich fixings.

START TO FINISH: 30 minutes

- 1 cup fresh basil (leaves only)
- 1/4 cup olive oil or salad oil
- 2 Tbsp. grated Parmesan cheese
- 1 Tbsp. capers, drained
- 1 Tbsp. white wine vinegar
- 2 tsp. Dijon-style mustard
- 1 clove garlic, quartered
- 1 16-oz. loaf unsliced French bread
- 1 14-oz. can artichoke hearts, drained and sliced
- 4 oz. sliced provolone cheese
- 1 medium tomato, thinly sliced
- 2 cups torn fresh spinach

1. In a blender or food processor combine basil, oil, Parmesan cheese, capers, vinegar, mustard, and garlic. Cover; blend or process until nearly smooth. Set aside.

2. Cut bread in half lengthwise. Hollow out each half, leaving a 1/2- to 1-inch-thick shell. (Save bread crumbs for another use.)

3. Spread basil mixture onto cut side of each bread half. On bottom half, layer artichoke hearts, provolone cheese, tomato, and spinach. Cover with top half of bread. To serve, cut sandwich crosswise into 6 slices. Makes 6 servings.

Each serving: 396 cal., 17 g total fat (5 g sat. fat), 14 mg chol., 887 mg sodium, 46 g carbo., 4 g fiber, 15 g pro. Daily Values: 18% vit. C, 24% calcium, 23% iron.

EASY SUBSTITUTES

DON'T DESPAIR WHEN YOU RUN OUT OF A KEY RECIPE INGREDIENT AND THE PANTRY HOLDS ONLY ITS DISTANT COUSIN. THIS HANDY CHART WILL HELP YOU REPLACE THE MISSING ITEM.

AIOLI (½ CUP): Mix ½ cup mayonnaise and 1 large garlic clove, minced.
APPLE CIDER (2 TBSP.): Combine 2 tablespoons apple juice and ¼ teaspoon cider vinegar.
BAKING POWDER (1 TSP.): Combine ½ teaspoon cream of tartar with ¼ teaspoon baking soda.
BALSAMIC VINEGAR (1 TBSP.): Combine 1 tablespoon cider vinegar or red wine vinegar and ½ teaspoon sugar.
CAKE FLOUR (1 CUP): Omit 2 tablespoons from 1 cup all-purpose flour.
CAPERS (1 TBSP): Use 1 tablespoon chopped green olives.
CHILI OIL (1 TBSP): Whisk a few drops of hot pepper sauce and/or red pepper flakes into 1 tablespoon olive oil or vegetable oil.
CHIVES: Substitute an equal amount of snipped green onion tops.
CILANTRO: For fresh, substitute an equal amount of fresh parsley. For dried, substitute equal parts dried parsley and dried coriander.
CRÉME FRAICHE (1 CUP): Combine ½ cup whipping cream and ½ cup sour cream. Let stand at room temperature for 30 minutes. Chill for longer storage. (Note: Do not use ultra-pasteurized whipping cream.)
EGGS (LARGE): If your egg size is different than large, try this:
Jumbo: For 1 or 2 eggs, substitute 1 jumbo egg for each egg called for. For 3 or more, use the number called for minus 1.
Extra large: Up to 4 eggs, substitute 1 for 1. For 5 or more, use the number called for minus 1.
Medium: Up to 3 eggs, substitute 1 for 1. For 4 or more, use the number called for plus one.
FRESH GARLIC (1 CLOVE): Use ½ teaspoon bottled minced garlic or ⅛ teaspoon garlic powder.
FRESH GINGERROOT (1 TSP.): Use ¼ teaspoon ground ginger.
HERBES DE PROVENCE: Mix together at least 5 of the following dried spices in a mortar and pestle: basil, fennel seeds, lavender, marjoram, rosemary, sage, savory, or thyme.
MADIERA (1 TBSP.): Stir together 1 tablespoon red wine and ½ teaspoon sugar.
MOLASSES (1 CUP): Substitute 1 cup of honey.
PRESERVED LEMON SLICES: Brush lemon slices with olive oil; sprinkle liberally with kosher salt. Cover with paper towel and let stand for 10 to 30 minutes.
SAFFRON: Substitute an equal amount of turmeric.
SESAME SEEDS (1 TBSP.): Substitute 1 tablespoon finely chopped blanched almonds.
SOUR CREAM: Use an equal amount of plain low-fat yogurt.
STAR ANISE: Substitute an equal amount of Chinese five-spice powder or ground anise seeds.
TAMARI (2 TEASPOONS): Substitute 1 tablespoon soy sauce.
TOMATO PASTE (½ CUP): Cook 1 cup tomato sauce, uncovered, until reduced to ½ cup.
VANILLA EXTRACT: Substitute an equal amount of almond extract plus a pinch of cream of tartar.

Moussaka

Check out the ingredient list for this Greek classic before you start cooking. If you don't have exactly what you need, there are some smart substitutions you can make, using the list opposite.

PREP: 40 minutes **BAKE:** 35 minutes **STAND:** 10 minutes

- 2 1-lb. eggplants, peeled and cut into 1/2-inch-thick slices
- 1/4 cup cooking oil
- 2 lb. ground lamb or ground beef
- 1 large onion, chopped (1 cup)
- 1 clove garlic, minced
- 1 8-oz. can tomato sauce
- 3/4 cup dry red wine
- 2 Tbsp. snipped fresh parsley
- 3/4 tsp. salt
- 1/4 tsp. dried oregano, crushed
- 1/4 tsp. ground cinnamon
- 1 beaten egg
- 1/4 cup butter or margarine
- 1/4 cup all-purpose flour
- 1/2 tsp. salt
- Dash ground black pepper
- 2 cups milk
- 3 eggs
- 1/4 cup grated Parmesan cheese

1. Preheat oven to 325° F. Brush both sides of eggplant slices with the oil. In a large skillet brown eggplant slices over medium heat about 2 minutes per side. Drain; set aside.

2. In the same skillet cook ground lamb, half at a time, until meat is brown, cooking onion and garlic with the second half of meat. Drain off fat. Stir in tomato sauce, wine, parsley, the 3/4 teaspoon salt, oregano, and cinnamon. Heat to boiling; reduce heat. Simmer, uncovered, for 10 minutes or until most of the liquid is absorbed. Cool mixture slightly. Stir 1/2 cup of the meat mixture into the 1 beaten egg. Stir egg mixture into meat mixture in skillet.

3. Meanwhile, in a medium saucepan melt butter. Stir in flour, the 1/2 teaspoon salt, and pepper. Add milk all at once. Cook and stir until thickened and bubbly. Cook and stir for 1 minute more. In a medium bowl beat the 3 eggs. Gradually stir the thickened milk mixture into the beaten eggs.

4. In a 3-quart rectangular baking dish arrange half of the eggplant sli... Spread meat mixture over eggplant slices; top ... eggplant slices. Pour hot egg mixture over all. Top ... cheese; sprinkle with additional cinnamon. Bake, ... for 35 to 40 minutes or until edges are bubbly. Let ... minutes. To serve, cut into squares. If desired, sprin-...tional parsley. Makes 8 to 10 servings.

...36 cal., 39 g total fat (16 g sat. fat), 207 mg chol., 764 mg sodium, ... g fiber, 27 g pro. Daliy Values: 19% vit. A, 14% vit. C, ...7% iron.

Banana Split Cake

You probably have all of the ingredients for this soda-fountain-inspired pound cake right on your shelf. But if not, the list opposite will help you pinch-hit your way to a home run.

PREP: 30 minutes **BAKE:** 55 minutes **STAND:** 30 minutes

- 1 cup butter
- 4 eggs
- 3 cups all-purpose flour
- 2 tsp. baking powder
- 1 tsp. salt
- 1/4 tsp. baking soda
- 1 1/2 cups sugar
- 1 large banana, mashed (1/2 cup)
- 1/2 cup dairy sour cream
- 1/2 cup milk
- 1 tsp. vanilla
- 1/2 cup strawberry preserves
- Few drops red food coloring
- 1/2 cup presweetened cocoa powder (not low calorie)
- 1 12-oz. jar chocolate fudge ice cream topping
- Vanilla ice cream (optional)

1. Let butter and eggs stand at room temperature for 30 minutes. Preheat oven to 350° F. Meanwhile, grease and flour a 10-inch fluted tube pan. In a medium bowl stir together flour, baking powder, salt, and baking soda. Set aside.

2. In a large bowl beat butter with an electric mixer on low to medium speed for 30 seconds. Add sugar; beat until fluffy. Add eggs, 1 at a time, beating well after each addition. In a small bowl, combine banana, sour cream, milk, and vanilla. Alternately add flour mixture and banana mixture to butter mixture, beating on low speed after each addition just until combined.

3. Stir 1/2 cup strawberry preserves and red food coloring into 1 cup of the batter. Stir cocoa powder into another 1 cup of the batter. Spoon half the remaining plain batter into prepared pan. Spoon strawberry batter over plain batter. Top with remaining plain, then chocolate batter.

4. Bake for 55 to 65 minutes or until a wooden toothpick inserted near center comes out clean. Cool in pan on a wire rack for 10 minutes; remove from pan. Cool on wire rack.

5. Before serving, in a small saucepan heat chocolate fudge ice cream topping until warm; drizzle onto cake. If desired, serve cake with ice cream; top with additional chocolate fudge topping. Makes 12 servings.

Each serving: 561 cal., 24 g total fat (14 g sat. fat), 121 mg chol., 635 mg sodium, 79 g carbo., 2 g fiber, 8 g pro. Daliy Values: 16% vit. A, 3% vit. C, 11% calcium, 10% iron..

SWEET AND SIMPLE

HERE'S HOW TO WOW A CELEBRATION CROWD IN THREE EASY STEPS. TAKE THE CAKE. FROST. EMBELLISH.

(Purchased cake and frosting from a can makes the project even simpler.)

SAY IT WITH A SUNFLOWER

Chocolate chips mimic sunflower seeds when arranged in a circle and surrounded by edible chrysanthemum petals and mint leaves. Be sure to use only edible flowers and herbs that have been grown organically (not those from a florist). Sunflower blossoms also are edible. So if you've still got some of the sunny flowers nodding on their stalks in your garden, borrow some of their petals. Let your guests know that mums and sunflower petals have a slightly bitter taste.

LOLLIPOP CAROUSEL

This brilliantly colored merry-go-round of a cake is gussied up in minutes. Use scissors to trim the sticks so the candies peek out above the edge of the cake. Remove the wrappers. Guide the lollipops in place by holding the top of the candy with your fingertips (plastic gloves, please) and pressing each lollipop into place.

SWEET LEAVES OF THE SEASON

Make melt-in-your-mouth leaves out of thinly rolled chocolate. Or stencil leaf patterns on top of the cake.

STENCILED LEAVES: Place leaf-shape cookie cutters on frosting; sprinkle sifted cocoa powder or colored decorative sugar inside. Remove cutters to reveal the pattern.

CHOCOLATE LEAVES: In a small saucepan melt 6 ounces semisweet chocolate over low heat, stirring often; cool slightly. Stir in 3 tablespoons light-colored corn syrup (do not overmix). Transfer to a large sheet of waxed paper. Cover; let stand at room temperature for 6 to 24 hours or until dry. (The mixture stiffens after standing, but kneading makes it pliable again.) Gently knead for 10 to 15 strokes or until smooth and pliable. If too soft, chill in the refrigerator about 15 minutes or until easy to handle. To make leaves, shape half of the chocolate mixture into a ball. Flatten slightly; place between 2 sheets of waxed paper dusted lightly with powdered sugar. Roll to 1/8-inch thickness. Use 2-inch leaf-shape cookie cutters to cut chocolate. Repeat with remaining half. Dust leaves with cocoa powder or colored decorative sugar. Store unused chocolate in a sealed plastic bag at room temperature for 3 to 4 weeks. Makes about thirty-six 2-inch leaves.

Best-Ever Chocolate Cake

PREP: 30 minutes **BAKE:** 30 minutes **COOL:** 1 hour

- 3/4 cup butter, softened
- 3 eggs
- 2 cups all-purpose flour
- 3/4 cup unsweetened cocoa powder
- 1 tsp. baking soda
- 3/4 tsp. baking powder
- 1/2 tsp. salt
- 2 cups sugar
- 2 tsp. vanilla
- 1 1/2 cups milk
- 1 recipe Chocolate-Sour Cream Frosting (below)

1. Let butter and eggs stand at room temperature for 30 minutes. Lightly grease bottoms of three 8×1 1/2- or 9×1 1/2-inch round cake pans. Line bottoms of pans with waxed paper. Grease and lightly flour bottoms and sides of pans. Set pans aside.

2. Preheat oven to 350° F. In a mixing bowl stir together flour, cocoa powder, baking soda, baking powder, and salt; set aside.

3. In a large mixing bowl beat butter with an electric mixer on medium to high speed for 30 seconds. Gradually add sugar, about 1/2 cup at a time, beating on medium speed for 3 to 4 minutes or until combined. Scrape side of bowl; continue beating on medium speed for 2 minutes. Add eggs, 1 at a time, beating after each addition (about 1 minute total). Beat in vanilla.

4. Alternately add flour mixture and milk to beaten mixture, beating on low speed after each addition just until combined. Beat on medium to high speed for 20 seconds more. Spread batter evenly in the prepared pans.

5. Bake for 30 to 35 minutes or until a wooden toothpick inserted in the centers comes out clean.

6. Cool cake layers in pans for 10 minutes. Remove from pans. Peel off waxed paper. Cool on a wire rack.

7. Prepare Chocolate-Sour Cream Frosting. Frost cake with frosting. Decorate cake as desired. Cut cake into wedges to serve. Cover and store any leftover cake in the refrigerator. Makes 12 to 16 servings.

CHOCOLATE-SOUR CREAM FROSTING: In a large saucepan melt one 12-ounce package semisweet chocolate pieces and 1/2 cup butter over low heat, stirring frequently. Cool for 5 minutes. Stir in one 8-ounce carton dairy sour cream. Gradually add 4 1/2 cups sifted powdered sugar, beating until smooth.

Each serving: 760 cal., 36 g total fat (20 g sat. fat), 118 mg chol., 475 mg sodium, 99 g carbo., 5 g fiber, 7 g pro. Daily Values: 21% vit. A, 14% calcium.

COOKING Together

IF SHARING TIME IN THE KITCHEN KEEPS US ALL CONNECED, THEN FALL IS THE TIME TO START. FALL WEEKENDS LEND THEMSELVES TO LAZY BRUNCHES, HEARTY STEW SUPPERS, AND QUICK-TO-FIX PASTA DINNERS.

Harvest Vegetable Stew

Harvest Vegetable Stew

A combination of hearty fall vegetables makes this meatless stew so satisfying, you can eat it as a main dish.

PREP: 25 minutes **COOK:** 30 minutes

- 5 cups water
- 3 beef bouillon cubes or 3 tsp. instant beef bouillon granules
- 2 medium Yukon gold potatoes, peeled and cut into 1-inch pieces (8 oz.)
- 3 plum tomatoes, chopped, or one 14½-oz. can diced tomatoes
- 2 stalks celery, chopped (1 cup)
- 1 small green sweet pepper, chopped (¼ cup)
- 1 small onion, chopped (¼ cup)
- 2 cups shredded cabbage
- 4 oz. fresh green beans, trimmed and cut in half (1 cup)
- 1 small zucchini, chopped (1 cup)
- 1 15-oz. can red kidney beans, rinsed and drained
- 8 to 10 fresh oregano sprigs, tied in a bunch with kitchen string
- ¼ cup catsup
- ¼ tsp. pepper
- Dash bottled hot pepper sauce
- Salt
- Pepper

1. In a Dutch oven combine water and bouillon cubes or granules; bring to boiling. Add potatoes, undrained tomatoes, celery, green pepper, and onion. Return to boiling; reduce heat. Simmer, uncovered, for 15 minutes.

2. Add remaining ingredients. Simmer, uncovered, about 15 minutes more or until vegetables are tender. Remove and discard oregano. Season to taste with salt and pepper. Makes 8 to 10 servings.

Each serving: 93 cal., 0 g total fat (0 g sat. fat), 0 mg chol., 702 mg sodium, 19 g carbo., 6 g dietary fiber, 4 g pro. Daily Values: 9% vit. A, 41% vit. C, 4% calcium, 8% iron.

STEW SUPPER

Harvest Vegetable Stew *(above)*
Dad's Rolls *(recipe, page 388)*
Hedy's Oatmeal Cookies *(page 389)*
Milk

THE FAMILY THAT COOKS TOGETHER...

Neil

Spending time in the kitchen together is a major part of the recipe for staying connnected, at least that's what one North Carolina family has found. The Leiters of Raleigh have found that cooking together is more than a creative outlet for family members who pursue writing, music, glassblowing, flower arranging, and acting. For them, time together in the kitchen is time to catch up and to show that they care. "It's not that we especially like to cook together," says son Neil, "so much as it is that we like to cook for each other."

Cole

That's not always easy to do. Family schedules are tight. Neil has college. His sister, Hedy, rows competitively, teaches fitness, and bakes for neighbors. Younger brother Cole plays baseball and is apprenticed to a glassblower. Mom Carrie Knowles writes and speaks on Alzheimer's nationally, often discussing her mother's battle with the disease. Dad Jeff is a sociology professor, who is involved in local politics.

Yet, making time to cook for each other is important. For Hedy, baking is a passion and dessert is her daily gift to her family. "I'm the kind of person who would rather give presents than get them," says Hedy. "It's the way I've always been."

Carrie, Hedy, and Jeff

Another key to finding time to cook together is finding foods that are quick to prepare or easy to put together, then leave to bake or simmer.

"Cooking can't take too long because we always have something else to do," says Neil.

For Jeff and Carrie, cooking meals with their kids lets them watch the lessons that they have tried to teach take hold.

"I get the sense that here are three people who are going to be able to take care of themselves in the kitchen," Jeff says.

Jeff

Beet and Blue Cheese Salad

Serve this salad as a starter or for a light lunch or outdoor dinner.

PREP: 20 minutes **COOK:** 40 minutes

- 6 medium beets (2 lb.)
- 1/4 cup balsamic vinegar
- 3 Tbsp. olive oil
- 2 tsp. Dijon-style mustard
- 1/4 tsp. salt
- 1/4 tsp. pepper
- 1 15-oz. can chickpeas (garbanzo beans), rinsed and drained
- 4 to 5 small green onions, sliced
- 5 cups torn mixed greens, such as baby spinach leaves, bibb lettuce, or mesclun mix
- 1/2 cup hazelnuts (filberts), toasted and coarsely chopped*
- 6 oz. blue cheese, cut into 5 or 6 wedges

1. Cut stems off beets, but leave roots; wash. Do not peel. Cook whole beets, covered, in boiling salted water for 40 to 50 minutes or until crisp-tender.

2. Meanwhile, for dressing, in a screw-top jar combine vinegar, olive oil, mustard, salt, and pepper. Cover; shake well. Set dressing aside.

3. Drain, cool, peel, and cut beets into wedges. Rinse beets until water runs almost clear. In a medium bowl combine beets, chickpeas, and green onions. Pour dressing over beet mixture; toss gently to coat. Cover and chill until serving time.

4. Arrange greens on six salad plates; spoon beet mixture onto greens. Sprinkle with hazelnuts. Serve with wedges of blue cheese. Makes 6 servings.

***TEST KITCHEN TIP:** To toast hazelnuts, spread them in a single layer on a shallow baking pan. Bake in a 350° F oven for 8 to 10 minutes or until golden, watching carefully and stirring once or twice so they don't overbrown. To remove skin from toasted nuts, roll warm nuts vigorously in a towel.

Each serving: 414 cal., 28 g total fat (8 g sat. fat), 26 mg chol., 957 mg sodium, 28 g carbo., 8 g dietary fiber, 16 g pro. Daily Values: 47% vit. A, 24% vit. C, 28% calcium, 18% iron.

DINNER ON THE QUICK

College Chicken and Pasta *(right)*
Beet and Blue Cheese Salad *(above)*
Pear-Peach Crisp *(page 391)*
Dry red wine or grape juice

College Chicken and Pasta

College Chicken and Pasta

START TO FINISH: 30 minutes

- 1 1/2 tsp. coarsely ground pepper blend
- 3/4 tsp. salt
- 1 clove garlic, minced
- 4 medium skinless, boneless chicken breast halves
- 2 large onions, sliced
- 2 Tbsp. olive oil
- 3 medium tomatoes, chopped (1 lb.)
- 1 Tbsp. tomato paste
- 2 to 3 tsp. grated fresh ginger
- 8 oz. dried spaghetti
- 1/4 cup Homemade Pesto (below) or purchased pesto
- Parmesan cheese (optional)

1. Combine 1 teaspoon of the pepper blend, 1/2 teaspoon of the salt, and the garlic. Rub onto chicken. In a 12-inch skillet cook chicken and onions in hot oil over medium heat about 15 minutes or until onions are tender and chicken is no longer pink and registers 170° F on an instant-read thermometer, turning chicken once and stirring onions occasionally.

2. Remove chicken from skillet; slice crosswise into strips. Return to pan; add tomatoes, tomato paste, ginger, remaining pepper blend, and remaining 1/4 teaspoon salt. Heat through.

3. Meanwhile, in a large saucepan cook spaghetti according to package directions; drain. Return spaghetti to pan; stir in pesto. Serve chicken and sauce over pesto-coated spaghetti. If desired, top with Parmesan cheese. Makes 6 servings.

HOMEMADE PESTO: In a blender container combine 2 cups firmly packed, fresh basil leaves; 1/2 cup chopped walnuts or pine nuts; 1/2 cup grated Parmesan cheese; 1/4 cup olive oil; 4 cloves peeled garlic; 1/4 teaspoon salt; and a dash pepper. Cover and blend until nearly smooth, stopping and scraping sides as necessary.

Each serving: 373 cal., 12 g total fat (2 g sat. fat), 56 mg chol., 444 mg sodium, 38 g carbo., 3 g dietary fiber, 29 g pro. Daily Values: 11% vit. A, 28% vit. C, 6% calcium, 14% iron.

Beet and Blue Cheese Salad

Shortcut Nutty Fruit Cinnamon Rolls

"COOKING CAN'T TAKE TOO LONG, BECAUSE WE ALWAYS HAVE SOMETHING ELSE TO DO."

–Neil Leiter

Zucchini Quiche

Shortcut Nutty Fruit Cinnamon Rolls

Shape these rolls the night before, then cover with plastic wrap and refrigerate overnight to bake them fresh for brunch.

PREP: 40 minutes **RISE:** 30 minutes **PREP:** 20 minutes

- **5 3/4 to 6 1/4 cups bread flour or all-purpose flour**
- **2 pkg. active dry yeast**
- **2 1/4 cups warm water (105° to 115° F)**
- **1 Tbsp. packed brown sugar**
- **1/4 cup butter, softened**
- **2 Tbsp. ground cinnamon**
- **2 tsp. salt**
- **1 cup packed brown sugar**
- **5 Tbsp. butter, softened**
- **1 cup chopped walnuts or pecans**
- **1 cup raisins or other dried fruit, such as apricots or cherries**
- **1 recipe Almond Icing(below)**

1. In a large mixing bowl stir together 1/2 cup of the bread flour, yeast, 1/2 cup of the warm water, and 1 tablespoon brown sugar. Let stand about 15 minutes or until surface is bubbly.

2. Add 1 3/4 cups of the warm water, 1 cup of the bread flour, 1/4 cup butter, 1 tablespoon cinnamon, and salt. Beat with a wooden spoon until smooth. Stir in as much of the remaining flour as you can. Turn out onto a lightly floured surface and knead in enough of the remaining flour to make a moderately soft dough that is smooth and elastic (3 to 5 minutes). (Or, to prepare dough in a stand mixer with a dough hook, beat on low speed until smooth. Add 4 cups of the flour, 1 cup at a time, beating with a dough hook on low speed about 5 minutes or until a moderately soft dough that is not sticky forms, adding additional flour, if necessary.) Let dough rise in bowl in a warm place for 15 minutes.

3. Preheat oven to 400° F. Meanwhile, for filling, in a bowl combine the 1 cup brown sugar, the 5 tablespoons softened butter, and 1 tablespoon cinnamon. Stir in nuts and fruit (if using dried apricots, cut into small pieces).

4. On a lightly floured surface, roll the dough into a 20×12-inch rectangle. Sprinkle with the filling, then carefully roll up into a spiral, starting from one of the long sides. Slice into 20 equal pieces. Place rolls in a greased 15×10×1-inch baking pan or two 9×9×2 baking pans.

5. Bake about 20 minutes or until tops are golden brown. Cool slightly; remove rolls from pans. Drizzle with Almond Icing. Serve warm. Makes 20 rolls.

ALMOND ICING: In a medium bowl stir together 1 cup sifted powdered sugar, 1 tablespoon light cream or half-and-half, 1 teaspoon vanilla, and 1/2 teaspoon almond extract. If necessary, stir in additional powered sugar until of drizzling consistency.

Each roll: 322 cal., 10 g total fat (4 g sat. fat), 15 mg chol., 296 mg sodium, 53 g carbo., 2 g dietary fiber, 6 g pro. Daily Values: 4% vit. A, 1% vit. C, 4% calcium, 15% iron.

LAZY DAY BRUNCH

Zucchini Quiche (*below*)
Shortcut Nutty Fruit Cinnamon Rolls (*left*)
Orange and grapefruit slices
Coffee or tea

Zucchini Quiche

The quickie for this quiche? There's no crust to roll and shape.

PREP: 20 minutes **BAKE:** 40 minutes **STAND:** 10 minutes

- **4 eggs**
- **3 cups finely shredded zucchini**
- **1 cup packaged biscuit mix**
- **1/2 cup grated Parmesan cheese**
- **2 oz. Gruyère cheese or Swiss cheese, shredded**
- **1/4 cup cooking oil**
- **4 green onions, cut diagonally into 1-inch pieces**
- **2 Tbsp. snipped fresh dill or 1 1/2 tsp. dried dillweed**
- **1 recipe Dill-Tomato Topper(below)(optional)**

1. Preheat oven to 350° F. In a large bowl beat eggs; stir in remaining ingredients except Dill-Tomato Topper. Pour into a greased 9-inch quiche dish.

2. Bake, uncovered, for 40 to 45 minutes or until a knife inserted near the center comes out clean.

3. Let stand for 10 minutes. If desired, top with Dill-Tomato Topper. Makes 6 servings.

DILL-TOMATO TOPPER: In a medium mixing bowl stir together 2 large tomatoes, chopped; 1 1/2 teaspoons snipped fresh dill; and a dash salt.

Each serving: 313 cal., 21 g total fat (7 g sat. fat), 158 mg chol., 527 mg sodium, 18 g carbo., 2 g dietary fiber, 13 g pro. Daily Values: 18% vit. A, 25% vit. C, 27% calcium, 10% iron.

Hedy's Black Walnut Cake

If you're not a fan of the black walnut's distinctive flavor, of course you can use regular walnuts.

PREP: 25 minutes **BAKE:** 65 minutes **COOL:** 1 hour

- 1½ cups chopped black walnuts or English walnuts, toasted
- 2 Tbsp. all-purpose flour
- 1¾ cups granulated sugar
- 1½ cups butter, melted
- 1 cup packed dark brown sugar
- 5 eggs
- 2 Tbsp. rum or milk
- ½ tsp. vanilla
- 2⅔ cups all-purpose flour
- ¾ cup carob powder* or unsweetened cocoa powder
- ½ tsp. baking powder
- ¼ tsp. salt
- 1 cup milk
- 1 recipe Rum Glaze (below) (optional)

1. Preheat oven to 325° F. Grease and flour a 10-inch square tube pan or a 10-inch fluted tube pan; set aside. In a small bowl stir together nuts and the 2 tablespoons flour; set aside.

2. In a large mixing bowl stir together granulated sugar, melted butter, and brown sugar until combined. Using a wooden spoon, beat in eggs, one at a time. Stir in 2 tablespoons rum or milk and vanilla.

3. In a medium bowl stir together the 2⅔ cups flour, carob or cocoa powder, baking powder, and salt. Stir flour mixture into egg mixture. Gradually stir in milk. Fold in nut mixture.

4. Pour batter into the prepared pan. Bake about 65 minutes or until a toothpick inserted near the center comes out clean. Let cool in pan on a wire rack for 10 minutes. Remove from pan. Let stand for 1 hour. If desired, drizzle with Rum Glaze. Cool completely. Makes 12 servings.

RUM GLAZE: In a small bowl combine 1⅓ cups sifted powdered sugar; 2 tablespoons butter, melted; and 1 tablespoon rum or milk. Stir in 1 tablespoon whipping cream or milk. If necessary, add additional cream or milk, 1 teaspoon at a time, until glaze reaches drizzling consistency.

***TEST KITCHEN TIP:** Carob powder has a sweet, mildly chocolaty flavor and is available at health food stores and the health-food aisles of some supermarkets.

Each serving: 540 cal., 29 g total fat (14 g sat. fat), 122 mg chol., 286 mg sodium, 66 g carbo., 3 g dietary fiber, 8 g pro. Daily Values: 19% vit. A, 1% vit. C, 8% calcium, 11% iron.

Dad's Rolls

To make these rolls extra crusty, put a baking pan of water in the oven along with the rolls to create steam.

PREP: 40 minutes **RISE:** 60 minutes **BAKE:** 25 minutes

- 1 Tbsp. active dry yeast
- 2 cups warm water (105° to 115° F)
- 1 Tbsp. sugar
- 1¼ tsp. salt
- 5¼ to 5¾ cups all-purpose flour
- Olive oil
- Yellow cornmeal
- Coarse salt (optional)

1. In a large mixing bowl dissolve yeast in the warm water. Stir in sugar and salt. With a wooden spoon, stir in as much of the flour as you can. Turn out onto a lightly floured surface and knead in enough of the remaining flour to make a moderately stiff dough that is smooth and elastic (6 to 8 minutes). (Or, to prepare dough in a stand mixer with a dough hook, add flour to yeast mixture, 1 cup at a time, beating with the dough hook on low speed until a moderately stiff, smooth dough forms.)

2. Lightly coat a large bowl with olive oil. Shape dough into a ball; place in oiled bowl. Turn dough once; cover with a clean kitchen towel. Let rise in a warm place until double in size (45 to 60 minutes).

3. Punch dough down. Turn dough out onto a lightly floured board or surface. Cover; let rest for 10 minutes.

4. Grease a very large baking sheet or two smaller baking sheets; sprinkle heavily with cornmeal. Shape dough into 14 round rolls. Place rolls on prepared baking sheet. Let rise for 5 minutes.

5. Preheat oven to 400° F. Slash roll tops in 2 or 3 places with a sharp knife. Brush rolls with water. If desired, sprinkle with coarse salt. Place an empty baking pan on the bottom rack of an unheated oven. Pour boiling water into the pan to a depth of 1 inch. Place rolls on second rack. Bake for 25 to 30 minutes or until crusty and golden brown. Remove from pan; cool slightly on a wire rack. Serve warm. Makes 14 rolls.

Each roll: 182 cal., 1 g total fat (0 g sat. fat), 0 mg chol., 417 mg sodium, 37 g carbo., 1 g dietary fiber, 5 g pro. Daily Values: 1% calcium 13% iron.

"IT'S NOT THAT WE LIKE TO COOK TOGETHER AS MUCH AS WE LIKE TO COOK FOR EACH OTHER." –Neil Leiter

Dad's Rolls

Hedy's Oatmeal Cookies

Choose any dried fruit, such as raisins, currants, cranberries, cherries, or snipped apricots, for this old-fashioned favorite.

PREP: 20 minutes **BAKE:** 9 minutes per batch

- 1/2 cup butter, softened
- 1/2 cup packed dark brown sugar
- 1/4 cup granulated sugar
- 1 tsp. baking soda
- 1/2 tsp. salt
- 1 egg
- 1/4 cup pure maple syrup or maple-flavored syrup
- 1 tsp. vanilla
- 1 1/2 cups all-purpose flour
- 2 cups quick-cooking rolled oats
- 1 cup dried blueberries

1. Preheat oven to 350° F. In a large mixing bowl beat butter with an electric mixer on medium to high speed for 30 seconds. Add brown and granulated sugars, baking soda, and salt. Beat until combined, scraping sides of bowl occasionally. Beat in egg, maple syrup, and vanilla until combined. Beat in as much of the flour as you can with the mixer. Stir in remaining flour with a wooden spoon. Stir in the rolled oats and blueberries.

2. Using a small cookie scoop (about 1 1/4 inches in diameter) or a spoon, drop dough 2 inches apart onto an ungreased cookie sheet. Bake for 9 to 11 minutes or until edges are golden brown. Let stand for 1 minute on the cookie sheet. Remove and cool on a wire rack. Makes about 48 cookies.

Each cookie: 80 cal., 2 g total fat (1 g sat. fat), 10 mg chol., 74 mg sodium, 13 g carbo., 1 g dietary fiber, 1 g pro. Daily Values: 2% vit. A, 1% calcium, 2% iron.

Hedy's Black Walnut Cake and Hedy's Oatmeal Cookies

Lemon-and-Spice Applesauce

Lemon-and-Spice Applesauce

Lightly mashing the apples keeps the applesauce chunky.

PREP: 45 minutes **COOK:** 40 minutes

- 4 3/4 to 5 1/2 lb. cooking apples, such as Granny Smith or Golden Delicious (15 cups), peeled, cored, and sliced
- 2 1/2 cups water
- 1 to 1 1/2 cups packed brown sugar
- 3 Tbsp. finely shredded lemon peel
- 3/4 cup lemon juice
- 1 1/2 tsp. apple pie spice or 2 tsp. ground cinnamon
- 1 Tbsp. vanilla

1. In a 6-quart heavy kettle or Dutch oven combine apples, water, brown sugar, lemon peel, lemon juice, and apple pie spice or cinnamon. Bring to boiling; reduce heat. Simmer, covered, for 40 minutes or until the apples are very soft, stirring occasionally.

2. Remove from heat. Stir in vanilla. Mash mixture lightly with the back of a large wooden spoon. Serve warm or cover and chill before serving. Makes about 8 1/2 cups (16 servings).

Each serving: 127 cal., 0 g total fat (0 g sat. fat), 0 mg chol., 7 mg sodium, 33 g carbo., 3 g dietary fiber, 0 g pro. Daily Values: 1% vit. A, 17% vit. C, 2% calcium, 3% iron.

Pear-Peach Crisp

Pear-Peach Crisp

Farmer's market fans: Try this luscious way to use the bumper crop of the week. For fall, the crisp also works well with apples.

PREP: 25 minutes **BAKE:** 55 minutes

- 6 cups peeled, sliced pears (about 6 medium)
- 2 cups peeled, pitted, and sliced fresh peaches (2 to 3 medium) or 2 cups frozen, unsweetened peach slices, thawed
- 1/2 cup raisins
- 3 Tbsp. packed brown sugar
- 3/4 tsp. ground ginger
- 1 1/2 cups quick-cooking rolled oats
- 1/2 cup Grape Nuts® cereal
- 1/2 cup chopped walnuts or pecans
- 1/4 cup granulated sugar
- 1/4 cup packed brown sugar
- 1/2 cup butter, melted
- 1 cup orange juice or apple juice
- Vanilla ice cream (optional)

1. Preheat oven to 350° F. In a large bowl toss together sliced pears and peaches, raisins, the 3 tablespoons brown sugar, and 1/2 teaspoon of the ginger. Spread in the bottom of a 3-quart rectangular baking dish.

2. For topping, in a small bowl combine oats, cereal, nuts, the granulated sugar, 1/4 cup brown sugar, and 1/4 teaspoon of the ginger. Stir in the butter. Spoon over the fruit. Pour orange or apple juice evenly over the topping.

3. Bake, uncovered, about 55 minutes or until topping is golden and filling is bubbly. Transfer to a wire rack. Cool slightly. Serve warm with ice cream, if desired. Makes 12 servings.

Each serving: 303 cal., 13 g total fat (6 g sat. fat), 22 mg chol., 116 mg sodium, 47 g carbo., 5 g dietary fiber, 4 g pro. Daily Values: 12% vit. A, 26% vit. C, 4% calcium, 10% iron.

"I ALWAYS COOK FROM WHAT REALLY LOOKS WONDERFUL. IT'S MORE FUN TO GET PUSHED TO DO DIFFERENT THINGS."

—Carrie Knowles

Celebration Roasts

AS ENTERTAINING SEASON REVS UP, CHANCES ARE A FAVORITE ROAST WILL BE MAKING ITS APPEARANCE at your dinner table. If you're investing time and money in one of these special cuts of meat, you'll want to be sure of two things: It's as handsome as can be, and it's as tasty as it is handsome.

No one can deny the convenience of cooking a roast—the oven does most of the work—but here's some savory advice: Don't wing it. Follow the roasting guidelines on page 395 using an oven-safe meat thermometer and you'll achieve spectacular results every time.

To go with that perfect roast, the produce aisle now offers a few new sidekicks for creating an exciting, mouth-watering presentation. That means you can set aside the traditional carrots, onions, and potatoes for their more exotic cousins.

Pork Rib Crown Roast

There's no denying it: This roast is a WOW. Pork roasts are leaner these days, so don't overcook them. Place your roast in a 325° F oven until the juices run clear and the center is pink and juicy. Before serving, fill the center with a favorite cooked bread stuffing sprinkled with red and green apples, then surround it with a barely-simmered compote of dried fruits (try apricots, plums, figs, and raisins) and fresh sage.

Beef Tenderloin Roast

Watch your cooking times with this roast. You'll be cooking at a higher temperature (425° F) than with other roasts. A tenderloin is oh-so-grown-up and elegant, so why not pull out all the stops with equally elegant baby vegetables (here, braised baby cauliflower and pearl carrots with dill) and a classic French sauce, such as peppercorn or bordelaise.

Beef Ribeye Roast

Trim the roast of some, but not all, of its fat, and roast the meat fat side up. As the beef cooks, the fat melts and adds its flavor. The naturally robust nature of this cut finds a happy match with such aromatic root vegetables as sweet potatoes and turnips, most of the onion family members (including garlic), wild mushrooms, and starchy squashes—all of which sweeten up as they caramelize in the roasting pan.

Veal Rib Roast

"Velvety" best describes the texture of a well-prepared veal roast. If you need to special order this roast from the butcher, ask for the chine bone (or backbone) to be removed. Toss on a mass of fresh herbs, such as thyme or basil, or rub the roast with garlic and olive oil.

Boneless Pork Double Top Loin Roast

A double top loin is simply two top loins tied together. Ask the butcher to do this for you. Cooking two loins together yields a tender, succulent roast, especially if you rub first with olive oil, dry mustard, and fresh herbs. Match with roasted fruits that have firm enough flesh to stand up to long cooking, such as apples and slightly under-ripe pears like the russet-hued Seckel pear shown.

Leg of Lamb

Be sure to remove the "fell," or thin outer skin, from the roast before cooking. Lamb benefits from pungent herb or spice rubs. Try caraway, marjoram, oregano, paprika, curry powder, or a mix of several of them. Or liven the mint-lamb relationship by using a fresh mint rub. A Mediterranean medley of steamed baby artichokes, tiny hard-cooked quail eggs, and fresh lemon makes an appealing accompaniment.

ROASTING BASICS

- Preheat oven to the desired temperature. Use meat taken directly from the refrigerator. Place the roast, fat side up, on a rack in a shallow roasting pan. Season as desired.
- Insert an oven-safe thermometer into the thickest portion of the roast, not resting on fat or bone. Do not add water. Do not cover.
- Roast the meat according to the Roasting Chart below, until the thermometer registers the Final Roasting Temperature. For accuracy, double-check the temperature with an instant-read thermometer.
- As a general rule of thumb, add vegetables and fruits to the roasting pan approximately 30 to 45 minutes before the end of the roasting time.
- Remove the roast from the oven; cover with foil. Let stand for 10 to 15 minutes until the temperature reaches the desired doneness.
- Figure on four servings per pound of boneless meat.

ROASTING CHART

CUT	OVEN TEMPERATURE	WEIGHT	APPROXIMATE ROASTING TIME	FINAL ROASTING TEMPERATURE	FINAL DONENESS AND TEMPERATURE
Pork rib crown roast	325° F	6 to 8 pounds	2½ to 3¼ hours	155°	160° medium
Boneless pork double top loin roast	325° F	3 to 4 pounds	1½ to 2¼ hours	155°	160° medium
		4 to 5 pounds	2 to 2½ hours	155°	160° medium
Beef ribeye roast	350° F	3 to 4 pounds	1½ to 1¾ hours	135°	145° medium rare
			1¾ to 2 hours	150°	160° medium
		4 to 6 pounds	1¾ to 2 hours	135°	145° medium rare
			2 to 2½ hours	150°	160° medium
Beef tenderloin roast	425° F	2 to 3 pounds	35 to 40 minutes	135°	145° medium rare
			45 to 50 minutes	150°	160° medium
		4 to 5 pounds	50 to 60 minutes	135°	145° medium rare
			60 to 70 minutes	150°	160° medium
Leg of lamb (whole leg with bone)	325° F	5 to 7 pounds	1¾ to 2¼ hours	140°	145° medium rare
			2¼ to 2¾ hours	155°	160° medium
		7 to 8 pounds	2¼ to 2¾ hours	140°	145° medium rare
			2½ to 3 hours	155°	160° medium
Veal rib roast	325° F	4 to 5 pounds	1½ to 2¼ hours	155°	160° medium

For information about roasting meat cuts not listed here, please contact the National Cattleman's Beef Association at www.beef.org or www.veal.org; the National Pork Board at www.otherwhitemeat.com; or the American Lamb Council at www.lambchef.com.

Better Breakfast Loaf

BEFORE BAKERY-FRESH ARTISANAL BREAD BECAME THE RISING STAR OF DISCERNING palates, the good old American homemade white loaf was king. That bread was easy on the baker. There was no need to make a starter three weeks ahead. The loaf yielded big, soft slices. And best of all, the bread was versatile: every bit as good served warm with soup as it was toasted for breakfast.

Our Rosemary-Raisin Bread is in the tradition of classic homemade loaves, only—we think—a little better. It has milk and butter for an extra-tender, tasty slice. An egg yolk leaves a creamy tint and acts as a natural preservative. The unlikely duet of raisins and rosemary strikes a savory-sweet chord that works as well with omelets as it does for French toast. Try it toasted and slathered with honey butter or topped with cream cheese and smoked salmon. It's also wonderful for scooping up the last of the scrambled eggs.

Rosemary-Raisin Bread

We were inspired to create this rosemary-raisin loaf by Sue and Julie Campoy, the mother and daughter team who own Julienne, a beautiful brasserie in San Marino, California. We feasted on a fabulous breakfast and sampled their rosemary-raisin bread. See if you agree.

PREP: 30 minutes **RISE:** 75 minutes **BAKE:** 40 minutes

- **6 to 6½ cups all-purpose flour**
- **2 pkg. active dry yeast**
- **2½ cups milk**
- **3 Tbsp. sugar**
- **2 Tbsp. butter**
- **2 tsp. salt**
- **1 egg yolk**
- **1½ cups golden or dark raisins**
- **4 tsp. dried rosemary, crushed**
- **1 egg yolk, beaten**
- **1 Tbsp. milk**

1. In a very large mixing bowl stir together 3 cups of the flour and the yeast; set aside. In a medium saucepan heat and stir the 2½ cups milk, the sugar, butter, and salt until warm (120° to 130° F) and butter is almost melted. Add warm milk mixture to flour mixture. Add 1 egg yolk; stir until combined.

2. Beat with an electric mixer on low speed for 30 seconds, scraping the side of the bowl constantly. Beat mixture on high speed for 3 minutes more. Sprinkle raisins and rosemary onto flour mixture (see photo 1). Using a wooden spoon, stir in as much of the remaining flour as you can (see photo 2).

3. Turn dough out onto a lightly floured surface. Knead in enough of the remaining flour to make a moderately stiff dough that is smooth and elastic (see photo 3), about 6 to 8 minutes total. Shape dough into a ball. Place dough in a lightly greased bowl; turn once to grease the surface. Cover and let rise in a warm place until double in size (about 45 to 60 minutes).

4. Punch dough down (see photo 4). Turn out onto a lightly floured surface. Divide dough in half. Cover and let rest for 10 minutes. Lightly grease two 8×4×2-inch or 9×5×3-inch loaf pans. Shape each half of the dough into a loaf. Place in prepared pans. Cover and let rise in a warm place until nearly double in size (30 to 40 minutes).

5. Meanwhile, preheat oven to 375° F. For the glaze, combine the remaining egg yolk and milk; brush lightly onto tops of risen dough. Using a serrated knife, make a long shallow cut down the length of dough in each pan.

6. Bake about 40 minutes or until the loaf is golden brown and crusty. The bread should sound hollow when tapped. Cover loosely with foil during the last 10 minutes of baking to prevent overbrowning, if necessary. Loosen bread and remove from pans immediately. Cool on wire racks. Makes 2 loaves (32 slices).

Each slice: 135 cal., 2 g total fat (1 g sat. fat), 13 mg chol., 166 mg sodium, 26 g carbo., 1 g dietary fiber, 4 g pro. Daily Values: 2% vit. A, 1% vit. C, 3% calcium, 8% iron.

1

2

3

4

Purely Persimmon

THE APPLE OF THE ORIENT IS WHAT SOME old-timers call this soft-textured winter fruit, although we think it looks more like a tomato in color and in shape. Ripe persimmons have a shiny, brilliant orange skin and red-orange meat. The flavor has a spicy sweetness, although people who've bitten into an unripe persimmon know that it can have an astringent, puckery quality. When cooking with persimmons, you usually mash and strain them to use the pulp, as we've done for the coffee cake and pudding recipes opposite. So pull out your strainer and rediscover an old favorite.

Persimmon-Walnut Coffee Cake

PREP: 45 minutes **BAKE:** 1 hour

- 4 fresh, very ripe Hachiya persimmons* (about $1^3/_4$ lb.) or 1 cup applesauce
- $^1/_3$ cup packed light brown sugar
- 1 Tbsp. all-purpose flour
- 2 cups all-purpose flour
- 2 tsp. baking powder
- $^1/_2$ tsp. baking soda
- $^1/_2$ tsp. salt
- $^1/_2$ cup butter, softened
- 1 cup granulated sugar
- 1 tsp. vanilla
- 2 eggs
- 1 8-oz. carton dairy sour cream
- 1 recipe Walnut Streusel(below)

1. Preheat oven to 350° F. Grease and flour a 9-inch springform pan; set aside.

2. Press persimmons into pulp (see below). (You should have 1 cup persimmon pulp.) In a small bowl stir together brown sugar and 1 tablespoon flour; stir in persimmon pulp or applesauce. Set aside.

3. In a medium bowl stir together the 2 cups flour, baking powder, baking soda, and salt; set aside. In a large bowl beat butter with an electric mixer on medium to high speed for 30 seconds. Beat in granulated sugar and vanilla. Add eggs, one at a time, beating after each addition. Add flour mixture and sour cream alternately to beaten mixture, beating just until combined after each addition. (The batter will be stiff.)

4. Spread half of the batter into prepared pan, building up a 1-inch rim of batter around edges of pan. Spoon persimmon mixture into center of pan. Carefully spoon remaining batter in small mounds, covering persimmon mixture. Sprinkle Walnut Streusel over batter.

5. Bake about 1 hour or until toothpick inserted into cake near center comes out clean. (The filling will sink as coffee cake bakes.) Cool in pan on a wire rack for 10 minutes. Loosen and remove sides. Cool completely on wire rack. Makes 12 servings.

WALNUT STREUSEL: In a medium bowl stir together $^1/_2$ cup all-purpose flour, $^1/_2$ cup granulated sugar, and $^1/_2$ teaspoon cinnamon. Cut in $^1/_4$ cup butter until mixture resembles coarse crumbs. Stir in $^1/_2$ cup chopped walnuts; set aside.

***TEST KITCHEN TIP:** Store ripe persimmons in the refrigerator. Let persimmons stand at room temperature about an hour before using. Peel persimmons or scrape pulp from peel with a metal spoon. Press persimmons through a coarse single-mesh strainer until you have pulp.

Nutrition facts per serving: 410 cal., 20 g total fat (11 g sat. fat), 77 mg chol., 364 mg sodium, 53 g carbo., 1 g dietary fiber, and 5 g pro. Daily Values: 10% vit. C, 9% calcium, and 10% iron.

THE VARIETIES

■ **Fuyu:** The smaller, tomato-shaped Fuyu persimmon is firm when ripe. Because its flesh is firm, it can be rinsed and eaten out-of-hand or may be peeled and sliced for salads.

■ **Hachiya:** This variety is the most widely available in the United States and is also called the Japanese persimmon or Kaki. Let the heart-shaped Hachiya ripen until very soft, when it has a smooth, creamy texture. It's great to use in baked goods.

Persimmon Pudding

Serve this warm, bready baked pudding in squares and top it with a spoonful of whipped cream.

PREP: 20 minutes **BAKE:** 35 minutes

- 4 fresh, very ripe Hachiya persimmons (about $1^3/_4$ lb.)
- 2 tsp. butter, melted
- 1 cup all-purpose flour
- 1 tsp. baking powder
- Dash ground cinnamon
- $^1/_2$ cup light cream or half-and-half
- $^1/_2$ cup buttermilk or sour milk**
- $^1/_2$ tsp. baking soda
- 1 egg
- 1 cup sugar
- $^1/_2$ tsp. finely shredded orange peel
- 2 Tbsp. butter, melted
- Whipped cream (optional)

1. Grease an 8×8×2-inch baking pan with the 2 teaspoons of butter. Set aside. Press persimmons* into pulp (see below left). (You should have 1 cup pulp.)

2. In a small bowl stir together flour, baking powder, and cinnamon; set aside. In another small bowl combine light cream, buttermilk, and baking soda; set aside.

3. In a medium bowl beat egg; stir in persimmon pulp, sugar, and orange peel. Add flour mixture and buttermilk mixture alternately to persimmon mixture, stirring well after each addition. Stir in 2 tablespoons melted butter. Pour into prepared pan.

4. Bake in a 325° F. oven for 35 minutes. Serve warm with whipped cream, if desired. Makes 6 to 8 servings.

****TEST KITCHEN TIP:** To make $^1/_2$ cup sour milk, place $1^1/_2$ teaspoons lemon juice or vinegar in a glass measuring cup. Add enough milk to make $^1/_2$ cup liquid; stir. Let the mixture stand for 5 minutes before using.

Each serving: 336 cal., 9 g total fat (5 g sat. fat), 58 mg chol., 268 mg sodium, 61 g carbo., 1 g dietary fiber, 5 g pro. Daily Values: 23% vit. A, 43% vit. C, 10% calcium, 11% iron.

Pumpkin Chocolate Cheesecake Bars

DO THE PUMPKIN MASH

Not all pumpkins are created equal. Cooking pumpkins weigh, on average, from 4 to 7 pounds. When you see them in the market, they're often called "sugar" or "pie" pumpkins.

From a 4- to $4\frac{1}{2}$-pound pie pumpkin, you will get about $3\frac{1}{2}$ cups cooked pumpkin puree. Cut a pumpkin into large pieces. Remove seeds and strings. Arrange pieces in a single layer, skin sides up, in a large shallow baking pan. Cover with foil. Bake in a 375° F oven for 1 to $1\frac{1}{2}$ hours or until tender. Cool. Remove pulp, discarding peel. Place pulp, half at a time, in a food processor bowl. Cover and process until smooth, scraping sides as needed. Line a strainer with a double layer of 100-percent-cotton cheesecloth. Transfer to a strainer; press to remove liquid. Use in recipes calling for cooked pumpkin puree.

IT'S A PRETTY SAFE BET THAT NO VEGETABLE TICKLES our kids' collective fancy like the pumpkin. Is it any wonder? While kids tend to view most vegetables as something you simply eat—oftentimes with less than relish—the colorful pumpkin is blessed with multiple personalities. In fact, it's literally a seasonal smorgasbord of edible and decorative possibilities.

Of course, a carved pumpkin is the candle-lit symbol of every child's favorite spooky day. But you can use one for a centerpiece and toast the seeds to make a snack. Furthermore, the pumpkin doesn't even take its role as a veggie all that seriously: about the only thing that stands between it and some delicious desserts is a little sugar and spice.

Pumpkin Chocolate Cheesecake Bars

These bars are special when they're made with your own homemade pumpkin puree. But canned pumpkin also works beautifully for this recipe, and no one is likely to be the wiser.

PREP: 1½ hours **BAKE:** 55 minutes

- 2 8-oz. pkg. cream cheese, softened
- 1¾ cups sugar
- 3 large eggs
- 1 cup cooked and pureed pumpkin (see left) or canned pumpkin
- ½ tsp. pumpkin pie spice
- ½ tsp. vanilla
- ½ tsp. salt
- 6 oz. semisweet chocolate, cut up
- 2 Tbsp. butter
- 1 recipe Graham Cracker Crust(below)
- 1¼ cups dairy sour cream
- ½ cup sugar
- Grated fresh nutmeg

1. Preheat oven to 325° F. For filling, in a large bowl combine cream cheese and 1¾ cups sugar; beat with an electric mixer on medium speed until mixed. Add eggs, one at a time, beating on low speed after each addition until just combined. Stir in the cooked or canned pumpkin, pumpkin pie spice, vanilla, and salt. Pour 1¼ cups of the filling into a medium bowl. Set both bowls of filling aside.

2. In a small saucepan melt chocolate and butter over very low heat, stirring frequently until smooth. Stir melted chocolate into the 1¼ cups reserved filling. Carefully spread the chocolate filling evenly over Graham Cracker Crust. Bake for 15 minutes. Remove from oven. Carefully pour remaining pumpkin filling over baked chocolate layer, spreading evenly.

3. Bake for 40 to 45 minutes or until mixture is slightly puffed around edges and just set in center. Remove from oven; cool for 30 minutes. Meanwhile, combine sour cream and ¼ cup sugar. Cover; let stand at room temperature while bars cool.

4. Gently spread the sour cream layer onto bars. Cool. Refrigerate for several hours or overnight before cutting. Sprinkle with nutmeg just before serving. To serve, loosen the edges by moving a knife around the pan. Keep any remaining bars refrigerated. Makes 24 servings.

GRAHAM CRACKER CRUST: Lightly grease a 13×9×2-inch baking pan. In a large mixing bowl stir together 1¼ cups graham cracker crumbs and ¼ cup sugar. Add ⅓ cup melted butter; mix thoroughly. Press evenly onto the bottom of the prepared pan; set aside.

Each serving: 256 cal., 16 g total fat (9 g sat. fat), 62 mg chol., 155 mg sodium, 27 g carbo., 1 g fiber, 3 g pro. Daily Values: 15% vit. A, 1% vit. C, 3% calcium, 5% iron.

MORE FUN IDEAS

Just one pumpkin will never do. You'll need several to sample all the fun ways you and your kids can make the most with pumpkins. For instance:

- **Create a centerpiece:** A hollowed pumpkin is a fitting place to tuck a small pot of mums or an arrangement of fresh or dried flowers. For fresh flowers, you can ease a glass of water inside to secretly house the blossoms. A bit of sand in the pumpkin helps stabilize dried flowers.
- **Toast the seeds:** First, separate the seeds from the pulp and gently rinse them to remove pulp and any strings. Drain seeds well. Place them in a bowl and toss with about a tablespoon of oil. Spread seeds onto a waxed-paper-lined 15×10×1-inch baking pan. Let stand for 24 to 48 hours or until seeds are dry. Remove the waxed paper from the baking pan. Toast seeds in a 325° F oven for 40 minutes, stirring once or twice. Season to taste with salt.

You Say Vanilla

WHOEVER COINED THE PHRASE "PLAIN VANILLA" obviously didn't know beans—vanilla beans, that is. The fruit of a tropical orchid, vanilla beans have an exotic aroma and a heavenly range of flavor notes.

For everyday cooking, vanilla extract is just fine. But when you want to pin a badge of vanilla authenticity on your cooking, use beans. Half a bean has about as much flavor as one teaspoon of vanilla extract. To use, cut as much of the bean (or seed pod, really) as you'll need, then slit it lengthwise. Scrape the seeds from the pod, and add both to your dish. Save the remainder for a future use. Store the whole beans in an airtight jar in a cool, dry place. Look for vanilla beans that are 5 to 7 inches long, a sure sign they've grown to full ripeness. Stay away from partial or cut beans, a sign the bean might have been moldy. The bean should glisten and be leathery but supple—never dry or brittle.

Creamy Desserts

Using between 1/2 to a whole bean, scrape the seeds into the milk when making your favorite custard, crème brûlée, or rice pudding. Cook the custard mixture to bring out the flavor of the seeds, then remove the seeds before cooling.

Hot Chocolate

Scrape the seeds from 1/4 of a vanilla bean into a single serving of hot chocolate. Whip the seeds from an additional 1/4 of a bean into some whipping cream to use as a topper for the hot chocolate. For fun, serve a vanilla bean as a stir stick.

Hot Cereals

Add 1/2 of a bean, split and seeded, to the water or milk when cooking four servings of oatmeal. Remove the bean before serving. You can also use vanilla to flavor cream of wheat, grits, cornmeal mush, and rice during cooking.

November

HOME IS WHERE THE HEART IS–ESPECIALLY WHEN IT'S TIME FOR THE FAMILY FEAST OF THE YEAR.

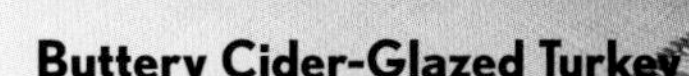

Buttery Cider-Glazed Turkey

Harvest Breadsticks

Maple-Pumpkin Cheesecake

Homecoming Feast

Plus...

Rosemary Roasted Vegetables

Sparkling Kumquat Salad

Keeping the Feast

Butterscotch Meringue Pie

Plus...

THE HARVEST IS IN WITH PUMPKINS, SQUASH, PEARS, AND APPLES, SO NOW IT'S TIME TO PLAN THE TRADITIONAL FEAST, WITH A FEW NEW TWISTS.

Roast Turkey with Roasted Garlic and Sweet Onion Jam

Pesto Rolls

homecoming FEAST

IT'S THAT TIME OF YEAR WHEN YOUR FAVORITE PEOPLE—AND FOOD—COME TOGETHER AGAIN. HERE'S HOW TO MAKE IT ALL HAPPEN.

Pomegranate Starter

Served in individual cups, this warm, sweet starter soup is a three-ingredient sensation. Look for pomegranate juice in the refrigerated produce section of grocery stores, health food stores, or online at www.pomwonderful.com.

PREP: 15 minutes **STAND:** 10 minutes

- **$3\frac{1}{2}$ cups pomegranate juice or red grape juice**
- **1 2-inch strip tangerine peel**
- **$\frac{1}{2}$ tsp. coriander seeds, lightly crushed, or $\frac{1}{4}$ tsp. ground coriander**

1. In a medium saucepan heat pomegranate juice just until simmering; remove from heat. Add tangerine peel and coriander; let stand, covered, for 10 minutes.

2. Strain juice through a fine-mesh sieve. Discard the solids. To serve, ladle juice into small heatproof cups. Makes 10 to 12 servings (about 3 ounces each).

Each serving: 53 cal., 0 g total fat, 0 mg chol., 4 mg sodium, 13 g carbo., 0 g fiber, 0 g pro. Daily Values: 16% vit. C, 2% iron.

Pomegranate Starter

A Time to Remember

From the sweet squeeze of a toddler's little arms around your neck to the comfy hold-tight hugs of your favorite uncle, when everyone comes home again, it's an experience to savor. No matter what event you're celebrating—a gathering of old college chums, Grandpa's 80th birthday, or the annual Thanksgiving dinner—your home is about to become a sanctuary for loved ones. Plan for good cheer and great food that will make this a homecoming to remember for years to come.

Be sure to serve foods that stir up warm memories—a few tried-and-true favorites and traditional family fare. The pièce de résistance? A turkey, of course, whetting appetites with the savory smells of the season as it roasts. Set out wines, glasses, and a cork puller, and let people help themselves. For the younger set, have a stash of soft drinks chilled. If the weather's nippy, a warm mulled cider simmering in a slow cooker is yummy.

Encourage those who want to help to step up to the stove and strut their stuffing. Put kids to work mashing potatoes—don't forget the extra aprons! Leave time to step back and bask in the warmth of your family's familiar routine of working as a crew: chopping and teasing, mashing and laughing, stirring and noshing. Better yet, capture those moments on film. (A teenager and a digital camera are incredible together.)

Forgotten anything? It's OK. You're with family and friends. Just have fun!

Greens with Spiced Corn Bread

Roasted Beet and Goat Cheese Salad

If you find fresh beets with the greens still attached, go ahead and include them as part of the mixed greens to add color.

PREP: 30 minutes **ROAST:** 40 minutes

- 1 lb. red baby beets or small beets, rinsed and trimmed
- 1 Tbsp. olive oil
- 1/3 cup olive oil
- 1/4 cup white wine vinegar
- 2 tsp. Dijon-style mustard
- 1/4 tsp. salt
- 1/8 tsp. ground black pepper
- 2 Tbsp. finely chopped shallots
- 10 cups baby salad greens (mesclun) or other mild salad greens
- 1 8-oz. tube semisoft goat cheese (chèvre or Montrachet), cut into 1/2-inch rounds

1. Preheat oven to 425° F. If using small beets, halve or quarter. Place beets in a single layer in a shallow baking pan. Drizzle with the 1 tablespoon olive oil; toss to coat. Season with salt and pepper; toss again. Cover with foil; roast for 25 minutes. Uncover; roast about 15 minutes more or until fork-tender. Cool; peel the small beets if using. (Baby beets do not need to be peeled.) Cut beets into 1/2-inch cubes. Place cubes in a medium bowl; set aside.

2. Meanwhile, for dressing, in a screw-top jar combine the 1/3 cup olive oil, the white wine vinegar, Dijon-style mustard, salt, and pepper. Cover; shake well.

3. Add shallots to beets; drizzle with 1 tablespoon of the dressing. Toss to coat; set aside. Place the greens in a very large bowl; drizzle with remaining dressing and toss to coat.

4. Divide salad greens among 8 salad plates. Top each serving with a slice of cheese and some beet mixture. Makes 8 servings.

MAKE-AHEAD TIP: Roast beets and make dressing up to 24 hours in advance. Cover and store in the refrigerator.

Each serving: 237 cal., 19 g total fat (7 g sat. fat), 22 mg chol., 350 mg sodium, 8 g carbo., 2 g fiber, 8 g pro. Daily Values: 21% vit. A, 11% vit. C, 12% calcium, 8% iron.

Greens with Spiced Corn Bread

Packaged corn muffin mix turns into oversized croutons for a fantastic flavor accent to a mix of salad greens. The croutons are dusted with sugar and spices.

PREP: 20 minutes **BAKE:** 20 minutes **COOL:** 10 minutes

- 1 recipe Buttermilk Corn Bread (below) or purchased corn bread
- 6 cups arugula, baby red lettuce, and/or baby mixed salad greens
- 1/4 cup olive oil
- 3 Tbsp. lemon juice
- 1/2 tsp. coarse salt or 1/4 tsp. salt
- 1/4 tsp. ground black pepper
- 2 Tbsp. butter or margarine
- 1 Tbsp. sugar
- 1/4 tsp. pumpkin pie spice

1. Prepare Buttermilk Corn Bread, if using. Wash greens; pat dry. For dressing, in a screw-top jar combine olive oil, lemon juice, salt, and pepper. Cover; shake well.

2. Cut corn bread in half crosswise to form two 5×4½-inch rectangles. In a large skillet melt 1 tablespoon of the butter over medium heat. Add one of the corn bread rectangles; cook until browned on top and bottom, turning once. Remove. Repeat with remaining 1 tablespoon butter and other corn bread rectangle.

3. In a small bowl stir together sugar and pumpkin pie spice; sprinkle onto corn bread rectangles. Cut each corn bread rectangle into six 5×3/4-inch croutons. (You will have 12 rectangular croutons total.)

4. To serve, shake dressing and toss with greens. Place a corn bread crouton on each of 12 salad plates. Top with greens. Makes 12 servings.

BUTTERMILK CORN BREAD: Preheat oven to 400° F. Prepare one 8½-ounce package corn muffin mix according to package directions, except add 1 egg and substitute 1/3 cup buttermilk for the liquid. Pour batter into a greased 9×5×3-inch loaf pan. Bake about 20 minutes or until a wooden toothpick inserted into the center comes out clean. Cool in pan on a wire rack for 10 minutes. Remove from pan. Cool on a wire rack. (Loaf will only be about 2 inches thick.)

MAKE-AHEAD TIP: Prepare and bake corn bread up to 24 hours in advance. Store tightly wrapped at room temperature. Just before serving, proceed with step 2.

Each serving: 155 cal., 9 g total fat (2 g sat. fat), 23 mg chol., 225 mg sodium, 16 g carbo., 0 g fiber, 2 g pro. Daily Values: 7% vit. A, 6% vit. C, 2% calcium, 4% iron.

Brown Bread Squash Stuffing

Buttery Cider-Glazed Turkey

Two all-American standards, turkey and apples, combine to provide a double dose of incredible taste. Try Golden Delicious, Gravenstein, Granny Smith, Winesap, Rhode Island Greening, or Braeburn apples. Use the apple-tinged drippings to make a gravy like none you've ever tasted.

PREP: 45 minutes **ROAST:** 3¼ hours **STAND:** 15 minutes

- 1 12- to 14-lb. turkey
- Kosher salt or salt
- Ground black pepper
- 4 large cloves garlic, peeled and halved
- 1 small onion, peeled and cut into wedges
- 1 medium baking apple, cored and cut into wedges
- 2 Tbsp. butter, melted
- 6 medium baking apples, cored and cut into eighths
- 2 Tbsp. lemon juice
- 1 recipe Cider Glaze (right)
- Fresh fruit, such as grapes, berries, and apples (optional)
- Fresh herb sprigs, such as flat-leaf parsley or variegated sage (optional)
- ⅓ cup all-purpose flour
- Chicken broth

1. Preheat oven to 325° F. Rinse turkey; pat dry with paper towels. Season inside cavity with salt and pepper. Rub 1 of the halved garlic cloves inside cavity. Place garlic cloves, onion, and 1 apple into the cavity.

2. Pull neck skin to back; fasten with skewer. If a band of skin crosses the tail, tuck drumsticks under band. If there isn't a band, tie drumsticks securely to tail with 100-percent-cotton string. Twist wing tips under back. Brush turkey with the 2 tablespoons melted butter. Season with additional salt and pepper.

3. Place bird, breast side up, on a rack in a shallow roasting pan. Insert an oven-safe meat thermometer into the center of an inside thigh muscle without letting thermometer touch bone. Cover bird loosely with foil. Roast for 2½ to 3½ hours or until thermometer registers 160° F. (Cut band of skin or string between drumsticks after 2½ hours.)

4. Toss apple wedges with lemon juice. Place apple wedges around turkey. Cover apple wedges with foil. Roast turkey and apples for 30 minutes more.

5. Meanwhile, prepare Cider Glaze. Remove foil from turkey; baste turkey and drizzle apples with Cider Glaze. Continue roasting, uncovered, until meat thermometer registers 180° F, basting bird and drizzling cider mixture onto apples every 10 minutes.

6. Remove turkey from oven; discard cavity ingredients. Transfer roasted bird to a large platter. Surround with roasted apples. Cover with foil; let stand for 15 to 20 minutes before carving turkey. If desired, garnish platter with fresh fruit and herbs.

7. Meanwhile, for gravy, pour pan drippings into a large measuring cup. Scrape browned bits from the pan into the cup. Skim and reserve fat from drippings. Pour ¼ cup of the fat into a medium saucepan (discard remaining fat). Stir in flour. Add enough broth to remaining drippings to measure 2½ cups total liquid; add broth mixture all at once to flour mixture. Cook and stir over medium heat until thickened and bubbly. Cook and stir for 1 minute more. Season to taste with salt and pepper. Makes 16 to 18 servings.

CIDER GLAZE: In a small saucepan bring 2 cups apple cider and five 3-inch cinnamon sticks to boiling. Reduce heat and boil steadily about 30 minutes or until cider is reduced to ⅔ cup. Add ⅓ cup butter, ⅓ cup brown sugar, and 1 teaspoon dried thyme, crushed. Heat and stir until brown sugar is dissolved. Remove and discard cinnamon sticks.

Each serving: 544 cal., 26 g total fat (9 g sat. fat), 196 mg chol., 359 mg sodium, 18 g carbo., 2 g fiber, 55 g pro. Daily Values: 5% vit. A, 6% vit. C, 7% calcium, 23% iron.

Buttery Cider-Glazed Turkey

THE SPREAD IS READY

Make the golden turkey the centerpiece of your buffet or dining room table. This year, carve a cider-glazed version decorated with roasted apples and eye-catching fresh fruits and herbs.

Brown Bread Squash Stuffing

Remember brown bread in a can? The super-moist, molasses-flavored bread adds a nostalgic twist to this baked stuffing. Pictured on page 413.

PREP: 35 minutes **BAKE:** 45 minutes

- **7 cups honey wheat bread cut into 1/2-inch cubes (7 to 9 slices)**
- **1 16-oz. can brown bread with raisins, cut into 1/2-inch cubes (5 cups)**
- **6 Tbsp. butter or margarine**
- **4 cups peeled and seeded winter squash, such as butternut or acorn squash, cut into 3/4-inch cubes,**
- **1 1/2 cups sliced celery with tops**
- **1 large red onion, cut into thin wedges**
- **2 1/4 to 2 3/4 cups chicken broth**
- **1/4 cup snipped fresh sage or 2 tsp. dried sage, crushed**
- **2 Tbsp. snipped fresh flat-leaf parsley**
- **1 tsp. ground nutmeg**
- **1/2 tsp. salt**
- **1/2 tsp. ground black pepper**
- **Fresh sage sprigs (optional)**

1. Preheat oven to 325° F. Spread wheat bread cubes and brown bread cubes in 2 shallow baking pans. Melt 4 tablespoons of the butter and drizzle evenly over bread cubes; toss to coat. Bake, uncovered, for 15 to 20 minutes or until lightly toasted, stirring once. Transfer to a very large mixing bowl.

2. In a very large skillet melt remaining 2 tablespoons butter over medium heat. Add squash. Cook, uncovered, 5 minutes, stirring occasionally. Add celery and onion; cover and cook 10 minutes more. Stir in 1/4 cup of the chicken broth. Cover and cook 5 minutes more or until squash is just tender, stirring occasionally. Remove from heat. Stir in snipped or dried sage, parsley, nutmeg, salt, and pepper.

3. Add squash mixture to bread in bowl. Add 2 cups of the remaining broth; toss lightly to coat. Add enough of the remaining broth to make a stuffing of desired moistness.

4. Grease a 3-quart casserole. Transfer stuffing mixture to casserole. Bake, covered, for 30 minutes. Uncover; bake for 15 to 20 minutes more or until stuffing is heated through. If desired, garnish with fresh sage sprigs. Makes 10 to 12 servings.

MAKE-AHEAD TIP: You can toast bread cubes up to 2 days in advance and keep them dry in an airtight container.

Each serving: 261 cal., 9 g total fat (5 g sat. fat), 20 mg chol., 823 mg sodium, 41 g carbo., 3 g fiber, 6 g pro. Daily Values: 90% vit. A, 21% vit. C, 6% calcium, 7% iron.

Rosemary Roasted Vegetables

The flavors jump to the foreground of this fresh spin on the classic green bean casserole. Brussels sprouts add welcome variety.

PREP: 30 minutes **ROAST:** 20 minutes

- **12 oz. fresh whole green beans**
- **1 lb. fresh brussels sprouts**
- **1 bunch green onions (6), trimmed and cut up**
- **12 fresh rosemary sprigs**
- **8 slices pancetta or bacon, partially cooked, drained, and cut up**
- **2 Tbsp. olive oil**
- **Salt**
- **Ground black pepper**
- **1 lemon, halved**

1. Preheat oven to 425° F. Wash beans and brussels sprouts; drain. Halve large brussels sprouts. In a covered large saucepan cook brussels sprouts in a small amount of boiling lightly salted water for 3 minutes. Add beans; cook for 5 minutes more.

2. Drain; place brussels sprouts and beans in a shallow roasting pan. Add green onions and rosemary sprigs; toss to combine. Top with partially cooked pancetta or bacon.

3. Drizzle vegetable mixture with olive oil. Sprinkle with salt and pepper. Roast, uncovered, about 20 minutes or until vegetables are crisp-tender and pancetta is crisp. Transfer to a platter. Squeeze lemon juice over vegetables. Makes 12 servings.

MAKE-AHEAD TIP: One day in advance, clean vegetables. Cut brussels sprouts in half. Place brussels sprouts, beans, and onions in separate sealed food-storage bags in the refrigerator.

Each serving: 143 cal., 10 g total fat (4 g sat. fat), 10 mg chol., 275 mg sodium, 6 g carbo., 3 g fiber, 4 g pro. Daily Values: 10% vit. A, 51% vit. C, 3% calcium, 6% iron.

THANKSGIVING DINNER

Pomegranate Starter *(page 409)*
Greens with Spiced Corn Bread *(page 411)*
or Roasted Beet and Goat Cheese Salad *(page 411)*
Buttery Cider-Glazed Turkey *(page 412)*
Brown Bread Squash Stuffing *(left)*
Rosemary Roasted Vegetables *(above)*
Mashed Potatoes with Caramelized Onions *(page 417)*
Harvest Breadsticks *(page 417)*
Maple-Pumpkin Cheesecake *(page 418)*
or Deep-Dish Cranberry Pie *(page 418)*

Rosemary Roasted Vegetables

A PICTURE'S WORTH

Give your family the special treatment by adding extras that show you care. A single wheat sheaf woven through holes in a menu card adds a touch of warm whimsy. Tuck a treasured family photo—perhaps an old picture of each guest—next to the menu to spark nostalgic memories and easy conversation. The kids will love helping you select the photos.

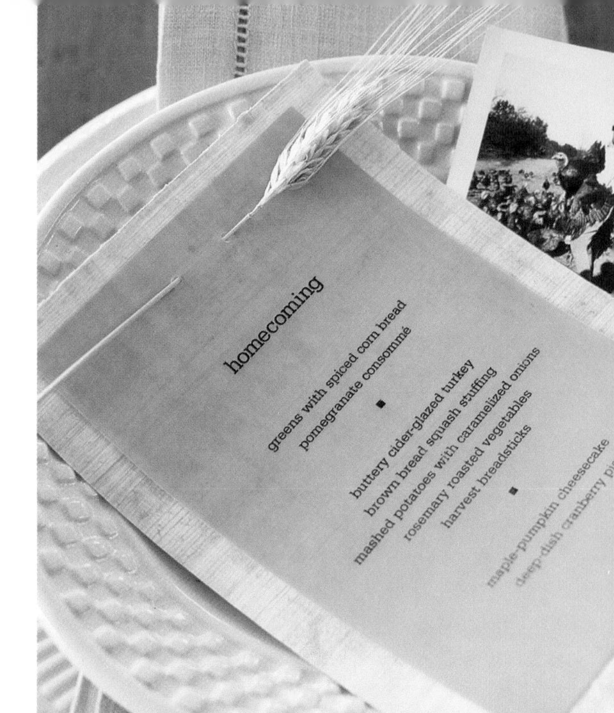

Mashed Potatoes with Caramelized Onions and Harvest Breadsticks

Harvest Breadsticks

Choose from a variety of toppings to flavor these extra-long breadsticks. Bundle them together on a long tray or stand them upright in a clean glass vase.

PREP: 45 minutes **RISE:** 50 minutes **BAKE:** 15 minutes per batch

- **1¼ cups water**
- **2 small russet (baking) potatoes, peeled and cubed (1⅓ cups)**
- **1 cup buttermilk**
- **2 Tbsp. sugar**
- **2 Tbsp. butter or margarine**
- **2 tsp. salt**
- **6 to 6½ cups all-purpose flour**
- **2 pkg. active dry yeast**
- **1 egg white**
- **1 Tbsp. water**
- **Desired toppings, such as sesame seeds, fennel seeds, cumin seeds, and/or crushed red peppercorns**

1. In a small saucepan bring water and cubed potatoes to boiling. Simmer, covered, about 15 minutes or until potatoes are tender; do not drain. Mash potatoes in the water. Measure potato mixture. If necessary, add additional water to make 1⅔ cups total.

2. Return potato mixture to saucepan. Add buttermilk, sugar, butter, and salt. Heat or cool as necessary until warm (120° F to 130° F), stirring constantly.

3. In a large mixing bowl combine 2 cups of the flour and the yeast. Add the potato mixture. Beat with an electric mixer on low to medium speed for 30 seconds, scraping the side of the bowl constantly. Beat on high speed for 3 minutes. Using a wooden spoon, stir in as much of the remaining flour as you can.

4. Turn dough out onto a lightly floured surface. Knead in enough of the remaining flour to make a moderately stiff dough that is smooth and elastic (6 to 8 minutes total). Shape dough into a ball. Place in a lightly greased bowl; turn once to grease the surface. Cover; let rise in warm place until double in size (30 to 45 minutes). Lightly grease baking sheets; set aside.

5. Punch dough down. Turn dough out onto a lightly floured surface; divide dough in half. Cover and let rest for 10 minutes. Roll one portion into a 15×8-inch rectangle. Cut into twenty 8×¾-inch pieces. Stretch and roll each piece to form a 15-inch-long breadstick. Place ¾ to 1 inch apart on prepared baking sheets. Repeat with remaining dough.

6. Preheat oven to 375° F. Cover and let breadsticks rise for 20 minutes. Stir together egg white and the water; brush onto breadsticks. Sprinkle with desired toppings. Bake about 15 minutes or until light brown. Transfer to wire racks. Serve warm or at room temperature. Makes 40 breadsticks.

MAKE-AHEAD TIP: To freeze these breadsticks or any yeast bread, place completely cooled breads in a freezer bag; freeze for up to 3 months. Thaw the wrapped bread at room temperature for 2 hours.

Each breadstick: 87 cal., 1 g total fat (0 g sat. fat), 2 mg chol., 131 mg sodium, 17 g carbo., 1 g fiber, 3 g pro. Daily Values: 1% vit. C, 1% calcium, 6% iron.

Mashed Potatoes with Caramelized Onions

The essential comfort food—mashed potatoes—forms the base of this dish. But by the time you top the mashed potatoes with sautéed onions and thin shards of white cheddar cheese, you won't need to add gravy. Melty cheese plays a big role in the appeal of this dish, so don't delay in getting the cheddar on the hot potatoes. And yes, orange cheddar can be substituted for the white.

START TO FINISH: 40 minutes

- **3 lb. russet (baking) potatoes, peeled and quartered**
- **1 tsp. salt**
- **2 Tbsp. olive oil**
- **2 large yellow onions, peeled and cut into thin wedges (about 2 cups)**
- **¼ cup butter or margarine, softened**
- **2 Tbsp. snipped fresh sage or 1 tsp. dried sage, crushed**
- **¼ tsp. ground black pepper**
- **½ to ¾ cup half-and-half, light cream, or milk**
- **1 oz. aged white cheddar cheese, shaved into thin shards**

1. In a covered large saucepan cook potatoes and ½ teaspoon of the salt in enough boiling water to cover for 20 to 25 minutes or until tender; drain.

2. Meanwhile, for caramelized onions, in a large skillet heat oil. Stir in the onion wedges. Cook, uncovered, over medium heat about 20 minutes or until onions are tender, stirring frequently. (If necessary, reduce heat to medium-low to prevent overbrowning before onions are tender.) Increase heat to medium-high and cook about 5 minutes more or until onions are golden brown, stirring frequently.

3. Mash drained potatoes with a potato masher. Add butter, sage, the remaining ½ teaspoon salt, and the pepper. Gradually beat in enough half-and-half to make mixture light and fluffy.

4. Mound potatoes in a serving dish. Top with caramelized onions and cheese shards; serve immediately. Makes 10 to 12 servings.

Each serving: 187 cal., 10 g total fat (5 g sat. fat), 21 mg chol., 309 mg sodium, 20 g carbo., 3 g fiber, 4 g pro. Daily Values: 5% vit. A, 29% vit. C, 5% calcium, 6% iron.

Maple-Pumpkin Cheesecake

Inspired by chef Joanne Bondy's individual pumpkin cheesecakes served at Ciudad Restaurant in Dallas, this full-size version is beautiful when embellished with glittering fruit. This time of year, look for currants, champagne grapes, raspberries, or other small fruit. It's also elegant served with just a drizzle of caramel sauce.

PREP: 35 minutes **BAKE:** 1 hour
COOL: 1¾ hours **CHILL:** 4 hours

- **1½ cups finely crushed graham crackers (about 20 squares)**
- **1⅓ cups maple sugar or granulated sugar**
- **½ cup butter (1 stick), melted**
- **3 8-oz. pkg. cream cheese, softened**
- **1 cup canned pumpkin**
- **1 Tbsp. whipping cream**
- **1½ tsp. vanilla**
- **¾ tsp. ground allspice**
- **3 eggs, slightly beaten**
- **½ cup caramel ice cream topping**
- **Fresh currants and/or small fruit (optional)**

1. Preheat oven to 325° F. For crust, in a medium bowl combine crushed graham crackers, ⅓ cup of the maple sugar, and the melted butter. Press crumb mixture onto the bottom and about 2 inches up the side of an ungreased 9-inch springform pan. Bake for 8 minutes. Remove from oven; cool on a wire rack.

2. For filling, in a medium mixing bowl beat cream cheese, the remaining 1 cup maple sugar, the pumpkin, cream, vanilla, and allspice with an electric mixer on medium speed until combined. Add eggs; beat on low speed just until combined.

3. Preheat oven to 325° F. Spoon filling into crust-lined pan. Place pan in a shallow baking pan. Bake about 1 hour or until center appears nearly set when gently shaken.

4. Cool in springform pan on a wire rack for 15 minutes. Using a thin-bladed knife or narrow spatula, loosen crust from side of pan; cool for 30 minutes more. Remove side of pan; cool for 1 hour. Cover and chill for 4 to 24 hours.

5. Just before serving, spoon caramel ice cream topping over cheesecake. If desired, garnish with fresh currants and/or small fruit. Makes 12 servings.

MAKE-AHEAD TIP: To store, before adding caramel ice cream topping, cover cheesecake with plastic wrap and refrigerate for up to 2 days. (Or carefully transfer cheesecake to a freezerproof plate or platter. Place cheesecake in a freezer bag or airtight container. Freeze for up to 1 month. Thaw frozen cheesecake in the refrigerator for 24 hours.) Continue with step 5.

Each serving: 475 cal., 31 g total fat (18 g sat. fat), 139 mg chol., 362 mg sodium, 44 g carbo., 1 g fiber, 7 g pro. Daily Values: 114% vit. A, 7% vit. C, 9% calcium, 11% iron.

Deep-Dish Cranberry Pie

We took traditional cranberry pie to the oooh-ahhh level by adding lots more filling and capping it with a pastry that drapes low over the edge of the bowl.

PREP: 40 minutes **BAKE:** 1¼ hours

- **¼ cup brandy or water**
- **2¾ cups dried tart cherries**
- **1 recipe Deep-Dish Pastry (below)**
- **1 12-oz. pkg. fresh cranberries (3½ cups)**
- **1½ cups granulated sugar**
- **3 Tbsp. all-purpose flour**
- **2 tsp. finely shredded lemon peel**
- **Milk**
- **Coarse sugar**
- **1 recipe Honey Cream Sauce (below)**

1. In a small saucepan combine ¾ cup water and the brandy or additional water. Heat until mixture starts to boil; add cherries. Remove from heat. Cover; let stand for 20 minutes.

2. Meanwhile, prepare Deep-Dish Pastry. Preheat oven to 375° F. On a lightly floured surface, roll out half of the pastry to a 13-inch circle if using a 1½-quart oven-safe bowl or an 18×14-inch oval or rectangle if using a 2-quart oval or rectangular casserole. Gently fit pastry onto bottom and up side of the bowl or casserole, letting excess pastry extend beyond edge of dish; fold pastry into pleats as needed to fit dish. Set aside.

3. In a large bowl stir together cranberries, undrained cherry mixture, granulated sugar, flour, and lemon peel. Turn into pastry-lined dish. Roll out remaining half of pastry to a 10-inch circle or a 14×10-inch oval or rectangle. Use a cookie cutter or knife to cut a design or circle in the center of the circle, oval, or rectangle. Place pastry over filling, allowing it to hang over the edge of the dish. Pinch top and bottom pastry together to seal. Brush with milk; sprinkle with coarse sugar. Place dish on a baking sheet.

4. Cover edge of pie with foil. Bake for 55 minutes; remove foil and bake for 20 to 25 minutes more or until juices bubble and pastry is light brown. Cool on a wire rack.

5. Serve pie with Honey Cream Sauce. Break off and serve pastry overhang with pie. Makes 10 servings.

DEEP-DISH PASTRY: In a large bowl combine 2¼ cups all-purpose flour and ¾ teaspoon salt. Cut in ⅔ cup shortening until pieces are pea-size. Sprinkle 1 tablespoon cold water over part of flour mixture; gently toss with a fork. Push moistened dough to side of bowl. Repeat, using 1 tablespoon water at a time (8 to 10 tablespoons cold water total), until all of the flour is moistened. Divide dough in half.

HONEY CREAM SAUCE: Stir together one 8-ounce carton dairy sour cream and 3 tablespoons wildflower or orange blossom honey; stir in 1 to 2 tablespoons half-and-half, light cream, or milk to make desired consistency. Cover and chill until serving time.

Each serving: 551 cal., 19 g total fat (7 g sat. fat), 11 mg chol., 190 mg sodium, 88 g carbo., 4 g fiber, 5 g pro. Daily Values: 4% vit. A, 9% vit. C, 4% calcium, 8% iron.

Maple-Pumpkin Cheesecake and Deep-Dish Cranberry Pie

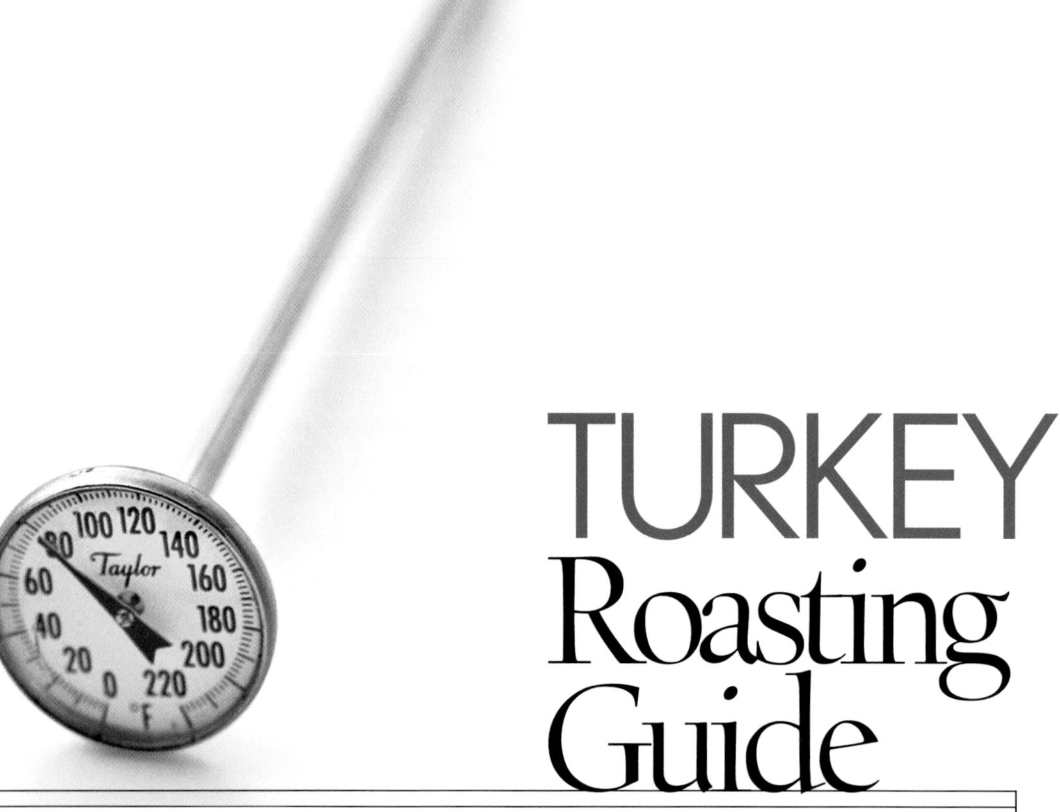

TURKEY Roasting Guide

HOW MUCH TO BUY

To make sure you have plenty of turkey, purchase 1 to 1½ pounds of bird per person. For each pound of bird you put into the oven, you'll get just under a half pound of meat. Fresh or frozen birds are about equal in quality. Fresh turkeys take up space for less time in the fridge; frozen turkeys must spend up to a week thawing.

For a fresh turkey, check the sell-by date. The unopened turkey will taste best and be safe to use up to 1 or 2 days after the date on the wrapper. If you're buying a frozen bird, look for one that is clean, undamaged, and free of ice crystals.

BEFORE YOU START

If you're serious about making a perfect turkey, invest in a meat thermometer. Turkey gets dry when it's overcooked, and for $10 to $20, you can be sure of serving a savory turkey. Meat thermometers are available both as instant-read and conventional. The main difference: conventionals stay in the bird; the smaller instant-reads can't be left in the oven.

Another key to success is to allow plenty of time. On average, it takes about an hour to stuff and prepare a turkey for roasting. The depth of your roasting pan may affect the roasting time. A depth of more than 3 inches can increase the roasting time by up to an hour.

THAWING

A sticking point for many cooks is allowing enough time to thaw the bird. For a whole frozen turkey, leave the bird in its wrapping and place it on a tray or platter in the refrigerator for 2 to 5 days. Plan on 24 hours for every 5 pounds and don't count the day you'll be cooking as part of the thawing time. For instance, a 15-pound bird should start thawing Sunday night to be ready for Thanksgiving. Thawed birds will keep for 2 days in the refrigerator.

The bird is ready for roasting if the giblets can be removed easily and there are no ice crystals in the body cavities. If the center is still frozen, the bird will cook unevenly.

If your turkey is not completely thawed on the day you plan to roast it, place the bird in a clean sink full of cold water and change the water every 30 minutes. This method works really well, so don't be tempted to thaw at room temperature, in the microwave, or in warm water; these methods can cause bacteria to grow.

After thawing, remove the giblets and neck. If you wish, rinse the bird. In either case, pat dry with paper towels.

STUFFING

Prepare the stuffing just before you put the bird in the oven. Measure out the amount of stuffing that will go into the bird, allowing ¾ cup per pound of bird. (That's 11 cups for a 15-pound bird.) Spoon some stuffing loosely into the neck cavity. Pull the neck skin over stuffing; fasten to the turkey's back with a short skewer.

The drumsticks are usually held in place by a band of skin or a plastic or metal clamp. Unhook the legs and loosely spoon the stuffing into the body cavity; don't pack it or the stuffing may not be fully cooked and safe to eat by the time the turkey is done. Spoon any remaining stuffing into a greased casserole; cover and chill until you're ready to bake it (about an hour before the turkey is scheduled to come out of the oven).

After stuffing, tuck the drumsticks under the band of skin that crosses the tail or reset them into the leg clamp. If there isn't a band or if you've removed the clamp, tie the drumsticks to the tail using kitchen string. Twist the wing tips under the back—this gives the turkey a nice stable base.

If you don't have an accurate thermometer, cook the stuffing in a covered casserole alongside the turkey, rather than inside the bird.

ROAST AND SERVE

Place your oven rack in its lowest position; preheat the oven to 325° F. Place turkey, breast side up, on a rack in a shallow pan. To promote browning, brush with cooking oil or melted butter. Push an oven-safe meat thermometer into the center of an inside thigh muscle without touching bone. Cover turkey loosely with foil, pressing it over the drumsticks and neck. Roast, using our timing chart *(below)* as a guide. Since most turkeys are self-basting, basting is not necessary, but it will add flavor.

When the bird has been in the oven for two-thirds of the time shown on the chart, cut the string between the drumsticks. Remove the foil for the last 30 to 45 minutes of roasting. The meat thermometer (or instant-read thermometer) in the thigh should register 180° F and the stuffing should be at least 165° F.

When the turkey is done, the drumsticks should move very easily in their sockets and their thickest parts should feel soft when pressed. In addition, juices from the thigh should run clear when pierced deeply with a long-tined fork. Remove from the oven and cover loosely with foil. Let stand for 20 minutes. Release legs from leg clamp, if present. To avoid burns or splatters, do not remove clamp until bird has cooled slightly. Remove stuffing before carving.

Pear-Pecan Stuffing

Pears, toasted pecans, and nutmeg create a festive holiday twist on old-fashioned stuffing. It's equally delicious when baked inside the bird or in a casserole.

PREP: 30 minutes **BAKE:** 40 minutes (in casserole)

- **1 lb. firm-textured white sandwich bread**
- **2 Tbsp. butter**
- **1 cup chopped onion**
- **2 large ripe, yet firm, Barlett pears, cored, peeled, and chopped**
- **½ cup water**
- **¼ cup butter**
- **1 cup coarsely chopped pecans, toasted**
- **2 Tbsp. snipped fresh flat-leaf parsley**
- **¼ tsp. ground nutmeg**
- **⅛ tsp. salt**
- **Dash ground black pepper**

1. Preheat oven to 350° F. Spread bread slices on baking sheets. Place baking sheets in the preheated oven about 20 minutes or until bread is dry.

2. In a large skillet melt the 2 tablespoons butter over medium heat. Add onion and pear; cook about 4 minutes or until tender. Set aside.

3. Break the dried bread into small pieces; place in a very large bowl. In a small saucepan combine the water and the ¼ cup butter; bring to boiling. Add to bread; toss just until moistened.

4. Stir in pear mixture, pecans, parsley, nutmeg, salt, and pepper. Add just enough additional water (about ¼ cup) to make desired moistness. Stuff turkey and roast according to directions at left. (Or transfer stuffing to a greased 2-quart casserole and bake, covered, in a 350° F oven about 40 minutes or until heated through.) Makes 12 to 14 servings.

Each serving: 243 cal., 15 g total fat (4 g sat. fat), 16 mg chol., 291 mg sodium, 26 g carbo., 2 g fiber, 4 g pro. Daily Values: 5% vit. A, 5% vit. C, 5% calcium, 8% iron.

STUFFED TURKEY ROASTING TIMES

READY-TO-COOK TURKEY WEIGHT	OVEN TEMPERATURE	ROASTING TIME
8 to 12 lb.	325° F	3 to 3¾ hours
12 to 14 lb.	325° F	3¼ to 4½ hours
14 to 18 lb.	325° F	4 to 5 hours
18 to 20 lb.	325° F	4½ to 5¼ hours
20 to 24 lb.	325° F	4¾ to 5¾ hours

FOR UNSTUFFED TURKEYS OF THE SAME WEIGHT, REDUCE THE TOTAL ROASTING TIME BY 15 TO 45 MINUTES. THE TURKEY IS DONE WHEN THE THIGH TEMPERATURE REACHES 180° F AND THE STUFFING IS 165° F.

LEFTOVERS go right

Turkey Benedict

CHEF-BROTHERS KENT AND KEVIN RATHBUN TRADE SIBLING RIVALRY FOR KITCHEN COOPERATION WHEN THEY DIG INTO LEFTOVERS FOR A POST-HOLIDAY SUNDAY BRUNCH.

Turkey Benedict

START TO FINISH: 1 hour

- $1\frac{3}{4}$ cups all-purpose flour
- 2 Tbsp. snipped fresh parsley
- 1 Tbsp. sugar
- 1 Tbsp. baking powder
- $\frac{3}{4}$ tsp. kosher salt or $\frac{1}{2}$ tsp. salt
- $\frac{1}{3}$ cup cold butter
- $\frac{1}{2}$ cup half-and-half or light cream
- $\frac{1}{4}$ cup buttermilk
- $\frac{1}{4}$ tsp. bottled minced roasted garlic
- 1 recipe Spicy Hollandaise Sauce (below)
- 8 to 10 oz. roasted turkey breast slices
- 8 eggs

1. For biscuits, preheat oven to 400° F. In a bowl stir together flour, parsley, sugar, baking powder, and salt. Cut in butter until mixture resembles coarse crumbs. Add half-and-half, buttermilk, and garlic. Use a fork to gently mix until a slightly sticky dough forms. Do not overmix. Turn out onto a floured surface. Knead a few times until nearly smooth. Roll or pat dough to a 6-inch square. Cut into 4 squares. Place on an ungreased cookie sheet. Bake for 18 to 20 minutes or until brown on tops; set aside.

2. Meanwhile, prepare Spicy Hollandaise Sauce; keep warm.

3. Heat a griddle or large skillet over medium-high heat. Add turkey; cook about 4 minutes or until brown, turning once.

4. Half fill a large saucepan with water. Bring to boiling; reduce heat to just simmering. Break 1 egg into custard cup. Carefully slide egg into the simmering water, holding the lip of the cup as close to the water as possible. Repeat with 3 more eggs, allowing each egg an equal amount of space. Simmer, uncovered, for 3 to 5 minutes or until yolks and whites are set. Using a slotted spoon, transfer eggs to an oven-safe shallow dish. Cover; keep warm in a 300° F oven. Repeat with remaining eggs.

5. To assemble, split biscuits; arrange on a platter. Top each half with turkey, a poached egg, and about 1 tablespoon sauce. Serve with remaining sauce. Makes 8 servings.

SPICY HOLLANDAISE SAUCE: In top of a double boiler whisk together 2 egg yolks, 2 tablespoons water, and 2 tablespoons lemon juice. Place over simmering water (the bottom of the pan should not touch the water) and whisk until the mixture thickens and doubles in volume ($1\frac{1}{2}$ to 2 minutes) and an instant-read thermometer inserted into the mixture registers 160° F (you may need to tilt the pan to get an accurate reading). Gradually add 1 cup cut-up and softened butter, whisking constantly after each addition until butter is melted. Remove double boiler from heat. Stir in 1 seeded and chopped serrano chile pepper (see note, page 121). Keep sauce warm over water.

Each serving: 535 cal., 41 g total fat (23 g sat. fat), 384 mg chol., 832 mg sodium, 23 g carbo., 1 g fiber, 19 g pro. Daily Values: 35% vit. A, 6% vit. C, 16% calcium, 15% iron.

Final feast

Everyone pitches in to prepare Thanksgiving dinner when the Rathbun clan gathers for the holiday. But come Sunday morning, brothers Kent and Kevin are on their own to prepare the final feast of the weekend, Sunday brunch. Even though the brothers—both professional chefs—serve haute cuisine daily, like most Americans, they've got leftovers to use—and they enjoy the challenge.

Kent Rathbun is chef/owner of Abacus restaurant in Dallas; Kevin opened Rathbun's in Atlanta. The brothers grew up in Kansas City. Traditionally, the family alternates between the three cities for Thanksgiving. On Sunday morning, Kent gets up first and starts cooking bacon so the aroma will get Kevin out of bed. After a cup of coffee, the two start opening up containers of leftover turkey, stuffing, gravy, and sweet potatoes.

"We get creative on the fly. We usually set out to do something that makes sense, like a strata, and just let it go. It doesn't always look great, but it always tastes great," Kent says.

Kevin joins in, "There's a very big mutual respect between us when we cook. We recognize the other may have a better idea. We bounce ideas as well as jokes."

When you're adapting an existing recipe to use up leftovers, or just making something up, the brothers stress confidence as a key ingredient.

By the time brunch gets on the table, Kevin and Kent have cleaned out the fridge. Do too many cooks spoil the broth in the Rathbun household? "Not if they're both good cooks," Kent jokes.

Portobello and Lemon Thyme Bread Pudding

"THERE'S A VERY BIG MUTUAL RESPECT BETWEEN US WHEN WE COOK."

Kevin Rathbun

Portobello and Lemon Thyme Bread Pudding

You can use any leftover bread from making the stuffing instead of the baguette. Just make sure you have 7 cups of bread total.

PREP: 45 minutes **BAKE:** 35 minutes **STAND:** 10 minutes

- Nonstick cooking spray
- 7 cups 1-inch cubes French-style baguette or other firm-textured bread (about 12 oz.)
- 4 4-oz. portobello mushrooms
- 3 Tbsp. butter
- 6 cloves garlic, minced
- 6 shallots, finely chopped
- 3 Tbsp. snipped fresh lemon thyme*
- 10 oz. Gruyère cheese, shredded (2½ cups)
- 1 cup cubed cooked turkey
- 6 eggs
- 1 14-oz. can chicken broth
- 1½ cups whipping cream
- 2 tsp. cracked black pepper
- ½ tsp. kosher salt or salt

1. Preheat oven to 350° F. Lightly coat eight 10-ounce ramekins or custard cups with nonstick cooking spray; set aside. Place bread cubes in a very large bowl; set aside.

2. Remove stems and gills from mushrooms; discard. Chop mushrooms (you should have about 5 cups). In a large skillet heat butter until melted. Add mushrooms, garlic, and shallots; cook about 3 minutes or until tender. Add lemon thyme. Cook and stir for 1 minute more.

3. Add mushroom mixture to bread cubes; toss to combine. Add 2 cups of the cheese and the turkey; toss to combine.

4. In a large bowl whisk together eggs, broth, cream, pepper, and salt. Add to bread mixture; fold gently to combine.

5. Divide bread mixture evenly among the prepared cups (cups will be full). Sprinkle remaining ½ cup cheese over the tops. Place cups in a foil-lined 15×10×1-inch baking pan or shallow roasting pan.

6. Bake, uncovered, for 35 to 40 minutes or until puffed and set. Let stand for 10 minutes before serving (top will deflate slightly). Makes 8 servings.

***NOTE:** If you cannot find lemon thyme, substitute 2 tablespoons snipped fresh thyme and 1 teaspoon finely shredded lemon peel.

Each serving: 585 cal., 40 g total fat (22 g sat. fat), 285 mg chol., 833 mg sodium, 30 g carbo., 2 g fiber, 28 g pro. Daily Values: 36% vit. A, 7% vit. C, 46% calcium, 16% iron.

LOWER FAT BREAD PUDDING: Prepare Portobello and Lemon Thyme Bread Pudding as above, except use only 8 ounces Gruyère cheese; substitute half-and-half for the whipping cream.

Each serving: 460 cal., 26 g total fat (13 g sat. fat), 233 mg chol., 811 mg sodium, 31 g carbo., 2 g fiber, 26 g pro. Daily Values: 25% vit. A, 7% vit. C, 41% calcium, 16% iron.

THANKS FOR THE LEFTOVERS

The brothers pinned down two recipes for leftover turkey—Turkey Benedict *(page 423)* and Portobello and Lemon Thyme Bread Pudding *(left)*. Then, they shared a few spontaneous thoughts on what to do with some common Thanksgiving leftovers.

OVERALL: "Take a risk. Start small. Add a little of something at a time," Kent suggests. "Once your dish is in the oven," Kevin adds, "check it along the way. Make sure it's not too wet or dry. Leftover gravy can go a long or little way, depending on how you use it."

CRANBERRY SAUCE: Kent and Kevin suggest boiling it down to make cranberry syrup or tossing the sauce into waffle, scone, or pancake batter.

FRESH OR FROZEN CRANBERRIES: For an easy cranberry dessert, Kent suggests pureeing 1 cup frozen cranberries in a blender with ½ cup sugar and ¼ cup orange juice. "Spoon it onto scoops of vanilla ice cream or yogurt and top with chocolate shaved from a bar with a vegetable peeler," he says.

Kevin offers a cranberry chutney by combining 1 cup lightly cooked cranberries with a peeled, chopped orange, 2 tablespoons brown sugar, and a dash of balsamic or sherry vinegar. "Serve it with ham or scones," he recommends.

GRAVY: The brothers wax ecstatic about the wonders of gravy. "Put it into soup. It's a great base for any kind you can think of. And speaking of soups, pumpkin soup made with leftover canned pumpkin is a brilliant idea, or turkey and dumpling soup made from the leftover turkey."

CANDIED SWEET POTATOES: Use them in sweet potato pie or in bread pudding. Or take them Mexican by mashing them, adding Monterey Jack cheese and diced fresh jalapeño chile pepper, and serving them in flour tortillas.

GREEN BEAN CASSEROLE: Use the casserole as the base for a filling for turkey potpie. Or mix the casserole with bread crumbs, form patties, and sauté them until crisp. Use the patties alone or top them with poached eggs. Top them off with some leftover cranberry sauce seasoned with a diced chile pepper.

read it and eat

COME ALONG AS FRIENDS GET TOGETHER TO DEVOUR A BOOK AND SHARE A MEAL INSPIRED BY THE PLOT.

A great book, great friends, great food, and a chance to ditch the guys, even if for just one evening—all in the name of fun and a little intellectual stimulation. The requisites? Each friend must bring the book and a dish or a bottle of wine to Kate Manchester's house in East Hampton, NY.

The book club members gather 'round the kitchen island, nosh on huge pimiento-stuffed olives and fresh veggies dunked in a thick homemade dip, and dish out their thoughts about the novel of the night. Nibble a little, dish a little, nibble some more, dish some more—it's all about fun.

"I try to get everybody to sit in the living room, but the girls prefer standing around the kitchen island, nibbling, drinking, and talking. I think it's the Big Girl Drinks, also known as martinis," laughs Kate.

Pastrami Panini

Marinated cucumbers and onions add crunch to the hearty sandwiches.

PREP: 40 minutes **CHILL:** 1 hour **COOK:** 6 minutes

- **1 medium cucumber, thinly sliced**
- **1 medium red onion, thinly sliced**
- **¼ cup vinegar**
- **1 Tbsp. sugar**
- **½ tsp. salt**
- **3 to 4 Tbsp. honey mustard**
- **2 tsp. prepared horseradish (optional)**
- **8 slices hearty wheat or rye bread**
- **6 oz. thinly sliced pastrami**
- **4 oz. Swiss cheese slices**
- **Olive oil**
- **Bottled Thousand Island salad dressing (optional)**

1. In a medium bowl stir together the cucumber, onion, vinegar, sugar, and salt. Cover and chill until serving time or up to 24 hours. Drain before using.

2. In a small bowl stir together honey mustard and, if desired, horseradish. To assemble sandwiches, spread one side of each bread slice with the mustard mixture. Top half of the bread slices, mustard sides up, with pastrami, cheese, and some of the drained cucumber mixture. Top with remaining bread slices. Brush outsides of sandwiches lightly with olive oil.

3. Heat a nonstick griddle or large skillet over medium heat. Wrap a brick completely in foil. Place a sandwich on griddle or in skillet and top with the foil-wrapped brick. Grill weighted sandwich about 3 minutes on each side or until golden brown and cheese is melted. Repeat for remaining sandwiches. (Or place sandwich on a covered indoor grill or panini grill. Close lid; grill 4 to 5 minutes or until golden brown and cheese is melted.) If desired, serve with Thousand Island salad dressing. Makes 4 sandwiches.

Each sandwich: 559 cal., 29 g total fat (11 g sat. fat), 66 mg chol., 1,423 mg sodium, 54 g carbo., 7 g fiber, 23 g pro. Daily Values: 8% vit. A, 10% vit. C, 33% calcium, 19% iron.

9 GREAT BOOKS FOR FOOD LOVERS

Death by Darjeeling, by Laura Childs
Fried Green Tomatoes at the Whistle Stop Cafe, by Fannie Flagg
Heartburn, by Nora Ephron
Like Water for Chocolate, by Laura Esquivel
Stuffed, by Patricia Volk
Tender at the Bone, by Ruth Reichl
The Art of Eating, by M. F. K. Fisher
The Soul of a Chef, by Michael Ruhlman
Under the Tuscan Sun, by Frances Mayes

BOOK CLUB BASICS

GOT THE E-INVITE: "There's no easier way!" says Kate who e-mails the invitations, including a menu based on food inspired by the group's current book. Sometimes, she even sends along recipes to keep the emphasis on simplicity. There's no need to throw anyone into a hissy fit. "It can't become homework; we're all too busy," says Kate, adding that the gathering is held every six or so weeks after work, midweek. "My whole schtick is to get people back in the kitchen sharing food together," says Kate.

ATTACK OF THE BOOK BEES: The girls break into groups of two or three, and the laughter and the pitch get louder and louder. "It seems like everybody talks at once. When we actually start talking about the book, watch out! We chatter our way through chapter after chapter It's a free-for-all. Everybody talks at once about their favorite parts. It's so intellectually stimulating," says Kate.

BOOK REVIEW NOTES: Rated "a very good read" by the group, *Stuffed,* by Patricia Volk, was a hit. The book is a memoir that chronicles the author's family, who introduced pastrami to America and gave birth to the first New York deli. "I thought it was hysterical—the way the family equated food with love, food with everything, and I could totally relate to all her diets over the years. It felt fun to be an observer in somebody else's crazy life with their crazy relatives," says Kate.

GETTING DISHY ABOUT THE MENU: In this case, the book inspired Kate to focus on pastrami, crudités, and chocolate cake. But every book is different. "When I'm deciding on recipes to suggest, I try to keep things pretty mainstream. If there are too many ingredients or steps, the group gets totally turned off," says Kate.

Who better to throw the party than Kate Manchester? Books are her passion; food is her forte. She's also a cookbook author and personal chef.

Everyone brings the book, a dish or a bottle of wine to Kate's house and comes ready to engage in wherever the conversation goes.

Triple Cranberry Spread

Cranberry's MORNING MAGIC

We love cranberries at holiday time, for a lot of reasons. As one of only a few edible fruits native to the United States, their roots are deep in American cuisine. They freeze like champions, so it's easy to keep a supply on hand. And they graciously bestow their sweet-sour tang on appetizers, main dishes, and desserts. Cranberries have long been favored at holiday time because they add a daring dash of color to the comfy browns of the buffet table. But, as much as we love them for dinner, cranberries make great eye openers in the morning too. Even better for holiday time, these two breakfast treats that can be made the night before.

The first is a toast topper that takes less than a half hour to stir together. It's a mix of three forms of cranberries—fresh, dried, and juice—and it's perfect for spooning onto toasted holiday breads, stollen, scones, and biscuits to get you through those early morning hours.

The second is a good-morning drink you can have waiting for guests as they drift downstairs, one by one. What a great way to toast the new day!

Triple Cranberry Spread

Prepare this tart cranberry spread several days ahead for a stress-free holiday morning. It tastes tangy and juicy when served on hearty raisin bread with a shard of provolone cheese.

PREP: 10 minutes **COOK:** 15 minutes **CHILL:** 4 hours

- **2/3 cup cranberry juice**
- **1/2 cup sugar**
- **1 1/2 cups fresh cranberries (6 oz.)**
- **1 lime, peeled and sectioned**
- **1 tsp. finely shredded lime peel**
- **1/2 cup dried cranberries**
- **Dash ground allspice**

1. In a medium saucepan combine cranberry juice and sugar. Bring to boiling; reduce heat. Simmer, uncovered, stirring occasionally, until sugar is dissolved.

2. Add fresh cranberries, lime sections, dried cranberries, and allspice. Return to boiling; reduce heat. Simmer, uncovered, about 15 minutes or until mixture is thickened (it will thicken more upon chilling).

3. Remove from heat; stir in lime peel. Cover and chill at least 4 hours or up to 3 days. Makes 1 1/2 cups.

Each tablespoon: 31 cal., 0 g total fat, 0 mg chol., 1 mg sodium, 8 g carbo., 1 g fiber, 0 g pro. Daily Values: 7% vit. C.

CRANBERRY COOKING TIPS

- Fresh cranberries are available in stores between October and December. Because their season is so short, it's a good idea to stock up. You can store them in their original bags, frozen, for up to a year.
- Count on a 12-ounce bag containing about 3 cups whole berries.
- Before cooking, discard any soft berries or stems. Rinse the remaining berries in cold water.
- If you're using frozen cranberries, don't thaw them before using. Sort and rinse, then use just as you would fresh cranberries.
- Cranberries can be time-consuming to chop on a cutting board, because they tend to roll. Instead, try chopping them in small batches in either the blender or food processor—short pulses only or you'll turn them to paste.
- Give muffins that unmistakable cranberry tang: For a recipe that makes a dozen muffins, take a cup of fresh cranberries, chop coarsely, and toss in a bowl with 3 tablespoons sugar. Add this sugar-cranberry mixture to your favorite muffin recipe. Fill the muffin cups slightly fuller than normal and you should be able to get the entire recipe into 12 muffin cups.
- Holiday math: You'll need 24 cranberries to make a foot of Christmas tree garland. That means about 10 feet per 12-ounce bag.

Mulled Cranberry Drink

Mulled Cranberry Drink

START TO FINISH: 20 minutes

- **5 cups cranberry juice**
- **1 1/2 cups fresh cranberries (6 oz.)**
- **1/3 cup honey**
- **1/4 cup crystallized ginger, chopped**
- **1 tsp. cardamom pods or 1/4 tsp. ground cardamom**
- **1/2 tsp. whole black pepper, cracked**
- **1 vanilla bean, split**

1. In a large saucepan stir together all ingredients. Heat over medium heat until mixture boils and cranberry skins pop. Remove from heat. Cover and let stand for 5 minutes.

2. Strain and discard solids. Serve warm. Makes 8 to 10 servings (about 4 ounces each).

TEST KITCHEN TIP: Cover and chill any leftovers. Reheat or, if desired, serve iced.

Each serving: 156 cal., 0 g total fat, 0 mg chol., 5 mg sodium, 40 g carbo., 1 g fiber, 0 g pro. Daily Values: 98% vit. C, 1% calcium, 3% iron.

The Apple MAN

AN APPLE OBSESSION KEPT MARK ROSENSTEIN IN HIS KITCHEN FOR MONTHS IN SEARCH OF LIQUID GOLD.

Chunky Apple-Sage Sauce

Create an appetizer by serving the chunky applesauce on biscuits or toasted pita wedges that have been topped with smoked ham, cheddar cheese, and fresh sage leaves.

PREP: 15 minutes **COOK:** 10 minutes

- 4 medium Rome Beauty or Jonathan apples, cored and chopped (about 3 cups)
- 1/4 cup finely chopped onion
- 3 Tbsp. snipped fresh sage
- 2 Tbsp. butter, cut up, or olive oil
- 2 Tbsp. lemon juice

1. In a medium saucepan combine apples, onion, sage, butter or olive oil, and lemon juice. Cook, covered, over medium heat for 10 minutes or until apples are softened, stirring occasionally.

2. If desired, mash slightly with a potato masher or fork. Let cool slightly. Serve warm or cover and chill for up to 24 hours. Let stand at room temperature for 20 minutes before serving. Makes 2½ cups.

Each ¼-cup serving: 57 cal., 3 g total fat (2 g sat. fat), 7 mg chol., 26 mg sodium, 9 g carbo., 2 g fiber, 0 g pro. Daily Values: 3% vit. A, 9% vit. C, 1% calcium, 1% iron.

Chunky Apple-Sage Sauce

Apple euphoria

There's a deep honey-brown syrup in Mark Rosenstein's kitchen that he cherishes. One taste and you'll know that it is, indeed, a treasure. The owner and chef of The Market Place restaurant in Asheville, North Carolina, has captured the essence of apples in a drizzly syrup that he uses whenever he wants to uniquely enhance a food he is preparing.

Mark created his prized syrup and many of his other delicious ideas at a time when he was at the height of his apple euphoria. It all began with an effort to include regional foods in his cooking.

"I started wondering if there was a cuisine in this neck of the woods where I live. But there wasn't really a western North Carolina cuisine," Mark says.

So he sought to find foods that epitomized the region. "We've got a lot of trout and apples around here, so I decided to start messing around with apples," he says.

His goal was to find something that would thicken and add rich flavor to vegetable stock. And he found it by gently simmering apple cider until it reduced to the consistency of maple syrup.

With a hint of cinnamon and cloves, the syrup is an incredible treat on ice cream or waffles, or drizzled over scones. Adding herbs or chile peppers gives the syrup a spicy-sweet kiss that enhances pork or seafood.

His concentration on apples resulted in enough recipes and information to fill his cookbook, *In Praise of Apples*. And he works apples and other seasonal produce into his menus. Part of his philosophy is to support local growers, something that began at his first restaurant 31 years ago. He continues to use fresh, organic local produce whenever possible. And he's still the apple man.

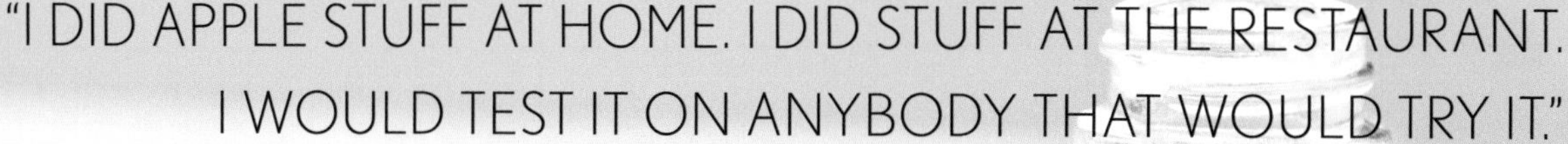

Mark Rosenstein

Apple Cider Syrup

Use fresh apple cider, not apple juice, when creating this reduction syrup. Start with 3 cups of apple cider, or double it as we did to get a bigger batch.

CINNAMON APPLE SYRUP: In a small stainless-steel or enamel saucepan bring 3 cups apple cider, a stick of cinnamon, and 2 whole cloves to boiling. Reduce heat; simmer over medium heat for 1 to 1¼ hours or until cider is thickened and reduced to ⅓ cup. Strain.

APPLE-AND-HERB SYRUP: In a small stainless-steel or enamel saucepan bring 3 cups apple cider, two 2-inch sprigs fresh thyme, one 2-inch sprig fresh rosemary, and one 2-inch sprig fresh marjoram to boiling. Reduce heat; simmer over medium heat for 1 to 1¼ hours or until cider is thickened and is reduced to ⅓ cup. Strain.

SPICY APPLE SYRUP: In a small stainless-steel or enamel saucepan bring 3 cups apple cider and 1 fresh serrano chile pepper, cut in half, to boiling. Reduce heat; simmer over medium heat for 1 to 1¼ hours or until cider is thickened and is reduced to ⅓ cup. Strain.

Each tablespoon: 70 cal., 0 g total fat, 0 mg chol., 4 mg sodium, 17 g carbo., 0 g fiber, 0 g pro. Daily Values: 2% vit. C, 1% calcium, 3% iron.

Apple Dumplings

PREP: 50 minutes **BAKE:** 40 minutes

- $1\frac{3}{4}$ **cups water**
- $1\frac{1}{4}$ **cups sugar**
- $\frac{1}{2}$ **tsp. ground cinnamon**
- $\frac{1}{2}$ **tsp. ground nutmeg**
- **Several drops red food coloring (optional)**
- 2 **Tbsp. butter**
- $2\frac{1}{4}$ **cups all-purpose flour**
- $\frac{1}{4}$ **tsp. salt**
- $\frac{2}{3}$ **cup shortening**
- 6 **to 8 Tbsp. cold water**
- 6 **small cooking apples (about $1\frac{1}{2}$ lb.), such as Granny Smith, Rome Beauty, Braeburn, or Gala**

1. For syrup, in a medium saucepan combine the $1\frac{3}{4}$ cups water, 1 cup of the sugar, $\frac{1}{4}$ teaspoon of the cinnamon, $\frac{1}{4}$ teaspoon of the nutmeg, and, if desired, the food coloring. Heat to boiling; reduce heat. Simmer, uncovered, about 10 minutes or until mixture is reduced to $1\frac{1}{2}$ cups. Remove saucepan from heat; stir in butter.

2. Meanwhile, for pastry, stir together flour and salt. Cut in shortening until pieces are pea-size. Add the 6 to 8 tablespoons water, a little at a time, mixing until flour mixture is moistened. Form dough into a ball. On a lightly floured surface, roll dough into an 18×12-inch rectangle; cut into six 6-inch squares.

3. Preheat oven to 375° F. Peel and core apples. Place an apple on each pastry square. Combine the remaining $\frac{1}{4}$ cup sugar, $\frac{1}{4}$ teaspoon cinnamon, and $\frac{1}{4}$ teaspoon nutmeg; sprinkle onto fruit. Moisten edges of pastry with water; fold corners to center over fruit. Pinch pastry corners together to seal. Place in a 13×9×2-inch baking pan. Pour syrup into pan around dumplings.

4. Bake, uncovered, for 40 to 45 minutes or until fruit is tender and pastry is golden. To serve, spoon syrup from baking pan over dumplings. Makes 6 servings.

Each serving: 611 cal., 26 g total fat (8 g sat. fat), 11 mg chol., 142 mg sodium, 90 g carbo., 3 g fiber, 5 g pro. Daily Values: 4% vit. A, 7% vit. C, 3% calcium, 15% iron.

THE APPEAL'S IN THE PEEL

Most of an apple's fiber and those good-for-you antioxidants are found in the peel, so leave it on if at all possible. Do wash the fruit well before eating it. Try Mark's top picks for starters.

BRAEBURN: A spicy-sweet variety that balances well with tart Granny Smiths in a pie or cobbler.

CAMEO: Subtle red stripes make this an apple to admire as much as to eat. It's a crisp and sweet-tart apple.

GINGER GOLD: Get this one while you can. Available through November, Ginger Gold is snappy-crisp and excellent for eating out of hand.

HONEY CRISP: Its name gives a hint of its flavor. Try it in salads.

Cranberry-Stuffed Pork Loin

ROOTED IN THE HEARTLAND

Judith Fertig (in photo, left, in 1962) and her family, with their Midwestern roots, celebrate the holidays with heartland foods inspired by the past. Her Pesto Rolls (*page* 442) evolved from a cloverleaf roll recipe passed on from her great-grandmother. Cloverleaf rolls often appear on the holiday table, although Judith, a Kansas City food writer and cookbook author, adds her own updates.

Her grown son and daughter always joke that their mother never serves the same dish twice. "Our family has a collective sense of humor, so we usually laugh down memory lane through Thanksgiving dinner," Judith says.

Because her children are not turkey fans, Judith created a Thanksgiving feast focusing on Cranberry-Stuffed Pork Loin, slathered with a garlic-onion jam. (If your family, like most, insists on turkey, you can use the jam on that too.) Judith also serves acorn squash, a hearty stuffing of freshly baked herb bread, and a make-ahead mashed potato casserole.

Making slight adjustments to traditional recipes has become part of the holiday dinner ritual at the Fertig home. The main ingredients may not change from year to year, but the flavors almost always do. "What matters most to me at Thanksgiving is celebrating the abundance we enjoy with the people I love," she says.

Holding memories and recipes close to the heart is a trait Judith inherited. Her great-grandmother's recipe collection was just the beginning. Her grandmother maintained the tradition, using a fountain pen to include recipes in a "household book"—now a torn and tattered family keepsake.

"Then my mother collected recipes and family photos and compiled a book for my sister and me, which I treasure," Judith says. That spiral notebook is called *The Family Heirloom Cookbook* (a page is shown below). Judith has started putting together a similar feast journal for her two children, now 26 and 21 years old. "I think the kids will appreciate it more when they have their own households," she says.

Judith also includes family anecdotes in the cookbooks she writes. Her latest books are *Prairie Home Cooking* and *Prairie Home Breads.*

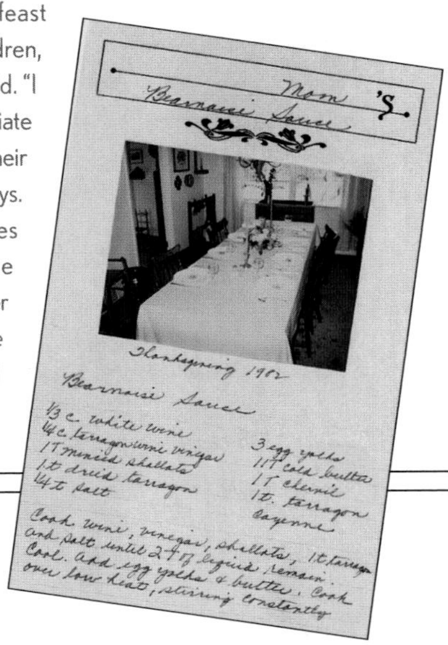

Mom's Bearnaise Sauce

Thanksgiving 1962

Bearnaise Sauce

1/3 c. white wine
1/4 c. tarragon wine vinegar
1 T minced shallots
1 t dried tarragon
1/4 t salt

3 egg yolks
1 1/2 T cold butter
1 T chervil
1 t. tarragon
Cayenne

Cook wine, vinegar, shallots, 1 t tarragon and salt until 2-4 T of liquid remain. Cool. Add egg yolks & butter. Cook over low heat, stirring constantly.

Cranberry-Stuffed Pork Loin

Ask your butcher to butterfly the pork loin for you, or do it yourself, using the directions below.

PREP: 30 minutes **ROAST:** 1¼ to 1½ hours **STAND:** 15 minutes

- **1 4½- to 5-lb. boneless pork center loin roast (single loin)**
- **Salt**
- **Pepper**
- **1 cup Roasted Garlic and Sweet Onion Jam (page 437)**
- **¾ cup dried cranberries**
- **1 tsp. garlic salt**
- **1 tsp. pepper**
- **¾ cup dry white wine or apple juice**
- **Chicken broth**
- **3 Tbsp. all-purpose flour**

1. Preheat the oven to 325° F. To butterfly the roast, turn the roast fat side down. Make a single lengthwise cut down the center of the loin, cutting to within ½ inch of the other side. Spread open like a book. Place knife in the "V" of the first cut. Make another cut—knife should be parallel to the table—to the right of the "V" to within ½ inch of the end (do not cut all the way through roast). Repeat the parallel cut to the left of the "V." Spread open the sections. Cover with plastic wrap. Working from center to edges, pound with flat side of meat mallet to ¾- to 1-inch thickness. Remove plastic wrap.

2. Sprinkle meat with salt and pepper; spread with ⅔ cup Roasted Garlic and Sweet Onion Jam. Sprinkle cranberries onto jam. Starting at a long side, roll meat up. Tie snugly at 3-inch intervals with 100-percent-cotton string. Place the rolled pork loin roast on a rack in a shallow roasting pan. Sprinkle with garlic salt and pepper. Insert a meat thermometer into center of roast. Roast, uncovered, for 1¼ to 1½ hours or until thermometer (or instant-read thermometer) registers 155° F, spreading with remaining jam the last 15 minutes of roasting.

3. Remove roast from pan. Cover with foil; let stand for 15 minutes before carving. (The temperature of the meat will rise 5° F during standing.)

4. Meanwhile, for gravy, carefully pour wine into roasting pan, stirring to scrape up browned bits from bottom of pan. Strain and measure pan juices. Add chicken broth, if necessary, to equal 1½ cups total. In a saucepan stir ¾ cup chicken broth into flour until smooth; stir in the wine mixture. Cook and stir until thickened and bubbly; cook and stir for 1 minute more.

5. To carve, cut string. Using a carving knife, cut roast into 1-inch-thick slices. Serve with gravy. Makes 10 to 12 servings.

Each serving: 404 cal., 11 g total fat (4 g sat. fat), 128 mg chol., 399 mg sodium, 24 g carbo., 1 g fiber, 46 g pro. Daily Values: 7% vit. C, 6% calcium, 12% iron.

Roast Turkey with Roasted Garlic and Sweet Onion Jam

Roast Turkey with Roasted Garlic and Sweet Onion Jam

If you don't have time to make the jam yourself, grab a jar in a specialty food market. We like Stonewall Kitchen's version.

Prep: 15 minutes **Roast:** 2$^3/_4$ hours **Stand:** 15 minutes

- 1 10- to 12-lb. turkey
- Salt
- Cooking oil
- 6 medium red and/or white onions, peeled and cut into wedges
- 10 to 12 cloves unpeeled garlic
- 1 recipe Roasted Garlic and Sweet Onion Jam (right) or 1 cup purchased roasted onion jam
- Chicken broth (optional)
- $^1/_4$ cup dry white wine or apple juice
- 3 Tbsp. all-purpose flour

1. Preheat oven to 325° F. Remove turkey neck from body cavity and giblets from neck cavity. Rinse inside and outside of turkey; pat dry with paper towels. If desired, season body cavity with salt. Pull the neck skin to the back; fasten with a skewer.

2. Tuck the ends of the drumsticks under the band of skin across the tail. If there is no band of skin, tie the drumsticks securely to the tail. Twist wing tips under the back.

3. Place turkey, breast side up, on a rack in a shallow roasting pan. Brush with cooking oil. Insert a meat thermometer into the center of an inside thigh muscle. The thermometer should not touch bone. Cover turkey loosely with foil. Place turkey in oven. Roast for 1 hour.

4. In a bowl toss onion wedges and unpeeled garlic cloves with 2 tablespoons cooking oil. Spoon the onion mixture around the turkey; roast for 1$^1/_4$ hours more.

5. Remove foil from turkey. (The thermometer should register 160° F.) Cut band of skin or string between drumsticks so that thighs cook evenly. Carefully spread Roasted Garlic and Sweet Onion Jam onto turkey. Roast for 30 to 45 minutes more or until the thermometer registers 180° F. (The juices should run clear and drumsticks should move easily in their sockets.)

6. Remove turkey from oven. Transfer turkey, garlic, and onions to a platter. Cover and let stand for 15 to 20 minutes.

7. Meanwhile, pour pan drippings into a large measuring cup. Skim fat from drippings and strain remaining broth. Add chicken broth, if necessary, to equal 1$^3/_4$ cups. In a medium saucepan, combine wine and flour. Stir in strained pan juices. Cook and stir until thickened and bubbly; cook and stir for 1 minute more. Serve with turkey. Makes 12 to 14 servings.

Each serving: 590 cal., 27 g total fat (7 g sat. fat), 202 mg chol., 199 mg sodium, 19 g carbo., 1 g fiber, 62 g pro. Daily Values: 8% vit. C, 8% calcium, 25% iron.

Roasted Garlic and Sweet Onion Jam

Prep: 15 minutes **Roast:** 45 minutes **Cook:** 30 minutes

- 1 bulb garlic
- 1 Tbsp. olive oil
- 1 large sweet onion, peeled and finely chopped (1 cup)
- $^1/_2$ cup finely chopped Granny Smith apple
- $^1/_2$ cup sugar
- $^1/_2$ cup balsamic vinegar

1. Preheat the oven to 350° F. Slice about $^1/_4$ inch off the pointed end of the garlic bulb so the individual cloves show. Place the bulb in a small baking dish, cut side up, and drizzle with olive oil. Cover and roast for 45 to 60 minutes or until the garlic cloves have softened. Cool.

2. Gently squeeze the garlic cloves and juices into a saucepan. Stir in the onion, apple, sugar, and balsamic vinegar. Bring to boiling over medium-high heat, stirring occasionally. Reduce heat; simmer about 30 minutes or until the onion and apple have softened and turned transparent and the mixture has thickened, stirring occasionally. Makes about 1 cup.

Each tablespoon: 46 cal., 1 g total fat (0 g sat. fat), 0 mg chol., 1 mg sodium, 10 g carbo., 1 g fiber, 0 g pro. Daily Values: 2% vit. C, 1% calcium.

Mashed Baked Potatoes with Garden Confetti

Crowned with autumn colors, this rustic version of an American classic can be made a day ahead.

PREP: 30 minutes **BAKE:** 40 minutes + 1¼ hours

- 5 lb. red potatoes (about 15 medium potatoes), baked*
- 1 8-oz. pkg. cream cheese or reduced-fat cream cheese (Neufchâtel), cut up and softened
- 1½ cups half-and-half, light cream, or fat-free evaporated milk
- 1 tsp. salt
- 1 tsp. cracked black pepper
- Nonstick cooking spray
- 1 recipe Garden Confetti (below)
- 2 Tbsp. butter, melted

1. Preheat oven to 325° F. While the potatoes are still hot, transfer half of the potatoes to a very large bowl. (Cut large potatoes in half for easier mashing.) Using a potato masher or an electric mixer, mash potatoes (with their skins still on) until slightly lumpy; transfer to another bowl. Use the same bowl to mash the remaining potatoes. Return all potatoes to the bowl.

2. Add cream cheese, half-and-half, salt, and pepper to potatoes; beat until combined. Coat a 3-quart casserole with cooking spray; spoon potato mixture into casserole. Top with Garden Confetti; drizzle with melted butter. Bake, uncovered, about 1¼ hours or until heated through. Makes 10 to 12 servings.

GARDEN CONFETTI: In a large skillet melt 2 tablespoons butter over medium heat. Add 2 medium carrots, shredded; 1 stalk celery, finely chopped; and 1 medium onion, thinly sliced. Cook and stir for 4 to 5 minutes or until vegetables are tender.

***TEST KITCHEN TIP:** To bake potatoes, scrub potatoes thoroughly with a brush; pat dry. Prick potatoes with a fork. Bake in a 425° F oven for 40 to 60 minutes or until tender.

MAKE-AHEAD DIRECTIONS: Prepare as above, except after drizzling with melted butter, cover and refrigerate overnight. Bake, covered, in the 325° F oven for 1 hour. Uncover and bake for 1 to 1¼ hours more or until heated through.

Each serving: 304 cal., 17 g total fat (11 g sat. fat), 51 mg chol., 386 mg sodium, 33 g carbo., 3 g fiber, 7 g pro. Daily Values: 75% vit. A, 42% vit. C, 9% calcium, 16% iron.

Artisanal Bread Stuffing

For this recipe, "artisanal" simply refers to any homemade or bakery-fresh loaf, typically with a burst of flavor from added ingredients, such as herbs, olives, or cheese.

PREP: 30 minutes **BAKE:** 1 hour

- 12 cups 1-inch cubes artisanal bread, such as rosemary, olive, or sun-dried tomato (about a 1¼-lb. loaf)
- ½ cup pine nuts
- 4½ cups coarsely chopped fennel (reserve leafy tops for another use)
- 1½ cups chopped onion
- 6 Tbsp. butter
- 1½ cups sliced, pitted kalamata olives
- 3 Tbsp. snipped fresh thyme or 1 Tbsp. dried thyme, crushed
- ¾ tsp. pepper
- 2¼ cups chicken broth
- Nonstick cooking spray

1. Preheat oven to 350° F. In a large roasting pan toast bread and pine nuts for 15 to 20 minutes or until bread is crisp and pine nuts are light brown, tossing once. Set aside.

2. Meanwhile, in a large skillet cook fennel and onion in butter over medium-high heat about 10 minutes or until tender, stirring occasionally.

3. Stir olives, thyme, and pepper into onion mixture; transfer to an extra-large bowl. Add bread cubes and pine nuts; toss to combine. Add chicken broth, stirring until moistened. Lightly coat a 3-quart casserole with cooking spray; spoon in bread mixture. Cover and bake for 45 minutes.

4. Remove cover; bake about 15 minutes more or until stuffing is heated through. Serve warm. Makes 10 to 12 servings.

Each serving: 319 cal., 16 g total fat (6 g sat. fat), 20 mg chol., 818 mg sodium, 38 g carbo., 5 g fiber, 8 g pro. Daily Values: 7% vit. A, 12% vit. C, 7% calcium, 14% iron.

"WHAT MATTERS MOST TO ME AT THANKSGIVING IS CELEBRATING THE ABUNDANCE WE ENJOY WITH THE PEOPLE I LOVE."

—Judith Fertig

Mashed Baked Potatoes with Garden Confetti and Artisanal Bread Stuffing

Pumpkin Rolls with Maple Streusel Filling and Caramelized Acorn Squash

Pumpkin Rolls with Maple Streusel Filling

There's a sweet surprise inside these pumpkin-flavored rolls: a crumbly combo of hickory nuts, apricots, and brown sugar.

PREP: 1 hour **CHILL:** overnight
RISE: 40 minutes **BAKE:** 12 minutes

- **$4\frac{1}{2}$ to 5 cups all-purpose flour**
- **1 pkg. active dry yeast**
- **$\frac{1}{2}$ cup milk**
- **$\frac{1}{2}$ cup water**
- **$\frac{1}{4}$ cup butter**
- **$\frac{1}{4}$ cup sugar**
- **$\frac{3}{4}$ tsp. salt**
- **1 egg**
- **$\frac{1}{2}$ cup canned pumpkin**
- **1 recipe Maple Streusel Filling (below)**

1. In a large mixing bowl stir together $1\frac{1}{2}$ cups of the flour and yeast; set aside.

2. In a medium saucepan heat and stir milk, water, butter, sugar, and salt just until warm (120° to 130° F) and butter almost melts.

3. Add milk mixture to dry mixture; add egg. Beat with an electric mixer on low to medium speed for 30 seconds, scraping side of bowl constantly. Beat on high speed for 3 minutes. Stir in canned pumpkin. Using a wooden spoon, stir in as much of the remaining flour as you can.

4. Turn dough out onto a lightly floured surface. Knead in enough of the remaining flour to make a moderately stiff dough that is smooth and elastic (6 to 8 minutes total). Shape dough into a ball. Place in a lightly greased large bowl; turn once to grease surface. Cover with plastic wrap; refrigerate overnight.

5. Punch dough down. Turn dough out onto a lightly floured surface. Divide dough in half. Cover; let rest for 10 minutes.

6. Meanwhile, lightly grease 2 baking sheets. Divide each half of dough into 8 pieces. On a lightly floured surface flatten each piece into a $3\frac{1}{2}$-inch round. For each roll, place the round of dough in the palm of your hand. Place 1 generous tablespoon of Maple Streusel Filling in the center of each round. Shape dough into a ball by pulling the edges of dough up and over streusel, pinching edges of dough to seal. Place rolls, smooth side up, on prepared baking sheets. Cover; let rise in a warm place until nearly double in size (30 to 40 minutes).

7. Preheat oven to 375° F. Bake rolls for 12 to 14 minutes or until golden brown. Immediately remove rolls from baking sheets. Cool on wire racks. Makes 16 rolls.

MAPLE STREUSEL FILLING: In a medium mixing bowl stir together $\frac{2}{3}$ cup chopped hickory nuts or hazelnuts (filberts), $\frac{1}{3}$ cup maple granulated sugar or packed brown sugar, $\frac{1}{3}$ cup all-purpose flour, and $\frac{1}{4}$ cup snipped dried apricots. Stir in $\frac{1}{3}$ cup melted butter until combined.

MAKE-AHEAD DIRECTIONS: Follow the same instructions for storing and reheating Pesto Rolls (recipe, page 442).

Each roll: 274 cal., 11 g total fat (5 g sat. fat), 33 mg chol., 191 mg sodium, 38 g carbo., 2 g fiber, 6 g pro. Daily Values: 43% vit. A, 1% vit. C, 3% calcium, 13% iron.

Caramelized Acorn Squash

PREP: 25 minutes **BAKE:** 40 minutes **CHILL:** overnight

- **4 1- to $1\frac{1}{2}$-lb. acorn squash**
- **$\frac{1}{2}$ cup sugar**
- **$\frac{1}{2}$ cup butter**
- **$\frac{1}{2}$ cup apple cider**
- **1 tsp. ground cinnamon**
- **$\frac{1}{2}$ tsp. ground nutmeg**
- **$\frac{1}{2}$ tsp. salt**

1. Preheat oven to 350° F. Carefully cut each squash into 4 rings; discard seeds and remove fibrous material. Line 2 shallow baking pans with parchment paper or foil. Arrange rings in a single layer on pans. Cover with foil; bake for 40 to 45 minutes or until squash is tender. Cool; place in a container, cover, and refrigerate overnight. (Let squash to come to room temperature before finishing recipe.)

2. Before serving, heat sugar in a 12-inch nonstick skillet over medium-high heat until it starts to melt, shaking occasionally. Do not stir. Reduce heat; cook and stir 3 minutes or until sugar is melted and medium caramel in color.

3. Whisk in the butter until completely melted. Whisk in cider, cinnamon, nutmeg, and salt. (The mixture will bubble up and sizzle before it reaches sauce consistency.)

4. Transfer a few rings to the skillet; turn to coat with caramel mixture. Warm rings in caramel for 3 minutes; transfer to an ovenproof platter. Keep warm in a 300° F oven. Repeat with remaining squash rings. Pour sauce over squash rings. Makes 10 to 12 servings.

Each serving: 185 cal., 10 g total fat (6 g sat. fat), 26 mg chol., 220 mg sodium, 26 g carbo., 2 g fiber, 1 g pro. Daily Values: 16% vit. A, 22% vit. C, 5% calcium, 6% iron.

THANKSGIVING DINNER

Cranberry-Raspberry Spinach Salad *(page 446)*
Roast Turkey with Roasted Garlic and Sweet Onion Jam *(page 437)*
Artisanal Bread Stuffing *(page 438)*
Mashed Baked Potatoes with Garden Confetti *(page 438)*
Caramelized Acorn Squash *(above)*
Pumpkin Rolls with Maple Streusel Filling *(left)*
Caramel-Pecan Pumpkin Pie *(page 450)*
Wine, coffee, or tea

Dill Batter Bread

If time is a little precious, remember this speedy yeast bread. It rises just once and requires no kneading or shaping.

PREP: 20 minutes **RISE:** 50 minutes **BAKE:** 25 minutes

- **2 cups all-purpose flour**
- **1 pkg. active dry yeast**
- **1/2 cup water**
- **1/2 cup cream-style cottage cheese**
- **1 Tbsp. sugar**
- **1 Tbsp. dill seed or caraway seed**
- **1 Tbsp. butter or margarine**
- **1 tsp. dried minced onion**
- **1 tsp. salt**
- **1 egg**
- **1/2 cup toasted wheat germ**

1. Grease a 9×1 1/2-inch round baking pan or a 1-quart casserole; set aside. In a large mixing bowl combine 1 cup of the flour and the yeast; set aside.

2. In a medium saucepan heat and stir water, cottage cheese, sugar, dillseed, butter, dried onion, and salt just until warm (120° to 130° F) and butter almost melts.

3. Add cottage cheese mixture to flour mixture; add egg. Beat with an electric mixer on low to medium speed for 30 seconds, scraping side of bowl constantly. Beat on high speed for 3 minutes. Using a wooden spoon, stir in the wheat germ and the remaining flour (the batter will be stiff).

4. Spoon batter into the prepared pan or casserole, spreading to edges. Cover and let rise in a warm place until double in size (50 to 60 minutes).

5. Preheat oven to 375° F. Bake for 25 to 30 minutes or until golden. Immediately remove from pan or casserole. Serve warm, or cool on a wire rack. Makes 1 loaf (8 servings).

Each slice: 185 cal., 4 g total fat (2 g sat. fat), 33 mg chol., 369 mg sodium, 30 g carbo., 2 g fiber, 8 g pro. Daily Values: 3% vit. A, 1% vit. C, 3% calcium, 13% iron.

Pesto Rolls

You can make these flavorful rolls a day ahead and store them in an airtight container. Or prepare them several weeks in advance and keep in freezer containers.

PREP: 35 minutes **CHILL:** overnight
RISE: 40 minutes **BAKE:** 12 minutes

- **4 1/2 to 5 cups all-purpose flour**
- **2 pkg. active dry yeast**
- **3/4 cup milk**
- **1/2 cup water**
- **1/3 cup butter**
- **1/3 cup sugar**
- **1 tsp. salt**
- **1 egg**
- **1/2 cup basil pesto**
- **1/2 cup finely shredded Parmesan cheese**

1. In a large mixing bowl stir together 1 3/4 cups of the flour and yeast; set aside.

2. In a medium saucepan heat and stir milk, water, butter, sugar, and salt just until warm (120° to 130° F) and butter almost melts.

3. Add milk mixture to dry mixture; add egg. Beat with an electric mixer on low to medium speed for 30 seconds, scraping side of bowl constantly. Beat on high speed for 3 minutes. Stir in pesto. Using a wooden spoon, stir in as much of the remaining flour as you can.

4. Turn dough out onto a lightly floured surface. Knead in enough of the remaining flour to make a moderately stiff dough that is smooth and elastic (6 to 8 minutes total). Shape dough into a ball. Place in a lightly greased large bowl; turn once to grease surface. Cover with plastic wrap; refrigerate overnight.

5. Punch dough down. Turn dough out onto a lightly floured surface. Divide dough in half. Cover; let rest for 10 minutes. Meanwhile, lightly grease eighteen 2 1/2-inch muffin cups.

6. Divide each half of dough into 9 equal portions. Divide each portion into 3 pieces. Shape each piece into a ball, pulling edges under to make a smooth top. Place 3 balls in each muffin cup, smooth sides up. Sprinkle with Parmesan cheese. Cover and let rise in a warm place until nearly double in size (about 30 minutes).

7. Preheat oven to 375° F. Bake for 12 to 14 minutes or until rolls are golden brown. Immediately remove rolls from pans. Serve warm, or cool on wire racks. Makes 18 rolls.

MAKE-AHEAD DIRECTIONS: To reheat rolls from room temperature, wrap in foil and warm in a 375° F oven about 7 minutes or until heated through. To reheat frozen rolls, wrap and warm in a 375° F oven about 20 minutes or until warm.

Each roll: 217 cal., 8 g total fat (4 g sat. fat), 26 mg chol., 258 mg sodium, 29 g carbo., 1 g fiber, 6 g pro. Daily Values: 5% vit. A, 6% calcium, 10% iron.

Pesto Rolls

Vegetable-Topped Mussels with Chardonnay Cream

Vegetable-Topped Mussels with Chardonnay Cream

You can store the bread mixture and sauce separately overnight in the refrigerator. Or steam the mussels in the wine mixture; cover and refrigerate overnight, then reheat just before serving.

PREP: 1 hour **COOK:** 30 minutes **BAKE:** 15 minutes

- 1/2 cup chopped zucchini
- 1/2 cup chopped fresh mushrooms
- 1/3 cup chopped red or yellow sweet pepper
- 1/4 cup chopped leek
- 2 tsp. olive oil
- 1 cup Chardonnay wine
- 1 Tbsp. finely chopped shallot
- 1 bay leaf
- 1 sprig fresh thyme
- 1 clove garlic, minced
- 20 green-lip mussels (about 2 lb.), cleaned*
- 1/2 tsp. curry powder
- Dash ground red pepper
- 1 recipe Herbed Bread Crumbs (below)
- 1/2 cup whipping cream
- Toasted baguette slices

1. In a 4-quart Dutch oven cook zucchini, mushrooms, sweet pepper, and leek in hot olive oil over medium heat for 2 to 3 minutes or until vegetables are crisp tender. Remove from pan.

2. Add wine, shallot, bay leaf, thyme, and garlic to pan. Bring to boiling. Add mussels; return to boiling. Reduce heat. Cook, covered, for 5 to 9 minutes or until mussels open.

3. Remove mussels, discarding any unopened shells; set aside. Strain remaining liquid; return to pan. Bring to boiling. Stir in curry powder and red pepper. Simmer, uncovered, about 10 minutes or until mixture is reduced by half (about 2/3 cup).

4. Meanwhile, pull apart mussel shells. Using a sharp knife, cut mussel loose, but do not remove from bottom shell. Discard empty shells. Place remaining mussel shells on a 15×10×1-inch baking pan. Spoon about 1 teaspoon of the vegetables over each mussel; top with about 2 teaspoons of the Herbed Bread Crumbs. Reserve remaining vegetables.

5. When curry liquid has been reduced, add cream; simmer, uncovered, for 5 minutes more. Stir in remaining vegetables.

6. Preheat oven to 425° F. Just before serving, bake mussels for 15 minutes or until heated through and bread crumbs are golden brown. Spoon some of the hot vegetable-cream mixture into ten shallow soup plates. Top each serving with 2 mussels. Serve with toasted baguette slices. Makes 10 appetizer servings.

HERBED BREAD CRUMBS: In a bowl combine 1 cup coarse bread crumbs, 4 teaspoons olive oil, 2 teaspoons snipped fresh thyme, and 2 teaspoons snipped fresh parsley. Season to taste.

***TEST KITCHEN TIP:** To clean mussels, scrub under cold running water. Remove beards. In an 8-quart Dutch oven combine 4 quarts cold water and 1/3 cup salt; add mussels. Soak for 15 minutes; drain and rinse. Discard water. Repeat soaking in salt water, draining, and rinsing twice.

Each serving: 346 cal., 13 g total fat (5 g sat. fat), 46 mg chol., 806 mg sodium, 29 g carbo., 2 g fiber, 23 g pro. Daily Values: 28% vit. A, 24% vit. C, 12% calcium, 26% iron.

A TOAST TO THE FAMILY

Jamie Davies (*at right* with her sister in 1943) believes in holding true to tradition, especially on Thanksgiving Day. As they've done for years, her three sons (*below*) and their families gather at her Calistoga, California, home—a majestic Victorian—where they grew up. "We celebrate Thanksgiving here because of the great memories," says Jamie, who purchased Schramsberg Vineyards in 1965 with her late husband, Jack. The Napa Valley winery is known for its sparkling wines.

Now the family includes grandchildren who take part in the pre-dinner hustle and bustle along with their parents. "Everyone gets an assignment. The prepping becomes a family experience," Jamie says. Someone picks the wine. Another chooses the china. Someone else mashes the potatoes.

The celebration begins with seafood, such as a mussel appetizer, followed by a salad of winter greens. Then there's the roast turkey with corn bread stuffing, plus mashed potatoes. Jamie might tweak the flavors and presentation of the remaining side dishes, but the basics are always there.

Dessert also reflects the season, typically featuring pumpkin and mincemeat. The pumpkin could flavor a crème brûlée and the mincemeat just might show up in a tart or turnover, or the two flavors might be melded.

Keeping the family's recipes neatly organized is second nature to Jamie, whose organizational skills are evident to those who know her. She oversees 60 vineyards that cover 200 acres and stretch across four counties. In fact, she has so many recipes that she keeps them categorized in file folders. Some come from the Napa Valley cooking class she founded with friends about 30 years ago.

Her photos, such as the holiday table setting (*right*), are just as cherished. She keeps them in photo albums, but pulls a few out every so often to display on her kitchen walls. "The photo walls are another way to share our family memories," Jamie says.

Sparkling Kumquat Salad

Jamie uses a sparkling wine from Schramsberg Vineyards, which we recommend. You can use another wine or even an alcohol-free version for the vinaigrette.

Start to Finish: 30 minutes

- 1/3 **cup walnut pieces, toasted**
- 1/3 **cup pomegranate seeds**
- 2 **Tbsp. snipped fresh fennel leafy tops**
- 1 **recipe Sparkling Vinaigrette (below)**
- 12 **cups torn mixed salad greens**
- 1 **fennel bulb, thinly sliced**
- 1/2 **cup kumquats, seeds removed and thinly sliced**
- 1/4 **tsp. salt**
- 1/8 **tsp. pepper**

1. In a small mixing bowl combine walnut pieces, pomegranate seeds, fennel tops, and 1 tablespoon of the Sparkling Vinaigrette; set aside.

2. In a large bowl combine salad greens, sliced fennel, kumquats, salt, and pepper. Drizzle with remaining Sparkling Vinaigrette. Toss gently to coat. Sprinkle with the walnut mixture. Makes 10 servings.

SPARKLING VINAIGRETTE: In a blender container or small food processor bowl combine 1/2 cup coarsely chopped and seeded kumquats, 1/2 cup chilled sparkling white wine or chilled alcohol-free sparkling white grape beverage, 1/4 cup walnut oil, 1 quartered shallot, 1/4 teaspoon salt, 1/8 teaspoon pepper, and 1/8 teaspoon ground coriander or ground cardamom. Cover and blend or process until nearly smooth.

Each serving: 130 cal., 8 g total fat (1 g sat. fat), 0 mg chol., 139 mg sodium, 12 g carbo., 4 g fiber, 2 g pro. Daily Values: 16% vit. A, 33% vit. C, 6% calcium, 5% iron.

THANKSGIVING WITH A TWIST

Vegetable-Topped Mussels with Chardonnay Cream *(page 445)*
Sparkling Kumquat Salad *(left)*
Cranberry-Stuffed Pork Loin *(page 435)*
Steamed pea pods
Pesto Rolls *(page 442)*
Chocolate-Pear Spice Cake *(page 449)*
Sparkling wine, coffee, or tea

Cranberry-Raspberry Spinach Salad

Prep: 35 minutes **Chill:** 1 hour

- 1 **10-oz. pkg. fresh spinach, stems removed and torn (8 cups)**
- 1/2 **cup broken walnuts**
- 1/3 **cup dried cranberries**
- 1/4 **cup sunflower seeds**
- 3 **green onions, thinly sliced**
- 1 **recipe Cranberry-Raspberry Vinaigrette (below)**

1. In a large bowl combine spinach, walnuts, cranberries, sunflower seeds, and green onions. Drizzle with some of the Cranberry-Raspberry Vinaigrette; toss gently to coat. Pass remaining dressing. Makes 6 servings.

CRANBERRY-RASPBERRY VINAIGRETTE: In a blender container or a food processor bowl place one 10-ounce package frozen red raspberries in syrup, thawed. Cover and blend or process until smooth; strain through a sieve to remove seeds. Discard seeds. In a medium saucepan combine 1/4 cup sugar and 2 teaspoons cornstarch. Stir in strained raspberries, 1/2 cup cranberry-raspberry juice cocktail, 1/4 cup red wine vinegar, 1/4 teaspoon celery seed, 1/4 teaspoon ground cinnamon, and 1/8 teaspoon ground cloves. Cook and stir over medium heat until thickened and bubbly; cook and stir for 2 minutes more. Transfer to a nonmetal container. Cover and chill for at least 1 hour.

Each serving: 195 cal., 10 g total fat (1 g sat. fat), 0 mg chol., 48 mg sodium, 25 g carbo., 4 g fiber, 4 g pro.Daily Values: 64% vit. A, 32% vit. C, 7% calcium, 14% iron.

"I MAY TWEAK THE TRADITIONAL THANKSGIVING DINNER, BUT THE BASIC FLAVORS ARE ALWAYS THERE."

—Jamie Davies

Sparkling Kumquat Salad

Chocolate-Pear Spice Cake

Chocolate-Pear Spice Cake

You'll get a pretty good idea of how this dessert is going to taste by breathing in its spicy aroma while it bakes.

PREP: 35 minutes **BAKE:** 1 hour
STAND: 45 minutes **COOL:** 10 minutes

- 2 cups all-purpose flour
- 1 Tbsp. ground cinnamon
- 2 tsp. baking soda
- 1 tsp. ground nutmeg
- 1/2 tsp. baking powder
- 1/2 tsp. salt
- 1/4 tsp. ground cloves
- 6 Tbsp. butter, softened
- 1 cup sugar
- 3 Tbsp. molasses
- 2 eggs
- 2 cups unsweetened applesauce
- 1 Tbsp. finely shredded orange peel
- 1 small Bosc pear, peeled, cored, and thinly sliced
- 2 oz. bittersweet and/or milk chocolate, coarsely chopped
- 1/2 cup coarsely chopped walnuts, hazelnuts (filberts), or pecans
- 1 recipe Pear Chips (below) (optional)
- Whipped cream (optional)

1. Preheat oven to 350° F. Grease and flour a 9-inch springform pan; set aside.

2. In a medium bowl stir together flour, cinnamon, baking soda, nutmeg, baking powder, salt, and cloves; set aside.

3. In a large mixing bowl combine butter, sugar, and molasses; beat with an electric mixer on medium speed until combined, scraping side of bowl constantly. Add eggs, one at a time, beating just until combined after each addition. Alternately add flour mixture and applesauce, beating on low speed until combined. Stir in orange peel.

4. Spoon the batter into the prepared pan. Arrange pear slices on top of the batter in one layer. Sprinkle with chopped chocolate and nuts. Bake about 1 hour or until the top springs back when gently touched and a toothpick inserted in the center comes out clean. Cool in pan on a wire rack for 10 minutes.

5. Remove side of pan. Serve cake warm with Pear Chips and whipped cream, if desired. Makes 10 servings.

PEAR CHIPS: Using a mandoline or sharp knife, very thinly slice a small Bosc pear. Place pear slices on a large baking sheet lined with parchment paper. Bake in a 300° F oven for 20 to 25 minutes until golden brown and crisp, turning once.

Each slice: 359 cal., 15 g total fat (6 g sat. fat), 62 mg chol., 480 mg sodium, 55 g carbo., 3 g dietary fiber, 5 g pro. Daily Values: 7% vit. A, 2% vit. C, 6% calcium, 13% iron.

FROM THE FAMILY GARDEN

Although Jim Fobel—a food writer—hails from Ohio, he now lives near Central Park in New York City where he has a close-up view of the annual Macy's Thanksgiving Day Parade. He's never sure what he might bump into when he steps outside to watch the festivities. "Last year I came out to find three human cupcakes sitting on my front steps," he says.

When Jim was a youngster, he reaped the benefits of his family's peach orchard and enormous garden. His mother always baked bread, churned butter, put up preserves and canned fruits and vegetables. His Chocolate-Pear Spice Cake was inspired by his grandmother's spice cake, the orchard, and his own inclination to add a bit of fruit to his cake batters.

His recipe for Butterscotch Meringue Pie (page 450) came from his grandmother (below) who was on the road with her husband, an orchestra leader, sometime in the early 1900s. They had stopped at a restaurant, probably in Pennsylvania, where she ordered pie for dessert. It was so good that she asked for the recipe. The chef complied and the pie has been a family favorite ever since.

"My grandmother and Aunt Irma were avid recipe collectors," Jim Fobel says. "I have an old composition notebook—dated 1917—full of Aunt Irma's handwritten recipes" (below).

The penchant for keeping recipes was passed on through the generations. Jim started compiling his own assortment when he was a boy. "I began collecting my favorite recipes on cards," he says. "I didn't know if we'd ever have enough money to buy a cookbook, so this was how I put one together."

Visits to his aunt's house were times to scout out new recipes, and it was in her California kitchen that he learned the best way to prepare Thanksgiving dinner. He treasures this and many similar memories, which he shares in his book *Jim Fobel's Old-Fashioned Baking Book*, providing snippets of family tales, along with favorite recipes and old pictures from his photo album. He has also written *Jim Fobel's Big Flavors.*

Caramel-Pecan Pumpkin Pie

Two favorite family pies—pecan and pumpkin—are layered in one flaky crust.

PREP: 25 minutes **BAKE:** 45 minutes

- 2 eggs
- 1 15-oz. can pumpkin
- 1/4 cup half-and-half, light cream, or milk
- 3/4 cup granulated sugar
- 1 Tbsp. all-purpose flour
- 1 tsp. finely shredded lemon peel
- 1/2 tsp. vanilla
- 1/4 tsp. salt
- 1/4 tsp. ground cinnamon
- 1/4 tsp. ground nutmeg
- 1/8 tsp. ground allspice
- 1 recipe Pastry for Single-Crust Pie (see recipe, page 334)
- 1/2 cup packed brown sugar
- 1/2 cup chopped pecans
- 2 Tbsp. butter, softened

1. Preheat oven to 375° F. In a large bowl beat eggs; stir in pumpkin and half-and-half. Stir in granulated sugar, flour, lemon peel, vanilla, salt, cinnamon, nutmeg, and allspice.

2. Pour pumpkin mixture into Pastry for Single-Crust Pie. To prevent overbrowning, cover edge of pie with foil. Bake for 25 minutes.

3. Meanwhile, for topping, in a medium bowl stir together brown sugar, pecans, and butter until combined.

4. Remove foil from pie. Sprinkle topping onto pie. Bake about 20 minutes more or until a knife inserted near the center comes out clean and topping is golden and bubbly. Cool on a wire rack. Cover; refrigerate within 2 hours. Makes 8 servings.

Each slice: 386 cal., 19 g total fat (5 g sat. fat), 64 mg chol., 204 mg sodium, 52 g carbo., 3 g fiber, 5 g pro. Daily Values: 239% vit. A, 5% vit C, 5% calcium, 12% iron.

"I BEGAN COLLECTING MY FAVORITE RECIPES ON CARDS AS A BOY SO I COULD PUT A COOKBOOK TOGETHER."

—Jim Fobel

Butterscotch Meringue Pie

Jim Fobel played with his grandmother's homey pie recipe by topping it with a brown sugar meringue, although he says a traditional meringue also works well. You can simplify it even more by topping it with whipped cream instead of meringue.

PREP: 50 minutes **BAKE:** 15 minutes **CHILL:** 3 hours

- 3 egg whites
- 1/4 tsp. cream of tartar
- 1/4 cup granulated sugar
- 1 cup packed brown sugar
- 1/4 cup cornstarch
- 1/4 tsp. salt
- 1 12-oz. can (1 1/2 cups) evaporated whole milk
- 3 egg yolks
- 1 cup milk
- 3 Tbsp. butter, sliced
- 1 tsp. vanilla
- 1 recipe Flaky Pecan Pastry (below)

1. Preheat oven to 350° F. For meringue, in a large bowl combine egg whites and cream of tartar; whisk to blend. In a small bowl combine granulated sugar and 1/4 cup brown sugar; set aside. Beat egg whites with an electric mixer on medium speed about 5 minutes or until peaks form (tips curl). Gradually add sugar mixture, 2 tablespoons at a time, beating on high speed about 5 minutes more or until stiff peaks form (tips stand straight). Let stand at room temperature while making filling.

2. For filling, in a medium saucepan combine remaining 3/4 cup brown sugar, cornstarch, and salt. Whisk in about 1/2 cup evaporated milk; whisk in the egg yolks. Whisk in remaining evaporated milk and the 1 cup milk. Cook over medium heat, whisking constantly, until mixture is thickened and bubbly.

3. Remove pan from heat; stir in butter and vanilla until blended. Pour into Flaky Pecan Pastry. Spoon meringue over top, spreading evenly and sealing to pie shell. Bake 15 minutes.

4. Cool pie on a wire rack away from drafts for 1 hour. Chill for 3 to 6 hours. Serve cold. Makes 8 servings.

FLAKY PECAN PASTRY: In a medium bowl stir together 1 1/3 cups flour and 1/4 teaspoon salt. Using a pastry blender, cut in 1/4 cup shortening and 1/4 cup butter until pieces are pea-size. Stir in 1/3 cup finely chopped pecans. Combine 2 tablespoons cold water and 2 teaspoons vinegar; sprinkle over flour mixture. Gently toss with a fork. Repeat with additional 2 tablespoons cold water until dough is moistened.

Form dough into a ball. Wrap and chill for 1 hour. Preheat oven to 425° F. On a lightly floured surface roll pastry into a circle about 12 inches in diameter. Wrap pastry around rolling pin. Unroll pastry into a 9-inch pie plate. Ease pastry into plate. Trim to 1/2 inch beyond edge of pie plate. Fold under extra pastry; flute edge. Line with double thickness of foil. Bake for 12 minutes. Carefully remove foil. Bake for 8 to 10 minutes more or until golden brown. Cool on a wire rack.

Each slice: 507 cal., 26 g total fat (12 g sat. fat), 125 mg chol., 354 mg sodium, 60 g carbo., 1 g fiber, 9 g pro. Daily Values: 14% vit. A, 3% vit. C, 21% calcium, 12% iron.

Butterscotch Meringue Pie

Winter Squash

SUMMER'S HEAT WAVE ACCELERATES THE GROWING SEASON FOR SQUASH, RESULTING IN AN ABUNDANCE of winter squash that'll stick around into the winter season. As pretty as it is, squash looks great piled up as a long-term centerpiece—the hard, thick shells act as "storage containers" for sweet flesh, lasting 30 to 180 days. But cook 'em up to take full advantage of this seasonal bounty—and don't forget to save the seeds for roasting. Here are some of the more popular varieties.

Red Kuri Squash

- **Red kuri squash:** The red-orange skin of this squash houses a finely textured flesh reminiscent of sweet potatoes. Red kuri is delicious baked or steamed. Its flesh is also a great candidate for puréeing for a soup. Scrape the cooked flesh into a blender, and add seasonings and a liquid such as chicken broth, water, or cream. Then just hit the "blend" button.
- **Acorn squash:** This favorite shows up in outfits of gold, green, and white, with wide ribs. It has tender, fine-textured flesh with a nutty, peppery taste. Serve this small, versatile squash quartered and baked, mashed, or puréed. Or create an edible bowl by halving it crosswise and baking, then filling it with cooked rice or stuffing.
- **Green buttercup squash:** Use this for stress relief: a knife should be lightly pounded into its thick skin to aid slicing. The rewards for this effort are worth it. Its deep yellow flesh eats like a sweet potato and holds up well through long cooking, so consider it for braising, roasting, and stewing.
- **Turban squash:** Here are more color variations—from bright orange to green or white. Its oversized cap can be sliced off, hollowed, and used for serving soup. The seed cavity is small, which leaves room for plenty of sweet, hazelnut-flavored flesh to bake into tarts, pies, and breads.

Squash, Pear, and Onion au Gratin

PREP: 25 minutes **BAKE:** 60 minutes

- 1½ lb. acorn, buttercup, or turban squash
- 1 large onion, sliced and separated into rings (1 cup)
- 1 Tbsp. butter or margarine
- 1 medium pear, peeled and thinly sliced (1 cup)
- Salt
- 3 Tbsp. fine dry bread crumbs
- 3 slices bacon, crisp cooked, drained, and crumbled
- 2 Tbsp. chopped walnuts
- 1 Tbsp. grated Romano cheese
- 1 Tbsp. melted butter or margarine
- 2 Tbsp. snipped fresh parsley (optional)

1. Preheat oven to 350° F. Slice squash in half lengthwise. Remove and discard seeds. Remove peel, if desired. Cut crosswise into ½-inch-thick slices. Set aside.

2. In a large skillet cook onion rings in 1 tablespoon hot butter for 5 to 10 minutes or until tender.

3. Arrange half of the squash slices in an 8×8×2-inch baking dish. Top with half of the pear slices. Repeat layers. Sprinkle with salt. Cover with the cooked onions. Bake, covered, about 45 minutes or until nearly tender.

4. Meanwhile, for topping, in a small bowl stir together bread crumbs, bacon, walnuts, Romano cheese, and 1 tablespoon melted butter.

5. Sprinkle topping over vegetables. Bake, uncovered, about 15 minutes more or until tender. If desired, sprinkle with parsley. Makes 6 servings.

Each serving: 153 cal., 8 g total fat (3 g sat. fat), 14 mg chol., 270 mg sodium, 20 g carbo., 1 g fiber, 3 g pro. Daily Values: 146% vit. A, 35% vit. C, 7% calcium, 6% iron.

SQUASH TIPS

- Choose a well-shaped squash with good color for the variety. It should be heavy for its size, dry, and free from heavy bruising or cracks.
- Store whole winter squash in a cool, dry place for up to 2 months.
- Once you cut it, you can tightly wrap winter squash and store it for up to 4 days in the refrigerator.
- Always scrape out the seed cavity before cooking.
- Pierce the skin with a knife.
- Whenever possible, cook squash, quartered or halved, in its skin. This makes it easier to peel or scrape the flesh out of the shell.
- Steaming, microwave cooking, baking, and braising are the most effective ways to get the biggest flavor out of winter squash. Avoid boiling it.
- In general, baked, cubed winter squash has about 40 calories for each ½-cup serving.

Nuts about Nuts

MUNCHING ON A HANDFUL OF NUTS NOT ONLY GETS YOU THROUGH A SNACK ATTACK BUT PROVIDES A batch of health benefits. Nuts—from almonds to pistachios—may protect your brain as well as your heart. They're a good source of dietary fiber, antioxidant vitamins, minerals, and other substances.

New studies suggest that chomping on nuts reduces your chances of developing heart disease and perhaps Alzheimer's disease. Researchers at Brigham and Women's Hospital in Boston recently reported that eating a handful of nuts two or more times a week may drop a person's risk of sudden cardiac death by 47 percent. The Boston researchers looked at more than 21,000 male physicians between the ages of 40 and 84. Researchers theorize that alpha-linolenic acid, a component of nuts (especially walnuts), may protect the heart by preventing a rhythm disturbance called ventricular fibrillation that causes sudden death.

The Chicago Health and Aging Project (CHAP) found that a diet rich in foods containing vitamin E may reduce the risk of Alzheimer's disease. Lead researcher Martha Clare Morris says the study showed that the more vitamin E a person consumed from food, the lower the risk of developing Alzheimer's disease. Nuts especially high in vitamin E include almonds, walnuts, hazelnuts, and pecans.

GO NUTS

Lola O'Rourke, a registered dietitian with the American Dietetic Association, recommends eating an ounce or so of nuts—a small handful—daily. Keep in mind that all nuts are high in total fat and calories. O'Rourke suggests using nuts to replace other fats in your diet. For example, try sprinkling toasted, slivered almonds onto green beans instead of butter. For an adult nut nosh, toast 2 cups of walnut pieces in a 350° F oven about 10 minutes.

- Toss with 1/3 cup or so of golden raisins.
- Serve with tiny wedges of cheese.
- Pair the nuts with your favorite red wine.
- Munch along with a beautiful bunch of grapes.

Toasted Nuts with Rosemary

Start to Finish: 20 minutes

- Nonstick cooking spray
- 1 egg white
- 2 tsp. snipped fresh rosemary or 1 tsp. dried rosemary, crushed
- 1/2 tsp. salt
- 1/2 tsp. coarsely ground black pepper
- 3 cups walnuts, hazelnuts (filberts), and/or whole almonds

1. Preheat oven to 350° F. Line a 13×9×2-inch pan with foil; lightly coat the pan with cooking spray and set aside.

2. In a medium bowl lightly beat egg white with a fork until frothy. Add rosemary, salt, and pepper; beat with the fork until combined. Add the nuts; toss to coat.

3. Spread nut mixture in an even layer in the prepared pan. Bake for 15 to 20 minutes or until golden brown, stirring once.

4. Remove foil with nuts from pan; set aside to cool. Break up any large pieces. Store in an airtight container in freezer for up to 1 month. Makes about 3 cups.

Nutrition facts per tablespoon: 50 cal., 5 g total fat (1 g sat. fat), 0 mg chol., 25 mg sodium, 1 g carbo., 1 g fiber, and 1 g pro. Daily Values: 1% calcium and 2% iron.

In a nutshell (per 1-ounce serving)

ALMONDS

175 calories, 14.4 g fat, 6 g protein, 3.1 g fiber, 73 mg calcium, 7.5 mg vit. E

CASHEWS

163 calories, 13.2 g fat, 4.4 g protein, .90 g fiber, 13 mg calcium, .41 mg vit. E

HAZELNUTS (FILBERTS)

179 calories, 17.8 g fat, 3.7 g protein, 1 g fiber, 53 mg calcium, 4.4 mg vit. E

MACADAMIA NUTS

199 calories, 20 g fat, 2.4 g protein, 2.2 g fiber, 20 mg calcium, .30 mg vit. E

PEANUTS

164 calories, 13.9 g fat, 8 g protein, 2.5 g fiber, 28 mg calcium, 2.1 mg vit. E

PECANS

187 calories, 18.4 g fat, 2.3 g protein, 2.6 g fiber, 10 mg calcium, 3.5 mg vit. E

PISTACHIOS

164 calories, 13.7 g fat, 5.8 g protein, 3 g fiber, 38 mg calcium, .60 mg vit. E

WALNUTS

172 calories, 16.1 g fat, 6.9 g protein, 1.7 g fiber, 16 mg calcium, 4 mg vit. E

Tapping Into Maple Sugar

THESE SWEETLY FLAVORED LITTLE CAKES AND COOKIES KNOW THEIR place: high on a pedestal. Just slather a generous pat of butter onto one of these spicy muffins while it's still warm, and call it dessert. Or grab a good cup of cappuccino, and start dunking the spritz cookies.

The sweet flavor comes from maple sugar, made from natural maple syrup. It may take a little effort to track down the maple sugar, but it's worth it. Look for the brownish granulated sugar in specialty food stores. Or you can order it from *The Baker's Catalogue* at 800/827-6836 or www.bakerscatalogue.com.

Once you buy a bag of maple sugar, you'll want to start playing with it. Try it in simple recipes to let the subtle maple flavor come through. Or stir it into tea. For starters, try these two naturally sweet recipes.

Maple Sugar Spritz

When making spritz, use only butter and do not chill the dough.

PREP: 25 minutes
BAKE: 8 minutes per batch

- $1\frac{1}{2}$ **cups butter, softened**
- 1 **cup maple granulated sugar**
- 1 **tsp. baking powder**
- 1 **egg**
- $3\frac{1}{2}$ **cups all-purpose flour**
- 1 **recipe Vanilla Glaze (recipe, page 459) (optional)**

1. Preheat oven to 375° F. In a large mixing bowl beat butter with an electric mixer on medium to high speed for 30 seconds. Add maple sugar and baking powder. Beat until combined, scraping side of bowl occasionally. Beat in egg until combined. Beat in as much of the flour as you can with mixer. Stir in any remaining flour.

2. Force unchilled dough through a cookie press onto an ungreased cookie sheet. Bake for 8 to 10 minutes or until edges are firm but not brown. Cool on a wire rack.

3. If desired, dip tops into Vanilla Glaze. Makes about 84 cookies.

Each cookie: 57 cal., 4 g total fat (2 g sat. fat), 12 mg chol., 41 mg sodium, 6 g carbo., 0 g fiber, 1 g pro. Daily Values: 3% vit. A, 1% calcium, 2% iron.

Maple Sugar Muffins

PREP: 15 minutes **BAKE:** 12 minutes

- $2\frac{1}{4}$ **cups all-purpose flour**
- $\frac{3}{4}$ **tsp. baking soda**
- $\frac{1}{8}$ **tsp. salt**
- 1 **egg**
- 1 **8-oz. carton dairy sour cream**
- 1 **cup maple granulated sugar or $\frac{3}{4}$ cup granulated sugar plus $\frac{1}{4}$ tsp. maple flavoring**
- $\frac{1}{2}$ **tsp. ground allspice**

1. Preheat oven to 375° F. Grease a large baking sheet. In a bowl stir together flour, baking soda, and salt. Set aside.

2. In a bowl beat egg; stir in sour cream, maple sugar, and allspice. Add flour mixture all at once; stir just until combined.

3. Turn dough out onto a well-floured surface. Knead for 10 to 12 strokes. Pat or lightly roll dough to a $\frac{1}{2}$-inch thickness. Cut dough with a floured $2\frac{1}{2}$-inch round cutter. Arrange muffins on the prepared baking sheet.

4. Bake for 12 to 15 minutes or until bottoms of muffins are brown. Transfer to a wire rack. Serve warm. Makes 14 muffins.

Each muffin: 148 cal., 4 g total fat (2 g sat. fat), 22 mg chol., 102 mg sodium, 25 g carbo., 1 g dietary fiber, 3 g pro. Daily Values: 2% calcium, 5% iron.

Apricot Cherry Slab Pie

Pie for a party

A BIT STURDIER THAN TYPICAL PIES, THIS OVERSIZED BAKING-SHEET VERSION CAN BE EATEN out of hand. Slice yourself a slab and sneak out of the kitchen without even dirtying a plate. An apple version has been around for decades, but this sweet and puckery apricot-cherry rendition will knock your socks off.

Making the fruity filling and the pastry is a snap. But rolling out the large, rectangular pastry and transferring it to the pan requires a little concentration.

A lightly floured pastry cloth is the ideal surface for rolling out the dough, but a countertop dusted with flour works too. Start by using your hands to pat the dough into a flat rectangle. Then let the rolling begin.

Flour the rolling pin, place it in the center of the dough, and roll from the center to the edges. Add just enough flour to the rolling surface to prevent the dough from sticking.

To transfer the dough to the pan, use the rolling pin method as directed in the recipe, right. Or try this: Sprinkle flour on top of the dough, brush off excess flour, then gently fold the dough in half; then foldin half again. Carefully place the dough into the pan and unfold. Patch any cracks with pastry scraps before adding the filling.

Apricot-Cherry Slab Pie

Keep a can of apricots and cherries on hand and you're ready to bake this when the pie mood strikes.

PREP: 30 minutes **BAKE:** 40 minutes

- 3¼ cups all-purpose flour
- 1 tsp. salt
- 1 cup shortening
- 1 egg yolk
- Milk
- ½ cup sugar
- 3 Tbsp. cornstarch
- 3 15¼-oz. cans unpeeled apricot halves, drained and cut into quarters
- 1 16-oz. can pitted tart red cherries, drained
- 1 recipe Vanilla Glaze (below)

1. For pastry, in a large mixing bowl stir together the flour and salt. Using a pastry blender, cut in shortening until pieces are pea-size. Set aside.

2. Lightly beat egg yolk in a glass measuring cup. Add enough milk to egg yolk to make ¾ cup total liquid; mix well. Stir egg yolk mixture into flour mixture; mix well. Shape one-third of the dough into a ball; set aside.

3. Form remaining two-thirds of dough into a ball. On a lightly floured surface use your hands to flatten dough. Roll dough from the center to edges into an 18×12-inch rectangle. Wrap pastry around the rolling pin; unroll into a 15×10×1-inch baking pan (pastry will hang over edges of pan).

4. Preheat oven to 375° F. In a large bowl combine sugar and cornstarch. Stir in apricots and cherries. Spoon into the crust.

5. Roll the remaining dough into a 16×11-inch rectangle; place over fruit. Bring bottom pastry up and over top pastry. Seal edges with the tines of a fork. Prick top pastry over entire surface with the tines of a fork.

6. Bake about 40 minutes or until golden brown. Cool in pan on a wire rack. Drizzle with Vanilla Glaze. Serve warm or cool. Cut into 2×3-inch bars. Makes 25 bars.

VANILLA GLAZE: In a small bowl stir together 1¼ cups sifted powdered sugar and ¼ teaspoon vanilla. Stir in enough milk (5 to 6 teaspoons) to make a glaze of drizzling consistency.

Each bar: 230 cal., 8 g total fat (2 g sat. fat), 9 mg chol., 104 mg sodium, 37 g carbo., 1 g dietary fiber, 2 g pro. Daily Values: 16% vit. A, 3% vit. C, 2% calcium, 8% iron.

Best-Ever Chocolate Cake

WE TESTED AND RETESTED CHOCOLATE CAKE RECIPES TO COME UP WITH THE MOISTEST, RICHEST, CHOCOLATIEST CAKE EVER. Then, we tasted chocolate frosting recipes and came up with the best of each. After we calmed down, we fine-tuned the recipe some more. Here's the result: our Best-Ever Chocolate Cake with your choice of frosting. It's so good, we made it THE chocolate cake in our 12th edition of the *Better Homes and Gardens® New Cook Book*. So if chocolate cravings are part of your family's genetic blueprint, you'll want to end your holiday feast with this incredible cake. After all, chocolate is thicker than water.

Best-Ever Chocolate Cake with Chocolate-Sour Cream Frosting

Best-Ever Chocolate Cake

We pictured our best-loved cake with the Chocolate-Sour Cream Frosting and chocolate curls, but you can choose any of the frostings to the right.

PREP: 30 minutes **BAKE:** 30 minutes **COOL:** 1 hour

- 3/4 cup butter, softened
- 3 eggs
- 2 cups all-purpose flour
- 3/4 cup unsweetened cocoa powder
- 1 tsp. baking soda
- 3/4 tsp. baking powder
- 1/2 tsp. salt
- 2 cups sugar
- 2 tsp. vanilla
- 1 1/2 cups milk
- 1 recipe desired frosting (see right)
- White and dark chocolate curls* (optional)
- 1 recipe Candied Nuts (below) (optional)

1. Allow butter and eggs to stand at room temperature for 30 minutes. Meanwhile, lightly grease bottoms of three 8×1 1/2-inch round cake pans or two 9×1 1/2-inch round cake pans or 8×8×2-inch cake pans. Line bottoms of pans with waxed paper. Grease and lightly flour bottoms and sides of pans. Or grease one 13×9×2-inch baking pan. Set pan(s) aside.

2. Preheat oven to 350° F. In a mixing bowl stir together flour, cocoa powder, baking soda, baking powder, and salt; set aside.

3. In a mixing bowl beat butter with an electric mixer on medium to high speed for 30 seconds. Gradually add sugar, about 1/4 cup at a time, beating on medium speed for 3 to 4 minutes or until combined. Scrape side of bowl; continue beating on medium speed for 2 minutes. Add eggs, one at a time, beating after each addition (1 minute total). Beat in vanilla.

4. Alternately add flour mixture and milk to beaten mixture, beating on low speed after each addition just until combined. Beat on medium to high speed for 20 seconds more. Spread batter evenly into the prepared pan(s).

5. Bake round cake pans for 30 to 35 minutes; bake square or rectangular pan(s) for 35 to 40 minutes. The cake is done when a wooden toothpick inserted in center comes out clean.

6. Cool cake layers in pans for 10 minutes. Remove from pans. Peel off waxed paper. Cool on wire racks. Or place 13×9×2-inch cake in pan on a wire rack; cool. Frost with desired frosting. Cover and store cake in refrigerator. If desired, top with chocolate curls and Candied Nuts. Makes 12 to 16 servings.

***TEST KITCHEN TIP:** To make chocolate curls, warm a chocolate bar in your apron pocket while frosting. Draw a vegetable peeler across the broad surface of the slightly warm bar.

CANDIED NUTS: In a 10-inch heavy skillet cook 1 1/2 cups nuts, 1/2 cup sugar, 2 tablespoons butter, and 1/2 teaspoon vanilla until sugar begins to melt, shaking occasionally (do not stir). Cook over low heat until sugar is golden brown, stirring often. Pour onto a well-greased baking sheet. Cool. Break up.

Each slice with Chocolate-Sour Cream Frosting: 760 cal., 35 g total fat (20 g sat. fat), 118 mg chol., 475 mg sodium, 99 g carbo., 5 g fiber, 7 g pro. Daily Values: 21% vit. A, 14% calcium.

OUR FAVORITE CHOCOLATE FROSTINGS

Chocolate-Sour Cream Frosting: In a large saucepan melt one 12-ounce package (2 cups) semisweet chocolate pieces and 1/2 cup butter over low heat, stirring frequently. Cool for 5 minutes. Stir in one 8-ounce carton dairy sour cream. Gradually add 4 1/2 cups sifted powdered sugar (about 1 pound), beating with an electric mixer until smooth. This frosts the tops and sides of two or three 8- or 9-inch cake layers. (Halve recipe to frost the top of a 13×9×2-inch cake.) Makes 4 1/2 cups.

Chocolate Butter Frosting: In a very large mixing bowl combine 3/4 cup softened butter and 1/2 cup unsweetened cocoa powder; beat with an electric mixer until smooth. Gradually add 2 cups sifted powdered sugar, beating well. Slowly beat in 1/4 cup milk and 2 teaspoons vanilla. Gradually beat in 6 1/2 cups sifted powdered sugar. Beat in enough additional milk to reach spreading consistency. This frosts the tops and sides of two or three 8- or 9-inch cake layers. (Halve the recipe to frost the top of a 13×9×2-inch cake.) Makes about 4 cups.

Chocolate-Buttermilk Frosting: In a medium saucepan combine 1/4 cup butter or margarine, 3 tablespoons unsweetened cocoa powder, and 3 tablespoons buttermilk. Bring to boiling. Remove from heat. Beat in 2 1/4 cups sifted powdered sugar and 1/2 teaspoon vanilla until smooth. If desired, stir in 3/4 cup chopped pecans. This frosts the tops of two or three 8- or 9-inch cake layers or a 13×9×2-inch cake. Makes about 3 cups.

Chocolate-Cream Cheese Frosting: In a large bowl combine one 8-ounce package softened cream cheese, 1/2 cup softened butter or margarine, 1/2 cup unsweetened cocoa powder, and 2 teaspoons vanilla; beat with an electric mixer until light and fluffy. Gradually add 2 cups sifted powdered sugar, beating well. Gradually beat in 3 1/4 to 3 3/4 cups sifted powdered sugar to reach spreading consistency. This frosts the tops and sides of two or three 8- or 9-inch layers. (Halve the recipe to frost a 13×9×2-inch cake.) Makes about 3 2/3 cups.

Coconut-Pecan Frosting: In a medium saucepan slightly beat 1 egg. Stir in one 5-ounce can (2/3 cup) evaporated milk, 2/3 cup sugar, and 1/4 cup butter. Cook and stir over medium heat for 6 to 8 minutes or until thickened and bubbly. Remove from heat; stir in 1 1/3 cups flaked coconut and 1/2 cup chopped pecans. Cover and cool thoroughly. This frosts the tops of two or three 8- or 9-inch cake layers or a 13×9×2-inch cake for a German chocolate-style cake. Makes about 3 cups.

a gift of HOT CHOCOLATE

FINISH OFF A CUP OF THIS OUTRAGEOUSLY CHOCOLATY hot chocolate,and you'll want to stretch out on the couch with a sigh. Or maybe you'd rather go back for another steamy cup. Either way, you'll want to keep a pretty good stash of this handy drink mix for yourself or your very, very good friends.

A sprinkling of cinnamon added to the mix of chocolate chunks plus cocoa powder intensifies the flavor big time. Include a little toasted anise seed for its subtle licorice hint, and you'll stir up a combo like none you've ever tasted. This was intended as a homemade holiday gift, but chances are you'll want it all for yourself. Or maybe you'll succumb to the spirit of the season and share it with someone special.

If you do decide to make a gift of it, package it prettily, perhaps in a shiny silver tin wrapped in an oversized ribbon. You can also tuck in some interesting and whimsical stir sticks. How about candy canes, or stick candy, cinnamon sticks, colorful plastic spoons dipped into chocolate, or stick-style rolled wafer cookies?

Be sure to include the simple instructions for preparing the hot chocolate mix. Or, if you forget, maybe the recipients of your gift will invite you over to show them exactly how it's made. Nice trick.

All-Is-Calm Hot Chocolate Mix

START TO FINISH: 20 minutes

- 8 oz. semisweet or bittersweet chocolate chunks or pieces
- 2/3 cup sugar
- 1/2 cup unsweetened cocoa powder
- 1/2 tsp. anise seeds, toasted* and crushed
- 1/2 tsp. ground cinnamon

1. For mix, in a large bowl combine chocolate chunks or pieces, sugar, cocoa powder, anise seeds, and cinnamon. Spoon into a container, jar, or self-sealing plastic bag. Cover or seal. Makes 12 servings. Include the following directions:

ALL-IS-CALM HOT CHOCOLATE: In a medium saucepan combine 2/3 cup mix and 1/4 cup water. Stir over medium heat until chocolate is melted and mixture is smooth. Whisk in 4 cups milk, half-and-half, or light cream (you'll get a richer result using half-and-half or light cream); heat through, whisking occasionally. Pour into four mugs. Makes 4 servings.

***TEST KITCHEN TIP:** To toast anise seeds, place anise in a shallow baking pan. Bake in a 350° F oven about 5 minutes or until toasted and aromatic.

Each serving: 272 cal., 11 g total fat (6 g sat. fat), 18 mg chol., 122 mg sodium, 30 g carbo., 3 g fiber, 9 g pro. Daily Values: 4% vit. C, 34% calcium, 4% iron.

All-Is-Calm Hot Chocolate

December

DURING THIS SEASON OF GOOD CHEER, GATHER FOR OUTDOOR FUN AND RELAX WITH COZY DOWN-HOME MEALS.

Chocolate-Cherry Bread Pudding

Hot Apple Cider with Calvados

Lamb and Black Bean Quesadillas

Come for a Sledding Supper

Mitten Cookies

Grits with Smoked Oysters

Smoky Mountain Holiday

Plus...

Cranberry Black Walnut Cake

Jackson's Cereal Blend

WITH THE HOLIDAYS COMING, OUR TO-DO LIST IS LONG: BAKING HOMEMADE GIFTS, GATHERING GREENS, TRIMMING THE TREE, AND MAKING IT ALL FUN

Spicy Bittersweet Coco

Come for a Sledding Supper

Hot Apple Cider with Calvados

HOST A WINTER WONDERLAND SLEDDING PARTY, FOLLOWED BY SNUG, WARM-YOU-UP ROCKY MOUNTAIN FARE.

Fire and Ice Nut Mix

This grab-a-gloveful snack balances the heat of peppery cashews with sweet and sugary maple-toasted pecans.

Prep: 15 minutes **Bake:** 45 minutes

- 1½ lb. lightly salted cashews (4½ cups)
- ¾ tsp. cayenne pepper
- 3 Tbsp. kecap manis (Indonesian sauce) or soy sauce
- 3 Tbsp. honey
- ¾ cup pure maple syrup
- 4 tsp. butter, melted
- 1½ lb. pecan halves (6 cups)

1. Preheat oven to 350° F. For cashews, line two 15×10×1-inch baking pans with foil. Grease foil; set aside. In a food processor or blender place 1½ cups of the cashews. Cover and process or blend until finely ground. Stir together ground cashews and cayenne pepper; set aside.

2. In a large bowl combine kecap manis and honey. Add remaining whole cashews; toss to coat. Stir in ground cashew mixture. Spread in the prepared pans. Bake for 15 to 20 minutes (25 to 30 minutes if using soy sauce) or until golden, stirring once.

3. For pecans, line the two 15×10×1-inch baking pans with clean foil. Grease foil; set aside. In a large bowl combine maple syrup and butter. Add pecans; toss to coat. Spread pecans in prepared pans. Bake for 20 minutes, stirring twice.

4. Cool both types of nuts completely. Break into chunks. To serve, in a bowl combine both types of nuts. Store in an airtight container at room temperature. Makes 13 cups.

Each ¼-cup serving: 188 cal., 16 g total fat (2 g sat. fat), 1 mg chol., 82 mg sodium, 9 g carbo., 2 g fiber, 4 g pro. Daily Values: 1% vit. A, 1% calcium, 7% iron.

Fire and Ice Nut Mix

Winter warming

Skiing takes a powder when Charles and Aimee Dale hear the weather forecast is predicting snow. Instead, they decide sledding is just the ticket. Hills soon pile high with fluffy white stuff near their Colorado home, and an opportunity to share the afternoon and supper with friends is too much to resist for the Dales and their two children, Lily and Lucien. All it takes is a few telephone calls to quickly fill the sled run.

Out come mittens and hats, mufflers and ski pants, toboggans and sleds. Then it's red noses and squeals of delight all the way to the very bottom of the hill.

"We live in a place that's world-renowned for skiing, but Lily and Lucien are too young for that, so sledding's a great alternative," Charles says. Charles is chef/owner of two popular restaurants in nearby Aspen—Rustique and Range. Both are known for their sophisticated, unfussy approach to French country and Western cooking, respectively. At home though, Charles and Aimee bring the down-home, casual side of cooking to their kitchen. "We want people to remember the hominess and coziness, the family feeling of good cheer," Aimee says.

Aimee and Charles' agenda for parties goes like this: Plan ahead, shop ahead, make ahead. They also build their menus around the kind of foods that kids will gobble up and adults will enjoy as well. "There's a handful of things the kids like. We tend to stick to classics or the tried-and-true. The holidays are about traditions anyway, so it's an easy road for us," Aimee says.

Cheese Fondue

For old-fashioned disposable tableware, take Charles' lead and find some clean twigs to spear and dunk the chunks of bread.

PREP: 30 minutes **STAND:** 30 minutes

- 12 oz. Emmentaler or Swiss cheese, shredded (3 cups)
- 12 oz. Beaufort or Gruyère cheese, shredded (3 cups)
- 4 tsp. cornstarch
- 1 clove garlic, halved
- 1 3/4 cups dry white wine, such as Sauvignon Blanc
- 1 Tbsp. Kirsch (optional)
- Dash ground black pepper
- Dash ground nutmeg
- 1 or 2 loaves country bread or Two-Tone Bread (right), torn into 1-inch chunks

1. Let shredded cheeses stand at room temperature for 30 minutes. Toss cheeses with cornstarch; set aside.

2. Rub the inside of a 4-quart Dutch oven with the halved garlic clove. Discard garlic. In Dutch oven heat wine over medium heat until small bubbles rise to the surface. Just before wine boils, reduce heat to low and stir in the cheeses, a little at a time, stirring constantly and making sure cheeses are melted before adding more. Heat and stir until the mixture bubbles gently.

3. Stir in Kirsch, if using, pepper, and nutmeg. If desired, transfer to fondue pot. Keep mixture bubbling gently over a burner. (If mixture becomes too thick, gradually stir in a little additional wine.) Serve with chunks of country bread threaded onto long skewers or clean small tree twigs. Makes 10 servings.

Each serving: 421 cal., 22 g total fat (13 g sat. fat), 68 mg chol., 467 mg sodium, 25 g carbo., 1 g fiber, 24 g pro. Daily Values: 14% vit. A, 70% calcium, 9% iron.

OUTDOOR SLEDDING PARTY

Fire and Ice Nut Mix *(page 469)*
Cheese Fondue *(above)* with bread cubes and vegetables
Lamb and Black Bean Quesadillas *(page 473)*
Oatmeal Jam Bars *(page 476)*
Hot Apple Cider with Calvados *(page 476)*

Two-Tone Bread

Cut up this swirled bread for white or sweet dark chunks to dunk into the fondue.

PREP: 1 hour **RISE:** 1 3/4 hours **BAKE:** 30 minutes

- 5 to 5 1/2 cups all-purpose flour
- 2 pkg. active dry yeast
- 3 cups milk
- 1/3 cup sugar
- 1/3 cup shortening
- 1 Tbsp. salt
- 3 Tbsp. molasses
- 2 1/2 cups whole wheat flour

1. In a large mixing bowl stir together 3 1/4 cups of the all-purpose flour and the yeast; set aside. In a medium saucepan heat and stir milk, sugar, shortening, and salt just until warm (120° F to 130° F) and shortening almost melts. Add milk mixture to flour mixture. Beat with an electric mixer on low to medium speed for 30 seconds, scraping the side of the bowl constantly. Beat on high speed for 3 minutes. Remove 2 1/2 cups of the batter.

2. To the 2 1/2 cups batter, use a wooden spoon to stir in as much of the remaining all-purpose flour as you can. Turn dough out onto a lightly floured surface. Knead in enough of the remaining all-purpose flour to make a moderately stiff dough that is smooth and elastic (6 to 8 minutes total). Shape into a ball. Place in a lightly greased bowl; turn once to grease surface. Cover; set aside.

3. To remaining batter, use a wooden spoon to stir in molasses; stir in whole wheat flour and as much of the remaining all-purpose flour as you can. Turn dough out onto a lightly floured surface. Knead in enough of the remaining all-purpose flour to make a moderately stiff dough that is smooth and elastic (6 to 8 minutes total). Shape dough into a ball. Place in another lightly greased bowl; turn once to grease surface. Cover.

4. Let both doughs rise in a warm place until double (1 to 1 1/4 hours). Punch doughs down. Turn out onto a lightly floured surface; divide each dough portion in half. Cover; let rest for 10 minutes.

5. Meanwhile, lightly grease two 9×5×3-inch loaf pans; set aside. Roll out half of the light dough and half of the dark dough, each to a 12×8-inch rectangle. Place dark dough on top of light dough. Starting from a short side, roll up tightly and shape into a loaf; seal seams. Repeat with remaining doughs to make a second loaf. Place in prepared loaf pans. Cover and let rise in a warm place until nearly double (45 to 60 minutes).

6. Preheat oven to 375° F. Bake for 30 to 35 minutes or until bread sounds hollow when lightly tapped. If necessary, cover loosely with foil the last 10 minutes to prevent overbrowning. Immediately remove loaves from pans. Cool on wire racks. Makes 2 loaves (32 servings).

Each serving: 150 cal., 3 g total fat (1 g sat. fat), 2 mg chol., 231 mg sodium, 27 g carbo., 2 g fiber, 4 g pro. Daily Values: 1% vit. A, 1% vit. C, 4% calcium, 9% iron.

Cheese Fondue

Lamb and Black Bean Quesadillas

Lamb and Black Bean Quesadillas

The Dales slow-cook the lamb filling the day before the party so they can enjoy the fun along with family and friends.

PREP: 35 minutes **COOK:** 4½ or 9 hours **GRILL:** 2 minutes

- 1 recipe Lamb-Black Bean Filling (below)
- 1 medium mango, sliced
- 10 8-inch flour tortillas
- 8 oz. Fontina cheese, shredded (2 cups)
- 1 Tbsp. olive oil (optional)
- 1 recipe Jalapeño Pepper Apple Jelly (right)
- Purchased avocado dip (guacamole)
- Bottled salsa

1. Prepare Lamb-Black Bean Filling. For quesadillas, divide filling and mango slices among 5 of the tortillas; sprinkle with cheese. Top with remaining 5 tortillas.

2. Place quesadillas on the rack of an uncovered grill directly over medium heat. Grill about 2 minutes or until tortillas are light brown and cheese is melted, carefully turning once. (Or in a 12-inch skillet or griddle cook quesadillas, one at a time, in hot oil over medium heat for 2 to 3 minutes or until tortilla is light brown and cheese is melted, carefully turning once. Remove the quesadilla from the skillet; place on a baking sheet. Keep warm in a 300° F oven while cooking remaining quesadillas, adding additional oil as needed.)

3. To serve, quarter quesadillas. Serve with Jalapeño Pepper Apple Jelly, avocado dip, and salsa. Makes 10 servings.

LAMB-BLACK BEAN FILLING: Trim fat from 2½ pounds lamb shoulder or 2 pounds boneless lamb leg; cut meat into bite-size strips. In a 3½- or 4-quart slow cooker stir together meat strips; one 15-ounce can black beans, rinsed and drained; one 12-ounce can mango nectar; 1½ cups water; 2 small red sweet peppers and/or Anaheim peppers, sliced; 1 small onion, sliced; ⅓ cup dry white wine; 8 cloves garlic, peeled; 1 teaspoon salt; and ½ teaspoon ground cumin. Cover and cook on low-heat setting for 9 to 10 hours or on high-heat setting for 4½ to 5 hours; drain. Stir 2 tablespoons tomato paste into lamb mixture.

LAMB AND BLACK BEAN BURRITOS: Fill the flour tortillas with lamb filling, mango slices, cheese, jalapeño jelly, and snipped fresh cilantro; roll up tortillas. Serve with avocado dip and salsa.

Each serving with toppings: 588 cal., 31 g total fat (14 g sat. fat), 104 mg chol., 796 mg sodium, 47 g carbo., 4 g fiber, 31 g pro. Daily Values: 47% vit. A, 77% vit. C, 21% calcium, 21% iron.

Jalapeño Pepper Apple Jelly

This simple jelly is perfect with the quesadillas, but it's also yummy spooned over cream cheese on bagels or crackers.

PREP: 10 minutes **CHILL:** 1 hour

- 1 small fresh jalapeño chile pepper, seeded and finely chopped*
- 1 small fresh red chile pepper, seeded and finely chopped*
- 1 tsp. butter
- 1 10-oz. jar apple jelly
- 2 Tbsp. snipped fresh cilantro
- Fresh cilantro leaves

1. In a small saucepan cook and stir chile peppers in hot butter over medium heat about 1 minute or until tender. Remove from heat; cool. Stir in apple jelly and snipped cilantro, leaving clumps of apple jelly.

2. Transfer jelly to a small jar or serving dish. Cover and chill for at least 1 hour. Sprinkle with cilantro leaves. Makes 1 cup.

***NOTE:** Because hot chile peppers, such as jalapeños, contain volatile oils that can burn your skin and eyes, avoid direct contact with chiles as much as possible. When working with chile peppers, wear plastic or rubber gloves. If your bare hands do touch the chile peppers, wash your hands well with soap and water.

Each tablespoon: 54 cal., 0 g total fat, 1 mg chol., 8 mg sodium, 13 g carbo., 0 g fiber, 0 g pro. Daily Values: 7% vit. A, 13% vit. C, 1% iron.

Winter White Vegetable Soup

Winter White Vegetable Soup

Chopped roasted beet and snipped chives give this creamy soup a celebratory touch of color.

PREP: 45 minutes **ROAST:** 1 hour

- 1 medium beet, trimmed (about 8 oz.)
- 1 medium onion, chopped
- 1 Tbsp. butter
- 1 small head cauliflower, coarsely chopped (4 cups)
- 2 medium turnips, peeled and cut into 1-inch pieces (3 cups)
- 1 medium celeriac, peeled and cut into 1-inch pieces (3 cups)
- 2 medium potatoes, peeled and cut into 1-inch pieces (2 cups)
- 1 large fennel bulb, sliced (discard leafy top) (2 cups)
- 2 medium parsnips, peeled and coarsely chopped (1 cup)
- 2 cloves garlic, halved
- 1/4 tsp. salt
- 4 cups water
- 1 1/2 cups milk
- Milk
- 1 Tbsp. snipped fresh chives (optional)

1. Preheat oven to 400° F. Wrap beet in foil. Roast about 1 hour or just until tender. Cool. Peel and chop or grate; set aside.

2. Meanwhile, in a 4- to 5-quart Dutch oven cook onion in hot butter over medium heat about 5 minutes or until tender, stirring occasionally. Add cauliflower, turnips, celeriac, potatoes, fennel, parsnips, garlic, and salt; stir in water. Bring to boiling; reduce heat. Simmer, covered, for 25 to 30 minutes or until vegetables are very tender. Remove from heat. Stir in the 1 1/2 cups milk. Let cool slightly, about 30 minutes.

3. Transfer soup mixture in batches to a blender or food processor; cover and blend or process until smooth. Return all soup to Dutch oven. Add enough additional milk to reach desired consistency. Heat through. Ladle into 10 soup bowls. Sprinkle with beet and, if desired, snipped chives. Makes 10 servings.

MAKE-AHEAD TIP: Roast, peel, and chop or grate beet up to 24 hours in advance. Store tightly wrapped in the refrigerator. Prepare soup through step 2. After cooling slightly, blend or process as in step 3. Do not return to Dutch oven. Transfer mixture to a storage container and chill for up to 24 hours. To serve, return mixture to Dutch oven and stir in enough additional milk to reach desired consistency. Heat through and serve as directed.

Each serving: 119 cal., 2 g total fat (1 g sat. fat), 6 mg chol., 199 mg sodium, 22 g carbo., 9 g fiber, 4 g pro. Daily Values: 3% vit. A, 57% vit. C, 11% calcium, 6% iron.

Citrus Salad with Honey Balsamic Vinaigrette

To tote this refreshing salad to the sledding spot, pack the dressing separately from the fruit. Toss it before serving.

PREP: 25 minutes **CHILL:** 30 minutes

- 1 recipe Honey Balsamic Vinaigrette (below)
- 3 medium pink grapefruits
- 3 medium oranges
- 1 1/2 cups red and/or green seedless grapes
- 3 Tbsp. pomegranate seeds (optional)
- 1 head red leaf lettuce

1. Prepare Honey Balsamic Vinaigrette; cover and chill until serving time.

2. Peel and section grapefruits and oranges, working over a large bowl to catch juices; set juices aside. Add grapes and pomegranate seeds, if using. Cover and chill until serving time.

3. Before serving, toss citrus mixture with Honey Balsamic Vinaigrette. Serve in a lettuce-lined bowl. Makes 12 servings.

HONEY BALSAMIC VINAIGRETTE: In a blender or food processor combine 1/3 cup salad oil, 1/3 cup orange juice, 1/4 cup balsamic vinegar, 4 teaspoons honey, and 1/4 teaspoon cracked black pepper. Cover; blend until combined. Chill for at least 30 minutes.

Each serving: 140 cal., 7 g total fat (1 g sat. fat), 0 mg chol., 5 mg sodium, 21 g carbo., 2 g fiber, 1 g pro. Daily Values: 76% vit. C.

Oatmeal Jam Bars

These ready-to-go cream cheese bars reward sledders with their berry-good flavor and a boost of energy.

PREP: 15 minutes **BAKE:** 35 minutes

- **1⅓ cups all-purpose flour**
- **¼ tsp. baking soda**
- **¼ tsp. salt**
- **¾ cup quick-cooking rolled oats**
- **⅓ cup packed brown sugar**
- **1 tsp. finely shredded lemon peel**
- **2 3-oz. pkg. cream cheese, softened**
- **¼ cup butter, softened**
- **¾ cup blackberry or red raspberry jam**
- **1 tsp. lemon juice**

1. Grease a 9×9×2-inch baking pan; set aside. In a medium bowl stir together flour, baking soda, and salt. Stir in oats, brown sugar, and lemon peel; set aside.

2. Preheat oven to 350° F. In a large mixing bowl beat cream cheese and butter with an electric mixer on medium to high speed for 30 seconds. Add the flour mixture; beat on low speed until mixture is crumbly. Reserve 1 cup of the crumb mixture. Pat remaining crumb mixture onto the bottom of prepared pan. Bake for 20 minutes.

3. Meanwhile, in a small bowl stir together jam and lemon juice. Spread onto baked crust. Sprinkle with the reserved crumb mixture. Bake about 15 minutes more or until light brown. Cool in pan on a wire rack. Cut into bars. Makes 36 bars.

Each bar: 78 cal., 3 g total fat (2 g sat. fat), 9 mg chol., 56 mg sodium, 11 g carbo., 0 g fiber, 1 g pro. Daily Values: 2% vit. A, 1% vit. C, 1% calcium, 2% iron.

OUTDOOR SLEDDING PARTY TOO

Fire and Ice Nut Mix *(page 469)*
Winter White Vegetable Soup *(page 475)*
Citrus Salad with Honey Balsamic Vinaigrette *(page 475)*
Giant Ginger Cookies or Mitten Cookies *(page 486)*
Minted Hot Chocolate *(page 476)*

Hot Apple Cider with Calvados

Sips of hot cider laced with apple brandy keep grown-ups warm while they're not slipping and sliding down the hill.

PREP: 15 minutes **COOK:** 20 minutes

- **1 gallon apple cider**
- **1 cup strong brewed tea**
- **4 cinnamon sticks**
- **1 cup Calvados or other apple brandy**
- **Crushed ice (optional)**
- **Crabapples (optional)**

1. In a 5- to 6-quart Dutch oven combine apple cider, tea, and the 4 cinnamon sticks. Bring just to simmering (do not boil). Simmer, uncovered, for 20 minutes. Remove cinnamon sticks. Stir in Calvados.

2. Serve hot cider in mugs over ice, if desired. If desired, garnish each serving with a crabapple. Makes 16 to 20 servings.

Each serving: 167 cal., 0 g total fat, 0 mg chol., 21 mg sodium, 28 g carbo., 0 g fiber, 0 g pro. Daily Values: 4% vit. C, 2% calcium, 4% iron.

Minted Hot Chocolate

Mugs of this hot chocolate flavored with fresh mint warm up frosty little fingers and bright red cheeks.

PREP: 15 minutes **COOK:** 35 minutes **STAND:** 15 minutes

- **6 sprigs fresh mint**
- **1 vanilla bean, split in half lengthwise, or 1 tsp. vanilla extract**
- **12 cups milk**
- **¾ cup sugar**
- **9 oz. bittersweet chocolate, chopped**
- **Peppermint sticks (optional)**

1. Using 100-percent-cotton string, tie together mint sprigs and, if using, vanilla bean. In a 4-quart Dutch oven combine mint bundle, milk, and sugar. Heat just to boiling (watch carefully as milk may foam), stirring occasionally. Remove from heat. Let stand for 15 minutes.

2. Remove mint bundle and discard. Whisk chocolate into milk. Heat and stir just until mixture returns to boiling and chocolate is melted. Remove from heat. If using, stir in vanilla extract.

3. Serve in mugs. If desired, garnish each serving with a peppermint stick. Makes 12 servings.

Each serving: 272 cal., 12 g total fat (7 g sat. fat), 20 mg chol., 124 mg sodium, 36 g carbo., 2 g fiber, 9 g pro. Daily Values: 10% vit. A, 4% vit. C, 31% calcium, 5% iron.

Hot Apple Cider with Calvados

Chicken Fricassee

Chicken Fricassee

Make this dish the day before so the flavors blend together and party day becomes a lot easier for you.

PREP: 1 hour **COOK:** 30 minutes

- 2 3- to 3½-lb. cut-up broiler-fryer chickens
- Salt
- Ground black pepper
- ½ cup all-purpose flour
- ¼ cup olive oil
- 4 medium carrots, bias-sliced ¼ inch thick
- 2 cups pearl onions, peeled*
- 12 cloves garlic, peeled
- ¼ cup red wine vinegar
- ¼ cup champagne vinegar
- 4 cups chicken broth
- ¼ cup snipped fresh thyme or 2 tsp. dried thyme, crushed, plus 2 Tbsp. snipped fresh parsley
- 1 lb. small Yukon gold potatoes, quartered

1. If desired, remove skin from chicken. Sprinkle chicken with salt and pepper. Place flour in a sturdy plastic bag. Add chicken pieces, a few at a time, shaking to coat. Heat two 10- to 12-inch skillets (or use one electric skillet and one 10- to 12-inch skillet) over medium-high heat. Add 2 tablespoons of the oil to each skillet. Cook chicken in hot oil for 10 to 15 minutes or until brown, turning occasionally to brown evenly. Remove the chicken from skillets; set one skillet aside.

2. Add carrots and onions to the other skillet, adding more oil if necessary. Cook and stir vegetables for 4 minutes. Add garlic cloves; cook for 1 minute. Add vinegars. Cook, uncovered, about 3 minutes more or until most of the liquid has evaporated, stirring occasionally. Transfer half of the vegetable mixture to the first skillet. Add 2 cups of the chicken broth and 1 tablespoon of the fresh thyme or parsley (or 1 teaspoon of the dried thyme) to each skillet. Bring mixture in each skillet to boiling.

3. Add light-meat chicken pieces to one skillet and dark-meat chicken pieces to other skillet. Divide potatoes between the 2 skillets. Return to boiling; reduce heat. Simmer, covered, for 30 to 40 minutes or until chicken is no longer pink (170° F for light-meat pieces, 180° F for dark-meat pieces). (Light-meat pieces may be done a few minutes before dark-meat pieces.)**

4. Transfer chicken pieces and vegetables to a serving platter; cover and keep warm. For sauce, boil mixture in both skillets, uncovered, until it reaches desired consistency. Skim off fat. Spoon sauce over chicken and vegetables. Sprinkle with remaining fresh thyme or parsley. Makes 10 servings.

***NOTE:** To peel onions, in a medium saucepan cook onions in boiling water for 30 seconds; drain. Rinse under cold running water; drain again. When cool enough to handle, cut a small slice from the root end of each onion. Squeeze from the other end to remove onion from peel.

****TO FINISH IN OVEN:** Use 2 oven-going skillets and preheat oven to 350° F. After adding potatoes and returning mixture to boiling in step 3, cover skillets and place in oven. Bake for 35 to 45 minutes or until chicken is no longer pink (170° F for light-meat pieces, 180° F for dark-meat pieces). Transfer chicken and vegetables to platter; cook sauce in skillets as directed.

Each serving: 535 cal., 33 g total fat (9 g sat. fat), 138 mg chol., 517 mg sodium, 19 g carbo., 2 g fiber, 38 g pro. Daily Values: 128% vit. A, 26% vit. C, 5% calcium, 16% iron.

"PLAN YOUR MENU AROUND
SOMETHING THAT MAKES YOU
THINK OF HOME AND HEARTH."
CHARLES DALE

Cornmeal Buns

Serve this big batch of homespun buns warm with softened butter and you'll be glad this recipe makes so many.

PREP: 45 minutes **RISE:** 1 hour 50 minutes **BAKE:** 12 minutes

- **6 to 6½ cups all-purpose flour**
- **1 pkg. active dry yeast**
- **2¼ cups milk**
- **½ cup sugar**
- **½ cup butter**
- **1 tsp. salt**
- **2 eggs**
- **1½ cups cornmeal**

1. In a large mixing bowl stir together 3 cups of the flour and the yeast. In a medium saucepan heat and stir milk, sugar, butter, and salt just until warm (120° F to 130° F) and butter almost melts. Add milk mixture to flour mixture; add eggs. Beat with an electric mixer on low speed for 30 seconds, scraping the side of the bowl constantly. Beat on high speed for 3 minutes. Add cornmeal, beating on low speed until combined. Using a wooden spoon, stir in as much of the remaining flour as you can.

2. Turn dough out onto a lightly floured surface. Knead in enough of the remaining flour to make a moderately stiff dough that is smooth and elastic (6 to 8 minutes total). Shape into a ball. Place in a lightly greased bowl; turn once to grease surface. Cover and let rise in a warm place until double (1 to 1¼ hours).

3. Meanwhile, grease thirty-six 2½-inch muffin cups; set aside. Punch dough down. Turn dough out onto a lightly floured surface. Shape into 72 balls. Place 2 balls in each prepared muffin cup. Cover and let rise in a warm place until nearly double (50 to 60 minutes).

4. Preheat oven to 375° F. Bake for 12 to 15 minutes or until buns are golden brown. Immediately transfer from pans to wire racks. Serve warm or cool. Makes 36 buns.

***NOTE:** If you don't have 36 muffin cups, place dough balls on a waxed-paper-lined baking sheet; cover with plastic wrap and chill while the first pan rises and bakes. After removing the baked buns from pan, wash pan, grease, and refill with chilled dough. Cover, let rise, and bake as directed.

Each bun: 144 cal., 4 g total fat (2 g sat. fat), 20 mg chol., 106 mg sodium, 24 g carbo., 1 g fiber, 4 g pro. Daily Values: 3% vit. A, 2% calcium, 7% iron.

Macaroni and Cheese with Mushrooms

Not only will kids love this double cheese version of one of their favorite foods, but adults will enjoy it too.

PREP: 35 minutes **BAKE:** 30 minutes **STAND:** 15 minutes

- **12 oz. dried cavatappi or penne pasta**
- **5 Tbsp. butter**
- **3 Tbsp. all-purpose flour**
- **1½ cups half-and-half or light cream**
- **4 oz. Gruyère cheese, shredded (1 cup)**
- **3 Tbsp. finely shredded Parmigiano-Reggiano cheese**
- **1 Tbsp. porcini mushroom powder* (optional)**
- **⅛ tsp. salt**
- **Dash ground nutmeg**
- **12 oz. assorted fresh mushrooms, sliced, such as porcini, chanterelle, hedgehog, shiitake, or button**
- **¼ cup dry white wine**
- **2 Tbsp. snipped fresh parsley**

1. Preheat oven to 350° F. Cook pasta according to package directions; drain. Rinse under cold running water; drain again. Return pasta to pan; set aside.

2. Meanwhile, in a medium saucepan heat 3 tablespoons of the butter over medium heat until melted. Stir in flour. Add half-and-half all at once. Cook and stir until thickened and bubbly. Add ¾ cup of the Gruyère cheese, the Parmigiano-Reggiano cheese, porcini mushroom powder (if desired), salt, and nutmeg, stirring until cheeses are melted. Set aside.

3. In a large skillet cook mushrooms in the remaining 2 tablespoons butter over medium heat about 6 minutes or until tender and most of the liquid has evaporated, stirring occasionally. Add wine and cook, uncovered, until wine has nearly evaporated. Stir in parsley.

4. Add cheese mixture and mushroom mixture to the cooked pasta; stir to coat. Transfer pasta mixture to a 2- to 2½-quart shallow baking dish. Top with remaining ¼ cup Gruyère cheese. Bake, uncovered, about 30 minutes or until light brown and heated through. Let stand for 15 minutes before serving. Makes 10 servings.

MAKE-AHEAD TIP: Prepare pasta dish up to 24 hours in advance. Store tightly covered in the refrigerator. To serve, bake, covered, for 25 minutes. Uncover and bake about 30 minutes more or until light brown and heated through. Let stand as directed.

***NOTE:** If you can't find porcini mushroom powder, use a spice mill to grind dried mushrooms into a powder.

Each serving: 336 cal., 18 g total fat (10 g sat. fat), 49 mg chol., 317 mg sodium, 30 g carbo., 1 g fiber, 14 g pro. Daily Values: 13% vit. A, 2% vit. C, 29% calcium, 8% iron.

Macaroni and Cheese with Mushrooms

Caramelized Brussels Sprouts

"WE WANT PEOPLE TO REMEMBER THE COZY FEELING OF SHARING A GOOD MEAL."

AIMEE DALE

Spinach with Sweet Red Onion

Simple spinach salad takes a surprising twist when punctuated with onions sautéed in grenadine syrup.

PREP: 15 minutes **COOK:** 15 minutes

- 2 large red onions, halved lengthwise and sliced (3 cups)
- 2 Tbsp. butter
- 1 cup dry or sweet red wine
- 1/4 cup grenadine syrup or boysenberry syrup
- 2 Tbsp. sugar
- 1/4 tsp. salt
- 2 5- to 6-oz. pkg. fresh baby spinach (16 cups)

1. In a large nonstick skillet cook onions in hot butter for 5 to 8 minutes or until tender, stirring occasionally. Add wine, syrup, sugar, and salt. Bring to boiling; reduce heat. Simmer gently, uncovered, about 15 minutes or until most of the liquid has evaporated and liquid is syrupy.

2. Meanwhile, place the baby spinach in a very large serving bowl. Spoon the onion mixture over spinach; toss to combine. Season to taste with salt and pepper. Serve immediately. Makes 10 servings.

Each serving: 88 cal., 3 g total fat (2 g sat. fat), 7 mg chol., 153 mg sodium, 12 g carbo., 3 g fiber, 1 g pro. Daily Values: 32% vit. A, 15% vit. C, 3% calcium, 12% iron.

Spinach with Sweet Red Onion

Caramelized Brussels Sprouts

Spoon up homey Brussels sprouts to serve alongside the root vegetables in Chicken Fricasee.

PREP: 25 minutes **COOK:** 21 minutes

- 10 cups small, firm fresh Brussels sprouts (about 2 3/4 lb.)
- 1/2 cup sugar
- 1/4 cup butter
- 1/2 cup red wine vinegar
- 3/4 cup water
- 3/4 tsp. salt

1. Prepare Brussels sprouts by peeling off 2 or 3 of the dark outer leaves; trim stem ends.

2. In a Dutch oven or 12-inch skillet heat the sugar over medium-high heat until it begins to melt, shaking pan occasionally to heat sugar evenly. Once sugar starts to melt, reduce heat and cook until sugar starts to turn brown. Add butter; stir until melted. Add vinegar. Cook and stir for 1 minute.

3. Carefully add the water and salt. Bring to boiling. Add the Brussels sprouts. Return to boiling; reduce heat. Simmer, covered, for 6 minutes. Uncover and cook about 15 minutes more or until most of the liquid has been absorbed and Brussels sprouts are coated with a golden glaze, gently stirring occasionally. Makes 16 servings.

Each serving: 76 cal., 3 g total fat (2 g sat. fat), 8 mg chol., 155 mg sodium, 11 g carbo., 2 g fiber, 2 g pro. Daily Values: 11% vit. A, 66% vit. C, 2% calcium, 5% iron.

ROCKY MOUNTAIN SUPPER

Chicken Fricassee *(page 478)*
Caramelized Brussels Sprouts *(above)*
Cornmeal Buns *(page 480)*
Chocolate-Cherry Bread Pudding *(page 485)*
Coffee or tea

Chocolate-Cherry Bread Pudding

Caramel Apple Crepes

Make the crepes ahead so you simply reheat them before serving.

START TO FINISH: 30 minutes

- 1 recipe Blender Crepes (below)
- 1 recipe Candied Nuts (below) or toasted pecan halves (optional)
- 1 cup packed brown sugar
- 4 tsp. cornstarch
- 1 cup whipping cream
- 2 Tbsp. apple brandy, brandy, or apple juice
- 1 Tbsp. butter softened
- 2 cups thinly sliced apples
- Vanilla ice crea m (optional)

1. Prepare Blender Crepes. To reheat or to keep warm, place stack of crepes in a 300° F oven until serving time. Prepare Candied Nuts, if using.

2. In a large saucepan stir together brown sugar and cornstarch. Stir in whipping cream, brandy, and butter. Add apples. Cook and stir over medium heat until thickened and bubbly. Cook and stir for 2 minutes more.

3. To serve, fold each crepe in half, brown side out. Fold in half again, forming a triangle. Place 2 crepes on each of 6 dessert plates. Pour warm apple mixture onto crepes.Sprinkle with some of the Candied Nuts. If desired, serve with vanilla ice cream. Makes 6 servings.

BLENDER CREPES: In a blender combine 3/4 cup all-purpose flour, 1/3 cup water, 1/3 cup milk, 2 eggs, 2 tablespoons sugar, and 4 teaspoons walnut oil or cooking oil. Cover and blend until smooth, stopping and scraping the sides as necessary. Heat a lightly greased 6-inch skillet over medium heat; remove from heat. Spoon 2 tablespoons of batter into skillet; lift and tilt skillet to spread batter evenly. Return skillet to heat; brown on 1 side only. Invert skillet over paper towels to remove crepe from pan. Repeat with remaining batter, making 12 crepes total.

CANDIED NUTS: Line a baking sheet with foil; butter the foil. Set aside. In a large heavy skillet combine 1 1/2 cups pecan halves, 1/2 cup sugar, 2 tablespoons butter, and 1/2 teaspoon vanilla. Cook over medium-high heat, shaking skillet occasionally, until sugar begins to melt; do not stir. Reduce heat to low; continue cooking until sugar is golden brown, stirring occasionally. Remove skillet from heat. Pour nut mixture onto the prepared baking sheet. Cook completely. Break into clusters.

MAKE-AHEAD TIP: To freeze crepes, stack with waxed paper between layers. Place in a moisture-proof freezer bag; freeze for up to 3 months. Thaw at room temperature for 1 hour before using. Before reheating, remove waxed paper. You can also store Candied Nuts tightly covered in the refrigerator for up to 3 weeks.

Each serving: 465 cal., 22 g total fat (11 g sat. fat), 132 mg chol., 79 mg sodium, 61 g carbo., 1 g fiber, 5 g pro. Daily Values: 16% vit. A, 4% vit. C, 9% calcium, 10% iron.

Chocolate-Cherry Bread Pudding

When guests lean back in their chairs, bring out this old-time dessert, studded with bits of dried cherries and bittersweet chocolate.

PREP: 25 minutes **STAND:** 1 hour **BAKE:** 1 hour **COOL:** 1 hour

- 2/3 cup Kirsch or orange juice
- 1 1/2 cups dried tart cherries or dried plums (prunes), snipped (about 8 oz.)
- 1 16-oz. loaf country Italian bread or baguette, cut into 1- to 1 1/2-inch pieces (about 11 cups)
- 1/4 cup butter, melted
- 8 oz. bittersweet chocolate, coarsely chopped
- 6 eggs
- 3 cups milk
- 2 cups half-and-half or light cream
- 1 cup sugar
- 1 tsp. vanilla

1. In a small saucepan heat Kirsch or orange juice over medium-low heat just to simmering; remove from heat. Stir in dried cherries or plums. Let stand, covered, for 1 hour. Do not drain.

2. Preheat oven to 350° F. In a very large bowl drizzle bread with melted butter; toss to coat. Divide bread evenly between two 1 1/2-quart casseroles or place in one 3-quart rectangular baking dish. Sprinkle half of the chocolate evenly over bread in casseroles or baking dish; reserve remaining half of chocolate. Spoon half of the fruit and liquid evenly over the chocolate layer; reserve remaining half of fruit and liquid. Top with remaining bread.

3. In a large bowl whisk eggs; whisk in milk, half-and-half, sugar, and vanilla until combined. Slowly pour egg mixture evenly over the layers in casseroles or baking dish. Press down lightly.

4. Bake, covered, for 45 minutes. Uncover and bake for 15 to 20 minutes more for the 1 1/2-quart casseroles or 30 minutes more for the baking dish or until egg portion in center appears set. Sprinkle with remaining chocolate and fruit with liquid. Let stand about 1 hour. Serve warm. Makes 12 servings.

Each serving: 506 cal., 20 g total fat (11 g sat. fat), 137 mg chol., 342 mg sodium, 67 g carbo., 3 g fiber, 11 g pro. Daily Values: 12% vit. A, 2% vit. C, 17% calcium, 12% iron.

Giant Ginger Cookies

Chewy and delicious, these cookies are giants in both size and snappy ginger flavor.

PREP: 20 minutes **BAKE:** 11 minutes per batch

- **4½ cups all-purpose flour**
- **4 tsp. ground ginger**
- **2 tsp. baking soda**
- **1½ tsp. ground cinnamon**
- **1 tsp. ground cloves**
- **¼ tsp. salt**
- **1½ cups shortening**
- **2 cups granulated sugar**
- **2 eggs**
- **½ cup molasses**
- **½ cup coarse or granulated sugar**

1. Preheat oven to 350° F. In a medium bowl stir together flour, ginger, baking soda, cinnamon, cloves, and salt; set aside.

2. In a large mixing bowl beat shortening with an electric mixer on medium to high speed for 30 seconds. Add the 2 cups sugar. Beat until combined, scraping side of bowl occasionally. Beat in eggs and molasses until combined. Beat in as much of the flour mixture as you can with the mixer. Stir in any remaining flour mixture.

3. Using ¼ cup dough for each cookie, shape dough into balls. Roll balls in the ½ cup sugar. Place 2½ inches apart on an ungreased cookie sheet.

4. Bake for 11 to 13 minutes or until bottoms are light brown and tops are puffed (do not overbake). Cool on the cookie sheet for 2 minutes. Transfer cookies to a wire rack; let cool. Makes about 24 cookies.

Each cookie: 306 cal., 13 g total fat (3 g sat. fat), 18 mg chol., 138 mg sodium, 45 g carbo., 1 g fiber, 3 g pro. Daily Values: 1% vit. A, 1% vit. C, 3% calcium, 10% iron.

Mitten Cookies

Plain big cookies become the talk of the sledding hill when Charles and Aimee sprinkle on mitten shapes with colored sugars.

PREP: 30 minutes **CHILL:** 2 hours **BAKE:** 14 minutes per batch

- **1½ cups butter, softened**
- **1⅔ cups granulated sugar**
- **2 tsp. baking powder**
- **½ tsp. salt**
- **2 eggs**
- **¼ cup buttermilk**
- **½ tsp. vanilla**
- **⅓ cup ground toasted almonds**
- **4 cups all-purpose flour**
- **Coarse colored sugars**

1. In a large mixing bowl beat butter with an electric mixer on medium to high speed for 30 seconds. Add granulated sugar, baking powder, and salt. Beat until combined, scraping side of bowl occasionally. Beat in eggs, buttermilk, and vanilla until combined. Beat in ground almonds. Beat in as much of the flour as you can with the mixer. Stir in any remaining flour. Cover and chill about 2 hours or until easy to handle.

2. Preheat oven to 375° F. Using ⅓ cup dough for each cookie, shape dough into balls. Place 3½ inches apart on an ungreased cookie sheet. Cover with plastic wrap and flatten with hand or bottom of a pie plate to 4- to 5-inch rounds.

3. Place a mitten cookie cutter or a stencil* on top of cookie; sprinkle colored sugar inside the cutter or stencil. Remove and repeat with remaining cookies. Bake about 14 minutes or until edges are firm and bottoms are brown. Cool on cookie sheet for 2 to 3 minutes. Transfer to a wire rack and let cool. Makes 16 large cookies.

***MITTEN STENCIL:** Draw a mitten shape about 3 inches long on heavy cardboard or on the back of a stiff paper plate. Cut out mitten with a sharp knife or scissors.

Each cookie: 426 cal., 21 g total fat (12 g sat. fat), 76 mg chol., 321 mg sodium, 57 g carbo., 1 g fiber, 5 g pro. Daily Values: 15% vit. A, 5% calcium, 10% iron.

ROCKY MOUNTAIN SUPPER TWO

Macaroni and Cheese with Mushrooms *(page 480)*
Spinach with Sweet Red Onion *(page 483)*
Cornmeal Buns *(page 480)*
Caramel Apple Crepes *(page 485)*
Milk

Mitten Cookies

Pack up some cookies for the car to see everyone home in good spirits. Little ones will giggle at the sugar-sprinkled mittens on cheery Mitten Cookies.

Smoky Mountain Holiday

GRAB A COAT AND A WALKING STICK. YOU'RE ALL SET TO ENJOY THE SIMPLE EARTHY CUISINE OF A COZY INN IN TENNESSEE, AND CELEBRATE THE HOLIDAYS WITH DOWN-HOME COUNTRY STYLE.

Braised Fresh Pork Hocks with Bourbon Gravy

Start the gravy by lifting the tasty browned bits from the pan with a generous splash of smooth Southern whiskey.

PREP: 30 minutes **BAKE:** 2½ hours

- 6 fresh pork hocks (about 5½ lb.)
- ¾ tsp. salt
- ¾ tsp. pepper
- ¾ cup all-purpose flour
- 3 Tbsp. olive oil
- ¼ cup bourbon whiskey
- 1 14-oz. can beef broth
- 3 Tbsp. (¼ of a 6-oz. can) tomato paste
- 1½ cups coarsely chopped sweet onion, such as Vidalia (see page 575)
- 1 small leek, coarsely chopped
- 1 small stalk celery, coarsely chopped
- 1 small carrot, coarsely chopped
- 4 cloves garlic, peeled
- 3 sprigs fresh thyme
- 1 bay leaf
- Fresh sage leaves (optional)
- Roasted garlic bulb (see page 437) (optional)

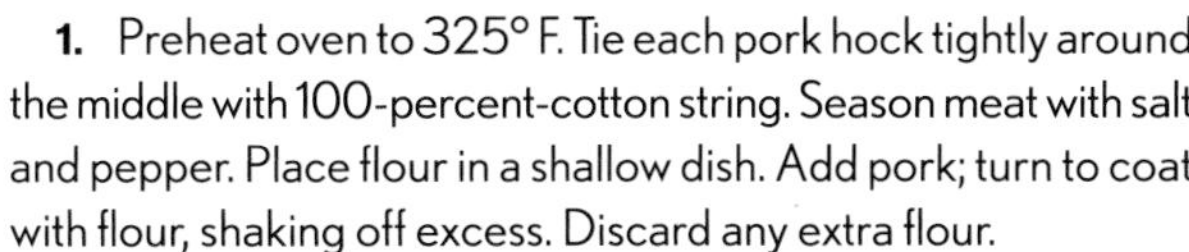

1. Preheat oven to 325° F. Tie each pork hock tightly around the middle with 100-percent-cotton string. Season meat with salt and pepper. Place flour in a shallow dish. Add pork; turn to coat with flour, shaking off excess. Discard any extra flour.

2. In a 10- to 12-quart stewpot brown pork on all sides in hot oil over medium heat; remove from pan. Drain off excess oil.

3. To deglaze pan, carefully add bourbon, using a wooden spoon to scrape browned bits off the bottom of the pan and continuing to cook until nearly all of the liquid is gone.

4. Add beef broth and tomato paste, whisking together until smooth. Bring to boiling. Return pork to pan along with onions, leek, celery, carrot, garlic, thyme, and bay leaf. Return to boiling. Cover with oven-going lid or foil; bake for 2½ to 3 hours or until meat pulls apart easily with a fork.

5. Transfer pork to a serving platter; remove string. For sauce, skim fat from vegetable mixture; discard bay leaf and thyme sprigs. Season meat with salt and pepper. Spoon sauce over pork. If desired, garnish with sage leaves and roasted garlic. Makes 6 servings.

Each serving: 351 cal., 19 g total fat (5 g sat. fat), 55 mg chol., 611 mg sodium, 20 g carbo., 2 g fiber, 19 g pro. Daily Values: 34% vit. A, 12% vit. C, 4% calcium, 13% iron.

Collard Greens with Tasso Ham

Tasso is a Louisianan ham—usually pork shoulder that's richly seasoned. You can substitute another spiced ham.

START TO FINISH: 30 minutes

- 4½ lb. collard greens
- 1½ cups finely chopped tasso ham or Cajun-spiced cooked ham
- 2 Tbsp. clarified butter or butter
- ⅓ cup packed brown sugar
- ⅓ cup red wine vinegar
- 1 tsp. salt
- 1 tsp. pepper

1. Remove stems and thick ribs from collard greens. In a 4-quart Dutch oven immerse greens, one-third at a time, in boiling water for 30 seconds. Remove with tongs or slotted spoon; drain well in a colander. Coarsely chop greens; set aside.

2. In a 12-inch skillet cook and stir tasso ham in hot butter over medium-high heat for 1 minute. Add brown sugar and vinegar; stir until sugar is dissolved. Add greens, salt, and pepper. Cook and stir until heated through. Serve warm. Makes 6 to 8 servings.

Each serving: 218 cal., 9 g total fat (1 g sat. fat), 22 mg chol., 998 mg sodium, 23 g carbo., 7 g fiber, 13 g pro. Daily Values: 141% vit. A, 63% vit. C, 28% calcium, 7% iron.

Grits with Smoked Oysters

Pictured upper left: Mary Celeste Beall and daughter Cameron. Above: Chef John Fleer. Right: Local storyteller, Willard M. Abbott, and guest, Sam Carroll.

Grits with Smoked Oysters

PREP: 45 minutes **BAKE:** 30 minutes

- 4 cups reduced-sodium chicken broth
- $1\frac{1}{3}$ cups stone ground yellow grits
- ½ tsp. ground red pepper
- $1\frac{1}{4}$ cups chopped red sweet pepper
- 1 cup chopped celery
- ½ cup bias-sliced green onions
- 1 Tbsp. snipped fresh parsley
- 6 Tbsp. butter
- 4 egg yolks
- ½ cup grated dry Monterey Jack or Parmesan cheese
- 2 Tbsp. all purpose flour
- 12 oz. smoked oysters*, canned or fresh, drained and coarsely chopped
- 4 egg whites
- Nonstick cooking spray

1. Preheat oven to 350° F. In a large saucepan bring chicken broth to boiling. Gradually whisk in grits and ground red pepper. Reduce heat. Cook, uncovered, about 25 minutes or until mixture is very thick, stirring frequently.

2. Meanwhile, in a large skillet cook and stir red sweet pepper, celery, green onions, and parsley in 1 tablespoon hot butter over medium heat about 5 minutes or just until tender; set aside.

3. In a small mixing bowl beat egg yolks; set aside. Remove cooked grits from heat; stir in remaining butter until melted. Gradually stir about 1 cup of the grits into the egg yolks. Return yolk mixture to the remaining grits. Stir in cooked vegetables, cheese, and flour. Gently stir in oysters; set aside.

4. In a mixing bowl beat egg whites with an electric mixer on high speed until stiff peaks form (tips stand straight); fold egg whites, one-third at a time, into the grits mixture. Lightly coat a 3-quart rectangular baking dish with cooking spray. Spoon grits mixture into baking dish.

5. Bake, uncovered, about 30 minutes or until a knife inserted off center comes out clean. Makes 10 to 12 servings.

***TEST KITCHEN TIP:** If smoked oysters are unavailable, you can smoke the oysters at home. Soak 2 cups hickory or mesquite wood chips in enough water to cover for 1 hour. Drain before using. Place $1\frac{1}{2}$ pounds drained, shucked oysters, half at a time, in a single layer in an 11×8-inch foil pan or grill pan. In a charcoal grill, arrange medium-hot coals around the outside edge of the grill. Test for medium heat in the center of the grill. Sprinkle the drained wood chips over the coals. Place the pan with the oysters in the center of the grill rack. Cover and smoke for 10 to 12 minutes or until edges of oysters begin to curl. Repeat with remaining oysters.

Each serving: 291 cal., 16 g total fat (8 g sat. fat), 114 mg chol., 513 mg sodium, 24 g carbo., 1 g fiber, 14 g pro. Daily Values: 35% vit. A, 54% vit. C, 8% calcium, 33% iron.

AT HOME ON THE FARM

Way down a winding hollow, along the foothills of the Great Smoky Mountains, there's a country house hotel in Walland, Tennessee, known as Blackberry Farm. Even when hunger beckons, there's plenty to do—a homey feast under a cottage roof, a luncheon hike up a rocky path, a cookie-and-nog storytelling session, and a quiet breakfast by a cozy crackling fire. After welcoming guests for nearly 30 years, proprietors Kreis and Sandy Beall want to make folks feel comfortable from the moment they arise from their fluffy feather beds until they've eaten their last bite of dessert. At Christmastime, this translates to greenery dripping from doorways, freshly cut trees, heirloom decorations, and heady aromas of baked breads, cookies, cider, and candies.

"A Tennessee Christmas is simple and relaxed. Ideally, it's about great food and how many extended kin you can gather in one place for great food," says executive chef John Fleer. "We believe that great cooking is nourishment for the soul. It should never intimidate and should always satisfy. My grandmother called it comfort food; I call it foothill's cuisine." Like Christmas at Blackberry, Fleer describes his cuisine as wandering a fine line between familiar and new, refined and rugged, and straightforward and simple. It's humble and always delicious. "We don't float up into the never land of gourmet but stay rooted in what makes sense."

Fleer often relies on an old Irish proverb, "The laughter is brightest where the food is best." He says, "While guests celebrate the holidays with us, we hope they experience the table as a place where the spirit of the season is rekindled."

Kreis Beall adds, "The main thing is: there is no right or wrong way to relish the season. It's the spirit behind the effort that becomes memory."

CHRISTMAS EVE FEAST

Braised Fresh Pork Hocks with Bourbon Gravy *(page 489)*

Grits with Smoked Oysters *(left)*

Collard Greens with Tasso Ham *(page 489)*

Orange Chess Pie *(page 495)*

Chocolate Chess Pie *(page 495)*

Wine or sparkling water

Peanut Soup

Even though it's native to Williamsburg, this soup has been a must-have for Chef Fleer's family and for Blackberry guests. "It's how my family has always started Christmas dinner," says Fleer.

PREP: 30 minutes **BAKE:** 25 minutes **COOK:** 30 minutes

- 1 cup chopped shallots (two 3-oz. pkg.)
- 1 cup finely chopped celery
- 1/4 cup butter
- 2 Tbsp. all-purpose flour
- 3/4 cup creamy peanut butter
- 2 Tbsp. chopped unsalted raw Spanish peanuts
- 1 49-oz. can chicken broth (6 cups)
- 1/2 cup whipping cream
- Ground red pepper
- 1 cup Red Spiced Peanuts (below)

1. In a large saucepan cook shallots and celery in hot butter over medium heat about 5 minutes or until tender, stirring occasionally. Stir flour into shallot mixture; cook and stir about 2 minutes or until flour starts to brown.

2. Stir in peanut butter and peanuts; cook until peanut butter melts. Gradually whisk in chicken broth. Bring to boiling (watch carefully to prevent soup from boiling over); reduce heat. Simmer, uncovered, for 30 minutes, stirring occasionally.

3. Stir in cream and ground red pepper. Garnish with Red Spiced Peanuts. Makes 8 servings.

Each serving: 396 cal., 34 g total fat (12 g sat. fat), 42 mg chol., 1,008 mg sodium, 17 g carbo., 3 g fiber, 12 g pro. Daily Values: 16% vit. A, 4% vit. C, 5% calcium, 8% iron.

RED SPICED PEANUTS: Preheat oven to 350° F. Line a 15×10×1-inch baking pan with foil; grease the foil and set aside. In a large skillet melt 1/4 cup butter over medium heat. Stir in 1/4 cup granulated sugar, 1/4 cup packed brown sugar, 1/2 teaspoon salt, and 1/4 teaspoon ground red pepper. Stir in 1/4 cup water. Cook and stir until sugars dissolve. Add 2 cups unsalted raw Spanish peanuts. Bring to boiling. Boil gently, uncovered, for 5 minutes. Transfer nut mixture to the prepared pan, spreading in an even layer. Bake, uncovered, for 25 minutes, stirring occasionally. Transfer foil lining to a wire rack. Cool completely. Break nut mixture into small clusters. Store in an airtight container for up to 2 weeks. Freeze for longer storage. Makes 3 1/2 cups (28 servings).

Each serving: 89 cal., 7 g total fat (2 g sat. fat), 5 mg chol., 62 mg sodium, 5 g carbo., 1 g fiber, 3 g pro. Daily Values: 1% vit. A, 1% calcium, 3% iron.

Smoked Trout Club Sandwiches

PREP: 20 minutes **CHILL:** up to 8 hours

- 12 slices firm-textured white bread (Pain de Mie), toasted
- 1 cup Scallion Mayonnaise (below)
- 1 lb. smoked trout or smoked white fish, bones removed and broken into chunks
- 8 slices bacon, crisp-cooked, drained, and halved crosswise
- 1 to 1 1/2 cups arugula
- 1/2 cup Pecan Sweet Hot Mustard Sauce(below) or honey mustard

1. Spread one side of 4 bread slices with 1/2 cup of the Scallion Mayonnaise. Top, mayonnaise side up, with half of the trout. Top each with 2 bacon half-pieces and half of the arugula.

2. Spread both sides of 4 more bread slices with Pecan Sweet Hot Mustard Sauce. Lay slices on top of the bacon layer. Top with remaining trout, bacon pieces, and arugula.

3. Spread one side of remaining 4 bread slices with remaining 1/2 cup of the Scallion Mayonnaise. Place, mayonnaise side down, onto bacon. Wrap in plastic wrap; chill for up to 8 hours. Before serving, cut sandwiches in half. Makes 8 servings.

Each serving: 419 cal., 26 g total fat (4 g sat. fat), 77 mg chol., 789 mg sodium, 33 g carbo., 1 g fiber, 15 g pro. Daily Values: 2% vit. A, 5% vit. C, 14% calcium, 10% iron.

SCALLION MAYONNAISE: In a small saucepan cook 6 chopped green onions in 1 teaspoon hot cooking oil for 1 to 2 minutes or until bright green and just tender. Remove from heat and cool. In a blender container or food processor bowl combine cooked green onions, 6 chopped fresh green onions, 1 cup mayonnaise or salad dressing, 1 1/2 teaspoons lemon juice, 1/2 teaspoon kosher salt, and 1/4 teaspoon pepper. Cover and blend or process until smooth. Cover and store in the refrigerator for up to 1 week. Makes 1 1/2 cups.

Each tablespoon: 70 cal., 8 g total fat (1 g sat. fat), 3 mg chol., 91 mg sodium, 1 g carbo., 0 g fiber, 0 g pro. Daily Values: 2% vit. C, 1% iron.

PECAN SWEET HOT MUSTARD SAUCE: In a medium bowl stir together 1 1/2 cups packed brown sugar; 1/2 cup chopped pecans, toasted; 1/2 cup Dijon-style mustard; 1/2 cup stone ground mustard; 2 tablespoons cider vinegar; and 1/2 teaspoon bottled hot pepper sauce. Cover and store in the refrigerator for up to 1 week. Makes 1 1/2 cups.

Each tablespoon: 44 cal., 2 g total fat (0 g sat. fat), 0 mg chol., 99 mg sodium, 6 g carbo., 0 g fiber, 1 g pro. Daily Values: 2% calcium, 2% iron.

Smoked Trout Club Sandwiches, Peanut Soup, and Pear Isaacs,

Orange and Chocolate Chess Pies

Orange Chess Pie

PREP: 25 minutes **BAKE:** 40 minutes

- 4 eggs
- 1¼ cups sugar
- ⅓ cup butter, melted
- ¼ cup buttermilk
- 2 Tbsp. cornmeal
- 2 Tbsp. vanilla
- 1 Tbsp. finely shredded orange peel
- 1 Tbsp. orange liqueur
- ¼ tsp. salt
- ⅛ tsp. ground nutmeg
- 1 recipe Sweet Pastry Crust(below)

1. Preheat oven to 325° F. For filling, in a medium mixing bowl slightly beat eggs with a rotary beater or fork. Stir in sugar, butter, buttermilk, cornmeal, vanilla, orange peel, orange liqueur, salt, and nutmeg.

2. Pour filling into partially baked Sweet Pastry Crust. Bake about 40 minutes or until edges are puffed and golden (center may still shake a bit). Cool in pan on a wire rack. Refrigerate within 2 hours; cover pie for longer storage. Makes 8 servings.

SWEET PASTRY CRUST: Preheat oven to 375° F. In a medium bowl stir together 1¼ cups all-purpose flour, 1 tablespoon sugar, and ¼ teaspoon salt. Using a pastry blender, cut in ⅓ cup shortening until pieces are pea-size. Sprinkle 1 tablespoon cold water over part of the mixture; gently toss with a fork. Push moistened dough to the side of the bowl. Repeat, using 1 tablespoon cold water at a time, until all the dough is moistened (4 to 5 tablespoons water total).

Form dough into a ball. On a lightly floured surface flatten dough. Roll out dough to a 12-inch circle. Transfer pastry to a 9-inch pie plate. (If stacking pies, line the bottom of the pie plate with foil. Lightly coat foil and sides of plate with cooking spray. Line the pie plate with pastry.)

Trim pastry to ½ inch beyond edge of pie plate. Fold extra pastry under and crimp edge as desired. Cover pastry with a double thickness of foil. Bake for 10 minutes. Remove foil cover from top. Bake about 5 minutes more or until set and dry.

Each slice: 401 cal., 19 g total fat (8 g sat. fat), 128 mg chol., 268 mg sodium, 50 g carbo., 1 g fiber, 6 g pro. Daily Values: 10% vit. A, 3% vit. C, 4% calcium, 8% iron.

Chocolate Chess Pie

PREP: 30 minutes **BAKE:** 40 minutes

- 3 oz. bittersweet chocolate, chopped
- 6 Tbsp. butter, cut up
- 4 eggs
- 1⅓ cups sugar
- 2 Tbsp. all-purpose flour
- ¼ tsp. salt
- 2 Tbsp. whipping cream
- 1 Tbsp. bourbon whiskey
- 1½ tsp. vanilla
- 1 recipe Sweet Pastry Crust (left)

1. Preheat oven to 325° F. For filling, in a small, heavy saucepan combine chocolate and butter; cook and stir over low heat until melted.

2. Meanwhile, in a medium mixing bowl slightly beat eggs with a rotary beater or fork. Beat in sugar, flour, and salt. Stir in whipping cream and melted chocolate mixture. Stir in bourbon and vanilla.

3. Pour filling into partially baked Sweet Pastry Crust. Bake about 40 minutes or until set (top will puff and fall on cooling, leaving a slightly crackled crust). Cool the pie in pan on a wire rack. Refrigerate within 2 hours; cover pie for longer storage. Makes 8 servings.

Each slice: 469 cal., 25 g total fat (12 g sat. fat), 136 mg chol., 273 mg sodium, 56 g carbo., 1 g fiber, 6 g pro. Daily Values: 11% vit. A, 1% vit. C, 3% calcium, 10% iron.

TEST KITCHEN TIP: For a tip-top serving idea, prepare 2 Orange Chess Pies and 1 Chocolate Chess Pie. Carefully remove whole pies from each pie plate, using foil liners. Stack the pies on a platter with the chocolate pie in the center; sprinkle with fresh blackberries.

Cranberry-Black Walnut Coffee Cake

PREP: 45 minutes **BAKE:** 1 hour 15 minutes

- 2 cups dried cranberries (8 oz.)
- 1 cup apple cider
- 1/2 cup packed brown sugar
- 1/2 cup water
- 1 2-inch piece stick cinnamon
- 3 cups all-purpose flour
- 1 cup granulated sugar
- 1 cup black or English walnuts, toasted and ground
- 2 tsp. baking powder
- 1 tsp. ground cinnamon
- 1/4 tsp. salt
- 4 eggs
- 1 cup whole milk
- 1 cup butter, melted
- 1 tsp. vanilla
- 1 recipe Walnut Streusel Topping(below)

1. In a medium saucepan combine cranberries, cider, brown sugar, water, and cinnamon stick. Bring to boiling, stirring to dissolve sugar. Remove from heat. Cover; let stand 10 minutes.

2. Preheat oven to 325° F. Grease a 10-inch springform pan; set aside. Drain cranberries; discard liquid and cinnamon stick. Coarsely chop cranberries; set aside.

3. In a large mixing bowl stir together flour, granulated sugar, nuts, baking powder, ground cinnamon, and salt. In a medium bowl lightly beat eggs; stir in milk, melted butter, and vanilla. Add egg mixture to flour mixture; stir just until moistened. Spoon batter into prepared pan. Sprinkle center with cranberries to within 1 inch of the outside edge.

4. Sprinkle Walnut Streusel Topping evenly over top. Bake, uncovered, for 1 hour and 15 minutes or until a wooden toothpick inserted near the center comes out clean. Remove and cool for 15 minutes in the pan on a wire rack. Before serving, remove side of springform pan. Serve warm. Makes 12 servings.

WALNUT STREUSEL TOPPING: In a food processor bowl combine 2/3 cup all-purpose flour, 1/3 cup packed brown sugar, 1/4 cup sugar, 3/4 teaspoon ground cinnamon, 1/4 teaspoon salt, and 1/4 teaspoon vanilla. Cover and process several seconds or until combined. Cut up 1/3 cup butter; add to flour mixture. Cover and process with several on-off turns until crumbly. (Or in a medium mixing bowl stir together flour, sugars, cinnamon, salt, and vanilla. Using a pastry blender, cut in butter until crumbly.) Stir in 1/4 cup chopped black or English walnuts.

Each slice: 619 cal., 32 g total fat (15 g sat. fat), 32 mg chol., 422 mg sodium, 77 g carbo., 3 g fiber, 10 g pro. Daily Values: 20% vit. A, 1% vit. C, 11% calcium, 16% iron.

Pear Issacs

Chef Fleer named these pear cookies "Isaacs" since "Newton" was already taken by figs.

PREP: 1 hour **CHILL:** 2 hours **BAKE:** 20 minutes per batch

- 6 medium pears, peeled, cored, and cut into eighths
- 1 tsp. finely shredded lemon peel
- 1 Tbsp. lemon juice
- 3 Tbsp. butter
- 1/2 cup sugar
- 1 tsp. finely chopped crystallized ginger
- 1/2 tsp. vanilla
- 1 recipe Cream Cheese Pastry (below)
- Coarse sugar

1. For filling, in a large bowl toss together pears, lemon peel, and juice. In a large skillet, melt butter. Add pear mixture, sugar, and ginger. Stir gently until sugar is dissolved. Cook over medium heat for 15 to 20 minutes or until pears are translucent, stirring occasionally. Strain pears in colander, reserving syrup; transfer pears to a bowl. Return syrup to skillet. Heat to boiling; reduce heat and simmer syrup, uncovered, about 5 minutes or until slightly thick and golden brown. Stir in 1/2 teaspoon vanilla. Stir into pears; cover and chill.

2. Preheat oven to 350° F. On a lightly floured surface roll one portion of Cream Cheese Pastry into a 9-inch square. Transfer to a cookie sheet, placing dough near one end of sheet. Spoon one-fourth of the pear mixture (about 1/2 cup) over half of the dough to within 1/2 inch of edges. Brush edges with water. Fold uncovered dough over filling; press edges to seal. Brush top of dough with water; sprinkle with coarse sugar. Repeat with another portion of dough and one-fourth of the filling, placing second rolled dough near the other end of cookie sheet. Bake for 20 minutes or until light brown and edges are firm. Cool on wire rack. Repeat with remaining dough and filling.

3. With a serrated knife, trim edges to make a smooth edge. Cut each portion crosswise into 6 cookies. Makes 24 cookies.

CREAM CHEESE PASTRY: In a medium bowl stir together 3 cups all-purpose flour, 1 teaspoon baking powder, 1/2 teaspoon salt, 1/2 teaspoon ground cinnamon, and 1/4 teaspoon baking soda. In a large mixing bowl combine one 3-ounce package cream cheese, softened, and 1/4 cup softened butter; beat with an electric mixer on medium speed for 30 seconds. Add 1 cup packed brown sugar; beat until fluffy. Beat in 2 egg whites and 1 teaspoon vanilla. Beat or stir in flour mixture. Divide dough into fourths; wrap each portion in plastic wrap. Chill for 2 to 3 hours or until firm enough to handle.

Each cookie: 182 cal., 5 g total fat (3 g sat. fat), 13 mg chol., 133 mg sodium, 32 g carbo., 1 g fiber, 2 g pro. Daily Values: 4% vit. A, 3% vit. C, 3% calcium, 6% iron.

Cranberry-Black Walnut Coffee Cake

Tennessee Orange Biscuits with Blackberry Gravy

Jackson's Cereal Blend

Wake-Up Smoothies

Tennessee Orange Biscuits with Blackberry Gravy

The farm uses its namesake blackberries in dishes year-round, including the sauce for these tender biscuits.

PREP: 30 minutes **BAKE:** 12 minutes

- 3½ cups sifted cake flour
- 3 Tbsp. sugar
- 4 tsp. baking powder
- 1 Tbsp. finely shredded orange peel
- 1 tsp. salt
- ½ cup butter, chilled
- 3 eggs
- ½ cup whole milk
- ¼ cup whipping cream
- 1 Tbsp. orange juice
- 1 Tbsp. water
- Granulated sugar or extra-fine granulated sugar
- 1 cup fresh or frozen blackberries, thawed
- 1 cup Fresh Blackberry Jam (below)
- ¼ cup butter, softened

1. Preheat oven to 400° F. In a large mixing bowl stir together cake flour, 3 tablespoons sugar, baking powder, orange peel, and salt. Using a pastry blender, cut in the ½ cup butter until mixture resembles coarse crumbs. In a medium bowl whisk together 2 of the eggs, milk, whipping cream, and orange juice. Add to dry ingredients; stir just to combine.

2. Turn dough out onto a well-floured surface (the dough will be slightly sticky). Knead by folding and pressing dough 10 to 12 strokes or until nearly smooth. Roll out dough to ¾ -inch thickness. Cut with a floured 2- or 3-inch round cutter.

3. On a greased baking sheet arrange cutouts 1 inch apart. In a small bowl beat the remaining egg and water. Brush tops of cutouts with egg mixture; sprinkle with additional sugar. Bake for 12 to 14 minutes or until golden.

4. For blackberry gravy, stir blackberries into blackberry jam. Transfer biscuits to a wire rack; cool slightly. To serve, spread tops of biscuits with softened butter; top with blackberry gravy. To store leftover gravy, cover and refrigerate for up to 2 weeks. Makes 12 small or 8 large biscuits.

Each small biscuit: 337 cal., 16 g total fat (9 g sat. fat), 94 mg chol., 475 mg sodium, 43 g carbo., 2 g fiber, 5 g pro. Daily Values: 13% vit. A, 6% vit. C, 13% calcium, 16% iron.

Fresh Blackberry Jam

START TO FINISH: 15 minutes

1. In a large saucepan combine 3 cups fresh or frozen blackberries, ⅓ cup sugar, ¼ cup sorghum or molasses, and 3 tablespoons blackberry brandy or orange juice. Bring to boiling; reduce heat. Cook, uncovered, over medium heat for 5 minutes, stirring occasionally. In a small bowl stir together ¼ cup orange juice and 3 tablespoons cornstarch; add to berry mixture in saucepan. Cook and stir until thickened and bubbly. Cook and stir for 2 minutes more. Remove from heat; cool slightly. To store, cover and chill for up to 2 weeks. Makes 2 cups.

Each tablespoon: 33 cal., 0 g total fat (0 g sat. fat), 0 mg chol., 1 mg sodium, 8 g carbo., 1 g fiber, 0 g pro. Daily Values: 2% vit. C, 1% calcium, 1% iron.

Jackson's Cereal Blend

John Fleer's 10-year-old son, Jackson, created the farm's most popular cereal—a mix of sweet crunch and healthful bran.

PREP: 10 minutes

- 1 18.3-oz. pkg. whole bran cereal (about 8 cups)
- 1 18-oz. pkg. low-fat granola (about 6 cups)
- 1 16-oz. pkg. Grape Nuts® cereal (about 4 cups)
- 1 14-oz. pkg. seven grain and sesame cereal (about 7 cups)
- 2 cups dried cranberries and/or raisins

1. In a very large storage container toss together cereals and cranberries. Cover tightly; store at room temperature for up to 2 weeks. For longer storage, seal in freezer bags and freeze for up to 3 months. Makes about 36 servings.

Each serving: 193 cal., 2 g total fat (0 g sat. fat), 0 mg chol.,143 mg sodium, 45 g carbo., 8 g fiber, 5 g pro. Daily Values: 10% vit. A, 12% vit. C, 8% calcium, 33% iron.

Wake-Up Smoothies

PREP: 10 minutes

- 1 cup plain low-fat yogurt
- 1 cup apple cider, chilled
- 1 cup fat-free milk
- 1 banana, sliced
- ½ cup fresh blackberries
- 2 Tbsp. honey
- ¼ tsp. ground white pepper (optional)
- ¼ tsp. ground cinnamon
- ¼ tsp. ground allspice
- ⅛ tsp. ground nutmeg

1. In a blender container combine all ingredients. Cover; blend until smooth. Pour into tall glasses. Makes 4 servings.

Each serving: 156 cal., 1 g total fat (1 g sat. fat), 5 mg chol.,74 mg sodium, 32 g carbo., 2 g fiber, 6 g pro. Daily Values: 4% vit. A, 14% vit. C, 19% calcium, 3% iron.

HOLIDAY BREAKFAST BUFFET

Jackson's Cereal Blend *(above)*
Tennessee Orange Biscuits with Blackberry Gravy *(left)*
Cranberry-Black Walnut Coffee Cake *(page 496)*
Fresh fruit plate
Wake-Up Smoothies *(above)*
Coffee or tea

White Chocolate and Jam S'Mores

White Chocolate and Jam S'Mores

PREP: 8 minutes

- 1 oz. white baking bar
- 2 Chocolate Graham Crackers (see recipe, right)
- 3 marshmallows, toasted*
- 2 Tbsp. Fresh Blackberry Jam (see recipe, page 499) or purchased blackberry jam

1. For each s'more, place the white baking bar on top of one of the Chocolate Graham Crackers. Place marshmallows on top of the bar. Spoon Fresh Blackberry Jam over the marshmallows; top with remaining cracker.

***TEST KITCHEN TIP:** To toast marshmallows, place marshmallows on the end of a long skewer and hold over a campfire flame or hot coals for 30 to 60 seconds, turning frequently. Makes 1 serving.

BROILER METHOD: For 4 s'mores, place 4 Chocolate Graham Crackers on a foil-lined baking sheet. Top each with 1 ounce white baking bar. Top each with 3 marshmallows. Broil 4 inches from the heat for 30 to 60 seconds or until marshmallows are toasted and chocolate softens and begins to melt. Remove from broiler; add 2 tablespoons Fresh Blackberry Jam to each. Top with another Chocolate Graham Cracker. Makes 4 servings.

Each serving: 465 cal., 14 g total fat (9 g sat. fat), 15 mg chol., 199 mg sodium, 80 g carbo., 1 g fiber, 4 g pro. Daily Values: 3% vit. A, 6% vit. C, 6% calcium, 5% iron.

Sorghum Gingersnaps

"I'm completely infatuated with sorghum," says Chef Fleer. It appears here and in his blackberry jam.

PREP: 25 minutes **BAKE:** 12 minutes per batch

- 2 cups sugar
- 1 cup shortening
- 2 eggs
- 1/2 cup sorghum or mild-flavored molasses
- 3 1/2 cups all-purpose flour
- 2 tsp. baking soda
- 2 tsp. ground ginger
- 1 1/4 tsp. ground cinnamon
- 1 tsp. ground cloves
- Sugar

1. Preheat oven to 350° F. In a large mixing bowl beat the 2 cups sugar and shortening with an electric mixer on medium speed until fluffy. Beat in eggs and sorghum.

2. In a medium mixing bowl stir together flour, baking soda, ginger, cinnamon, and cloves. Gradually beat or stir flour mixture into egg mixture. Shape dough into 1-inch balls; roll in additional sugar.

3. Arrange dough balls on an ungreased cookie sheet. Bake about 12 minutes or until bottoms are light brown. Cool on wire racks. Makes about 7 dozen cookies.

Each cookie: 66 cal., 3 g total fat (1 g sat. fat), 5 mg chol., 32 mg sodium, 10 g carbo., 0 g fiber, 1 g pro. Daily Values: 1% calcium, 2% iron.

Alphabet Chocolate Graham Crackers

Chocolate Graham Crackers

PREP: 30 minutes **CHILL:** 1 hour **BAKE:** 8 minutes per batch

- 1/3 cup milk
- 1/4 cup honey
- 2 oz. bittersweet chocolate, chopped
- 2 cups all-purpose flour
- 1 cup packed brown sugar
- 1/2 cup whole wheat flour
- 1 tsp. baking soda
- 1/2 tsp. salt
- 1/2 cup butter
- 1 Tbsp. vanilla

1. In a small saucepan combine milk, honey, and chocolate; cook and stir over low heat just until chocolate is melted. Let cool about 15 minutes.

2. Meanwhile, in a food processor bowl combine all-purpose flour, brown sugar, whole wheat flour, baking soda, and salt. Cover; pulse to combine. Add butter; pulse until mixture resembles coarse crumbs. (Or place in a large bowl; cut in butter using a pastry blender until it resembles coarse crumbs.)

3. Stir vanilla into chocolate mixture; add to flour mixture. Pulse (or stir) until just combined. If necessary, knead dough gently to form a ball. Divide into fourths. Wrap each portion in plastic wrap; chill about 1 hour or until easy to handle.

4. Preheat oven to 350° F. On a lightly floured surface roll one portion of dough to 1/8-inch thickness. Cut with a 3-inch scalloped round cutter. Arrange on ungreased cookie sheets. Mark cracker tops in a snowflake pattern, using tines of a fork.

5. Bake for 8 to 10 minutes or until edges are firm. Transfer to a wire rack; cool. Makes about 4 1/2 dozen crackers.

ALPHABET CHOCOLATE GRAHAM CRACKERS: Prepare as directed above, except cut dough using 3-inch letter-shaped cutters. Bake as directed for 8 to 10 minutes.

Each cracker: 63 cal., 2 g total fat (1 g sat. fat), 5 mg chol., 66 mg sodium, 10 g carbo., 0 g fiber, 1 g pro. Daily Values: 1% vit. A, 1% calcium, 2% iron.

Spicy Bittersweet Cocoa

START TO FINISH: 25 minutes

- 1/2 cup unsweetened cocoa powder
- 1/2 cup sugar
- 6 1/2 cups whole milk
- 1 1/2 cups whipping cream
- 5 oz. bittersweet chocolate, chopped
- 1 2-inch piece stick cinnamon
- 1 1/2 tsp. vanilla
- Whipped cream (optional)

1. In a large saucepan stir together cocoa powder and sugar. Using a whisk, stir in milk, cream, chocolate, and cinnamon stick. Heat and stir over medium heat until just boiling. Remove cinnamon stick. Stir in vanilla. Serve warm topped with whipped cream, if desired. Makes 10 servings.

Each serving: 348 cal., 24 g total fat (15 g sat. fat), 71 mg chol., 92 mg sodium, 28 g carbo., 1 g fiber, 8 g pro. Daily Values: 15% vit. A, 3% vit. C, 27% calcium, 6% iron.

Holiday Blackberry Nog

PREP: 15 minutes **CHILL:** 4 hours

- 4 egg yolks
- 1 3/4 cups milk
- 1/3 cup sugar
- 1/4 tsp. ground nutmeg
- 1 cup whipping cream
- 2 tsp. vanilla
- 1 1/2 cups fresh blackberries (6 oz.) (optional)

1. In a medium, heavy saucepan beat egg yolks; stir in milk, sugar, and nutmeg. Cook and stir over medium heat until mixture just coats a metal spoon. Remove from heat.

2. Place pan in a sink or bowl of ice water; stir for 2 minutes. Stir in whipping cream and vanilla. Cover and chill for 4 to 24 hours.

3. To serve, place berries in gift bottles or a glass pitcher, if desired. Pour eggnog over berries. Serve immediately. Makes 8 servings.

Each serving: 194 cal., 15 g total fat (8 g sat. fat), 151 mg chol., 42 mg sodium, 12 g carbo., 0 g fiber, 4 g pro. Daily Values: 14% vit. A, 1% vit. C, 10% calcium, 2% iron.

Buttery Blackberry or Green Apple Lollipops

PREP: 20 minutes **COOK:** 45 minutes **COOL:** 20 minutes

- 1 cup water
- 2 cups sugar
- 3/4 cup light-colored corn syrup
- 1 Tbsp. butter
- 1/4 tsp. blackberry flavoring oil or 1/2 tsp. apple flavoring
- 6 drops purple or 2 drops green gel food coloring (optional)
- 18 to 20 lollipop sticks or clean maple twigs

1. In a medium saucepan bring the 1 cup water to boiling. Stir in sugar, corn syrup, and butter. Cook and stir over medium-high heat until mixture boils, stirring to dissolve sugar (about 7 minutes).

2. Clip a candy thermometer to the side of the pan. Reduce heat to medium; continue boiling at a moderate, steady rate, stirring occasionally until thermometer registers 300° F, hard-crack stage (45 to 50 minutes).

3. Remove saucepan from heat; stir in blackberry flavoring oil or apple flavoring and gel food coloring, if desired. Let stand until candy thermometer registers 220° F (about 20 minutes). Meanwhile, butter 2 large baking sheets. Place lollipop sticks 4 inches apart on the prepared baking sheets.

4. Working quickly, spoon 1 tablespoon of the candy mixture over the top 1 inch of each lollipop stick (do not spread; mixture will flow out). Cool completely. To store, wrap each lollipop in plastic wrap. Store at room temperature for up to 2 weeks. Makes 18 to 20 lollipops.

Each lollipop: 127 cal., 1 g total fat (0 g sat. fat), 2 mg chol., 24 mg sodium, 32 g carbo., 0 g fiber, 0 g pro. Daily Values: 1% vit. A.

Buttery Blackberry or Green Apple Lollipops

Holiday Blackberry Nog

Spicy Bittersweet Cocoa

Pistachios with a Kick

Add Pizzazz to Pistachios

THANKS TO THE VENDING MACHINE, pistachio nuts are pretty plentiful in America. When the machines began offering up nuts for coins—around about the 1930s—pistachios gained in popularity. However, it wasn't until 40 years later that the first commercial crop of pistachios was harvested in this country. Up until that time, most pistachios were imported from the Middle East.

Lucky for you, pistachio nuts today are readily available in supermarkets across the country—shelled and unshelled. Pistachio shells split open naturally as the nut inside grows to maturity. So if you find a shell that has no split, throw it away. The nut inside is not mature. Store pistachio nuts in a covered container or sealed plastic bag because they tend to absorb moisture from the air and may lose their crunch. Count on two cups of pistachios in their shells giving you about a cup of shelled nuts when you're making any of the pistachio recipes below.

Pistachios with a Kick

PREP: 5 minutes **BAKE:** 20 minutes

- 2 Tbsp. butter or margarine, melted
- 1 tsp. ground coriander
- 1/2 tsp. salt
- 1/4 tsp. ground cloves
- 1/4 tsp. ground red pepper
- 1 1/2 cups pistachio nuts

1. Preheat oven to 350° F. In a 9×9×2-inch baking pan combine melted butter, coriander, salt, cloves, and ground red pepper. Add nuts; toss to coat.

2. Bake, uncovered, for 20 to 25 minutes or until toasted, stirring occasionally. Spread on foil; cool. Store in an airtight container. Makes 1 1/2 cups nuts.

Each 1/4-cup serving: 212 cal., 18 g total fat (2 g sat. fat), 0 mg chol., 239 mg sodium, 9 g carbo., 3 g fiber, 7 g pro. Daily Values: 3% vit. C, 4% calcium, 8% iron.

Smoky Cheese Ball

STAND: 30 + 15 minutes
PREP: 15 minutes **CHILL:** 4 hours

- 2 8-oz. pkg. cream cheese
- 2 cups finely shredded smoked Swiss, cheddar, or Gouda cheese
- 1/2 cup butter or margarine
- 2 Tbsp. milk
- 2 tsp. steak sauce
- 1 cup finely chopped pistachio nuts, toasted
- Assorted crackers

1. In a large bowl let cream cheese, shredded cheese, and butter stand at room temperature for 30 minutes. Add milk and steak sauce; beat until fluffy. Cover and chill for 4 to 24 hours.

2. Shape mixture into a ball; roll in nuts. Let stand for 15 minutes. Serve with crackers. Makes 3 1/2 cups spread.

FREEZE-AHEAD DIRECTIONS: Prepare as above, except do not roll in nuts. Wrap cheese ball in moisture- and vaporproof plastic wrap. Freeze for up to 1 month. To serve, thaw cheese ball in the refrigerator overnight. Roll in nuts. Let stand for 30 minutes at room temperature before serving.

Each 1 tablespoon spread: 73 cal., 7 g total fat (4 g sat. fat), 17 mg chol, 71 mg sodium, 1 g carbo., 0 g fiber, 2 g pro. Daily Values: 5% vit. A, 4% calcium, 1% iron.

Lemon-Pistachio Biscotti

PREP: 35 minutes **BAKE:** 36 minutes
COOL: 30 minutes

- 1/3 cup butter, softened
- 2/3 cup sugar
- 2 tsp. baking powder
- 1/2 tsp. salt
- 2 eggs
- 1 tsp. vanilla
- 2 cups all-purpose flour
- 4 tsp. finely shredded lemon peel
- 1 1/4 cups pistachio nuts
- 1 recipe Lemon Icing (below)

1. Preheat oven to 375° F. Lightly grease 2 cookie sheets; set aside. In a large bowl beat butter with an electric mixer on medium to high speed for 30 seconds. Add sugar, baking powder, and salt. Beat until combined, scraping side of bowl occasionally. Beat in eggs and vanilla. Beat in as much flour as you can. Stir in any remaining flour and lemon peel. Stir in pistachio nuts.

2. Divide dough into 3 equal portions. Shape each portion into an 8-inch-long roll. Place at least 3 inches apart on prepared cookie sheets; flatten slightly until about 2 1/2 inches wide.

3. Bake for 20 to 25 minutes or until golden brown and tops are cracked (loaves will spread slightly). Cool on cookie sheet for 30 minutes.

4. Reduce oven temperature to 325° F. Use a serrated knife to cut each roll diagonally into 1/2-inch-thick slices. Place slices, cut sides down, on ungreased cookie sheets. Bake for 16 to 18 minutes or until dry and crisp (do not overbake), turning after 8 minutes. Cool a wire rack.

5. Drizzle cookies with Lemon Icing. Makes about 36 cookies.

LEMON ICING: Prepare Lime Icing as directed on page 295, except substitute lemon peel and juice for the lime.

Each cookie: 95 cal., 4 g total fat (1 g sat. fat),17 mg chol., 76 mg sodium, 13 g carbo., 1 g fiber, 2 g pro. Daily Values: 2% vit. A, 1% vit. C, 2% calcium, 3% iron.

Easy Phyllo Pastries

REPEAT AFTER ME: PHYLLO (FEE-LOH) IS FUN.

It really is. And festive too. These finished phyllo bundles, full of sliced pears and caramel, have phyllo's characteristic flaky-crisp crunch. And, you've got to admit, the presentation is pretty darn stunning too.

There's no need to fear phyllo dough, especially when you use packaged phyllo, available in most supermarkets. Here are tips to bear in mind while fooling with phyllo.

- Allow frozen phyllo dough to thaw while it is still wrapped and sealed. It's best to let it thaw overnight in the refrigerator.
- Once you unwrap them, sheets of phyllo dough dry out quickly and crumble. If that starts to happen, keep the opened stack of phyllo sheets covered with a slightly damp cloth or plastic wrap until you need it.
- If a phyllo sheet tears a little, don't worry; just gently brush tear with butter to seal the edges back together. With so many layers, the tear will soon be covered by another flaky layer.

Santa's Pear Pouches

Looking a little like Santa's sack, these flaky phyllo bundles bulge with a pleasant present of spiced pears.

PREP: 30 minutes **BAKE:** 20 minutes

- **3 medium red or green skinned pears, cored and thinly sliced (about 3½ cups)**
- **1 Tbsp. sugar**
- **1 Tbsp. all-purpose flour**
- **¼ tsp. ground cardamom**
- **⅓ cup butter, melted**
- **4 sheets frozen phyllo dough (18×14-inch rectangles), thawed**
- **¼ cup caramel ice cream topping**
- **Sugar or coarse sugar**
- **Bay leaves (optional)***
- **Dried cranberries (optional)**

1. Preheat oven to 375° F. For filling, in a medium mixing bowl combine pears, 1 tablespoon sugar, flour, and cardamom. Toss to combine; set aside.

2. Brush four 6-ounce custard cups with some of the melted butter; set aside. Place 1 sheet of phyllo dough on a flat surface. (Cover remaining phyllo with plastic wrap to prevent it from becoming dry.) Lightly brush the sheet with some of the melted butter. Place another phyllo sheet on top; brush with butter. Repeat with 2 more phyllo sheets. Cut stack in half lengthwise and then in half crosswise to form 4 rectangles.

3. Ease a stack of phyllo into bottom and up sides of a custard cup (phyllo will hang over edge). Spoon about ¾ cup pear filling into center. Drizzle 1 tablespoon of caramel topping over pears. Bring phyllo up over filling, pinching together to form a ruffled edge. Secure pouch with 100-percent-cotton string. Brush again with butter. Sprinkle with sugar. Repeat to make 3 more pouches. Place custard cups in a 15×10×1-inch baking pan.

4. Bake for 20 minutes or until phyllo is golden brown. Cool for 5 minutes; remove bundles from cups. Serve warm. If desired, tuck bay leaves under string; arrange cranberries on plate. Makes 4 servings.

***TEST KITCHEN TIP:** Bay leaves are for decorative purposes only in this recipe. Do not eat them.

Each serving: 364 cal., 18 g total fat (10 g sat. fat), 43 mg chol., 310 mg sodium, 51 g carbo., 4 g fiber, 2 g pro. Daily Values: 13% vit. A, 8% vit. C, 3% calcium, 6% iron.

Santa's Pear Pouches

Prize Tested Recipes

OUR MONTHLY RECIPE CONTEST HAS BEEN GOING SINCE 192
HERE ARE SOME OF OUR FAVORITE WINNERS.

Lemon-Blackberry Mini Tarts

Mexican Polenta Pie

Terrific Toffee

Stuffed Foccacia

SEAFOOD APPETIZERS

PRIZE TESTED RECIPES® $400 WINNER

L.D. MONTGOMERY, NASHVILLE, TENN.

Calypso Shrimp Skewers

PREP: 30 minutes **GRILL:** 5 minutes

- 1/3 cup honey
- 1 tsp. grated fresh ginger
- 2/3 cup shredded coconut
- 2/3 cup finely chopped peanuts
- 1 lb. large shrimp, peeled and deveined (about 30)
- 1 3-oz. pkg. very thinly sliced prosciutto, cut into 7×1/2-inch strips
- 1 7-oz. container crème fraîche
- 1 tsp. finely shredded lime peel
- Lime juice

1. Soak 30 short wooden skewers in water for 30 minutes. Meanwhile, in a shallow dish combine honey and ginger. In another shallow dish combine coconut and peanuts. Set aside.

2. Drain skewers. Thread shrimp lengthwise on skewers, beginning at tail end. Brush each shrimp with honey mixture; roll in coconut mixture. Wrap a strip of prosciutto around each shrimp.

3. For a charcoal grill, arrange medium-hot coals around a drip pan. Test for medium heat above the pan. Place shrimp on grill rack over the drip pan. Cover and grill for 5 to 8 minutes or until shrimp turn opaque. (For a gas grill, preheat grill. Reduce heat to medium. Adjust for indirect cooking. Grill as above.)

4. Mix crème fraîche, peel, and enough juice to make of dipping consistency. Serve with shrimp. Makes 30 appetizers.

BAKING DIRECTIONS: Preheat oven to 375° F. Arrange the shrimp on a foil-lined baking sheet. Bake for 4 to 6 minutes or until shrimp turn opaque.

Each appetizer: 72 cal., 5 g total fat (2 g sat. fat), 25 mg chol., 111 mg sodium, 4 g carbo., 0 g fiber, 4 g pro. Daily Values: 1% vit. C, 2% calcium, 2% iron.

PRIZE TESTED RECIPES® $200 WINNER

DONNA FEUERSTEIN, NEENAH, WIS.

Smoked Salmon Roll-Ups

PREP: 30 minutes **CHILL:** 1 hour

- 2 cups cooked short grain rice, cooled
- 2 Tbsp. toasted sesame seeds
- 2 Tbsp. rice vinegar
- 2 tsp. sugar
- 1 tsp. salt
- 1/4 cup mayonnaise or salad dressing
- 1/8 tsp. cayenne pepper
- 4 10-inch spinach-flavored flour tortillas
- 2 3-oz. pkg. thinly sliced, smoked salmon (lox-style)
- 1 medium avocado, halved, seeded, peeled, and sliced
- 1/2 of a medium cucumber, halved lengthwise, seeded, and cut into thin sticks
- Shredded lettuce (optional)

1. Combine rice and sesame seeds. Combine vinegar, sugar, and salt; stir until sugar is dissolved. Pour vinegar mixture over rice; toss to coat. Combine mayonnaise and cayenne. Set aside.

2. Spread 1 tablespoon mayonnaise mixture onto each tortilla. Top half of each tortilla with rice mixture, salmon, avocado, and cucumber. Carefully roll each tortilla tightly, starting at the filled sides. Wrap each in plastic wrap. Chill for 1 to 4 hours.

3. To serve, trim ends. Cut rolls crosswise into 1-inch-thick slices. If necessary, secure with toothpicks. If desired, arrange on shredded lettuce. Makes 28 appetizers.

Each appetizer: 77 cal., 4 g total fat (1 g sat. fat), 5 mg chol., 146 mg sodium, 8 g carbo., 1 g fiber, 2 g pro. Daily Values: 1% vit. A, 1% vit. C, 2% calcium, 3% iron.

Peppered Shrimp over Spicy Cheese Grits

PREP: 25 minutes **BAKE:** 25 minutes

- 1 recipe Spicy Cheese Grits (below)
- 8 oz. medium shrimp, peeled and deveined (about 24)
- 1/2 tsp. chili powder
- 1/4 tsp. ground black pepper
- 2 slices bacon
- 4 cups cremini mushrooms, quartered
- 2 cloves garlic, minced
- 2 Tbsp. dry white wine or chicken broth
- 1 Tbsp. olive oil
- 1/4 cup sliced green onions

1. Preheat oven to 350° F. Prepare Spicy Cheese Grits. Spoon the grits into a 1-quart casserole. Bake for 25 minutes; keep warm.

2. Meanwhile, toss shrimp with chili powder and black pepper; set aside. In a large skillet cook bacon until crisp. Remove bacon; drain on paper towels. Reserve 2 tablespoons of the drippings in skillet.

3. Add mushrooms and garlic to drippings; cook and stir until mushrooms are tender. Stir in wine or broth. Meanwhile, in a medium skillet cook shrimp in hot oil 4 to 5 minutes or until shrimp turn opaque.

4. Divide grits among 8 appetizer plates; top with mushroom and shrimp mixtures. Crumble bacon on top; sprinkle with green onion. Makes 8 appetizer servings.

SPICY CHEESE GRITS: In a medium saucepan bring 2 1/2 cups water to boiling. Slowly add 3/4 cup quick-cooking (hominy) grits, stirring constantly. Gradually stir 1/2 cup of the hot mixture into 1 beaten egg. Return egg mixture to saucepan; stir to combine. Remove from heat. Stir in 4 ounces Monterey Jack cheese with jalapeño peppers, shredded (1 cup); 2 tablespoons butter or margarine; 1/8 teaspoon salt; and, if desired, 1/8 teaspoon cayenne pepper.

Each serving: 247 cal., 15 g total fat (7 g sat. fat), 97 mg chol., 353 mg sodium, 14 g carbo., 1 g fiber, 14 g pro. Daily Values: 9% vit. A, 2% vit. C, 13% calcium, 10% iron.

Mahi Mahi Spring Rolls

PREP: 40 minutes

GRILL: 4 minutes per 1/2-inch thickness

- 2 tsp. sesame oil
- 1 tsp. cooking oil
- 12 oz. mahi mahi, monkfish, or red snapper fillets
- 12 8-inch rice papers
- 1 recipe Hoisin Dipping Sauce (below)
- 1 1/2 cups shredded cabbage
- 2/3 cup shredded carrot
- 1/3 cup shredded coconut
- 1/4 cup thinly sliced green onions

1. In a bowl combine sesame oil and cooking oil; brush onto both sides of fish. Place fish in a well-greased grill basket. Place on rack of an uncovered grill directly over medium coals. Grill for 4 to 6 minutes per 1/2-inch thickness or until fish flakes easily, turning fish once halfway through grilling. (Or, place on greased unheated rack of a broiler pan. Broil 4 to 6 minutes per 1/2-inch thickness, turning once.) Cool slightly.

2. Pour 1 cup warm water into a pie plate. Carefully dip rice papers into water, 1 at a time. Place papers, without touching, on clean dry kitchen towels. Let soften a few minutes until pliable.

3. For filling, prepare Hoisin Dipping Sauce. Gently flake fish; place in a large bowl. Add 6 tablespoons of the dipping sauce. Gently fold in cabbage, carrot, coconut, and green onion.

4. Spoon about 1/3 cup of the fish mixture onto a softened rice paper, just below center of paper. Tightly roll rice paper up from bottom around filling, tucking in opposite sides as you roll. Repeat with remaining papers and fish mixture, covering rolls as you make them to prevent drying. Serve with remaining Hoisin Dipping Sauce. Makes 12 appetizers.

HOISIN DIPPING SAUCE: Combine 1/2 cup hoisin sauce, 3 tablespoons unsweetened pineapple juice, 1 tablespoon rice vinegar, and 1/8 teaspoon cayenne pepper.

Each appetizer: 120 cal., 3 g total fat (1 g sat.fat), 21 mg chol., 160 mg sodium, 16 g carbo., 1 g fiber, 7 g pro. Daily Values: 42% vit. A, 7% vit. C, 2% calcium, 4% iron.

Seafood-Melon Cocktail

PREP: 35 minutes **CHILL:** 1 hour

- 1 recipe Cilantro-Lime Salad Dressing (below)
- 8 oz. sea scallops
- 8 oz. medium shrimp, peeled and deveined (about 24)
- 2 cups cubed cantaloupe and/or honeydew melon
- 1/4 of a medium English cucumber (3 oz.), quartered lengthwise and sliced (about 1 cup)
- 1 medium avocado, halved, seeded, peeled, and chopped (about 1 cup)
- 1/4 cup finely chopped red onion
- Red leaf lettuce
- Lime slices (optional)
- Fresh cilantro sprigs (optional)

1. Prepare Cilantro-Lime Salad Dressing; set aside. Quarter the scallops. In a large saucepan cook the scallops and shrimp in boiling water for 1 to 2 minutes or until opaque. Drain and rinse with cold water; drain again.

2. In a large bowl stir together the scallops, shrimp, melon, cucumber, avocado, and onion. Add dressing; gently toss until coated. Cover and chill for 1 to 4 hours.

3. To serve, line martini or margarita glasses with lettuce. Stir seafood mixture; spoon into glasses. If desired, garnish with lime slices and cilantro sprigs. Makes 8 to 10 appetizer servings.

CILANTRO-LIME SALAD DRESSING: In a small bowl combine 1/2 cup mayonnaise; 2 tablespoons snipped fresh cilantro; 1 fresh jalapeño chile pepper, seeded and finely chopped; 1/2 teaspoon finely shredded lime peel; 1 tablespoon lime juice; 1 clove garlic, minced; 1/2 teaspoon salt; 1/4 teaspoon ground cumin; and 1/8 teaspoon ground black pepper.

Each serving: 207 cal., 15 g total fat (2 g sat. fat), 57 mg chol., 316 mg sodium, 8 g carbo., 2 g fiber, 12 g pro. Daily Values: 34% vit. A, 44% vit. C, 4% calcium, 7% iron.

SUMMER COOLERS

PRIZE TESTED RECIPES® $400 WINNER

ERICA GRADWELL, ARVADA, COLO.

White Strawberry Sangria

For unbeatable flavor, select a white wine such as Pinot Grigio or Sauvignon Blanc.

Prep: 10 minutes **Chill:** 1 hour

- 1 750-ml bottle dry white wine
- ½ cup strawberry schnapps
- ¼ cup sugar
- 2 cups sliced fresh strawberries
- Ice cubes
- Whole fresh strawberries (optional)

1. In a 2-quart pitcher stir together wine, strawberry schnapps, and sugar until sugar is dissolved. Add sliced strawberries; chill for 1 to 4 hours.

2. Serve over ice in 5 or 6 glasses. If desired, garnish each serving with a whole strawberry. Makes 5 or 6 servings.

Each serving: 221 cal., 0 g total fat. 0 mg chol., 8 mg sodium, 22 g carbo., 1 g fiber, 1 g pro. Daily Values: 54% vit. C, 2% calcium, 4% iron.

PRIZE TESTED RECIPES® $200 WINNER

MARY BAYRAMIAN, LAGUNA BEACH, CALIF.

Cranberry-Pineapple Cooler

Prep: 10 minutes **Chill:** 1 hour

- ½ cup sugar
- ½ cup water
- 2 cups cranberry juice, chilled
- 1 cup orange juice, chilled (about 3 oranges)
- 1 cup unsweetened pineapple juice, chilled
- ¾ cup lemon juice, chilled (about 4 lemons)
- 1 2-liter bottle ginger ale, chilled
- Fresh cranberries (optional)
- Lemon slices (optional)

1. For syrup, in a small saucepan combine sugar and the water. Cook and stir over medium heat until sugar is dissolved. Transfer to a 1-cup glass measure. Cover and chill for 1 hour.

2. In a large punch bowl stir together cranberry juice, orange juice, pineapple juice, lemon juice, and chilled syrup. Slowly add ginger ale, pouring down side of bowl; stir gently to mix. Serve immediately. If desired, garnish with cranberries and lemon slices. Makes 14 servings.

Each serving: 118 cal., 0 g total fat, 0 mg chol., 12 mg sodium, 30 g carbo., 0 g fiber, 0 g pro. Daily Values: 1% vit. A, 49% vit. C, 1% calcium, 2% iron.

Mango-Ginger Coladas

START TO FINISH: 15 minutes

- 3/4 cup ginger brandy
- 3/4 cup mango or apricot nectar
- 1/2 cup cream of coconut
- 3 Tbsp. lime juice
- 4 1/2 to 5 cups ice cubes
- Fresh mango wedges (optional)

1. In a blender combine ginger brandy, mango nectar, cream of coconut, and lime juice. Cover; blend until combined.

2. Add ice, 1 cup at a time, blending well after each addition. Blend until mixture becomes slushy. Pour into 6 tall glasses. If desired, garnish with mango wedges. Makes 6 servings.

Each serving: 160 cal., 7 g total fat, 0 mg chol., 4 mg sodium, 7 g carbo., 0 g fiber, 1 g pro. Daily Values: 11% vit. C, 1% calcium, 3% iron.

Raspberry Delight Punch

START TO FINISH: 15 minutes

- 1 qt. raspberry sorbet or sherbet
- 1 12-oz. can frozen raspberry juice blend concentrate, thawed
- 3 cups unsweetened pineapple juice, chilled
- 1/4 cup lemon juice
- 1/2 of a 2-liter bottle club soda, chilled

1. In a chilled large bowl stir 1 cup of the raspberry sorbet to soften; stir in thawed juice concentrate. Add pineapple juice and lemon juice.

2. Transfer to a punch bowl. Add remaining sorbet in small scoops. Slowly add club soda, pouring down side of bowl; stir gently to mix. Serve immediately. Makes 10 servings.

MAKE-AHEAD TIP: Scoop the sorbet or sherbet ahead onto a 15×10×1-inch baking pan or into a large freezer container. Cover and freeze until just before serving.

Each serving: 200 cal., 0 g total fat, 0 mg chol., 25 mg sodium, 50 g carbo., 2 g fiber, 0 g pro. Daily Values: 93% vit. C, 2% calcium, 1% iron.

Frozen Strawberry-Mango Margaritas

PREP: 10 minutes **FREEZE:** 1 hour

- 2 medium mangoes*
- 1/2 cup gold (oro) tequila
- 1/3 cup orange liqueur
- 1/4 cup lime juice
- 2 Tbsp. sugar
- 2 cups frozen unsweetened whole strawberries
- 2 cups ice cubes

1. Seed, peel, and cube mangoes. Place cubes in a single layer in a shallow baking pan lined with plastic wrap. Cover and freeze for 1 hour. Transfer to a freezer bag or container for longer storage.

2. In a blender combine tequila, orange liqueur, lime juice, sugar, strawberries, and mango chunks. Cover; blend until smooth. With blender running, add ice cubes, 1 at a time, through opening in lid, blending until mixture becomes slushy. Pour mixture into 5 glasses. Makes 5 servings.

***NOTE:** If mangoes are not available, use 2 cups frozen unsweetened peach slices and skip step 1.

Each serving: 176 cal., 0 g total fat, 0 mg chol., 3 mg sodium, 26 g carbo., 3 g fiber, 1 g pro. Daily Values: 52% vit. A, 91% vit. C, 2% calcium, 2% iron.

Icy Cranberry Margaritas

START TO FINISH: 10 minutes

- 1/2 cup frozen cranberry-raspberry juice cocktail concentrate, thawed
- 1/2 cup tequila
- 1/4 cup orange liqueur
- 3 Tbsp. melon liqueur
- 5 cups ice cubes

1. In a blender combine juice concentrate, tequila, orange liqueur, and melon liqueur. Cover; blend until combined.

2. With blender running, add ice cubes, 1 at a time, through opening in lid, blending until slushy. Pour into 6 margarita glasses. Makes 6 servings.

Each serving: 147 cal., 0 g total fat, 0 mg chol., 2 mg sodium, 18 g carbo., 0 g fiber, 0 g pro. Daily Values: 19% vit. C.

Peaches and Cream Sunrise

This frosty dessert resembles soft-serve ice cream.

PREP: 15 minutes **FREEZE:** 1 hour

- 2 medium fresh peaches,* peeled, pitted, and sliced, or 2 cups frozen unsweetened peach slices
- 1 15 1/2-oz. can pineapple chunks (juice pack)
- 1 cup vanilla yogurt
- 1/4 cup mascarpone cheese
- 1 cup milk
- 2 Tbsp. honey
- 2 tsp. grenadine syrup
- Fresh peach slices, strawberries, and/or peeled kiwifruit slices (optional)

1. Place the 2 sliced fresh peaches on a plastic wrap-lined 15×10×1-inch baking pan. Drain pineapple, reserving juice. Add pineapple chunks to the baking pan. Cover; freeze for 1 to 2 hours or until frozen. Cover and chill juice.

2. In a blender combine reserved pineapple juice, yogurt, mascarpone, milk, and honey. Add half of the frozen peaches and half of the pineapple. Cover and blend until smooth. Add the remaining frozen fruit; cover and blend until smooth.

3. Place 1/2 teaspoon of the grenadine in each of 4 glasses; swirl slightly to coat glasses. Pour in peach mixture. If desired, garnish each with fresh fruit on a skewer. Serve immediately. Makes 4 servings.

***NOTE:** If using fresh peaches, brush with lemon juice before freezing.

Each serving: 270 cal., 9 g total fat (5 g sat. fat), 26 mg chol., 79 mg sodium, 45 g carbo., 2 g fiber, 9 g pro. Daily Values: 9% vit. A, 25% vit. C, 19% calcium, 3% iron.

SUNDAY POT ROASTS

PRIZE TESTED RECIPES® $400 WINNER

GAIL L. JENNER, ETNA, CALIF.

"Can't Be Beat" Pot Roast

PREP: 20 minutes **ROAST:** 1½ hours + 45 minutes

- 1 3- to 4-lb. boneless beef chuck pot roast
- 1 Tbsp. cooking oil
- ⅓ cup sweet Marsala wine
- 2 tsp. dried basil, crushed
- 1 tsp. garlic salt
- ½ cup plum preserves
- 4 medium potatoes, peeled and cut lengthwise into sixths
- 4 medium carrots, peeled, halved lengthwise, and halved crosswise
- 1 large rutabaga, peeled and cut into 1-inch chunks
- 1 medium onion, cut into large wedges
- 1 Tbsp. cold water
- 2 tsp. cornstarch

1. Preheat oven to 350° F. Trim fat from meat. In a 6- to 8-quart Dutch oven brown meat in hot oil. Drain off fat. In a small bowl stir together ⅓ cup water, wine, basil, garlic salt, and ½ teaspoon ground black pepper; pour over meat. Cover; roast for 1½ hours.

2. In a small saucepan melt preserves; pour over roast. Arrange vegetables around meat. Cover; roast 45 minutes to 1 hour more or until meat and vegetables are tender, stirring vegetables once.

3. Transfer meat and vegetables to a platter; cover to keep warm. For gravy, measure pan juices and skim off fat. If necessary, add enough water to juices to equal 1½ cups. Return to Dutch oven. Stir together the cold water and cornstarch. Stir into juices in Dutch oven. Cook and stir until thickened and bubbly; cook and stir for 2 minutes more. Serve with meat and vegetables. Makes 8 to 10 servings.

Each serving: 388 cal., 10 g total fat (3 g sat. fat), 108 mg chol., 222 mg sodium, 33 g carbo., 4 g fiber, 38 g pro. Daily Values: 160% vit. A, 36% vit. C, 6% calcium, 29% iron.

PRIZE TESTED RECIPES® $200 WINNER

CONSTANCE MOYLAN, WILMETTE, ILL.

Mediterranean Pot Roast

PREP: 20 minutes **COOK:** 2 + 1 hour

- 1 3-lb. fresh beef brisket
- 3 Tbsp. all-purpose flour
- 1 tsp. dried oregano, crushed
- 1 tsp. dried thyme, crushed
- ¾ tsp. salt
- ½ tsp. ground black pepper
- 2 Tbsp. olive oil
- 1 28-oz. can crushed tomatoes
- ¾ cup beef broth
- 1 large onion, chopped
- 4 cloves garlic, minced
- ½ tsp. sugar
- 2 medium fennel bulbs, cut into wedges
- ¼ cup pitted ripe and/or green olives
- ½ tsp. finely shredded lemon peel
- Hot cooked noodles or rice (optional)
- Pitted ripe and/or green olives (optional)

1. Trim fat from meat. In a small bowl combine flour, oregano, thyme, salt, and black pepper. Rub onto both sides of meat. In a 4- to 6-quart Dutch oven brown meat in hot oil. Combine undrained tomatoes, broth, onion, garlic, and sugar. Pour over meat. Bring to boiling; reduce heat. Cover; simmer for 2 hours.

2. Add fennel wedges and the ¼ cup olives. Simmer, covered, about 1 hour more or until meat is tender.

3. Transfer meat to a platter. For sauce, stir lemon peel into fennel mixture. Serve sauce and vegetables with meat and noodles or rice, if desired. If desired, garnish with additional olives. Makes 8 to 10 servings.

Each serving: 520 cal., 36 g total fat (13 g sat. fat), 110 mg chol., 689 mg sodium, 13 g carbo., 8 g fiber, 32 g pro. Daily Values: 1% vit. A, 24% vit. C, 7% calcium, 21% iron.

Beef and Sweet Potato Pot Roast

PREP: 20 minutes
COOK: 1¾ hours + 15 minutes

- 1 3-lb. boneless beef chuck pot roast
- 2 Tbsp. cooking oil
- 1 14-oz. can beef broth
- 1 Tbsp. Worcestershire sauce
- 3 medium sweet potatoes, peeled and cut into ½-inch-thick slices
- 1 14-oz. pkg. frozen whole green beans
- 1 large onion, cut into wedges
- ¼ tsp. ground cinnamon
- Apple juice
- 2 Tbsp. cornstarch
- ¼ tsp. salt

1. Trim fat from meat. Season with salt and ground black pepper. In a 4- to 6-quart Dutch oven brown roast in hot oil. Drain off fat. Pour broth and Worcestershire over roast. Bring to boiling; reduce heat. Simmer, covered, for 1¾ hours. Add vegetables and cinnamon. Return to boiling; reduce heat. Simmer, covered, 15 to 20 minutes or until meat and vegetables are tender.

2. Transfer meat and vegetables to a platter. For gravy, measure juices; skim off fat. Add enough apple juice to equal 1¾ cups; add to Dutch oven. Stir together ¼ cup apple juice, cornstarch, and salt. Stir into juices in Dutch oven. Cook and stir over medium heat until thickened and bubbly. Cook and stir for 2 minutes more. Serve over roast and vegetables. Makes 8 servings.

Each serving: 456 cal., 25 g total fat (9 g sat. fat), 109 mg chol., 441 mg sodium, 21 g carbo., 3 g fiber, 34 g pro. Daily Values: 180% vit. A, 23% vit. C, 5% calcium, 26% iron.

Reuben Pot Roast

PREP: 20 minutes **ROAST:** 1 + 1 hours
STAND: 10 minutes

- 1 3-lb. corned beef brisket
- ⅓ cup bottled Russian salad dressing
- 1 16-oz. can sauerkraut, drained
- 4 medium russet potatoes, peeled and quartered
- 2 cups packaged peeled baby carrots
- 2 oz. Swiss cheese, shredded (½ cup)
- Crusty rye bread (optional)

1. Preheat oven to 350° F. Discard seasoning packet from corned beef brisket. Trim fat from meat; place meat in a roasting pan. Spread dressing onto meat. Spoon sauerkraut around meat. Pour 1 cup water into pan. Cover; roast for 1 hour.

2. Arrange potatoes and carrots around the roast. Cover; roast for 1 to 1¼ hours more or until meat and vegetables are tender.

3. Transfer meat and vegetables to a platter; sprinkle vegetables with cheese. Let stand 10 minutes. Thinly slice meat across the grain. If desired, serve with bread. Serves 8.

Each serving: 407 cal., 27 g total fat (8 g sat. fat), 95 mg chol., 610 mg sodium, 10 g carbo., 4 g fiber, 29 g pro. Daily Values: 156% vit. A, 91% vit. C, 11% calcium, 25% iron.

Balsamic Pork Pot Roast

PREP: 15 minutes **COOK:** 2 hours

- 1 2½- to 3-lb. boneless pork shoulder roast
- 1 Tbsp. olive oil
- 1 large onion, sliced
- 2 cloves garlic, minced
- 1 14½-oz. can Italian-style stewed tomatoes
- ¼ cup dry red wine
- ¼ cup balsamic vinegar
- 1½ tsp. fines herbes or dried basil, crushed
- 1 bay leaf
- Hot cooked spaetzle or pasta
- ¼ cup shredded Parmesan cheese (optional)

1. Trim fat from meat. Season with salt and ground black pepper. In a 4-quart Dutch oven brown roast in hot oil. Remove meat. Add onion and garlic to Dutch oven; cook about 5 minutes or until tender.

2. Stir in undrained tomatoes, wine, vinegar, herbs, and bay leaf. Return meat to the Dutch oven. Bring to boiling; reduce heat. Simmer, covered, about 2 hours or until meat is tender.

3. Transfer meat to a platter; cover to keep warm. Skim fat from pan juices. Discard bay leaf.

4. For sauce, in a blender blend juices, half at a time, until smooth. Top spaetzle with meat, sauce, and cheese, if desired. Makes 8 servings.

Each serving: 420 cal., 15 g total fat (5 g sat. fat), 136 mg chol., 590 mg sodium, 27 g carbo., 3 g fiber, 38 g pro. Daily Values: 5% vit. A, 12% vit. C, 8% calcium, 19% iron.

Caribbean Pork Pot Roast

PREP: 20 minutes **ROAST:** 2½ hours

- 1 3½- to 4-lb. boneless pork shoulder roast
- 2 tsp. chili powder
- 1 tsp. packed brown sugar
- ½ tsp. salt
- ½ tsp. ground black pepper
- ¼ tsp. cayenne pepper
- 2 4-oz. cans whole green chile peppers, drained
- 1 20-oz. can pineapple tidbits
- 1 to 2 fresh jalapeño chile peppers, seeded and finely chopped (see note, page 554) (optional)
- 2 Tbsp. cornstarch
- 1 Tbsp. packed brown sugar
- 2 tsp. cider vinegar

1. Preheat oven to 325° F. Remove netting from roast, if present. Trim fat from meat. Combine chili powder, the 1 teaspoon brown sugar, the salt, and black and cayenne peppers; rub onto roast. Cut pocket down center of the roast. Stuff green chile peppers into pocket; tie with clean string, if necessary.

2. In a 6-quart Dutch oven arrange half of the undrained pineapple and, if desired, jalapeños. Add meat, stuffed side up. Cover; roast about 2½ hours or until tender.

3. Transfer meat to a platter. Skim fat from pan juices. Measure juices; add water, if necessary, to equal 1½ cups. Combine the 2 tablespoons cornstarch and remaining pineapple; stir into pan juices. Stir in the 1 tablespoon brown sugar and the vinegar. Cook and stir until thickened and bubbly. Cook and stir for 2 minutes more. Serve with meat. Makes 10 to 12 servings.

Each serving: 391 cal., 24 g total fat (8 g sat. fat), 111 mg chol., 287 mg sodium, 13 g carbo., 1 g fiber, 29 g pro. Daily Values: 5% vit. A, 23% vit. C, 8% calcium, 12% iron.

MOTHER'S DAY ENTRÉES

PRIZE TESTED RECIPES® $400 WINNER

JACQUELYN CLARK, SAN ANTONIO, TEXAS

Roast Rack of Lamb

PREP: 20 minutes **MARINATE:** 4 hours
ROAST: 25 minutes **STAND:** 15 minutes

- 2 1-lb. French-style lamb rib roasts (each rack about 8 ribs)
- 1 cup Merlot or other dry red wine
- 2 cloves garlic, minced
- ½ tsp. ground nutmeg
- 3 Tbsp. olive oil
- 1 Tbsp. butter
- 1 Tbsp. snipped fresh rosemary
- 2 cups soft bread crumbs
- 3 Tbsp. dried cranberries
- 1 Tbsp. dried lavender*

1. Peel off the lamb's layer of fell (membrane) and fat, if present, down to the silver skin. Place lamb in a large resealable plastic bag set in a shallow dish. Add wine, 1 clove of the garlic, and the nutmeg. Seal bag. Refrigerate for 4 to 24 hours; turn bag occasionally.

2. In a skillet heat 1 tablespoon oil and butter. Add rosemary and remaining garlic; cook for 1 minute. Add crumbs; cook and stir for 3 minutes. Remove from heat. Stir in remaining oil, cranberries, lavender, ½ teaspoon salt, and ½ teaspoon ground black pepper.

3. Preheat oven to 450° F. Remove lamb from marinade; reserve marinade. Place lamb, bone side down, in a foil-lined shallow roasting pan. Pat crumb mixture evenly onto lamb. Insert a meat thermometer. Pour reserved marinade into roasting pan.

4. Roast for 25 to 30 minutes or until meat thermometer registers 140° F (medium-rare) or 155° F (medium). Cover loosely with foil for last 5 minutes of roasting. Let stand 15 minutes. Serves 8.

***NOTE:** Look for dried lavender at health food stores.

Each serving: 212 cal., 11 g total fat (3 g sat. fat), 36 mg chol., 255 mg sodium, 9 g carbo., 1 g fiber, 11 g pro. Daily Values: 4% vit. A, 1% vit. C, 3% calcium, 10% iron.

PRIZE TESTED RECIPES® $200 WINNER

TINA FERDINAND, TAMARAC, FLA.

Sausage and Apple Torta

PREP: 25 minutes **BAKE:** 35 minutes **STAND:** 10 minutes

- ½ of a 15-oz. pkg. folded refrigerated unbaked piecrust (1 crust)
- 2 large tart apples, peeled and thinly sliced
- ½ cup chopped onion
- 1 Tbsp. sugar (optional)
- 3 Tbsp. butter
- 12 oz. bulk sweet Italian sausage
- 1 clove garlic, minced
- 2 eggs
- 2 cups shredded Italian-style cheese blend (8 oz.)
- 1 cup ricotta cheese
- 1 oz. garlic-and-herb feta cheese, crumbled (¼ cup)

1. Preheat oven to 450° F. Unfold piecrust and use to line a 9-inch pie plate. Bake according to package directions. Set aside. Reduce oven temperature to 350° F.

2. In a large skillet cook apples, onion, and sugar (if using) in hot butter over medium heat about 5 minutes or until tender. Transfer to a medium bowl. In the same skillet cook sausage and garlic until done. Drain in a colander; pat dry with clean paper towels.

3. Spoon sausage into prebaked crust. Top with the cooked apple mixture. In a bowl beat eggs; stir in cheeses. Spoon evenly over apple mixture.

4. Bake for 35 to 40 minutes or until a knife inserted near the center comes out clean. Let stand for 10 minutes on a wire rack before serving. Makes 8 servings.

Each serving: 486 cal., 34 g total fat (17 g sat. fat), 138 mg chol., 641 mg sodium, 23 g carbo., 2 g fiber, 19 g pro. Daily Values: 9% vit. A, 7% vit. C, 27% calcium, 5% iron.

Portobello and Spinach Brunch Tart

PREP: 25 minutes **BAKE:** 12 minutes

- 1 recipe Thyme Pastry (below)
- 3 cups fresh baby portobello mushrooms, quartered
- 2 cloves garlic, minced
- 1 Tbsp. butter
- 5 cups torn fresh spinach
- 1/2 cup sliced green onions
- 2 Tbsp. butter
- 5 eggs
- 1/4 cup half-and-half, light cream, or milk
- 1 tsp. snipped fresh thyme
- 1/4 tsp. ground nutmeg
- 1/4 tsp. salt
- 1/8 tsp. ground black pepper
- 4 oz. Gruyère cheese, cut into small cubes
- 1/4 cup shredded Parmesan cheese

1. Prepare and bake Thyme Pastry. Reduce oven temperature to 325° F.

2. Meanwhile, in a large skillet cook and stir mushrooms and garlic in 1 tablespoon butter over medium heat about 4 minutes or until tender. Add spinach and green onion; cover and cook about 2 minutes or until spinach is wilted. Drain in a colander.

3. In the same skillet melt the 2 tablespoons butter over medium heat. In a large bowl beat eggs; stir in half-and-half, thyme, nutmeg, salt, and pepper. Add to skillet. Cook, without stirring, until mixture begins to set on the bottom and around edges. With a spatula or large spoon, lift and fold the partially cooked egg mixture so the uncooked portion flows underneath. Continue cooking over medium heat for 2 to 3 minutes or until egg mixture is cooked through but still glossy and moist.

4. Remove from heat; fold in mushroom mixture and Gruyère cheese. Spoon into baked pastry shell. Sprinkle Parmesan cheese atop egg mixture. Bake for 12 to 15 minutes or until filling is heated through and cheese is melted. Makes 6 servings.

THYME PASTRY: Preheat oven to 450° F. Stir together 1 1/4 cups all-purpose flour, 2 teaspoons snipped fresh thyme, and 1/4 teaspoon salt; cut in 1/2 cup butter until pieces are pea-size. Add 4 to 5 tablespoons cold water, 1 tablespoon at a time, until dough forms, tossing with a fork to moisten evenly. Form dough into a ball. On a lightly floured surface, roll dough to 12-inch circle. Ease into 9-inch pie plate. Trim to 1/2 inch beyond edge of pie plate. Fold under extra pastry; flute as desired. Prick bottom and sides with a fork. Line pastry with double thickness of foil. Bake 8 minutes. Remove foil. Bake 5 to 6 minutes more or until golden. Cool on a wire rack.

Each serving: 438 cal., 36 g total fat (20 g sat. fat), 265 mg chol., 657 mg sodium, 22 g carbo., 4 g fiber, 18 g pro. Daily Values: 57% vit. A, 15% vit. C, 32% calcium, 23% iron.

Smothered Chicken

PREP: 30 minutes **BAKE:** 45 minutes

- 4 chicken breast halves (2 1/2 lb. total)
- 1/2 cup crumbled feta cheese (2 oz.)
- 1/4 cup pitted kalamata olives, chopped
- 2 Tbsp. snipped fresh basil
- 1/2 tsp. lemon-pepper seasoning
- 1 large onion, thinly sliced
- 2 cloves garlic, minced
- 1 Tbsp. olive oil
- 1 green sweet pepper, cut into strips
- 1 cup cherry tomatoes, halved

1. Preheat oven to 375° F. Loosen skin from chicken. In a small bowl combine half of the cheese, olives, and half of the basil; spread under skin of each breast half. Place chicken, skin sides up, in a lightly greased 2-quart rectangular baking dish. Sprinkle with seasoning. Bake, uncovered, for 40 minutes.

2. Meanwhile, in a large skillet cook onion and garlic in hot oil until onion is tender. Add sweet pepper, tomatoes, and remaining basil; cook for 1 minute more.

3. Drain fat. Top with onion mixture and remaining cheese. Bake 5 minutes more or until done (170° F). Makes 4 servings.

Each serving: 491 cal., 27 g total fat (8 g sat. fat), 156 mg chol., 506 mg sodium, 9 g carbo., 2 g fiber, 51 g pro. Daily Values: 14% vit. A, 60% vit. C, 11% calcium, 12% iron.

Warm Gorgonzola and Beef Salad

PREP: 35 minutes **FREEZE:** 1 hour

- 4 oz. Gorgonzola cheese
- 1 Tbsp. honey
- 1 1/2 tsp. packed brown sugar
- 1/4 cup toasted panko (Japanese-style) bread crumbs
- 1 recipe Dijon Vinaigrette (below)
- 12 oz. boneless beef sirloin steak, cut 1 inch thick
- 6 cups torn mixed salad greens
- 1/4 cup thinly sliced red onion, separated into rings
- 1/3 cup hazelnuts (filberts), toasted and chopped

1. Slice cheese into 4 pieces. In a small microwave-safe bowl combine honey and brown sugar. Microwave on 100% power (high) for 30 seconds. Brush honey mixture onto both sides of each slice of cheese; coat slices with crumbs. Place on a baking sheet. Freeze for 1 hour.

2. Prepare Dijon Vinaigrette. Set aside half for the dressing. Brush remaining vinaigrette onto steak.

3. Preheat oven to 375° F. Preheat a large nonstick skillet over medium-high heat until very hot. Add steak. Reduce heat to medium and cook for 15 to 18 minutes or until medium-rare (145° F), turning once. Remove from skillet; thinly slice.

4. Meanwhile, bake cheese for 4 to 5 minutes or just until cheese starts to melt. Toss salad greens and red onion with the reserved vinaigrette. Divide dressed greens among 4 dinner plates. Top with steak slices, warmed cheese, and nuts. Serve immediately. Makes 4 servings.

DIJON VINAIGRETTE: In a bowl whisk together 1/3 cup hazelnut or walnut oil, 1/4 cup balsamic vinegar, 2 teaspoons Dijon-style mustard, 1/2 teaspoon ground black pepper, and 1/4 teaspoon sea salt.

Each serving: 506 cal., 36 g total fat (8 g sat. fat), 61 mg chol., 620 mg sodium, 18 g carbo., 3 g fiber, 27 g pro. Daily Values: 10% vit. A, 7% vit. C, 20% calcium, 17% iron.

MAIN DISHES FROM THE GRILL

PRIZE TESTED RECIPES® $400 WINNER

CATHERINE A. BODI, WESTERVILLE, OHIO

Burgers with Jicama Slaw

PREP: 30 minutes **GRILL:** 10 minutes

- 1 recipe Jicama Slaw (below)
- 1/4 cup bottled fire-roasted chunky salsa
- 1 clove garlic, minced
- 2 tsp. chili powder
- 1/2 tsp. salt
- 1/4 tsp. ground black pepper
- 1 1/2 lb. lean ground beef
- 1/2 cup canned black beans, rinsed and drained
- 6 kaiser rolls, split and toasted

1. Prepare Jicama Slaw; cover and set aside. In a small bowl combine salsa, garlic, chili powder, salt, and black pepper; add beef and beans. Mix well. Shape into six 1/2-inch-thick patties.

2. For a charcoal grill, grill patties on the rack of an uncovered grill directly over medium coals for 10 to 13 minutes or until an instant-read thermometer registers 160° F, turning once halfway through grilling. (For a gas grill, preheat grill. Reduce heat to medium. Place patties on rack over heat. Cover and grill as above.) Place burger on bottom half of each roll. Add about 1/4 cup of the slaw and the top half of roll. Makes 6 servings.

JICAMA SLAW: In a small food processor or blender combine 1 canned chipotle pepper in adobo sauce, 1/4 cup lime juice, and 1/2 teaspoon salt. Cover; process or blend until smooth. Transfer to a bowl; stir in 1/3 cup snipped fresh cilantro, 1/4 cup dairy sour cream, and 2 tablespoons mayonnaise or salad dressing. Add 2 cups shredded peeled jicama; toss to combine.

Each serving: 448 cal., 19 g total fat (6 g sat. fat), 77 mg chol., 870 mg sodium, 41 g carbo., 3 g fiber, 29 g pro. Daily Values: 12% vit. A, 33% vit. C, 9% calcium, 28% iron.

PRIZE TESTED RECIPES® $200 WINNER

SHARON ROBERTSON, RENTON, WASH.

Grilled Teriyaki Tuna Wraps

PREP: 25 minutes **MARINATE:** 1 hour **GRILL:** 8 + 2 minutes

- 3 8-oz. tuna steaks, cut 1 inch thick
- 1/3 cup soy sauce
- 2 cloves garlic, minced
- 1 1/2 tsp. packed brown sugar
- 1 1/2 tsp. grated fresh ginger
- 8 10-inch flour tortillas
- 1 Tbsp. cooking oil
- 3/4 cup fat-free dairy sour cream
- 3/4 cup bottled honey-Dijon salad dressing
- 2 cups arugula leaves
- 1 large red onion, sliced
- 1 medium tomato, chopped

1. Place fish in resealable plastic bag set in shallow dish. Combine soy sauce, garlic, brown sugar, and ginger; pour over fish. Seal bag. Marinate in refrigerator 1 to 2 hours, turning often.

2. Drain; discard marinade. For a charcoal grill, grill fish on greased rack of uncovered grill directly over medium coals for 8 to 12 minutes or until fish flakes easily (may be slightly pink in center), turning once. (For gas grill, preheat grill. Reduce heat to medium. Place fish on greased rack over heat. Cover; grill as above.) Brush both sides of each tortilla with cooking oil; place 2 at a time on grill rack for 30 to 45 seconds or just until warm.

3. In a medium bowl stir together sour cream and salad dressing. Spread 3 tablespoons sour cream mixture onto each tortilla. Cut tuna into 1/2-inch chunks; place some near an edge of each tortilla. Top each with arugula, onion, and tomato. Fold edges over filling; fold in the sides and roll up. Makes 8 wraps.

Each wrap: 384 cal., 15 g total fat (3 g sat. fat), 42 mg chol., 610 mg sodium, 35 g carbo., 2 g fiber, 25 g pro. Daily Values: 46% vit. A, 11% vit. C, 10% calcium, 14% iron.

Grilled Salmon with Citrus Sauce

PREP: 15 minutes **MARINATE:** 1 hour
GRILL: 4 to 6 minutes per 1/2-inch thickness

- 1½ lb. boneless salmon fillet (with skin)
- 1 recipe Citrus Marinade (below)
- 1 Tbsp. orange peel cut into thin strips* (set aside)
- 1 Tbsp. lemon peel cut into thin strips* (set aside)
- ½ cup orange juice
- 3 Tbsp. lemon juice
- 1 Tbsp. olive oil

1. Place salmon in a shallow glass dish. Prepare Citrus Marinade; pour over fish. Cover and marinate in the refrigerator for 1 hour, turning often.

2. For sauce, in a small saucepan combine peel strips, orange juice, and lemon juice. Bring to boiling; reduce heat to medium. Simmer, uncovered, about 10 minutes or until mixture is reduced by half and slightly syrupy.

3. Remove salmon from marinade, reserving marinade. Measure thickness of fish. Brush salmon with olive oil. For a charcoal grill, place fish, skin side up, on the greased rack of an uncovered grill directly over medium coals; grill for 4 to 6 minutes per ½-inch thickness or until fish flakes easily when tested with a fork, brushing once with reserved marinade and gently turning halfway through grilling. (For a gas grill, preheat grill. Reduce heat to medium. Place fish on greased grill rack over heat. Cover and grill as above.)

4. Use a large spatula to transfer fish from grill to a platter, leaving skin behind; discard skin. Discard any remaining marinade. To serve, pour sauce over fish. Makes 6 servings.

CITRUS MARINADE: Combine 1 tablespoon shredded orange peel, ¼ cup orange juice, 1 tablespoon shredded lemon peel, 2 tablespoons lemon juice, 2 tablespoons snipped fresh basil, 1 tablespoon snipped fresh lemon thyme, 1 tablespoon snipped fresh chives, ½ teaspoon salt, and ⅛ teaspoon ground black pepper.

***NOTE:** To make orange and lemon peel strips, use a vegetable peeler to peel orange and lemon. Use a sharp knife to cut peels into thin strips.

Each serving: 172 cal., 6 g total fat (1 g sat. fat), 59 mg chol., 270 mg sodium, 5 g carbo., 1 g fiber, 23 g pro. Daily Values: 5% vit. A, 46% vit. C, 3% calcium, 6% iron.

Tennessee Pork Ribs

PREP: 20 minutes **CHILL:** 6 hours
GRILL: 1½ hours

- 1 Tbsp. paprika
- 1 Tbsp. packed brown sugar
- 1 tsp. ground black pepper
- 1 tsp. ground cumin
- 1 tsp. dry mustard
- ½ tsp. garlic powder
- ½ tsp. cayenne pepper
- ¼ tsp. celery seeds
- 4 to 5 lb. pork loin back ribs or meaty pork spareribs
- 1½ cups hickory wood chips
- ½ cup cider vinegar
- 2 Tbsp. prepared mustard
- ¼ tsp. salt

1. In a small bowl combine paprika, brown sugar, black pepper, cumin, dry mustard, garlic powder, cayenne pepper, and celery seeds. Sprinkle evenly over all sides of ribs; rub onto the surface of the meat. Wrap with plastic wrap; refrigerate for 6 to 24 hours.

2. Meanwhile, at least 1 hour before grilling, soak wood chips in enough water to cover. Drain wood chips. For a charcoal grill, arrange medium-hot coals around a drip pan. Test for medium heat above the pan. Sprinkle drained wood chips over coals. Place ribs, bone sides down, on grill rack over drip pan. Cover and grill for 1 hour, adding additional charcoal as necessary.

3. Meanwhile, stir together vinegar, prepared mustard, and salt. Brush onto ribs. Grill for 30 to 45 minutes more or until tender, brushing with mustard mixture every 10 minutes. Makes 4 to 6 servings.

Each serving: 485 cal., 21 g total fat (7 g sat. fat), 135 mg chol., 336 mg sodium, 8 g carbo., 1 g fiber, 63 g pro. Daily Values: 23% vit. A, 4% vit. C, 5% calcium, 18% iron.

Grilled Pork Tenderloin with Blackberry Sauce

PREP: 40 minutes **MARINATE:** 2 hours
GRILL: 30 minutes

- 1 1-lb. pork tenderloin
- ¼ cup olive oil
- ⅓ cup dry white wine
- 3 Tbsp. balsamic vinegar
- 2 Tbsp. Dijon-style mustard
- ½ tsp. soy sauce
- 2 cloves garlic, minced
- 1 tsp. snipped fresh rosemary
- ¼ tsp. ground black pepper
- Dash cayenne pepper
- ¼ cup seedless blackberry jam
- 1 tsp. finely shredded lemon peel

1. Trim fat from meat. Place meat in a resealable plastic bag set in a shallow dish. For marinade, combine olive oil, white wine, vinegar, mustard, soy sauce, garlic, rosemary, black pepper, and cayenne pepper. Pour over meat; seal bag. Marinate in the refrigerator for 2 to 4 hours, turning bag occasionally.

2. Drain meat, reserving marinade. For a charcoal grill, arrange medium-hot coals around a drip pan. Test for medium heat above the pan. Place meat on the grill rack over the drip pan. Cover and grill for 30 to 45 minutes or until done (160° F). (For a gas grill, preheat grill. Reduce heat to medium. Adjust for indirect cooking. Place meat on a rack in a roasting pan; place on grill rack and grill as above.)

3. Meanwhile, in small saucepan bring reserved marinade to boiling; reduce heat. Simmer, uncovered, for 8 to 10 minutes or until reduced by about half. Strain mixture. Return strained mixture to saucepan. Stir in jam and lemon peel; heat through.

4. To serve, arrange sliced meat on a platter; spoon jam mixture over meat. Makes 4 servings.

Each serving: 347 cal., 17 g total fat (3 g sat. fat), 73 mg chol., 266 mg sodium, 18 g carbo., 0 g fiber, 24 g pro. Daily Values: 6% vit. C, 2% calcium, 10% iron.

WINTER GRILLING

PRIZE TESTED RECIPES® $200 WINNER

JUDY L. HENDERSON, CHATTANOOGA, TENN.

PRIZE TESTED RECIPES® $200 WINNER

ANDREA CUNNINGHAM, LOS ALAMOS, N.M.

Blue Cheese Vidalia Onions

Grill burgers or steaks alongside the vegetable packet.

PREP: 15 minutes **GRILL:** 25 minutes

- 2 large Vidalia onions or other sweet onions, cut into 1/2-inch-thick slices
- 1 Tbsp. butter
- 4 oz. blue cheese, crumbled (1 cup)
- 1/2 of an 8-oz. pkg. cream cheese, cut up
- 2 tsp. Worcestershire sauce
- 1/2 tsp. ground black pepper
- 1/2 tsp. dried dill weed

1. Fold a 36×18-inch piece of heavy-duty foil in half to make an 18-inch square. Place onion slices in center of foil. Dot with butter. Bring up opposite edges of the foil; seal with a double fold. Seal remaining edges with double folds to completely enclose the onions, leaving space for steam to build.

2. For a charcoal grill, place the packet on the rack of a covered grill directly over medium coals. Cover and grill for 25 to 30 minutes or until onions are just tender, turning packet once or twice during cooking. (For a gas grill, preheat the grill. Reduce heat to medium. Grill as above.)

3. Meanwhile, in a large bowl combine the crumbled blue cheese, cream cheese, Worcestershire sauce, pepper, and dill weed. Use a slotted spoon to add onions to the cheese mixture; toss to coat. Makes 8 servings.

Each serving: 130 cal., 11 g total fat (7 g sat. fat), 30 mg chol., 273 mg sodium, 5 g carbo., 1 g fiber, 5 g pro. Daily Values: 7% vit. A, 4% vit. C, 10% calcium, 3% iron.

Football Chicken Fajitas

PREP: 20 minutes **MARINATE:** 1 hour **GRILL:** 12 minutes

- 4 skinless, boneless chicken breast halves (about 1 1/4 lb.)
- 1/2 cup bottled Italian salad dressing
- 1/2 tsp. chili powder
- 1/2 tsp. ground cumin
- 2 small sweet peppers
- 1 small red onion
- 8 10-inch flour tortillas
- 1 recipe Jicama Relish (below)
- 1 16-oz. jar salsa

1. Place chicken in resealable plastic bag. For marinade, combine dressing, chili powder, and cumin. Pour over chicken; seal bag. Marinate in refrigerator 1 to 24 hours; turn bag often.

2. Drain chicken, reserving marinade. Quarter and seed sweet peppers. Slice onion 1/2 inch thick. Brush with marinade.

3. For a charcoal grill, place chicken, peppers, and onion on the rack of an uncovered grill directly over medium coals. Grill until chicken is no longer pink (170° F) and vegetables are crisp-tender, turning once halfway through grilling (allow 12 to 15 minutes for chicken and 8 to 10 minutes for vegetables).

4. Meanwhile, prepare Jicama Relish. Warm tortillas. Slice chicken and vegetables into bite-size strips; spoon onto tortillas. Top with Jicama Relish and salsa. Roll up. Makes 8 servings.

JICAMA RELISH: In a large bowl toss together one 15-ounce can black beans, rinsed and drained; 1 cup chopped, peeled jicama; 1 large tomato, chopped; 1 medium avocado, halved, seeded, peeled, and chopped; and 1/2 cup snipped fresh cilantro.

Each serving: 396 cal., 16 g total fat (3 g sat. fat), 41 mg chol., 720 mg sodium, 42 g carbo., 6 g fiber, 25 g pro. Daily Values: 38% vit. A, 91% vit. C, 11% calcium, 22% iron.

Grilled Steak House Salad

Prep: 45 minutes **Marinate:** 8 hours
Grill: 17 minutes

- 1 1½-lb. beef flank steak
- 2 Tbsp. soy sauce
- 2 Tbsp. toasted sesame oil
- 1 Tbsp. grated fresh ginger
- 2 tsp. finely shredded lemon peel
- 2 cloves garlic, minced
- ½ tsp. ground black pepper
- 1 recipe Honey-Lemon Dressing (right)
- 1 large Vidalia onion or other sweet onion, cut into ½-inch-thick slices
- 1 Tbsp. cooking oil
- 2 hearts of romaine lettuce, torn (about 8 cups)
- 1 5-oz. pkg. arugula
- ½ cup chopped walnuts, toasted
- 2 oz. Gorgonzola cheese, crumbled

1. Trim fat from steak. Score steak on both sides by making shallow cuts at 1-inch intervals in a diamond pattern. Place steak in a resealable plastic bag set in a shallow dish. For marinade, combine soy sauce, sesame oil, ginger, lemon peel, garlic, and pepper. Pour over steak; seal bag. Marinate in the refrigerator for 8 to 24 hours, turning the bag occasionally. Prepare Honey-Lemon Dressing; chill.

2. Remove steak from marinade; discard marinade. Brush onion slices with cooking oil. For a charcoal grill, grill steak and onion slices on the rack of an uncovered grill directly over medium coals for 17 to 21 minutes for medium doneness (160° F), turning once halfway through grilling. (For a gas grill, preheat grill. Reduce heat to medium. Place steak on grill rack over heat. Cover and grill as above.)

3. Remove onion slices when they are tender and slightly charred. Thinly slice the steak diagonally across the grain.

4. In a very large bowl toss together the torn romaine and arugula. Drizzle with half of the Honey-Lemon Dressing; toss to coat. Add sliced steak, grilled onion, walnuts, and remaining dressing; toss to coat. Divide among 8 plates. Sprinkle with cheese. Makes 8 servings.

HONEY-LEMON DRESSING: In a small bowl whisk ¾ cup olive oil, ¼ cup white balsamic vinegar, 3 tablespoons lemon juice, 2 tablespoons finely chopped shallots, 1 tablespoon honey, 1 tablespoon Dijon-style mustard, ½ teaspoon ground black pepper, and ¼ teaspoon salt.

Each serving: 482 cal., 39 g total fat (8 g sat. fat), 39 mg chol., 502 mg sodium, 11 g carbo., 2 g fiber, 24 g pro. Daily Values: 39% vit. A, 35% vit. C, 11% calcium, 16% iron.

Cheesy Meat Loaf

Prep: 30 minutes **Grill:** 60 minutes

- 1 egg
- 1¼ cups soft bread crumbs
- ¼ cup milk
- 1 cup shredded taco cheese (4 oz.)
- ½ cup shredded carrot
- ¼ cup bottled steak sauce
- 1 to 2 Tbsp. prepared horseradish
- ½ tsp. seasoned salt
- ½ tsp. ground black pepper
- 1 lb. ground beef
- 8 oz. ground pork

1. In a large bowl beat egg; stir in bread crumbs, milk, cheese, carrot, 2 tablespoons of the steak sauce, the horseradish, seasoned salt, and pepper. Add ground meats; mix well. Shape meat mixture into an 8×4-inch loaf.

2. Fold a 24×18-inch piece of heavy-duty foil in half crosswise. Trim to a 12-inch square. Cut several large slits in the foil. Place the meat loaf on foil.

3. For a charcoal grill, arrange medium coals around a drip pan. Test for medium-low heat above pan. Place foil with meat loaf on grill rack over pan. Cover; grill for 60 to 70 minutes or until meat is done (160° F), brushing with remaining 2 tablespoons steak sauce during the last 5 minutes. To check doneness, insert an instant-read thermometer through the side of the loaf to a depth of 2 to 3 inches. (For a gas grill, preheat grill. Reduce heat to medium-low. Adjust for indirect cooking. Cover and grill as above.)

4. Carefully remove meat loaf from grill. Cover with foil; let stand for 15 minutes before serving. Makes 6 to 8 servings.

Each serving: 305 cal., 13 g total fat (9 g sat. fat), 117 mg chol., 534 mg sodium, 8 g carbo., 1 g fiber, 22 g pro. Daily Values: 64% vit. A, 6% vit. C, 14% calcium, 12% iron.

Marinated Mint Lamb

Prep: 25 minutes **Marinate:** 8 hours
Grill: 1½ hours **Stand:** 15 minutes

- 1 3- to 4-lb. boneless leg of lamb, rolled and tied
- ¾ cup snipped fresh mint
- ½ cup white wine vinegar
- ¼ cup cooking oil
- 2 Tbsp. honey
- 1 Tbsp. Worcestershire sauce
- 3 cloves garlic, minced
- ½ tsp. salt
- ½ tsp. ground black pepper

1. Untie roast and trim fat. Place lamb in a resealable plastic bag set in a shallow dish. For marinade, combine mint, vinegar, oil, honey, Worcestershire sauce, garlic, salt, and pepper. Pour marinade over lamb; seal bag. Marinate in the refrigerator for 8 to 24 hours, turning bag occasionally.

2. Drain lamb; discard marinade. Retie meat with butcher's string. Insert an oven-going meat thermometer into center.

3. For a charcoal grill, arrange medium coals around a drip pan. Test for medium-low heat above pan. Place meat on a grill rack over drip pan. Cover and grill until meat thermometer registers 140° F for medium-rare (1½ to 2¼ hours) or 155° F for medium doneness (1¾ to 2½ hours). (For a gas grill, preheat grill. Reduce heat to medium. Adjust for indirect cooking. Cover and grill as above, except place meat on rack in a roasting pan.)

4. Remove meat from grill. Cover with foil; let stand for 15 minutes (the meat's temperature will rise 5° F during standing). To serve, remove string and thinly slice meat. Makes 8 servings.

Each serving: 358 cal., 23 g total fat (9 g sat. fat), 111 mg chol., 158 mg sodium, 3 g carbo., 0 g fiber, 32 g pro. Daily Values: 4% vit. C, 2% calcium, 20% iron.

SUMMER FRIED CHICKEN

PRIZE TESTED RECIPES® $400 WINNER

JANET TEAS, ZANESVILLE, OHIO

Green Chile Fried Chicken

PREP: 25 minutes **MARINATE:** 8 hours **COOK:** 40 minutes

- 1 2½- to 3-lb. cut-up broiler-fryer chicken, skinned, if desired
- 1 8-oz. carton dairy sour cream
- ¼ cup milk
- 1 4-oz. can diced green chile peppers
- 2 Tbsp. snipped fresh cilantro
- 2 Tbsp. lime juice
- 1 clove garlic, minced
- ¾ tsp. ground cumin
- ½ tsp. salt
- ¼ tsp. ground black pepper
- ¾ cup all-purpose flour
- Cooking oil
- Bottled hot pepper sauce (optional)
- Lime wedges (optional)

1. Place chicken in resealable plastic bag set in shallow dish. For marinade, in a medium bowl combine sour cream, milk, chile peppers, cilantro, lime juice, garlic, cumin, salt, and black pepper. Pour over chicken; seal bag. Refrigerate for 8 to 24 hours, turning bag occasionally. Place flour in a shallow dish. Remove chicken from bag; discard marinade. Add chicken pieces to flour, a few at a time, turning to coat.

2. Add oil to a 12-inch heavy skillet to a depth of ¼ to ½ inch. Heat over medium-high heat until hot (350° F). Reduce heat. Carefully add chicken to the skillet. Cook, uncovered, over medium heat about 40 minutes or until chicken is no longer pink (170° F for breasts; 180° F for thighs and drumsticks), turning occasionally to brown evenly. Drain on paper towels. If desired, serve with bottled hot pepper sauce and lime wedges. Serves 4 to 6.

Each serving: 608 cal., 42 g total fat (14 g sat. fat), 125 mg chol., 501 mg sodium, 22 g carbo., 1 g fiber, 36 g pro. Daily Values: 12% vit. A, 25% vit. C, 15% calcium, 15% iron.

PRIZE TESTED RECIPES® $200 WINNER

MARCY ARMITAGE, MOBILE, ALA.

Pecan Crust Chicken

Marmalade and maple syrup lend a hint of sweetness while pecans provide the crunch.

PREP: 20 minutes **COOK:** 12 minutes

- 2 Tbsp. orange marmalade
- 2 Tbsp. pure maple syrup
- 1 cup finely chopped pecans
- 3 Tbsp. all-purpose flour
- ¼ tsp. salt
- 4 skinless, boneless chicken breast halves (1¼ lb. total)
- 2 Tbsp. cooking oil
- 1 Tbsp. butter

1. In a small bowl stir together orange marmalade and maple syrup; set aside. In a shallow dish combine pecans, flour, and salt. Brush marmalade mixture onto both sides of each chicken breast half. Dip chicken into pecan mixture, turning to coat; press pecan mixture onto chicken, if necessary.

2. In a 12-inch skillet heat oil and butter over medium heat until butter is melted and mixture begins to bubble. Carefully add chicken to skillet. Cook for 6 minutes. Turn chicken. Cook for 6 to 9 minutes more or until golden brown and no longer pink (170° F). Watch closely and reduce heat if chicken browns too quickly. Makes 4 servings.

Each serving: 506 cal., 32 g total fat (5 g sat. fat), 90 mg chol., 279 mg sodium, 21 g carbo., 3 g fiber, 36 g pro. Daily Values: 4% vit. A, 4% vit. C, 5% calcium, 12% iron.

Dilled Chicken and Jicama-Potato Salad

PREP: 45 minutes **CHILL:** 4 hours

- 1 recipe Jicama-Potato Salad (below)
- 1 lb. skinless, boneless chicken breasts
- 1 egg
- 1 Tbsp. dill mustard or Dijon-style mustard
- 1 Tbsp. water
- 1/4 cup all-purpose flour
- 1/4 cup seasoned fine dry bread crumbs
- 2 Tbsp. finely chopped almonds
- 3 Tbsp. garlic-flavored olive oil or olive oil
- Fresh dill sprigs (optional)

1. Prepare Jicama-Potato Salad; cover and chill for 4 to 24 hours.

2. Cut chicken into bite-size strips. In a shallow bowl beat egg; stir in mustard and water. Place flour in a second shallow bowl. In a third shallow bowl combine bread crumbs and almonds. Coat chicken with flour; dip into egg mixture, then into bread crumb mixture, turning to coat.

3. In a 12-inch skillet cook chicken in hot oil over medium-high heat about 6 minutes or until tender and no longer pink, turning once. Serve chicken with Jicama-Potato Salad. If desired, garnish with dill sprigs. Makes 6 servings.

JICAMA-POTATO SALAD: In a large saucepan place 5 medium potatoes, peeled and cubed, and 1/2 teaspoon salt; add enough water to cover. Bring to boiling; reduce heat. Simmer, covered, for 10 to 15 minutes or just until tender. Drain well; cool slightly. In a large bowl combine potatoes; 1/2 of a small jicama, peeled and cut into 3/4-inch pieces; 2 stalks celery, sliced; and 3 green onions, sliced. Gently fold in 3/4 cup bottled cucumber ranch salad dressing and 1 tablespoon snipped fresh dill or 1 teaspoon dried dill weed.

Each serving: 462 cal., 26 g total fat (4 g sat. fat), 79 mg chol., 673 mg sodium, 34 g carbo., 3 g fiber, 24 g pro. Daily Values: 2% vit. A, 45% vit. C, 5% calcium, 17% iron.

Parmesan-Sesame Chicken Strips

START TO FINISH: 30 minutes

- 1 lb. chicken breast tenderloins or skinless, boneless chicken breasts
- 1 egg
- 2 Tbsp. light mayonnaise dressing or salad dressing
- 3/4 cup fine dry bread crumbs
- 1/4 cup grated Parmesan cheese
- 3 Tbsp. sesame seeds, toasted
- 1/4 tsp. salt
- 1/4 tsp. ground black pepper
- 1 1/2 cups cooking oil
- 1 recipe Tahini-Lemon Dipping Sauce (below)

1. With a sharp knife, cut the white membrane away from each of the chicken tenderloins or breasts; cut chicken into bite-size strips. Set aside.

2. In a small bowl beat egg; stir in mayonnaise dressing. In a shallow bowl combine bread crumbs, Parmesan cheese, sesame seeds, salt, and pepper. Dip each chicken strip into egg mixture, then into bread crumb mixture, turning to coat.

3. In a large skillet heat cooking oil and sesame oil to 350° F. Add chicken strips, a few at a time, to hot oil. Cook for 4 to 5 minutes or until no longer pink. Remove chicken with a slotted spoon; drain on paper towels.

4. Make Tahini-Lemon Dipping Sauce; serve with chicken. Makes 4 to 6 servings.

TAHINI-LEMON DIPPING SAUCE: In a small bowl combine 1/3 cup light mayonnaise dressing or salad dressing, 2 tablespoons tahini (sesame seed paste), 2 tablespoons toasted sesame oil, and 1 1/2 teaspoons lemon juice.

Each serving: 633 cal., 48 g total fat (9 g sat. fat), 133 mg chol., 900 mg sodium, 18 g carbo., 2 g fiber, 35 g pro. Daily Values: 3% vit. A, 4% vit. C, 14% calcium, 15% iron.

Curried Oven-Fried Chicken

PREP: 30 minutes **BAKE:** 45 minutes

- 1/3 cup all-purpose flour
- 1 tsp. onion powder
- 1/2 tsp. salt
- 1/2 tsp. ground coriander
- 1/2 tsp. curry powder
- 1/2 tsp. cayenne pepper
- 1/2 tsp. ground black pepper
- 1/4 tsp. ground cinnamon
- 1/4 tsp. garlic powder
- 1/8 tsp. ground allspice
- 1/3 cup orange juice
- 2 Tbsp. honey
- 2 1/2 lb. meaty chicken pieces (breast halves, thighs, and drumsticks), skinned
- 2 Tbsp. butter, melted
- 1 recipe Yogurt Curry Sauce (below)

1. Preheat oven to 375° F. Line a 15×10×1-inch baking pan with foil; grease the foil. In a shallow dish stir together flour, onion powder, salt, coriander, curry powder, cayenne pepper, black pepper, cinnamon, garlic powder, and allspice; set aside. Pour orange juice into another shallow bowl; whisk in honey. Dip chicken pieces into orange juice mixture, then into flour mixture, turning to coat.

2. Arrange the chicken on the prepared baking pan, bone sides down, so pieces aren't touching. Drizzle chicken with the melted butter.

3. Bake chicken, uncovered, for 45 to 55 minutes or until no longer pink (170° F for breasts; 180° F for thighs and drumsticks). Do not turn chicken pieces while baking. Prepare Yogurt Curry Sauce; serve with chicken. Makes 4 servings.

YOGURT CURRY SAUCE: In a small bowl stir together 1 cup plain yogurt, 1/2 cup seeded and chopped cucumber, 1/2 teaspoon curry powder, and 1/4 teaspoon salt. Cover and chill until serving time.

Each serving: 414 cal., 16 g total fat (7 g sat. fat), 135 mg chol., 644 mg sodium, 24 g carbo., 1 g fiber, 41 g pro. Daily Values: 9% vit. A, 20% vit. C, 14% calcium, 13% iron.

OVEN DINNERS

PRIZE TESTED RECIPES® $400 WINNER

DARLENE GODSCHALX, PRESCOTT, ARIZ.

PRIZE TESTED RECIPES® $200 WINNER

KATHY BERKEY, WHITEHOUSE, OHIO

Moroccan-Style Short Ribs

PREP: 30 minutes **ROAST:** 1 hour + 45 minutes

- 1 Tbsp. dried thyme, crushed
- 1 tsp. salt
- 1 tsp. ground ginger
- 1 tsp. ground black pepper
- ½ tsp. ground cinnamon
- 5 lb. beef short ribs
- 2 Tbsp. olive oil
- 3 cups beef broth
- 1 14½-oz. can diced tomatoes
- 4 cloves garlic, minced
- 1 15-oz. can chickpeas (garbanzo beans), rinsed and drained
- 1 large onion, cut into wedges
- 1 medium fennel bulb, trimmed and cut into wedges
- 1 cup chopped carrot
- 1 recipe Nut-Olive Couscous (below)

1. Preheat oven to 350° F. In a small bowl combine thyme, salt, ginger, pepper, and cinnamon. Sprinkle over ribs; rub in. In a 4-quart Dutch oven brown ribs, half at a time, in hot oil over medium-high heat. Drain off fat. Add beef broth, undrained tomatoes, and garlic. Bring to boiling. Cover; roast for 1 hour.

2. Add chickpeas, onion, fennel, and carrot; stir. Cover; roast 45 to 60 minutes more or until meat and vegetables are tender.

3. Prepare Nut-Olive Couscous; spoon couscous onto a platter. Transfer ribs to platter. Pour remaining mixture into a colander, reserving liquid. Top ribs and couscous with vegetables. If desired, moisten with cooking liquid. Makes 8 servings.

NUT-OLIVE COUSCOUS: Prepare one 10-ounce package quick-cooking couscous according to package directions. Stir in ½ cup sliced almonds, toasted, and ½ cup pitted kalamata olives, halved.

Each serving: 506 cal., 20 g total fat (5 g sat. fat), 53 mg chol., 1,046 mg sodium, 46 g carbo., 10 g fiber, 34 g pro. Daily Values: 79% vit. A, 17% vit. C, 11% calcium, 23% iron.

Pork with Parsnips and Pears

PREP: 45 minutes **ROAST:** 2 hours

- 1 3½- to 4-lb. boneless pork top loin roast (double loin, tied)
- 2 Tbsp. cooking oil
- 6 cloves garlic, minced
- 1 tsp. snipped fresh rosemary
- 1 tsp. snipped fresh thyme
- ½ tsp. salt
- ¼ tsp. ground black pepper
- 2 lb. parsnips and/or carrots, peeled and cut into 1½- to 2-inch-long pieces
- 5 to 6 medium fresh pears, peeled, quartered, and cored
- 1½ cups port wine
- 2 Tbsp. cold water
- 1 Tbsp. cornstarch

1. Preheat oven to 325° F. In a large skillet brown meat on all sides in hot oil. Transfer to a shallow roasting pan. Sprinkle meat with garlic, rosemary, thyme, salt, and pepper. Place parsnips and/or carrots and pears around meat. Pour wine over all. Loosely cover with foil; roast 2 to 2½ hours or until meat is done (160° F).

2. Transfer meat to a platter, reserving cooking liquid; transfer parsnips and pears to platter. Cover with foil; set aside.

3. For sauce, measure 1½ cups of the cooking liquid; skim off fat. In a medium saucepan stir together cold water and cornstarch; add cooking liquid. Cook and stir over medium heat until thickened and bubbly; cook and stir for 2 minutes more. Season to taste with additional salt and pepper. Remove string from roast; slice meat. Serve sauce with meat and vegetables. Makes 10 to 12 servings.

Each serving: 417 cal., 12 g total fat (3 g sat. fat), 93 mg chol., 238 mg sodium, 33 g carbo., 6 g fiber, 35 g pro. Daily Values: 1% vit. A, 27% vit. C, 7% calcium, 15% iron.

Mexican Fiesta Casserole

PREP: 30 minutes **BAKE:** 23 minutes
STAND: 5 minutes

1 recipe Cornmeal Pastry (below)
12 oz. uncooked chorizo sausage
8 oz. lean ground beef
1 small onion, chopped (1/3 cup)
1 small red sweet pepper, chopped
2 cloves garlic, minced
1 16-oz. jar fire-roasted salsa or salsa
1 15-oz. can black beans, rinsed and drained
1 cup frozen whole kernel corn
1 tsp. chili powder
Dash bottled hot pepper sauce
2 oz. sharp cheddar cheese, shredded (1/2 cup)

1. Prepare Cornmeal Pastry; set aside. In a large skillet crumble chorizo and beef. Add onion, sweet pepper, and garlic; cook until meat is brown. Drain off fat. Stir in salsa, beans, corn, chili powder, hot pepper sauce, and 1/4 teaspoon salt. Cook and stir for 5 minutes. Spoon into baked pastry shell. Lay pastry strips atop. Bake for 20 to 25 minutes or until pastry is golden.

2. Sprinkle with cheese. Bake about 3 minutes more or until cheese is melted. Let stand 5 minutes before serving. Serves 8.

CORNMEAL PASTRY: Preheat oven to 425° F. In a large bowl stir together 2 cups all-purpose flour, 2/3 cup yellow cornmeal, and 1/2 teaspoon salt. Cut in 3/4 cup butter until pieces are pea-size. Using 1/3 to 1/2 cup cold water total, sprinkle water over flour mixture, 1 tablespoon at a time, gently tossing with a fork until all of the flour mixture is moistened. Form dough into a ball. Set aside one-third of the dough. On a lightly floured surface, roll remaining dough to 12×7-inch rectangle; place in lightly greased 2-quart rectangular baking dish. Bake for 8 minutes. Meanwhile, on a lightly floured surface, roll reserved dough to a 10×6-inch rectangle; cut into 8 strips. Cover strips.

Each serving: 650 cal., 41 g total fat (20 g sat. fat), 112 mg chol., 1,366 mg sodium, 48 g carbo., 6 g fiber, 26 g pro. Daily Values: 36% vit. A, 46% vit. C, 11% calcium, 22% iron.

Baked Chicken And Artichoke Risotto

PREP: 30 minutes **BAKE:** 1 hour + 5 minutes
STAND: 5 minutes

3 cups sliced fresh mushrooms, such as cremini, oyster, shiitake (stems removed), and/or button
1 small onion, chopped (1/3 cup)
2 cloves garlic, minced
1 Tbsp. olive oil
3/4 cup arborio or long grain rice
2 9-oz. pkg. frozen artichoke hearts, thawed, drained, and halved
1 14 1/2-oz. can Italian-style stewed tomatoes
1 tsp. dried thyme, crushed
1/4 tsp. ground black pepper
1 cup chicken broth
2/3 cup milk, half-and-half, or light cream
3 cups cubed cooked chicken (about 1 lb.)
1/2 cup finely shredded Parmesan or Romano cheese (2 oz.)
1/4 cup seasoned fine dry bread crumbs
1 Tbsp. olive oil
1/2 tsp. finely shredded lemon peel

1. Preheat oven to 350° F. In a 12-inch skillet cook mushrooms, onion, and garlic in 1 tablespoon hot oil over medium-high heat until onion is tender. Add uncooked rice; cook and stir for 1 minute more.

2. Add artichoke hearts, tomatoes, thyme, and pepper. Stir in broth and milk. Bring just to boiling. Stir in chicken and 1/4 cup of the Parmesan cheese. Transfer to a 2 1/2-quart ungreased casserole. Bake, covered, about 1 hour or until rice is tender.

3. Meanwhile, for topping, combine remaining 1/4 cup cheese, the bread crumbs, 1 tablespoon oil, and lemon peel. Uncover casserole and sprinkle with topping; bake for 5 minutes more. Let stand for 5 minutes before serving. Makes 6 servings.

Each serving: 563 cal., 25 g total fat (10 g sat. fat), 96 mg chol., 1,316 mg sodium, 38 g carbo., 6 g fiber, 45 g pro. Daily Values: 10% vit. A, 12% vit. C, 67% calcium, 19% iron.

Orange-Spinach Stuffed Snapper

PREP: 30 minutes **BAKE:** 10 + 8 minutes

8 oz. fresh mushrooms, sliced (3 cups)
1 large onion, chopped (1 cup)
2 cloves garlic, minced
2 Tbsp. butter
2 10-oz. pkg. frozen chopped spinach, thawed and well drained
2 cups herb-seasoned stuffing mix
1 tsp. finely shredded orange peel (set aside)
1/3 cup orange juice
2 lb. red snapper fillets, skinned and cut into 8 serving-size portions
1 cup whipping cream
2 Tbsp. Dijon-style mustard
1/2 cup thinly sliced green onions
1 Tbsp. butter, melted
1/4 cup finely shredded Parmesan cheese

1. Preheat oven to 375° F. Grease a 3-quart rectangular baking dish; set aside.

2. In a large skillet cook mushrooms, onion, and garlic in the 2 tablespoons hot butter until mushrooms and onion are tender. Remove from heat; set aside half of the onion mixture (about 1/2 cup). Stir spinach, 1 1/2 cups of the stuffing mix, and the orange juice into mixture remaining in skillet. Heat through.

3. Transfer to prepared baking dish. Top with fish fillets; sprinkle fish with salt and pepper. Bake, uncovered, for 10 minutes.

4. Meanwhile, for sauce, in the same skillet combine the reserved onion mixture, the whipping cream, mustard, and orange peel. Bring to boiling; reduce heat. Simmer, uncovered, about 2 minutes or until slightly thickened. Stir in green onion.

5. For topping, crush remaining stuffing mix; place in a small bowl. Add melted butter; stir to coat.

6. Spoon sauce over fish. Sprinkle with topping and Parmesan. Bake, uncovered, about 8 minutes more or until fish flakes easily with a fork. Makes 8 servings.

Each serving: 426 cal., 23 g total fat (13 g sat. fat), 107 mg chol., 837 mg sodium, 18 g carbo., 4 g fiber, 35 g pro. Daily Values: 223% vit. A, 25% vit. C, 34% calcium, 9% iron.

PRIZE TESTED RECIPES® $400 WINNER

MARY ALCIERE, HINGHAM, MASS.

PRIZE TESTED RECIPES® $200 WINNER

CATHERINE MARTIN, PERRIS, CALIF.

Mexican-Style Pasta Bake

PREP: 35 minutes **BAKE:** 15 minutes **STAND:** 5 minutes

- 12 oz. dried bow tie pasta
- 1/2 cup chopped onion
- 1/2 cup chopped red sweet pepper
- 3 Tbsp. butter
- 1/3 cup all-purpose flour
- 1 tsp. dried cilantro, crushed
- 1/2 tsp. ground cumin
- 3 cups milk
- 6 oz. colby cheese, cubed
- 1 1/2 cups shredded Monterey Jack cheese (6 oz.)
- 1 cup bottled salsa
- 2/3 cup halved pitted green and/or ripe olives
- Chili powder

1. Preheat oven to 350° F. Butter six 12- to 16-ounce individual casserole dishes or one 3-quart baking dish; set aside. In a 4-quart Dutch oven cook pasta according to package directions. Drain; return to pan. In a large saucepan cook onion and sweet pepper in hot butter over medium heat about 5 minutes or until tender. Stir in flour, cilantro, cumin, and 1 teaspoon salt. Add milk all at once. Cook and stir until thickened and bubbly. Reduce heat to low. Stir in colby cheese and 1 cup of the Monterey Jack cheese; stir until cheese is melted. Pour over pasta; stir to combine.

2. Layer half of the pasta mixture, all of the salsa, and remaining pasta mixture in prepared casserole(s). Sprinkle with remaining 1/2 cup Jack cheese, the olives, and chili powder. Bake for 15 to 20 minutes or until bubbly around the edges and heated through. (If using large casserole, bake in a 400° F oven about 20 minutes.) Let stand for 5 minutes. Makes 6 servings.

Each serving: 604 cal., 31 g total fat (17 g sat. fat), 132 mg chol., 1,293 mg sodium, 56 g carbo., 3 g fiber, 27 g pro. Daily Values: 40% vit. A, 42% vit. C, 59% calcium, 19% iron.

Cheese 'n' Nut Stuffed Shells

PREP: 45 minutes **BAKE:** 45 minutes

- 24 dried jumbo shell macaroni*
- 2 eggs
- 1 15-oz. carton ricotta cheese
- 1 1/2 cups shredded mozzarella cheese (6 oz.)
- 1 cup shredded Parmesan cheese (4 oz.)
- 1 cup chopped walnuts
- 1 Tbsp. snipped fresh parsley
- 1/2 tsp. salt
- 1/4 tsp. ground black pepper
- 1/8 tsp. ground nutmeg
- 1 26-oz. jar thick-and-chunky pasta sauce

1. Preheat oven to 350° F. Cook shells according to package directions. Drain shells; rinse with cold water and drain well.

2. Meanwhile, for filling, in a large bowl beat eggs; stir in ricotta cheese, 1 cup of the mozzarella cheese, 3/4 cup of the Parmesan cheese, the walnuts, parsley, salt, pepper, and nutmeg.

3. Spread 1 cup of the pasta sauce in the bottom of a 3-quart baking dish. Spoon a heaping tablespoon of the filling into each cooked shell. Arrange filled shells in the baking dish. Pour remaining sauce over shells. Sprinkle with the remaining mozzarella and Parmesan cheeses. Bake, covered, about 45 minutes or until heated through. Makes 6 servings.

***NOTE:** Cook a few extra shells so you can replace any that tear during cooking.

Each serving: 549 cal., 32 g total fat (12 g sat. fat), 132 mg chol., 1,072 mg sodium, 36 g carbo., 4 g fiber, 30 g pro. Daily Values: 18% vit. A, 19% vit. C, 60% calcium, 15% iron.

Greek Orzo and Pepper Casserole

PREP: 50 minutes **BAKE:** 45 minutes
STAND: 5 minutes

- 6 oz. dried orzo (1 cup)
- 1/2 of a 10-oz. pkg. frozen chopped spinach, thawed
- 3 medium red and/or green sweet peppers, halved lengthwise, seeded, and membranes removed
- 8 oz. bulk pork sausage
- 1 cup sliced fresh mushrooms
- 1 small onion, chopped (1/3 cup)
- 1 clove garlic, minced
- 2 cups shredded Italian-style cheese blend (8 oz.)
- 1/2 cup ricotta cheese
- 2 oz. feta or kasseri cheese, crumbled (1/2 cup)
- 2 Tbsp. seasoned fine dry bread crumbs
- 1 egg, slightly beaten
- 6 pitted kalamata olives, chopped (1 Tbsp.)
- 1 26-oz. jar marinara sauce

1. Preheat oven to 350° F. Grease 6 individual au gratin or casserole dishes; set aside. Cook orzo according to package directions; drain. Stir in spinach. Divide evenly among prepared dishes. Place a sweet pepper half, cut side up, in each dish. Set aside.

2. In a large skillet cook sausage, mushrooms, onion, and garlic until meat is done and onion is tender. Drain off fat. Stir 1 cup of the Italian cheese, the ricotta, feta, bread crumbs, egg, and olives into mushroom-sausage mixture. Spoon mixture into pepper halves. Pour marinara sauce evenly over stuffed peppers and orzo mixture.

3. Cover with foil. Bake about 45 minutes or until heated through. Uncover; sprinkle with remaining 1 cup Italian cheese. Let stand for 5 minutes before serving. Makes 6 servings.

Each serving: 526 cal., 28 g total fat (13 g sat. fat), 102 mg chol., 1,200 mg sodium, 42 g carbo., 5 g fiber, 25 g pro. Daily Values: 126% vit. A, 168% vit. C, 39% calcium, 17% iron.

Green Lasagna

PREP: 30 minutes **BAKE:** 25 + 10 minutes
STAND: 10 minutes

- 1 10-oz. pkg. frozen cut broccoli, thawed
- 1 9-oz. pkg. frozen artichoke hearts, thawed and cut up
- 1 recipe Basil Cream Sauce (below)
- 6 no-boil lasagna noodles
- 6 oz. mozzarella cheese, shredded (1 1/2 cups)
- 1/4 cup grated Parmesan cheese (1 oz.)

1. Preheat oven to 375° F. In a medium bowl stir together broccoli and artichoke hearts; set aside.

2. Prepare Basil Cream Sauce. In a 2-quart square baking dish spread about 1/2 cup of Basil Cream Sauce. Arrange 2 of the lasagna noodles on the sauce. Top with half of the broccoli mixture, a third of the remaining sauce, and half of the mozzarella cheese. Add 2 more noodles, the remaining broccoli mixture, a third of the remaining sauce, and the remaining mozzarella cheese. Top with the remaining noodles and the remaining sauce. Sprinkle with Parmesan cheese.

3. Bake, covered, for 25 minutes. Uncover; bake about 10 minutes more or until top begins to brown. Let stand for 10 minutes before serving. Serves 6.

BASIL CREAM SAUCE: In a medium saucepan melt 3 tablespoons butter or margarine over medium heat. Add 1/2 cup sliced green onions and 6 cloves garlic, minced; cook and stir about 5 minutes or until green onion is almost tender. Stir in 1/4 cup all-purpose flour and 1/2 teaspoon salt; cook and stir for 1 minute. Add 2 1/2 cups milk all at once; cook and stir until thickened and bubbly. Remove from heat. Stir in 1/2 cup snipped fresh basil.

Each serving: 313 cal., 14 g total fat (9 g sat. fat), 43 mg chol., 541 mg sodium, 30 g carbo., 5 g fiber, 17 g pro. Daily Values: 35% vit. A, 49% vit. C, 42% calcium, 11% iron.

Nutty Gorgonzola Roll-Ups

Two convenient products—Italian cheese blend and bottled pasta sauce—make these cheesy roll-ups extra easy.

PREP: 45 minutes **BAKE:** 40 minutes

- 8 dried lasagna noodles
- 12 oz. cream cheese (four 3-oz. or 1 1/2 8-oz. pkg.), softened
- 2 cups shredded Italian-style cheese blend (8 oz.)
- 4 oz. Gorgonzola or other blue cheese, crumbled (1 cup)
- 1 cup chopped walnuts, toasted
- 2 Tbsp. snipped fresh basil or 2 tsp. dried basil, crushed
- 1 26-oz. jar tomato-basil pasta sauce
- 6 cups shredded fresh spinach

1. Preheat oven to 375° F. Cook lasagna noodles according to package directions; drain well. Rinse with cold water; drain.

2. In a large bowl combine cream cheese, Italian cheese, Gorgonzola, 3/4 cup of the walnuts, and the basil. Spread some of the cheese mixture onto one side of each lasagna noodle. Roll up noodles; place, seam sides down, in an ungreased 2-quart rectangular baking dish. Pour pasta sauce over all.

3. Cover and bake about 40 minutes or until heated through.

4. Divide spinach evenly among 8 dinner plates. Place a roll-up on top of spinach on each plate. Spoon sauce evenly over lasagna rolls. Sprinkle with remaining 1/4 cup walnuts. Makes 8 servings.

Each serving: 513 cal., 37 g total fat (17 g sat. fat), 77 mg chol., 813 mg sodium, 28 g carbo., 4 g fiber, 21 g pro. Daily Values: 49% vit. A, 17% vit. C, 37% calcium, 17% iron.

PRIZE TESTED RECIPES® $400 WINNER

CAMILLA SORENSON, ADA, MINN.

PRIZE TESTED RECIPES® $200 WINNER

STEPHEN ALEXANDER, CINCINNATI, OHIO

Curried Butternut Chicken Bisque

PREP: 30 minutes **BAKE:** 30 + 20 minutes

- 2 lb. butternut squash
- 1 medium onion, chopped
- 1 Tbsp. olive oil
- 2 cloves garlic, minced
- 2 Tbsp. grated fresh ginger
- 2 cups cubed cooked chicken
- 1 14-oz. can chicken broth
- 1 13½-oz. can unsweetened coconut milk
- ¼ cup water
- 2 to 3 tsp. curry powder
- ½ tsp. salt
- ⅛ tsp. ground black pepper
- 2 cups hot cooked brown rice
- ¼ cup snipped fresh cilantro
- ¼ cup chopped cashews

1. Preheat oven to 350° F. Cut squash in half lengthwise; remove and discard seeds. Arrange squash halves, cut sides down, in a 3-quart rectangular baking dish. Bake for 30 minutes. Turn squash cut sides up. Bake, covered, for 20 to 25 minutes more or until tender. Cool slightly. Carefully scoop squash pulp into bowl; discard shells. Use a potato masher to mash squash slightly; set aside.

2. In a large saucepan cook onion in hot oil for 3 to 4 minutes or until tender. Add garlic and ginger; cook and stir for 1 minute more. Carefully stir in mashed squash, chicken, broth, coconut milk, water, curry powder, salt, and pepper. Cook over medium heat until heated through, stirring occasionally.

3. To serve, spoon hot rice and chicken mixture into bowls. Sprinkle with cilantro and cashews. Makes 5 or 6 servings.

Each serving: 465 cal., 26 g total fat (15 g sat. fat), 50 mg chol., 684 mg sodium, 37 g carbo., 4 g fiber, 24 g pro. Daily Values: 103% vit. A, 32% vit. C, 7% calcium, 18% iron.

Zydeco Soup

PREP: 25 minutes **COOK:** 30 minutes

- 2 stalks celery, chopped (1 cup)
- 1 large onion, chopped (1 cup)
- 1 medium green sweet pepper, chopped (¾ cup)
- 2 cloves garlic, minced
- 2 Tbsp. olive oil
- 6 oz. cooked ham, diced (1¼ cups)
- 1 tsp. paprika
- ½ tsp. dry mustard
- ½ tsp. ground cumin
- ½ tsp. sugar
- ½ tsp. dried basil, crushed
- ½ tsp. dried oregano, crushed
- ½ tsp. dried thyme, crushed
- ¼ tsp. ground cloves
- ¼ tsp. ground black pepper
- ⅛ tsp. cayenne pepper
- 1 15-oz. can black-eyed peas, rinsed and drained
- 1 14½-oz. can golden hominy, rinsed and drained
- 1 14½-oz. can diced tomatoes
- 1 14-oz. can chicken broth
- 1 Tbsp. snipped fresh parsley
- 1 Tbsp. mild-flavored molasses

1. In a 4-quart Dutch oven cook celery, onion, sweet pepper, and garlic in hot oil over medium heat for 5 minutes. Stir in ham, paprika, mustard, cumin, sugar, basil, oregano, thyme, cloves, black pepper, and cayenne pepper. Cook and stir 5 minutes more.

2. Stir in black-eyed peas, hominy, undrained tomatoes, chicken broth, parsley, and molasses. Bring to boiling; reduce heat. Cover and simmer for 30 minutes. Makes 4 servings.

Each serving: 384 cal., 14 g total fat (3 g sat. fat), 24 mg chol., 1,627 mg sodium, 47 g carbo., 10 g fiber, 17 g pro. Daily Values: 16% vit. A, 69% vit. C, 13% calcium, 15% iron.

Brie, Crab, and Mushroom Soup

Serve this elegant soup as a first course for a dinner party or a main dish for a luncheon.

Start to Finish: 35 minutes

- 8 oz. fresh mushrooms, thinly sliced
- 1 medium onion, finely chopped
- 3 Tbsp. butter or margarine
- 1/4 cup all-purpose flour
- 1/4 tsp. ground white pepper
- 1/8 tsp. salt
- 1 14-oz. can vegetable broth
- 2 cups milk
- 1 4 1/2-oz. round Brie cheese, rind removed and cut into 1-inch pieces
- 3 plum tomatoes, chopped
- 2 6-oz. cans crabmeat, drained, flaked, and cartilage removed
- 2 Tbsp. snipped fresh parsley
- 4 tsp. finely shredded Romano cheese

1. In large saucepan cook mushrooms and onion in hot butter about 5 minutes or until tender. Stir in flour, pepper, and salt. Add vegetable broth all at once. Cook and stir until thickened and bubbly.

2. Stir in milk, Brie, and tomatoes. Cook and stir about 7 minutes more or until Brie is melted. Stir in crabmeat; heat through.

3. To serve, spoon into 4 bowls; top with parsley and shredded Romano cheese. Makes 4 main-dish servings or 8 first-course servings.

Each serving: 419 cal., 24 g total fat (13 g sat. fat), 150 mg chol., 1,183 mg sodium, 19 g carbo., 2 g fiber, 35 g pro. Daily Values: 28% vit. A, 33% vit. C, 33% calcium, 12% iron.

Dilly Dijon Salmon Bisque

Bisques are noted for being rich and creamy. This one lives up to that reputation, even though it uses evaporated fat-free milk.

Start to Finish: 35 minutes

- 1 medium onion, chopped
- 1 Tbsp. olive oil
- 1 1/4 cups water
- 1/2 cup long grain rice
- 1 14-oz. can chicken broth
- 8 oz. salmon fillet, cut into 1-inch pieces
- 2 cups fresh or frozen whole kernel corn
- 1 12-oz. can (1 1/2 cups) evaporated fat-free milk
- 1 Tbsp. Dijon-style mustard
- 1 tsp. snipped fresh dill or 1/2 tsp. dried dill weed
- 1/2 tsp. salt
- 1/2 tsp. ground black pepper
- Fresh dill sprigs (optional)

1. In a large saucepan cook onion in hot olive oil over medium heat until tender. Add the water; bring to boiling. Stir in uncooked rice. Reduce heat. Simmer, covered, for 15 minutes.

2. Add chicken broth; return to boiling. Add salmon and corn; simmer about 5 minutes or until rice is tender and salmon flakes easily with a fork.

3. Stir in evaporated milk, mustard, dill, salt, and pepper; heat through. To serve, spoon into 4 bowls. If desired, garnish with fresh dill sprigs. Makes 4 main-dish servings.

Each serving: 348 cal., 8 g total fat (1 g sat. fat), 33 mg chol., 944 mg sodium, 48 g carbo., 3 g fiber, 23 g pro. Daily Values: 13% vit. A, 14% vit. C, 27% calcium, 13% iron.

Seafood Salsa Soup

For a little extra kick, opt for medium salsa instead of mild.

Prep: 30 minutes **Cook:** 25 minutes

- 1 cup chopped peeled potato
- 1 cup chopped onion
- 1 cup chopped carrot
- 1/2 cup chopped celery
- 1 clove garlic, minced
- 2 Tbsp. olive oil
- 1 14-oz. can chicken or vegetable broth
- 1 1/4 cups bottled mild salsa
- 1/2 tsp. lemon-pepper seasoning
- 12 oz. orange roughy fillets, cut into 1-inch pieces
- 2 cups shredded fresh spinach
- Snipped fresh cilantro or parsley

1. In a large saucepan cook potato, onion, carrot, celery, and garlic in hot oil for 5 minutes. Stir in broth, salsa, and lemon-pepper seasoning. Bring to boiling; reduce heat. Cover and simmer for 15 minutes.

2. Add the orange roughy and spinach. Cook, uncovered, about 5 minutes more or until fish flakes easily with a fork. To serve, spoon into 4 bowls. Top with cilantro or parsley. Makes 4 main-dish servings.

Each serving: 206 cal., 9 g total fat (1 g sat. fat), 17 mg chol., 818 mg sodium, 17 g carbo., 5 g fiber, 16 g pro. Daily Values: 178% vit. A, 36% vit. C, 8% calcium, 13% iron.

Cheesy Cream of Roasted Red Pepper and Jalapeño Soup

Prep: 45 minutes **Cook:** 15 minutes

- 1 7-oz. jar roasted red pepper, drained and chopped
- 1 cup finely chopped sweet onion
- 1/2 cup finely chopped celery
- 2 cloves garlic, minced
- 2 14-oz. cans chicken broth
- 1/8 tsp. seasoned salt
- 1/8 tsp. ground black pepper
- 4 tsp. finely chopped seeded jalapeño peppers (see note, page 554)
- 3 Tbsp. butter or margarine
- 3 Tbsp. all-purpose flour
- 1 cup milk
- 6 oz. smoked cheddar or Swiss cheese, shredded
- 1 cup half-and-half, light cream, or milk
- 1/2 cup finely chopped cooked ham

1. In a large saucepan combine sweet pepper, onion, celery, garlic, broth, seasoned salt, black pepper, and half of the finely chopped jalapeño peppers. Bring to boiling; reduce heat. Cover and simmer for 7 minutes or until onion and celery are tender. Remove from heat; cool slightly.

2. Place broth mixture, half at a time, in a blender or food processor. Cover and blend or process until smooth.

3. In same pan melt butter. Stir in flour. Add milk and pureed mixture; cook and stir until thickened and bubbly. Add cheese, half-and-half, remaining jalapeño, and ham; cook and stir until cheese is melted. Makes 4 main-dish servings.

Each serving: 473 cal., 35 g total fat (21 g sat. fat), 105 mg chol., 1,549 mg sodium, 20 g carbo., 2 g fiber, 21 g pro. Daily Values: 89% vit. A, 171% vit. C, 47% calcium, 7% iron.

COOKING WITH WINE

PRIZE TESTED RECIPES® $400 WINNER

VIOLET KOSCICA, HOBART, IND.

PRIZE TESTED RECIPES® $200 WINNER

RALANE AUGUSTINE, MANVEL, TEXAS

Croatian Nut Tart

Wine in the pastry is a delightfully delicious surprise.

PREP: 30 minutes **BAKE:** 40 minutes

- 1 recipe White Wine Pastry (see recipe, page 533)
- 3 egg whites
- 1¼ cups finely chopped walnuts (about 5 oz.)
- ¼ cup granulated sugar
- ¼ cup packed brown sugar
- 3 egg yolks, slightly beaten
- 1½ tsp. finely shredded lemon peel
- ½ tsp. vanilla

1. Prepare the White Wine Pastry. Let egg whites stand at room temperature for 30 minutes. Preheat oven to 350° F.

2. For filling, in a medium bowl combine walnuts, granulated sugar, and brown sugar. Stir in egg yolks, lemon peel, and vanilla. Set aside. In a small bowl beat egg whites with an electric mixer on medium to high speed until stiff peaks form (tips stand straight). Fold beaten egg whites, a third at a time, into walnut mixture.

3. Pour filling into partially baked pastry, spreading evenly. Roll remaining dough ball into a circle about 11 inches in diameter. Cut slits to allow steam to escape. Place pastry on filling; trim edges even with edges of pan.

4. Bake for 40 to 45 minutes or until pastry is golden. Cool completely in pan on a wire rack. To serve, remove sides of pan; cut into wedges. Makes 12 servings.

Each serving: 354 cal., 26 g total fat (11 g sat. fat), 97 mg chol., 232 mg sodium, 25 g carbo., 1 g fiber, 6 g pro. Daily Values: 14% vit. A, 1% vit. C, 3% calcium, 9% iron.

Wine-Balsamic Glazed Steak

START TO FINISH: 30 minutes

- 2 tsp. cooking oil
- 1 lb. boneless beef top loin or top sirloin steak, cut ½ to ¾ inch thick
- 3 cloves garlic, minced
- ⅛ tsp. crushed red pepper
- ¾ cup dry red wine
- 2 cups sliced fresh mushrooms
- 3 Tbsp. balsamic vinegar
- 2 Tbsp. soy sauce
- 4 tsp. honey
- 2 Tbsp. butter

1. In a large skillet heat oil over medium-high heat until very hot. Add steak(s). Do not add any liquid and do not cover the skillet. Reduce heat to medium; cook for 10 to 13 minutes or until desired doneness (145° F for medium-rare doneness or 160° F for medium doneness), turning meat occasionally. If meat browns too quickly, reduce heat to medium-low. Transfer meat to a platter; keep warm.

2. For sauce, add garlic and crushed red pepper to skillet; cook for 10 seconds. Remove skillet from heat. Carefully add wine. Return to heat. Boil, uncovered, about 5 minutes or until most of the liquid is evaporated. Add mushrooms, balsamic vinegar, soy sauce, and honey; return to simmer. Cook and stir about 4 minutes or until mushrooms are tender. Stir in butter until melted. Spoon sauce over steak. Makes 4 servings.

Each serving: 377 cal., 21 g total fat (9 g sat. fat), 82 mg chol., 588 mg sodium, 12 g carbo., 0 g fiber, 27 g pro. Daily Values: 5% vit. A, 1% vit. C, 2% calcium, 15% iron.

White Wine Pastry

PREP: 10 minutes **BAKE:** 8 + 4 minutes

- 2 cups all-purpose flour
- 1/4 tsp. salt
- 1 cup cold butter
- 7 to 9 Tbsp. dry or sweet white wine, chilled

1. In a large bowl stir together flour and salt. Using a pastry blender, cut in butter until mixture resembles coarse cornmeal. Sprinkle 1 tablespoon of the wine over part of the flour mixture; gently toss with a fork. Push moistened dough to side of bowl. Repeat, using 1 tablespoon wine at a time, until all the flour mixture is moistened. Divide dough in half; form each half into a ball. If necessary, wrap dough in plastic wrap and chill for 30 minutes until easy to handle.

2. Preheat oven to 450° F. On a floured surface, slightly flatten 1 dough ball. Roll dough from center to edges into a circle 11 inches in diameter. Transfer pastry to a 9-inch round tart pan with a removable bottom. Ease pastry into pan without stretching it. Press pastry into fluted sides of tart pan; trim edges even with pan. Prick bottom and sides of pastry with tines of a fork. Line pastry with a double thickness of foil. Bake for 8 minutes. Remove foil; bake 4 to 5 minutes more or until set and dry. Cool slightly on wire rack. Use tart shell and remaining dough for Croatian Nut Tart (see recipe, page 532). Makes 12 servings.

Swiss Cheese and Olive Spread

PREP: 10 minutes

STAND: 30 minutes + 1 hour **CHILL:** 2 hours

- 12 oz. Swiss cheese, shredded (3 cups)
- 1 3-oz. pkg. cream cheese, cubed
- 1/4 cup dry sherry or dry white wine
- 3 Tbsp. mayonnaise or salad dressing
- 1 tsp. Worcestershire sauce
- 1/3 cup chopped pitted ripe olives, drained
- 3 Tbsp. snipped flat-leaf parsley
- 3 Tbsp. finely chopped green onions
- Toasted baguette slices or crackers

1. Place cheeses in a large bowl; let stand, covered, at room temperature for 30 minutes. Add sherry, mayonnaise, and Worcestershire. Beat with electric mixer until combined. Stir in olives, parsley, and green onion. Transfer to serving bowl. Cover; chill for 2 to 24 hours.

2. Let stand at room temperature for 1 hour. Serve with baguette slices. Makes 2 1/2 cups (10 to 12 servings).

Each serving: 201 cal., 16 g total fat (8 g sat. fat), 42 mg chol., 181 mg sodium, 2 g carbo., 0 g fiber, 10 g pro. Daily Values: 10% vit. A, 3% vit. C, 34% calcium, 3% iron.

Spiced Pork and Sweet Potatoes

PREP: 20 minutes

COOK: 10 hours (low) or 5 hours (high)

- 1 3- to 3 1/2-lb. boneless pork shoulder roast
- 2 cloves garlic, minced
- 1 Tbsp. cooking oil
- 1 lb. sweet potatoes, peeled and cut into 1-inch cubes (3 1/2 cups)
- 2 stalks celery, sliced (1 cup)
- 1 cup dried cranberries
- 1 medium onion, cut into thin wedges
- 1 small cooking apple, coarsely chopped
- 2 Tbsp. quick-cooking tapioca
- 1/2 cup chicken broth
- 1/2 cup Merlot or other dry red wine
- 1/2 teaspoon apple pie spice
- 1/4 teaspoon ground sage

1. Trim fat from meat. If necessary, cut meat to fit into a 4- to 6-quart electric slow cooker. Sprinkle pork with salt and black pepper; rub with garlic. In a large skillet brown meat on all sides in hot oil; drain.

2. Place sweet potatoes, celery, cranberries, onion, and apple in the slow cooker. Sprinkle with tapioca. In a medium bowl combine broth, wine, apple pie spice, and sage; pour over mixture in cooker. Place meat on top of mixture. Cover; cook on low-heat setting for 10 to 12 hours or on high-heat setting for 5 to 6 hours.

3. To serve, transfer meat and vegetable mixture to a platter. Drizzle with some of the cooking liquid. Makes 8 servings.

Each serving: 381 cal., 12 g total fat (4 g sat. fat), 110 mg chol., 260 mg sodium, 29 g carbo., 3 g fiber, 35 g pro. Daily Values: 148% vit. A, 17% vit. C, 3% calcium, 15% iron.

Five-Spice Beef Soup

PREP: 25 minutes **COOK:** 1 1/4 hours

- 1 1/2 lb. beef stew meat
- 2 Tbsp. cooking oil
- 1 tsp. Five-Spice Powder (below)
- 2 green onions, sliced
- 4 cloves garlic, minced
- 1 1-inch piece fresh ginger
- 1/2 tsp. crushed red pepper
- 3 medium tomatoes, chopped (1 lb.)
- 1 cup chopped daikon
- 1 cup chopped carrot
- 1 1/3 cups rice wine
- 1 cup water
- 3 Tbsp. soy sauce
- 4 cups hot cooked rice

1. In a 4-quart Dutch oven brown meat, half at a time, in the hot oil. Meanwhile, prepare Five-Spice Powder. Remove meat from Dutch oven. Cook green onion, garlic, ginger, and crushed red pepper in drippings for 1 minute. Stir in tomatoes, daikon, carrot, and browned meat. Stir in rice wine, the water, soy sauce, and Five-Spice Powder.

2. Bring to boiling; reduce heat. Simmer, covered, about 1 1/4 hours or until meat and vegetables are tender. Skim off fat. Discard fresh ginger. Serve over hot cooked rice. Makes 6 servings.

FIVE-SPICE POWDER: In a blender combine 3 tablespoons ground cinnamon; 2 teaspoons anise seeds or 6 star anise; 1 1/2 teaspoons fennel seeds; 1 1/2 teaspoons whole Szechwan pepper or whole black peppercorns; and 3/4 teaspoon ground cloves. Cover and process until powdery. Store in a covered container.

Each serving: 480 cal., 10 g total fat (3 g sat. fat), 68 mg chol., 608 mg sodium, 51 g carbo., 2 g fiber, 31 g pro. Daily Values: 111% vit. A, 24% vit. C, 16% calcium, 34% iron.

TAILGATE FAVORITES

PRIZE TESTED RECIPES® $400 WINNER

AARON A. FAIRFIELD, PORT SAINT LUCIE, FLA.

PRIZE TESTED RECIPES® $200 WINNER

TARA RINEHART, MERCER, WIS.

Hot and Spicy Sloppy Joes

PREP: 25 minutes **COOK:** 40 + 10 minutes

- 2 lb. ground beef
- 4 medium green sweet peppers, chopped (3 cups)
- 2 medium red sweet peppers, chopped (1½ cups)
- 4 medium onions, chopped (2 cups)
- 2 cups strong coffee
- 1 cup cider vinegar
- 1½ cups ketchup
- 2 tsp. chili powder
- 2 tsp. paprika
- ½ tsp. salt
- ½ tsp. ground black pepper
- 1 fresh Scotch bonnet chile pepper, seeded and finely chopped (see note, page 554), or ¼ tsp. cayenne pepper
- 14 to 16 hamburger or hot dog buns, split

1. In a 4-quart Dutch oven cook ground beef, green and red sweet peppers, and onions until meat is brown and vegetables are tender. Drain off fat.

2. Stir in coffee and vinegar. Bring to boiling. Boil gently, uncovered, over medium heat about 40 minutes or until liquid is almost all evaporated, stirring occasionally.

3. Stir in ketchup, chili powder, paprika, salt, black pepper, and Scotch bonnet or cayenne pepper. Cook and stir for 10 to 15 minutes more or until desired consistency. Keep hot while transporting. If desired, toast hamburger or hot dog buns. Serve meat in buns. Makes 14 to 16 servings.

Each serving: 283 cal., 9 g total fat (3 g sat. fat), 41 mg chol., 658 mg sodium, 36 g carbo., 3 g fiber, 17 g pro. Daily Values: 35% vit. A, 111% vit. C, 8% calcium, 18% iron.

Carrot Dip

Serve a colorful assortment of vegetable dippers alongside the horseradish-sparked dip.

PREP: 15 minutes **CHILL:** 4 hours

- ½ of an 8-oz. carton dairy sour cream
- ½ of an 8-oz. pkg. cream cheese, softened
- ¼ cup mayonnaise or salad dressing
- 2 tsp. soy sauce
- 1½ tsp. prepared horseradish (optional)
- ¼ tsp. salt
- ¼ tsp. ground black pepper
- 1½ cups shredded carrots
- ⅓ cup chopped green onions

1. In a medium mixing bowl combine sour cream, cream cheese, mayonnaise, soy sauce, horseradish (if using), salt, and pepper; beat with an electric mixer until smooth. Stir in shredded carrot and green onion.

2. Cover and chill for 4 to 24 hours. Keep chilled while transporting. Stir before serving. Makes 2 cups.

Each tablespoon: 110 cal., 10 g total fat (4 g sat. fat), 19 mg chol., 195 mg sodium, 3 g carbo., 1 g fiber, 2 g pro. Daily Values: 107% vit. A, 4% vit. C, 3% calcium, 2% iron.

Hearty Sausage Gumbo

Smoked turkey sausage stars in this hearty Cajun-style stew.

Prep: 45 minutes **Cook:** 30 minutes

- 1 medium Vidalia onion or other sweet onion, chopped (1 cup)
- 1 small red sweet pepper, chopped
- 1 small green sweet pepper, chopped
- 1 stalk celery, chopped
- 1 clove garlic, minced
- 1 Tbsp. olive oil
- 5½ cups water
- 1 lb. smoked turkey sausage links, quartered lengthwise and sliced
- 1 16-oz. pkg. frozen cut okra
- 1 14½-oz. can diced tomatoes
- 1 7-oz. pkg. gumbo mix with rice
- 1 tsp. snipped fresh rosemary
- ½ tsp. snipped fresh thyme
- ⅛ tsp. cayenne pepper (optional)

1. In a 4-quart Dutch oven cook onion, red and green sweet pepper, celery, and garlic in hot oil over medium heat until tender, stirring frequently.

2. Stir in the water, sausage, okra, undrained tomatoes, gumbo mix, rosemary, thyme, and, if desired, cayenne pepper. Bring to boiling; reduce heat. Simmer, covered, about 20 minutes or until rice is tender. Keep stew hot while transporting. Makes 8 servings.

Each serving: 224 cal., 7 g total fat (1 g sat. fat), 38 mg chol., 1,329 mg sodium, 29 g carbo., 3 g fiber, 13 g pro. Daily Values: 13% vit. A, 53% vit. C, 8% calcium, 11% iron.

Mushroom Deluxe Hamburgers

Set up a grill at your tailgate site and bring on the burgers.

Prep: 25 minutes **Grill:** 14 minutes

- 1 cup assorted fresh mushrooms, chopped
- ¼ cup chopped green sweet pepper
- ¼ cup chopped onion
- 1 Tbsp. butter
- 1 egg
- 3 Tbsp. garlic-flavored fine dry bread crumbs
- 3 Tbsp. grated Parmesan cheese
- 2 Tbsp. ketchup
- ½ tsp. celery salt
- ⅛ tsp. ground coriander
- ⅛ tsp. cayenne pepper
- 1 lb. ground beef
- 1 medium onion, cut into 4 slices
- 1 Tbsp. olive oil
- 4 hamburger buns, split and toasted
- Sliced Swiss cheese (optional)
- Sliced tomatoes (optional)

1. In a medium skillet cook mushrooms, green sweet pepper, and onion in hot butter until tender; cool.

2. In a large bowl beat egg; stir in bread crumbs, Parmesan cheese, ketchup, celery salt, coriander, and cayenne pepper. Add mushroom mixture and ground beef; mix well. Shape into four ¾-inch-thick patties. Brush onion slices with olive oil.

3. At the party, grill patties and onion slices on the rack of an uncovered grill directly over medium coals for 14 to 18 minutes or until an instant-read thermometer inserted in the burgers registers 160° F, turning once halfway through grilling. Serve burgers topped with onion slices on buns. If desired, add cheese and tomato slices. Makes 4 servings.

Each serving: 483 cal., 26 g total fat (10 g sat. fat), 136 mg chol., 845 mg sodium, 32 g carbo., 2 g fiber, 31 g pro. Daily Values: 8% vit. A, 19% vit. C, 14% calcium, 22% iron.

Onion Chili Sauce

Adjust the heat to suit your taste by using small, medium, or large jalapeños and your favorite Louisiana hot sauce.

Prep: 20 minutes **Cook:** 30 minutes

- 1½ lb. Vidalia onions or other sweet onions, halved lengthwise and sliced (about 6 cups)
- 1 Tbsp. cooking oil
- 1 medium green sweet pepper, cut into thin strips (1 cup)
- 2 fresh jalapeño chile peppers, halved, seeded, and thinly sliced (see note, page 554)
- ¾ cup bottled chili sauce
- 1 Tbsp. bottled Louisiana hot sauce
- 1 Tbsp. honey
- ½ tsp. salt
- ½ tsp. ground cinnamon
- ¼ tsp. ground black pepper
- ⅛ tsp. ground cloves

1. In a large skillet cook onion slices, covered, in hot oil over medium heat for 20 minutes, stirring occasionally. (Reduce heat to medium-low if onion slices begin to brown.)

2. Add sweet and hot peppers; cover and cook about 5 minutes more or just until peppers are tender. Stir in chili sauce, Louisiana hot sauce, honey, salt, cinnamon, black pepper, and cloves. Bring to boiling; reduce heat. Simmer, uncovered, for 5 minutes. Cool; chill to store. Keep cold while transporting.

3. Serve chili sauce over grilled bratwurst, hot dogs, or burgers. Makes about 3 cups sauce (enough sauce for 12 sandwiches).

Each serving: 54 cal., 1 g total fat (0 g sat. fat), 0 mg chol., 307 mg sodium, 10 g carbo., 2 g fiber, 1 g pro. Daily Values: 4% vit. A, 23% vit. C, 2% calcium, 2% iron.

BAG LUNCH SPECIALS

PRIZE TESTED RECIPES® $400 WINNER

SHOBA HAVALAD, GLENVIEW, ILL.

Cucumber Sandwiches

START TO FINISH: 20 minutes

- 1 cup packed fresh cilantro leaves
- ½ cup packed fresh mint leaves
- 1 Tbsp. lime juice
- 1 fresh jalapeño pepper, quartered (seeded, if desired) (see note, page 554)
- 1 clove garlic, quartered
- 2 Tbsp. grated Parmesan cheese
- 4 slices whole wheat or white bread
- 2 Tbsp. butter, softened
- 4 1-oz. slices provolone cheese
- ½ of a medium cucumber, thinly sliced (1 cup)

1. In a food processor combine cilantro, mint, lime juice, jalapeño pepper, and garlic. Cover and process until finely chopped. (If you do not have a food processor, finely chop the herbs, jalapeño, and garlic; combine with the lime juice.) Stir in Parmesan cheese.

2. If desired, remove crusts from bread. Spread one side of each bread slice with softened butter. Top 2 of the bread slices with 2 of the cheese slices. Top with cucumber slices. Carefully top with cilantro mixture, remaining cheese slices, and remaining bread slices, buttered sides down. Cut sandwiches in half. Serve immediately or wrap in plastic wrap and pack with an ice pack and chill up to 4 hours before eating. Makes 2 sandwiches.

Each sandwich: 485 cal., 31 g total fat (19 g sat. fat), 75 mg chol., 992 mg sodium, 30 g carbo., 4 g fiber, 23 g pro. Daily Values: 53% vit. A, 104% vit. C, 62% calcium, 43% iron.

PRIZE TESTED RECIPES® $200 WINNER

ELLEN BURR, LOS ANGELES, CALIF.

Stuffed Focaccia

Mascarpone cheese, artichoke hearts, capers, salami, and arugula layered on focaccia add up to one tremendous sandwich.

START TO FINISH: 20 minutes

- ½ of a 9- to 10-inch garlic-flavored, onion-flavored, or plain Italian flatbread (focaccia), split horizontally
- ½ of an 8-oz. container mascarpone cheese
- 1 6-oz. jar marinated artichoke hearts, drained and chopped
- 1 Tbsp. capers, drained
- 4 oz. thinly sliced Genoa salami
- 1 cup arugula leaves

1. Spread cut sides of focaccia with mascarpone cheese. Sprinkle bottom half of focaccia with artichoke hearts and capers; top with salami and arugula leaves. Add top of focaccia, mascarpone side down.

2. Cut sandwich into thirds. Serve immediately or wrap in plastic wrap and pack with an ice pack and chill up to 4 hours before eating. Makes 3 sandwiches.

Each sandwich: 545 cal., 36 g total fat (16 g sat. fat), 83 mg chol., 970 mg sodium, 43 g carbo., 3 g fiber, 23 g pro. Daily Values: 3% vit. A, 24% vit. C, 10% calcium, 8% iron.

Asian-Style Pork and Noodle Salad

Look for bottled Thai peanut sauce in your supermarket's Asian foods section or at an Asian market.

PREP: 30 minutes **BROIL:** 9 minutes
CHILL: 4 hours

- 1 3-oz. pkg. pork- or chicken-flavored ramen noodles
- 1/2 cup salad oil
- 1/3 cup rice vinegar
- 3 cloves garlic, minced
- 3 Tbsp. Thai peanut sauce
- 1/4 tsp. crushed red pepper
- 12 oz. boneless pork loin chops, cut 3/4 inch thick
- 4 cups shredded cabbage
- 1 cup broccoli florets
- 1/2 cup sliced almonds, toasted
- 1/2 cup sliced green onions

1. Measure out 3/4 teaspoon of the seasoning packet (half of the packet); reserve the remaining for another use. In a medium bowl whisk together the 3/4 teaspoon seasoning, salad oil, rice vinegar, garlic, peanut sauce, and red pepper. Remove 2 tablespoons of the mixture; brush onto pork chops.

2. Preheat broiler. Place pork on the unheated rack of a broiler pan. Broil 3 to 4 inches from the heat for 9 to 12 minutes or until meat juices run clear (160° F), turning chops once. Cool slightly. Thinly slice across the grain into bite-size strips.

3. Meanwhile, cook noodles in a large saucepan in boiling water for 2 minutes; drain. Transfer to a large bowl. Add the pork, cabbage, broccoli, almonds, green onion, and remaining oil mixture. Toss to coat. Cover and chill for 4 to 24 hours.

4. To tote, spoon into 5 individual containers; pack each with an ice pack. Eat within 5 hours. Makes 5 servings.

Each serving: 505 cal., 38 g total fat (6 g sat. fat), 40 mg chol., 490 mg sodium, 22 g carbo., 4 g fiber, 22 g pro. Daily Values: 8% vit. A, 63% vit. C, 10% calcium, 11% iron.

Cucumber and Corn Chicken Salad

Transform leftover cooked chicken into a refreshing main-dish salad. No leftovers on hand? Use frozen diced cooked chicken.

PREP: 25 minutes **BAKE:** 6 minutes
CHILL: 4 hours

- 1 10-oz. pkg. frozen whole kernel corn
- 1 large cucumber, seeded and chopped
- 1 1/2 cups cubed cooked chicken (about 8 oz.)
- 1/2 of a medium red, yellow, or green sweet pepper, seeded and chopped
- 1/3 cup bottled creamy Italian salad dressing
- 1 Tbsp. snipped fresh dill or 1 tsp. dried dill weed
- 1/4 tsp. salt
- 1 recipe Toasted Wheat Pita Triangles (below)

1. Cook corn according to package directions; drain well. In a large bowl combine corn, cucumber, chicken, sweet pepper, salad dressing, dill, and salt. Toss to mix. Cover and chill for 4 to 24 hours.

2. To tote, spoon into 4 individual containers; pack each with an ice pack. Pack pita wedges separately. Eat within 5 hours. Makes 4 servings.

TOASTED WHEAT PITA TRIANGLES: Preheat oven to 375° F. Split 2 whole wheat pita rounds in half horizontally. Cut each half into 6 wedges. Place, cut sides up, on a large baking sheet. Brush with 1 tablespoon olive oil. In a small bowl stir together 1/4 cup finely shredded Parmesan cheese; 1/4 teaspoon dried Italian seasoning, crushed; and 1/8 teaspoon cayenne pepper. Sprinkle Parmesan mixture over pita wedges. Bake for 6 to 8 minutes or until wedges are toasted.

Each serving: 379 cal., 17 g total fat (4 g sat. fat), 50 mg chol., 614 mg sodium, 37 g carbo., 4 g fiber, 23 g pro. Daily Values: 22% vit. A, 57% vit. C, 9% calcium, 11% iron.

Greek Chicken Salad Sub with Olive Salsa

Another time, serve the Olive Salsa as a dip with tortilla chips.

START TO FINISH: 20 minutes

- 1 recipe Olive Salsa (below)
- 1 16-oz. loaf French bread
- 1 9-oz. pkg. frozen cooked chicken breast strips, thawed
- 3/4 cup thinly sliced cucumber
- 3 oz. feta cheese, coarsely crumbled (3/4 cup)

1. Prepare Olive Salsa; set aside. Horizontally split loaf of bread. Hollow out inside of each half, leaving a 3/4-inch-thick shell. Fill the bottom half of the loaf with chicken, cucumber, feta, and the Olive Salsa. Top with hollowed-out top half.

2. To serve, cut sandwich into 4 to 6 pieces. To tote, wrap each slice in plastic wrap. Pack each with an ice pack. Eat within 5 hours. Makes 4 to 6 servings.

OLIVE SALSA: In a food processor* combine 1/2 cup pitted kalamata olives; 1/2 cup pepperoncini salad peppers, stems and seeds removed; 1/4 cup chopped red onion; 1/4 cup olive oil; 2 tablespoons red wine vinegar; 2 teaspoons snipped fresh oregano; 1/8 teaspoon salt; and 1/8 teaspoon ground black pepper. Cover and process until coarsely chopped. Stir in 1 medium tomato, diced; set aside.

***NOTE:** If you don't have a food processor, finely chop the ingredients and combine by hand.

Each serving: 611 cal., 24 g total fat (6 g sat. fat), 60 mg chol., 2,206 mg sodium, 65 g carbo., 5 g fiber, 13 g pro. Daily Values: 7% vit. A, 13% vit. C, 20% calcium, 21% iron.

TAKE-ALONG SIDE DISHES

PRIZE TESTED RECIPES® $400 WINNER

BECKI HAGERMAN, NOWATA, OKLA

Squash Gratin with Spinach

PREP: 40 minutes **BAKE:** 10 minutes

- 1¾ to 2 lb. butternut squash
- 1 Tbsp. olive oil
- Salt
- Ground black pepper
- 16 cups fresh spinach
- 1 cup half-and half or light cream
- 1 Tbsp. cornstarch
- 1 cup finely shredded Parmesan cheese
- ½ cup purchased crème fraîche

1. Preheat oven to 425° F. Lightly grease a 2-quart rectangular baking dish; set aside. Peel squash; slice ¼ inch thick. Discard seeds; halve large slices. Brush both sides with olive oil. Arrange in a 15×10×1-inch baking pan. Sprinkle with salt and pepper. Bake, uncovered, for 20 minutes.

2. In a 4- to 6-quart Dutch oven cook spinach, half at a time, in lightly salted boiling water for 1 minute or until wilted. Drain and cool slightly; squeeze out excess liquid. Coarsely chop the spinach; set aside.

3. Meanwhile, in a medium saucepan stir together half-and-half and cornstarch; cook and stir until thickened and bubbly. Stir in spinach. Spread in prepared dish; arrange squash on top.

4. Increase oven temperature to 475° F. In a small bowl stir together Parmesan and crème fraîche; spread onto squash. Bake, uncovered, for 10 to 15 minutes or until squash is tender and Parmesan mixture is light brown. Makes 8 servings.

Each serving: 408 cal., 28 g total fat (17 g sat. fat), 72 mg chol., 1,297 mg sodium, 11 g carbo., 7 g fiber, 29 g pro. Daily Values: 130% vit. A, 28% vit. C, 95% calcium, 28% iron.

PRIZE TESTED RECIPES® $200 WINNER

PATRICIA SAMUELSON, EDINA, MINN.

Buffet Wild Rice

PREP: 30 minutes **COOK:** 45 minutes

- 2 14-oz. cans chicken or vegetable broth
- ¾ cup uncooked wild rice, rinsed and drained
- ⅓ cup regular barley
- 1 cup fresh pea pods, halved crosswise
- 1 cup golden raisins
- 6 green onions, sliced (¾ cup)
- 2 tsp. finely shredded orange peel
- ½ cup orange juice
- ¼ cup snipped fresh mint
- 2 Tbsp. olive oil
- ½ tsp. curry powder

1. In a large saucepan bring broth to boiling; stir in wild rice and barley. Return to boiling; reduce heat. Simmer, covered, about 40 minutes or until rice and barley are tender. Drain off liquid. Return rice and barley to pan.

2. Stir in pea pods, raisins, green onions, orange peel, orange juice, mint, olive oil, and curry powder. Cook and stir over medium heat until heated through. Serve warm or at room temperature. Makes 6 to 8 servings.

Each serving: 271 cal., 6 g total fat (1 g sat. fat), 0 mg chol., 562 mg sodium, 50 g carbo., 6 g fiber, 7 g pro. Daily Values: 3% vit. A, 30% vit. C, 5% calcium, 13% iron.

Roasted Potatoes with Goat Cheese Sauce

PREP: 25 minutes **BAKE:** 40 + 45 minutes

- 3 lb. tiny red potatoes, scrubbed and quartered, or medium round red potatoes, cut into eighths
- 3 cloves garlic, minced
- 3 Tbsp. olive oil
- ½ tsp. salt
- ½ tsp. ground black pepper
- 4 oz. chèvre (soft goat cheese)
- ¾ cup milk
- 1 Tbsp. all-purpose flour
- 2 tsp. snipped fresh rosemary or ½ tsp. dried rosemary, crushed
- 1 recipe Walnut-Rosemary Topper (below)

1. Preheat oven to 450° F. In an extra-large mixing bowl toss together potatoes, garlic, olive oil, ¼ teaspoon of the salt, and ¼ teaspoon of the pepper. Spread mixture in a greased 15×10×1-inch baking pan. Place pan on bottom oven rack; roast for 40 to 45 minutes or until golden brown and tender, turning once. Transfer to a 2-quart baking dish. If making ahead, cool slightly, then cover and chill.

2. Meanwhile, for sauce, in a blender combine cheese, milk, flour, rosemary, remaining ¼ teaspoon salt, and ¼ teaspoon pepper. Cover and blend until smooth. If making ahead, transfer to a container; cover and chill. Prepare Walnut-Rosemary Topper; cover and chill.

3. To serve, bake potatoes, covered, at 350° F for 30 minutes. Pour sauce onto potatoes; stir gently. Sprinkle with topper. Bake, uncovered, about 15 minutes or until heated through. Makes 6 to 8 servings.

WALNUT-ROSEMARY TOPPER: In a small bowl combine ¼ cup finely chopped walnuts, ¼ cup fine dry bread crumbs, and 1 teaspoon fresh rosemary or ¼ teaspoon crushed dried rosemary. Toss with 2 teaspoons olive oil. Cover and chill until needed.

Each serving: 318 cal., 16 g total fat (5 g sat. fat), 11 mg chol., 379 mg sodium, 34 g carbo., 3 g fiber, 10 g pro. Daily Values: 2% vit. A, 43% vit. C, 10% calcium, 17% iron.

Paradise Bread

PREP: 30 minutes **RISE:** 2 hours **BAKE:** 30 minutes

- 5 to 5½ cups all-purpose flour
- 2 pkg. active dry yeast
- 2 tsp. finely shredded orange peel
- ⅓ cup butter
- ⅓ cup honey
- 3 Tbsp. granulated sugar
- 1½ tsp. anise seeds, crushed
- 1 tsp. salt
- 1 tsp. ground mace
- 1 egg
- 1 cup raisins
- 1 cup coarsely chopped pecans
- 1 Tbsp. butter, melted
- ½ cup sifted powdered sugar
- 1 to 2 tsp. orange juice

1. In a large bowl combine 2½ cups flour, the yeast, and orange peel; set aside.

2. In a medium saucepan heat and stir 1¼ cups water, ⅓ cup butter, honey, granulated sugar, anise seeds, salt, and mace just until warm (120° F to 130° F) and butter almost melts. Add butter mixture and egg to flour mixture. Beat with an electric mixer on low to medium speed for 30 seconds, scraping bowl constantly. Beat on high speed for 3 minutes. Stir in raisins, pecans, and as much remaining flour as you can.

3. Turn dough out onto a lightly floured surface. Knead in enough of the remaining flour to make a moderately stiff dough that is smooth and elastic (6 to 8 minutes total). Shape into a ball. Place in a lightly greased bowl; turn once. Cover; let rise in a warm place until double (1¼ to 1½ hours).

4. Punch dough down. Turn dough out onto a lightly floured surface; divide in half. Cover; let rest for 10 minutes.

5. Lightly grease two 8×4×2-inch loaf pans. Shape dough into loaves; place in pans. Cover; let rise in a warm place until nearly double in size (about 45 minutes).

6. Preheat oven to 350° F. Bake for 30 to 35 minutes or until bread sounds hollow when lightly tapped (if necessary, cover loosely with foil the last 10 minutes of baking). Remove from pans. Brush with melted butter. Cool on wire racks.

7. In a small bowl combine powdered sugar and enough orange juice to make of drizzling consistency. Drizzle onto cooled loaves. Makes 2 loaves (24 servings).

Each serving: 198 cal., 9 g total fat (2 g sat. fat), 17 mg chol., 134 mg sodium, 32 g carbo., 1 g fiber, 4 g pro. Daily Values: 3% vit. A, 1% vit. C, 1% calcium, 9% iron.

Corn and Fig Spoon Bread

PREP: 35 minutes **BAKE:** 45 minutes

- 3 egg whites
- Nonstick cooking spray
- ½ cup chopped dried figs
- ½ cup apple juice
- 2 cups milk
- 1½ cups buttermilk
- 1¼ cups cornmeal
- 1 Tbsp. sugar
- 1 tsp. salt
- 1½ cups frozen whole kernel corn, thawed
- ¼ cup butter, cut up
- 3 egg yolks
- 1 tsp. baking powder

1. Let egg whites stand at room temperature for 30 minutes. Preheat oven to 375° F. Lightly coat a 2½-quart casserole with nonstick cooking spray; set aside. In a small saucepan combine figs and apple juice. Bring to boiling; remove from heat. Set aside.

2. In a large saucepan combine milk, buttermilk, cornmeal, sugar, and salt. Cook and stir over medium heat for 10 to 15 minutes or until very thick and bubby, stirring often. Remove from heat. Stir in corn, butter, and fig-apple juice mixture.

3. In a small bowl combine egg yolks and baking powder. Slowly stir in 1 cup hot cornmeal mixture. Return mixture to pan.

4. In a large bowl beat egg whites until stiff peaks form. Fold egg whites into the corn mixture. Transfer to the prepared dish.

5. Bake, uncovered, for 45 minutes or until slightly puffed and center appears set. Makes 8 servings.

Each serving: 272 cal., 11 g total fat (6 g sat. fat), 103 mg chol., 514 mg sodium, 38 g carbo., 4 g fiber, 9 g pro. Daily Values: 13% vit. A, 5% vit. C, 19% calcium, 8% iron.

GOING WITH GRAINS

PRIZE TESTED RECIPES® $400 WINNER

MELISSA BARTON, TALLAHASSEE, FLA.

Mom's Bread

PREP: 30 minutes **RISE:** $1\frac{1}{2}$ hours **BAKE:** 30 minutes

1. Place $\frac{1}{2}$ cup bulgur in a small bowl. Add boiling water to cover. Let stand 15 minutes; drain well. Meanwhile, in a large mixing bowl combine 2 cups all-purpose flour and 1 package active dry yeast; set aside. In medium saucepan heat and stir $1\frac{1}{4}$ cups milk, $\frac{1}{4}$ cup honey, $\frac{1}{4}$ cup butter, and 1 teaspoon salt just until warm (120° F to 130° F) and butter almost melts. Add milk mixture to flour mixture. Add 1 egg. Beat with electric mixer on low to medium speed for 30 seconds, scraping sides of bowl. Beat on high speed 3 minutes. Using a wooden spoon, stir in bulgur, 1 cup whole wheat flour, $\frac{1}{2}$ cup all-purpose flour, $\frac{1}{2}$ cup rolled oats, $\frac{1}{2}$ cup wheat cereal flakes, and $\frac{1}{2}$ cup toasted wheat germ.

2. Turn out onto lightly floured surface. Knead in $\frac{1}{4}$ to $\frac{3}{4}$ cup whole wheat flour to make a moderately stiff dough that is smooth and elastic (6 to 8 minutes total). Shape dough into a ball. Place in lightly greased bowl; turn once. Cover; let rise in warm place until double in size (about 1 hour). Punch down dough. Turn out onto lightly floured surface; divide in half. Cover; let rest 10 minutes. Lightly grease two 8×4×2-inch loaf pans. Shape dough into 2 loaves; place in prepared pans. Mix 1 egg white and 1 tablespoon water; brush onto loaves. Sprinkle with coarsely crushed wheat cereal flakes. Cover; let rise until nearly double (about 30 minutes).

3. Preheat oven to 375° F. Bake about 30 minutes or until bread sounds hollow when lightly tapped. If desired, cover with foil the last 10 minutes of baking to prevent overbrowning. Remove from pans; cool on wire racks. Makes 2 loaves (24 slices).

Each slice: 134 cal., 3 g total fat (2 g sat. fat), 15 mg chol., 136 mg sodium, 23 g carbo., 2 g fiber, 4 g pro. Daily Values: 3% vit. A, 3% vit. C, 3% calcium, 10% iron.

PRIZE TESTED RECIPES® $200 WINNER

DAWN K. MURPHY, RENO, NEV.

Orzo and Bulgur Salad

PREP: 30 minutes **STAND:** 45 minutes **CHILL:** 4 hours

- 1 cup dried orzo
- 1 cup bulgur
- 1 recipe Parsley-Fennel Vinaigrette (below)
- $\frac{1}{2}$ cup finely chopped celery
- $\frac{1}{2}$ cup shredded carrot
- $\frac{1}{2}$ cup chopped, seeded cucumber
- $\frac{1}{2}$ cup dried cranberries
- $\frac{1}{4}$ cup bias-sliced green onions
- $\frac{1}{4}$ cup crumbled feta cheese (1 oz.)

1. Cook orzo according to package directions. Drain orzo, reserving cooking water. Place bulgur in a 2-cup glass measure. Add enough of the hot cooking water to bulgur to equal 2 cups total mixture. Let bulgur stand about 45 minutes or until all liquid is absorbed. Meanwhile, prepare Parsley-Fennel Vinaigrette.

2. In a large bowl combine orzo, bulgur, celery, carrot, cucumber, and cranberries. Add Parsley-Fennel Vinaigrette; toss to coat. Cover and chill for 4 to 24 hours. Stir before serving. Top with green onion and feta cheese. Makes 10 to 12 servings.

PARSLEY-FENNEL VINAIGRETTE: In a bowl whisk together $\frac{1}{2}$ cup snipped fresh parsley, $\frac{1}{3}$ cup olive oil, $\frac{1}{4}$ cup balsamic vinegar, 2 tablespoons finely chopped shallot, 1 teaspoon sugar, 1 teaspoon salt, 1 teaspoon dry mustard, $\frac{1}{2}$ teaspoon crushed fennel seeds, and $\frac{1}{4}$ teaspoon ground black pepper.

Each serving: 217 cal., 9 g total fat (2 g sat. fat), 3 mg chol., 288 mg sodium, 31 g carbo., 4 g fiber, 5 g pro. Daily Values: 35% vit. A, 10% vit. C, 4% calcium, 8% iron.

Asparagus Barley Pilaf

START TO FINISH: 50 minutes

- 1 cup quick-cooking barley
- 1 Tbsp. olive oil
- 1/2 cup finely chopped onion
- 1 Tbsp. butter
- 1 large clove garlic, minced
- 1 14-oz. can chicken broth or vegetable broth
- 8 oz. fresh asparagus, cut into 1-inch pieces
- 1/2 cup shredded carrot
- 1/4 cup shredded Asiago cheese or Parmesan cheese (1 oz.)
- 1/4 cup snipped fresh basil

1. In a large saucepan cook barley in hot olive oil over medium heat about 5 minutes or until lightly toasted, stirring often. Add onion, butter, and garlic; cook until onion is tender.

2. In a small saucepan heat broth. Slowly add 3/4 cup of the broth to barley mixture, stirring constantly. Continue to cook and stir over medium heat until liquid is absorbed. Add another 1/2 cup of the broth, stirring constantly. Continue to cook and stir until the liquid is absorbed. Add another 1/2 cup of the broth; cook and stir until liquid is almost all absorbed.

3. Add asparagus and carrot; continue cooking until all the liquid is absorbed and the barley is tender. (Should take about 30 minutes total.)

4. Remove from heat. Stir in cheese and basil; season to taste with salt and ground black pepper. Makes 3 main-dish servings or 6 side-dish servings.

Each main-dish serving: 334 cal., 15 g total fat (6 g sat. fat), 21 mg chol., 836 mg sodium, 44 g carbo., 7 g fiber, 10 g pro. Daily Values: 103% vit. A, 14% vit. C, 9% calcium, 9% iron.

Fiesta Quinoa Salad

PREP: 30 minutes **CHILL:** 2 hours

- 1 cup quinoa
- 1 15-oz. can black beans, rinsed and drained
- 1 medium jicama, peeled and cut into bite-size strips (2 cups)
- 1 medium yellow or red sweet pepper, chopped (3/4 cup)
- 1/3 cup chopped red onion
- 1/4 cup snipped fresh cilantro
- 1 fresh jalapeño chile pepper, seeded and finely chopped (see note, page 554)
- 1 recipe Spiced Lime Dressing (below)

1. Place quinoa in a fine-mesh strainer. Rinse under cold running water; drain. In a medium saucepan bring 2 1/2 cups water to boiling. Add quinoa. Return to boiling; reduce heat. Cover; simmer for 10 minutes. Drain in fine-mesh strainer. Rinse with cold water; drain again. Place in large bowl.

2. Stir in beans, jicama, sweet pepper, onion, cilantro, and jalapeño. Prepare Spiced Lime Dressing; add to quinoa mixture. Toss to coat. Cover and chill for 2 to 24 hours. Makes 4 main-dish servings or 8 side-dish servings.

SPICED LIME DRESSING: In a small bowl stir together 1/4 cup olive oil, 1 teaspoon finely shredded lime peel, 3 tablespoons lime juice, 1 teaspoon salt, and 1 teaspoon ground cumin.

Each main-dish serving: 406 cal., 17 g total fat (2 g sat. fat), 0 mg chol., 858 mg sodium, 57 g carbo., 9 g fiber, 14 g pro. Daily Values: 6% vit. A, 188% vit. C, 8% calcium, 35% iron.

Feta Tabbouleh Salad

PREP: 20 minutes **CHILL:** 30 minutes

- 1 5.25-oz. pkg. tabbouleh (wheat salad) mix
- 1 cup boiling water
- 1 1/2 cups chopped tomato
- 4 oz. feta cheese with garlic and herb, crumbled (1 cup)
- 1 cup chopped yellow, red, and/or green sweet pepper
- 2 oz. hard salami, chopped (1/2 cup)
- 1/2 cup sliced green onions
- 1/2 cup snipped fresh parsley
- 1/2 cup snipped fresh mint
- 3 Tbsp. lemon juice
- 2 Tbsp. olive oil
- 1/2 tsp. ground black pepper
- Lettuce leaves

1. In a large bowl combine tabbouleh mix with spice packet. Stir in the boiling water. Cover and chill for 30 minutes or up to 24 hours.

2. Stir in tomato, 1/2 cup of the feta cheese, the sweet pepper, salami, green onion, parsley, mint, lemon juice, olive oil, and black pepper.

3. To serve, spoon onto lettuce leaves. (Or cover and chill up to 24 hours.) Sprinkle with remaining feta cheese. Makes 6 side-dish servings or 4 main-dish servings.

Each side-dish serving: 229 cal., 12 g total fat (5 g sat. fat), 24 mg chol., 627 mg sodium, 25 g carbo., 6 g fiber, 9 g pro. Daily Values: 21% vit. A, 135% vit. C, 14% calcium, 11% iron.

Jeweled Bulgur Salad

PREP: 10 minutes **COOK:** 20 minutes
STAND: 30 minutes **CHILL:** 2 hours

- 1 3/4 cups water
- 2/3 cup bulgur
- 1/2 cup dried cranberries
- 1/2 cup dried apricot halves, quartered
- 1 8-oz. can pineapple tidbits
- 1 recipe Apricot-Dijon Dressing (below)
- 1 cup seedless green grapes, halved
- 1/4 cup broken pecans, toasted

1. In a medium saucepan combine the water and bulgur. Bring to boiling; reduce heat. Simmer, covered, about 20 minutes or until liquid is absorbed. Remove from heat. Stir in cranberries and apricots; let stand, covered, for 30 minutes. Transfer bulgur to a medium bowl.

2. Stir in undrained pineapple. Cover and chill for 2 to 24 hours. Prepare Apricot-Dijon Dressing; add to salad. Add grapes and pecans. Toss to coat. Makes 6 side-dish servings.

APRICOT-DIJON DRESSING: In a screw-top jar combine 1/4 cup apricot nectar, 3 tablespoons cider vinegar, 3 tablespoons salad oil, 1 teaspoon Dijon-style mustard, and 1/4 teaspoon salt. Cover and shake well to mix.

Each serving: 253 cal., 11 g total fat (1 g sat. fat), 0 mg chol., 125 mg sodium, 41 g carbo., 6 g fiber, 3 g pro. Daily Values: 19% vit. A, 12% vit. C, 3% calcium, 8% iron.

TOMATO IDEAS

PRIZE TESTED RECIPES® $400 WINNER

MAUREEN SPRINGFIELD, DEPTFORD, N.J.

PRIZE TESTED RECIPES® $200 WINNER

LYNN NEFF, CLINTON, CONN.

Tomato-Cucumber Soup

START TO FINISH: 25 minutes

- 3 medium cucumbers, peeled, seeded, and cut up (1½ lb.)
- 3 medium tomatoes, cored, seeded, and cut up (1 lb.)
- ½ cup coarsely sliced green onions or scallions
- ¼ cup snipped fresh parsley
- 3 Tbsp. cider vinegar
- 1 clove garlic, minced
- 1 cup chicken broth
- 2 8-oz. cartons dairy sour cream
- ½ tsp. salt
- ½ tsp. ground black pepper
- Cucumber slices (optional)
- Cherry tomato or grape tomato wedges (optional)

1. In a food processor or blender combine cut-up cucumbers, tomatoes, green onion, parsley, vinegar, and garlic; cover and process until nearly smooth. (If using a blender, blend half of the vegetables at a time.) Transfer puree to a bowl; stir in chicken broth.

2. Serve immediately or cover and chill for up to 4 hours. Before serving, add sour cream, salt, and pepper; whisk until smooth. Spoon into 6 bowls. If desired, garnish with cucumber slices and tomato wedges. Makes 6 side-dish servings.

Each serving: 203 cal., 17 g total fat (10 g sat. fat), 33 mg chol., 413 mg sodium, 11 g carbo., 2 g fiber, 4 g pro. Daily Values: 29% vit. A, 43% vit. C, 12% calcium, 6% iron.

Tomato-Corn Pudding

PREP: 45 minutes **BAKE:** 25 minutes **COOL:** 10 minutes

- 12 small tomatoes (about 4 oz. each)
- Nonstick cooking spray
- ½ cup light dairy sour cream
- ½ cup milk
- 2 eggs
- 1 Tbsp. butter, melted
- ¼ cup finely crushed saltine crackers (7)
- 1 Tbsp. all-purpose flour
- 1 Tbsp. sugar
- ½ tsp. baking powder
- 1 cup fresh corn kernels or frozen whole kernel corn, thawed
- 1 Tbsp. finely chopped onion
- 2 oz. Havarti cheese with dill, shredded (½ cup)
- Fresh dill sprigs (optional)

1. Cut a ¼-inch slice from stem end of each tomato. Using a spoon, scoop out pulp of each, leaving about a ¼-inch-thick shell. Sprinkle cavities with salt and pepper. Turn upside down on a paper towel-lined baking sheet; let drain for 30 minutes.

2. Meanwhile, lightly coat twelve 2½-inch muffin cups with cooking spray; set aside. Preheat oven to 350° F. In a medium bowl whisk together sour cream, milk, eggs, and butter. Whisk in crackers, flour, sugar, baking powder, and ¼ teaspoon salt until smooth. Stir in corn and onion.

3. Place tomatoes, cut sides up, in prepared muffin cups. Fill each with about 3 tablespoons corn mixture. Top with cheese. Bake, uncovered, for 25 to 30 minutes or until puffed and set.

4. Cool in pan on a wire rack for 10 minutes. Use a large spoon to remove from cups. Serve warm. If desired, trim with dill sprigs. Makes 12 side-dish servings.

Each serving: 107 cal., 5 g total fat (2 g sat. fat), 48 mg chol., 204 mg sodium, 11 g carbo., 2 g fiber, 5 g pro. Daily Values: 17% vit. A, 35% vit. C, 8% calcium, 4% iron.

Cheesy Cavatappi with Tomatoes and Olives

START TO FINISH: 35 minutes

- 12 oz. dried cavatappi or mostaccioli pasta
- 4 cups red pear tomatoes, yellow pear tomatoes, and/or cherry tomatoes, halved
- 1 tsp. kosher salt or salt
- 1½ cups half-and-half or light cream
- 3 oz. Gorgonzola cheese, crumbled (¾ cup)
- ¾ cup finely shredded Parmesan cheese (3 oz.)
- Dash ground white pepper
- Dash cayenne pepper
- ¼ cup snipped fresh parsley
- 2 Tbsp. snipped fresh basil
- 1 Tbsp. snipped fresh lemon thyme or thyme
- ⅔ cup pitted kalamata olives, halved
- ¼ cup sliced green onions
- ¼ cup shredded fresh basil

1. In a 4-quart Dutch oven cook pasta according to package directions; drain. Return to Dutch oven.

2. Meanwhile, in a large bowl toss together tomatoes and salt; set aside. In a small saucepan bring half-and-half just to boiling. Reduce heat; stir in Gorgonzola cheese, Parmesan cheese, white pepper, and cayenne pepper until cheese is melted. Stir in parsley, the 2 tablespoons snipped basil, and the thyme.

3. Add the tomato mixture and cheese mixture to the pasta; toss gently to coat. Transfer the pasta mixture to a platter. Sprinkle with olives, green onion, and shredded basil. Makes 8 side-dish servings.

Each serving: 182 cal., 13 g total fat (7 g sat. fat), 32 mg chol., 724 mg sodium, 9 g carbo., 2 g fiber, 9 g pro. Daily Values: 22% vit. A, 36% vit. C, 25% calcium, 5% iron.

Rosemary Potatoes and Tomatoes

PREP: 10 minutes **BAKE:** 25 minutes

- 1 lb. tiny new potatoes, scrubbed and quartered (10 to 12)
- 2 Tbsp. olive oil
- 1 tsp. snipped fresh rosemary
- ¼ tsp. salt
- ¼ tsp. ground black pepper
- 4 plum tomatoes, quartered lengthwise (2 cups)
- ½ cup pitted kalamata olives, halved
- 3 cloves garlic, minced
- ¼ cup grated Parmesan cheese

1. Preheat oven to 450° F. Lightly grease a 15×10×1-inch baking pan; place potatoes in pan. In a small bowl combine oil, rosemary, salt, and pepper; drizzle over potatoes, tossing to coat.

2. Bake for 20 minutes, stirring once. Add tomatoes, olives, and garlic, tossing to combine. Bake for 5 to 10 minutes more or until potatoes are tender and brown on the edges and tomatoes are soft. Transfer to a serving dish. Sprinkle with Parmesan cheese. Makes 6 to 8 side-dish servings.

Each serving: 144 cal., 7 g total fat (1 g sat. fat), 3 mg chol., 295 mg sodium, 17 g carbo., 2 g fiber, 4 g pro. Daily Values: 8% vit. A, 39% vit. C, 6% calcium, 8% iron.

Tomatoes with Smoked Salmon

START TO FINISH: 15 minutes

- 2 small yellow or red tomatoes (6 to 8 oz. total)
- 3 oz. thinly sliced, smoked salmon (lox-style), cut into strips
- 1 recipe Horseradish Dill Cream (right)
- 4 small fresh dill sprigs

1. Core tomatoes; cut a thin slice from top and bottom ends so tomato slices will be even thickness. Cut tomatoes in half crosswise to make 4 thick slices. Arrange tomato slices on a platter; set aside.

2. Arrange smoked salmon on tomatoes. Prepare Horseradish Dill Cream; spoon onto salmon. Top with dill sprigs. Makes 4 appetizer servings.

HORSERADISH DILL CREAM: In a small bowl stir together ¼ cup dairy sour cream, 1½ teaspoons snipped fresh dill or ¼ teaspoon dried dill weed, 1 teaspoon finely chopped shallot, ½ teaspoon prepared horseradish, ½ teaspoon white wine Worcestershire sauce, dash salt, and dash ground white pepper.

Each serving: 61 cal., 4 g total fat (2 g sat. fat), 10 mg chol., 479 mg sodium, 3 g carbo., 0 g fiber, 5 g pro. Daily Values: 8% vit. A, 13% vit. C, 2% calcium, 2% iron.

Sweet Summer Tomato Relish

PREP: 15 minutes **CHILL:** 4 hours

- 3 medium plum tomatoes, chopped
- 1 small zucchini, chopped
- 1 stalk celery, chopped
- 4 tsp. lemon juice
- 1 Tbsp. sugar
- 1 Tbsp. finely chopped red onion
- 1 Tbsp. strawberry balsamic vinegar or balsamic vinegar
- 1½ tsp. olive oil
- ½ tsp. salt
- ½ tsp. dry mustard
- ½ tsp. poppy seeds

1. In a medium bowl combine the tomatoes, zucchini, and celery; set aside.

2. In a screw-top jar combine lemon juice, sugar, onion, vinegar, olive oil, salt, mustard, and poppy seeds. Cover; shake well. Pour over vegetable mixture. Cover; chill for 4 to 24 hours.

3. Serve with a slotted spoon as a relish for bratwurst, burgers, or ham. Makes 2½ cups relish.

Each ¼-cup serving: 23 cal., 1 g total fat (0 g sat. fat), 0 mg chol., 125 mg sodium, 4 g carbo., 1 g fiber, 0 g pro. Daily Values: 4% vit. A, 12% vit. C, 1% calcium, 1% iron.

ZUCCHINI FROM APPETIZERS TO DESSERTS

PRIZE TESTED RECIPES® $400 WINNER

CHRISTINE FORTNEY, CARMICHAELS, PA.

Zucchini Alfredo

PREP: 30 minutes **STAND:** 1 hour

- 5 large zucchini (about 2½ lb. total)
- 1 tsp. salt
- 2 to 3 cloves garlic, minced
- 2 Tbsp. olive oil
- 1 8-oz. pkg. cream cheese, cubed and softened
- ¾ cup half-and-half or light cream
- ½ cup finely shredded Parmesan cheese (2 oz.)
- Ground black pepper
- Ground nutmeg
- Finely shredded Parmesan cheese

1. Cut zucchini in half crosswise. Cut lengthwise into ¼-inch-thick slices; cut slices lengthwise into long, thin strips about ¼ inch wide (resembling strips of fettuccine). You should have about 8 cups. In a large colander toss the zucchini with the salt. Let stand to drain for 1 hour. Rinse and drain. Pat dry.

2. In a 12-inch skillet cook zucchini and garlic in hot oil over medium-high heat for 2 to 4 minutes or until crisp-tender. Transfer mixture to a large bowl.

3. In the same skillet heat and stir the cream cheese and half-and-half over medium-low heat until smooth. Stir in the ½ cup Parmesan cheese. Stir in zucchini; heat through. Transfer to a serving dish. Sprinkle with pepper, nutmeg, and additional Parmesan cheese. Makes 8 side-dish servings.

Each serving: 351 cal., 27 g total fat (16 g sat. fat), 69 mg chol., 876 mg sodium, 7 g carbo., 2 g fiber, 20 g pro. Daily Values: 25% vit. A, 21% vit. C, 59% calcium, 7% iron.

PRIZE TESTED RECIPES® $200 WINNER

LILLIAN KAYTE, GAINESVILLE, FLA.

Zucchini-Olive Couscous

START TO FINISH: 30 minutes

- 2 cloves garlic, minced
- 1 Tbsp. olive oil
- 3 cups chicken broth
- 1 cup pimiento-stuffed green olives, pitted green olives, and/or pitted ripe olives, cut up
- 3 medium zucchini, halved lengthwise and thinly sliced (about 3¾ cups)
- 1 10-oz. pkg. quick-cooking couscous
- 2 tsp. finely shredded lemon peel
- ¼ tsp. ground black pepper
- 4 green onions, sliced
- 2 Tbsp. snipped fresh parsley
- Thin strips lemon peel (optional)
- Lemon wedges

1. In a large saucepan cook garlic in hot oil for 1 minute, stirring frequently. Add broth and olives; bring to boiling. Stir in zucchini, couscous, shredded lemon peel, and pepper. Cover; remove from heat. Let stand for 5 minutes.

2. To serve, gently stir in green onion and parsley. If desired, top with thin strips of lemon peel. Serve with lemon wedges. Makes 8 side-dish servings.

Each serving: 190 cal., 5 g total fat (1 g sat. fat), 0 mg chol., 762 mg sodium, 31 g carbo., 3 g fiber, 6 g pro. Daily Values: 7% vit. A, 18% vit. C, 4% calcium, 6% iron.

Shrimp and Zucchini with Basil-Chive Cream Sauce

PREP: 40 minutes **GRILL:** 8 minutes

- 1 recipe Basil-Chive Cream Sauce (below)
- 1¼ lb. large shrimp in shells
- 2 medium zucchini, halved lengthwise and cut into 1-inch-thick slices (about 1 lb. total)
- 2 Tbsp. olive oil
- ½ tsp. finely shredded orange peel or lime peel
- 1 Tbsp. orange juice or lime juice
- ¼ tsp. salt
- ¼ tsp. cayenne pepper
- 5 cups shredded fresh spinach, arugula, and/or romaine

1. Prepare Basil-Chive Cream Sauce. Cover and store in the refrigerator until ready to serve.

2. Peel and devein shrimp, leaving tails intact. Rinse shrimp; pat dry. Thread shrimp and zucchini alternately onto 6 long metal skewers, leaving a ½-inch space between pieces. In a small bowl combine olive oil, orange or lime peel, orange or lime juice, salt, and cayenne pepper; brush evenly onto shrimp and zucchini.

3. For a charcoal grill, grill kabobs on the greased rack of an uncovered grill directly over medium coals for 8 to 10 minutes or until shrimp turn opaque, turning once. (For a gas grill, preheat grill. Reduce heat to medium. Cover and grill as above.)

4. Arrange shredded greens on a platter. Top with shrimp and zucchini; serve with sauce. Makes 4 to 6 servings.

BASIL-CHIVE CREAM SAUCE: In a food processor or blender combine one 8-ounce carton dairy sour cream, ½ cup snipped fresh basil, 3 tablespoons snipped fresh chives, ½ teaspoon salt, and ⅛ teaspoon ground black pepper. Cover and process or blend until nearly smooth.

Each serving: 283 cal., 20 g total fat (9 g sat. fat), 174 mg chol., 670 mg sodium, 7 g carbo., 3 g fiber, 20 g pro. Daily Values: 76% vit. A, 41% vit. C, 16% calcium, 23% iron.

Triple-Nut Zucchini Cake

PREP: 35 minutes **BAKE:** 35 minutes
COOL: 1 hour **BROIL:** 1½ minutes

- ¾ cup chopped walnuts
- ¾ cup chopped pecans
- ¾ cup slivered almonds, chopped
- ¾ cup rolled oats
- 2 cups all-purpose flour
- 2 cups granulated sugar
- 1 tsp. baking powder
- 1 tsp. salt
- ¼ tsp. baking soda
- 3 cups shredded zucchini
- 1 cup cooking oil
- 3 eggs, slightly beaten
- 1 tsp. vanilla
- ⅓ cup butter
- 3 Tbsp. half-and-half, light cream, or milk
- ⅔ cup packed brown sugar

1. Preheat oven to 350° F. Grease a 13×9×2-inch baking pan; set aside. In a 15×10×1-inch baking pan combine ½ cup of the walnuts, ½ cup of the pecans, ½ cup of the almonds, and all of the rolled oats. Bake about 12 minutes or until toasted, stirring several times. Set aside on a wire rack.

2. In a large bowl stir together the flour, granulated sugar, baking powder, salt, and baking soda. Stir in zucchini, oil, eggs, and vanilla until combined. Stir in toasted nut mixture. Spread in prepared baking pan.

3. Bake for 35 to 40 minutes or until a wooden toothpick inserted near the center comes out clean. Cool in pan on a wire rack for 1 hour.

4. In a small saucepan combine butter and half-and-half. Cook and stir until butter is melted. Add brown sugar; stir until sugar is dissolved. Remove from heat. Stir in remaining nuts.

5. Spread nut mixture onto cake in pan. Broil 4 inches from the heat for 1½ to 2 minutes or until topping is bubbly and golden. Cool in pan on wire rack before serving. Makes 20 servings.

Each serving: 388 cal., 24 g total fat (5 g sat. fat), 41 mg chol., 199 mg sodium, 41 g carbo., 2 g fiber, 5 g pro. Daily Values: 5% vit. A, 4% vit. C, 6% calcium, 9% iron.

Zucchini Spoon Bread

PREP: 20 minutes **BAKE:** 35 minutes

- 3 cups shredded zucchini
- 1 8½-oz. pkg. corn muffin mix
- 1⅓ cups shredded Italian-style or Mexican-style cheese blend
- 4 eggs
- ½ cup cooking oil
- ½ cup finely chopped onion
- ¼ cup buttermilk or sour milk*
- ½ tsp. dried Italian seasoning
- Dash bottled hot pepper sauce
- ⅔ cup chopped almonds

1. Preheat oven to 350° F. In a large bowl combine zucchini, dry muffin mix, 1 cup of the cheese, the eggs, oil, onion, buttermilk, Italian seasoning, and hot pepper sauce. Spoon into a greased 2- to 2½-quart baking dish. Sprinkle with almonds and remaining ⅓ cup cheese.

2. Bake, uncovered, about 35 minutes or until a wooden toothpick inserted in the center comes out clean.

3. To serve, spoon warm spoon bread onto plates. Makes 12 side-dish servings.

***NOTE:** To make ¼ cup sour milk, place 1 teaspoon lemon juice or vinegar in a glass measuring cup. Add enough milk to make ¼ cup total liquid; stir. Let mixture stand for 5 minutes before using.

Each serving: 277 cal., 20 g total fat (4 g sat. fat), 80 mg chol., 250 mg sodium, 17 g carbo., 1 g fiber, 9 g pro. Daily Values: 4% vit. A, 4% vit. C, 11% calcium, 6% iron.

FRESH FRUIT DESSERTS

PRIZE TESTED RECIPES® $400 WINNER

MARY LOU COOK, WELCHES, ORE.

PRIZE TESTED RECIPES® $200 WINNER

MARTHA MELLINGER, RADNOR, PA.

Lemon-Blackberry Mini Tarts

PREP: 20 minutes **BAKE:** 10 minutes
COOL: 30 minutes **CHILL:** 2 hours

- 1/2 of a 15-oz. pkg. folded refrigerated unbaked piecrust (1 crust)
- 1/2 of an 8-oz. pkg. cream cheese, softened
- 1/4 cup lemon curd
- 1 cup fresh blackberries
- 2 Tbsp. seedless blackberry spreadable fruit
- 2 tsp. lemon juice
- Fresh mint sprigs (optional)
- Powdered sugar

1. Let piecrust stand at room temperature for 15 minutes. Preheat oven to 400° F. Unfold piecrust. Cut four 4 1/2- to 5-inch rounds from piecrust. Press rounds firmly onto bottom and up sides of four 3 1/2- to 4-inch individual tart pans with removable bottoms. Trim crusts even with tops of tart pans. Prick bottom of each crust several times with tines of a fork. Place tart pans on a baking sheet. Bake for 10 to 12 minutes or until golden brown. Cool in pan on a wire rack.

2. For filling, in a small mixing bowl beat cream cheese and lemon curd with an electric mixer on medium speed until smooth. Divide filling among pastry shells, spreading evenly. Cover and chill for 2 to 24 hours.

3. Before serving, remove tarts from pans; place on 4 plates. Arrange berries in each tart. Combine spreadable fruit and lemon juice; spoon over tarts. If desired, garnish with mint sprigs. Sift powdered sugar over tops. Makes 4 servings.

Each serving: 448 cal., 25 g total fat (13 g sat. fat), 56 mg chol., 299 mg sodium, 54 g carbo., 4 g fiber, 3 g pro. Daily Values: 9% vit. A, 15% vit. C, 3% calcium, 3% iron.

Minty Summer Shortcake

PREP: 25 minutes **BAKE:** 12 minutes **STAND:** 30 minutes

- 1 2/3 cups all-purpose flour
- 1/4 cup sugar
- 1 1/2 tsp. baking powder
- 1/4 tsp. baking soda
- 1/4 tsp. salt
- 1/2 cup butter
- 2/3 cup buttermilk
- 3 Tbsp. finely chopped crystallized ginger
- 1 recipe Minty Fruit Topper (below)
- 1 7-oz. container purchased crème fraîche
- 1 Tbsp. sugar

1. Preheat oven to 425° F. Stir together flour, the 1/4 cup sugar, the baking powder, soda, and salt. Cut in butter until coarse crumbs. Make a well in center of flour mixture. Add buttermilk all at once. Using a fork, stir in ginger. Stir just until moistened. Turn out onto lightly floured surface. Knead gently 4 to 6 strokes or just until dough holds together. Lightly roll to a 7 1/2×6-inch rectangle (about 3/4 inch thick). Cut into six 3×2 1/2-inch rectangles. Place 1 inch apart on ungreased baking sheet. Bake about 12 minutes or until golden. Cool on wire rack; split biscuits.

2. Prepare Minty Fruit Topper. Place biscuit bottom halves on 6 dessert plates. Combine crème fraîche and the 1 tablespoon sugar; spoon onto biscuit bottoms. Spoon on Minty Fruit Topper; add biscuit tops. Makes 6 servings.

MINTY FRUIT TOPPER: Combine 3 cups chopped, seeded, and peeled mangoes or peaches; 1 1/2 cups sliced fresh strawberries; 1/4 cup lightly packed fresh mint, finely chopped; 2 tablespoons honey; and 2 teaspoons lemon juice. Let stand for 30 minutes.

Each serving: 553 cal., 32 g total fat (20 g sat. fat), 98 mg chol., 460 mg sodium, 64 g carbo., 3 g fiber, 5 g pro. Daily Values: 98% vit. A, 74% vit. C, 12% calcium, 11% iron.

Tropical Fruit Strudel

PREP: 40 minutes **BAKE:** 25 minutes
COOL: 1¼ hours

- 2 medium fresh pears, peeled and chopped
- ⅔ cup apricot or mango nectar
- ⅓ cup tropical blend mixed dried fruit bits
- 1 3-oz. pkg. cream cheese, softened
- 2 Tbsp. packed brown sugar
- ½ tsp. vanilla
- ⅓ cup chopped macadamia nuts, toasted
- 1 to 2 Tbsp. finely chopped crystallized ginger
- 1 tsp. finely shredded lemon peel
- 12 sheets frozen phyllo dough (14×9-inch rectangles), thawed
- ⅓ cup butter, melted
- 2 tsp. granulated sugar

1. Preheat oven to 375° F. In a medium saucepan combine pears, nectar, and dried fruit bits. Bring to boiling; reduce heat. Cover; simmer for 5 minutes. Drain well. Cool completely.

2. For filling, in a medium bowl stir together cream cheese, brown sugar, and vanilla. Stir in cooled pear mixture, nuts, ginger, and lemon peel; set aside.

3. Line a baking sheet with parchment paper or foil; set aside. On a work surface, place 1 sheet of phyllo. (Keep remaining covered with plastic wrap to keep it from drying.) Brush phyllo sheet with some of the melted butter. Repeat layering, using 5 more sheets and most of the remaining butter. Spoon half of the filling about 2 inches from a long side of phyllo. Fold in short sides; roll into a spiral. Repeat with remaining phyllo and filling. Place, seam side down, on prepared baking sheet. Brush with remaining butter; sprinkle with granulated sugar.

4. Bake for 25 to 30 minutes or until golden. Cool on baking sheet on a wire rack for 45 minutes. Serve warm. Serves 8.

Each serving: 273 cal., 17 g total fat (8 g sat. fat), 33 mg chol., 219 mg sodium, 28 g carbo., 2 g fiber, 3 g pro. Daily Values: 16% vit. A, 4% vit. C, 3% calcium, 6% iron.

Macaroon Fruit Tart

PREP: 30 minutes **BAKE:** 15 minutes
CHILL: 2 hours

- Nonstick cooking spray
- 1 13-oz. pkg. soft macaroon cookies (16)
- 1 cup ground pecans
- ⅓ cup miniature semisweet chocolate pieces (2 oz.)
- ¾ cup whipping cream
- 12 oz. cream cheese (four 3-oz. pkg. or 1½ 8-oz. pkg.), softened
- ½ cup sugar
- 1 Tbsp. orange juice
- 1½ tsp. vanilla
- 2 cups strawberries, halved
- 2 medium kiwifruit, peeled, halved lengthwise, and sliced
- ⅓ cup apricot preserves or jam

1. Chill a medium mixing bowl and beaters of an electric mixer. Preheat oven to 350° F.

2. For crust, lightly coat the bottom and sides of a 12-inch tart pan with removable bottom with nonstick cooking spray. Set aside. In a medium bowl crumble cookies. Add pecans; mix well. Press onto bottom of prepared tart pan. Bake for 15 to 20 minutes or until golden. Immediately sprinkle with chocolate pieces; cool.

3. In chilled bowl beat whipping cream with the chilled beaters on medium speed until soft peaks form (tips curl); set aside. In large mixing bowl beat cream cheese and sugar until smooth; beat in orange juice and vanilla. Fold in whipped cream. Spread in prepared crust. Cover surface with plastic wrap; chill for 2 to 24 hours.

4. Arrange fruit on tart. Melt preserves or jam; gently brush onto fruit. Serve immediately or chill for up to 2 hours. Makes 12 servings.

Each serving: 442 cal., 28 g total fat (15 g sat. fat), 52 mg chol., 170 mg sodium, 47 g carbo., 3 g fiber, 5 g pro. Daily Values: 14% vit. A, 46% vit. C, 5% calcium, 6% iron.

Blackberry-Coconut Dessert

PREP: 30 minutes **FREEZE:** 4 hours
STAND: 10 minutes

- 1 recipe Nut Crust (below)
- 3 cups fresh or frozen blackberries, thawed and drained
- ⅓ cup sugar
- 1½ tsp. cornstarch
- ¼ cup orange juice
- ¾ cup flaked coconut
- ¾ cup chopped walnuts
- 1 qt. vanilla bean ice cream

1. Prepare and bake Nut Crust. Meanwhile, in a blender place half of the blackberries; cover and blend until smooth. In a small saucepan combine sugar and cornstarch; add berry puree and orange juice. Cook and stir until thickened and bubbly; cook and stir for 2 minutes more. Cool slightly. Stir in remaining whole blackberries. Cover and cool.

2. In a shallow baking pan combine coconut and walnuts. Bake in the 350° F oven about 8 minutes or until toasted, stirring once. Cool.

3. In a large chilled bowl stir ice cream to soften; swirl in ¾ cup of the blackberry mixture and 1 cup of the coconut mixture. Spoon over baked crust. Sprinkle with remaining coconut mixture. Cover and freeze at least 4 hours or until firm. Cover and chill remaining berry mixture.

4. Before serving, let stand at room temperature for 10 minutes. Spoon some of the remaining blackberry mixture onto each serving. Makes 12 servings.

NUT CRUST: Preheat oven to 350° F. In large bowl combine ½ cup all-purpose flour, ⅓ cup chopped walnuts, and ¼ cup sugar. Add ⅓ cup softened butter; beat with an electric mixer on low to medium speed until mixture resembles fine crumbs. Press onto the bottom of a 2-quart rectangular baking dish. Bake about 20 minutes or until golden.

Each serving: 348 cal., 23 g total fat (11 g sat. fat), 45 mg chol., 105 mg sodium, 34 g carbo., 3 g fiber, 5 g pro. Daily Values: 12% vit. A, 18% vit. C, 8% calcium, 4% iron.

LEMON DESSERTS

PRIZE TESTED RECIPES® $400 WINNER

BETSY DIJULIO, VIRGINIA BEACH, VA.

PRIZE TESTED RECIPES® $200 WINNER

JUNE HERKE, WATERTOWN, S.D.

Citrus Shortbread Torte

PREP: 30 minutes **BAKE:** 20 minutes **CHILL:** 2 hours

- 1 recipe Nut Shortbread (below)
- 1½ cups whipping cream
- 1 14-oz. can sweetened condensed milk
- 1½ tsp. finely shredded lemon peel
- 1½ tsp. finely shredded lime peel
- 3 Tbsp. lemon juice
- 2 Tbsp. lime juice
- 2 drops yellow food coloring
- 1 10-oz. jar (about ¾ cup) lemon curd

1. Prepare and bake Nut Shortbread. Whip cream to stiff peaks. Stir together milk, 1 teaspoon of each peel, lemon and lime juices, and food coloring. Fold in 2 cups of the whipped cream.

2. To assemble, on a platter layer shortbread rounds with lemon curd and cream mixture. Spread remaining cream mixture on top. Sprinkle with remaining peels. Cover and refrigerate for 2 to 6 hours before serving. Makes 12 servings.

NUT SHORTBREAD: Preheat oven to 325° F. In large bowl beat ¾ cup softened butter and ¾ cup sifted powdered sugar until combined. Gradually beat in 1¼ cups all-purpose flour and 2 tablespoons cornmeal. Stir in ½ cup macadamia nuts, toasted and finely chopped. Divide dough in half. On 2 large ungreased baking sheets, press each half of dough into an 8-inch circle. Prick each circle several times with tines of a fork. Bake about 20 minutes or until edges are light brown. Cool on baking sheets for 10 minutes. Transfer to wire racks; cool completely.

Each serving: 513 cal., 32 g total fat (18 g sat. fat), 103 mg chol., 210 mg sodium, 55 g carbo., 3 g fiber, 5 g pro. Daily Values: 20% vit. A, 7% vit. C, 12% calcium, 5% iron.

Good Thyme Lemon Cups

PREP: 25 minutes **BAKE:** 35 minutes

- ½ cup sugar
- 2 Tbsp. all-purpose flour
- 2 tsp. snipped fresh thyme or ½ tsp. dried thyme, crushed
- 1 tsp. finely shredded lemon peel
- ⅛ tsp. salt
- 2 egg yolks
- 3 Tbsp. lemon juice
- 1 Tbsp. butter, melted
- ¾ cup milk
- 2 egg whites
- Whipped cream
- Fresh thyme sprigs (optional)

1. Preheat oven to 325° F. For batter, in a medium bowl combine sugar, flour, thyme, lemon peel, and salt. In a small bowl beat egg yolks; stir in lemon juice and butter. Stir in milk until combined. Stir milk mixture into flour mixture; set aside.

2. In another medium bowl beat egg whites with an electric mixer on medium to high speed until stiff peaks form (tips stand straight). Fold egg whites into batter (batter will be thin).

3. Place four 6-ounce custard cups in a 9×9×2-inch baking pan. Divide batter evenly among custard cups. Place pan on oven rack. Pour hot water into pan around cups to depth of 1 inch. Bake 35 to 40 minutes or until tops are light brown and puffed (tops may be cracked).

4. Carefully transfer cups to a wire rack. Serve warm, or cover and chill for up to 24 hours. Top with whipped cream. If desired, garnish with fresh thyme sprigs. Makes 4 servings.

Each serving: 250 cal., 12 g total fat (7 g sat. fat), 139 mg chol., 164 mg sodium, 31 g carbo., 0 g fiber, 5 g pro. Daily Values: 12% vit. A, 12% vit. C, 8% calcium, 3% iron.

Lemon-Lime Mascarpone Trifle

PREP: 25 minutes **CHILL:** 1 + 4 hours

- 1 recipe Citrus Curd (below)
- 2 8-oz. cartons mascarpone cheese
- 3/4 cup sugar
- 1/2 cup milk
- 1 10 3/4-oz. frozen pound cake, thawed and cubed
- 1/2 cup orange juice or 1/4 cup orange liqueur plus 1/4 cup orange juice
- 1/3 cup sliced almonds, toasted, or purchased glazed nuts

1. Prepare Citrus Curd. In a medium bowl beat mascarpone cheese, sugar, and milk with a wooden spoon until smooth.

2. In a 2-quart clear straight-sided bowl layer half of the cake cubes. Sprinkle with half of the orange juice (or a mixture of the juice and liqueur). Add half of the Citrus Curd and half of the mascarpone mixture. Repeat layers. Cover and chill for 4 to 24 hours.

3. Before serving, sprinkle with nuts. Makes 12 servings.

CITRUS CURD: In a medium saucepan stir together 1 cup sugar and 2 tablespoons cornstarch. Stir in 2/3 cup water, 2 teaspoons finely shredded lemon peel, 1/4 cup lemon juice, 1 teaspoon finely shredded lime peel, and 2 tablespoons lime juice. Cook and stir over medium heat until thickened and bubbly. Stir half of the lemon mixture into 4 egg yolks. Return the egg yolk mixture to the saucepan. Cook and stir over medium heat until mixture comes to a gentle boil. Cook and stir for 2 minutes more. Remove from heat. Add 1/2 cup butter, cut up, stirring until melted. Cover surface with plastic wrap. Chill for 1 to 2 hours.

Each serving: 511 cal., 34 g total fat (19 g sat. fat), 170 mg chol., 206 mg sodium, 47 g carbo., 1 g fiber, 11 g pro. Daily Values: 12% vit. A, 15% vit. C, 4% calcium, 4% iron.

Lemon Cream Coffee Cake

PREP: 25 minutes **BAKE:** 45 minutes

- 1 recipe Lemon Cream (below)
- 3 cups all-purpose flour
- 1 cup sugar
- 1 Tbsp. baking powder
- 1/4 tsp. salt
- 1/4 tsp. ground nutmeg or mace
- 1 cup butter
- 2 eggs
- 1 cup milk
- 1/2 tsp. almond extract
- 1/2 cup sugar
- 1/2 cup all-purpose flour
- 1/4 cup butter
- 1/2 cup chopped pecans or sliced almonds

1. Prepare Lemon Cream; set aside. Preheat oven to 350° F. Grease a 13×9×2-inch baking pan; set aside.

2. In a large mixing bowl stir together the 3 cups flour, the 1 cup sugar, the baking powder, salt, and nutmeg. Using a pastry blender, cut in the 1 cup butter until mixture resembles fine crumbs. Beat eggs; stir in milk and almond extract. Add to flour mixture, stirring until mixed. Spread half of the batter in the prepared pan.

3. Spoon Lemon Cream onto batter. Spoon remaining batter into small mounds on cream, spreading as much as possible.

4. For topping, combine the 1/2 cup sugar and the 1/2 cup flour; cut in the 1/4 cup butter until mixture resembles coarse crumbs. Stir in nuts. Sprinkle over batter.

5. Bake for 45 to 50 minutes or until cake is golden and toothpick inserted in dough mounds comes out clean. Cool on a wire rack at least 45 minutes before serving. Chill to store. Makes 12 servings.

LEMON CREAM: In a medium mixing bowl beat one 8-ounce package cream cheese, softened, with an electric mixer on medium speed until fluffy. Beat in 1/4 cup sugar. Fold in 1 cup lemon yogurt and 1 1/2 teaspoons finely shredded lemon peel.

Each serving: 559 cal., 32 g total fat (18 g sat. fat), 114 mg chol., 447 mg sodium, 61 g carbo., 1 g fiber, 8 g pro. Daily Values: 23% vit. A, 1% vit. C, 15% calcium, 12% iron.

Strawberry-Lemon Bars

PREP: 20 minutes **BAKE:** 35 minutes
CHILL: 1 hour

- 1 cup all-purpose flour
- 1/4 cup sifted powdered sugar
- 1/2 cup butter
- 2 eggs
- 3/4 cup granulated sugar
- 2 tsp. finely shredded lemon peel (set aside)
- 3 Tbsp. lemon juice
- 2 Tbsp. all-purpose flour
- 1/4 tsp. baking soda
- 1/3 cup strawberry jelly
- 1 tsp. lemon juice
- 5 whole fresh strawberries, hulled and quartered

1. Preheat oven to 350° F. In a medium bowl stir together the 1 cup flour and the powdered sugar. Using a pastry blender, cut in the butter until mixture resembles coarse crumbs (mixture will be dry). Press mixture onto the bottom of an ungreased 8×8×2-inch baking pan. Bake for 15 to 18 minutes or just until golden.

2. Meanwhile, for filling, in a large mixing bowl beat the eggs, the granulated sugar, the 3 tablespoons lemon juice, the 2 tablespoons flour, and the baking soda with an electric mixer on medium speed about 2 minutes or until combined. Stir in lemon peel. Pour filling over hot crust. Bake about 20 minutes more or until light brown around the edges and center is set. Cool on a wire rack.

3. In a small saucepan heat and stir jelly and the 1 teaspoon lemon juice just until jelly is melted; spoon over bars in pan and spread evenly. Arrange berry quarters on top of bars so that each cut bar will have a berry on top. Cover and chill for 1 to 2 hours. Cut into bars. Makes 20 bars.

Each bar: 125 cal., 5 g total fat (3 g sat. fat), 34 mg chol., 73 mg sodium, 18 g carbo., 0 g fiber, 1 g pro. Daily Values: 4% vit. A, 5% vit. C, 1% calcium, 2% iron.

EASTER DESSERTS

PRIZE TESTED RECIPES® $400 WINNER

JAUNEEN HOSKING, WIND LAKE, WIS.

Orange Chiffon Cake

PREP: 30 minutes **BAKE:** 30 minutes **CHILL:** 1 hour

- 2 eggs
- 3 medium oranges
- 1½ cups sugar
- 2¼ cups all-purpose flour
- 2 tsp. baking powder
- ½ cup milk
- ⅓ cup cooking oil
- 1 recipe Fluff Frosting (below)

1. Let eggs stand at room temperature for 30 minutes. Preheat oven to 350° F. Grease and flour two 9×1½-inch round cake pans. Finely shred 1 tablespoon peel. Squeeze juice from 2 oranges to measure ½ cup. Section remaining orange; set aside.

2. Separate eggs; set yolks aside. Beat egg whites to soft peaks. Gradually add ½ cup of the sugar, beating to stiff peaks.

3. In another large mixing bowl combine remaining 1 cup sugar, the flour, baking powder, and 1 teaspoon salt. Add milk and oil. Beat on until combined. Add orange juice and egg yolks; beat for 1 minute. Gently fold in egg white mixture until combined. Fold in peel. Divide batter between pans. Bake for 30 to 35 minutes or until toothpick inserted near centers comes out clean.

4. Cool in pans on wire racks; remove from pans. Frost with Fluff Frosting. Top with orange sections. Chill. Makes 12 servings.

FLUFF FROSTING: Finely shred 2 tablespoons orange peel; set aside. In a small saucepan stir together ⅓ cup sugar and 4 teaspoons cornstarch. Stir in ½ cup orange juice. Cook and stir until thickened. Cook and stir for 2 minutes more. Remove from heat; stir in reserved peel. Cover and chill for 1 hour. Beat 2 cups whipping cream to stiff peaks; fold into chilled mixture.

Each serving: 417 cal., 22 g total fat (11 g sat. fat), 91 mg chol., 292 mg sodium, 51 g carbo., 1 g fiber, 5 g pro. Daily Values: 14% vit. A, 26% vit. C, 9% calcium, 7% iron.

PRIZE TESTED RECIPES® $200 WINNER

JANE SHAPTON, TUSTIN, CALIF.

Coconut-Lemon Puffs

PREP: 35 minutes **BAKE:** 25 minutes

- 5 eggs, separated
- ¼ cup butter
- ¼ cup all-purpose flour
- ⅛ tsp. salt
- 1 cup canned unsweetened coconut milk or whole milk
- ⅓ cup sugar
- ⅓ cup shredded coconut
- 2 Tbsp. finely shredded lemon peel
- ¼ cup lemon juice
- Shredded coconut, toasted

1. Let egg whites stand at room temperature for 30 minutes. Preheat oven to 350° F. Butter sides of six 6-ounce soufflé dishes or custard cups; set aside. In small saucepan melt the ¼ cup butter over medium heat. Stir in flour and salt. Add coconut milk all at once. Cook and stir until very thick and bubbly around edges; set aside.

2. In a medium bowl beat egg yolks and sugar with an electric mixer on high speed about 3 minutes or until light and lemon-colored. Stir in the ⅓ cup coconut, the lemon peel, and lemon juice. Stir in flour mixture.

3. Wash beaters. In a large mixing bowl beat egg whites with electric mixer on medium speed until stiff peaks form (tips stand straight). Fold about 1 cup of the beaten egg white into lemon mixture. Fold lemon mixture into remaining beaten white. Transfer to prepared dishes (dishes will be full). Bake, uncovered, for 25 to 30 minutes or until a knife inserted near centers comes out clean. Serve immediately. If desired, sprinkle with toasted coconut. Makes 6 servings.

Each serving: 337 cal., 25 g total fat (18 g sat. fat), 199 mg chol., 221 mg sodium, 23 g carbo., 2 g fiber, 8 g pro. Daily Values: 11% vit. A, 14% vit. C, 3% calcium, 9% iron.

Easter Ricotta Pie

PREP: 45 minutes **BAKE:** 30 minutes
COOL: 1 hour **CHILL:** 2 hours

- **1 cup water**
- **1/4 cup long grain rice**
- **1 recipe Lemon Pastry (right)**
- **1 15-oz. carton ricotta cheese**
- **2/3 cup granulated sugar**
- **1 1/2 tsp. finely shredded lemon peel**
- **3/4 tsp. vanilla**
- **Dash ground cinnamon**
- **4 eggs, slightly beaten**
- **1/3 cup dried tart cherries**
- **1/4 cup dried apricot halves, snipped**
- **Milk**
- **Coarse sugar**

1. In a small saucepan bring the water and rice to boiling; reduce heat. Simmer, covered, about 25 minutes or until rice is very tender. Pour into a fine-mesh sieve; rinse with cold water. Drain well; let cool.

2. Preheat oven to 375° F. Prepare Lemon Pastry. On lightly floured surface, roll half of the pastry to 12-inch circle. Transfer to 9-inch pie plate. Trim pastry to 1/2 inch beyond edge of pie plate; set aside.

3. For filling, in a large bowl combine ricotta, the 2/3 cup sugar, the lemon peel, vanilla, and cinnamon. Add eggs; mix well. Fold rice and dried fruit into ricotta mixture. Pour filling into pastry-lined pie plate.

4. On a lightly floured surface, roll remaining pastry to 12-inch circle. Cut into 1/2-inch-wide strips. Dampen the edge of the pie with water and place strips over the filling in lattice-fashion, laying a strip in one direction, then overlapping in the other direction; repeat until pie is covered. Press edges of strips into bottom pastry rim. Fold pastry under; seal and crimp edge. Brush pastry strips with milk. Sprinkle with coarse sugar. To prevent overbrowning, cover edge of pie with foil.

5. Bake for 30 to 35 minutes or until filling is set, removing foil for the last 15 minutes of baking. Cool on a wire rack for 1 hour. Cover and chill before serving. Makes 10 servings.

LEMON PASTRY: In a medium bowl stir together 2 1/4 cups all-purpose flour and 2 tablespoons sugar. Cut in 2/3 cup cold butter until pieces are pea-size. Stir in 1 1/2 teaspoons finely shredded lemon peel. Beat 1 egg yolk and 6 tablespoons ice water; stir into flour mixture with a fork. Using your fingers, gently knead dough just until a ball forms. Divide in half. Cover with plastic wrap; let rest for 15 minutes.

Each serving: 423 cal., 21 g total fat (12 g sat. fat), 163 mg chol., 197 mg sodium, 47 g carbo., 1 g fiber, 11 g pro. Daily Values: 22% vit. A, 1% vit. C, 11% calcium, 12% iron.

Italian Cheesecake

PREP: 25 minutes **BAKE:** 50 minutes
COOL: 2 hours **CHILL:** 4 hours

- **1 recipe Crumb Crust (right)**
- **1 15-oz. carton ricotta cheese**
- **1 8-oz. pkg. cream cheese, softened**
- **3/4 cup sugar**
- **1/2 cup dairy sour cream**
- **2 Tbsp. all-purpose flour**
- **4 eggs, slightly beaten**
- **2 tsp. vanilla**
- **1 1/2 tsp. finely shredded orange peel**
- **1/3 cup golden raisins**
- **1/2 cup semisweet chocolate pieces**
- **1/2 cup pistachio nuts, chopped**

1. Preheat oven to 350° F. Prepare Crumb Crust. Set aside.

2. In a large mixing bowl combine the ricotta and cream cheese. Beat with an electric mixer on medium speed until smooth. Add sugar, sour cream, and flour; beat on low speed until combined. Stir in eggs, vanilla, and orange peel. Stir in raisins. Spoon over crust in pan. Place the roasting pan on the oven rack. Add boiling water to roasting pan to a depth of 1 inch.

3. Bake for 50 to 55 minutes or until center appears nearly set when gently shaken. Remove roasting pan from oven. Remove springform pan; place on a wire rack. Remove foil. Cool for 15 minutes. Loosen from sides of pan; cool for 30 minutes more. Remove sides of pan; cool completely. Cover and chill at least 4 hours before serving.

4. An hour before serving, in a small saucepan heat chocolate pieces over low heat, stirring until smooth. Sprinkle pistachio nuts over cheesecake; drizzle with melted chocolate. Return to refrigerator. Makes 12 to 16 servings.

CRUMB CRUST: Lightly grease a 9-inch springform pan. Wrap outside of the pan with heavy foil. Place springform pan in a large roasting pan; set aside. In a medium bowl combine 3/4 cup crushed zwieback (9 slices), 1/4 cup sugar, and 2 tablespoons all-purpose flour. Stir in 1/4 cup butter, melted. Press onto bottom of prepared springform pan.

Each serving: 374 cal., 23 g total fat (13 g sat. fat), 125 mg chol., 165 mg sodium, 34 g carbo., 2 g fiber, 10 g pro. Daily Values: 16% vit. A, 2% vit. C, 12% calcium, 7% iron.

Hazelnut Poached Pears and Strawberries

PREP: 30 minutes **COOL:** 2 hours

- **1 cup dark-colored corn syrup**
- **1/4 cup hazelnut liqueur (Frangelico)**
- **1/2 tsp. ground cinnamon**
- **1/2 tsp. ground nutmeg**
- **4 small pears, peeled, cored, and sliced**
- **3 cups small fresh strawberries, halved**
- **1 qt. vanilla ice cream**
- **1/2 cup hazelnuts (filberts) or almonds, toasted and finely chopped**

1. In a medium saucepan combine corn syrup, hazelnut liqueur, cinnamon, and nutmeg. Bring mixture to boiling. Add pears; cook, covered, about 5 minutes or just until pears are tender. Use a slotted spoon to transfer pears to a large bowl. Boil mixture in saucepan, uncovered, for 5 to 7 minutes or until syruplike (about 1 cup); pour over pears. Cover and cool about 2 hours or until room temperature.

2. To serve, stir strawberries into pear mixture. Divide evenly among 8 serving bowls. Top with ice cream and hazelnuts. Makes 8 servings.

Each serving: 396 cal., 14 g total fat (5 g sat. fat), 25 mg chol., 98 mg sodium, 66 g carbo., 4 g fiber, 4 g pro. Daily Values: 9% vit. A, 56% vit. C, 10% calcium, 6% iron.

CHOCOLATE CHIPS BEYOND THE COOKIE

PRIZE TESTED RECIPES® $400 WINNER

CAROL GILLESPIE, CHAMBERSBURG, PA.

Terrific Toffee

PREP: 15 minutes **COOK:** 15 minutes **COOL:** 1 hour

- 1 cup unblanched whole almonds, toasted and coarsely chopped
- 3/4 cup semisweet chocolate pieces
- 3/4 cup milk chocolate pieces
- 1/3 cup white baking pieces
- 2 Tbsp. instant malted milk powder
- 1 cup butter
- 1 cup sugar
- 3 Tbsp. water

1. Line a 13×9×2-inch baking pan with foil, extending foil over edges of pan. In a bowl combine almonds, semisweet and milk chocolate pieces, and white baking pieces. Sprinkle half (about 1 1/2 cups) of the mixture onto prepared baking pan. Sprinkle malted milk powder over mixture.

2. In a heavy 2-quart saucepan combine butter, sugar, and water. Cook over medium heat until boiling, stirring to dissolve sugar. Clip a candy thermometer to side of pan. Cook, stirring often, until thermometer registers 290° F, soft-crack stage (about 15 minutes). Mixture should boil at a steady rate over the entire surface. (Adjust heat as necessary to maintain a steady boil.)

3. Remove from heat; remove thermometer. Quickly pour mixture over nuts and chocolate pieces in pan. Immediately sprinkle remaining nut-chocolate piece mixture over toffee. Cool for 1 hour; break into pieces. If necessary, chill about 15 minutes or until chocolate is firm. Makes about 2 pounds (36 servings).

Each serving: 137 cal., 10 g total fat (5 g sat. fat), 16 mg chol., 65 mg sodium, 12 g carbo., 1 g fiber, 2 g pro. Daily Values: 4% vit. A, 2% calcium, 2% iron.

PRIZE TESTED RECIPES® $200 WINNER

GLORIA T. BOVE, BETHLEHEM, PA.

Chocolate-Kissed Date Puffs

PREP: 30 minutes **BAKE:** 12 minutes

- 1 egg
- 1 Tbsp. water
- 1 17 1/4-oz. pkg. frozen puff pastry (2 sheets), thawed
- 1 13-oz. jar chocolate-hazelnut spread
- 1/2 cup coarsely chopped hazelnuts (filberts), toasted
- 1/3 cup chopped pitted dates
- 1/3 cup large milk chocolate pieces

1. Preheat oven to 400° F. Lightly grease 2 baking sheets; set aside. In a small bowl beat egg and the water; set aside. On a lightly floured surface unfold each pastry sheet. Roll each into a 12-inch square. Cut each into nine 4-inch squares (18 total).

2. Spread the center of each square with about 1 tablespoon of the chocolate-hazelnut spread, leaving a 1-inch border around edges. Divide hazelnuts, dates, and chocolate pieces evenly among the prepared pastry squares, placing atop spread. Brush edges of squares with egg mixture. Fold each to form a triangle; crimp edges with a fork to seal. Prick tops with the fork. Transfer to prepared baking sheets. Brush with egg mixture.

3. Bake for 12 to 15 minutes or until golden brown. Cool slightly on wire racks. Serve warm. Makes 18 puffs.

Each puff: 282 cal., 18 g total fat (1 g sat. fat), 13 mg chol., 128 mg sodium, 27 g carbo., 1 g fiber, 4 g pro. Daily Values: 1% calcium, 2% iron.

Coffee and Chocolate Gingerbread

PREP: 20 minutes **BAKE:** 40 minutes

- 2¼ cups all-purpose flour
- 1 Tbsp. finely chopped crystallized ginger
- 2 tsp. ground cinnamon
- 1 tsp. baking soda
- 1 tsp. ground ginger
- ½ cup butter, softened
- ⅓ cup sugar
- 1 egg
- ¾ cup mild-flavored molasses
- 1 cup strong coffee, cooled
- 1 cup semisweet chocolate pieces
- 1 recipe Coffee Whipped Cream (below)
- Finely chopped crystallized ginger (optional)

1. Preheat oven to 350° F. Grease an 8×8×2-inch baking pan; set aside. In a bowl stir together flour, 1 tablespoon crystallized ginger, the cinnamon, soda, ground ginger, and ¼ teaspoon salt; set aside.

2. In a large bowl beat butter with an electric mixer on medium speed for 30 seconds. Add sugar; beat until combined. Add egg and molasses; beat for 1 minute on medium speed. Alternately add flour mixture and coffee to beaten mixture, beating on low speed after each addition until combined. Stir in chocolate pieces. Pour batter into prepared pan.

3. Bake about 40 minutes or until a wooden toothpick inserted near center comes out clean. Cool slightly in pan on a wire rack. Serve warm with Coffee Whipped Cream. If desired, sprinkle with crystallized ginger. Makes 9 servings.

COFFEE WHIPPED CREAM: In a chilled medium mixing bowl combine 1 cup whipping cream, 1 tablespoon sugar, and ½ teaspoon instant coffee crystals. Beat with chilled beaters of an electric mixer on low to medium speed until soft peaks form (tips curl).

Each serving: 510 cal., 27 g total fat (17 g sat. fat), 89 mg chol., 345 mg sodium, 65 g carbo., 2 g fiber, 5 g pro. Daily Values: 17% vit. A, 1% vit. C, 10% calcium, 20% iron.

Nutty Berry-Chip Squares

PREP: 30 minutes **BAKE:** 50 minutes

- 1⅓ cups all-purpose flour
- ½ cup ground almonds
- 1¼ tsp. baking powder
- ⅛ tsp. salt
- ¼ cup butter, softened
- 1 cup sugar
- 1 tsp. vanilla
- 1 egg
- ⅔ cup half-and-half, light cream, or milk
- 1 cup white baking pieces
- 1 cup dried blueberries or dried cranberries
- 1 recipe Creamy Frosting (below)
- ¼ cup sliced almonds, toasted

1. Preheat oven to 350° F. Grease and lightly flour an 8×8×2-inch or 9×9×2-inch baking pan. In a bowl stir together flour, ground almonds, baking powder, and salt. Set aside.

2. In a large mixing bowl beat butter with an electric mixer on medium to high speed for 30 seconds. Add sugar and vanilla; beat until combined. Beat in egg. Alternately add flour mixture and half-and-half to beaten mixture, beating on low speed after each addition just until combined. Fold in white baking pieces and dried fruit. Spread batter in prepared pan.

3. Bake for 50 to 55 minutes for 8-inch pan, 40 to 45 minutes for 9-inch pan, or until wooden toothpick inserted in center comes out clean. Cool in pan on a wire rack.

4. Spread Creamy Frosting onto cooled cake. Sprinkle with sliced almonds. Chill to store. Makes 12 servings.

CREAMY FROSTING: In a medium mixing bowl combine one 3-ounce package softened cream cheese, ¼ cup softened butter, and 1 teaspoon vanilla; beat for 30 seconds. Gradually beat in 2¼ to 2½ cups sifted powdered sugar until mixture reaches spreading consistency.

Each serving: 490 cal., 22 g total fat (11 g sat. fat), 55 mg chol., 197 mg sodium, 69 g carbo., 2 g fiber, 6 g pro. Daily Values: 10% vit. A, 9% calcium, 6% iron.

Frozen Praline Chocolate Torte

PREP: 25 minutes **COOL:** 30 minutes **FREEZE:** 4 hours **STAND:** 15 minutes

- 1⅓ cups crushed chocolate wafers (about 24)
- 3 Tbsp. butter, melted
- 1 12-oz. pkg. miniature semisweet chocolate pieces
- 2 cups whipping cream
- 1 8-oz. pkg. cream cheese or mascarpone cheese
- ¼ cup sugar
- ½ cup caramel ice cream topping
- 1½ tsp. vanilla
- ¾ cup coarsely chopped pecans, toasted

1. For crust, lightly butter an 8- or 9-inch springform pan. In a small bowl combine crushed wafers and melted butter. Sprinkle half of the crumb mixture onto bottom of prepared pan; set aside.

2. In a small saucepan combine 1½ cups of the chocolate pieces and ½ cup of the whipping cream. Cook and stir over low heat until chocolate is melted. Cool for 30 minutes.

3. Chill a medium bowl and beaters of an electric mixer. Beat remaining 1½ cups whipping cream until soft peaks form (tips curl); fold into chocolate mixture.

4. In a large bowl beat cream cheese, sugar, ¼ cup of the caramel ice cream topping, and the vanilla. Stir in remaining chocolate and ½ cup of the pecans.

5. Drop half of the chocolate mixture by spoonfuls into the prepared pan; spread carefully. Spoon the cheese mixture over top. Sprinkle with remaining crumbs. Top with remaining chocolate mixture.

6. Cover; freeze for 4 to 24 hours. Before serving, remove sides of pan. Let stand for 15 minutes. To serve, cut into wedges. Top with remaining ¼ cup caramel topping and ¼ cup pecans. Makes 12 servings.

Each serving: 514 cal., 38 g total fat (20 g sat. fat), 85 mg chol., 227 mg sodium, 44 g carbo., 3 g fiber, 6 g pro. Daily Values: 20% vit. A, 5% calcium, 8% iron.

FROZEN HOMEMADE TREATS

PRIZE TESTED RECIPES® $400 WINNER

AMELIA BEONDE, DENVER, COLO.

PRIZE TESTED RECIPES® $200 WINNER

MAX DOCKEN, SANDPOINT, IDAHO

Frozen Berry-Melon Pops

PREP: 20 minutes **FREEZE:** several hours

- 2½ cups cubed, seeded watermelon, cantaloupe, or honeydew melon
- ½ cup fresh or frozen red raspberries, thawed
- ¼ cup sugar
- 5 tsp. lemon juice
- 1 Tbsp. light-colored corn syrup

1. In a blender combine melon, berries, sugar, lemon juice, and corn syrup. Cover and blend until smooth. Press fruit mixture through a fine-mesh sieve, holding sieve over a bowl to catch juices. Discard solids. Pour strained juices into 3-ounce paper or plastic drink cups or pop molds. Cover cups with foil; cut a slit in the foil over each cup and insert wooden sticks. Freeze several hours or overnight until pops are firm.

2. To serve, remove from cups or molds. Makes 8 pops.

Each pop: 50 cal., 0 g total fat, 0 mg chol., 4 mg sodium, 12 g carbo., 1 g fiber, 0 g pro. Daily Values: 4% vit. A, 13% vit. C, 1% calcium, 1% iron.

Cucumber-Chile Granité

PREP: 20 minutes **FREEZE:** 3 + 2 hours

- 2 14-oz. cucumbers, peeled, seeded, and cut into 1-inch chunks (3 cups)
- 1 fresh jalapeño pepper, seeded and cut up*
- ⅔ cup sugar
- ⅓ cup lemon juice
- ¼ of a small cucumber, cut into matchstick-size pieces (optional)

1. In a food processor or blender combine cucumber chunks, jalapeño pepper, sugar, and lemon juice. Cover and process or blend until nearly smooth. Press mixture through a fine-mesh sieve, one-third at a time, holding sieve over a bowl to catch juices (you should have about 1⅔ cups strained juices). Discard solids. Transfer strained juices to a shallow 2-quart freezer container. Cover and freeze for 3 to 4 hours or until firm.

2. Break up frozen mixture. Transfer mixture to a chilled large mixing bowl. Beat with an electric mixer until slushy, but not melted. Return to freezer container; cover and freeze for 2 to 3 hours or until firm.

3. To serve, scoop into 8 small dessert dishes. If desired, top with cucumber pieces. Makes 8 servings.

***NOTE:** Because hot peppers contain volatile oils that can burn your skin and eyes, avoid direct contact with chile peppers as much as possible. When working with chile peppers, wear plastic or rubber gloves. If your bare hands do touch the chile peppers, wash your hands well with soap and water.

Each serving: 70 cal., 0 g total fat, 0 mg chol., 1 mg sodium, 18 g carbo., 0 g fiber, 0 g pro. Daily Values: 2% vit. A, 12% vit. C, 1% calcium, 1% iron.

Frozen White Chocolate Cranberry Cheese Pie

PREP: 20 minutes **COOL:** 30 minutes
FREEZE: 15 minutes + 6 hours
STAND: 15 minutes

- 2 oz. white chocolate baking squares or white baking bars, coarsely chopped
- 1 3-oz. pkg. cream cheese, cut up
- 1 butter-flavored crumb pie shell
- 1 qt. vanilla ice cream
- ½ cup dried cranberries, chopped
- ¼ cup chopped pecans, toasted
- Dried cranberries (optional)
- Chopped pecans, toasted (optional)

1. In a small saucepan combine white chocolate and cream cheese; cook and stir over low heat until melted and smooth. Cool to room temperature. Spread white chocolate mixture onto bottom of the pie shell. Freeze about 15 minutes or until firm.

2. In a chilled medium bowl stir ice cream to soften; fold in the ½ cup chopped cranberries and the ¼ cup chopped pecans. Spoon ice cream mixture into pie shell. Cover and freeze about 6 hours or until firm.

3. Before serving, let stand at room temperature for 15 minutes. If desired, top with additional dried cranberries and pecans. To serve, slice into 8 wedges. Makes 8 servings.

Each serving: 419 cal., 28 g total fat (13 g sat. fat), 67 mg chol., 195 mg sodium, 38 g carbo., 1 g fiber, 5 g pro. Daily Values: 17% vit. A, 1% vit. C, 12% calcium, 4% iron.

Lemon-Avocado Sorbet

Serve this refreshing sorbet as a palate cleanser between courses.

PREP: 10 minutes **FREEZE:** 4 hours
STAND: 15 minutes

- 1 large avocado, halved, seeded, peeled, and coarsely chopped
- 1 cup half-and-half or light cream
- ⅔ cup sifted powdered sugar
- ½ tsp. finely shredded lemon peel
- ⅓ cup lemon juice

1. In a blender combine avocado, half-and-half, powdered sugar, lemon peel, and lemon juice. Cover and blend until smooth. Pour mixture into a shallow 2-quart freezer container. Cover and freeze at least 4 hours or until firm.

2. Before serving, let stand at room temperature for 15 minutes. To serve, scrape mixture with a small scoop into 8 small dishes. Makes 8 servings.

Each serving: 112 cal., 7 g total fat (3 g sat. fat), 11 mg chol., 15 mg sodium, 12 g carbo., 1 g fiber, 1 g pro. Daily Values: 5% vit. A, 11% vit. C, 3% calcium, 2% iron.

Pistachio-Coconut Sorbet

PREP: 20 minutes **FREEZE:** 5 + 8 hours

- 1 recipe Glazed Pistachios (below)
- 1 13½-oz. can unsweetened coconut milk
- 1 cup cream of coconut
- 1 cup half-and-half or light cream
- 1 tsp. finely shredded lemon peel

1. Prepare Glazed Pistachios; set aside. In a large bowl whisk together the coconut milk, cream of coconut, half-and-half, and lemon peel. Pour into a shallow 2-quart freezer container. Cover; freeze for 5 to 6 hours or until nearly firm, stirring once.

2. Break up frozen mixture. Transfer to a chilled large mixing bowl. Beat with an electric mixer on low to medium speed until smooth but not melted. Stir in glazed pistachio pieces. Return to freezer container. Cover and freeze about 8 hours or overnight until firm.

3. To serve, scoop into 8 small dessert dishes. Makes 8 servings.

GLAZED PISTACHIOS: Butter a 12-inch piece of foil; set aside. In a heavy medium skillet combine ½ cup pistachio nuts, coarsely chopped; ¼ cup sugar; and 1 tablespoon butter. Cook and stir over medium heat for 4 to 6 minutes or until sugar melts and turns a rich brown color. Spread on prepared foil. Cool. Break apart and coarsely crush.

Each serving: 307 cal., 28 g total fat (21 g sat. fat), 15 mg chol., 41 mg sodium, 13 g carbo., 2 g fiber, 4 g pro. Daily Values: 5% vit. A, 3% vit. C, 4% calcium, 8% iron.

Tropical Sorbet

PREP: 30 minutes **FREEZE:** 4 hours
STAND: 10 minutes

- ½ cup water
- ⅓ cup sugar
- ¼ cup light-colored corn syrup
- ½ of a small pineapple, peeled, cored, and chopped (1½ cups)
- 1 medium papaya, peeled, seeded, and chopped (1½ cups)
- 1 medium mango, seeded, peeled, and chopped (1 cup)
- 1 cup unsweetened pineapple juice
- 2 Tbsp. lemon juice

1. In a small saucepan combine the water, sugar, and corn syrup. Bring just to boiling, stirring to dissolve sugar; remove from heat. Cool to room temperature.

2. In a food processor or blender combine half of the fruits and half of the pineapple juice; cover and process or blend until smooth. Transfer to a shallow 3-quart freezer container. Repeat with remaining fruits and pineapple juice; add to container. Stir in the cooled syrup mixture and the lemon juice. Cover and freeze for 4 to 5 hours or just until firm.

3. For a fluffier texture, break up frozen mixture and transfer to a chilled large mixing bowl. Beat with an electric mixer until fluffy but not melted. Return to freezer container. Cover and freeze until firm.

4. Before serving, let stand at room temperature for 10 minutes. To serve, scoop fruit mixture into 8 small dessert dishes. Makes 8 servings.

Each serving: 131 cal., 0 g total fat, 0 mg chol., 17 mg sodium, 34 g carbo., 2 g fiber, 1 g pro. Daily Values: 22% vit. A, 70% vit. C, 2% calcium, 2% iron.

CANDY & FUDGE

PRIZE TESTED RECIPES® $400 WINNER

ELIZABETH WRIGHT, LAS VEGAS, NEV.

Spiced Brandy Truffles

PREP: 30 minutes **CHILL:** 2 hours **STAND:** 30 minutes

- 1 11½-oz. pkg. milk chocolate pieces
- ½ cup chopped walnuts, toasted
- ¼ cup dairy sour cream
- 2 tsp. brandy or ¼ tsp. brandy extract
- ½ tsp. ground nutmeg
- ¼ cup sifted powdered sugar
- ¼ tsp. ground cinnamon

1. In a small heavy saucepan melt chocolate pieces over low heat, stirring constantly. Remove from heat. Stir in walnuts, sour cream, brandy, and ¼ teaspoon of the ground nutmeg. Transfer mixture to a bowl. Cover and chill for at least 2 hours or until chocolate mixture is firm enough to shape into balls.

2. Line a baking sheet with waxed paper; set aside. In a small bowl stir together powdered sugar, cinnamon, and remaining ¼ teaspoon ground nutmeg; set aside.

3. Shape chilled truffle mixture into ¾-inch balls. Roll each ball in the powdered sugar mixture; place on the prepared baking sheet. Cover and chill until firm. Store truffles tightly covered in the refrigerator for up to 2 weeks. Before serving, let stand at room temperature about 30 minutes. Makes about 30 truffles.

Each truffle: 79 cal., 5 g total fat (2 g sat. fat), 3 mg chol., 9 mg sodium, 7 g carbo., 1 g fiber, 1 g pro. Daily Values: 2% iron.

PRIZE TESTED RECIPES® $200 WINNER

DIANNA YOUNGBLOOD, KEENES, ILL.

Pretzel Yummies

PREP: 40 minutes **COOK:** 10 minutes

- 2 cups walnuts (8 oz.)
- 1 cup peanut butter-flavored pieces
- 1 cup milk chocolate pieces
- 1 cup packed brown sugar
- ½ cup light-colored corn syrup
- ¼ cup butter
- ½ of a 14-oz. can (⅔ cup) sweetened condensed milk
- ½ tsp. vanilla
- 20 to 25 pretzel s

1. In a food processor combine walnuts, peanut butter pieces, and chocolate pieces. Cover; process until coarsely chopped. Transfer nut mixture to a large bowl; set aside.

2. In a heavy small saucepan combine brown sugar, corn syrup, and butter. Cook over medium heat until boiling, stirring constantly. Stir in condensed milk. Return to boiling, stirring constantly. Reduce heat to medium-low. Clip a candy thermometer to side of pan. Cook, stirring constantly, until 236° F, soft-ball stage (about 10 minutes). (Adjust heat to maintain a steady boil.) Remove from heat; remove thermometer. Stir in vanilla. Cool for 15 to 20 minutes or until slightly thickened.

3. Dip each pretzel into caramel mixture, covering about ⅔ of the pretzel. Let caramel drip off slightly. Spoon nut mixture onto caramel, pressing lightly with back of a spoon. Let stand on nonstick foil until set. Store in an airtight container between layers of waxed paper in refrigerator for up to 4 days or freeze for up to 1 month. Makes about 25 pretzels.

Each pretzel: 298 cal., 15 g total fat (7 g sat. fat), 10 mg chol., 192 mg sodium, 37 g carbo., 1 g fiber, 6 g pro. Daily Values: 2% vit.A, 1% vit. C, 1% calcium, 2% iron.

Coconut Cashew Pralines

PREP: 15 minutes **COOK:** 21 minutes
COOL: 30 minutes

- 1½ **cups granulated sugar**
- 1½ **cups packed brown sugar**
- 1 **cup half-and-half or light cream**
- 3 **Tbsp. butter**
- 2 **cups lightly salted roasted cashews**
- 1 **cup flaked coconut, toasted***

1. Butter the sides of a heavy 2-quart saucepan. In the saucepan combine the granulated sugar, brown sugar, and half-and-half. Cook over medium-high heat until boiling, stirring to dissolve sugar. Clip a candy thermometer to side of pan. Reduce heat to medium-low; continue boiling at a moderate steady rate, stirring occasionally, until thermometer registers 234° F, soft-ball stage (16 to 18 minutes).

2. Remove saucepan from heat. Add butter, but do not stir. Cool, without stirring, to 150° F (about 30 minutes).

3. Remove thermometer from pan. Stir in cashews and coconut. Beat vigorously with a clean wooden spoon until mixture just begins to thicken but is still glossy (about 3 minutes).

4. Working quickly, drop candy by spoonfuls onto waxed paper. Let stand until firm. Store tightly covered for up to 1 week. Makes about 60 candies.

***NOTE:** To toast coconut, spread the coconut in a single layer in a shallow baking pan. Bake in a 350° F oven for 5 to 8 minutes or until light golden brown, watching carefully and stirring once or twice so the coconut doesn't burn.

Each candy: 83 cal., 4 g total fat (2 g sat. fat), 3 mg chol., 23 mg sodium, 12 g carbo., 0 g fiber, 1 g pro. Daily Values: 1% vit. A, 1% calcium, 2% iron.

Peanut Granola Balls

PREP: 1 hour **FREEZE:** 40 minutes

- 2 **cups low-fat granola (without raisins), coarsely crushed**
- 1 **cup creamy peanut butter**
- ¼ **cup honey**
- 1 **lb. vanilla-flavored candy wafers or candy coating, chopped**
- 3 **cups finely chopped lightly salted peanuts**

1. In a medium bowl stir together granola, peanut butter, and honey. Drop from a teaspoon onto a waxed paper-lined cookie sheet. Freeze for 20 minutes.

2. Meanwhile, in a medium saucepan melt candy wafers or candy coating over very low heat, stirring constantly. Remove from heat.

3. Shape granola mixture into smooth balls. Dip balls in melted candy to coat; lift with a fork, allowing excess candy to drip off. Roll balls in peanuts; return to waxed paper-lined cookie sheet. Freeze for 20 minutes more or until set. Store tightly covered in the refrigerator for up to 1 week or in the freezer for up to 1 month. Makes about 60 pieces.

Each piece: 128 cal., 8 g total fat (3 g sat. fat), 0 mg chol., 28 mg sodium, 11 g carbo., 1 g fiber, 3 g pro. Daily Values: 1% vit. A, 1% calcium, 2% iron.

Coconut-Cranberry Bark

PREP: 15 minutes **CHILL:** 10 minutes

- 1 **11- to 12-oz. pkg. white baking pieces**
- ⅓ **cup coconut**
- ⅓ **cup toasted slivered almonds**
- ¼ **cup raisins**
- ¼ **cup dried cranberries or coarsely chopped dried tart cherries**

1. Line a baking sheet with foil. Melt baking pieces according to package directions. Quickly stir in coconut, almonds, raisins, and dried fruit. Spread on prepared baking sheet. If necessary, place in the refrigerator about 10 minutes or until set.

2. When ready to serve, break candy into irregular pieces. Store tightly covered at room temperature for up to 1 week. Makes about 1 pound (36 pieces).

Each piece: 67 cal., 4 g total fat (2 g sat. fat), 2 mg chol., 13 mg sodium, 7 g carbo., 0 g fiber, 1 g pro. Daily Values: 2% calcium.

Double-Chocolate Raspberry Creams

PREP: 40 minutes **CHILL:** 3 hours
STAND: 15 minutes

- 1 **lb. vanilla-flavored candy coating, chopped**
- ½ **of a 14-oz. can (⅔ cup) sweetened condensed milk**
- ¼ **cup seedless raspberry preserves**
- 4 **drops raspberry oil or ¼ tsp. raspberry flavoring**
- 14 **oz. chocolate-flavored candy coating, chopped**

1. In a medium saucepan combine vanilla-flavored candy coating, sweetened condensed milk, and preserves. Cook and stir over low heat until melted. Remove from heat; stir in raspberry oil or flavoring. Transfer to a bowl. Cover and chill for 2 to 3 hours or until just firm.

2. Line a 15×10×1-inch baking pan with waxed paper. With damp hands, shape candy mixture into ¾-inch balls; place on the prepared pan. Chill for 1 hour.

3. In a small saucepan melt chocolate-flavored candy coating over low heat until smooth. Dip raspberry balls into chocolate mixture to coat; allow excess chocolate to drip off. Arrange on the waxed paper-lined baking sheet; let stand until chocolate is set, about 15 minutes. Makes 4 dozen.

Each candy: 118 cal., 6 g total fat (5 g sat. fat), 1 mg chol., 6 mg sodium, 15 g carbo., 0 g fiber, 0 g pro. Daily Values: 2% calcium.

CHEESY APPETIZERS

PRIZE TESTED RECIPES® $400 WINNER

DEBBIE VANNI, LIBERTYVILLE, ILL.

Feta Custard in Phyllo Cups

PREP: 30 minutes **BAKE:** 15 minutes

- 30 Phyllo Cups (see page 559) or $1^3/_4$-inch baked miniature phyllo shells (two 2.1-oz. pkg.)
- 1 4-oz. pkg. crumbled feta cheese
- 1 3-oz. pkg. cream cheese, softened
- 1 egg
- 2 tsp. lemon juice
- 1 tsp. all-purpose flour
- ⅓ cup pitted kalamata olives, chopped
- ½ tsp. dried oregano, crushed
- ½ tsp. olive oil
- ¼ tsp. balsamic vinegar
- 1 clove garlic, minced
- Dash ground cumin
- Dash ground red pepper

1. Preheat oven to 325° F. Place Phyllo Cups on a large baking sheet. Set aside.

2. For filling, in a bowl combine feta cheese, cream cheese, egg, lemon juice, and flour. Beat with an electric mixer until nearly smooth. Spoon into cups, using a scant 2 teaspoons for each cup. Bake for 15 to 17 minutes or until golden and crisp.

3. For topping, in a bowl stir together olives, oregano, olive oil, vinegar, garlic, cumin, and red pepper; sprinkle evenly over custards. Serve warm. If desired, sprinkle with snipped fresh parsley or oregano. Makes 30 appetizers.

Each appetizer: 49 cal., 3 g total fat (1 g sat. fat), 14 mg chol., 79 mg sodium, 3 g carbo., 1 g pro. Daily Values: 2% vit. A, 1% vit. C, 2% calcium, 1% iron.

PRIZE TESTED RECIPES® $200 WINNER

LAURIE ROBINSON, TONASKET, WASH.

Fruited Cheese Log

PREP: 20 minutes **STAND:** 1 hour **CHILL:** 4 hours

- ½ cup snipped dried apricots
- 8 oz. shredded Monterey Jack cheese (2 cups)
- ½ of an 8-oz. pkg. cream cheese
- 2 Tbsp. orange juice
- ⅓ cup golden raisins, chopped
- ¼ cup pitted whole dates, snipped
- ¼ tsp. salt
- Chopped toasted almonds (optional)
- Assorted crackers and/or apple slices

1. In a bowl soak apricots in 1 cup water about 1 hour or until softened. Drain well; set aside. Let cheeses stand in a bowl 30 minutes or until room temperature.

2. Add orange juice to cheese mixture. Beat with an electric mixer on medium speed until combined. Stir in apricots, raisins, dates, and salt. Divide mixture in half.

3. On a large piece of waxed paper, shape each portion into a 5-inch-long log. Wrap in plastic wrap; chill for 4 to 24 hours. If desired, roll in nuts before serving. Serve with assorted crackers and/or apple slices. Makes 32 servings.

Each serving: 53 cal., 3 g total fat (2 g sat. fat), 10 mg chol., 67 mg sodium, 4 g carbo., 0 g fiber, 2 g pro. Daily Values: 5% vit. A, 1% vit. C, 6% calcium, 1% iron.

Phyllo Cups

PREP: 30 minutes **BAKE:** 8 minutes

1. Preheat oven to 350° F. Grease thirty-six 1¾-inch muffin cups; set aside. Cover 4 sheets of frozen phyllo dough (18×14-inch rectangles), thawed, with plastic wrap to prevent them from becoming dry and brittle. Lightly brush 1 sheet of phyllo dough with some of ¼ cup melted butter. Stack 3 more sheets, brushing between each layer with melted butter.

2. Cut phyllo stack lengthwise into six 18-inch-long strips. Cut each strip crosswise into six 3-inch-long rectangles. Press each rectangle into a prepared cup, pleating as needed to fit. Bake for 8 to 10 minutes or until golden. Fill and bake as directed for Feta Custard in Phyllo Cups (see page 558). (Wrap and freeze any leftover cups for up to 3 months.) Makes 36.

Savory Baked Brie

PREP: 20 minutes **BAKE:** 20 minutes

- 1 **13½-oz. round Brie cheese**
- 2 **Tbsp. snipped fresh thyme or oregano**
- ¼ **cup pine nuts, toasted**
- 3 **slices provolone cheese (about 2½ oz.)**
- **Crackers, toasted baguette slices, and/or apple or pear slices**

1. Unwrap Brie. Using a sharp knife, slice off the top of the rind. Set in a 9-inch glass pie plate. Sprinkle with thyme and pine nuts. Overlap provolone slices on Brie; tuck ends underneath, if necessary.

2. Place pie plate in a cool oven. Turn oven to 325° F. Bake for 20 to 25 minutes or cheese is softened.

3. Serve with crackers, baguette slices, and apple or pear slices*. Makes 8 servings.

***TEST KITCHEN TIP:** To prevent discoloration, treat apple or pear slices with citric acid color keeper or dip into a mixture of lemon juice and water.

Each serving: 215 cal., 18 g total fat (10 g sat. fat), 53 mg chol., 374 mg sodium,

Feta-Olive Wafers

PREP: 20 minutes **CHILL:** 4 hours **BAKE:** about 15 minutes

- 1 **4-oz. pkg. crumbled feta cheese (1 cup)**
- ½ **cup butter, softened**
- 1 **egg**
- 1 **Tbsp. dried Greek seasoning, crushed**
- 1⅔ **cups all-purpose flour**
- ¼ **cup pitted kalamata olives (about 10 olives), drained and finely chopped**
- 1 **Tbsp. oil-packed dried tomatoes, drained and finely chopped**

1. In a large mixing bowl beat feta cheese and butter with an electric mixer on medium speed until combined. Beat in egg and Greek seasoning. Beat in as much of the flour as you can with the mixer. Stir in the remaining flour.

2. With your hands, knead in the olives and tomatoes. Divide dough in half; shape each portion into a 5¾-inch-long log. Wrap in plastic wrap or waxed paper; chill for 4 to 24 hours.

3. Preheat oven to 375° F. Cut each log into ¼-inch-thick slices. Place 1 inch apart on an ungreased baking sheet. Bake about 15 minutes or until edges begin to brown. Serve warm or at room temperature. Makes about 40 wafers.

Each wafer: 50 cal., 3 g total fat (2 g sat. fat), 14 mg chol., 74 mg sodium, 4 g carbo., 0 g fiber, 1 g pro. Daily Values: 2% vit. A, 2% calcium, 1% iron.

Goat Cheese and Spinach Pesto Bites

PREP: 25 minutes **BAKE:** 12 minutes

- ¾ **cup packed fresh basil leaves**
- ⅔ **cup packed fresh spinach leaves**
- 2 **Tbsp. pine nuts**
- 1 **Tbsp. olive oil**
- 4 **oz. soft goat cheese (chèvre)**
- ¼ **cup hazelnuts, toasted and very finely chopped**
- 2 **Tbsp. grated Parmesan cheese**
- 8 **sheets frozen phyllo dough (18×12-inch rectangles), thawed**
- ⅓ **cup butter, melted**

1. Preheat oven to 400° F. For filling, in a food processor bowl or blender container combine basil, spinach, and pine nuts. Cover and process or blend with several on/off turns until paste forms, stopping machine several times and scraping sides down as needed. With machine running, slowly add the olive oil and process until almost smooth. Transfer to a bowl; stir in goat cheese, hazelnuts, and Parmesan cheese. Set aside.

2. Cover phyllo with plastic wrap to prevent it from becoming dry and brittle. Lightly brush a sheet of phyllo with some of the melted butter. Place another sheet of phyllo on top; brush with butter. Cut crosswise into eight 12-inch-long strips. Spoon a well rounded teaspoon of filling about 1 inch from an end of each dough strip. To fold into a triangle, bring a corner over filling so it lines up with the other side of the strip. Continue folding strip in a triangular shape. Repeat with remaining sheets of phyllo, melted butter, and filling.

3. Place triangles on an ungreased baking sheet; brush with any remaining butter. Bake for 12 to 15 minutes or until golden. Serve warm. Makes 24 servings.

Each serving: 76 cal., 6 g total fat (3 g sat. fat), 10 mg chol., 84 mg sodium, 4 g carbo., 0 g fiber, 2 g pro. Daily Values: 4% vit. A, 1% vit. C, 2% calcium, 3% iron.

BEST BREAD MACHINE BREADS

PRIZE TESTED RECIPES® $400 WINNER

GAIL ST. MARIE, PINE RIVER, MINN.

Cranberry-Peanut Butter Bread

No bread machine? No worries. Just follow the conventional directions on page 561.

PREP: 10 minutes

- 3/4 cup water
- 1/2 cup milk
- 1 egg
- 1/2 cup creamy peanut butter
- 3 Tbsp. honey
- 1 Tbsp. butter or margarine
- 3 cups whole wheat flour
- 2 Tbsp. gluten flour*
- 1 1/2 tsp. salt
- 2 1/4 tsp. active dry yeast or bread machine yeast
- 1 cup dried cranberries

1. Add ingredients to a 1 1/2- or 2-pound loaf bread machine according to manufacturer's directions. (The pan must have a capacity of 10 cups or more.) Select the basic white bread cycle and, if available, the light setting. Makes 1 loaf (16 slices).

***TEST KITCHEN TIP:** Look for gluten flour in health food stores or the baking aisle. You need this high-protein, hard-wheat flour to give the bread elasticity.

Each slice: 179 cal., 6 g total fat (2 g sat. fat), 16 mg chol., 274 mg sodium, 28 g carbo., 4 g fiber, 6 g pro. Daily Values: 1% vit. A, 2% calcium, 7% iron.

PRIZE TESTED RECIPES® $200 WINNER

TODD HOPKINS, VANCOUVER, WASH.

Salsa Bread

Make a tasty Tex-Mex sandwich with cream cheese, chicken, and roasted peppers. See page 561 for conventional directions.

PREP: 10 minutes

- 1 cup bottled chunky salsa
- 1/3 cup water
- 1 Tbsp. cooking oil
- Dash bottled hot pepper sauce
- 3 cups bread flour
- 1 Tbsp. sugar
- 1/2 tsp. ground cumin
- 1/2 tsp. chili powder
- 1/4 to 1/2 tsp. ground red pepper
- 2 tsp. active dry yeast or bread machine yeast

1. Add ingredients to a 1 1/2- or 2-pound loaf bread machine according to manufacturer's directions. Select the basic white bread cycle and desired color setting. Makes 1 loaf (10 to 12 slices).

Each slice: 172 cal., 2 g total fat (0 g sat. fat), 0 mg chol., 59 mg sodium, 32 g carbo., 1 g fiber, 5 g pro. Daily Values: 3% vit. A, 3% vit. C, 1% calcium, 12% iron.

Cranberry-Peanut Butter Bread

Prep: 30 minutes **Stand:** 2 hours
Bake: 30 minutes

CONVENTIONAL METHOD:

1. In a large mixing bowl stir together 1¼ cups all-purpose flour and yeast; set aside (omit the gluten flour).

2. In a small saucepan heat and stir the water, milk, only ⅓ cup peanut butter, the honey, butter, and salt just until warm (120° to 130° F) and butter almost melts.

3. Add warm mixture to dry mixture; add egg. Beat with an electric mixer on low to medium speed for 30 seconds, scraping bowl. Beat on high speed for 3 minutes. Using a wooden spoon, stir in only 1½ cups whole wheat flour, cranberries, and enough all-purpose flour (about ½ cup) to make dough easy to handle.

4. Turn out onto a floured surface. Knead in ⅓ to ⅔ cup more all-purpose flour to make a moderately soft dough that is smooth and elastic (3 to 5 minutes total). Shape into a ball. Place in a greased bowl; turn once. Cover; let rise in a warm place until double in size (1 to 1¼ hours).

5. Punch dough down. Turn out onto a lightly floured surface. Cover and let rest 10 minutes. Lightly grease an 9×5×3-inch loaf pan. Shape dough into a loaf. Place in pan. Cover; let rise in a warm place until nearly double (about 45 minutes).

6. Preheat oven to 375° F; bake for 30 to 35 minutes or until top sounds hollow when tapped (if necessary, cover loosely with foil the last 10 minutes of baking to prevent overbrowning). Immediately remove from pan. Cool on a wire rack. Makes 1 loaf (16 slices).

Salsa Bread

Prep: 30 minutes **Stand:** 1½ hours
Bake: 30 minutes

CONVENTIONAL METHOD:

1. In a large mixing bowl combine 1 cup of the bread flour (use 2½ to 3 cups total bread flour), yeast, cumin, chili powder, and ground red pepper; set aside.

2. In a small saucepan heat and stir salsa, water, sugar, oil, and hot pepper sauce just until warm (120° to 130° F).

3. Add to dry mixture. Beat with an electric mixer on low to medium speed for 30 seconds, scraping side of bowl constantly. Beat on high speed for 3 minutes. Using a wooden spoon, stir in as much of the remaining flour as you can.

4. Turn the dough out onto a lightly floured surface. Knead in enough of the remaining flour to make a moderately stiff dough that is smooth and elastic (6 to 8 minutes total). Shape into a ball. Place in a lightly greased bowl; turn once to grease surface. Cover; let rise in a warm place until double (45 to 60 minutes).

5. Punch dough down. Turn dough out onto a lightly floured surface. Cover; let rest 10 minutes. Meanwhile, lightly grease one 8×4×2-inch loaf pan. Shape dough into a loaf. Place in the prepared pan. Cover and let rise in a warm place until nearly double in size (about 30 minutes).

6. Preheat oven to 375° F; bake about 30 minutes or until bread sounds hollow when lightly tapped (if necessary, cover loosely with foil the last 10 minutes of baking to prevent overbrowning). Immediately remove from pan. Cool on a wire rack. Makes 1 loaf (10 to 12 slices).

Stout Asiago Foccacia Bread

Prep: 15 minutes **Stand:** 20 minutes
Bake: 20 minutes

- 1 **cup stout or dark beer**
- 1 **Tbsp. butter**
- 2½ **cups bread flour**
- 2 **Tbsp. sugar**
- 1 **tsp. salt**
- 2¾ **tsp. active dry yeast**
- 2 **tsp. olive oil**
- ¼ **cup finely shredded Asiago cheese**
- ½ **tsp. dried Italian seasoning, crushed**
- 1 **clove garlic, minced**
- ¼ **tsp. coarsely ground black pepper**

1. Add beer, butter, flour, sugar, salt, and yeast to a 1½- or 2-pound loaf bread machine according to manufacturer's directions. Select the dough cycle. When the cycle is complete, transfer dough to a lightly floured surface. Cover and let rest for 10 minutes.

2. Preheat oven to 350° F. Transfer dough to a large greased baking sheet or 14-inch pizza pan. Pat dough into a 12-inch circle. Brush with olive oil. With floured fingers, make ½-inch-deep indentations every 2 inches on the surface.

3. In a small mixing bowl combine cheese, Italian seasoning, garlic, and pepper. Sprinkle onto dough. Cover and let stand in a warm place for 20 minutes (for conventional method, let stand for 30 to 40 minutes or until puffed).

4. Bake in the preheated oven for 20 to 25 minutes or until golden brown. Serve warm. Makes 8 to 10 servings.

CONVENTIONAL METHOD:

1. In a large mixing bowl stir together 1 cup of the bread flour (use 2½ to 2¾ cups total flour) and yeast.

2. In a medium saucepan heat and stir stout, butter, sugar, and salt until warm (120° to 130° F) and butter almost melts.

3. Add to flour mixture. Beat with an electric mixer on low speed for 30 seconds, scraping side of bowl. Beat on high speed for 3 minutes. Using a wooden spoon, stir in as much of the flour as you can.

4. Turn dough out onto a lightly floured surface. Knead in enough of the remaining flour to make a moderately stiff dough that is smooth and elastic (6 to 8 minutes total). Shape into a ball. Place in a lightly greased bowl; turn once to grease surface. Cover; let rise in a warm place until double in size (about 1 hour).

5. Punch dough down. Cover and let rest for 10 minutes. Continue as directed from step 2 of the recipe above.

Each slice: 225 cal., 5 g total fat (2 g sat. fat), 8 mg chol., 347 mg sodium, 36 g carbo., 1 g fiber, 7 g pro. Daily Values: 1% vit. A, 3% calcium, 12% iron.

WAFFLES & FRENCH TOAST

PRIZE TESTED RECIPES® $400 WINNER

JOAN KOVACH, ORANGE PARK, FLA.

PRIZE TESTED RECIPES® $200 WINNER

SHELLY PLATTEN, AMHERST, WIS.

Berry-Nut French Toast

PREP: 10 minutes **COOK:** 4 minutes

- 2 cups multi-grain flakes with oat clusters, cranberries, and almonds
- 4 eggs
- 1/2 tsp. ground cinnamon
- 1/4 tsp. ground nutmeg
- 4 3/4-inch-thick slices French or Italian bread
- 2 Tbsp. butter
- Fruit-flavored syrup, maple syrup, or apricot preserves, warmed

1. In a shallow dish coarsely crush cereal; set aside. In another dish beat eggs; stir in cinnamon and nutmeg. Dip bread slices into egg mixture until moistened, turning to coat. Dip both sides into crushed cereal until coated.

2. In a large skillet or griddle cook bread in hot butter over medium-low heat about 2 minutes on each side or until golden. Serve with syrup. Makes 2 servings.

Each serving: 606 cal., 27 g total fat (11 g sat. fat), 458 mg chol., 765 mg sodium, 72 g carbo., 5 g fiber, 21 g pro. Daily Values: 37% vit. A, 26% iron.

Waffles with Salsa

PREP: 25 minutes **BAKE:** 3 minutes per waffle

- 1 cup all-purpose flour
- 1/2 cup yellow cornmeal
- 2 Tbsp. sugar
- 1 Tbsp. baking powder
- 2 tsp. chili powder
- 1/2 tsp. salt
- 1 egg
- 1 cup buttermilk
- 2 Tbsp. cooking oil
- 1 4-oz. can diced green chile peppers, drained
- 1 recipe Jicama-Bean Salsa (below)
- 3/4 cup bottled salsa
- Dairy sour cream (optional)

1. Combine flour, cornmeal, sugar, baking powder, chili powder, and salt. Beat together egg, buttermilk, and oil; add to flour mixture. Stir until mixed. Stir in peppers.

2. Pour batter onto grids of a preheated, lightly greased waffle baker. Bake according to manufacturer's directions. Serve warm with Jicama-Bean Salsa and bottled salsa. If desired, top with sour cream. Makes 10 to 12 (4-inch) waffles.

JICAMA-BEAN SALSA: Halve, seed, peel, and chop 1 avocado. Coarsely chop 1 medium tomato. In a medium bowl combine avocado; tomato; 1/2 of a 15-ounce can black beans, rinsed and drained; 1/4 cup chopped, peeled jicama; 1/4 cup chopped red onion; and 1 tablespoon snipped fresh cilantro. Makes about 2 1/2 cups.

Each waffle with salsa: 174 cal., 7 g total fat (1 g sat. fat), 22 mg chol., 403 mg sodium, 24 g carbo., 3 g fiber, 6 g pro. Daily Values: 10% vit. A, 17% vit. C, 13% calcium, 9% iron.

Peaches-and-Cream Stuffed French Toast

PREP: 30 minutes
COOK: 4 minutes per batch

- 1/4 cup butter
- 1 8-oz. pkg. reduced-fat or regular cream cheese, softened
- 1/4 cup sifted powdered sugar
- 1 tsp. vanilla
- 1 29-oz. can peach slices, drained
- 16 1/2-inch-thick slices challah bread or French bread
- 6 eggs
- 1 cup half-and-half, light cream, or whipping cream
- 1/4 tsp. ground cinnamon
- 2 Tbsp. butter or cooking oil
- 1 recipe Spiced Peach Sauce (below)

1. In a saucepan melt 1/4 cup butter over medium heat. Cook and stir about 5 minutes until golden brown. Let cool.

2. For filling, in a medium mixing bowl combine cream cheese, powdered sugar, and vanilla; beat until smooth. Gradually beat in cooled butter. Chop enough of the peaches to equal 1/2 cup; stir into filling. Reserve remaining peaches for sauce.

3. Spread about 3 tablespoons filling onto one side of half of the bread slices. Top with remaining bread slices. (You will have eight "sandwiches" total.)

4. In a shallow dish beat eggs; stir in half-and-half and cinnamon. Dip sandwiches into egg mixture about 15 seconds on each side or until moistened.

5. In a large skillet or griddle cook sandwiches in the 2 tablespoons hot butter or oil over medium heat for 2 to 3 minutes on each side or until golden, adding more butter, if needed. Serve warm with Spiced Peach Sauce. Makes 8 servings.

SPICED PEACH SAUCE: In a medium saucepan stir together 1/4 cup packed brown sugar, 2 tablespoons cornstarch, and 1/4 teaspoon ground cinnamon. Stir in 2 cups peach nectar. Cook and stir over medium heat until thickened and bubbly. Cook and stir for 2 minutes more. Stir in 1/2 teaspoon vanilla and reserved peach slices. Heat through. Makes 2 1/4 cups.

TEST KITCHEN TIP: To keep French toast warm, place it on a baking sheet in a 300° F oven.

Each serving with sauce: 505 cal., 25 g total fat (14 g sat. fat), 237 mg chol., 494 mg sodium, 58 g carbo., 3 g fiber, 13 g pro. Daily Values: 31% vit. A, 10% vit. C, 13% calcium, 14% iron.

Baked French Toast with Orange-Maple Sauce

PREP: 15 minutes **BAKE:** 11 minutes

- 2 Tbsp. butter, cut up
- 3 eggs
- 1/4 cup milk
- 2 Tbsp. sugar
- 2 Tbsp. frozen orange juice concentrate, thawed
- 1/4 tsp. ground cinnamon
- 1/4 tsp. almond extract
- 8 3/4-inch-thick slices firm-textured French bread
- 1 recipe Orange-Maple Sauce (below)
- 1 recipe Almond Whipped Cream (below) (optional)
- 1/4 cup sliced almonds, toasted

1. Preheat oven to 400° F. Place butter in a 15×10×1-inch baking pan. Heat in oven for 2 to 3 minutes or until butter is melted. Carefully remove from oven with pot holders, tilting pan to coat.

2. Meanwhile, in a shallow dish beat eggs; stir in milk, juice concentrate, sugar, cinnamon, and almond extract. Dip bread into egg mixture about 30 seconds on each side or until moistened.

3. Arrange bread in a single layer in the prepared pan. Bake, uncovered, about 6 minutes or until golden. Turn bread; bake 5 to 8 minutes more or until golden.

4. Serve warm with Orange-Maple Sauce. If desired, top with Almond Whipped Cream. Sprinkle with almonds. Makes 8 servings.

ORANGE-MAPLE SAUCE: In saucepan heat and stir 1 cup pure maple syrup or maple-flavored syrup, 1/4 cup orange marmalade, and a dash ground cinnamon. Stir in one 11-ounce can mandarin orange sections, drained; heat through. Makes 2 cups.

ALMOND WHIPPED CREAM: In a chilled bowl combined 1/2 cup whipping cream, 1 tablespoon sifted powdered sugar, and several drops almond extract. Beat with chilled beaters of an electric mixer until soft peaks form (tips curl). Makes 1 cup.

Each serving with sauce: 324 cal., 8 g total fat (3 g sat. fat), 88 mg chol., 222 mg sodium, 59 g carbo., 2 g fiber, 6 g pro.Daily Values: 12% vit. A, 24% vit. C, 8% calcium, 10% iron.

Praline-Glazed French Toast

PREP: 20 minutes
COOK: 4 minutes per batch
BROIL: 2 minutes

- 6 1-inch-thick slices French bread
- 1/4 cup butter, softened
- 1/4 cup packed brown sugar
- 1 Tbsp. light-colored corn syrup
- 1/8 tsp. ground cinnamon
- 1/4 cup chopped pecans
- 3 eggs
- 1 cup half-and-half, light cream, or whipping cream
- 1/2 tsp. vanilla
- 1/4 tsp. ground cinnamon
- 1/4 tsp. ground nutmeg
- Fresh peach slices (optional)
- Whipped cream (optional)

1. Preheat broiler. Arrange bread slices on a baking sheet. Broil 4 inches from the heat about 1 minute per side or until toasted. Set aside.

2. For topping, in a small bowl stir together softened butter, brown sugar, corn syrup, and 1/8 teaspoon cinnamon. Stir in pecans; set aside.

3. In a shallow dish beat eggs; stir in 1 cup half-and-half, vanilla, 1/4 teaspoon cinnamon, and nutmeg until blended. Dip bread into egg mixture about 30 seconds on each side or until moistened.

4. In a lightly buttered skillet or griddle cook bread slices over medium heat for 2 to 3 minutes on each side or until golden. Arrange cooked slices on baking sheet. Spread with topping.

5. Broil slices 4 inches from the heat about 2 minutes or until topping is golden and bubbly. Serve warm with fresh peach slices and whipped cream, if desired. Makes 6 servings.

Each serving: 306 cal., 19 g total fat (9 g sat. fat), 143 mg chol., 290 mg sodium, 27 g carbo., 1 g fiber, 7 g pro. Daily Values: 13% vit. A, 1% vit. C, 9% calcium, 8% iron.

CHICKEN SALADS

PRIZE TESTED RECIPES® $400 WINNER

JULIA GROVER, TUCSON, ARIZ.

Grilled Chicken Salad

PREP: 15 minutes **COOK:** 12 minutes

- 4 skinless, boneless chicken breast halves (1¼ to 1½ lb.)
- Montreal or Kansas City steak seasoning
- 8 cups torn mixed salad greens
- ¾ cup seedless red grapes, halved
- ⅓ cup crumbled goat cheese (chèvre)
- ¼ cup pine nuts, toasted
- 1 recipe Dill Vinaigrette (below)

1. Sprinkle chicken with seasoning. Grill on rack of uncovered grill directly over medium coals for 12 to 15 minutes or until no longer pink (170° F), turning once.

2. Arrange greens on four plates; top with grapes, cheese, and nuts. Slice chicken; arrange on salads. Shake Dill Vinaigrette; drizzle over salads. Makes 4 servings.

DILL VINAIGRETTE: In a screw-top jar combine ¼ cup grapeseed oil or olive oil; 3 tablespoons balsamic vinegar; 1 tablespoon dried dillweed; 1 large clove garlic, minced; ¼ teaspoon pepper; and ¼ teaspoon dried oregano, crushed. Cover and shake well to mix; let stand for 1 hour. Makes ½ cup.

Each serving: 400 cal., 23 g total fat (4 g sat. fat), 86 mg chol., 167 mg sodium, 12 g carbo., 2 g fiber, 38 g pro. Daily Values: 22% vit. A, 21% vit. C, 9% calcium, 18% iron.

PRIZE TESTED RECIPES® $200 WINNER

CAMILLA SORENSON, ADA, MINN.

Mediterranean Chicken Salad

PREP: 30 minutes **CHILL:** up to 2 hours

- 1 lb. cooked chicken, shredded or cut into bite-size strips (3 cups)
- ½ of a medium cucumber, halved lengthwise, seeded, and sliced
- 1 cup chopped celery
- ½ cup sliced pitted kalamata olives
- ½ cup chopped walnuts
- 1 13¾-oz. can artichoke hearts, drained and quartered
- ⅓ cup sliced green onion
- 1 recipe Sherry-Lemon Vinaigrette (below)
- 2 cups fresh spinach leaves
- Snipped fresh parsley (optional)

1. In a large mixing bowl combine chicken, cucumber, celery, olives, walnuts, artichokes, and green onion. Stir Sherry-Lemon Vinaigrette; pour over chicken mixture. Toss gently to coat. Cover and chill for up to 2 hours.

2. Arrange spinach on six salad plates. Top with chicken mixture. If desired, sprinkle with parsley. Makes 6 servings.

SHERRY-LEMON VINAIGRETTE: 1. In a blender container or food processor bowl combine ½ of a small lemon, seeded and cut into 6 wedges; ½ cup olive oil; ¼ cup sugar; ¼ cup sherry vinegar or white wine vinegar; ½ teaspoon salt; and ¼ teaspoon pepper. Cover; blend until nearly smooth. Makes 1 cup

Each serving: 451 cal., 32 g total fat (5 g sat. fat), 67 mg chol., 628 mg sodium, 17 g carbo., 5 g fiber, 25 g pro. Daily Values: 18% vit. A, 25% vit. C, 7% calcium, 18% iron.

Cherry-Cashew Chicken Salad

PREP: 25 minutes **CHILL:** 2 hours

- **1/2 cup light mayonnaise dressing or salad dressing**
- **1/4 cup orange marmalade**
- **1 Tbsp. lemon juice**
- **1/4 tsp. salt**
- **1/4 tsp. ground nutmeg**
- **1/4 tsp. pepper**
- **5 cups cubed cooked chicken**
- **1/3 cup dried tart red cherries**
- **1/4 cup thinly sliced green onion**
- **1 1/2 cups cubed cantaloupe**
- **1/2 cup cashews**
- **1 medium orange, peeled and sliced**
- **6 cups shredded fresh spinach**

1. In a large bowl stir together dressing, marmalade, lemon juice, salt, nutmeg, and pepper. Fold in chicken, cherries, and green onion. Cover; chill for 2 to 24 hours.

2. Before serving, fold in cantaloupe and cashews. Quarter orange slices; fold in. Serve atop spinach. Makes 8 servings.

Each serving: 329 cal., 16 g total fat (4 g sat. fat), 83 mg chol., 277 mg sodium, 20 g carbo., 3 g fiber, 28 g pro. Daily Values: 47% vit. A, 48% vit. C, 5% calcium, 19% iron.

Thai Chicken Salad

For this and many other salads, you can make the dressing ahead and let it chill for up to two days to blend the flavors.

PREP: 30 minutes **MARINATE:** 2 hours **COOK:** 12 minutes

- **4 skinless, boneless chicken breast halves (1 1/4 to 1 1/2 lb.)**
- **2 Tbsp. rice vinegar**
- **1 Tbsp. reduced-sodium soy sauce**
- **1 tsp. toasted sesame oil**
- **1/4 tsp. grated fresh ginger**
- **1/8 tsp. ground white pepper**
- **2 cups fresh pea pods, trimmed and strings removed**
- **8 cups torn mixed salad greens**
- **1 recipe Peanut-Sesame Vinaigrette (below)**
- **Toasted sesame seed (optional)**

1. Place chicken breast halves in a plastic bag. For marinade, combine rice vinegar, soy sauce, sesame oil, ginger, and white pepper; pour over chicken. Close bag; marinate in the refrigerator for 2 to 24 hours, turning bag occasionally.

2. Drain chicken; discard marinade. Grill chicken on the rack of an uncovered grill directly over medium coals for 12 to 15 minutes or until tender and no longer pink (170° F), turning once.

3. Meanwhile, in a saucepan cook pea pods in a small amount of boiling water for 1 to 2 minutes or until crisp-tender; drain.

4. To serve, diagaonally cut chicken breast halves into thin slices. Arrange greens on a serving platter or four salad plates. Top with sliced chicken and pea pods. Stir Peanut-Sesame Vinaigrette; pour over salad. If desired, sprinkle with sesame seed. Makes 4 servings.

PEANUT-SESAME VINAIGRETTE: In a small bowl whisk 1/4 cup salad oil into 2 tablespoons peanut butter. Stir in 3 tablespoons rice vinegar, 1 tablespoon reduced-sodium soy sauce, 1 teaspoon brown sugar, 1/2 teaspoon toasted sesame oil, and 1/4 to 1/2 teaspoon crushed red pepper. Makes 1/2 cup.

Each serving: 407 cal., 23 g total fat (4 g sat. fat), 82 mg chol., 419 mg sodium, 9 g carbo., 3 g fiber, 38 g pro. Daily Values: 11% vit. A, 14% vit. C, 7% calcium, 13% iron.

Greek Chicken Salad

PREP: 30 minutes **CHILL:** up to 2 hours

- **1 9-oz. pkg. frozen artichoke hearts**
- **2 cups cubed cooked chicken**
- **1 cup cherry tomatoes, halved**
- **1 small red onion, cut into slivers**
- **1 recipe Honey-Mustard Vinaigrette (right)**
- **8 cups torn mixed salad greens**
- **3 Tbsp. pine nuts, toasted**
- **1/4 cup crumbled feta cheese**

1. Cook artichokes according to package direction; drain. In a large salad bowl combine artichokes, chicken, tomatoes, and red onion. Shake Honey-Dijon Vinaigrette; pour over salad and toss to coat. Cover and chill for up to 2 hours.

2. Toss chicken mixture with greens and pine nuts. Sprinkle with feta cheese. Makes 4 servings.

HONEY MUSTARD VINAIGRETTE: In a screw-top jar combine 1/4 cup olive oil; 1/4 cup balsamic vinegar; 2 tablespoons honey mustard; 1 clove garlic, minced; 1/4 teaspoon salt; and 1/8 teaspoon pepper. Cover; shake well to mix. Makes 2/3 cup.

Each serving: 405 cal., 24 g total fat (5 g sat. fat), 69 mg chol., 363 mg sodium, 22 g carbo., 6 g fiber, 27 g pro. Daily Values: 16% vit. A, 34% vit. C, 10% calcium, 18% iron.

Orange-Barley Chicken Salad

PREP: 25 minutes **CHILL:** 1 hour

- **1/2 cup quick-cooking barley**
- **Leaf lettuce**
- **1 9-oz. pkg. frozen cooked chicken breast strips, thawed**
- **1 cup halved seedless grapes**
- **1 1/2 cups cubed fresh pineapple**
- **1 recipe Orange-Basil Vinaigrette (below)**
- **2 Tbsp. chopped pecans, toasted**

1. Cook barley according to package directions. Drain. Rinse under cold water; drain again. Cover; chill for at least 1 hour.

2. Line four plates with lettuce. Top with chicken, grapes, and pineapple. Shake Orange-Basil Vinaigrette; pour on salad. Top with pecans. Makes 4 servings.

ORANGE-BASIL VINAIGRETTE: In a screw- top jar combine 1 teaspoon finely shredded orange peel; 1/4 cup orange juice; 1/4 cup salad oil; 2 tablespoons white balsamic vinegar or white wine vinegar; 2 tablespoons snipped fresh basil or 1 teaspoon dried basil, crushed; and 1 tablespoon honey. Cover and shake to mix. Makes 1/2 cup.

Each serving: 381 cal., 20 g total fat (3 g sat. fat), 45 mg chol., 379 mg sodium, 36 g carbo., 4 g fiber, 19 g pro. Daily Values: 6% vit. A, 41% vit. C, 4% calcium, 7% iron.

DINNER IN A BOWL

PRIZE TESTED RECIPES® $400 WINNER

JULIE DEMATTEO, CLEMENTON, N.J.

PRIZE TESTED RECIPES® $200 WINNER

LAURI SADORUS, EVERETT, WASH.

Confetti Chicken Big Bowl

PREP: 30 minutes **COOK:** 6 minutes

- 1 lb. skinless, boneless chicken breasts, cut into 1-inch cubes
- 2 Tbsp. cooking oil
- 4 tsp. minced garlic (8 cloves)
- 4 tsp. grated fresh ginger
- 1 Tbsp. red curry paste
- 1 tsp. ground cumin
- 1 14-oz. can unsweetened coconut milk
- 2 cups shredded carrot
- 2 cups small broccoli florets
- 1 medium red sweet pepper, cut into bite-size strips
- 2 3-oz. pkg. chicken-flavored ramen noodles, coarsely broken
- 2 cups snow pea pods, halved
- 2 Tbsp. soy sauce
- 4 tsp. lime juice
- 1 cup slivered fresh basil
- 1/3 cup snipped fresh cilantro

1. In a 4-quart Dutch oven cook chicken in 1 tablespoon hot oil for 3 to 4 minutes or until no longer pink. Remove; set aside. Add remaining oil to pan. Add garlic, ginger, curry paste, and cumin; cook and stir for 30 seconds.

2. Stir in 4 cups water, milk, carrot, broccoli, pepper, and noodles (reserve seasoning). Bring to boiling; reduce heat. Simmer, covered, 3 minutes. Stir in chicken, pea pods,seasoning, soy, and lime. Stir in basil and cilantro. Makes 6 servings.

Each serving: 454 cal., 25 g total fat (12 g sat. fat), 44 mg chol., 1,087 mg sodium, 33 g carbo., 4 g fiber, 26 g pro. Daily Values: 246% vit. A, 143% vit. C, 8% calcium, 15% iron.

Italian Three-Bean Chili

PREP: 20 minutes **COOK:** 30 minutes

- 1/2 cup chopped red onion
- 1 clove garlic, minced
- 2 Tbsp. olive oil
- 1 15-oz. can tomato sauce
- 1 15-oz. can black beans, rinsed
- 1 15- to 16-oz. can Great Northern beans, rinsed and drained
- 1 14 1/2-oz. can diced tomatoes
- 1 cup frozen green soybeans
- 1 4 1/2-oz. can diced chile peppers
- 1 Tbsp. balsamic vinegar
- 1/3 cup sliced pitted ripe olives
- 2 Tbsp. snipped fresh cilantro
- Hot cooked rice, pasta, or couscous

1. Cook and stir onion and garlic in hot oil until tender. Add 1/2 cup water, tomato sauce, beans, tomatoes, soybeans, peppers, and vinegar. Bring to boiling; reduce heat. Simmer, covered, 20 minutes, stirring often. Stir in olives and cilantro; simmer 5 minutes. Serve over rice; top with cheese, if desired. Makes 6 servings.

Each serving: 436 cal., 12 g total fat (3 g sat. fat), 11 mg chol., 828 mg sodium, 62 g carbo., 10 g fiber, 23 g pro. Daily Values: 6% vit. A, 42% vit. C, 33% calcium, 29% iron.

Sausage Tortellini Soup

PREP: 15 minutes **COOK:** 20 minutes

Nonstick cooking spray
- 1 lb. smoked, fully cooked chicken sausage, halved lengthwise, then sliced crosswise into 1-inch pieces
- 1 large onion, cut into thin wedges
- 2 cloves garlic, minced
- 2 14-oz. cans chicken broth
- 1 14½-oz. can diced tomatoes with basil, oregano, and garlic
- 1 cup water
- 2 9-oz. pkg. refrigerated mushroom or cheese tortellini
- 1 10-oz. pkg. frozen baby lima beans
- ¼ cup slivered fresh basil
- 2 Tbsp. freshly shredded Parmesan cheese

1. Lightly coat a Dutch oven with nonstick cooking spray. Cook sausage, onion, and garlic over medium heat until sausage is brown and onion is tender. Drain off fat.

2. Add broth, tomatoes, and water. Bring to boiling; reduce heat. Simmer, covered, for 10 minutes. Add tortellini and lima beans. Return to boiling; reduce heat. Simmer, uncovered, for 5 to 6 minutes or until pasta and beans are tender.

3. Stir in basil. Ladle into six bowls. Sprinkle each serving with Parmesan cheese. Makes 6 to 8 servings.

Each serving: 527 cal., 18 g total fat (6 g sat. fat), 62 mg chol., 1.636 mg sodium, 60 g carbo., 4 g fiber, 32 g pro. Daily Values: 12% vit. A, 18% vit. C, 25% calcium, 26% iron.

Easy Moroccan Stew

PREP: 40 minutes **BAKE:** 1 hour 20 minutes

- 2 lb. boneless pork shoulder
- 3 Tbsp. all-purpose flour
- 1 tsp. ground cumin
- 2 Tbsp. cooking oil
- ½ cup chopped onion
- 2 14½-oz. cans diced tomatoes
- 1 tsp. salt
- 1 tsp. ground ginger
- 1 tsp. ground cinnamon
- ½ tsp. sugar
- ½ tsp. pepper
- 2 medium carrots, sliced
- 2 medium red potatoes, chopped
- 1 medium sweet potato, peeled and chopped
- 2 cups frozen cut green beans
- 1½ cups frozen baby lima beans
- 2 Tbsp. snipped fresh cilantro or parsley
- ½ cup plain yogurt

Pita bread (optional)

1. Preheat oven to 350° F. Trim fat; cut pork into ¾-inch pieces. Combine flour and cumin; toss meat cubes with flour mixture. In a 4- to 5-quart oven-proof Dutch oven brown meat and onion, half at a time, in hot oil. Drain fat. Return all meat and onion to the pan.

2. Stir in ⅓ cup water, undrained tomatoes, salt, ginger, cinnamon, sugar, and pepper. Add carrot, potatoes, green beans, and lima beans. Bring just to boiling.

3. Cover; bake 1 hour and 20 minutes or until meat and vegetables are tender. Spoon into six bowls. Top with cilantro or parsley; top with yogurt. If desired, serve with bread. Makes 6 servings.

Each serving: 400 cal. 23 g total fat (4 g sat. fat), 86 mg chol., 167 mg sodium, 12 g carbo., 2 g fiber, 38 g pro. Daily Values: 22% vit. A, 21% vit. C, 9% calcium, 18% iron.

Green Chile Stew

This Tex-Mex favorite won hands down in October of 1998, and it's still a champion.

PREP: 15 minutes **COOK:** 1¾ hours

- 2 lb. beef stew meat
- ¼ cup all-purpose flour
- ¼ cup margarine or butter
- 6 cloves garlic, minced
- 3 cups beef broth
- 1 12-oz. bottle dark (Mexican) beer
- 1 cup bottled green salsa
- 2 Tbsp. snipped fresh oregano or 2 tsp. dried oregano, crushed
- 1 tsp. ground cumin
- 3 medium potatoes, cubed
- 1 14½-oz. can hominy, drained
- 2 4½-oz. cans diced green chile peppers, drained
- 12 green onions, bias-sliced into 1-inch pieces
- ½ cup snipped fresh cilantro

1. Toss beef cubes with flour. In a 4½-quart Dutch oven brown beef cubes, half at a time, in hot margarine or butter. Using a slotted spoon, remove meat from Dutch oven.

2. Add garlic to Dutch oven; cook for 1 minute. Stir in broth, beer, salsa, oregano, and cumin. Return meat to Dutch oven. Bring to boiling; reduce heat. Cover and simmer about 1¼ hours or until meat is nearly tender.

3. Add potatoes; simmer about 30 minutes more or until meat and potatoes are tender. Stir in hominy, chile peppers, green onions, and cilantro; heat through. Spoon into eight bowls. Makes 8 servings.

Each serving: 392 cal., 16 g total fat (4 g sat. fat), 82 mg chol., 720 mg sodium, 28 g carbo., 1 g fiber, 32 g pro. Daily Values: 189% vit. A, 49% vit. C, 7% calcium, 38% iron.

Turnip and Barley Stew

PREP: 25 minutes **COOK:** 15 minutes

- 1 large onion, cut into wedges
- 4 cloves garlic, minced
- 1 Tbsp. olive oil or cooking oil
- 2 tsp. dried sage, crushed
- 1 tsp. ground cumin
- 2 medium turnips, peeled and cut into ½-inch cubes
- 1 small rutabaga, peeled and cut into ½-inch cubes
- 3 14-oz. cans vegetable broth
- ¾ cup quick-cooking barley
- 1 15-oz. can white kidney beans, rinsed and drained
- ⅓ cup snipped fresh parsley
- ½ tsp. pepper

1. In a 4-quart Dutch oven cook onion and garlic in hot oil over medium heat until onion is tender. Stir in sage, cumin, turnips, and rutabaga; cook and stir for 1 minute more.

2. Add broth and barley; bring to boiling. Reduce heat; simmer, covered, about 15 minutes or until tender.

3. Stir in beans, parsley, and pepper; heat through. To serve, spoon into six bowls. Makes 6 servings.

Each serving: 157 cal., 4 g total fat (0 g sat. fat), 0 mg chol., 955 mg sodium, 34 g carbo., 7 g fiber, 7 g pro. Daily Values: 6% vit. A, 26% vit. C, 6% calcium, 11% iron.

DINNERTIME SANDWICHES

PRIZE TESTED RECIPES® $400 WINNER

LINDA MORTEN, KATY, TEXAS

Spanish Grilled Sandwiches

PREP: 30 minutes **CHILL:** 8 minutes **COOK:** 8 minutes

- 4 sandwich rolls, such as pan cubano, bolillos, teleras (about 6½×3 inches), hoagie buns, or two 8-inch Italian flatbreads (focaccia), split in half horizontally
- 1 recipe Artichoke-Pepper Relish (below)
- 1 lb. thinly sliced deli roast beef or roast pork
- 8 oz. sliced provolone cheese
- 4 tsp. olive oil

1. If using focaccia, cut in half crosswise. Arrange Artichoke-Pepper Relish, meat, and cheese over bottom halves of rolls. Add tops of rolls.

2. Coat a very large skillet with 2 teaspoons of the oil; heat. Add 2 sandwiches; cover with foil; press with a heavy skillet. Cook for 8 to 10 minutes or until heated through, turning once. Cut in half; keep warm. Repeat. Makes 8 servings.

ARTICHOKE-PEPPER RELISH: Drain one 6½-ounce jar marinated artichoke hearts, reserving marinade; thinly slice artichokes. Combine artichokes; reserved marinade; one 7-ounce jar roasted red sweet peppers, drained and cut into strips; ⅔ cup jalapeño-stuffed olives, sliced; 1 medium onion, thinly sliced into rings; 1 clove garlic, minced; 1 tablespoon snipped fresh parsley; ⅛ teaspoon dried oregano, crushed; and ⅛ teaspoon ground cumin. Cover; chill 2 to 24 hours, tossing often.

Each serving: 417 cal., 16 g total fat (7 g sat. fat), 59 mg chol., 794 mg sodium, 38 g carbo., 2 g fiber, 30 g pro. Daily Values: 7% vit. A, 97% vit. C, 24% calcium, 22% iron.

PRIZE TESTED RECIPES® $200 WINNER

ELAINE SWEET, DALLAS, TEXAS

Cobb Salad Hoagies

START TO FINISH: 35 minutes

- 1⅓ cups cubed cooked chicken
- 2 plum tomatoes, chopped
- 4 slices bacon, crisp-cooked, drained, and crumbled
- ½ cup crumbled blue cheese
- 1 recipe Avocado Vinaigrette (below)
- 4 Boston lettuce leaves
- 4 hoagie buns, split, hollowed out, and toasted
- 2 hard-cooked eggs, chopped

1. In a bowl combine chicken, tomatoes, bacon, and blue cheese. Add Avocado Vinaigrette; toss to coat. Place lettuce leaves on bottom halves of buns. Add chicken mixture; top with chopped eggs and top halves of buns. Makes 4 sandwiches.

AVOCADO VINAIGRETTE: Whisk together 3 tablespoons olive oil, 1 tablespoon white wine vinegar, 1 teaspoon Dijon-style mustard, ½ teaspoon salt, and ½ teaspoon pepper. Stir in 1 avocado, halved, seeded, peeled, and finely chopped; set aside.

Each: 659 cal., 35 g total fat (9 g sat. fat), 165 mg chol., 1,214 mg sodium, 55 g carbo., 5 g fiber, 32 g pro. Daily Values: 18% vit. A, 18% calcium, 21% iron.

Roast Beef and Mango Hoagies

START TO FINISH: 25 minutes

- 1 medium onion, thinly sliced
- 1/4 cup olive oil
- 1/2 of a medium red and/or green sweet pepper, cut into thin strips
- 1/2 tsp. curry powder
- 1/4 cup red wine vinegar or cider vinegar
- 1/4 tsp. dried thyme, crushed
- 1/8 tsp. ground black pepper
- 1/4 cup tub light cream cheese
- 6 kaiser rolls, split and toasted
- 2 cups arugula
- 12 oz. thinly sliced fully cooked roast beef
- 1 mango, seeded, peeled, and sliced

1. In a medium skillet cook onion in olive oil until tender. Add sweet pepper and curry powder; cook and stir for 1 minute more. Stir in vinegar, thyme, and black pepper. Set aside.

2. Spread cream cheese onto cut side of each bun bottom. Line with arugula. Divide beef and mango slices among sandwiches. Top with curry mixture; add bun tops. Makes 6 sandwiches.

Each sandwich: 399 cal., 16 g total fat (4 g sat. fat), 44 mg chol., 399 mg sodium, 39 g carbo., 2 g fiber, 24 g pro. Daily Values: 44% vit. A, 46% vit. C, 9% calcium, 19% iron.

Reuben Quesadillas

PREP: 15 minutes **BAKE:** 10 minutes

- 1/2 of a sweet onion, such as Vidalia or Walla Walla, halved and thinly sliced (about 1 1/2 cups)
- 2 Tbsp. cooking oil
- 1 cup sauerkraut, drained
- 1 tsp. caraway seed
- 4 10-inch flour tortillas
- 1/4 cup bottled Thousand Island salad dressing
- 8 oz. thinly sliced corned beef, cut into strips
- 1 cup shredded Swiss cheese (4 oz.)

1. Preheat oven to 375° F. In a medium skillet cook onion in 1 tablespoon of the cooking oil until tender. Add sauerkraut and 1/2 teaspoon of the caraway seed; cook for 2 to 3 minutes or until any liquid is evaporated.

2. Brush some of the remaining oil onto 2 of the tortillas. Place, oiled side down, on two large pizza pans or baking sheets. Spread salad dressing onto tortillas. Top with corned beef, onion mixture, and Swiss cheese. Top with remaining tortillas. Brush with remaining oil; sprinkle with remaining caraway seed.

3. Bake about 10 minutes or until cheese is melted. Cut into wedges to serve. Makes 16 wedges.

Each wedge: 132 cal., 9 g total fat (3 g sat. fat), 21 mg chol., 304 mg sodium, 8 g carbo., 1 g fiber, 6 g pro. Daily Values: 1% vit. A, 3% vit. C, 8% calcium, 4% iron.

Asian Chicken Wraps

START TO FINISH: 30 minutes

- 1 2- to 2 1/4-lb. cooked roasted chicken (from deli)
- 8 8- to 10-inch flour tortillas
- 1/2 cup hoisin sauce
- 1/4 cup finely chopped peanuts
- 1/4 cup finely chopped green onion
- 1/2 cup shredded daikon, well drained
- 1 recipe Soy Dipping Sauce (below)

1. Remove skin from chicken and discard. Remove chicken from bones; shred chicken (you should have about 4 cups). Set aside.

2. Spread one side of each tortilla with some of the hoisin sauce; sprinkle with peanuts and green onion. Top with shredded chicken and daikon. Roll up; halve crosswise. Serve with Soy Dipping Sauce. Makes 8 servings.

SOY DIPPING SAUCE: In a small bowl combine 3 tablespoons soy sauce, 3 tablespoons Chinese black vinegar or rice vinegar, 1 tablespooon water, and 1 teaspoon chili oil or toasted sesame oil. Makes 1/3 cup.

Each sandwich: 283 cal., 9 g total fat (2 g sat. fat), 50 mg chol., 869 mg sodium, 26 g carbo., 1 g fiber, 20 g pro. Daily Values: 1% vit. A, 5% vit. C, 5% calcium, 10% iron.

Grilled Chicken Sausage Sandwiches

START TO FINISH: 30 minutes

- 1 medium sweet onion, such as Vidalia or Walla Walla, halved and thinly sliced (1/2 cup)
- 4 cloves garlic, minced
- 2 Tbsp. olive oil
- 1 large yellow summer squash, halved lengthwise and thinly sliced (about 2 cups)
- 1 cup sliced fresh mushrooms
- 2 Tbsp. balsamic vinegar
- 2 tsp. snipped fresh rosemary or 1/2 tsp. dried rosemary, crushed
- 1/2 cup quartered cherry tomatoes
- 6 cooked chicken sausage links or cooked smoked sausage links
- 6 hoagie buns
- 1/2 cup shredded fresh spinach

1. In a large skillet cook onion and garlic in hot oil over medium-high heat for 3 minutes. Stir in squash and mushrooms. Cook and stir for 4 to 5 minutes more or until vegetables are tender. Stir in vinegar and rosemary. Remove from heat. Stir in quartered cherry tomatoes.

2. Meanwhile, pierce skin of sausage several times with a fork. Grill sausages on the rack of an uncovered grill directly over medium coals about 7 minutes or until sausages are browned and heated through, turning once halfway through grilling.

3. Halve the buns lengthwise, cutting to but not through the other side. Toast cut sides of hoagie buns alongside the sausage.

4. Place a grilled sausage in each bun; top with mushroom mixture. Sprinkle with spinach. Makes 6 sandwiches.

Each sandwich: 466 cal., 19 g total fat (5 g sat. fat), 20 mg chol., 1,007 mg sodium, 55 g carbo., 4 g fiber, 20 g pro. Daily Values: 6% vit. A, 18% vit. C, 10% calcium, 16% iron.

EGG STRATAS & CASSEROLES

PRIZE TESTED RECIPES® $400 WINNER

VIV RAIVES, CAMBRIA, CALIF.

PRIZE TESTED RECIPES® $200 WINNER

MARGARET PACHE, MESA, ARIZ.

Bagel, Lox, and Egg Strata

PREP: 30 minutes **CHILL:** 4 hours
BAKE: 45 minutes **STAND:** 10 minutes

- 1/4 cup butter or margarine, melted
- 4 to 6 plain bagels, cut into bite-size pieces (8 cups)
- 1 3-oz. pkg. thinly sliced smoked salmon (lox-style), cut into small pieces
- 8 oz. Swiss cheese or Monterey Jack cheese, shredded (2 cups)
- 1/4 cup snipped fresh chives
- 8 eggs
- 2 cups milk
- 1 cup cream-style cottage cheese
- 1/4 tsp. pepper

1. Place melted butter in a 3-quart rectangular baking dish; spread to cover the bottom. Spread bagel pieces evenly in the prepared dish. Sprinkle lox, cheese, and chives evenly over bagel pieces.

2. In a large bowl beat eggs; stir in milk, cottage cheese, and pepper. Pour over layers in dish; press down gently with the back of a wooden spoon to moisten all of the ingredients. Cover and chill for 4 to 24 hours.

3. Preheat oven to 350° F. Bake, uncovered, about 45 minutes or until center is set and edges are puffed and golden. Let stand for 10 minutes. Makes 12 servings.

Each serving: 267 cal., 14 g total fat (8 g sat. fat), 176 mg chol., 497 mg sodium, 16 g carbo., 1 g fiber, 17 g pro. Daily Values: 13% vit. A, 2% vit. C, 28% calcium, 8% iron.

Margaret's Citrus Raisin Strata

PREP: 10 minutes **BAKE:** 45 minutes **STAND:** 15 minutes

- 10 slices cinnamon-raisin bread
- 3 eggs
- 2 cups half-and-half or light cream
- 2/3 cup sugar
- 1 1/2 tsp. finely shredded orange peel
- 1 tsp. vanilla
- Vanilla yogurt (optional)

1. Preheat oven to 350° F. Tear bread into bite-size pieces. Place in a greased 2-quart square baking dish. In a medium bowl beat eggs; stir in half-and-half, sugar, orange peel, and vanilla. Pour over bread in baking dish.

2. Bake, uncovered, about 45 minutes or until a knife inserted near the center comes out clean. Let stand for 15 minutes before serving. If desired, serve with vanilla yogurt. Makes 6 servings.

Each serving: 345 cal., 14 g total fat (7 g sat. fat), 136 mg chol., 233 mg sodium, 48 g carbo., 2 g fiber, 9 g pro. Daily Values: 10% vit. A, 2% vit. C, 13% calcium, 9% iron.

Artichoke and Mushroom Bake

Turn this Greek-inspired dish into brunch by serving with a Greek salad.

PREP: 25 minutes **BAKE:** 35 minutes

- Nonstick cooking spray
- 1½ cups sliced fresh mushrooms
- ½ cup finely chopped onion
- 1 Tbsp. olive oil
- 8 eggs
- 2 cups cream-style cottage cheese
- ½ cup all-purpose flour
- 4 oz. crumbled feta cheese
- 1 14-oz. can artichoke hearts, rinsed, drained, and chopped
- ½ cup grated Parmesan cheese
- Tomato wedges (optional)

1. Preheat oven to 350° F. Lightly coat a 2-quart rectangular baking dish with cooking spray; set aside.

2. In a large skillet cook mushrooms and onion in hot oil until tender; set aside.

3. In a large bowl beat eggs; stir in cottage cheese and flour. Stir in feta cheese, artichoke hearts, Parmesan cheese, and mushroom mixture. Pour mixture into the prepared dish.

4. Bake about 35 minutes or until a knife inserted near the center comes out clean. If desired, top with tomato wedges. Makes 8 servings.

Each serving: 257 cal., 14 g total fat (7 g sat. fat), 238 mg chol., 707 mg sodium, 12 g carbo., 2 g fiber, 20 g pro. Daily Values: 12% vit. A, 2% vit. C, 23% calcium, 13% iron.

Potato and Onion Breakfast Casserole

Serve with fresh tomatoes or melon or scramble a few eggs for a heartier meal.

PREP: 25 minutes **CHILL:** Overnight
BAKE: 40 minutes **STAND:** 15 minutes

- 4 slices bacon
- 3 cups thinly sliced sweet onion, such as Vidalia or Walla Walla
- 3 cups frozen loose-pack diced hash brown potatoes with onion and peppers (12 oz.)
- 1 Tbsp. balsamic vinegar
- Nonstick cooking spray
- 6 eggs
- 1½ cups milk
- 1 cup shredded Swiss cheese (4 oz.)
- ½ tsp. salt
- ¼ tsp. pepper

1. In a large skillet cook bacon until crisp. Drain on paper towels; reserve 2 tablespoons drippings in the skillet.

2. Add onion; cover and cook over medium-low heat for 10 minutes, stirring occasionally. Uncover; cook for 3minutes more or until onions are tender.

3. Stir in hash brown potatoes. Remove from heat. Crumble bacon; stir bacon and balsamic vinegar into potato mixture.

4. Lightly coat a 2-quart rectangular baking dish with cooking spray. Spread potato mixture in the baking dish.

5. In a medium mixing bowl beat eggs; stir in milk, cheese, salt, and pepper. Pour evenly over potato mixture. Cover and chill overnight.

6. Preheat oven to 350° F. Uncover potato mixture. Bake about 40 minutes or until a knife inserted near the center comes out clean. Let stand for 15 minutes before serving. Makes 6 to 8 servings.

Each serving: 263 cal., 14 g total fat (6 g sat. fat), 238 mg chol., 412 mg sodium, 18 g carbo., 2 g fiber, 16 g pro. Daily Values: 12% vit. A, 13% vit. C, 29% calcium, 7% iron.

Southwestern Breakfast Casserole

PREP: 30 minutes **CHILL:** 2 hours
BAKE: 45 minutes **STAND:** 10 minutes

- Nonstick cooking spray
- 6 cups cubed firm-textured white bread
- 6 oz. uncooked chorizo sausage or bulk pork sausage*, crumbled
- 1 cup chopped onion
- ½ cup chopped red sweet pepper
- 1 cup frozen whole kernel corn
- ½ tsp. ground cumin (optional)
- ¼ tsp. salt
- Dash bottled hot pepper sauce
- 6 eggs
- 2 cups milk
- 4 oz. Queso Fresco, crumbled, or Monterey Jack cheese, shredded, (1 cup)
- 1 to 2 Tbsp. snipped fresh cilantro or parsley (optional)
- Bottled salsa, dairy sour cream, chopped tomato, and/or sliced jalapeño peppers (optional)

1. Lightly coat a 2-quart rectangular baking dish with cooking spray; set aside. Place bread in a large bowl; set aside.

2. In a large skillet cook sausage, onion, and sweet pepper until meat is brown and onion is tender, stirring to break up sausage. Drain off any fat. Stir in corn, cumin (if using), salt, and hot pepper sauce; cook for 1 minute more. Add sausage mixture to bread mixture.

3. In a large bowl beat eggs; stir in milk. Pour egg mixture over bread mixture. Toss gently to moisten. (The mixture will be wet.) Spoon half of the bread mixture into prepared dish; sprinkle with half of the cheese. Cover with remaining bread mixture. Cover; chill for 2 to 24 hours.

4. Preheat oven to 350° F. Uncover baking dish; bake for 30 minutes. Sprinkle with remaining cheese; bake for 15 to 20 minutes more or until a knife inserted near the center comes out clean. Let stand 10 minutes before serving. If desired, sprinkle with cilantro; serve with salsa, sour cream, chopped tomato, and sliced jalapeño peppers. Makes 8 servings.

***TEST KITCHEN TIP:** If using pork sausage, add ½ teaspoon ground cumin.

Each serving: 302 cal., 16 g total fat (6 g sat. fat), 187 mg chol., 569 mg sodium, 24 g carbo., 1 g fiber, 16 g pro. Daily Values: 20% vit. A, 30% vit. C, 16% calcium, 10% iron.

ENTRÉES FOR ENTERTAINING

PRIZE TESTED RECIPES® $400 WINNER

DIANE HALFERTY, CORPUS CRISTI, TEXAS

PRIZE TESTED RECIPES® $200 WINNER

MARY JARSON, BATTLE GROUND, WASH.

Citrus Duck with Orange-Ginger Glaze

MARINATE: 4 hours **PREP:** 25 minutes
COOK: 35 minutes **ROAST:** 15 minutes

- 6 6- to 8-oz. duck breast halves
- 1 Tbsp. finely shredded orange peel
- 1 cup orange juice
- 1 cup dry white wine
- 6 Tbsp. honey
- 4 Tbsp. grated fresh ginger
- 1/4 cup chicken broth
- 1 Tbsp. soy sauce
- 1 Tbsp. olive oil
- 3 cups hot cooked rice

1. Trim duck fat; score skin. In a bag mix peel, juice, 1/2 cup wine, 1/4 cup honey, and 3 tablespoons ginger. Add duck; seal. Marinate 4 to 24 hours, turning often.

2. In a saucepan combine 1 3/4 cups marinade and 1/2 cup wine; bring to boiling. Reduce heat; simmer, uncovered, for 20 to 25 minutes or until reduced to 1 1/4 cups. Add 2 tablespoons honey, 1 tablespoon ginger, broth, and soy sauce. Return to boiling; cook and stir about 15 minutes or until reduced to 2/3 cup. Meanwhile, in a 12-inch skillet cook duck in hot oil about 10 minutes or until brown, turning once.

3. Preheat oven to 425° F. In 13×9×2-inch baking pan roast duck about 15 minutes or until 170° F. Serve sliced duck and glaze with rice. Makes 6 servings.

Each serving: 469 cal., 15 g total fat (4 g sat. fat), 154 mg chol., 402 mg sodium, 46 g carbo., 1 g fiber, 31 g pro. Daily Values: 3% vit. A, 45% vit. C, 28% iron.

Apricot Chicken Roll-Ups

PREP: 40 minutes **BAKE:** 35 minutes

- Nonstick cooking spray
- 1 6- or 7-oz. pkg. dried apricots, snipped (about 1 1/3 cups)
- 1/2 cup dried cranberries
- 3 Tbsp. honey
- 6 medium skinless, boneless chicken breast halves (about 2 lb.)
- 1 1/2 tsp. ground ginger
- 2 eggs, beaten
- 1 recipe Herb Coating (below)

1. Preheat oven to 350° F. Coat a 3-quart rectangular baking dish with spray; set aside. For filling, stir together apricots, cranberries, honey, and ginger; set aside.

2. Pound breasts to 1/4-inch thickness. Spoon 1/4 cup filling in centers. Fold in bottoms and sides; roll up. Secure with toothpicks. Dip into egg; coat in Herb Coating. Arrange in dish. Bake 35 to 40 minutes or until no pink remains. Serves 6.

HERB COATING: Stir together 2/3 cup fine dry bread crumbs; 2 tablespoons snipped fresh parsley; 1 tablespoon all-purpose flour; 1 tablespoon finely shredded Parmesan cheese; 1 teaspoon paprika; 1/2 teaspoon sugar; 1/2 teaspoon dried oregano, crushed; 1/2 teaspoon salt; 1/4 teaspoon garlic powder; 1/4 teaspoon onion powder; and 1/4 teaspoon pepper. Cut in 2 tablespoons shortening to resemble fine crumbs.

Each serving: 405 cal., 9 g total fat (2 g sat. fat), 159 mg chol., 546 mg sodium, 43 g carbo., 4 g fiber, 40 g pro. Daily Values: 50% vit. A, 8% calcium, 20% iron.

Stuffed Pork Tenderloin with Apple-Cranberry Glaze

PREP: 20 minutes **ROAST:** 20 minutes

- 2 cups torn fresh spinach
- 1/2 cup frozen artichoke hearts, thawed and chopped
- 1/3 cup finely shredded Parmesan cheese
- 1 tsp. snipped fresh rosemary or 1/4 tsp. dried rosemary, crushed
- 1 1-lb. pork tenderloin
- 1/2 cup frozen apple-cranberry juice concentrate, thawed
- 1/4 cup balsamic vinegar

1. Preheat oven to 425° F. For stuffing, in a large skillet cook spinach in a small amount of water until just wilted; drain well. In a small bowl combine spinach, artichoke hearts, cheese, and rosemary.

2. Slice tenderloin lengthwise, almost all the way through, making a pocket. Spoon stuffing into the pocket (the filling will be exposed). Place in a shallow roasting pan, stuffing side up. Insert a meat thermometer. Roast, uncovered, for 20 to 25 minutes or until thermometer registers 160° F. (The temperature of the meat will rise 5° to 10° F during standing.)

3. Meanwhile, for glaze, in a small saucepan combine apple-cranberry juice concentrate and balsamic vinegar. Bring to boiling. Simmer, uncovered, about 15 minutes or until mixture measures 1/3 cup. Spoon over pork during the last 10 minutes of roasting. Makes 4 servings.

Each serving: 270 cal., 6 g total fat (3 g sat. fat), 81 mg chol., 181 mg sodium, 24 g carbo., 3 g fiber, 28 g pro. Daily Values: 20% vit. A,58% vit. C, 12% calcium, 15% iron.

Chicken Chile Rellenos

PREP: 45 minutes **BAKE:** 20 minutes

- 6 fresh poblano peppers*
- 2 cups shredded or chopped cooked chicken
- 1 cup shredded Monterey Jack cheese (4 oz.)
- 1/2 cup frozen whole kernel corn, thawed
- 1/2 of an 8-oz. tub cream cheese with chives
- 2 Tbsp. snipped fresh cilantro
- 1 cup thinly sliced sweet onion
- 3 cloves garlic, thinly sliced
- 1 Tbsp. olive oil
- 1 15-oz. can tomato sauce
- 1 1/2 tsp. ground cumin
- 1/2 tsp. ground coriander
- 1/4 tsp. salt
- 1/4 tsp. ground red pepper
- 2 Tbsp. snipped fresh cilantro

1. Preheat oven to 350° F. Cut a lengthwise slice from one side of each pepper, leaving stems intact. Chop pepper slices; set aside. Remove seeds and membranes from peppers. In a large saucepan cook peppers, half at a time, in boiling water for 2 minutes. Drain well.

2. Meanwhile, for filling, combine chicken, 1/2 cup shredded cheese, corn, cream cheese, and 2 tablespoons cilantro.

3. For sauce, in a skillet cook chopped pepper, onion, and garlic in hot oil over medium-low heat about 5 minutes or until tender, stirring occasionally. Stir in tomato sauce, cumin, coriander, salt, and ground red pepper. Cook and stir until bubbly.

4. Spoon filling into poblano peppers; arrange in a greased 3-quart rectangular baking dish. Top with sauce. Bake, covered, for 20 to 25 minutes or until heated through. Sprinkle with remaining 1/2 cup cheese. Bake, uncovered, 2 minutes more or until cheese is melted. Before serving, sprinkle with remaining 2 tablespoons cilantro. Makes 6 servings.

***TEST KITCHEN TIP:** Because chile peppers, such as poblanos, contain volatile oils that can burn your skin and eyes, wear plastic or rubber gloves when working with them. If your bare hands do touch the chile peppers, wash your hands well with soap and water.

Each serving: 327 cal., 18 g total fat (8 g sat. fat), 78 mg chol., 657 mg sodium, 20 g carbo., 2 g fiber, 23 g pro. Daily Values: 28% vit. A, 553% vit. C, 20% calcium, 24% iron.

Beer-Brined Turkey

Soaking turkey overnight in beer, salt, and herbs really adds flavor before roasting.

PREP: 25 minutes **CHILL:** overnight
ROAST: 1 1/4 hours **STAND:** 15 minutes

- 1 1 3/4- to 2-lb. bone-in turkey breast portion
- 3 12-oz. cans beer
- 1/4 cup coarse salt
- 4 cloves garlic, peeled and sliced
- 4 fresh rosemary sprigs
- 6 bay leaves
- Water
- 1 Tbsp. butter, melted
- 2 cloves garlic, minced
- 1 tsp. dried thyme, crushed
- 1 tsp. paprika
- 1/2 tsp. onion powder
- 1/2 tsp. ground sage
- 1/4 tsp. pepper

1. Place turkey in a very large bowl. Pour beer over turkey. Add salt, sliced garlic, rosemary sprigs, and bay leaves. If necessary, add enough water to just cover. Cover; chill overnight in the refrigerator.

2. Preheat oven to 325° F. Remove turkey from brine; discard the brine. Place turkey on a rack in a shallow roasting pan. In a small bowl stir together butter and minced garlic; brush onto roast. In another small bowl stir together thyme, paprika, onion powder, sage, and pepper; sprinkle onto turkey.

3. Insert a meat thermometer into thickest part of the breast, without touching bone. Roast turkey, uncovered, for 1 1/4 to 1 3/4 hours or until thermometer registers 170° F. Cover and let stand for 15 minutes. Makes 6 servings.

Each serving: 198 cal., 10 g total fat (3 g sat. fat), 78 mg chol., 846 mg sodium, 1 g carbo., 1 g fiber, 25 g pro. Daily Values: 7% vit. A, 1% vit. C, 3% calcium, 9% iron.

GRILLED CHOPS & STEAKS

PRIZE TESTED RECIPES® $400 WINNER
GLORIA BRADLEY, NAPERVILLE, ILL.

PRIZE TESTED RECIPES® $200 WINNER
SUSAN M. DAVIES-POU[illegible]NE, [illegible]LO, MINN.

Ribeye Steaks with Chipotle Butter

PREP: 20 minutes **GRILL:** 14 minutes

- 2 tsp. ground cumin
- 1 tsp. paprika
- 1/2 tsp. salt
- 1/2 tsp. pepper
- 1 Tbsp. olive oil
- 1/4 tsp. adobo sauce
- 4 8- to 10-oz. boneless beef ribeye steaks, cut 1 inch thick
- 1 recipe Chipotle Butter (below)
- Fresh basil or cilantro

1. In a bowl stir together cumin, paprika, salt, and pepper. Stir in olive oil and adobo sauce (from the canned chipotle pepper used in Chipotle Butter) until a paste forms. Spread spice mixture onto both sides of steaks.

2. Grill steaks on rack of an uncovered grill directly over medium coals to desired doneness, turning once. Allow 14 to 18 minutes for medium. Serve with Chipotle Butter. If desired, garnish with fresh basil or cilantro. Makes 4 servings.

CHIPOTLE BUTTER: Stir together 1/4 cup butter, softened; 1 tablespoon finely chopped shallots; 2 teaspoons snipped fresh basil or cilantro; 1 1/2 teaspoons lime juice; and 1 teaspoon finely chopped chipotle pepper in adobo sauce (reserve sauce for meat).

Each serving: 416 cal., 27 g total fat (12 g sat. fat), 118 mg chol., 519 mg sodium, 2 g carbo., 1 g fiber, 40 g pro. Daily Values: 17% vit. A, 4% vit. C, 19% iron.

Mustard-Rosemary Grilled Lamb

PREP: 20 minutes **MARINATE:** 2 hours **GRILL:** 12 minutes

- 8 lamb rib or loin chops, cut 1 inch thick (about 2 lb.)
- 1/4 cup stone-ground mustard
- 2 green onions, thinly sliced (1/4 cup)
- 2 Tbsp. dry white wine
- 1 Tbsp. balsamic vinegar
- 3 cloves garlic, minced
- 1 tsp. snipped fresh rosemary
- 1 tsp. honey
- 1/2 tsp. salt
- 1/2 tsp. pepper

1. Trim fat from chops; set chops aside. In a small bowl stir together mustard, green onion, wine, vinegar, garlic, rosemary, honey, salt, and pepper. Spread mixture evenly onto both sides of chops. Place chops on a large plate; cover loosely with plastic wrap. Chill for 2 to 3 hours.

2. Grill chops on the rack of an uncovered grill directly over medium coals to desired doneness, turning chops once halfway through grilling. Allow 12 to 14 minutes for medium-rare and 15 to 17 minutes for medium. Makes 4 servings.

Each serving: 194 cal., 9 g total fat (3 g sat. fat), 64 mg chol., 557 mg sodium, 4 g carbo., 21 g pro. Daily Values: 1% vit. A, 4% vit. C, 4% calcium, 12% iron.

Curried Steaks with Mango-Cucumber Relish

PREP: 35 minutes **GRILL:** 11 minutes

- 1/2 tsp. curry powder
- 1/8 tsp. salt
- 1/8 tsp. crushed red pepper
- 1 Tbsp. cooking oil
- 4 boneless beef top loin steaks, cut 1 inch thick (2 1/4 lb. total)
- 1 recipe Mango-Cucumber Relish (below)

1. In a small bowl stir curry powder, salt, and red pepper into oil; set aside.

2. Grill steaks on rack of uncovered grill directly over medium coals to desired doneness, turning once halfway through cooking and brushing steak lightly with oil mixture. Turn steaks; brush again with oil mixture. Grill to desired doneness. Allow 11 to 15 minutes for medium-rare or 14 to 18 minutes for medium.

3. Serve steaks with Mango-Cucumber Relish. Makes 4 servings.

MANGO-CUCUMBER RELISH: In a bowl combine 1 small ripe mango, seeded, peeled, and chopped (3/4 cup); 1 small cucumber, seeded and coarsely chopped (1 1/4 cups); 1/3 cup chopped red onion; 1/3 cup chopped red or green sweet pepper; 1/3 cup chopped, peeled jicama; 2 tablespoons snipped fresh mint or parsley; 2 tablespoons seasoned rice vinegar; 1/2 teaspoon curry powder; 1/8 teaspoon salt; and 1/8 teaspoon crushed red pepper. Cover; chill up to 8 hours. Makes 3 cups.

Each serving: 391 cal., 14 g total fat (4 g sat. fat), 155 mg chol., 348 mg sodium, 9 g carbo., 1 g fiber, 55 g pro. Daily Values: 32% vit. A, 60% vit. C, 3% calcium, 41% iron.

Ribeye Steaks with Glazed Sweet Onions

Most sweet onions are grown from fall to spring in warm-weather states. Look for Vidalia, Maui, Walla Walla, AmeriSweet, Imperial, Oso, or Texas sweet onions.

PREP: 25 minutes **GRILL:** 11 minutes

- 1 tsp. coarse salt
- 3/4 tsp. cracked black pepper
- 1/2 tsp. mustard seeds, coarsely ground
- 4 8- to 10-oz. boneless beef ribeye steaks, cut 1 inch thick
- 1 Tbsp. olive oil
- 1 medium sweet onion, halved and thinly sliced
- 1 clove garlic, minced
- 1/4 cup chopped red sweet pepper
- 1 fresh jalapeño pepper*, seeded and finely chopped
- 2 Tbsp. balsamic vinegar
- 1 tsp. brown sugar
- 1/2 tsp. dried sage, crushed

1. In a small bowl combine salt, pepper, and mustard seeds; divide mixture in half. Rub half of the mustard mixture onto one side of the steaks; set aside.

2. In a large skillet heat olive oil; add onion and garlic. Cook and stir over medium heat about 5 minutes or until onion is tender. Add red sweet pepper and jalapeño pepper; cook and stir for 1 minute more. Add balsamic vinegar, brown sugar, sage, and remaining half of the mustard mixture; cook and stir for 1 minute more. Cover and keep warm.

3. Meanwhile, for a charcoal grill, grill steaks on the rack of an uncovered grill directly over medium coals until desired doneness, turning once halfway through grilling. Allow 11 to 15 minutes for medium-rare and 14 to 18 minutes for medium. (For a gas grill, preheat grill. Reduce heat to medium. Place steaks on rack over heat. Cover; grill as above.) Serve with onion mixture. Makes 4 servings.

***TEST KITCHEN TIP:** Because chile peppers, such as jalapeños, contain volatile oils that can burn your skin and eyes, avoid direct contact with them as much as possible. Wear plastic or rubber gloves. If your bare hands do touch the peppers, wash your hands well with soap and water.

Each serving: 320 cal., 14 g total fat (4 g sat. fat), 81 mg chol., 575 mg sodium, 8 g carbo., 1 g fiber, 38 g pro. Daily Values: 11% vit. A, 38% vit. C, 3% calcium, 18% iron.

Grilled Steak and Mango Salad

CHILL: 4 hours **PREP:** 20 minutes **COOK:** 15 minutes

- 12 oz. boneless beef top loin steak, cut 1 inch thick
- 1 Tbsp. olive oil or cooking oil
- 1/2 tsp. salt
- 1/4 tsp. cracked black pepper
- 1 10-oz. pkg. torn mixed salad greens
- 2 medium mangoes, seeded, peeled, and chopped
- 1 medium pear, peeled, cored, and chopped
- 1 recipe Blue Cheese Dressing (below)
- Cracked black pepper

1. Rub steak with oil; sprinkle both sides with salt and 1/4 teaspoon pepper.

2. Grill steak on rack of an uncovered grill directly over medium coals to desired doneness, turning once. Allow 11 to 15 minutes for medium-rare; 14 to 18 minutes for medium.

3. To serve, thinly slice steak across grain. Arrange greens on a platter; top with meat, mangoes, and pear. Stir Blue Cheese Dressing; pour over salad. Sprinkle with pepper. Makes 4 servings.

BLUE CHEESE DRESSING: Stir together 1/2 cup light mayonnaise dressing or salad dressing; 2 tablespoons dairy sour cream; 1 1/2 teaspoons snipped fresh parsley; 3/4 teaspoon lemon juice; 3/4 teaspoon Worcestershire sauce; 1 clove garlic, minced; dash pepper; and dash bottled hot pepper sauce. Gently stir in 1/4 cup crumbled blue cheese. Cover and chill for 4 to 6 hours. Makes 3/4 cup.

Each serving: 456 cal., 30 g total fat (10 g sat. fat), 73 mg chol., 632 mg sodium, 30 g carbo., 4 g fiber, 19 g pro. Daily Values: 88% vit. A, 58% vit. C, 8% calcium, 12% iron.

FIVE-INGREDIENT DINNERS

PRIZE TESTED RECIPES® $400 WINNER

HYUN C. EOM, SUNNYVALE, CALIF.

Spicy Jalapeño-Shrimp Pasta

START TO FINISH: 30 minutes

- 12 oz. fresh or frozen large shrimp in shells
- 8 oz. dried linguine
- 1 or 2 fresh jalapeño chile peppers
- 2 Tbsp. olive oil
- 2 cloves garlic, minced
- 1/2 tsp. salt
- 1/4 tsp. pepper
- 2 cups chopped tomatoes and/or cherry tomatoes, quartered
- Finely shredded Parmesan cheese (optional)

1. Thaw shrimp, if frozen. Peel and devein shrimp. Cook linguine according to package directions. Chop jalapeños finely (see tip, page 575).

2. In a large skillet heat oil over medium-high heat. Add jalapeños, garlic, salt, and pepper; cook and stir for 1 minute. Add shrimp; cook and stir about 3 minutes more or until shrimp turn opaque. Stir in tomatoes; heat through.

3. Drain linguine; toss with shrimp mixture. If desired, top with Parmesan cheese. Makes 4 servings.

Each serving: 363 cal., 9 g total fat (1 g sat. fat), 97 mg chol., 396 mg sodium, 48 g carbo., 3 g fiber, 21 g pro. Daily Values: 14% vit. A, 39% vit. C, 5% calcium, 20% iron.

PRIZE TESTED RECIPES® $200 WINNER

SHANNON MARTINEZ, WINTERS, CALIF.

Southwest Pork Chops

PREP: 15 minutes **COOK:** 2 1/2 hours(high) or 5 hours(low), plus 30 minutes(high)

- 6 pork rib chops, cut 3/4 inch thick (about 2 1/2 lb.)
- 1 15 1/2-oz. can Mexican-style or Tex-Mex-style chili beans
- 1 1/4 cups bottled salsa
- 1 cup fresh or frozen whole kernel corn
- 2 cups hot cooked rice
- Snipped fresh cilantro (optional

1. Trim excess fat from chops. Place chops in a 3 1/2- or 4-quart crockery cooker. Add chili beans and salsa. Cover; cook on high-heat setting for 2 1/2 hours or on low-heat setting for 5 hours. Turn to high-heat setting. Stir in corn. Cover and cook for 30 minutes more. Serve over rice. If desired, sprinkle each serving with cilantro. Makes 6 servings.

TEST KITCHEN TIP: To cook all day, substitute 8 boneless pork chops for the 6 rib chops. Cover and cook on low-heat setting for 9 1/2 hours. Turn to high-heat setting. Stir in corn. Cover and cook for 30 minutes more. Serve as above.

Each serving: 334 cal., 7 g total fat (2 g sat. fat), 77 mg chol., 716 mg sodium, 34 g carbo., 4 g fiber, 33 g pro. Daily Values: 5% vit. A, 13% vit. C, 6% calcium, 19% iron.

Salmon with Oriental Noodles

PREP: 15 minutes **BROIL:** 8 minutes

- 4 **fresh or frozen skinless, boneless salmon fillets, cut 1 inch thick (about 1¼ lb.)**
- 1 **Tbsp. olive oil**
- ¼ **tsp. pepper**
- 5 **Tbsp. bottled plum sauce**
- 1 **3-oz. pkg. ramen noodles (any flavor)**
- 5 **cups coarsely shredded Chinese cabbage**
- 2 **Tbsp. sliced almonds, toasted**

1. Thaw fish, if frozen. Preheat broiler. Rinse salmon fillets; pat dry. Arrange fillets on the greased unheated rack of a broiler pan, tucking under any thin edges. Brush with the olive oil. Sprinkle with pepper. Broil 4 inches from the heat for 5 minutes. Using a wide spatula, carefully turn fish. Remove 1 tablespoon of the plum sauce; lightly brush onto salmon. Broil for 3 to 7 minutes more or until fish flakes easily with a fork.

2. Meanwhile, cook noodles according to package directions; drain.

3. Place shredded cabbage in a large bowl. Toss hot cooked noodles and remaining plum sauce with cabbage until combined. Serve salmon fillets over noodle mixture; sprinkle with sliced almonds. Makes 4 servings.

Each serving: 439 cal., 23 g total fat (3 g sat. fat), 87 mg chol., 464 mg sodium, 25 g carbo., 4 g fiber, 36 g pro. Daily Values: 28% vit. A, 44% vit. C, 10% calcium, 8% iron.

Salmon with Pesto Mayo

Make your own pesto or buy some for this September 2000 champion.

START TO FINISH: 20 minutes

- 4 **5- to 6-oz. fresh or frozen skinless, boneless salmon fillets**
- 2 **Tbsp. crumbled firm-textured bread**
- ¼ **cup mayonnaise or salad dressing**
- 3 **Tbsp. basil pesto**
- 1 **Tbsp. grated Parmesan cheese**

1. Thaw fish, if frozen. Preheat broiler. Place the bread crumbs in a shallow baking pan. Broil 4 inches from heat for 1 to 2 minutes or until lightly toasted, stirring once. Set bread crumbs aside.

2. Measure thickness of fish. Arrange fish on the greased unheated rack of broiler pan, tucking under any thin edges. Broil 4 inches from heat for 4 to 6 minutes per ½-inch thickness or until fish begins to flake easily with a fork. Turn 1-inch-thick fillets halfway through broiling.

3. Meanwhile, in a small bowl stir together mayonnaise and pesto; set aside. Combine toasted bread crumbs and cheese. Spoon mayonnaise mixture over fillets. Sprinkle with crumb mixture. Broil 1 to 2 minutes more or until crumbs are light brown. Makes 4 servings.

Each serving: 363 cal., 24 g total fat (3 g sat. fat), 84 mg chol., 309 mg sodium, 5 g carbo., 0 g fiber, 31g pro. Daily Values: 6% vit. A, 4% calcium, 7% iron.

Curried Shrimp on Rice

START TO FINISH: 25 minutes

- 1 **10-oz. container refrigerated Alfredo sauce (1⅛ cup)**
- 2 **to 3 tsp. curry powder**
- 12 **oz. peeled, deveined, cooked medium shrimp***
- 3 **cups hot cooked rice**
- ¼ **cup slivered almonds, toasted**

1. In a large saucepan combine Alfredo sauce and curry powder. If necessary, add 1 or 2 tablespoons water to thin. Cook and stir over medium heat just until boiling. Add shrimp. Cook and stir 2 to 3 minutes more or until heated through. Serve shrimp mixture over rice; sprinkle with almonds. Makes 4 servings.

***TEST KITCHEN TIP:** If tails are present on the shrimp, remove them before using.

Each serving: 550 cal., 29 g total fat (1 g sat. fat), 206 mg chol., 426 mg sodium, 41 g carbo., 2 g fiber, 32 pro. Daily Values: 4% vit. A, 4% vit. C, 10% calcium, 27% iron.

Lamb and Peppers

Toss some couscous with a little butter and some finely shredded lemon peel to serve alongside.

START TO FINISH: 25 minutes

- 8 **lamb rib or loin chops, cut 1 inch thick**
- 3 **small green, red, and/or yellow sweet peppers, cut into 1-inch pieces**
- 2 **cloves garlic, minced**
- 1 **Tbsp. snipped fresh oregano**
- 1 **Tbsp. olive oil or cooking oil**
- ¼ **cup sliced pitted green or ripe olives**

1. Preheat broiler. Place chops on the unheated rack of a broiler pan. Broil 3 to 4 inches from heat for 10 to 15 minutes for medium (160° F), turning meat over after half of the broiling time. Transfer to a serving platter.

2. Meanwhile, in a large skillet cook sweet peppers, garlic, and oregano in hot oil for 8 to 10 minutes or until sweet peppers are crisp-tender. Add olives. Cook and stir until heated through. Spoon over chops. Makes 4 servings.

Each serving: 186 cal., 10 g total fat (2 g sat. fat), 60 mg chol., 257 mg sodium, 4 g carbo., 1 g fiber, 20 g pro. Daily Values: 7% vit. A, 72% vit. C, 3% calcium, 12% iron.

TAKE FIVE

For our five-ingredient category, we decided not to count optional ingredients or very common staples, since we all have them in the kitchen. So when you see six ingredients in a recipe, chances are one of them might be cooking oil, nonstick cooking spray, salt, pepper, water, or ice. Any other ingredients count for this easy-on-the-shopper category.

HOLIDAY HAM

PRIZE TESTED RECIPES® $400 WINNER

BETTY NICHOLS, EUGENE, OREGON

PRIZE TESTED RECIPES® $200 WINNER

BETTY NICHOLS, EUGENE, OREGON

Harvest Holiday Ham with Cider Glaze

PREP: 20 minutes **BAKE:** 1½ hours **COOK:** 20 minutes

- 1 5- to 6-lb. cooked ham, rump or shank portion
- 2 cups apple cider or apple juice
- 1 cup honey
- ½ cup cider vinegar
- ¼ cup Dijon-style mustard
- 2 tsp. chili powder
- 1 Tbsp. butter
- ½ tsp. apple pie spice

1. Preheat oven to 325° F. Trim fat from ham. Score with diagonal cuts in a diamond pattern. Place on a rack in a shallow roasting pan. Insert a meat thermometer. Roast, uncovered, about 1½ to 2¼ hours or until thermometer registers 140° F.

2. Meanwhile, for sauce, in a large saucepan combine apple cider, honey, vinegar, mustard, and chili powder. Bring to boiling; reduce heat. Simmer, uncovered, about 15 minutes or until reduced to 2 cups, stirring frequently. Transfer half of the mixture to a small bowl; stir in butter and ¼ teaspoon apple pie spice. Set aside.

3. For glaze, return remaining mixture in saucepan to boiling; reduce heat. Simmer gently about 5 minutes or until mixture is thickened and reduced to about ½ cup, stirring frequently. Stir in remaining ¼ teaspoon apple pie spice.

4. Brush ham with glaze the last 20 to 30 minutes of roasting. Transfer to a platter. Reheat sauce, if necessary; pass with ham. Makes 16 to 20 servings.

Each serving: 384 cal., 13 g total fat (5 g sat. fat), 138 mg chol., 126 mg sodium, 22 g carbo., 0 g fiber, 44 g pro. Daily Values: 3% vit. A, 2% vit. C, 2% calcium, 11% iron.

Ham with Ginger-Pear Relish

PREP: 25 minutes **CHILL:** 1 hour

- ⅓ cup dried cranberries
- 2 pears, cored and chopped
- 4 green onions, thinly sliced
- 3 Tbsp.. finely chopped crystallized ginger
- 1 Tbsp. olive oil
- 1 Tbsp. lime juice
- 1 Tbsp. honey
- 1 tsp. snipped fresh rosemary
- 1 2-lb. cooked boneless ham

1. Place cranberries in a small bowl; add boiling water to cover. Let stand for 10 minutes; drain and return to bowl.

2. Add remaining ingredients; toss gently to coat. Cover and chill for 1 to 3 hours. Heat ham, if desired; serve with relish. Makes 8 servings (2⅓ cups).

Each serving: 279 cal., 14 g total fat (4 g sat. fat), 65 mg chol., 1,496 mg sodium, 18 g carbo., 0 g fiber, 20 g pro. Daily Values: 1% vit. A, 6% vit. C, 2% calcium, 8% iron.

Ham Bites with Cranberry-Apple Sauce

Remember fondue? Ham cubes make the perfect dipper. You can also serve the fondue as a sauce for baked ham.

START TO FINISH: 30 minutes

- 1 cup fresh or frozen cranberries
- 1 tsp. finely shredded orange peel
- 1 cup orange juice
- 1 medium apple, cored and finely chopped (1 cup)
- 1/3 cup packed brown sugar
- 1 jalapeño pepper, seeded and finely chopped (1 to 2 Tbsp.) (see tip, page 575)
- 1/8 tsp. ground cloves
- 1 2-lb. cooked boneless ham, cut into 3/4-inch cubes
- 1/2 of a medium fresh pineapple, peeled, cored, and cut into 1-inch cubes

1. For sauce, in a medium saucepan combine cranberries, orange peel, and juice. Bring to boiling; reduce heat. Simmer gently, uncovered, for 1 minute. Add apple, brown sugar, jalapeño pepper, and cloves. Return to boiling; reduce heat and boil gently, uncovered, for 2 minutes more. Let cool for 10 minutes.

2. Place cranberry mixture in a food processor or blender; cover and process or blend until nearly smooth. Transfer to a fondue pot or chafing dish to keep warm.

3. Dip ham and pineapple cubes into warm sauce. Makes 16 appetizer servings.

Each serving: 141 cal., 5 g total fat (2 g sat. fat), 33 mg chol., 853 mg sodium, 10 g carbo., 1 g fiber, 13 g pro. Daily Values: 1% vit. A, 20% vit. C, 1% calcium, 5% iron.

Marinated Ham with Spiced Pineapple Sauce

PREP: 15 minutes **MARINATE:** 4 hours
ROAST: 1 hour

- 1 1/4 cups pineapple juice
- 3/4 cup packed brown sugar
- 3 Tbsp. white wine vinegar
- 2 Tbsp. Dijon-style mustard
- 1/2 tsp. chili powder
- 1/8 to 1/4 tsp. ground cloves
- 1 3- to 4-lb. cooked boneless ham
- 2 Tbsp. cornstarch

1. For marinade, in a medium bowl combine 1 1/4 cups pineapple juice, brown sugar, vinegar, mustard, chili powder, and cloves. Prick the ham all over with a long-tined fork. Place ham in an extra-large self-sealing plastic bag set in a shallow dish. Pour marinade over meat; close bag. Refrigerate for 4 to 24 hours.

2. Preheat oven to 325° F. Remove ham from marinade. Set aside 1 3/4 cups of the marinade for sauce. Place ham on a rack in a shallow roasting pan. Insert a meat thermometer into the thickest portion of the ham. Roast, uncovered, for 1 to 1 3/4 hours or until the thermometer registers 140° F, spooning some of the remaining marinade over the ham twice.

3. Meanwhile, for sauce, in a medium saucepan stir together reserved marinade and cornstarch. Cook and stir over medium heat until thickened and bubbly. Cook and stir for 2 minutes more.

4. Transfer ham to a serving platter. Spoon some sauce over ham; pass remaining sauce. Makes 12 to 16 servings.

Each serving: 278 cal., 10 g total fat (4 g sat. fat), 67 mg chol., 1,722 mg sodium, 19 g carbo., 0 g fiber, 26 g pro. Daily Values: 1% vit. A, 5% vit. C, 3% calcium, 11% iron.

Ham and Sweet Potatoes with Cranberry-Raspberry Sauce

PREP: 25 minutes **ROAST:** 1 1/4 hours

- 1 3- to 4-lb. cooked boneless ham
- 6 medium (about 3 lb.) sweet potatoes, peeled and halved lengthwise
- 2 medium onions, cut into wedges
- 1/2 cup packed brown sugar
- 1/2 cup Champagne
- 1 recipe Cranberry-Raspberry Sauce (right)

1. Preheat oven to 325° F. Slice ham into 1/4-inch-thick slices. Arrange in the center of a shallow roasting pan. Arrange sweet potatoes and onion wedges around ham. Pour 1/4 cup Champagne over ham. In a cup stir together brown sugar and 1/4 cup Champagne; drizzle over potatoes and onion. Cover tightly with foil. Bake about 1 1/4 hours or until potatoes and onion are tender.

2. Transfer ham and vegetables to a serving platter. Pass Cranberry-Raspberry Sauce. Makes 12 to 16 servings.

CRANBERRY-RASPBERRY SAUCE: Drain one thawed 10-ounce package frozen red raspberries in syrup, reserving liquid. Set the raspberries aside. In a small saucepan combine 1/3 cup packed brown sugar, 4 teaspoons cornstarch, and 1/4 teaspoon ground allspice. Stir in the reserved raspberry liquid, 1/2 cup Champagne, and 1 3/4 cups fresh or frozen cranberries. Cook and stir over medium heat until thickened and bubbly. Cook and stir for 2 minutes more. Remove from heat. Stir in 1/2 cup chopped walnuts and reserved raspberries.

Each serving: 480 cal., 14 g total fat (4 g sat. fat), 67 mg chol., 1,729 mg sodium, 57 g carbo., 5 g fiber, 29g pro. Daily Values: 432% vit. A, 41% vit. C, 26% calcium, 17% iron.

Prosciutto-Stuffed Mushrooms

PREP: 25 minutes **BAKE:** 8 minutes

- 24 large fresh mushrooms, 1 1/2 to 2 inches in diameter
- 1/4 cup sliced green onion
- 1 clove garlic, minced
- 1/4 cup butter or margarine
- 2/3 cup fine dry bread crumbs
- 1/3 cup chopped prosciutto or cooked ham
- 1/4 cup shredded provolone cheese
- 1/2 tsp. dried Italian seasoning, crushed

1. Preheat oven to 425° F. Rinse and drain mushrooms. Remove stems; reserve caps. Chop enough stems to make 1 cup.

2. In a medium saucepan cook chopped stems, green onion, and garlic in hot butter until tender. Stir in bread crumbs, prosciutto or ham, cheese, and seasoning. Spoon mixture into mushroom caps.

3. Arrange stuffed mushrooms in a 15×10×1-inch baking pan. Bake for 8 to 10 minutes or until heated through. Makes 24 mushrooms.

Each mushroom: 42 cal., 3 g total fat (2 g sat. fat), 7 mg chol., 97 mg sodium, 2 g carbo., 0 g fiber, 2 g pro. Daily Values: 2% vit. A, 2% calcium, 2% iron.

SKILLET DINNERS

PRIZE TESTED RECIPES® $400 WINNER\

KRISTYNN O. KRANER, TUCSON, ARIZ.

Pesce Italiano

START TO FINISH: 30 minutes

- 1 cup dried penne pasta
- 1 cup sliced fresh mushrooms
- 1/3 cup dry white wine
- 2 Tbsp. basil pesto
- 1 Tbsp. lemon juice
- 2 tsp. drained capers
- 2 6-oz. salmon, tuna, or swordfish steaks, cut 3/4 inch thick
- 1 tsp. Creole seasoning
- 1 Tbsp. olive oil

1. In a large saucepan cook pasta in lightly salted boiling water for 4 minutes. Drain pasta (it will not be tender). In a medium bowl combine partially cooked pasta, mushrooms, wine, pesto, lemon juice, and capers; set aside.

2. Rinse fish; pat dry. Sprinkle fish with Creole seasoning. (If seasoning is salt free, sprinkle with 1/4 teaspoon salt.) In a large skillet cook fish in hot oil over medium-high heat for 1 minute; turn and cook 1 minute more. Reduce heat to medium.

3. Spoon pasta mixture around fish in skillet. Bring to boiling; reduce heat. Simmer, covered, for 6 to 9 minutes or until fish flakes easily. Makes 2 servings.

Each serving: 627 cal., 30 g total fat (5 g sat. fat), 109 mg chol., 352 mg sodium, 36 g carbo., 2 g fiber, 46 g pro. Daily Values: 6% vit. A, 7% vit. C, 11% calcium, 17% iron.

PRIZE TESTED RECIPES® $200 WINNER

MARGIE TYLER STALZER, PALM COAST, FLA.

Tortellini and Veggies

START TO FINISH: 40 minutes

- 1 large onion, coarsely chopped
- 1 8-oz. pkg. fresh mushrooms, such as cremini or white, halved
- 1 medium red sweet pepper, cut into 3/4-inch pieces (3/4 cup)
- 2 cloves garlic, minced
- 2 Tbsp. olive oil
- 1 14 1/2-oz. can diced tomatoes
- 1/4 cup dry red wine
- 2 tsp. dried Italian seasoning, crushed
- 1/4 tsp. ground black pepper
- 1 9-oz. pkg. refrigerated cheese-filled tortellini
- 4 small zucchini, halved lengthwise and cut into 1/2-inch-thick slices
- 1/2 cup shredded Asiago or Parmesan cheese (2 oz.)

1. In a large skillet cook onion, mushrooms, sweet pepper, and garlic in hot oil until tender. Stir in 1/2 cup water, undrained tomatoes, wine, seasoning, and black pepper. Add tortellini. Bring to boiling; reduce heat. Simmer, covered, 10 minutes.

2. Stir in zucchini. Cook, uncovered, about 5 minutes more or until zucchini is crisp-tender. Remove from heat. Sprinkle with cheese. Makes 4 to 6 servings.

Each serving: 414 cal., 18 g total fat (6 g sat. fat), 45 mg chol., 566 mg sodium, 46 g carbo., 4 g fiber, 18 g pro. Daily Values: 38% vit. A, 118% vit.C, 32% calcium, 19% iron.

Flounder Mediterranean

PREP: 15 minutes **COOK:** 25 minutes

- 8 oz. sliced fresh mushrooms
- 2 shallots or half of a small onion, sliced (1/4 cup)
- 4 cloves garlic, minced
- 2 Tbsp. olive oil
- 2 14 1/2-oz. cans diced tomatoes with basil, oregano, and garlic
- 1/2 cup dry white wine
- 3/4 cup roasted red sweet peppers, cut into strips (about 3/4 of a 7-oz. jar)
- 1/4 cup oil-packed dried tomatoes, drained and chopped
- 1 Tbsp. capers
- 6 4-oz. flounder, haddock, or cod fillets, cut 1/2 inch thick
- 1/4 tsp. crushed red pepper
- 3 cups hot cooked rice
- Snipped fresh Italian flat-leaf parsley

1. In a 10-inch skillet cook mushrooms, shallots, and garlic in hot olive oil about 4 minutes or until tender.

2. Stir in undrained diced tomatoes and wine. Bring to boiling; reduce heat. Simmer, uncovered, for 15 minutes. Stir in sweet peppers, dried tomatoes, and capers.

3. Rinse fish. Place atop sauce; sprinkle with red pepper. Simmer, covered, for 4 to 6 minutes more or until fish flakes easily.

4. Divide rice among six shallow bowls. Place a fish fillet on rice. Divide tomato mixture among bowls. Sprinkle with parsley. Makes 6 servings.

Each serving: 345 cal., 7 g total fat (1 g sat. fat), 64 mg chol., 845 mg sodium, 40 g carbo., 2 g fiber, 28 g pro. Daily Values: 21% vit. A, 113% vit. C, 15% calcium, 28% iron.

Curried Chicken and Couscous

PREP: 15 minutes **COOK:** 17 minutes
STAND: 5 minutes

- 1 Tbsp. curry powder
- 1/2 tsp. ground ginger
- 1/4 tsp. ground cumin
- 1/8 tsp. salt
- 1/8 tsp. pepper
- 1 6-oz. pkg. quick-cooking roasted garlic-flavored couscous or 1 cup plain couscous
- 4 skinless, boneless chicken breast halves (about 1 1/4 to 1 1/2 lb.)
- 1 Tbsp. lime juice
- 2 Tbsp. cooking oil
- 1/2 cup sliced fresh mushrooms
- 1/4 cup thinly sliced carrot
- 1/4 cup sliced celery
- 1/4 cup chopped red onion
- 2 cloves garlic, minced
- 1 14-oz. can reduced-sodium chicken broth
- 1/4 cup mango chutney
- 1 Tbsp. snipped fresh cilantro
- Lime wedges (optional)

1. In a small mixing bowl stir together curry powder, ginger, cumin, salt, pepper, and the seasoning packet from the couscous mix, if using.

2. Drizzle chicken with lime juice. Sprinkle 1 1/2 teaspoons of the spice mixture onto both sides of chicken. Set remaining spice mixture aside.

3. In a large skillet brown chicken breasts on both sides in hot oil; set aside. Add mushrooms, carrot, celery, onion, garlic, and remaining spice mixture; cook 5 minutes or until vegetables are tender. Return chicken to skillet. Carefully add broth. Heat to boiling; reduce heat. Simmer, covered, for 12 to 15 minutes or until chicken is tender and no longer pink; remove chicken.

4. Stir couscous and chutney into cooking liquid. Return chicken to skillet. Remove from heat. Cover and let stand for 5 minutes or until couscous is done. Sprinkle with cilantro. If desired, serve with lime wedges. Makes 4 servings.

Each serving: 439 cal., 10 g total fat (2 g sat. fat), 82 mg chol., 796 mg sodium, 48 g carbo., 4 g fiber, 41 g pro. Daily Values: 55% vit. A, 23% vit. C, 6% calcium, 13% iron.

Corn and Beans with Cornmeal Dumplings

START TO FINISH: 35 minutes

- 2 14 1/2-oz. cans diced tomatoes with onions and garlic
- 1 15-oz. can black beans, rinsed and drained
- 1 cup frozen whole kernel corn
- 1 4-oz. can chopped green chile peppers
- 1/2 cup chopped green sweet pepper
- 1/2 cup chopped carrot
- 1/2 tsp. ground cumin
- 1/4 tsp. ground black pepper
- 1 recipe Cornmeal Dumplings (below)
- 1/2 cup shredded Monterey Jack cheese with jalapeño peppers
- Dairy sour cream (optional)

1. In a very large skillet combine undrained tomatoes, beans, corn, green chili peppers, green sweet pepper, carrot, cumin, and black pepper. Bring to boiling.

2. Drop Cornmeal Dumplings from a tablespoon to make 10 to 12 mounds atop bubbling mixture in skillet. Reduce heat and simmer, covered, for 10 to 15 minutes or until a toothpick inserted in dumpling comes out clean. Sprinkle with cheese.

3. If desired, serve with a dollop of sour cream. Makes 5 to 6 servings.

CORNMEAL DUMPLINGS: In a medium bowl stir together 1/2 cup all-purpose flour, 1/3 cup cornmeal, 1/4 cup shredded Monterey Jack cheese with jalapeño peppers, 2 tablespoons thinly sliced green onion, 1 teaspoon baking powder, 1/4 teaspoon salt, and a dash ground black pepper. In a small mixing bowl beat 1 egg. Stir in 2 tablespoons milk and 2 tablespoons cooking oil; add all at once to the flour mixture. Stir just until combined.

Each serving: 375 cal., 13 g total fat (5 g sat. fat), 61 mg chol., 1,481 mg sodium, 54 g carbo., 7 g fiber, 17 g pro. Daily Values: 91% vit. A, 57% vit. C, 34% calcium, 29% iron.

CANNED & FROZEN VEGETABLES

PRIZE TESTED RECIPES® $400 WINNER

DENNIS MILLER, HAWTHORNE, CALIF.

PRIZE TESTED RECIPES® $200 WINNER

SABRINA DANA, EULESS, TEXAS

East-West Veggies

START TO FINISH: 20 minutes

- 1 medium onion, cut into thin wedges (1/2 cup)
- 1 Tbsp. butter or margarine
- 1 Tbsp. olive oil
- 6 green onions, cut into 1-inch pieces (1/2 cup)
- 3 Tbsp. hoisin sauce
- 1 tsp. paprika
- 1 15 1/4-oz. can whole kernel corn, drained
- 1 15-oz. can black beans, rinsed and drained
- 3/4 cup chopped celery
- 1/2 cup finely chopped red sweet pepper

1. In a large skillet cook and stir onion wedges in hot butter and oil over medium heat about 4 minutes or until tender but not brown. Stir in green onions, hoisin sauce, and paprika. Cook and stir for 1 minute more.

2. Add corn, beans, celery, and red sweet pepper. Cook and stir until heated through. Transfer to a serving bowl. Makes 6 servings.

Each serving: 166 cal., 5 g total fat (2 g sat. fat), 5 mg chol., 574 mg sodium, 28 g carbo., 5 g fiber, 6 g pro. Daily Values: 21% vit. A, 47% vit. C, 4% calcium, 6% iron.

Great Greek Green Beans

START TO FINISH: 25 minutes

- 1/2 cup chopped onion
- 1 clove garlic, minced
- 2 Tbsp. olive oil
- 1 28-oz. can diced tomatoes
- 1/4 cup sliced pitted ripe olives
- 1 tsp. dried oregano, crushed
- 2 9-oz. pkg. or one 16-oz. pkg. frozen French-cut green beans, thawed and drained
- 1/2 cup crumbled feta cheese (2 oz.)

1. In a large skillet cook onion and garlic in hot olive oil about 5 minutes or until tender but not brown. Add undrained tomatoes, olives, and oregano. Bring to boiling; reduce heat. Simmer gently, uncovered, for 10 minutes.

2. Add beans. Return to boiling. Boil gently, uncovered, about 8 minutes or until desired consistency and beans are tender.

3. Transfer to a serving bowl; sprinkle with feta cheese. If desired, serve with a slotted spoon. Makes 6 servings.

Each serving: 132 cal., 7 g total fat (2 g sat. fat), 8 mg chol., 419 mg sodium, 15 g carbo., 5 g fiber, 4 g pro. Daily Values: 9% vit. A, 32% vit. C, 11% calcium, 8% iron.

Brussels Sprouts with Lemon-Dijon Sauce

START TO FINISH: 20 minutes

- 1 10-oz. pkg. frozen brussels sprouts or cut broccoli or one 9-oz. pkg. frozen cut green beans
- 2 slices bacon
- 1/2 cup thinly sliced green onion (6 onions)
- 2 cloves garlic, minced
- 2 Tbsp. Dijon-style mustard
- 2 tsp. all-purpose flour
- 1/2 tsp. finely shredded lemon peel
- 1/4 tsp. pepper
- 1 cup half-and-half, light cream, or milk

1. Cook brussels sprouts, broccoli, or green beans in lightly salted water according to package directions. Drain; set aside.

2. Meanwhile, in a medium skillet cook bacon until crisp. Drain bacon on paper towels, reserving 1 tablespoon drippings in skillet. Crumble bacon; set aside.

3. Add green onion and garlic to drippings in skillet; cook over medium heat for 1 minute. Stir in mustard, flour, lemon peel, and pepper. Add half-and-half, light cream, or milk all at once. Cook and stir until thickened and bubbly. (Sauce may appear slightly curdled before it bubbles.) Cook and stir for 1 minute more.

4. Add vegetables to lemon sauce; heat through, tossing gently to combine. Transfer to a serving bowl. Sprinkle with crumbled bacon. Makes 4 servings.

Each serving: 175 cal., 13 g total fat (6 g sat. fat), 28 mg chol., 126 mg sodium, 12 g carbo., 3 g fiber, 6 g pro. Daily Values: 17% vit. A, 71% vit. C, 10% calcium, 7% iron.

Golden Sunset Soup

PREP: 15 minutes **COOK:** 10 minutes

- 1 15-oz. can pumpkin
- 1 14-oz. can unsweetened light coconut milk
- 1 14-oz. can chicken broth
- 2 Tbsp. brown sugar
- 1 medium jalapeño pepper, seeded and finely chopped (see tip, page 575)
- 3/4 tsp. salt
- 1 16-oz. pkg. frozen yellow, red, and green peppers and onion stir-fry vegetables, thawed and drained
- 3 Tbsp. snipped fresh cilantro or parsley
- Toasted large flaked coconut (optional)

1. In a large saucepan stir together pumpkin, coconut milk, broth, brown sugar, jalapeño pepper, and salt.

2. Coarsely chop thawed vegetables; add to saucepan. Bring mixture to boiling; reduce heat. Simmer, uncovered, for 10 minutes or until vegetables are heated through, stirring frequently.

3. Stir in cilantro or parsley. Spoon soup into eight to twelve soup bowls. If desired, garnish with toasted coconut. Makes 8 to 12 appetizer servings.

Each serving: 83 cal., 3 g total fat (2 g sat. fat), 0 mg chol., 397 mg sodium, 12 g carbo., 2 g fiber, 2 g pro. Daily Values: 243% vit. A, 40% vit. C, 2% calcium, 9% iron.

Artichoke-Spinach Dip

PREP: 30 minutes **BAKE:** 25 minutes

- 2 10-oz. pkg. frozen chopped spinach, thawed and well drained
- 1 6-oz. jar marinated artichoke hearts, drained and finely chopped
- 1 1/2 cups shredded Monterey Jack cheese (6 oz.)
- 1 8-oz. carton dairy sour cream
- 3/4 cup mayonnaise or salad dressing
- 1/4 cup thinly sliced green onion
- 1/4 cup finely shredded or grated Parmesan cheese
- 2 Tbsp. finely shredded or grated Romano cheese
- 2 cloves garlic, minced
- 1/2 tsp. fajita seasoning
- 1 recipe Fajita Pitas (below)

1. Preheat oven to 350° F. Grease a 2-quart square baking dish; set aside.

2. In a large bowl combine spinach, chopped artichoke hearts, Monterey Jack cheese, sour cream, mayonnaise, green onion, Parmesan cheese, Romano cheese, garlic, and fajita seasoning. Transfer to prepared baking dish.

3. Bake, uncovered, for 25 to 30 minutes or until bubbly. Serve with Fajita Pitas. Makes 64 servings (4 cups).

FAJITA PITAS: Preheat oven to 400° F. Using a sharp knife, split 4 large pita rounds in half horizontally (8 rounds total). Brush tops of pita bread rounds evenly with 2 tablespoons olive oil. Sprinkle with 1/4 cup finely shredded Parmesan cheese, 1 teaspoon fajita seasoning, and 1 teaspoon cracked black pepper. Using a sharp knife, carefully cut each pita round into 8 wedges (64 wedges total). Arrange wedges on ungreased baking sheets. Bake for 6 to 8 minutes or until golden brown. Let cool. (Pita chips will crisp upon standing.)

Each tablespoon with wedge: 59 cal., 5 g total fat (2 g sat. fat), 6 mg chol., 82 mg sodium, 3 g carbo., 0 g fiber, 2 g pro. Daily Values: 14% vit. A, 3% vit. C, 5% calcium, 2% iron.

Menus

FOR PARTY AND MEAL IDEAS TO MARK YOUR MILESTONES ANY TIME OF YEAR, TRY OUR MENUS OF DELICIOUS RECIPES.

Orzo and Bulgur Salad

Cranberry-Pineapple Cooler

Moroccan-Style Short Ribs

Winning Menus for Family and Friends

Menus often suit the mood of the season, as you've seen throughout this book, but other times a menu must rise to the occasion, no matter what time of year. On the following pages, you'll find timeless party and meal suggestions for special celebrations, for dietary concerns, and for the adventurous, all based on Prize Tested Recipes from *Better Homes and Gardens*® magazine. The planning's been done. All you need to do is shop, cook a little, and enjoy good meal times.

Coconut-Lemon Puffs

celebration menus

WE ALL HAVE REASONS TO CELEBRATE, NO MATTER WHAT THE SEASON. PERHAPS IT'S A PROMOTION, A NEW HOUSE, OR A BIG ANNIVERSARY. OR MAYBE JUST GETTING EVERYONE TOGETHER IS REASON ENOUGH.

TROPICAL BUFFET

Mahi Mahi Spring Rolls *(page 511)*
Calypso Shrimp Skewers *(page 510)*
Asian-Style Pork and Noodle Salad *(page 537)*
Tropical fruit platter (pineapple, mango, papaya, kiwifruit)
Tropical Fruit Strudel *(page 547)*
Pistachio Coconut Sorbet *(page 555)*
Mango-Ginger Coladas *(page 513)*

SOUTHERN-STYLE COOKOUT

Tennessee Pork Ribs *(page 519)*
Blue Cheese Vidalia Onions *(page 520)*
Jicama-Potato Salad *(page 523)*
Baked beans
Corn and Fig Spoon Bread *(page 539)*
Minty Summer Shortcake *(page 546)*
Iced tea

TAILGATE TIME-OUT

Carrot Dip *(page 534)*
Assorted snack chips, crackers, vegetable dippers
Hot and Spicy Sloppy Joes *(page 534)*
Orzo and Bulgur Salad *(page 540)*
Triple-Nut Zucchini Cake *(page 545)*
Hot or cold cider or beer

AUTUMN CANDLELIGHT DINNER

Brie, Crab, and Mushroom Soup *(page 531)*
Roast Rack of Lamb *(page 353 or 516)*
Squash Gratin with Spinach *(page 538)*
Buffet Wild Rice *(page 538)*
Dinner rolls
Frozen White Chocolate Cranberry Cheese Pie *(page 555)*
Merlot or other red wine
Coffee

Minty Summer Shortcake

Orzo and Bulgur Salad

Roast Rack of Lamb

Mai Tai Me

Lavender Créme Brûlée

Good Ol' Buttermilk Fried Chicken

Guacamole Rice Salad

PACIFIC RIM BUFFET

Pork and Chicken BBQ Sticks *(page 28)*
Soy-Glazed Squash *(page 31)*
Egg Rolls *(page 94)*
Chilled Thai Tenderloin and Pasta with Tons of Basil *(page 273)*
Curried Green and Yellow Bean Salad *(page 473)*
Mango Cream Tart *(page 305)*
Mai Tai Me *(page 242)*
Tea or coffee

ELEGANT SIT-DOWN DINNER

Golden Sunset Soup *(page 583)*
Apple-Fennel Salad with Spiced Cider Vinaigrette *(page 289)*
Grilled Pork Chops with Honey-Orange Glaze *(page 279)*
Bulgur-Wild Rice Casserole *(page 293)*
Asparagus with Almond Sauce *(page 101)*
Dinner rolls
Lavender Crème Brûlée *(page 57)*
Wine or coffee

HOT-STUFF SUPPER

Jalapeño Popper Pizza *(page 302)*
Beef and Red Bean Chili *(page 89)*
Guacamole Rice Salad *(page 292)*
Salsa Bread *(page 560)*
Praline Crunch Cake *(page 295)*
Mojito Sparklers *(page 242)*

POTLUCK IN THE PARK

Artichoke-Spinach Dip *(page 583)*
Good Ol' Buttermilk Fried Chicken *(page 143)*
Tangy Barbecue Beef *(page 90)*
Onion Gratin with Country Ham *(page 307)*
Spinach Beet Salad with Roasted Shallot Dressing *(page 289)*
Red Pepper and Brussels Sprout Salad *(page 288)*
Sauerkraut-Rye Bread *(page 287)*
Rhubarb Pie *(page 199)*
Chocolate Caramel-Nut Bars *(page 298)*
Hit-the-Spot Lemon Water *(page 231)*

shower & wedding menus

ADDING PEOPLE WE LOVE TO OUR LIVES IS CAUSE FOR GREAT JOY AND LOTS OF PARTIES, WHETHER IT'S A BRIDE OR A BABY WE'RE WELCOMING. YOU PICK HOW AND WHEN, THEN CHOOSE THE MENU TO SUIT.

RECEPTION BUFFET

Smoked Salmon Roll-Ups *(page 510)*
Swiss Cheese and Olive Spread *(page 533)* with crackers
Grilled Pork Tenderloin with Blackberry Sauce *(page 519)*
Rosemary Potatoes and Tomatoes *(page 543)* with mixed greens
Spiced Brandy Truffles *(page 556)*
Double-Chocolate Raspberry Creams *(page 557)*
Champagne or other sparkling wine
Cranberry-Pineapple Cooler *(page 512)*

SHOWER FOR BUSY HOSTS

Antipasto tray (olives, sausages, cheeses, marinated peppers)
Focaccia or crackers
Baked Chicken and Artichoke Risotto *(page 527)*
Mixed green salad
Lemon-Lime Mascarpone Trifle *(page 549)*
Red or white wine
Cappuccino or espresso

AFTERNOON HIGH TEA

Cucumber Sandwiches *(page 536)*
Tomatoes with Smoked Salmon *(page 543)*
Assorted tea breads
Lemon-Blackberry Mini Tarts *(page 546)*
Citrus Shortbread Torte *(page 548)*
Hot tea or iced tea

WEEKEND BRUNCH

Portobello and Spinach Brunch Tart *(page 517)*
Sliced melons and berries
Paradise Bread *(page 539)*
Lemon Cream Coffee Cake *(page 549)*
White Strawberry Sangria *(page 512)*
Hot coffee or tea

White Strawberry Sangria

Smoked Salmon Roll-Ups

Lemon-Blackberry Mini Tarts

Jam Roly-Polys

Deviled Eggs with Spicy Crab

Chocolate Tartlettes

Filled-Up Phyllo Logs

AFTERNOON TEA

Nutty Cucumber Sandwiches *(page 269)*
Pear-Walnut Cheese Spirals *(page 263)*
Easy Lemon Sugar Snaps *(page 294)*
Chocolate Shortbread Bites *(page 63)*
Date-with-an-Angel Cookies *(page 299)*
Tea or coffee

WEEKDAY GATHERING

Deviled Eggs with Spicy Crab *(page 25)*
Brie-Pear Canapés *(page 307)*
Mini Cherry Pepper Quiches *(page 302)*
Jam Roly-Polys *(page 53)*
Chocolate Tartlettes *(page 61)*
Lemonade or punch

WEEKEND BRUNCH

Artichoke and Mushroom Bake *(page 571)*
Fruit Salad Bowl Turnover *(page 317)*
Mango Coffee Cake *(page 305)*
Bloody Mary Swizzlers *(page 21)*
Coffee or tea

COCKTAIL BUFFET

Caesar Salad Cracker Cups *(page 21)*
Goat Cheese and Spinach Pesto Bites *(page 559)*
Filled-Up Phyllo Logs *(page 27)*
Savory Baked Brie *(page 559)*
Toasted baguette slices
Mediterranean Chicken Salad *(page 564)*
Horseradish-Radish Sandwiches *(page 22)*
The Mount Everest of Spice Cake *(page 351)*
Best-Ever Chocolate Cake *(page 381 & 461)*
Champagne or punch

birthday menus

IT'S SO EASY TO MAKE SPECIAL PEOPLE FEEL SPECIAL ON THEIR DAY, AS THE MENUS BELOW PROVE. YOUNG CHILDREN, TEENS, PARENTS, AND GRANDPARENTS WILL ALL BE AS PLEASED AS PUNCH.

BALLERINA BIRTHDAY

Pretzel Yummies *(page 556)*
Parmesan-Sesame Chicken Strips *(page 523)*
Carrot and celery sticks
Orange Chiffon Cake *(page 550)*
Raspberry Delight Punch *(page 513)*

BACKYARD BASH

Snack chips and dips
Mushroom Deluxe Hamburgers *(page 535)*
Onion Chili Sauce *(page 535)*
Sweet Summer Tomato Relish *(page 543)*
Corn on the cob
Frozen Praline Chocolate Torte *(page 553)*
Cranberry-Pineapple Cooler *(page 512)*

ON HER DAY

Tomato-Cucumber Soup *(page 542)*
Shrimp and Zucchini with Basil-Chive Cream Sauce *(page 545)*
Breadsticks*(page* 189)
Blackberry Coconut Dessert *(page 547)*
Dry white wine
Hot tea or iced tea

ON HIS DAY

Wine-Balsamic Glazed Steak *(page 532)*
Roasted Potatoes with Goat Cheese Sauce *(page 539)*
Steamed green beans
Coffee and Chocolate Gingerbread *(page 553)*
Dry red wine
Coffee

Orange Chiffon Cake

Tomato-Cucumber Soup

Cranberry-Pineapple Cooler

The Mount Everest of Spice Cake

Lumpy PB&J Rooster

Tandoori Chicken Burgers

Strawberry-Mango Milk Shakes

SWEET SIXTEEN PARTY

Chicken and Sausage Kabobs *(page 144)*
Hot cooked rice
Cut-up vegetables and dip
Easy Chocolate-Peanut Butter Bars *(page 298)*
Sweetheart Shakes *(page 63)*

FUN FARMYARD FEST

Lumpy PB&J Roosters *(page 236)*
Shoestring potato chips
Carrots with Dried Fruit Confetti *(page 236)*
Lemon-Lime Cake *(page 295)*
Strawberry-Mango Milk Shakes *(page 308)*

BACKYARD COOKOUT

Pear, Mango, and Radish Salsa *(page 306)*
Tortilla chips
Ribeye Steaks with Glazed Sweet Onions *(page 575)*
Texas toast
Caramel-Bourbon Upside-Down Cake *(page 54)*
Basil Martinis *(page 242)*

SPACE-AGE BASH

Tandoori Chicken Burgers *(page 147)*
Sliced cucumbers and tomatoes
Double Chocolate Cake *(page 295)*
Mad Mad Martian Juice *(page 274)*

LADIES' NIGHT IN

Feta-Olive Wafers *(page 559)*
Thai Chicken Salad *(page 565)*
Grilled Steak and Mango Salad *(page 575)*
Crusty whole-grain rolls
White Chocolate Cheesecake Peardise *(page 307)*
Ultra Alexanders *(page 243)*

low-fat menus

EATING SMART CAN TASTE GREAT FOR THE WHOLE FAMILY, AS YOU CAN SEE FROM THE MENUS BELOW. THEY'RE SO CREATIVE, SATISFYING, AND FULL OF FLAVOR, YOU'LL NEVER MISS THE FAT!

TASTE OF THE NORTHWEST

Grilled Salmon with Citrus Sauce *(page 519)*
Asparagus Barley Pilaf *(page 541)*
Dinner rolls
Hazelnut Poached Pears and Strawberries over frozen low-fat yogurt *(page 551)*
Northwest wines

COMFORTING SOUP SUPPER

Hearty Sausage Gumbo *(page 535)*
Mom's Bread *(page 540)*
Frozen Berry-Melon Pops *(page 554)*
Fat-free milk

TEX-MEX FIESTA

Baked tortilla chips and salsa
Fiesta Quinoa Salad *(page 541)*
Tijuana Taco Beef Borracho *(page 525)*
Hot cooked rice
Cucumber-Chile Granité *(page 554)*
Frozen Strawberry-Mango Margaritas *(page 513)* and/or
Icy Cranberry Margaritas *(page 513)*

POT ROAST PLEASER

Pork with Parsnips and Pears *(page 524)*
Mashed potatoes
Dinner rolls
Tropical Sorbet *(page 555)*
Coffee or fat-free milk

Mom's Bread

Frozen Berry-Melon Pops

Cucumber-Chile Granité

Strawberry Soufflé

East-West Veggies

Strawberry Italian Ice

Big Green Salad with Two-Pepper Dressing

HEARTLAND DINNER

Pork with Pears and Barley *(page 306)*
Big Green Salad with Two-Pepper Dressing *(page 349)*
Berry Good Banana Bread *(page 294)*
Skim milk

SOUTHWEST SAMPLER

Green Chile Stew *(page 567)*
Warm tortillas
Jicama, carrot, and pepper sticks
Strawberry Italian Ice *(page 308)*
Limeade

THE ORIENT EXPRESS

Asian Chicken Wraps *(page 569)*
East-West Veggies *(page 582)*
Hot cooked rice
Easy Gingerbread Bars *(page 299)*
Hot green tea

NORTHWEST SOUP SUPPER

Salmon Confetti Chowder *(page 65)*
Fruit, Wild Rice, and Spinach Salad *(page 293)*
Sourdough bread
Mango-Raspberry Pie *(page 304)*
Cider or coffee

A TASTE OF FRANCE

Flounder Mediterranean *(page 581)*
Honey Dijon Bread *(page 265)*
Strawberry Soufflé *(page 53)*
Red wine or grape juice

global flavor menus

TAKE YOUR FAMILY AROUND THE WORLD JUST SITTING AT YOUR DINNER TABLE. THESE MENUS BORROW INSPIRATION FROM THE CUISINES OF FARAWAY PLACES. LET THEIR SEASONINGS TICKLE YOUR TASTE BUDS.

CARIBBEAN CAPER

Tropical fruit salad
Caribbean Pork Pot Roast *(page 515)*
Black beans
Hot cooked rice
Coconut-Lemon Puffs *(page 550)*
Mango-Ginger Coladas *(page 261)*

GREEK ODYSSEY

Feta Tabbouleh Salad *(page 541)*
Greek Orzo and Pepper Casserole *(page 529)*
Toasted pita bread
Good Thyme Lemon Cups *(page 548)*
Sparkling water

ITALIAN ARIA

Green salad with balsamic vinaigrette
Ham-Spinach Lasagna *(page 525)*
Italian bread with olive oil
Easter Ricotta Pie *(page 551)*
Red wine
Cappuccino or espresso

MOROCCAN CRUSADE

Orange-almond spinach salad
Moroccan-Style Short Ribs *(page 524)*
Zucchini-Olive Couscous *(page 544)*
Chocolate-Kissed Date Puffs *(page 552)*
Coffee or tea

Moroccan-Style Short Ribs

Coconut-Lemon Puffs

Zucchini-Olive Couscous

recipeindex

a

b

index

index

C

index

index

d

index

e

f

index

i

index

j

k

l

index

n

O

index

index

index

S

index

index

t

index

index

z

tips

Nutrition information.

With each recipe, we give you useful nutrition information you easily can apply to your own needs. First, read "What you need" *(below)* to determine your dietary requirements. Then refer to the nutrition information listed after each recipe. You'll find the calorie count and the amount of fat, saturated fat, cholesterol, sodium, carbohydrates, fiber, and protein for each serving. You'll find the amount of vitamin A, vitamin C, calcium, and iron noted as a percentage of the Daily Values, if they are present. The Daily Values are dietary standards set by the Food and Drug Administration. To stay in line with the nutrition breakdown of each recipe, follow the suggested number of servings.

How we analyze.

The *Better Homes and Gardens®* Test Kitchen computer analyzes each recipe for the nutritional value of a single serving.

- The analysis does not include optional ingredients.
- We use the first serving size listed when a range is given. For example: If we say a recipe "Makes 4 to 6 servings," the nutrition information is based on 4 servings.
- When ingredient choices (such as margarine or butter) appear in a recipe, we use the first one mentioned for analysis. The ingredient order does not mean we prefer one ingredient over another.
- When milk and eggs are recipe ingredients, the analysis is calculated using 2-percent (reduced-fat) milk and large eggs.

What you need.

The dietary guidelines below suggest nutrient levels that moderately active adults should strive to eat each day. As your calorie levels change, adjust your fat intake too. Try to keep the percentage of calories from fat to no more than 30 percent. There's no harm in occasionally going over or under these guidelines, but the key to good health is maintaining a balanced diet most of the time.

Calories: About 2,000
Total fat: Less than 65 grams
Saturated fat: Less than 20 grams
Cholesterol: Less than 300 milligrams
Carbohydrates: About 300 grams
Sodium: Less than 2,400 milligrams
Dietary fiber: 20 to 30 grams

Low-fat recipes.

For recipes that meet our low-fat criteria, each serving must contain three or fewer grams of fat for every 100 calories. These recipes are flagged with a low-fat symbol.

Metric information.

The charts on this page provide a guide for converting measurements from the U.S. customary system, which is used throughout this book, to the metric system.

Product Differences

Most of the ingredients called for in the recipes in this book are available in most countries. However, some are known by different names. Here are some common American ingredients and their possible counterparts:

- Sugar (white) is granulated, fine granulated, or castor sugar.
- Powdered sugar is icing sugar.
- All-purpose flour is enriched, bleached or unbleached white household flour. When self-rising flour is used in place of all-purpose flour in a recipe that calls for leavening, omit the leavening agent (baking soda or baking powder) and salt.
- Light-colored corn syrup is golden syrup.
- Cornstarch is cornflour.
- Baking soda is bicarbonate of soda.
- Vanilla or vanilla extract is vanilla essence.
- Green, red, or yellow sweet peppers are capsicums or bell peppers.
- Golden raisins are sultanas.

Volume and Weight

The United States traditionally uses cup measures for liquid and solid ingredients. The chart below shows the approximate imperial and metric equivalents. If you are accustomed to weighing solid ingredients, the following approximate equivalents will be helpful.

- 1 cup butter, castor sugar, or rice = 8 ounces = ½ pound = 250 grams
- 1 cup flour = 4 ounces = ¼ pound = 125 grams
- 1 cup icing sugar = 5 ounces = 150 grams

Canadian and U.S. volume for a cup measure is 8 fluid ounces (237 ml), but the standard metric equivalent is 250 ml.

1 British imperial cup is 10 fluid ounces.

In Australia, 1 tablespoon equals 20 ml, and there are 4 teaspoons in the Australian tablespoon.

Spoon measures are used for smaller amounts of ingredients. Although the size of the tablespoon varies slightly in different countries, for practical purposes and for recipes in this book, a straight substitution is all that's necessary. Measurements made using cups or spoons always should be level unless stated otherwise.

Common Weight Range Replacements

Imperial / U.S.	Metric
½ ounce	15 g
1 ounce	25 g or 30 g
4 ounces (¼ pound)	115 g or 125 g
8 ounces (½ pound)	225 g or 250 g
16 ounces (1 pound)	450 g or 500 g
1¼ pounds	625 g
1½ pounds	750 g
2 pounds or 2¼ pounds	1,000 g or 1 Kg

Oven Temperature Equivalents

Fahrenheit Setting	Celsius Setting*	Gas Setting
300°F	150°C	Gas Mark 2 (very low)
325°F	160°C	Gas Mark 3 (low)
350°F	180°C	Gas Mark 4 (moderate)
375°F	190°C	Gas Mark 5 (moderate)
400°F	200°C	Gas Mark 6 (hot)
425°F	220°C	Gas Mark 7 (hot)
450°F	230°C	Gas Mark 8 (very hot)
475°F	240°C	Gas Mark 9 (very hot)
500°F	260°C	Gas Mark 10 (extremely hot)
Broil	Broil	Grill

*Electric and gas ovens may be calibrated using celsius. However, for an electric oven, increase celsius setting 10 to 20 degrees when cooking above 160°C. For convection or forced air ovens (gas or electric), lower the temperature setting 25°F/10°C when cooking at all heat levels.

Baking Pan Sizes

Imperial / U.S.	Metric
9×1½-inch round cake pan	22- or 23×4-cm (1.5 L)
9×1½-inch pie plate	22- or 23×4-cm (1 L)
8×8×2-inch square cake pan	20×5-cm (2 L)
9×9×2-inch square cake pan	22- or 23×4.5-cm (2.5 L)
11×7×1½-inch baking pan	28×17x4-cm (2 L)
2-quart rectangular baking pan	30×19×4.5-cm (3 L)
13×9×2-inch baking pan	34×22×4.5-cm (3.5 L)
15×10×1-inch jelly roll pan	40×25×2-cm
9×5×3-inch loaf pan	23×13×8-cm (2 L)
2-quart casserole	2 L

U.S. / Standard Metric Equivalents

⅛ teaspoon = 0.5 ml	⅓ cup = 3 fluid ounces = 75 ml
¼ teaspoon = 1 ml	½ cup = 4 fluid ounces = 125 ml
½ teaspoon = 2 ml	⅔ cup = 5 fluid ounces = 150 ml
1 teaspoon = 5 ml	¾ cup = 6 fluid ounces = 175 ml
1 tablespoon = 15 ml	1 cup = 8 fluid ounces = 250 ml
2 tablespoons = 25 ml	2 cups = 1 pint = 500 ml
¼ cup = 2 fluid ounces = 50 ml	1 quart = 1 litre

Emergency substitutions.

If you don't have:	Substitute:
Bacon, 1 slice, crisp-cooked, crumbled	1 tablespoon cooked bacon pieces
Baking powder, 1 teaspoon	$^1/_2$ teaspoon cream of tartar plus $^1/_4$ teaspoon baking soda
Balsamic vinegar, 1 tablespoon	1 tablespoon cider vinegar or red wine vinegar plus $^1/_2$ teaspoon sugar
Bread crumbs, fine dry, $^1/_4$ cup	$^3/_4$ cup soft bread crumbs, or $^1/_4$ cup cracker crumbs, or $^1/_4$ cup cornflake crumbs
Broth, beef or chicken, 1 cup	1 teaspoon or 1 cube instant beef or chicken bouillon plus 1 cup hot water
Butter, 1 cup	1 cup shortening plus $^1/_4$ teaspoon salt, if desired
Buttermilk, 1 cup	1 tablespoon lemon juice or vinegar plus enough milk to make 1 cup (let stand 5 minutes before using), or 1 cup plain yogurt
Chocolate, semisweet, 1 ounce	3 tablespoons semisweet chocolate pieces, or 1 ounce unsweetened chocolate plus 1 tablespoon granulated sugar, or 1 tablespoon unsweetened cocoa powder plus 2 teaspoons sugar and 2 teaspoons shortening
Chocolate, sweet baking, 4 ounces	$^1/_4$ cup unsweetened cocoa powder plus $^1/_3$ cup granulated sugar and 3 tablespoons shortening
Chocolate, unsweetened, 1 ounce	3 tablespoons unsweetened cocoa powder plus 1 tablespoon cooking oil or shortening, melted
Cornstarch, 1 tablespoon (for thickening)	2 tablespoons all-purpose flour
Corn syrup (light), 1 cup	1 cup granulated sugar plus $^1/_4$ cup water
Egg, 1 whole	2 egg whites, or 2 egg yolks, or $^1/_4$ cup refrigerated or frozen egg product, thawed
Flour, cake, 1 cup	1 cup minus 2 tablespoons all-purpose flour
Flour, self-rising, 1 cup	1 cup all-purpose flour plus 1 teaspoon baking powder, $^1/_2$ teaspoon salt, and $^1/_4$ teaspoon baking soda
Garlic, 1 clove	$^1/_2$ teaspoon bottled minced garlic or $^1/_8$ teaspoon garlic powder
Ginger, grated fresh, 1 teaspoon	$^1/_4$ teaspoon ground ginger
Half-and-half or light cream, 1 cup	1 tablespoon melted butter or margarine plus enough whole milk to make 1 cup
Molasses, 1 cup	1 cup honey
Mustard, dry, 1 teaspoon	1 tablespoon prepared (in cooked mixtures)
Mustard, prepared, 1 tablespoon	$^1/_2$ teaspoon dry mustard plus 2 teaspoons vinegar
Onion, chopped, $^1/_2$ cup	2 tablespoons dried minced onion or $^1/_2$ teaspoon onion powder
Sour cream, dairy, 1 cup	1 cup plain yogurt
Sugar, granulated, 1 cup	1 cup packed brown sugar or 2 cups sifted powdered sugar
Sugar, brown, 1 cup packed	1 cup granulated sugar plus 2 tablespoons molasses
Tomato juice, 1 cup	$^1/_2$ cup tomato sauce plus $^1/_2$ cup water
Tomato sauce, 2 cups	$^3/_4$ cup tomato paste plus 1 cup water
Vanilla bean, 1 whole	2 teaspoons vanilla extract
Wine, red, 1 cup	1 cup beef or chicken broth in savory recipes; cranberry juice in desserts
Wine, white, 1 cup	1 cup chicken broth in savory recipes; apple juice or white grape juice in desserts
Yeast, active dry, 1 package	about $2^1/_4$ teaspoons active dry yeast

Seasonings

Apple pie spice, 1 teaspoon	$^1/_2$ teaspoon ground cinnamon plus $^1/_4$ teaspoon ground nutmeg, $^1/_8$ teaspoon ground allspice, and dash ground cloves or ginger
Cajun seasoning, 1 tablespoon	$^1/_2$ teaspoon white pepper, $^1/_2$ teaspoon garlic powder, $^1/_2$ teaspoon onion powder, $^1/_2$ teaspoon ground red pepper, $^1/_2$ teaspoon paprika, and $^1/_2$ teaspoon black pepper
Herbs, snipped fresh, 1 tablespoon	$^1/_2$ to 1 teaspoon dried herb, crushed, or $^1/_2$ teaspoon ground herb
Poultry seasoning, 1 teaspoon	$^3/_4$ teaspoon dried sage, crushed, plus $^1/_4$ teaspoon dried thyme or marjoram, crushed
Pumpkin pie spice, 1 teaspoon	$^1/_2$ teaspoon ground cinnamon plus $^1/_4$ teaspoon ground ginger, $^1/_4$ teaspoon ground allspice, and $^1/_8$ teaspoon ground nutmeg